IP Header

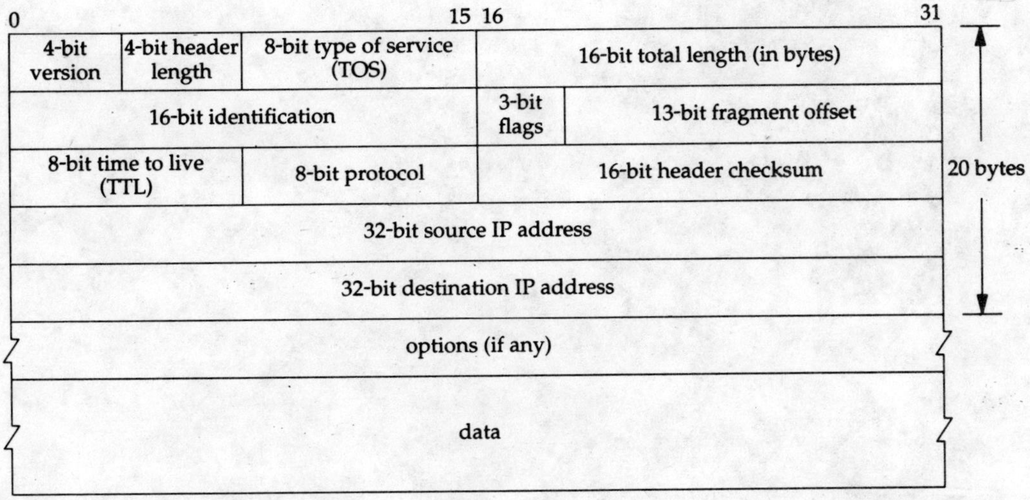

UDP Header

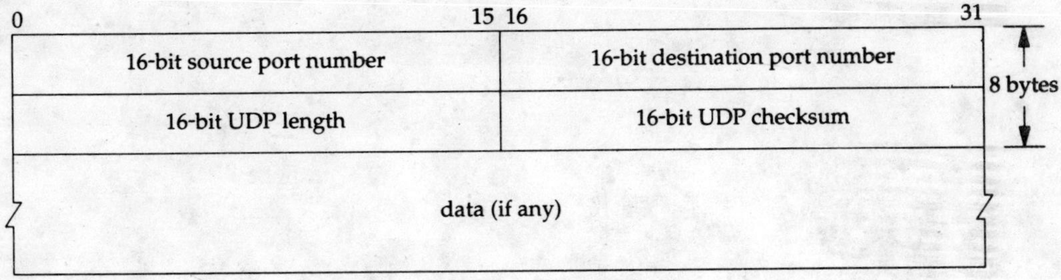

TCP Header

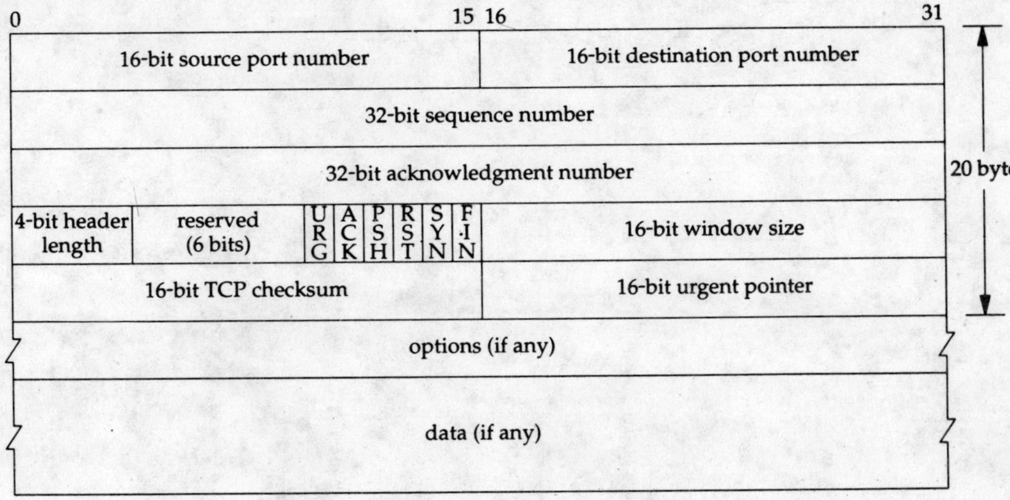

TCP/IP Illustrated, Volume 1

Addison-Wesley Professional Computing Series

Brian W. Kernighan, Consulting Editor

Ken Arnold/John Peyton, *A C User's Guide to ANSI C*
David R. Butenhof, *Programming with POSIX® Threads*
Tom Cargill, *C++ Programming Style*
William R. Cheswick/Steven M. Bellovin, *Firewalls and Internet Security: Repelling the Wily Hacker*
David A. Curry, *UNIX® System Security: A Guide for Users and System Administrators*
Erich Gamma/Richard Helm/Ralph Johnson/John Vlissides, *Design Patterns: Elements of Reusable Object-Oriented Software*
Erich Gamma/Richard Helm/Ralph Johnson/John Vlissides, *Design Patterns CD: Elements of Reusable Object-Oriented Software.*
David R. Hanson, *C Interfaces and Implementations: Techniques for Creating Reusable Software*
S. Keshav, *An Engineering Approach to Computer Networking: ATM Networks, the Internet, and the Telephone Network*
John Lakos, *Large Scale C++ Software Design*
Scott Meyers, *Effective C++: 50 Specific Ways to Improve Your Programs and Designs*
Scott Meyers, *More Effective C++: 35 New Ways to Improve Your Programs and Designs*
Robert B. Murray, *C++ Strategies and Tactics*
David R. Musser/Atul Saini, *STL Tutorial and Reference Guide: C++ Programming with the Standard Template Library*
John K. Ousterhout, *Tcl and the Tk Toolkit*
Craig Partridge, *Gigabit Networking*
J. Steven Pendergrast Jr., *Desktop KornShell Graphical Programming*
Radia Perlman, *Interconnections: Bridges and Routers*
David M. Piscitello/A. Lyman Chapin, *Open Systems Networking: TCP/IP and OSI*
Stephen A. Rago, *UNIX® System V Network Programming*
Curt Schimmel, *UNIX® Systems for Modern Architectures: Symmetric Multiprocessing and Caching for Kernel Programmers*
W. Richard Stevens, *Advanced Programming in the UNIX® Environment*
W. Richard Stevens, *TCP/IP Illustrated, Volume I: The Protocols*
W. Richard Stevens, *TCP/IP Illustrated, Volume 3: TCP for Transactions, HTTP, NNTP, and the UNIX® Domain Protocols*
Gary R. Wright/W. Richard Stevens, *TCP/IP Illustrated, Volume 2: The Implementation*

TCP/IP Illustrated, Volume 1

The Protocols

W. Richard Stevens

Pearson Education Asia

UNIX is a technology trademark of X/Open Company, Ltd.

ISBN 81-7808-101-6

First ISE Reprint, 1999
Second Indian Reprint, 2000
Third Indian Reprint, 2000
Fourth Indian Reprint, 2001
Fifth Indian Reprint, 2001
Sixth Indian Reprint, 2001

Published by Pearson Education (Singapore) Pte. Ltd., Indian Branch, 482 F.I.E. Patparganj, Delhi 110 092, India

Printed in India by Rashtriya Printers.

To Brian Kernighan and John Wait,
for their encouragement, faith, and support
over the past 5 years.

Praise for *TCP/IP Illustrated, Volume 1: The Protocols*

"This is sure to be the bible for TCP/IP developers and users. Within minutes of picking up the text, I encountered several scenarios which had tripped-up both my colleagues and myself in the past. Stevens reveals many of the mysteries once held tightly by the ever-elusive networking gurus. Having been involved in the implementation of TCP/IP for some years now, I consider this by far the finest text to date."

— Robert A. Ciampa, Network Engineer, Synernetics, division of 3COM

"While all of Stevens' books are readable and technically excellent, this new opus is awesome. Although many books describe the TCP/IP protocols, Stevens provides a level of depth and real-world detail lacking from the competition. He puts the reader inside TCP/IP using a visual approach and shows the protocols in action."

— Steven Baker, Networking Columnist, *Unix Review*

"*TCP/IP Illustrated, Volume 1* is an excellent reference for developers, network administrators, or anyone who needs to understand TCP/IP technology. *TCP/IP Illustrated* is comprehensive in its coverage of TCP/IP topics, providing enough details to satisfy the experts while giving enough background and commentary for the novice."

— Bob Williams, V.P. Marketing, NetManage, Inc.

"... the difference is that Stevens wants to show as well as tell about the protocols. His principal teaching tools are straight-forward explanations, exercises at the ends of chapters, byte-by-byte diagrams of headers and the like, and listings of actual traffic as examples."

— Walter Zintz, *UnixWorld*

"Much better than theory only ... W. Richard Stevens takes a multihost-based configuration and uses it as a travelogue of TCP/IP examples with illustrations. *TCP/IP Illustrated, Volume 1* is based on practical examples that reinforce the theory — distinguishing this book from others on the subject, and making it both readable and informative."

— Peter M. Haverlock, Consultant, IBM TCP/IP Development

"The diagrams he uses are excellent and his writing style is clear and readable. In sum, Stevens has made a complex topic easy to understand. This book merits everyone's attention. Please read it and keep it on your bookshelf."

— Elizabeth Zinkann, *Sys Admin*

"W. Richard Stevens has produced a fine text and reference work. It is well organized and very clearly written with, as the title suggests, many excellent illustrations exposing the intimate details of the logic and operation of IP, TCP, and the supporting cast of protocols and applications."

— Scott Bradner, Consultant, Harvard University OIT/NSD

Contents

Preface

Introduction

This book describes the TCP/IP protocol suite, but from a different perspective than other texts on TCP/IP. Instead of just describing the protocols and what they do, we'll use a popular diagnostic tool to watch the protocols in action. Seeing how the protocols operate in varying circumstances provides a greater understanding of how they work and why certain design decisions were made. It also provides a look into the implementation of the protocols, without having to wade through thousands of lines of source code.

When networking protocols were being developed in the 1960s through the 1980s, expensive, dedicated hardware was required to see the packets going "across the wire." Extreme familiarity with the protocols was also required to comprehend the packets displayed by the hardware. Functionality of the hardware analyzers was limited to that built in by the hardware designers.

Today this has changed dramatically with the ability of the ubiquitous workstation to monitor a local area network [Mogul 1990]. Just attach a workstation to your network, run some publicly available software (described in Appendix A), and watch what goes by on the wire. While many people consider this a tool to be used for *diagnosing* network problems, it is also a powerful tool for *understanding* how the network protocols operate, which is the goal of this book.

This book is intended for anyone wishing to understand how the TCP/IP protocols operate: programmers writing network applications, system administrators responsible for maintaining computer systems and networks utilizing TCP/IP, and users who deal with TCP/IP applications on a daily basis.

Organization of the Book

The following figure shows the various protocols and applications that are covered. The italic number by each box indicates the chapter in which that protocol or application is described.

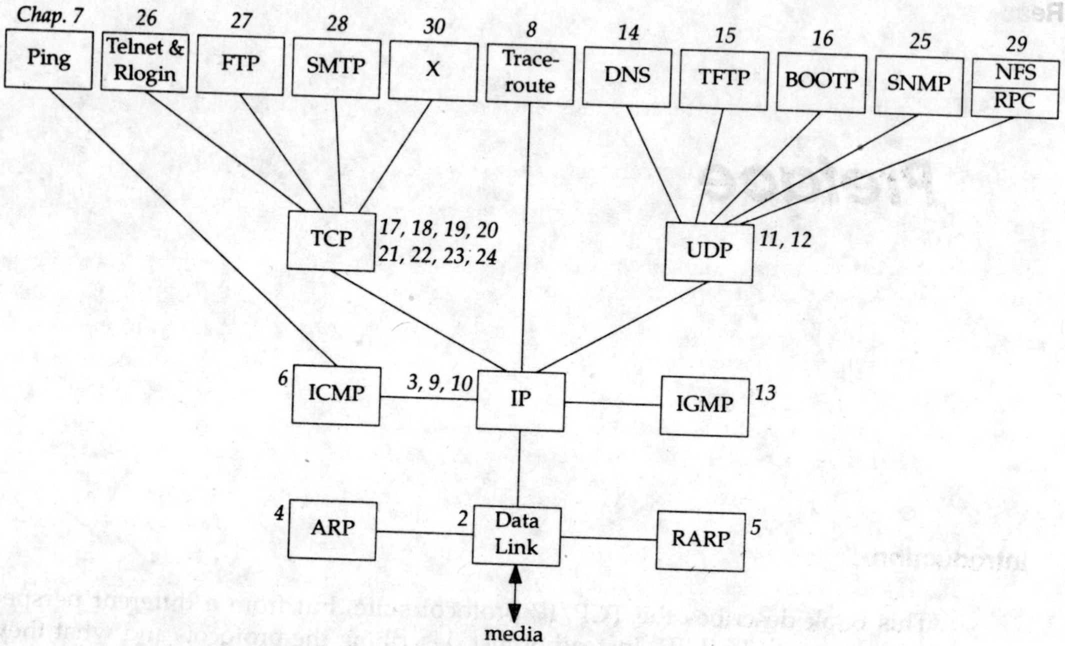

(Numerous fine points are missing from this figure that will be discussed in the appropriate chapter. For example, both the DNS and RPC use TCP, which we don't show.)

We take a bottom-up approach to the TCP/IP protocol suite. After providing a basic introduction to TCP/IP in Chapter 1, we will start at the link layer in Chapter 2 and work our way up the protocol stack. This provides the required background for later chapters for readers who aren't familiar with TCP/IP or networking in general.

This book also uses a functional approach instead of following a strict bottom-to-top order. For example, Chapter 3 describes the IP layer and the IP header. But there are numerous fields in the IP header that are best described in the context of an application that uses or is affected by a particular field. Fragmentation, for example, is best understood in terms of UDP (Chapter 11), the protocol often affected by it. The time-to-live field is fully described when we look at the Traceroute program in Chapter 8, because this field is the basis for the operation of the program. Similarly, many features of ICMP are described in the later chapters, in terms of how a particular ICMP message is used by a protocol or an application.

We also don't want to save all the good stuff until the end, so we describe TCP/IP applications as soon as we have the foundation to understand them. Ping and Traceroute are described after IP and ICMP have been discussed. The applications built on UDP (multicasting, the DNS, TFTP, and BOOTP) are described after UDP has been examined. The TCP applications, however, along with network management, must be saved until the end, after we've thoroughly described TCP. This text focuses on how these applications use the TCP/IP protocols. We do not provide all the details on running these applications.

Readers

This book is self-contained and assumes no specific knowledge of networking or TCP/IP. Numerous references are provided for readers interested in additional details on specific topics.

This book can be used in many ways. It can be used as a self-study reference and covered from start to finish by someone interested in all the details on the TCP/IP protocol suite. Readers with some TCP/IP background might want to skip ahead and start with Chapter 7, and then focus on the specific chapters in which they're interested. Exercises are provided at the end of the chapters, and most solutions are in Appendix D. This is to maximize the usefulness of the text as a self-study reference.

When used as part of a one- or two-semester course in computer networking, the focus should be on IP (Chapters 3 and 9), UDP (Chapter 11), and TCP (Chapters 17–24), along with some of the application chapters.

Many forward and backward references are provided throughout the text, along with a thorough index, to allow individual chapters to be studied by themselves. A list of all the acronyms used throughout the text, along with the compound term for the acronym, appears on the inside back covers.

If you have access to a network you are encouraged to obtain the software used in this book (Appendix F) and experiment on your own. Hands-on experimentation with the protocols will provide the greatest knowledge (and make it more fun).

Systems Used for Testing

Every example in the book was run on an actual network and the resulting output saved in a file for inclusion in the text. Figure 1.11 (p. 18) shows a diagram of the different hosts, routers, and networks that are used. (This figure is also duplicated on the inside front cover for easy reference while reading the book.) This collection of networks is simple enough that the topology doesn't confuse the examples, and with four systems acting as routers, we can see the error messages generated by routers.

Most of the systems have a name that indicates the type of software being used: `bsdi`, `svr4`, `sun`, `solaris`, `aix`, `slip`, and so on. In this way we can identify the type of software that we're dealing with by looking at the system name in the printed output.

A wide range of different operating systems and TCP/IP implementations are used:

- BSD/386 Version 1.0 from Berkeley Software Design, Inc., on the hosts named `bsdi` and `slip`. This system is derived from the BSD Networking Software, Release 2.0. (We show the lineage of the various BSD releases in Figure 1.10 on p. 17.)

- Unix System V/386 Release 4.0 Version 2.0 from U.H. Corporation, on the host named `svr4`. This is vanilla SVR4 and contains the standard implementation of TCP/IP from Lachman Associates used with most versions of SVR4.
- SunOS 4.1.3 from Sun Microsystems, on the host named `sun`. The SunOS 4.1.x systems are probably the most widely used TCP/IP implementations. The TCP/IP code is derived from 4.2BSD and 4.3BSD.
- Solaris 2.2 from Sun Microsystems, on the host named `solaris`. The Solaris 2.x systems have a different implementation of TCP/IP from the earlier SunOS 4.1.x systems, and from SVR4. (This operating system is really SunOS 5.2, but is commonly called Solaris 2.2.)
- AIX 3.2.2 from IBM on the host named `aix`. The TCP/IP implementation is based on the 4.3BSD Reno release.
- 4.4BSD from the Computer Systems Research Group at the University of California at Berkeley, on the host `vangogh.cs.berkeley.edu`. This system has the latest release of TCP/IP from Berkeley. (This system isn't shown in the figure on the inside front cover, but is reachable across the Internet.)

Although these are all Unix systems, TCP/IP is operating system independent, and is available on almost every popular non-Unix system. Most of this text also applies to these non-Unix implementations, although some programs (such as Traceroute) may not be provided on all systems.

Typographical Conventions

When we display interactive input and output we'll show our typed input in a **`bold font`**, and the computer output `like this`. *Comments are added in italics.*

```
bsdi % telnet svr4 discard          connect to the discard server
Trying 140.252.13.34...             this line and next output by Telnet client
Connected to svr4.
```

Also, we always include the name of the system as part of the shell prompt (`bsdi` in this example) to show on which host the command was run.

> Throughout the text we'll use indented, parenthetical notes such as this to describe historical points or implementation details.

We sometimes refer to the complete description of a command in the Unix manual as in `ifconfig`(8). This notation, the name of the command followed by a number in parentheses, is the normal way of referring to Unix commands. The number in parentheses is the section number in the Unix manual of the "manual page" for the command, where additional information can be located. Unfortunately not all Unix systems organize their manuals the same, with regard to the section numbers used for various groupings of commands. We'll use the BSD-style section numbers (which is the same for BSD-derived systems such as SunOS 4.1.3), but your manuals may be organized differently.

Acknowledgments

Although the author's name is the only one to appear on the cover, the combined effort of many people is required to produce a quality text book. First and foremost is the author's family, who put up with the long and weird hours that go into writing a book. Thank you once again, Sally, Bill, Ellen, and David.

The consulting editor, Brian Kernighan, is undoubtedly the best in the business. He was the first one to read various drafts of the manuscript and mark it up with his infinite supply of red pens. His attention to detail, his continual prodding for readable prose, and his thorough reviews of the manuscript are an immense resource to a writer.

Technical reviewers provide a different point of view and keep the author honest by catching technical mistakes. Their comments, suggestions, and (most importantly) criticisms add greatly to the final product. My thanks to Steve Bellovin, Jon Crowcroft, Pete Haverlock, and Doug Schmidt for comments on the entire manuscript. Equally valuable comments were provided on portions of the manuscript by Dave Borman, Tony DeSimone, Bob Gilligan, Jeff Gitlin, John Gulbenkian, Tom Herbert, Mukesh Kacker, Barry Margolin, Paul Mockapetris, Burr Nelson, Steve Rago, James Risner, Chris Walquist, Phil Winterbottom, and Gary Wright. A special thanks to Dave Borman for his thorough review of all the TCP chapters, and to Bob Gilligan who should be listed as a coauthor for Appendix E.

An author cannot work in isolation, so I would like to thank the following persons for lots of small favors, especially by answering my numerous e-mail questions: Joe Godsil, Jim Hogue, Mike Karels, Paul Lucchina, Craig Partridge, Thomas Skibo, and Jerry Toporek.

This book is the result of my being asked lots of questions on TCP/IP for which I could find no quick, immediate answer. It was then that I realized that the easiest way to obtain the answers was to run small tests, forcing certain conditions to occur, and just watch what happens. I thank Pete Haverlock for asking the probing questions and Van Jacobson for providing so much of the publicly available software that is used in this book to answer the questions.

A book on networking needs a real network to work with along with access to the Internet. My thanks to the National Optical Astronomy Observatories (NOAO), especially Sidney Wolff, Richard Wolff, and Steve Grandi, for providing access to their networks and hosts. A special thanks to Steve Grandi for answering lots of questions and providing accounts on various hosts. My thanks also to Keith Bostic and Kirk McKusick at the U.C. Berkeley CSRG for access to the latest 4.4BSD system.

Finally, it is the publisher that pulls everything together and does whatever is required to deliver the final product to the readers. This all revolves around the editor, and John Wait is simply the best there is. Working with John and the rest of the professionals at Addison-Wesley is a pleasure. Their professionalism and attention to detail show in the end result.

Camera-ready copy of the book was produced by the author, a Troff die-hard, using the Groff package written by James Clark. I welcome electronic mail from any readers with comments, suggestions, or bug fixes.

W. Richard Stevens

Tucson, Arizona
October 1993

`rstevens@noao.edu`
`http://www.noao.edu/~rstevens`

Acknowledgments

Although the author's name is the only one to appear on the cover, the combined effort of many people is required to produce a quality text book. First and foremost is the author's family, who put up with the long and weird hours that go into writing a book. Thank you once again, Sally, Bill, Ellen, and David.

The consulting editor, Brian Kernighan, is undoubtedly the best in the business. He was the first one to read various drafts of the manuscript and mark it up with his infinite supply of red pens. His attention to detail, his continual prodding for readable prose, and his thorough reviews of the manuscript are an immense resource to a writer.

Technical reviewers provide a different point of view and keep the author honest by catching technical mistakes. Their comments, suggestions, and (most importantly) criticisms add greatly to the final product. My thanks to Steve Bellovin, Jon Crowcroft, Pete Haverlock, and Doug Schmidt for comments on the entire manuscript. Equally valuable comments were provided on portions of the manuscript by Dave Borman, Tony DeSimone, Bob Gilligan, Jeff Gitlin, John Gulbenkian, Tom Herbert, Mukesh Kacker, Barry Margolin, Paul Mockapetris, Burr Nelson, Steve Rago, James Risner, Chris Walquist, Phil Winterbottom, and Gary Wright. A special thanks to Dave Borman for his thorough review of all the TCP chapters, and to Bob Gilligan who should be listed as a coauthor for Appendix E.

An author cannot work in isolation, so I would like to thank the following persons for lots of small favors, especially by answering my numerous e-mail questions: Joe Godsil, Jim Hogue, Mike Karels, Paul Lucchina, Craig Partridge, Thomas Skibo, and Jerry Toporek.

This book is the result of my being asked lots of questions on TCP/IP for which I could find no quick, immediate answer. It was then that I realized that the easiest way to obtain the answers was to run small tests, forcing certain conditions to occur, and just watch what happens. I thank Pete Haverlock for asking the probing questions and Van Jacobson for providing so much of the publicly available software that is used in this book to answer the questions.

A book on networking needs a real network to work with along with access to the Internet. My thanks to the National Optical Astronomy Observatories (NOAO), especially Sidney Wolff, Richard Wolff, and Steve Grandi, for providing access to their networks and hosts. A special thanks to Steve Grandi for answering lots of questions and providing accounts on various hosts. My thanks also to Keith Bostic and Kirk McKusick at the U.C. Berkeley CSRG for access to the latest 4.4BSD system.

Finally, it is the publisher that pulls everything together and does whatever is required to deliver the final product to the readers. This all revolves around the editor, and John Wait is simply the best there is. Working with John and the rest of the professionals at Addison-Wesley is a pleasure. Their professionalism and attention to detail show in the end result.

Camera-ready copy of the book was produced by the author, a Troff diehard, using the Groff package written by James Clark. I welcome electronic mail from any readers with comments, suggestions, or bug fixes.

W. Richard Stevens
Tucson, Arizona
October 1993

1

Introduction

1.1 Introduction

The TCP/IP protocol suite allows computers of all sizes, from many different computer vendors, running totally different operating systems, to communicate with each other. It is quite amazing because its use has far exceeded its original estimates. What started in the late 1960s as a government-financed research project into packet switching networks has, in the 1990s, turned into the most widely used form of networking between computers. It is truly an *open system* in that the definition of the protocol suite and many of its implementations are publicly available at little or no charge. It forms the basis for what is called the *worldwide Internet*, or the *Internet*, a wide area network (WAN) of more than one million computers that literally spans the globe.

This chapter provides an overview of the TCP/IP protocol suite, to establish an adequate background for the remaining chapters. For a historical perspective on the early development of TCP/IP see [Lynch 1993].

1.2 Layering

Networking *protocols* are normally developed in *layers*, with each layer responsible for a different facet of the communications. A *protocol suite*, such as TCP/IP, is the combination of different protocols at various layers. TCP/IP is normally considered to be a 4-layer system, as shown in Figure 1.1.

Application	Telnet, FTP, e-mail, etc.
Transport	TCP, UDP
Network	IP, ICMP, IGMP
Link	device driver and interface card

Figure 1.1 The four layers of the TCP/IP protocol suite.

Each layer has a different responsibility.

1. The *link* layer, sometimes called the *data-link* layer or *network interface* layer, normally includes the device driver in the operating system and the corresponding network interface card in the computer. Together they handle all the hardware details of physically interfacing with the cable (or whatever type of media is being used).

2. The *network* layer (sometimes called the *internet* layer) handles the movement of packets around the network. Routing of packets, for example, takes place here. IP (Internet Protocol), ICMP (Internet Control Message Protocol), and IGMP (Internet Group Management Protocol) provide the network layer in the TCP/IP protocol suite.

3. The *transport* layer provides a flow of data between two hosts, for the application layer above. In the TCP/IP protocol suite there are two vastly different transport protocols: TCP (Transmission Control Protocol) and UDP (User Datagram Protocol).

   TCP provides a reliable flow of data between two hosts. It is concerned with things such as dividing the data passed to it from the application into appropriately sized chunks for the network layer below, acknowledging received packets, setting timeouts to make certain the other end acknowledges packets that are sent, and so on. Because this reliable flow of data is provided by the transport layer, the application layer can ignore all these details.

   UDP, on the other hand, provides a much simpler service to the application layer. It just sends packets of data called *datagrams* from one host to the other, but there is no guarantee that the datagrams reach the other end. Any desired reliability must be added by the application layer.

   There is a use for each type of transport protocol, which we'll see when we look at the different applications that use TCP and UDP.

4. The *application* layer handles the details of the particular application. There are many common TCP/IP applications that almost every implementation provides:

   - Telnet for remote login,
   - FTP, the File Transfer Protocol,
   - SMTP, the Simple Mail Transfer protocol, for electronic mail,
   - SNMP, the Simple Network Management Protocol,

   and many more, some of which we cover in later chapters.

If we have two hosts on a local area network (LAN) such as an Ethernet, both running FTP, Figure 1.2 shows the protocols involved.

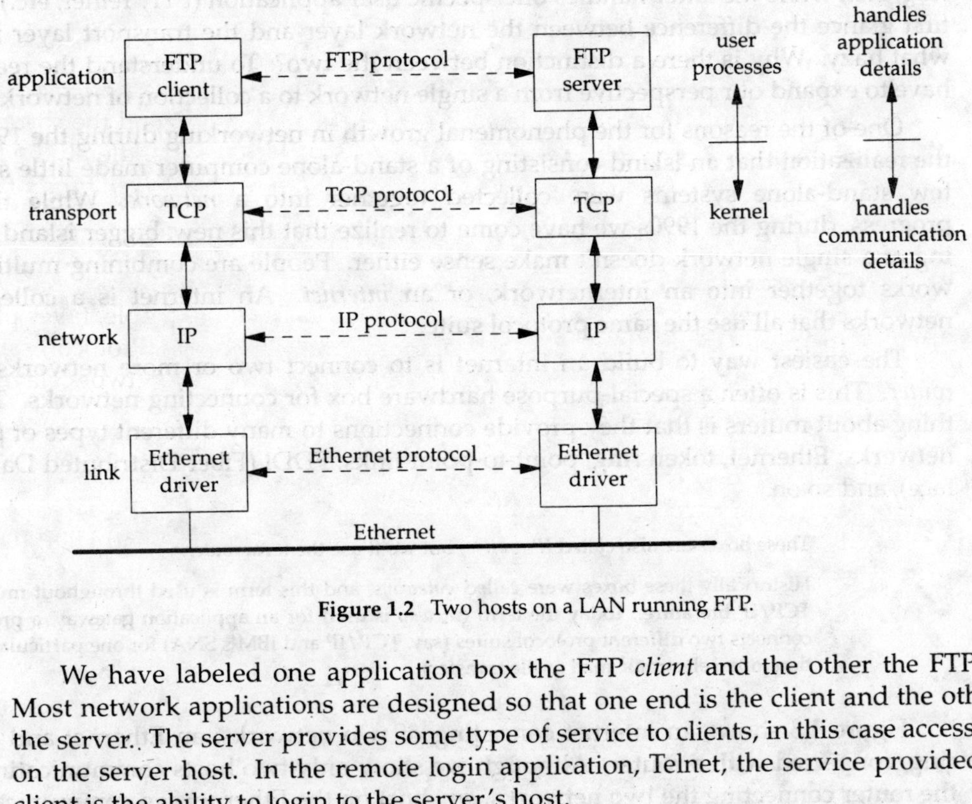

Figure 1.2 Two hosts on a LAN running FTP.

We have labeled one application box the FTP *client* and the other the FTP *server*. Most network applications are designed so that one end is the client and the other side the server. The server provides some type of service to clients, in this case access to files on the server host. In the remote login application, Telnet, the service provided to the client is the ability to login to the server's host.

Each layer has one or more protocols for communicating with its *peer* at the same layer. One protocol, for example, allows the two TCP layers to communicate, and another protocol lets the two IP layers communicate.

On the right side of Figure 1.2 we have noted that normally the application layer is a user process while the lower three layers are usually implemented in the kernel (the operating system). Although this isn't a requirement, it's typical and this is the way it's done under Unix.

There is another critical difference between the top layer in Figure 1.2 and the lower three layers. The application layer is concerned with the details of the application and not with the movement of data across the network. The lower three layers know nothing about the application but handle all the communication details.

We show four protocols in Figure 1.2, each at a different layer. FTP is an application layer protocol, TCP is a transport layer protocol, IP is a network layer protocol, and the Ethernet protocols operate at the link layer. The *TCP/IP protocol suite* is a combination of many protocols. Although the commonly used name for the entire protocol suite is TCP/IP, TCP and IP are only two of the protocols. (An alternative name is the *Internet Protocol Suite.*)

The purpose of the network interface layer and the application layer are obvious—the former handles the details of the communication media (Ethernet, token ring, etc.) while the latter handles one specific user application (FTP, Telnet, etc.). But on first glance the difference between the network layer and the transport layer is somewhat hazy. Why is there a distinction between the two? To understand the reason, we have to expand our perspective from a single network to a collection of networks.

One of the reasons for the phenomenal growth in networking during the 1980s was the realization that an island consisting of a stand-alone computer made little sense. A few stand-alone systems were collected together into a *network.* While this was progress, during the 1990s we have come to realize that this new, bigger island consisting of a single network doesn't make sense either. People are combining multiple networks together into an internetwork, or an *internet*. An internet is a collection of networks that all use the same protocol suite.

The easiest way to build an internet is to connect two or more networks with a *router*. This is often a special-purpose hardware box for connecting networks. The nice thing about routers is that they provide connections to many different types of physical networks: Ethernet, token ring, point-to-point links, FDDI (Fiber Distributed Data Interface), and so on.

These boxes are also called *IP routers*, but we'll use the term *router*.

Historically these boxes were called *gateways*, and this term is used throughout much of the TCP/IP literature. Today the term *gateway* is used for an application gateway: a process that connects two different protocol suites (say, TCP/IP and IBM's SNA) for one particular application (often electronic mail or file transfer).

Figure 1.3 shows an internet consisting of two networks: an Ethernet and a token ring, connected with a router. Although we show only two hosts communicating, with the router connecting the two networks, *any* host on the Ethernet can communicate with *any* host on the token ring.

In Figure 1.3 we can differentiate between an *end system* (the two hosts on either side) and an *intermediate system* (the router in the middle). The application layer and the transport layer use *end-to-end* protocols. In our picture these two layers are needed only on the end systems. The network layer, however, provides a *hop-by-hop* protocol and is used on the two end systems and every intermediate system.

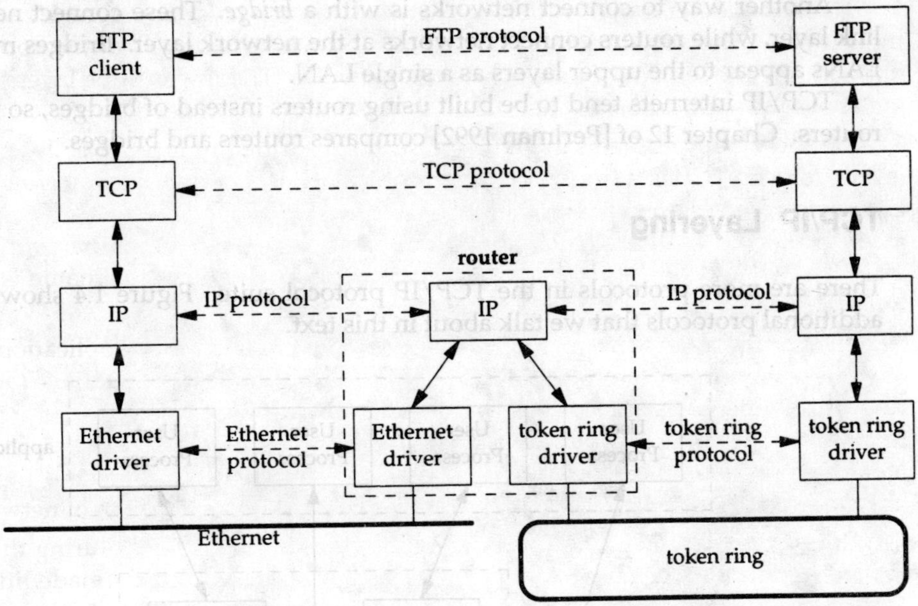

Figure 1.3 Two networks connected with a router.

In the TCP/IP protocol suite the network layer, IP, provides an unreliable service. That is, it does its best job of moving a packet from its source to its final destination, but there are no guarantees. TCP, on the other hand, provides a reliable transport layer using the unreliable service of IP. To provide this service, TCP performs timeout and retransmission, sends and receives end-to-end acknowledgments, and so on. The transport layer and the network layer have distinct responsibilities.

A router, by definition, has two or more network interface layers (since it connects two or more networks). Any system with multiple interfaces is called *multihomed*. A host can also be multihomed but unless it specifically forwards packets from one interface to another, it is not called a router. Also, routers need not be special hardware boxes that only move packets around an internet. Most TCP/IP implementations allow a multihomed host to act as a router also, but the host needs to be specifically configured for this to happen. In this case we can call the system either a host (when an application such as FTP or Telnet is being used) or a router (when it's forwarding packets from one network to another). We'll use whichever term makes sense given the context.

One of the goals of an internet is to hide all the details of the physical layout of the internet from the applications. Although this isn't obvious from our two-network internet in Figure 1.3, the application layers can't care (and don't care) that one host is on an Ethernet, the other on a token ring, with a router between. There could be 20 routers between, with additional types of physical interconnections, and the applications would run the same. This hiding of the details is what makes the concept of an internet so powerful and useful.

Another way to connect networks is with a *bridge*. These connect networks at the link layer, while routers connect networks at the network layer. Bridges makes multiple LANs appear to the upper layers as a single LAN.

TCP/IP internets tend to be built using routers instead of bridges, so we'll focus on routers. Chapter 12 of [Perlman 1992] compares routers and bridges.

1.3 TCP/IP Layering

There are more protocols in the TCP/IP protocol suite. Figure 1.4 shows some of the additional protocols that we talk about in this text.

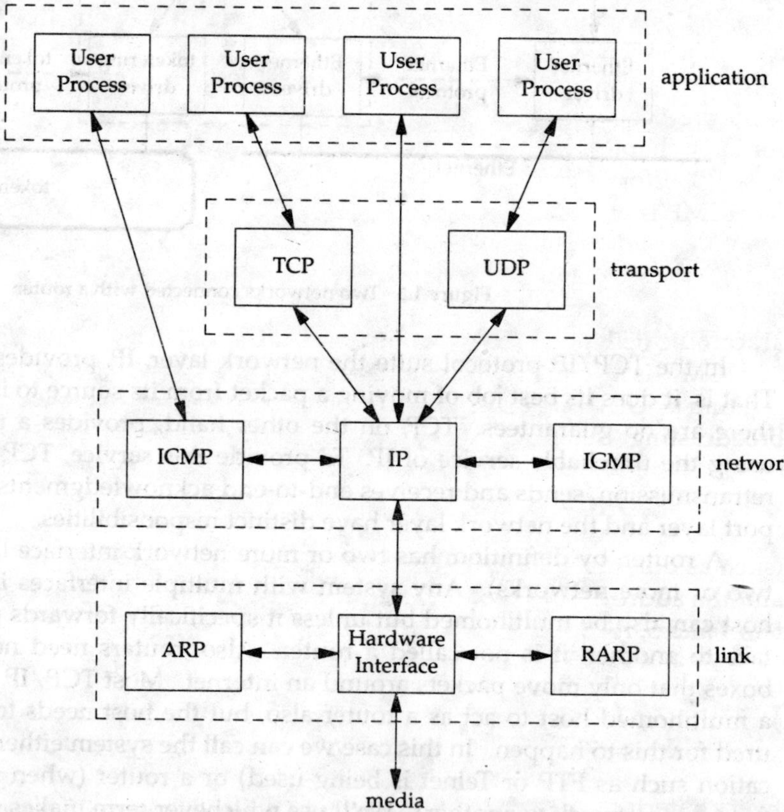

Figure 1.4 Various protocols at the different layers in the TCP/IP protocol suite.

TCP and UDP are the two predominant transport layer protocols. Both use IP as the network layer.

TCP provides a reliable transport layer, even though the service it uses (IP) is unreliable. Chapters 17 through 22 provide a detailed look at the operation of TCP. We then look at some TCP applications: Telnet and Rlogin in Chapter 26, FTP in Chapter 27, and SMTP in Chapter 28. The applications are normally user processes.

UDP sends and receives *datagrams* for applications. A datagram is a unit of information (i.e., a certain number of bytes of information that is specified by the sender) that travels from the sender to the receiver. Unlike TCP, however, UDP is unreliable. There is no guarantee that the datagram ever gets to its final destination. Chapter 11 looks at UDP, and then Chapter 14 (the Domain Name System), Chapter 15 (the Trivial File Transfer Protocol), and Chapter 16 (the Bootstrap Protocol) look at some applications that use UDP. SNMP (the Simple Network Management Protocol) also uses UDP, but since it deals with many of the other protocols, we save a discussion of it until Chapter 25.

IP is the main protocol at the network layer. It is used by both TCP and UDP. Every piece of TCP and UDP data that gets transferred around an internet goes through the IP layer at both end systems and at every intermediate router. In Figure 1.4 we also show an application accessing IP directly. This is rare, but possible. (Some older routing protocols were implemented this way. Also, it is possible to experiment with new transport layer protocols using this feature.) Chapter 3 looks at IP, but we save some of the details for later chapters where their discussion makes more sense. Chapters 9 and 10 look at how IP performs routing.

ICMP is an adjunct to IP. It is used by the IP layer to exchange error messages and other vital information with the IP layer in another host or router. Chapter 6 looks at ICMP in more detail. Although ICMP is used primarily by IP, it is possible for an application to also access it. Indeed we'll see that two popular diagnostic tools, Ping and Traceroute (Chapters 7 and 8), both use ICMP.

IGMP is the Internet Group Management Protocol. It is used with multicasting: sending a UDP datagram to multiple hosts. We describe the general properties of broadcasting (sending a UDP datagram to every host on a specified network) and multicasting in Chapter 12, and then describe IGMP itself in Chapter 13.

ARP (Address Resolution Protocol) and RARP (Reverse Address Resolution Protocol) are specialized protocols used only with certain types of network interfaces (such as Ethernet and token ring) to convert between the addresses used by the IP layer and the addresses used by the network interface. We examine these protocols in Chapters 4 and 5, respectively.

1.4 Internet Addresses

Every interface on an internet must have a unique *Internet address* (also called an *IP address*). These addresses are 32-bit numbers. Instead of using a flat address space such as 1, 2, 3, and so on, there is a structure to Internet addresses. Figure 1.5 shows the five different classes of Internet addresses.

These 32-bit addresses are normally written as four decimal numbers, one for each byte of the address. This is called *dotted-decimal* notation. For example, the class B address of the author's primary system is 140.252.13.33.

The easiest way to differentiate between the different classes of addresses is to look at the first number of a dotted-decimal address. Figure 1.6 shows the different classes, with the first number in boldface.

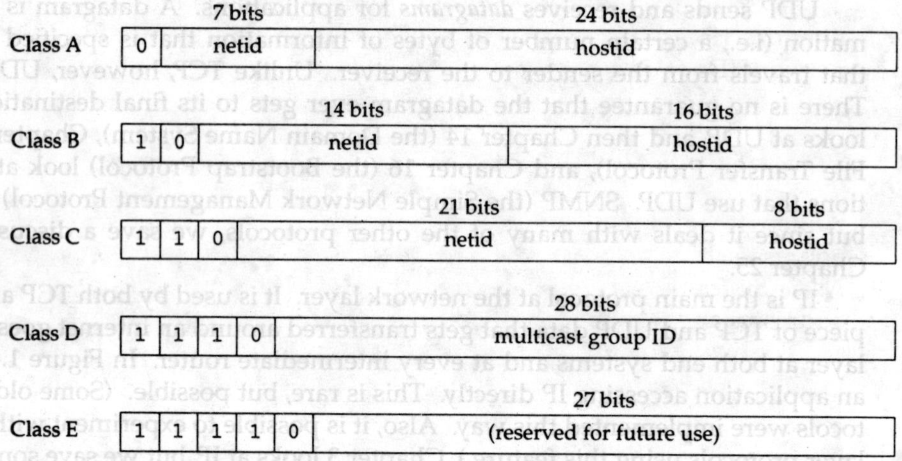

Figure 1.5 The five different classes of Internet addresses.

Class	Range
A	**0**.0.0.0 to **127**.255.255.255
B	**128**.0.0.0 to **191**.255.255.255
C	**192**.0.0.0 to **223**.255.255.255
D	**224**.0.0.0 to **239**.255.255.255
E	**240**.0.0.0 to **247**.255.255.255

Figure 1.6 Ranges for different classes of IP addresses.

It is worth reiterating that a multihomed host will have multiple IP addresses: one per interface.

Since every interface on an internet must have a unique IP address, there must be one central authority for allocating these addresses for networks connected to the worldwide Internet. That authority is the *Internet Network Information Center*, called the InterNIC. The InterNIC assigns only network IDs. The assignment of host IDs is up to the system administrator.

> Registration services for the Internet (IP addresses and DNS domain names) used to be handled by the NIC, at `nic.ddn.mil`. On April 1, 1993, the InterNIC was created. Now the NIC handles these requests only for the *Defense Data Network* (DDN). All other Internet users now use the InterNIC registration services, at `rs.internic.net`.
>
> There are actually three parts to the InterNIC: registration services (`rs.internic.net`), directory and database services (`ds.internic.net`), and information services (`is.internic.net`). See Exercise 1.8 for additional information on the InterNIC.

There are three types of IP addresses: *unicast* (destined for a single host), *broadcast* (destined for all hosts on a given network), and *multicast* (destined for a set of hosts that belong to a multicast group). Chapters 12 and 13 look at broadcasting and multicasting in more detail.

In Section 3.4 we'll extend our description of IP addresses to include subnetting, after describing IP routing. Figure 3.9 shows the special case IP addresses: host IDs and network IDs of all zero bits or all one bits.

1.5 The Domain Name System

Although the network interfaces on a host, and therefore the host itself, are known by IP addresses, humans work best using the *name* of a host. In the TCP/IP world the *Domain Name System* (DNS) is a distributed database that provides the mapping between IP addresses and hostnames. Chapter 14 looks into the DNS in detail.

For now we must be aware that any application can call a standard library function to look up the IP address (or addresses) corresponding to a given hostname. Similarly a function is provided to do the reverse lookup—given an IP address, look up the corresponding hostname.

Most applications that take a hostname as an argument also take an IP address. When we use the Telnet client in Chapter 4, for example, one time we specify a hostname and another time we specify an IP address.

1.6 Encapsulation

When an application sends data using TCP, the data is sent down the protocol stack, through each layer, until it is sent as a stream of bits across the network. Each layer adds information to the data by prepending headers (and sometimes adding trailer information) to the data that it receives. Figure 1.7 shows this process. The unit of data that TCP sends to IP is called a *TCP segment*. The unit of data that IP sends to the network interface is called an *IP datagram*. The stream of bits that flows across the Ethernet is called a *frame*.

The numbers at the bottom of the headers and trailer of the Ethernet frame in Figure 1.7 are the typical sizes of the headers in bytes. We'll have more to say about each of these headers in later sections.

A physical property of an Ethernet frame is that the size of its data must be between 46 and 1500 bytes. We'll encounter this minimum in Section 4.5 and we cover the maximum in Section 2.8.

All the Internet standards and most books on TCP/IP use the term *octet* instead of byte. The use of this cute, but baroque term is historical, since much of the early work on TCP/IP was done on systems such as the DEC-10, which did not use 8-bit bytes. Since almost every current computer system uses 8-bit bytes, we'll use the term *byte* in this text.

To be completely accurate in Figure 1.7 we should say that the unit of data passed between IP and the network interface is a *packet*. This packet can be either an IP datagram or a fragment of an IP datagram. We discuss fragmentation in detail in Section 11.5.

We could draw a nearly identical picture for UDP data. The only changes are that the unit of information that UDP passes to IP is called a *UDP datagram*, and the size of the UDP header is 8 bytes.

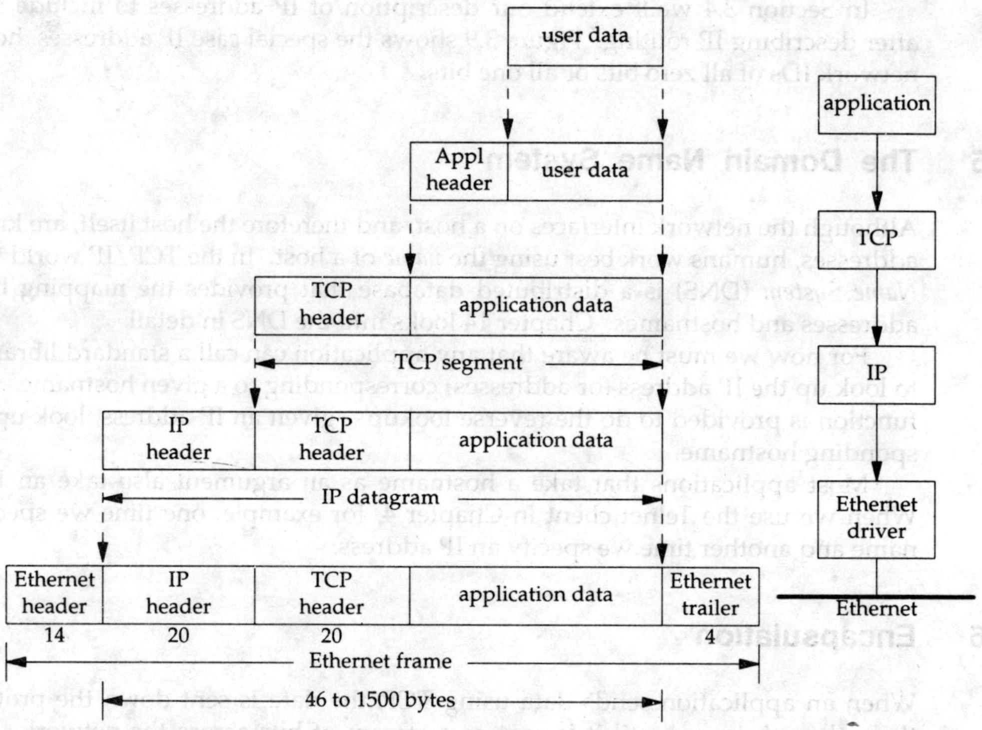

Figure 1.7 Encapsulation of data as it goes down the protocol stack.

Recall from Figure 1.4 (p. 6) that TCP, UDP, ICMP, and IGMP all send data to IP. IP must add some type of identifier to the IP header that it generates, to indicate the layer to which the data belongs. IP handles this by storing an 8-bit value in its header called the *protocol* field. A value of 1 is for ICMP, 2 is for IGMP, 6 indicates TCP, and 17 is for UDP.

Similarly, many different applications can be using TCP or UDP at any one time. The transport layer protocols store an identifier in the headers they generate to identify the application. Both TCP and UDP use 16-bit *port numbers* to identify applications. TCP and UDP store the source port number and the destination port number in their respective headers.

The network interface sends and receives frames on behalf of IP, ARP, and RARP. There must be some form of identification in the Ethernet header indicating which network layer protocol generated the data. To handle this there is a 16-bit frame type field in the Ethernet header.

1.7 Demultiplexing

When an Ethernet frame is received at the destination host it starts its way up the protocol stack and all the headers are removed by the appropriate protocol box. Each protocol box looks at certain identifiers in its header to determine which box in the next upper layer receives the data. This is called *demultiplexing*. Figure 1.8 shows how this takes place.

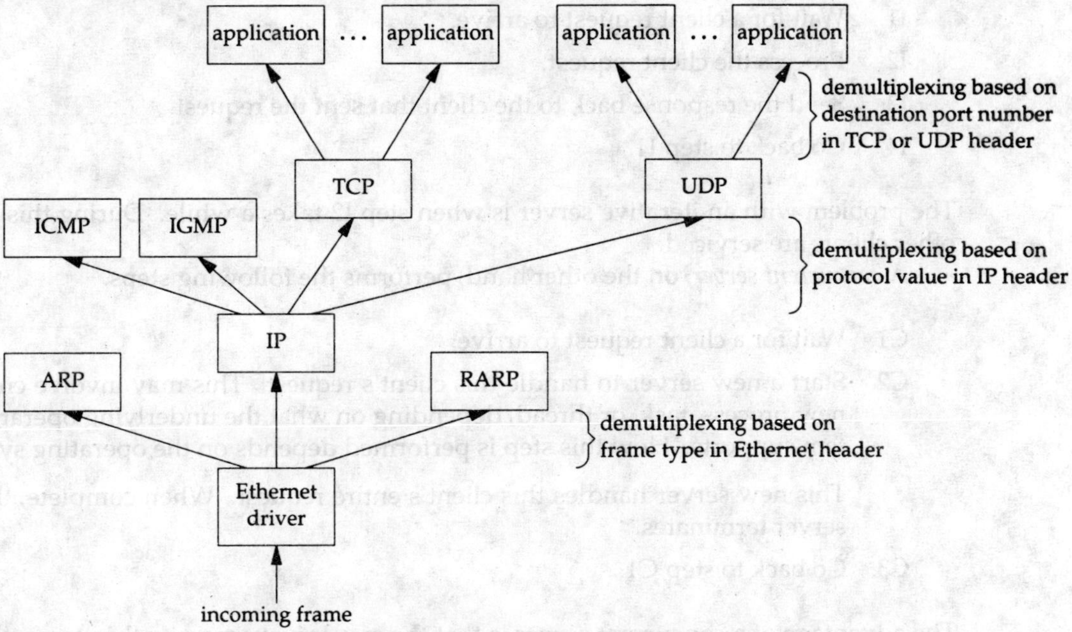

Figure 1.8 The demultiplexing of a received Ethernet frame.

Positioning the protocol boxes labeled "ICMP" and "IGMP" is always a challenge. In Figure 1.4 we showed them at the same layer as IP, because they really are adjuncts to IP. But here we show them above IP, to reiterate that ICMP messages and IGMP messages are encapsulated in IP datagrams.

We have a similar problem with the boxes "ARP" and "RARP." Here we show them above the Ethernet device driver because they both have their own Ethernet frame types, like IP datagrams. But in Figure 2.4 we'll show ARP as part of the Ethernet device driver, beneath IP, because that's where it logically fits.

Realize that these pictures of layered protocol boxes are not perfect.

When we describe TCP in detail we'll see that it really demultiplexes incoming segments using the destination port number, the source IP address, and the source port number.

1.8 Client–Server Model

Most networking applications are written assuming one side is the client and the other the server. The purpose of the application is for the server to provide some defined service for clients.

We can categorize servers into two classes: iterative or concurrent. An *iterative server* iterates through the following steps.

I1. Wait for a client request to arrive.

I2. Process the client request.

I3. Send the response back to the client that sent the request.

I4. Go back to step I1.

The problem with an iterative server is when step I2 takes a while. During this time no other clients are serviced.

A *concurrent server*, on the other hand, performs the following steps.

C1. Wait for a client request to arrive.

C2. Start a new server to handle this client's request. This may involve creating a new process, task, or thread, depending on what the underlying operating system supports. How this step is performed depends on the operating system.

This new server handles this client's entire request. When complete, this new server terminates.

C3. Go back to step C1.

The advantage of a concurrent server is that the server just spawns other servers to handle the client requests. Each client has, in essence, its own server. Assuming the operating system allows multiprogramming, multiple clients are serviced concurrently.

The reason we categorize servers, and not clients, is because a client normally can't tell whether it's talking to an iterative server or a concurrent server.

As a general rule, TCP servers are concurrent, and UDP servers are iterative, but there are a few exceptions. We'll look in detail at the impact of UDP on its servers in Section 11.12, and the impact of TCP on its servers in Section 18.11.

1.9 Port Numbers

We said that TCP and UDP identify applications using 16-bit port numbers. How are these port numbers chosen?

Servers are normally known by their *well-known* port number. For example, every TCP/IP implementation that provides an FTP server provides that service on TCP port

21. Every Telnet server is on TCP port 23. Every implementation of TFTP (the Trivial File Transfer Protocol) is on UDP port 69. Those services that can be provided by any implementation of TCP/IP have well-known port numbers between 1 and 1023. The well-known ports are managed by the *Internet Assigned Numbers Authority* (IANA).

Until 1992 the well-known ports were between 1 and 255. Ports between 256 and 1023 were normally used by Unix systems for Unix-specific services—that is, services found on a Unix system, but probably not found on other operating systems. The IANA now manages the ports between 1 and 1023.

An example of the difference between an Internet-wide service and a Unix-specific service is the difference between Telnet and Rlogin. Both allow us to login across a network to another host. Telnet is a TCP/IP standard with a well-known port number of 23 and can be implemented on almost any operating system. Rlogin, on the other hand, was originally designed for Unix systems (although many non-Unix systems now provide it also) so its well-known port was chosen in the early 1980s as 513.

A client usually doesn't care what port number it uses on its end. All it needs to be certain of is that whatever port number it uses be unique on its host. Client port numbers are called *ephemeral ports* (i.e., short lived). This is because a client typically exists only as long as the user running the client needs its service, while servers typically run as long as the host is up.

Most TCP/IP implementations allocate ephemeral port numbers between 1024 and 5000. The port numbers above 5000 are intended for other servers (those that aren't well known across the Internet). We'll see many examples of how ephemeral ports are allocated in the examples throughout the text.

Solaris 2.2 is a notable exception. By default the ephemeral ports for TCP and UDP start at 32768. Section E.4 details the configuration options that can be modified by the system administrator to change these defaults.

The well-known port numbers are contained in the file `/etc/services` on most Unix systems. To find the port numbers for the Telnet server and the Domain Name System, we can execute

```
sun % grep telnet /etc/services
telnet      23/tcp                       says it uses TCP port 23

sun % grep domain /etc/services
domain      53/udp                       says it uses UDP port 53
domain      53/tcp                       and TCP port 53
```

Reserved Ports

Unix systems have the concept of *reserved ports*. Only a process with superuser privileges can assign itself a reserved port.

These port numbers are in the range of 1 to 1023, and are used by some applications (notably Rlogin, Section 26.2), as part of the authentication between the client and server.

1.10 Standardization Process

Who controls the TCP/IP protocol suite, approves new standards, and the like? There are four groups responsible for Internet technology.

1. The *Internet Society* (ISOC) is a professional society to facilitate, support, and promote the evolution and growth of the Internet as a global research communications infrastructure.
2. The *Internet Architecture Board* (IAB) is the technical oversight and coordination body. It is composed of about 15 international volunteers from various disciplines and serves as the final editorial and technical review board for the quality of Internet standards. The IAB falls under the ISOC.
3. The *Internet Engineering Task Force* (IETF) is the near-term, standards-oriented group, divided into nine areas (applications, routing and addressing, security, etc.). The IETF develops the specifications that become Internet standards. An additional *Internet Engineering Steering Group* (IESG) was formed to help the IETF chair.
4. The *Internet Research Task Force* (IRTF) pursues long-term research projects.

Both the IRTF and the IETF fall under the IAB. [Crocker 1993] provides additional details on the standardization process within the Internet, as well as some of its early history.

1.11 RFCs

All the official standards in the internet community are published as a *Request for Comment*, or *RFC*. Additionally there are lots of RFCs that are not official standards, but are published for informational purposes. The RFCs range in size from 1 page to almost 200 pages. Each is identified by a number, such as RFC 1122, with higher numbers for newer RFCs.

All the RFCs are available at no charge through electronic mail or using FTP across the Internet. Sending electronic mail as shown here:

```
To: rfc-info@ISI.EDU
Subject: getting rfcs

help: ways_to_get_rfcs
```

returns a detailed listing of various ways to obtain the RFCs.

The latest RFC index is always a starting point when looking for something. This index specifies when a certain RFC has been replaced by a newer RFC, and if a newer RFC updates some of the information in that RFC.

There are a few important RFCs.

1. The *Assigned Numbers RFC* specifies all the magic numbers and constants that are used in the Internet protocols. At the time of this writing the latest version

of this RFC is 1340 [Reynolds and Postel 1992]. All the Internet-wide well-known ports are listed here.

When this RFC is updated (it is normally updated at least yearly) the index listing for 1340 will indicate which RFC has replaced it.

2. The *Internet Official Protocol Standards*, currently RFC 1600 [Postel 1994]. This RFC specifies the state of standardization of the various Internet protocols. Each protocol has one of the following states of standardization: standard, draft standard, proposed standard, experimental, informational, or historic. Additionally each protocol has a requirement level: required, recommended, elective, limited use, or not recommended.

   Like the Assigned Numbers RFC, this RFC is also reissued regularly. Be sure you're reading the current copy.

3. The *Host Requirements RFCs*, 1122 and 1123 [Braden 1989a, 1989b]. RFC 1122 handles the link layer, network layer, and transport layer, while RFC 1123 handles the application layer. These two RFCs make numerous corrections and interpretations of the important earlier RFCs, and are often the starting point when looking at any of the finer details of a given protocol. They list the features and implementation details of the protocols as either "must," "should," "may," "should not," or "must not."

   [Borman 1993b] provides a practical look at these two RFCs, and RFC 1127 [Braden 1989c] provides an informal summary of the discussions and conclusions of the working group that developed the Host Requirements RFCs.

4. The *Router Requirements RFC*. The official version of this is RFC 1009 [Braden and Postel 1987], but a new version is nearing completion [Almquist 1993]. This is similar to the host requirements RFCs, but specifies the unique requirements of routers.

1.12 Standard, Simple Services

There are a few standard, simple services that almost every implementation provides. We'll use some of these servers throughout the text, usually with the Telnet client. Figure 1.9 describes these services. We can see from this figure that when the same service is provided using both TCP and UDP, both port numbers are normally chosen to be the same.

If we examine the port numbers for these standard services and other standard TCP/IP services (Telnet, FTP, SMTP, etc.), most are odd numbers. This is historical as these port numbers are derived from the NCP port numbers. (NCP, the Network Control Protocol, preceded TCP as a transport layer protocol for the ARPANET.) NCP was simplex, not full-duplex, so each application required two connections, and an even–odd pair of port numbers was reserved for each application. When TCP and UDP became the standard transport layers, only a single port number was needed per application, so the odd port numbers from NCP were used.

Name	TCP port	UDP port	RFC	Description
echo	7	7	862	Server returns whatever the client sends.
discard	9	9	863	Server discards whatever the client sends.
daytime	13	13	867	Server returns the time and date in a human-readable format.
chargen	19	19	864	TCP server sends a continual stream of characters, until the connection is terminated by the client. UDP server sends a datagram containing a random number of characters each time the client sends a datagram.
time	37	37	868	Server returns the time as a 32-bit binary number. This number represents the number of seconds since midnight January 1, 1900, UTC.

Figure 1.9 Standard, simple services provided by most implementations.

1.13 The Internet

In Figure 1.3 we showed an *internet* composed of two networks—an Ethernet and a token ring. In Sections 1.4 and 1.9 we talked about the worldwide *Internet* and the need to allocate IP addresses centrally (the InterNIC) and the well-known port numbers (the IANA). The word *internet* means different things depending on whether it's capitalized or not.

The lowercase *internet* means multiple networks connected together, using a common protocol suite. The uppercase *Internet* refers to the collection of hosts (over one million) around the world that can communicate with each other using TCP/IP. While the Internet is an internet, the reverse is not true.

1.14 Implementations

The de facto standard for TCP/IP implementations is the one from the Computer Systems Research Group at the University of California at Berkeley. Historically this has been distributed with the 4.x BSD system (Berkeley Software Distribution), and with the "BSD Networking Releases." This source code has been the starting point for many other implementations.

Figure 1.10 shows a chronology of the various BSD releases, indicating the important TCP/IP features. The BSD Networking Releases shown on the left side are publicly available source code releases containing all of the networking code: both the protocols themselves and many of the applications and utilities (such as Telnet and FTP).

Throughout the text we'll use the term *Berkeley-derived implementation* to refer to vendor implementations such as SunOS 4.x, SVR4, and AIX 3.2 that were originally developed from the Berkeley sources. These implementations have much in common, often including the same bugs!

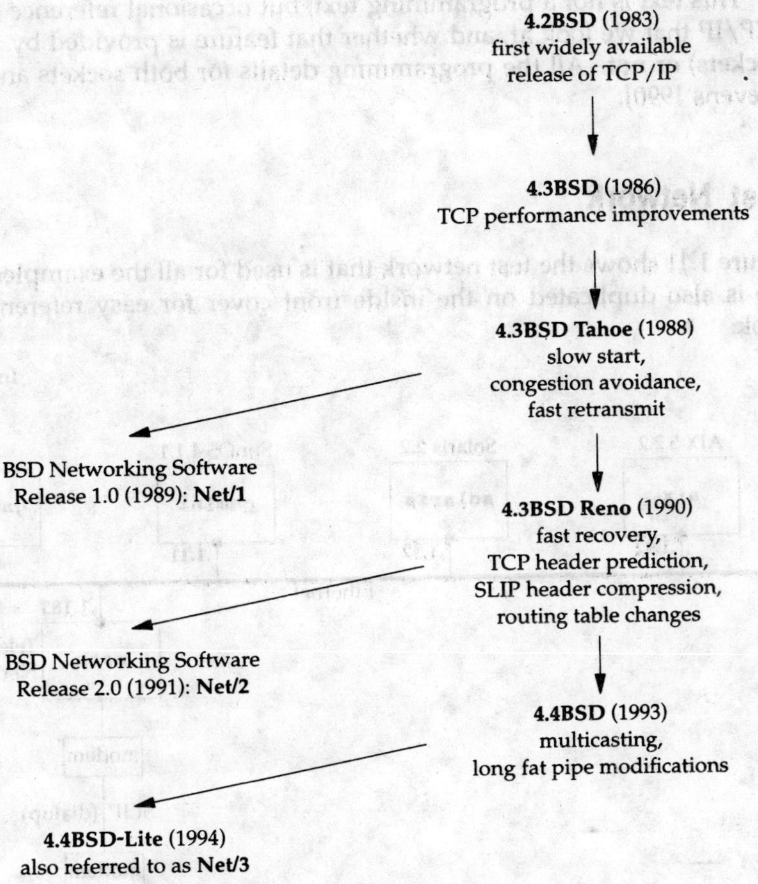

Figure 1.10 Various BSD releases with important TCP/IP features.

Much of the original research in the Internet is still being applied to the Berkeley system—new congestion control algorithms (Section 21.7), multicasting (Section 12.4), "long fat pipe" modifications (Section 24.3), and the like.

1.15 Application Programming Interfaces

Two popular *application programming interfaces* (APIs) for applications using the TCP/IP protocols are called *sockets* and *TLI* (Transport Layer Interface). The former is sometimes called "Berkeley sockets," indicating where it was originally developed. The latter, originally developed by AT&T, is sometimes called *XTI* (X/Open Transport Interface), recognizing the work done by X/Open, an international group of computer vendors that produce their own set of standards. XTI is effectively a superset of TLI.

This text is not a programming text, but occasional reference is made to features of TCP/IP that we look at, and whether that feature is provided by the most popular API (sockets) or not. All the programming details for both sockets and TLI are available in [Stevens 1990].

1.16 Test Network

Figure 1.11 shows the test network that is used for all the examples in the text. This figure is also duplicated on the inside front cover for easy reference while reading the book.

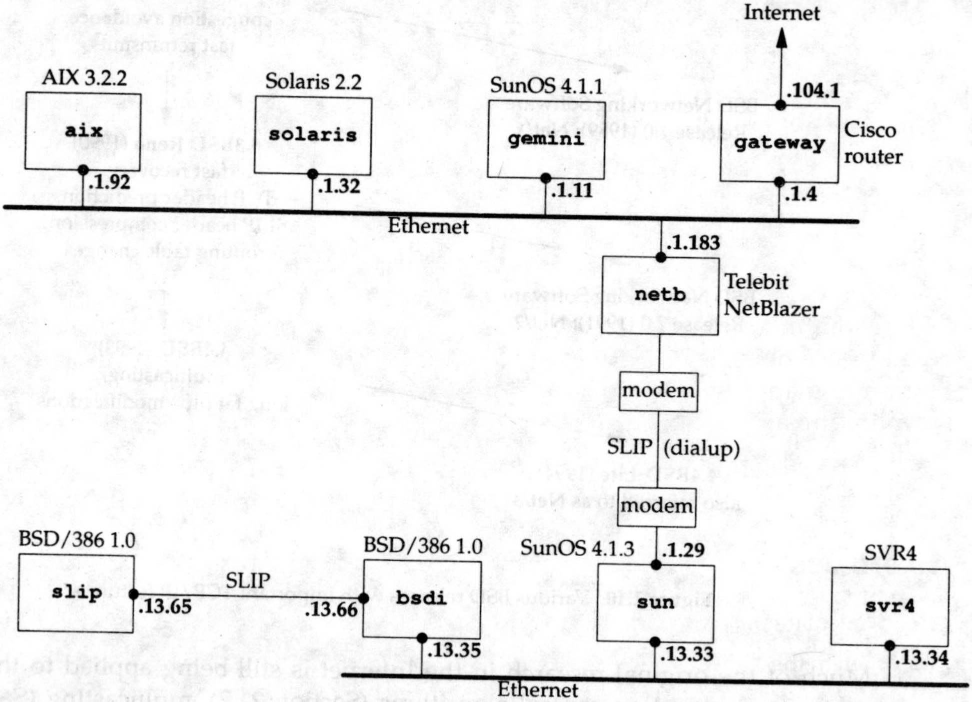

Figure 1.11 Test network used for all the examples in the text. All IP addresses begin with 140.252.

Most of the examples are run on the lower four systems in this figure (the author's subnet). All the IP addresses in this figure belong to the class B network ID 140.252. All the hostnames belong to the `.tuc.noao.edu` domain. (`noao` stands for "National Optical Astronomy Observatories" and `tuc` stands for Tucson.) For example, the lower right system has a complete hostname of `svr4.tuc.noao.edu` and an IP address of 140.252.13.34. The notation at the top of each box is the operating system running on that system. This collection of systems and networks provides hosts and routers running a variety of TCP/IP implementations.

It should be noted that there are many more networks and hosts in the noao.edu domain than we show in Figure 1.11. All we show here are the systems that we'll encounter throughout the text.

In Section 3.4 we describe the form of subnetting used on this network, and in Section 4.6 we'll provide more details on the dialup SLIP connection between sun and netb. Section 2.4 describes SLIP in detail.

1.17 Summary

This chapter has been a whirlwind tour of the TCP/IP protocol suite, introducing many of the terms and protocols that we discuss in detail in later chapters.

The four layers in the TCP/IP protocol suite are the link layer, network layer, transport layer, and application layer, and we mentioned the different responsibilities of each. In TCP/IP the distinction between the network layer and the transport layer is critical: the network layer (IP) provides a hop-by-hop service while the transport layers (TCP and UDP) provide an end-to-end service.

An internet is a collection of networks. The common building block for an internet is a router that connects the networks at the IP layer. The capital-I Internet is an internet that spans the globe and consists of more than 10,000 networks and more than one million computers.

On an internet each interface is identified by a unique IP address, although users tend to use hostnames instead of IP addresses. The Domain Name System provides a dynamic mapping between hostnames and IP addresses. Port numbers are used to identify the applications communicating with each other and we said that servers use well-known ports while clients use ephemeral ports.

Exercises

1.1 Calculate the maximum number of class A, B, and C network IDs.

1.2 Fetch the file nsfnet/statistics/history.netcount using anonymous FTP (Section 27.3) from the host nic.merit.edu. This file contains the number of domestic and foreign networks announced to the NSFNET infrastructure. Plot these values with the year on the x-axis and a logarithmic y-axis with the total number of networks. The maximum value for the y-axis should be the value calculated in the previous exercise. If the data shows a visual trend, extrapolate the values to estimate when the current addressing scheme will run out of network IDs. (Section 3.10 talks about proposals to correct this problem.)

1.3 Obtain a copy of the Host Requirements RFC [Braden 1989a] and look up the *robustness principle* that applies to every layer of the TCP/IP protocol suite. What is the reference for this principle?

1.4 Obtain a copy of the latest Assigned Numbers RFC. What is the well-known port for the "quote of the day" protocol? Which RFC defines the protocol?

1.5 If you have an account on a host that is connected to a TCP/IP internet, what is its primary IP address? Is the host connected to the worldwide Internet? Is it multihomed?

1.6 Obtain a copy of RFC 1000 to learn where the term RFC originated.

1.7 Contact the Internet Society, `isoc@isoc.org` or +1 703 648 9888, to find out about joining.

1.8 Fetch the file `about-internic/information-about-the-internic` using anonymous FTP from the host `is.internic.net`.

2

Link Layer

2.1 Introduction

From Figure 1.4 (p. 6) we see that the purpose of the link layer in the TCP/IP protocol suite is to send and receive (1) IP datagrams for the IP module, (2) ARP requests and replies for the ARP module, and (3) RARP requests and replies for the RARP module. TCP/IP supports many different link layers, depending on the type of networking hardware being used: Ethernet, token ring, FDDI (Fiber Distributed Data Interface), RS-232 serial lines, and the like.

In this chapter we'll look at some of the details involved in the Ethernet link layer, two specialized link layers for serial interfaces (SLIP and PPP), and the loopback driver that's part of most implementations. Ethernet and SLIP are the link layers used for most of the examples in the book. We also talk about the MTU (Maximum Transmission Unit), a characteristic of the link layer that we encounter numerous times in the remaining chapters. We also show some calculations of how to choose the MTU for a serial line.

2.2 Ethernet and IEEE 802 Encapsulation

The term *Ethernet* generally refers to a standard published in 1982 by Digital Equipment Corp., Intel Corp., and Xerox Corp. It is the predominant form of local area network technology used with TCP/IP today. It uses an access method called CSMA/CD, which stands for Carrier Sense, Multiple Access with Collision Detection. It operates at 10 Mbits/sec and uses 48-bit addresses.

A few years later the IEEE (Institute of Electrical and Electronics Engineers) 802 Committee published a sightly different set of standards. 802.3 covers an entire set of

CSMA/CD networks, 802.4 covers token bus networks, and 802.5 covers token ring networks. Common to all three of these is the 802.2 standard that defines the logical link control (LLC) common to many of the 802 networks. Unfortunately the combination of 802.2 and 802.3 defines a different frame format from true Ethernet. ([Stallings 1987] covers all the details of these IEEE 802 standards.)

In the TCP/IP world, the encapsulation of IP datagrams is defined in RFC 894 [Hornig 1984] for Ethernets and in RFC 1042 [Postel and Reynolds 1988] for IEEE 802 networks. The Host Requirements RFC requires that every Internet host connected to a 10 Mbits/sec Ethernet cable:

1. Must be able to send and receive packets using RFC 894 (Ethernet) encapsulation.
2. Should be able to receive RFC 1042 (IEEE 802) packets intermixed with RFC 894 packets.
3. May be able to send packets using RFC 1042 encapsulation. If the host can send both types of packets, the type of packet sent must be configurable and the configuration option must default to RFC 894 packets.

RFC 894 encapsulation is most commonly used. Figure 2.1 shows the two different forms of encapsulation. The number below each box in the figure is the size of that box in bytes.

Both frame formats use 48-bit (6-byte) destination and source addresses. (802.3 allows 16-bit addresses to be used, but 48-bit addresses are normal.) These are what we call *hardware addresses* throughout the text. The ARP and RARP protocols (Chapters 4 and 5) map between the 32-bit IP addresses and the 48-bit hardware addresses.

The next 2 bytes are different in the two frame formats. The 802 *length* field says how many bytes follow, up to but not including the *CRC* at the end. The Ethernet *type* field identifies the type of data that follows. In the 802 frame the same *type* field occurs later in the SNAP (Sub-network Access Protocol) header. Fortunately none of the valid 802 *length* values is the same as the Ethernet *type* values, making the two frame formats distinguishable.

In the Ethernet frame the data immediately follows the *type* field, while in the 802 frame format 3 bytes of 802.2 LLC and 5 bytes of 802.2 SNAP follow. The *DSAP* (Destination Service Access Point) and *SSAP* (Source Service Access Point) are both set to `0xaa`. The *ctrl* field is set to 3. The next 3 bytes, the *org code* are all 0. Following this is the same 2-byte *type* field that we had with the Ethernet frame format. (Additional type field values are given in RFC 1340 [Reynolds and Postel 1992].)

The *CRC* field is a cyclic redundancy check (a checksum) that detects errors in the rest of the frame. (This is also called the *FCS* or frame check sequence.)

There is a minimum size for 802.3 and Ethernet frames. This minimum requires that the data portion be at least 38 bytes for 802.3 or 46 bytes for Ethernet. To handle this, pad bytes are inserted to assure that the frame is long enough. We'll encounter this minimum when we start watching packets on the wire.

In this text we'll display the Ethernet encapsulation when we need to, because this is the most commonly used form of encapsulation.

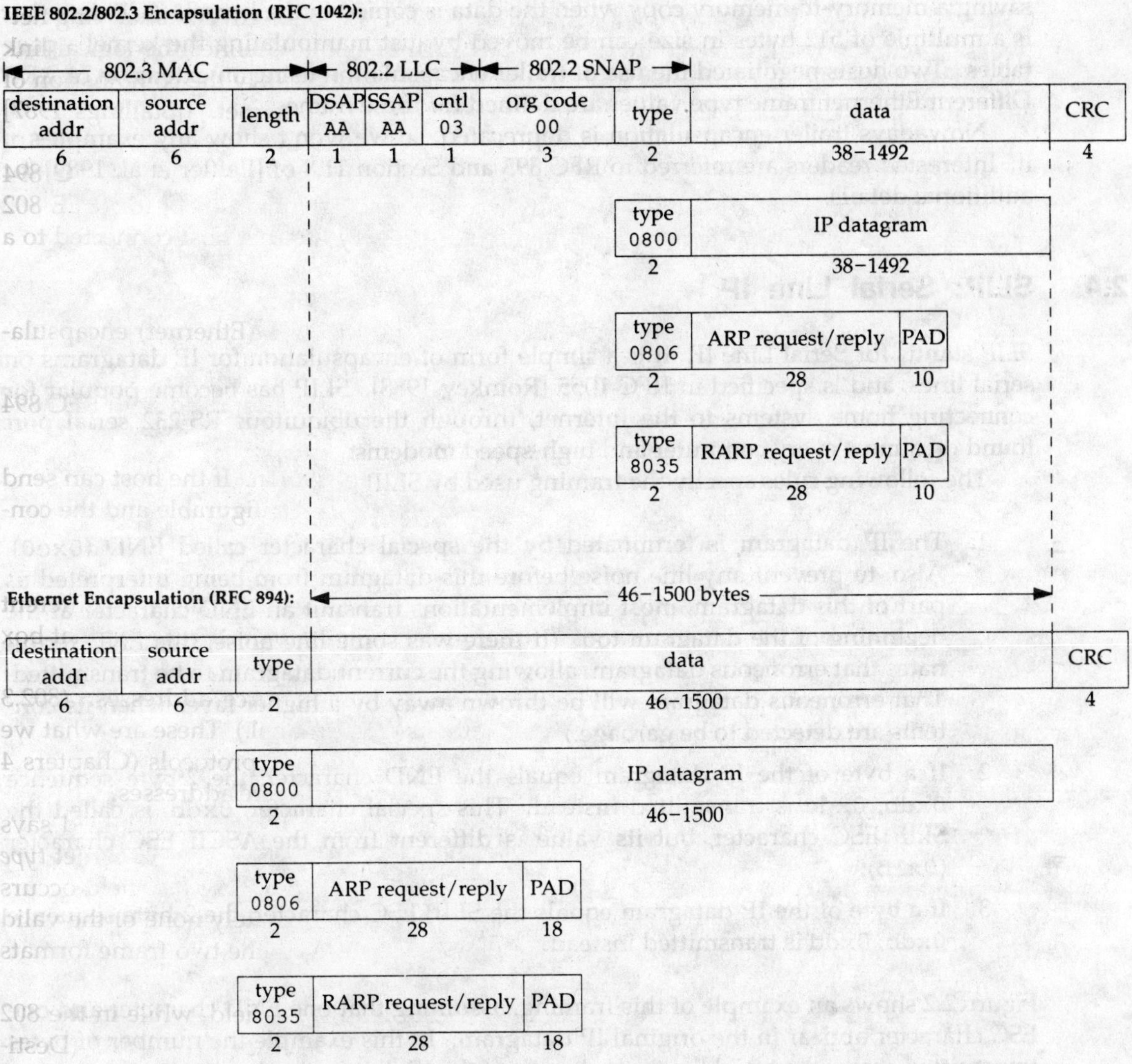

Figure 2.1 IEEE 802.2/802.3 encapsulation (RFC 1042) and Ethernet encapsulation (RFC 894).

2.3 Trailer Encapsulation

RFC 893 [Leffler and Karels 1984] describes another form of encapsulation used on Ethernets, called *trailer encapsulation*. It was an experiment with early BSD systems on DEC VAXes that improved performance by rearranging the order of the fields in the IP datagram. The variable-length fields at the beginning of the data portion of the Ethernet frame (the IP header and the TCP header) were moved to the end (right before the CRC). This allows the data portion of the frame to be mapped to a hardware page, saving a memory-to-memory copy when the data is copied in the kernel. TCP data that is a multiple of 512 bytes in size can be moved by just manipulating the kernel's page tables. Two hosts negotiated the use of trailer encapsulation using an extension of ARP. Different Ethernet frame type values are defined for these frames.

Nowadays trailer encapsulation is deprecated, so we won't show any examples of it. Interested readers are referred to RFC 893 and Section 11.8 of [Leffler et al. 1989] for additional details.

2.4 SLIP: Serial Line IP

SLIP stands for Serial Line IP. It is a simple form of encapsulation for IP datagrams on serial lines, and is specified in RFC 1055 [Romkey 1988]. SLIP has become popular for connecting home systems to the Internet, through the ubiquitous RS-232 serial port found on almost every computer and high-speed modems.

The following rules specify the framing used by SLIP.

1. The IP datagram is terminated by the special character called END (`0xc0`). Also, to prevent any line noise before this datagram from being interpreted as part of this datagram, most implementations transmit an END character at the beginning of the datagram too. (If there was some line noise, this END terminates that erroneous datagram, allowing the current datagram to be transmitted. That erroneous datagram will be thrown away by a higher layer when its contents are detected to be garbage.)
2. If a byte of the IP datagram equals the END character, the 2-byte sequence `0xdb`, `0xdc` is transmitted instead. This special character, `0xdb`, is called the SLIP ESC character, but its value is different from the ASCII ESC character (`0x1b`).
3. If a byte of the IP datagram equals the SLIP ESC character, the 2-byte sequence `0xdb`, `0xdd` is transmitted instead.

Figure 2.2 shows an example of this framing, assuming that one END character and one ESC character appear in the original IP datagram. In this example the number of bytes transmitted across the serial line is the length of the IP datagram plus 4.

SLIP is a simple framing method. It has some deficiencies that are worth noting.

1. Each end must know the other's IP address. There is no method for one end to inform the other of its IP address.
2. There is no type field (similar to the frame type field in Ethernet frames). If a serial line is used for SLIP, it can't be used for some other protocol at the same time.
3. There is no checksum added by SLIP (similar to the CRC field in Ethernet frames). If a noisy phone line corrupts a datagram being transferred by SLIP, it s up to the higher layers to detect this. (Alternately, newer modems can detect

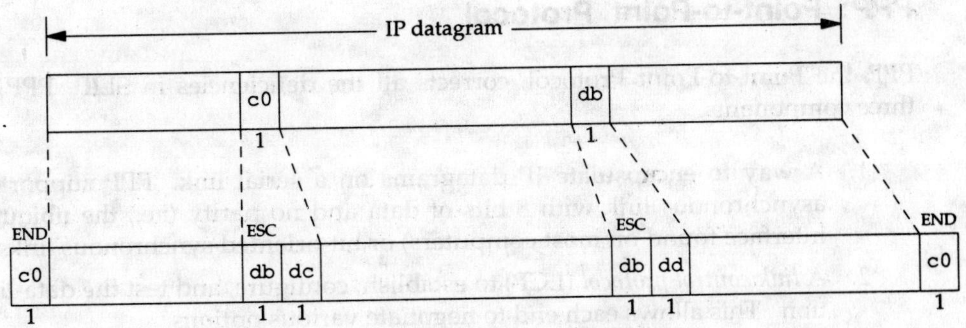

Figure 2.2 SLIP encapsulation.

and correct corrupted frames.) This makes it essential that the upper layers provide some form of CRC. In Chapters 3 and 17 we'll see that there is always a checksum for the IP header, and for the TCP header and the TCP data. But in Chapter 11 we'll see that the checksum that covers the UDP header and UDP data is optional.

Despite these shortcomings, SLIP is a popular protocol that is widely used.

The history of SLIP dates back to 1984 when Rick Adams implemented it in 4.2BSD. Despite its self-description as a nonstandard, it is becoming more popular as the speed and reliability of modems increase. Publicly available implementations abound, and many vendors support it today.

2.5 Compressed SLIP

Since SLIP lines are often slow (19200 bits/sec or below) and frequently used for interactive traffic (such as Telnet and Rlogin, both of which use TCP), there tend to be many small TCP packets exchanged across a SLIP line. To carry 1 byte of data requires a 20-byte IP header and a 20-byte TCP header, an overhead of 40 bytes. (Section 19.2 shows the flow of these small packets when a simple command is typed during an Rlogin session.)

Recognizing this performance drawback, a newer version of SLIP, called CSLIP (for compressed SLIP), is specified in RFC 1144 [Jacobson 1990a]. CSLIP normally reduces the 40-byte header to 3 or 5 bytes. It maintains the state of up to 16 TCP connections on each end of the CSLIP link and knows that some of the fields in the two headers for a given connection normally don't change. Of the fields that do change, most change by a small positive amount. These smaller headers greatly improve the interactive response time.

Most SLIP implementations today support CSLIP. Both SLIP links on the author's subnet (see inside front cover) are CSLIP links.

2.6 PPP: Point-to-Point Protocol

PPP, the Point-to-Point Protocol, corrects all the deficiencies in SLIP. PPP consists of three components.

1. A way to encapsulate IP datagrams on a serial link. PPP supports either an asynchronous link with 8 bits of data and no parity (i.e., the ubiquitous serial interface found on most computers) or bit-oriented synchronous links.
2. A *link control protocol* (LCP) to establish, configure, and test the data-link connection. This allows each end to negotiate various options.
3. A family of *network control protocols* (NCPs) specific to different network layer protocols. RFCs currently exist for IP, the OSI network layer, DECnet, and AppleTalk. The IP NCP, for example, allows each end to specify if it can perform header compression, similar to CSLIP. (The acronym NCP was also used for the predecessor to TCP.)

RFC 1548 [Simpson 1993] specifies the encapsulation method and the link control protocol. RFC 1332 [McGregor 1992] specifies the network control protocol for IP.

The format of the PPP frames was chosen to look like the ISO HDLC standard (high-level data link control). Figure 2.3 shows the format of PPP frames.

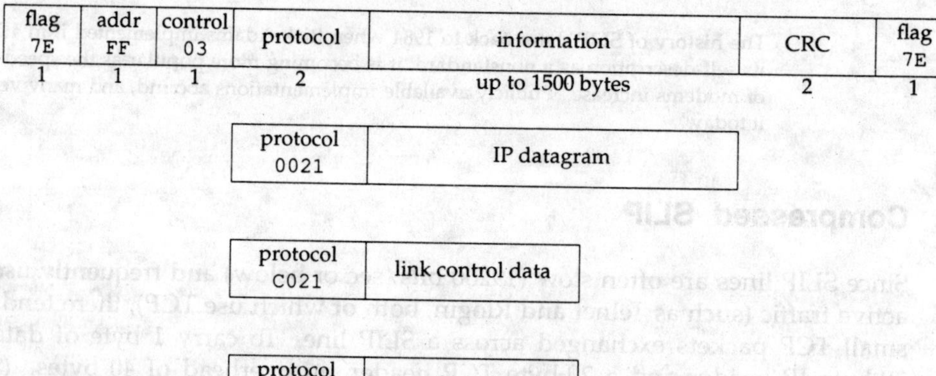

Figure 2.3 Format of PPP frames.

Each frame begins and ends with a *flag* byte whose value is `0x7e`. This is followed by an *address* byte whose value is always `0xff`, and then a *control* byte, with a value of `0x03`.

Next comes the *protocol* field, similar in function to the Ethernet *type* field. A value of `0x0021` means the *information* field is an IP datagram, a value of `0xc021` means the *information* field is link control data, and a value of `0x8021` is for network control data.

The *CRC* field (or FCS, for frame check sequence) is a cyclic redundancy check, to detect errors in the frame.

Since the byte value `0x7e` is the *flag* character, PPP needs to escape this byte when it appears in the *information* field. On a synchronous link this is done by the hardware using a technique called *bit stuffing* [Tanenbaum 1989]. On asynchronous links the special byte `0x7d` is used as an escape character. Whenever this escape character appears in a PPP frame, the next character in the frame has had its sixth bit complemented, as follows:

1. The byte `0x7e` is transmitted as the 2-byte sequence `0x7d, 0x5e`. This is the escape of the *flag* byte.
2. The byte `0x7d` is transmitted as the 2-byte sequence `0x7d, 0x5d`. This is the escape of the escape byte.
3. By default, a byte with a value less than `0x20` (i.e., an ASCII control character) is also escaped. For example, the byte `0x01` is transmitted as the 2-byte sequence `0x7d, 0x21`. (In this case the complement of the sixth bit turns the bit on, whereas in the two previous examples the complement turned the bit off.)

   The reason for doing this is to prevent these bytes from appearing as ASCII control characters to the serial driver on either host, or to the modems, which sometimes interpret these control characters specially. It is also possible to use the link control protocol to specify which, if any, of these 32 values must be escaped. By default, all 32 are escaped.

Since PPP, like SLIP, is often used across slow serial links, reducing the number of bytes per frame reduces the latency for interactive applications. Using the link control protocol, most implementations negotiate to omit the constant *address* and *control* fields and to reduce the size of the *protocol* field from 2 bytes to 1 byte. If we then compare the framing overhead in a PPP frame, versus the 2-byte framing overhead in a SLIP frame (Figure 2.2), we see that PPP adds three additional bytes: 1 byte for the *protocol* field, and 2 bytes for the *CRC*. Additionally, using the IP network control protocol, most implementations then negotiate to use Van Jacobson header compression (identical to CSLIP compression) to reduce the size of the IP and TCP headers.

In summary, PPP provides the following advantages over SLIP: (1) support for multiple protocols on a single serial line, not just IP datagrams, (2) a cyclic redundancy check on every frame, (3) dynamic negotiation of the IP address for each end (using the IP network control protocol), (4) TCP and IP header compression similar to CSLIP, and (5) a link control protocol for negotiating many data-link options. The price we pay for all these features is 3 bytes of additional overhead per frame, a few frames of negotiation when the link is established, and a more complex implementation.

Despite all the added benefits of PPP over SLIP, today there are more SLIP users than PPP users. As implementations become more widely available, and as vendors start to support PPP, it should (eventually) replace SLIP.

2.7 Loopback Interface

Most implementations support a *loopback interface* that allows a client and server on the same host to communicate with each other using TCP/IP. The class A network ID 127 is reserved for the loopback interface. By convention, most systems assign the IP address of 127.0.0.1 to this interface and assign it the name `localhost`. An IP datagram sent to the loopback interface must not appear on any network.

Although we could imagine the transport layer detecting that the other end is the loopback address, and short circuiting some of the transport layer logic and all of the network layer logic, most implementations perform complete processing of the data in the transport layer and network layer, and only loop the IP datagram back to itself when the datagram leaves the bottom of the network layer.

Figure 2.4 shows a simplified diagram of how the loopback interface processes IP datagrams.

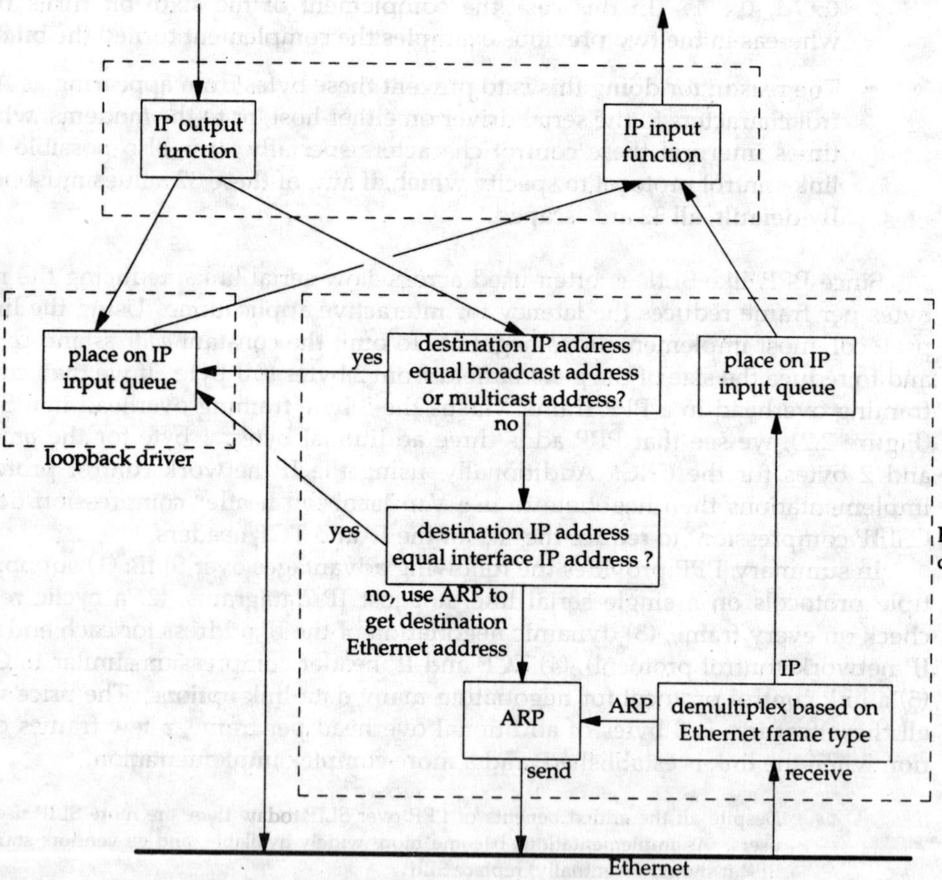

Figure 2.4 Processing of IP datagrams by loopback interface.

The key points to note in this figure are as follows:

1. Everything sent to the loopback address (normally 127.0.0.1) appears as IP input.
2. Datagrams sent to a broadcast address or a multicast address are copied to the loopback interface and sent out on the Ethernet. This is because the definition of broadcasting and multicasting (Chapter 12) includes the sending host.
3. Anything sent to one of the host's own IP addresses is sent to the loopback interface.

While it may seem inefficient to perform all the transport layer and IP layer processing of the loopback data, it simplifies the design because the loopback interface appears as just another link layer to the network layer. The network layer passes a datagram to the loopback interface like any other link layer, and it happens that the loopback interface then puts the datagram back onto IP's input queue.

Another implication of Figure 2.4 is that IP datagrams sent to the one of the host's own IP addresses normally do not appear on the corresponding network. For example, on an Ethernet, normally the packet is not transmitted and then read back. Comments in some of the BSD Ethernet device drivers indicate that many Ethernet interface cards are not capable of reading their own transmissions. Since a host must process IP datagrams that it sends to itself, handling these packets as shown in Figure 2.4 is the simplest way to accomplish this.

The 4.4BSD implementation defines the variable `useloopback` and initializes it to 1. If this variable is set to 0, however the Ethernet driver sends local packets onto the network instead of sending them to the loopback driver. This may or may not work, depending on your Ethernet interface card and device driver.

2.8 MTU

As we can see from Figure 2.1, there is a limit on the size of the frame for both Ethernet encapsulation and 802.3 encapsulation. This limits the number of bytes of data to 1500 and 1492, respectively. This characteristic of the link layer is called the *MTU*, its maximum transmission unit. Most types of networks have an upper limit.

If IP has a datagram to send, and the datagram is larger than the link layer's MTU, IP performs *fragmentation*, breaking the datagram up into smaller pieces (fragments), so that each fragment is smaller than the MTU. We discuss IP fragmentation in Section 11.5.

Figure 2.5 lists some typical MTU values, taken from RFC 1191 [Mogul and Deering 1990]. The listed MTU for a point-to-point link (e.g., SLIP or PPP) is not a physical characteristic of the network media. Instead it is a logical limit to provide adequate response time for interactive use. In the Section 2.10 we'll see where this limit comes from.

In Section 3.9 we'll use the `netstat` command to print the MTU of an interface.

Network	MTU (bytes)
Hyperchannel	65535
16 Mbits/sec token ring (IBM)	17914
4 Mbits/sec token ring (IEEE 802.5)	4464
FDDI	4352
Ethernet	1500
IEEE 802.3/802.2	1492
X.25	576
Point-to-point (low delay)	296

Figure 2.5 Typical maximum transmission units (MTUs).

2.9 Path MTU

When two hosts on the same network are communicating with each other, it is the MTU of the network that is important. But when two hosts are communicating across multiple networks, each link can have a different MTU. The important numbers are not the MTUs of the two networks to which the two hosts connect, but rather the smallest MTU of any data link that packets traverse between the two hosts. This is called the *path MTU.*

The path MTU between any two hosts need not be constant. It depends on the route being used at any time. Also, routing need not be symmetric (the route from A to B may not be the reverse of the route from B to A), hence the path MTU need not be the same in the two directions.

RFC 1191 [Mogul and Deering 1990] specifies the "path MTU discovery mechanism," a way to determine the path MTU at any time. We'll see how this mechanism operates after we've described ICMP and IP fragmentation. In Section 11.6 we'll examine the ICMP unreachable error that is used with this discovery mechanism and in Section 11.7 we'll show a version of the `traceroute` program that uses this mechanism to determine the path MTU to a destination. Sections 11.8 and 24.2 show how UDP and TCP operate when the implementation supports path MTU discovery.

2.10 Serial Line Throughput Calculations

If the line speed is 9600 bits/sec, with 8 bits per byte, plus 1 start bit and 1 stop bit, the line speed is 960 bytes/sec. Transferring a 1024-byte packet at this speed takes 1066 ms. If we're using the SLIP link for an interactive application, along with an application such as FTP that sends or receives 1024-byte packets, we have to wait, on the average, half of this time (533 ms) to send our interactive packet.

This assumes that our interactive packet will be sent across the link before any further "big" packets. Most SLIP implementations do provide this type-of-service queueing, placing interactive traffic ahead of bulk data traffic. The interactive traffic is normally Telnet, Rlogin, and the control portion (the user commands, not the data) of FTP.

This type of service queueing is imperfect. It cannot affect noninteractive traffic that is already queued downstream (e.g., at the serial driver). Also newer modems have large buffers so non-interactive traffic may already be buffered in the modem.

Waiting 533 ms is unacceptable for interactive response. Human factors studies have found that an interactive response time longer than 100–200 ms is perceived as bad [Jacobson 1990a]. This is the round-trip time for an interactive packet to be sent and something to be returned (normally a character echo).

Reducing the MTU of the SLIP link to 256 means the maximum amount of time the link can be busy with a single frame is 266 ms, and half of this (our average wait) is 133 ms. This is better, but still not perfect. The reason we choose this value (as compared to 64 or 128) is to provide good utilization of the line for bulk data transfers (such as large file transfers). Assuming a 5-byte CSLIP header, 256 bytes of data in a 261-byte frame gives 98.1% of the line to data and 1.9% to headers, which is good utilization. Reducing the MTU below 256 reduces the maximum throughput that we can achieve for bulk data transfers.

The MTU value listed in Figure 2.5, 296 for a point-to-point link, assumes 256 bytes of data and the 40-byte TCP and IP headers. Since the MTU is a value that IP queries the link layer for, the value must include the normal TCP and IP headers. This is how IP makes its fragmentation decision. IP knows nothing about the header compression that CSLIP performs.

Our average wait calculation (one-half the time required to transfer a maximum sized frame) only applies when a SLIP link (or PPP link) is used for both interactive traffic and bulk data transfer. When only interactive traffic is being exchanged, 1 byte of data in each direction (assuming 5-byte compressed headers) takes around 12.5 ms for the round trip at 9600 bits/sec. This is well within the 100–200 ms range mentioned earlier. Also notice that compressing the headers from 40 bytes to 5 bytes reduces the round-trip time for the 1 byte of data from 85 to 12.5 ms.

Unfortunately these types of calculations are harder to make when newer error correcting, compressing modems are being used. The compression employed by these modems reduces the number of bytes sent across the wire, but the error correction may increase the amount of time to transfer these bytes. Nevertheless, these calculations give us a starting point to make reasonable decisions.

In later chapters we'll use these serial line calculations to verify some of the timings that we see when watching packets go across a serial link.

2.11 Summary

This chapter has examined the lowest layer in the Internet protocol suite, the link layer. We looked at the difference between Ethernet and IEEE 802.2/802.3 encapsulation, and the encapsulation used by SLIP and PPP. Since both SLIP and PPP are often used on slow links, both provide a way to compress the common fields that don't often change. This provides better interactive response.

The loopback interface is provided by most implementations. Access to this interface is either through the special loopback address, normally 127.0.0.1, or by sending IP datagrams to one of the host's own IP addresses. Loopback data has been completely processed by the transport layer and by IP when it loops around to go up the protocol stack.

We described an important feature of many link layers, the MTU, and the related concept of a path MTU. Using the typical MTUs for serial lines, we calculated the latency involved in SLIP and CSLIP links.

This chapter has covered only a few of the common data-link technologies used with TCP/IP today. One reason for the success of TCP/IP is its ability to work on top of almost any data-link technology.

Exercises

2.1 If your system supports the `netstat(1)` command (see Section 3.9 also), use it to determine the interfaces on your system and their MTUs.

3

IP: Internet Protocol

3.1 Introduction

IP is the workhorse protocol of the TCP/IP protocol suite. All TCP, UDP, ICMP, and IGMP data gets transmitted as IP datagrams (Figure 1.4). A fact that amazes many newcomers to TCP/IP, especially those from an X.25 or SNA background, is that IP provides an unreliable, connectionless datagram delivery service.

By *unreliable* we mean there are no guarantees that an IP datagram successfully gets to its destination. IP provides a best effort service. When something goes wrong, such as a router temporarily running out of buffers, IP has a simple error handling algorithm: throw away the datagram and try to send an ICMP message back to the source. Any required reliability must be provided by the upper layers (e.g., TCP).

The term *connectionless* means that IP does not maintain any state information about successive datagrams. Each datagram is handled independently from all other datagrams. This also means that IP datagrams can get delivered out of order. If a source sends two consecutive datagrams (first A, then B) to the same destination, each is routed independently and can take different routes, with B arriving before A.

In this chapter we take a brief look at the fields in the IP header, describe IP routing, and cover subnetting. We also look at two useful commands: `ifconfig` and `netstat`. We leave a detailed discussion of some of the fields in the IP header for later when we can see exactly how the fields are used. RFC 791 [Postel 1981a] is the official specification of IP.

3.2 IP Header

Figure 3.1 shows the format of an IP datagram. The normal size of the IP header is 20 bytes, unless options are present.

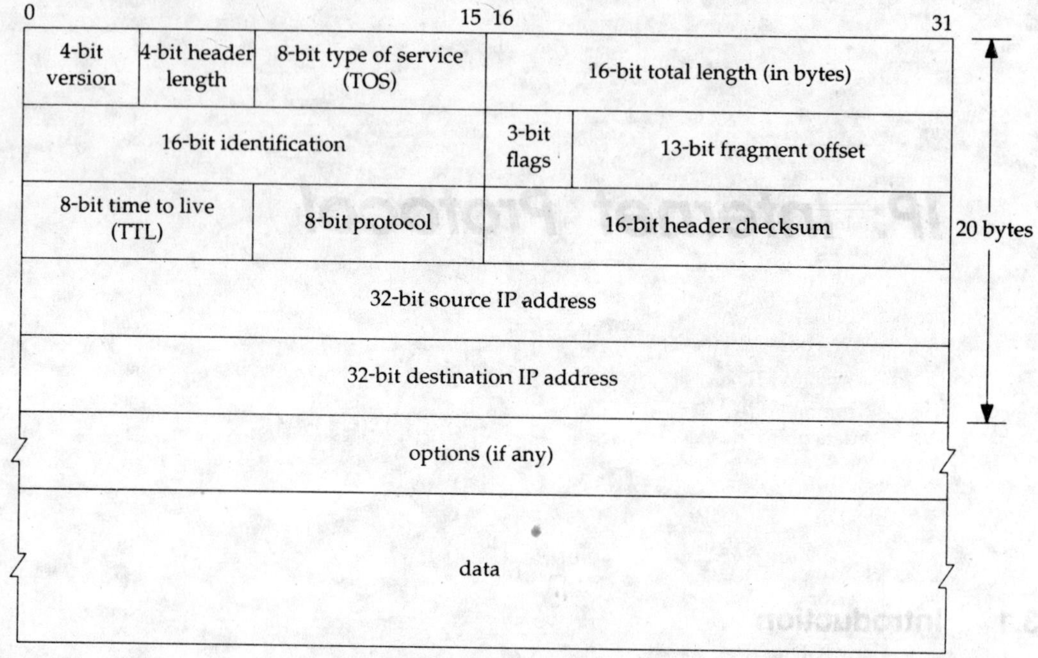

Figure 3.1 IP datagram, showing the fields in the IP header.

We will show the pictures of protocol headers in TCP/IP as in Figure 3.1. The most significant bit is numbered 0 at the left, and the least significant bit of a 32-bit value is numbered 31 on the right.

The 4 bytes in the 32-bit value are transmitted in the order: bits 0–7 first, then bits 8–15, then 16–23, and bits 24–31 last. This is called *big endian* byte ordering, which is the byte ordering required for all binary integers in the TCP/IP headers as they traverse a network. This is called the *network byte order*. Machines that store binary integers in other formats, such as the *little endian* format, must convert the header values into the network byte order before transmitting the data.

The current protocol *version* is 4, so IP is sometimes called IPv4. Section 3.10 discusses some proposals for a new version of IP.

The *header length* is the number of 32-bit words in the header, including any options. Since this is a 4-bit field, it limits the header to 60 bytes. In Chapter 8 we'll see that this limitation makes some of the options, such as the record route option, useless today. The normal value of this field (when no options are present) is 5.

The *type-of-service* field (TOS) is composed of a 3-bit precedence field (which is ignored today), 4 TOS bits, and an unused bit that must be 0. The 4 TOS bits are: minimize delay, maximize throughput, maximize reliability, and minimize monetary cost.

Only 1 of these 4 bits can be turned on. If all 4 bits are 0 it implies normal service. RFC 1340 [Reynolds and Postel 1992] specifies how these bits should be set by all the standard applications. RFC 1349 [Almquist 1992] contains some corrections to this RFC, and a more detailed description of the TOS feature.

Figure 3.2 shows the recommended values of the TOS field for various applications. In the final column we show the hexadecimal value, since that's what we'll see in the `tcpdump` output later in the text.

Application	Minimize delay	Maximize throughput	Maximize reliability	Minimize monetary cost	Hex value
Telnet/Rlogin	1	0	0	0	0x10
FTP					
control	1	0	0	0	0x10
data	0	1	0	0	0x08
any bulk data	0	1	0	0	0x08
TFTP	1	0	0	0	0x10
SMTP					
command phase	1	0	0	0	0x10
data phase	0	1	0	0	0x08
DNS					
UDP query	1	0	0	0	0x10
TCP query	0	0	0	0	0x00
zone transfer	0	1	0	0	0x08
ICMP					
error	0	0	0	0	0x00
query	0	0	0	0	0x00
any IGP	0	0	1	0	0x04
SNMP	0	0	1	0	0x04
BOOTP	0	0	0	0	0x00
NNTP	0	0	0	1	0x02

Figure 3.2 Recommended values for type-of-service field.

The interactive login applications, Telnet and Rlogin, want a minimum delay since they're used interactively by a human for small amounts of data transfer. File transfer by FTP, on the other hand, wants maximum throughput. Maximum reliability is specified for network management (SNMP) and the routing protocols. Usenet news (NNTP) is the only one shown that wants to minimize monetary cost.

The TOS feature is not supported by most TCP/IP implementations today, though newer systems starting with 4.3BSD Reno are setting it. Additionally, new routing protocols such as OSPF and IS–IS are capable of making routing decisions based on this field.

In Section 2.10 we mentioned that SLIP drivers normally provide type-of-service queueing, allowing interactive traffic to be handled before bulk data. Since most implementations don't use the TOS field, this queueing is done ad hoc by SLIP, with the driver looking at the protocol field (to determine whether it's a TCP segment or not) and then checking the source and destination TCP port numbers to see if the port number corresponds to an interactive service. One driver comments that this "disgusting hack" is required since most implementations don't allow the application to set the TOS field.

The *total length* field is the total length of the IP datagram in bytes. Using this field and the header length field, we know where the data portion of the IP datagram starts, and its length. Since this is a 16-bit field, the maximum size of an IP datagram is 65535 bytes. (Recall from Figure 2.5 [p. 30] that a Hyperchannel has an MTU of 65535. This means there really isn't an MTU—it uses the largest IP datagram possible.) This field also changes when a datagram is fragmented, which we describe in Section 11.5.

Although it's possible to send a 65535-byte IP datagram, most link layers will fragment this. Furthermore, a host is not required to receive a datagram larger than 576 bytes. TCP divides the user's data into pieces, so this limit normally doesn't affect TCP. With UDP we'll encounter numerous applications in later chapters (RIP, TFTP, BOOTP, the DNS, and SNMP) that limit themselves to 512 bytes of user data, to stay below this 576-byte limit. Realistically, however, most implementations today (especially those that support the Network File System, NFS) allow for just over 8192-byte IP datagrams.

The total length field is required in the IP header since some data links (e.g., Ethernet) pad small frames to be a minimum length. Even though the minimum Ethernet frame size is 46 bytes (Figure 2.1), an IP datagram can be smaller. If the total length field wasn't provided, the IP layer wouldn't know how much of a 46-byte Ethernet frame was really an IP datagram.

The *identification* field uniquely identifies each datagram sent by a host. It normally increments by one each time a datagram is sent. We return to this field when we look at fragmentation and reassembly in Section 11.5. Similarly, we'll also look at the *flags* field and the *fragmentation offset* field when we talk about fragmentation.

RFC 791 [Postel 1981a] says that the identification field should be chosen by the upper layer that is having IP send the datagram. This implies that two consecutive IP datagrams, one generated by TCP and one generated by UDP, can have the same identification field. While this is OK (the reassembly algorithm handles this), most Berkeley-derived implementations have the IP layer increment a kernel variable each time an IP datagram is sent, regardless of which layer passed the data to IP to send. This kernel variable is initialized to a value based on the time-of-day when the system is bootstrapped.

The *time-to-live* field, or *TTL*, sets an upper limit on the number of routers through which a datagram can pass. It limits the lifetime of the datagram. It is initialized by the sender to some value (often 32 or 64) and decremented by one by every router that handles the datagram. When this field reaches 0, the datagram is thrown away, and the sender is notified with an ICMP message. This prevents packets from getting caught in routing loops forever. We return to this field in Chapter 8 when we look at the Traceroute program.

We talked about the *protocol* field in Chapter 1 and showed how it is used by IP to demultiplex incoming datagrams in Figure 1.8. It identifies which protocol gave the data for IP to send.

The *header checksum* is calculated over the IP header only. It does *not* cover any data that follows the header. ICMP, IGMP, UDP, and TCP all have a checksum in their own headers to cover their header and data.

To compute the IP checksum for an outgoing datagram, the value of the checksum field is first set to 0. Then the 16-bit one's complement sum of the header is calculated (i.e., the entire header is considered a sequence of 16-bit words). The 16-bit one's complement of this sum is stored in the checksum field. When an IP datagram is received, the 16-bit one's complement sum of the header is calculated. Since the receiver's calculated checksum contains the checksum stored by the sender, the receiver's checksum is all one bits if nothing in the header was modified. If the result is not all one bits (a checksum error), IP discards the received datagram. No error message is generated. It is up to the higher layers to somehow detect the missing datagram and retransmit.

ICMP, IGMP, UDP, and TCP all use the same checksum algorithm, although TCP and UDP include various fields from the IP header, in addition to their own header and data. RFC 1071 [Braden, Borman, and Partridge 1988] contains implementation techniques for computing the Internet checksum. Since a router often changes only the TTL field (decrementing it by 1), a router can incrementally update the checksum when it forwards a received datagram, instead of calculating the checksum over the entire IP header again. RFC 1141 [Mallory and Kullberg 1990] describes an efficient way to do this.

The standard BSD implementation, however, does not use this incremental update feature when forwarding a datagram.

Every IP datagram contains the *source IP address* and the *destination IP address*. These are the 32-bit values that we described in Section 1.4.

The final field, the *options*, is a variable-length list of optional information for the datagram. The options currently defined are:

- security and handling restrictions (for military applications, refer to RFC 1108 [Kent 1991] for details),
- record route (have each router record its IP address, Section 7.3),
- timestamp (have each router record its IP address and time, Section 7.4),
- loose source routing (specifying a list of IP addresses that must be traversed by the datagram, Section 8.5), and
- strict source routing (similar to loose source routing but here only the addresses in the list can be traversed, Section 8.5).

These options are rarely used and not all host and routers support all the options.

The options field always ends on a 32-bit boundary. Pad bytes with a value of 0 are added if necessary. This assures that the IP header is always a multiple of 32 bits (as required for the *header length* field).

3.3 IP Routing

Conceptually, IP routing is simple, especially for a host. If the destination is directly connected to the host (e.g., a point-to-point link) or on a shared network (e.g., Ethernet or token ring), then the IP datagram is sent directly to the destination. Otherwise the host sends the datagram to a default router, and lets the router deliver the datagram to its destination. This simple scheme handles most host configurations.

In this section and in Chapter 9 we'll look at the more general case where the IP layer can be configured to act as a router in addition to acting as a host. Most multiuser systems today, including almost every Unix system, can be configured to act as a router. We can then specify a single routing algorithm that both hosts and routers can use. The fundamental difference is that a host *never* forwards datagrams from one of its interfaces to another, while a router forwards datagrams. A host that contains embedded router functionality should never forward a datagram unless it has been specifically configured to do so. We say more about this configuration option in Section 9.4.

In our general scheme, IP can receive a datagram from TCP, UDP, ICMP, or IGMP (that is, a locally generated datagram) to send, or one that has been received from a network interface (a datagram to forward). The IP layer has a routing table in memory that it searches each time it receives a datagram to send. When a datagram is received from a network interface, IP first checks if the destination IP address is one of its own IP addresses or an IP broadcast address. If so, the datagram is delivered to the protocol module specified by the protocol field in the IP header. If the datagram is not destined for this IP layer, then (1) if the IP layer was configured to act as a router the packet is forwarded (that is, handled as an outgoing datagram as described below), else (2) the datagram is silently discarded.

Each entry in the routing table contains the following information:

- Destination IP address. This can be either a complete *host address* or a *network address*, as specified by the flag field (described below) for this entry. A host address has a nonzero host ID (Figure 1.5) and identifies one particular host, while a network address has a host ID of 0 and identifies all the hosts on that network (e.g., Ethernet, token ring).
- IP address of a *next-hop router*, or the IP address of a directly connected network. A next-hop router is one that is on a directly connected network to which we can send datagrams for delivery. The next-hop router is not the final destination, but it takes the datagrams we send it and forwards them to the final destination.
- Flags. One flag specifies whether the destination IP address is the address of a network or the address of a host. Another flag says whether the next-hop router field is really a next-hop router or a directly connected interface. (We describe each of these flags in Section 9.2.)
- Specification of which network interface the datagram should be passed to for transmission.

IP routing is done on a hop-by-hop basis. As we can see from this routing table information, IP does not know the complete route to any destination (except, of course, those destinations that are directly connected to the sending host). All that IP routing provides is the IP address of the next-hop router to which the datagram is sent. It is assumed that the next-hop router is really "closer" to the destination than the sending host is, and that the next-hop router is directly connected to the sending host.

IP routing performs the following actions:

1. Search the routing table for an entry that matches the complete destination IP address (matching network ID and host ID). If found, send the packet to the indicated next-hop router or to the directly connected interface (depending on the flags field). Point-to-point links are found here, for example, since the other end of such a link is the other host's complete IP address.
2. Search the routing table for an entry that matches just the destination network ID. If found, send the packet to the indicated next-hop router or to the directly connected interface (depending on the flags field). All the hosts on the destination network can be handled with this single routing table entry. All the hosts on a local Ethernet, for example, are handled with a routing table entry of this type.

   This check for a network match must take into account a possible subnet mask, which we describe in the next section.
3. Search the routing table for an entry labeled "default." If found, send the packet to the indicated next-hop router.

If none of the steps works, the datagram is undeliverable. If the undeliverable datagram was generated on this host, a "host unreachable" or "network unreachable" error is normally returned to the application that generated the datagram.

A complete matching host address is searched for before a matching network ID. Only if both of these fail is a default route used. Default routes, along with the ICMP redirect message sent by a next-hop router (if we chose the wrong default for a datagram), are powerful features of IP routing that we'll come back to in Chapter 9.

The ability to specify a route to a network, and not have to specify a route to every host, is another fundamental feature of IP routing. Doing this allows the routers on the Internet, for example, to have a routing table with thousands of entries, instead of a routing table with more than one million entries.

Examples

First consider a simple example: our host `bsdi` has an IP datagram to send to our host `sun`. Both hosts are on the same Ethernet (see inside front cover). Figure 3.3 shows the delivery of the datagram.

When IP receives the datagram from one of the upper layers it searches its routing table and finds that the destination IP address (140.252.13.33) is on a directly connected network (the Ethernet 140.252.13.0). A matching network address is found in the routing table. (In the next section we'll see that because of subnetting the network address of this Ethernet is really 140.252.13.32, but that doesn't affect this discussion of routing.)

The datagram is passed to the Ethernet device driver, and sent to `sun` as an Ethernet frame (Figure 2.1). The destination address in the IP datagram is Sun's IP address (140.252.13.33) and the destination address in the link-layer header is the 48-bit Ethernet address of `sun`'s Ethernet interface. This 48-bit Ethernet address is obtained using ARP, as we describe in the next chapter.

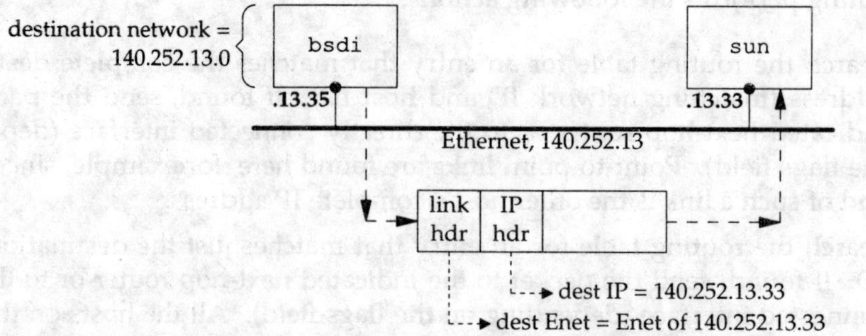

Figure 3.3 Delivery of IP datagram from bsdi to sun.

Now consider another example: bsdi has an IP datagram to send to the host ftp.uu.net, whose IP address is 192.48.96.9. Figure 3.4 shows the path of the datagram through the first three routers. First bsdi searches its routing table but doesn't find a matching host entry or a matching network entry. It uses its default entry, which tells it to send datagrams to sun, the next-hop router. When the datagram travels from bsdi to sun the destination IP address is the final destination (192.48.96.9) but the link-layer address is the 48-bit Ethernet address of sun's Ethernet interface. Compare this datagram with the one in Figure 3.3, where the destination IP address and the destination link-layer address specified the same host (sun).

When sun receives the datagram it realizes that the datagram's destination IP address is not one of its own, and sun is configured to act as a router, so it forwards the datagram. Its routing table is searched and the default entry is used. The default entry on sun tells it to send datagrams to the next-hop router netb, whose IP address is 140.252.1.183. The datagram is sent across the point-to-point SLIP link, using the minimal encapsulation we showed in Figure 2.2. We don't show a link-layer header, as we do on the Ethernets, because there isn't one on a SLIP link.

When netb receives the datagram it goes through the same steps that sun just did: the datagram is not destined for one of its own IP addresses, and netb is configured to act as a router, so the datagram is forwarded. The default routing table entry is used, sending the datagram to the next-hop router gateway (140.252.1.4). ARP is used by netb on the Ethernet 140.252.1 to obtain the 48-bit Ethernet address corresponding to 140.252.1.4, and that Ethernet address is the destination address in the link-layer header.

gateway goes through the same steps as the previous two routers and its default routing table entry specifies 140.252.104.2 as the next-hop router. (We'll verify that this is the next-hop router for gateway using Traceroute in Figure 8.4.)

A few key points come out in this example.

1. All the hosts and routers in this example used a default route. Indeed, most hosts and some routers can use a default route for everything other than destinations on local networks.

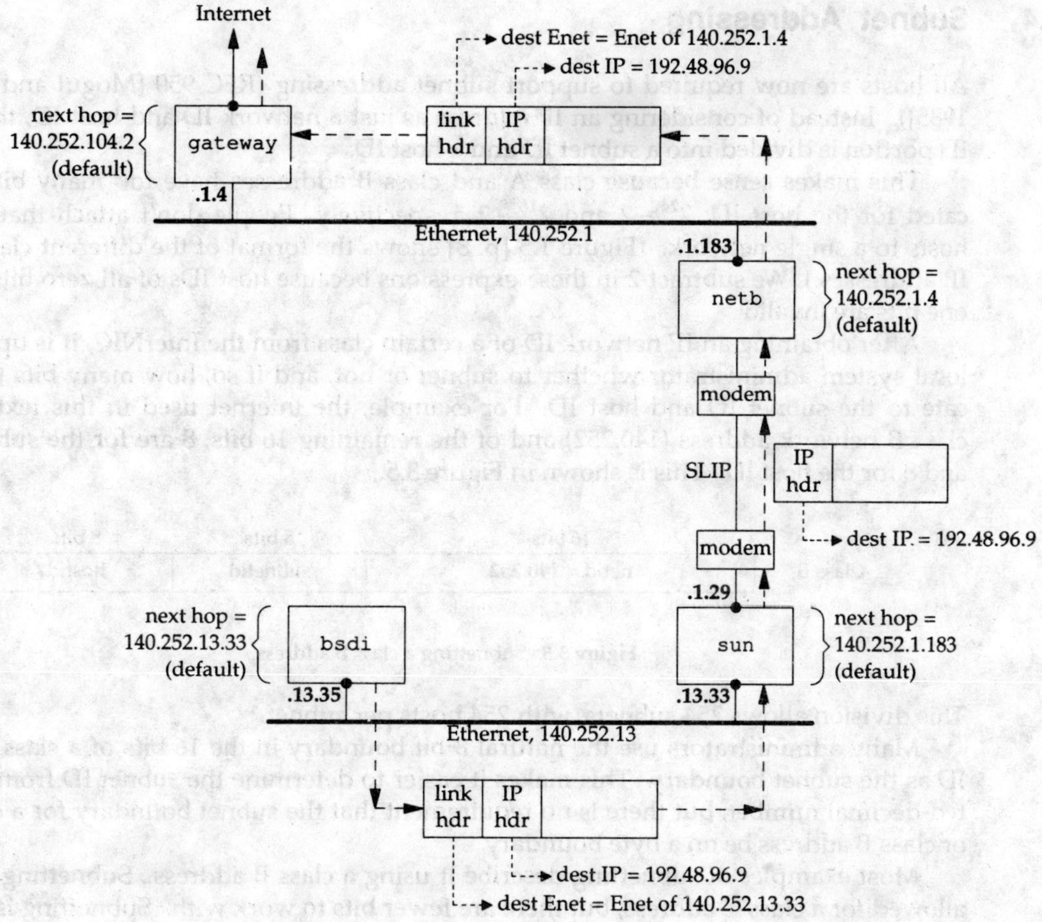

Figure 3.4 Initial path of datagram from `bsdi` to `ftp.uu.net` (192.48.96.9).

2. The destination IP address in the datagram never changes. (In Section 8.5 we'll see that this is not true only if source routing is used, which is rare.) All the routing decisions are based on this destination address.
3. A different link-layer header can be used on each link, and the link-layer destination address (if present) always contains the link-layer address of the next hop. In our example both Ethernets encapsulated a link-layer header containing the next-hop's Ethernet address, but the SLIP link did not. The Ethernet addresses are normally obtained using ARP.

In Chapter 9 we'll look at IP routing again, after describing ICMP. We'll also look at some sample routing tables and how they're used for routing decisions.

3.4 Subnet Addressing

All hosts are now required to support subnet addressing (RFC 950 [Mogul and Postel 1985]). Instead of considering an IP address as just a network ID and host ID, the host ID portion is divided into a subnet ID and a host ID.

This makes sense because class A and class B addresses have too many bits allocated for the host ID: $2^{24} - 2$ and $2^{16} - 2$, respectively. People don't attach that many hosts to a single network. (Figure 1.5 [p. 8] shows the format of the different classes of IP addresses.) We subtract 2 in these expressions because host IDs of all zero bits or all one bits are invalid.

After obtaining an IP network ID of a certain class from the InterNIC, it is up to the local system administrator whether to subnet or not, and if so, how many bits to allocate to the subnet ID and host ID. For example, the internet used in this text has a class B network address (140.252) and of the remaining 16 bits, 8 are for the subnet ID and 8 for the host ID. This is shown in Figure 3.5.

	16 bits	8 bits	8 bits
Class B	netid = 140.252	subnetid	hostid

Figure 3.5 Subnetting a class B address.

This division allows 254 subnets, with 254 hosts per subnet.

Many administrators use the natural 8-bit boundary in the 16 bits of a class B host ID as the subnet boundary. This makes it easier to determine the subnet ID from a dotted-decimal number, but there is no requirement that the subnet boundary for a class A or class B address be on a byte boundary.

Most examples of subnetting describe it using a class B address. Subnetting is also allowed for a class C address, but there are fewer bits to work with. Subnetting is rarely shown with a class A address because there are so few class A addresses. (Most class A addresses are, however, subnetted.)

Subnetting hides the details of internal network organization (within a company or campus) to external routers. Using our example network, all IP addresses have the class B network ID of 140.252. But there are more than 30 subnets and more than 400 hosts distributed over those subnets. A single router provides the connection to the Internet, as shown in Figure 3.6.

In this figure we have labeled most of the routers as R*n*, where *n* is the subnet number. We show the routers that connect these subnets, along with the nine systems from the figure on the inside front cover. The Ethernets are shown as thicker lines, and the point-to-point links as dashed lines. We do *not* show all the hosts on the various subnets. For example, there are more than 50 hosts on the 140.252.3 subnet, and more than 100 on the 140.252.1 subnet.

The advantage to using a single class B address with 30 subnets, compared to 30 class C addresses, is that subnetting reduces the size of the Internet's routing tables. The fact that the class B address 140.252 is subnetted is transparent to all Internet routers other than the ones within the 140.252 subnet. To reach any host whose IP

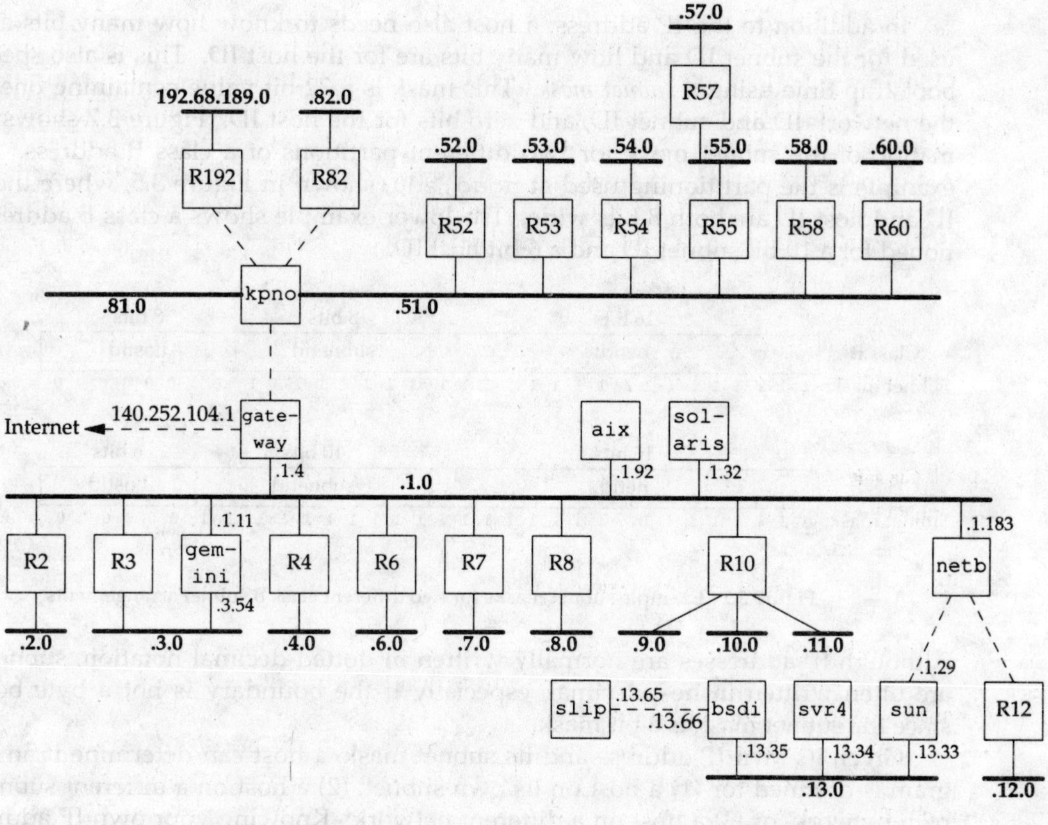

Figure 3.6 Arrangement of most of the noao.edu 140.252 subnets.

address begins with 140.252, the external routers only need to know the path to the IP address 140.252.104.1. This means that only one routing table entry is needed for all the 140.252 networks, instead of 30 entries if 30 class C addresses were used. Subnetting, therefore, reduces the size of routing tables. (In Section 10.8 we'll look at a new technique that helps reduce the size of routing tables even if class C addresses are used.)

To show that subnetting is not transparent to routers within the subnet, assume in Figure 3.6 that a datagram arrives at `gateway` from the Internet with a destination address of 140.252.57.1. The router `gateway` needs to know that the subnet number is 57, and that datagrams for this subnet are sent to `kpno`. Similarly `kpno` must send the datagram to R55, who then sends it to R57.

3.5 Subnet Mask

Part of the configuration of any host that takes place at bootstrap time is the specification of the host's IP address. Most systems have this stored in a disk file that's read at bootstrap time, and we'll see in Chapter 5 how a diskless system can also find out its IP address when it's bootstrapped.

In addition to the IP address, a host also needs to know how many bits are to be used for the subnet ID and how many bits are for the host ID. This is also specified at bootstrap time using a *subnet mask*. This mask is a 32-bit value containing one bits for the network ID and subnet ID, and zero bits for the host ID. Figure 3.7 shows the formation of the subnet mask for two different partitions of a class B address. The top example is the partitioning used at `noao.edu`, shown in Figure 3.5, where the subnet ID and host ID are both 8 bits wide. The lower example shows a class B address partitioned for a 10-bit subnet ID and a 6-bit host ID.

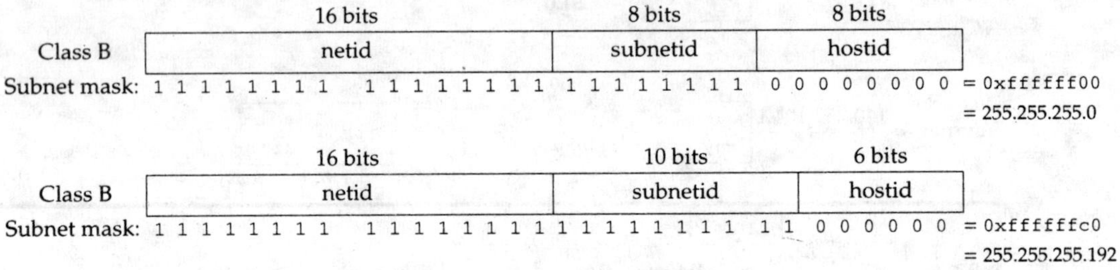

Figure 3.7 Example subnet masks for two different class B subnet arrangements.

Although IP addresses are normally written in dotted-decimal notation, subnet masks are often written in hexadecimal, especially if the boundary is not a byte boundary, since the subnet mask is a bit mask.

Given its own IP address and its subnet mask, a host can determine if an IP datagram is destined for (1) a host on its own subnet, (2) a host on a different subnet on its own network, or (3) a host on a different network. Knowing your own IP address tells you whether you have a class A, B, or C address (from the high-order bits), which tells you where the boundary is between the network ID and the subnet ID. The subnet mask then tells you where the boundary is between the subnet ID and the host ID.

Example

Assume our host address is 140.252.1.1 (a class B address) and our subnet mask is 255.255.255.0 (8 bits for the subnet ID and 8 bits for the host ID).

- If a destination IP address is 140.252.4.5, we know that the class B network IDs are the same (140.252), but the subnet IDs are different (1 and 4). Figure 3.8 shows how this comparison of two IP addresses is done, using the subnet mask.
- If the destination IP address is 140.252.1.22, the class B network IDs are the same (140.252), and the subnet IDs are the same (1). The host IDs, however, are different.
- If the destination IP address is 192.43.235.6 (a class C address), the network IDs are different. No further comparisons can be made against this address.

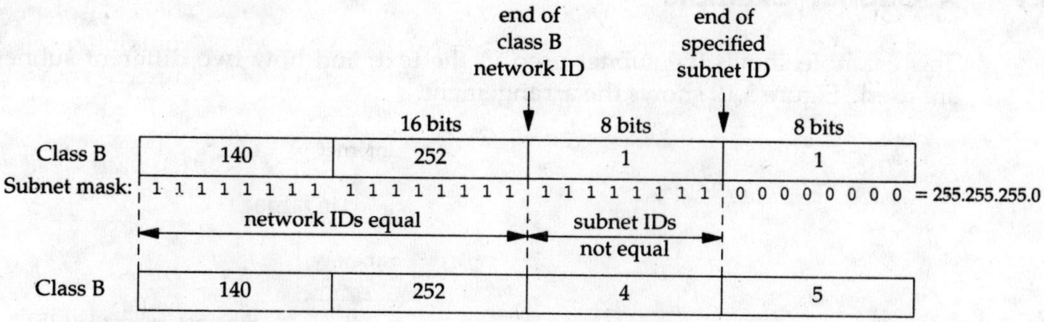

Figure 3.8 Comparison of two class B addresses using a subnet mask.

The IP routing function makes comparisons like this all the time, given two IP addresses and a subnet mask.

3.6 Special Case IP Addresses

Having described subnetting we now show the seven special case IP addresses in Figure 3.9. In this figure, 0 means a field of all zero bits, –1 means a field of all one bits, and *netid*, *subnetid*, and *hostid* mean the corresponding field that is neither all zero bits nor all one bits. A blank subnet ID column means the address is not subnetted.

IP address			Can appear as		Description
net ID	subnet ID	host ID	source?	destination?	
0		0	OK	never	this host on this net (see restrictions below)
0		*hostid*	OK	never	specified host on this net (see restrictions below)
127		*anything*	OK	OK	loopback address (Section 2.7)
–1		–1	never	OK	limited broadcast (never forwarded)
netid		–1	never	OK	net-directed broadcast to *netid*
netid	*subnetid*	–1	never	OK	subnet-directed broadcast to *netid, subnetid*
netid	–1	–1	never	OK	all-subnets-directed broadcast to *netid*

Figure 3.9 Special case IP addresses.

We have divided this table into three sections. The first two entries are special case source addresses, the next one is the special loopback address, and the final four are the broadcast addresses.

The first two entries in the table, with a network ID of 0, can only appear as the source address as part of an initialization procedure when a host is determining its own IP address, for example, when the BOOTP protocol is being used (Chapter 16).

In Section 12.2 we'll examine the four types of broadcast addresses in more detail.

3.7 A Subnet Example

This example shows the subnet used in the text, and how two different subnet masks are used. Figure 3.10 shows the arrangement.

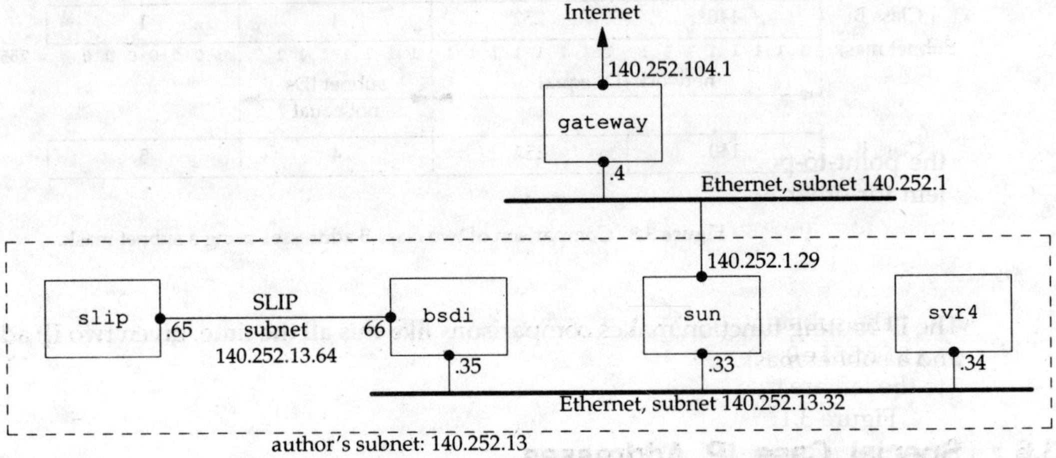

Figure 3.10 Arrangement of hosts and networks for author's subnet.

If you compare this figure with the one on the inside front cover, you'll notice that we've omitted the detail that the connection from the router sun to the top Ethernet in Figure 3.10 is really a dialup SLIP connection. This detail doesn't affect our description of subnetting in this section. We'll return to this detail in Section 4.6 when we describe proxy ARP.

The problem is that we have two separate networks within subnet 13: an Ethernet and a point-to-point link (the hardwired SLIP link). (Point-to-point links always cause problems since each end normally requires an IP address.) There could be more hosts and networks in the future, but not enough hosts across the different networks to justify using another subnet number. Our solution is to extend the subnet ID from 8 to 11 bits, and decrease the host ID from 8 to 5 bits. This is called *variable-length subnets* since most networks within the 140.252 network use an 8-bit subnet mask while our network uses an 11-bit subnet mask.

> RFC 1009 [Braden and Postel 1987] allows a subnetted network to use more than one subnet mask. The new Router Requirements RFC [Almquist 1993] requires support for this.
>
> The problem, however, is that not all routing protocols exchange the subnet mask along with the destination network ID. We'll see in Chapter 10 that RIP does not support variable-length subnets, while RIP Version 2 and OSPF do. We don't have a problem with our example, since RIP isn't required on the author's subnet.

Figure 3.11 shows the IP address structure used within the author's subnet. The first 8 bits of the 11-bit subnet ID are always 13 within the author's subnet. For the remaining 3 bits of the subnet ID, we use binary 001 for the Ethernet, and binary 010 for

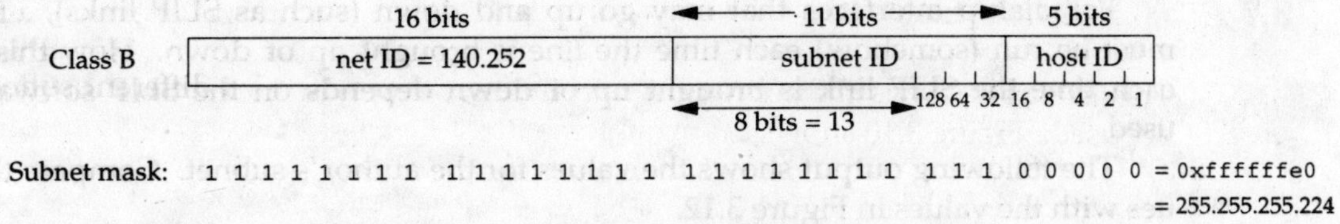

Figure 3.11 Using variable-length subnets.

the point-to-point SLIP link. This variable-length subnet mask does not cause a problem for other hosts and routers in the 140.252 network—as long as all datagrams destined for the subnet 140.252.13 are sent to the router sun (IP address 140.252.1.29) in Figure 3.10, and if sun knows about the 11-bit subnet ID for the hosts on its subnet 13, everything is fine.

The subnet mask for all the interfaces on the 140.252.13 subnet is 255.255.255.224, or 0xffffffe0. This indicates that the rightmost 5 bits are for the host ID, and the 27 bits to the left are the network ID and subnet ID.

Figure 3.12 shows the allocation of IP addresses and subnet masks for the interfaces shown in Figure 3.10.

Host	IP address	Subnet mask	Net ID/Subnet ID	Host ID	Comment
sun	140.252.1.29	255.255.255.0	140.252.1	29	on subnet 1
	140.252.13.33	255.255.255.224	140.252.13.32	1	on author's Ethernet
svr4	140.252.13.34	255.255.255.224	140.252.13.32	2	
bsdi	140.252.13.35	255.255.255.224	140.252.13.32	3	on Ethernet
	140.252.13.66	255.255.255.224	140.252.13.64	2	point-to-point
slip	140.252.13.65	255.255.255.224	140.252.13.64	1	point-to-point
	140.252.13.63	255.255.255.224	140.252.13.32	31	broadcast addr on Ethernet

Figure 3.12 IP addresses on author's subnet.

The first column is labeled "Host," but both sun and bsdi also act as routers, since they are multihomed and route packets from one interface to another.

The final row in this table notes that the broadcast address for the bottom Ethernet in Figure 3.10 is 140.252.13.63: it is formed from the subnet ID of the Ethernet (140.252.13.32) and the low-order 5 bits in Figure 3.11 set to 1 $(16+8+4+2+1=31)$. (We'll see in Chapter 12 that this address is called the subnet-directed broadcast address.)

3.8 ifconfig Command

Now that we've described the link layer and the IP layer we can show the command used to configure or query a network interface for use by TCP/IP. The ifconfig(8) command is normally run at bootstrap time to configure each interface on a host.

For dialup interfaces that may go up and down (such as SLIP links), `ifconfig` must be run (somehow) each time the line is brought up or down. How this is done each time the SLIP link is brought up or down depends on the SLIP software being used.

The following output shows the values for the author's subnet. Compare these values with the values in Figure 3.12.

```
sun % /usr/etc/ifconfig -a          SunOS -a option says report on all interfaces
le0: flags=63<UP,BROADCAST,NOTRAILERS,RUNNING>
        inet 140.252.13.33 netmask ffffffe0 broadcast 140.252.13.63
sl0: flags=1051<UP,POINTOPOINT,RUNNING,LINK0>
        inet 140.252.1.29 --> 140.252.1.183 netmask ffffff00
lo0: flags=49<UP,LOOPBACK,RUNNING>
        inet 127.0.0.1 netmask ff000000
```

The loopback interface (Section 2.7) is considered a network interface. Its class A address is not subnetted.

Other things to notice are that trailer encapsulation (Section 2.3) is not used on the Ethernet, and that the Ethernet is capable of broadcasting, while the SLIP link is a point-to-point link.

The flag `LINK0` for the SLIP interface is the configuration option that enables compressed slip (CSLIP, Section 2.5). Other possible options are `LINK1`, which enables CSLIP if a compressed packet is received from the other end, and `LINK2`, which causes all outgoing ICMP packets to be thrown away. We'll look at the destination address of this SLIP link in Section 4.6.

A comment in the installation instructions gives the reason for this last option: "This shouldn't have to be set, but some cretin pinging you can drive your throughput to zero."

`bsdi` is the other router. Since the -a option is a SunOS feature, we have to execute `ifconfig` multiple times, specifying the interface name as an argument:

```
bsdi % /sbin/ifconfig we0
we0: flags=863<UP,BROADCAST,NOTRAILERS,RUNNING,SIMPLEX>
        inet 140.252.13.35 netmask ffffffe0 broadcast 140.252.13.63
bsdi % /sbin/ifconfig sl0
sl0: flags=1011<UP,POINTOPOINT,LINK0>
        inet 140.252.13.66 --> 140.252.13.65 netmask ffffffe0
```

Here we see a new option for the Ethernet interface (`we0`): `SIMPLEX`. This 4.4BSD flag specifies that the interface can't hear its own transmissions. It is set in BSD/386 for all the Ethernet interfaces. When set, if the interface is sending a frame to the broadcast address, a copy is made for the local host and sent to the loopback address. (We show an example of this feature in Section 6.3.)

On the host `slip` the configuration of the SLIP interface is nearly identical to the output shown above on `bsdi`, with the exception that the IP addresses of the two ends are swapped:

```
slip % /sbin/ifconfig sl0
sl0: flags=1011<UP,POINTOPOINT,LINK0>
        inet 140.252.13.65 --> 140.252.13.66 netmask ffffffe0
```

The final interface is the Ethernet interface on the host `svr4`. It is similar to the Ethernet output shown earlier, except that SVR4's version of `ifconfig` doesn't print the `RUNNING` flag:

```
svr4 % /usr/sbin/ifconfig emd0
emd0: flags=23<UP,BROADCAST,NOTRAILERS>
        inet 140.252.13.34 netmask ffffffe0 broadcast 140.252.13.63
```

The `ifconfig` command normally supports other protocol families (other than TCP/IP) and has numerous additional options. Check your system's manual for these details.

3.9 netstat Command

The `netstat(1)` command also provides information about the interfaces on a system. The `-i` flag prints the interface information, and the `-n` flag prints IP addresses instead of hostnames.

```
sun % netstat -in
Name  Mtu  Net/Dest       Address        Ipkts  Ierrs Opkts  Oerrs Collis Queue
le0   1500 140.252.13.32  140.252.13.33  67719   0    92133   0     1      0
sl0   552  140.252.1.183  140.252.1.29   48035   0    54963   0     0      0
lo0   1536 127.0.0.0      127.0.0.1      15548   0    15548   0     0      0
```

This command prints the MTU of each interface, the number of input packets, input errors, output packets, output errors, collisions, and the current size of the output queue.

We'll return to the `netstat` command in Chapter 9 when we use it to examine the routing table, and in Chapter 13 when we use a modified version to see active multicast groups.

3.10 IP Futures

There are three problems with IP. They are a result of the phenomenal growth of the Internet over the past few years. (See Exercise 1.2 also.)

1. Over half of all class B addresses have already been allocated. Current estimates predict exhaustion of the class B address space around 1995, if they continue to be allocated as they have been in the past.
2. 32-bit IP addresses in general are inadequate for the predicted long-term growth of the Internet.
3. The current routing structure is not hierarchical, but flat, requiring one routing table entry per network. As the number of networks grows, amplified by the allocation of multiple class C addresses to a site with multiple networks, instead of a single class B address, the size of the routing tables grows.

CIDR (Classless Interdomain Routing) proposes a fix to the third problem that will extend the usefulness of the current version of IP (IP version 4) into the next century. We discuss it in more detail in Section 10.8.

Four proposals have been made for a new version of IP, often called *IPng*, for the next generation of IP. The May 1993 issue of *IEEE Network* (vol. 7, no. 3) contains overviews of the first three proposals, along with an article on CIDR. RFC 1454 [Dixon 1993] also compares the first three proposals.

1. SIP, the Simple Internet Protocol. It proposes a minimal set of changes to IP that uses 64-bit addresses and a different header format. (The first 4 bits of the header still contain the version number, with a value other than 4.)
2. PIP. This proposal also uses larger, variable-length, hierarchical addresses with a different header format.
3. TUBA, which stands for "TCP and UDP with Bigger Addresses," is based on the OSI CLNP (Connectionless Network Protocol), an OSI protocol similar to IP. It provides much larger addresses: variable length, up to 20 bytes. Since CLNP is an existing protocol, whereas SIP and PIP are just proposals, documentation already exists on CLNP. RFC 1347 [Callon 1992] provides details on TUBA. Chapter 7 of [Perlman 1992] contains a comparison of IPv4 and CLNP. Many routers already support CLNP, but few hosts do.
4. TP/IX, which is described in RFC 1475 [Ullmann 1993]. As with SIP, it uses 64 bits for IP addresses, but it also changes the TCP and UDP headers: 32-bit port number for both protocols, along with 64-bit sequence numbers, 64-bit acknowledgment numbers, and 32-bit windows for TCP.

The first three proposals use basically the same versions of TCP and UDP as the transport layers.

Since only one of these four proposals will be chosen as the successor to IPv4, and since the decision may have been made by the time you read this, we won't say any more about them. With the forthcoming implementation of CIDR to handle the short-term problem, it will take many years to implement the successor to IPv4.

3.11 Summary

We started this chapter with a description of the IP header and briefly described all the fields in this header. We also gave an introduction to IP routing, and saw that host routing can be simple: the destination is either on a directly connected network, in which case the datagram is sent directly to the destination, or a default router is chosen.

Hosts and routers have a routing table that is used for all routing decisions. There are three types of routes in the table: host specific, network specific, and optional default routes. There is a priority to the entries in a routing table. A host route will be chosen over a network router, and a default route is used only when no other route exists to the destination.

IP routing is done on a hop-by-hop basis. The destination IP address never changes as the datagram proceeds through all the hops, but the encapsulation and destination link-layer address can change on each hop. Most hosts and many routers use a default next-hop router for all nonlocal traffic.

Class A and B addresses are normally subnetted. The number of bits used for the subnet ID is specified by the subnet mask. We gave a detailed example of this, using the author's subnet, and introduced variable-length subnets. The use of subnetting reduces the size of the Internet routing tables, since many networks can often be accessed through a single point. Information on the interfaces and networks is available through the `ifconfig` and `netstat` commands. This includes the IP address of the interface, its subnet mask, broadcast address, and MTU.

We finished the chapter with a discussion of potential changes to the Internet protocol suite–the next generation of IP.

Exercises

3.1 Must the loopback address be 127.0.0.1?

3.2 Identify the routers in Figure 3.6 with more than two network interfaces.

3.3 What's the difference in the subnet mask for a class A address with 16 bits for the subnet ID and a class B address with 8 bits for the subnet ID?

3.4 Read RFC 1219 [Tsuchiya 1991] for a recommended technique for assigning subnet IDs and host IDs.

3.5 Is the subnet mask 255.255.0.255 valid for a class A address?

3.6 Why do you think the MTU of the loopback interface printed in Section 3.9 is set to 1536?

3.7 The TCP/IP protocol suite is built on a datagram network technology, the IP layer. Other protocol suites are built on a connection-oriented network technology. Read [Clark 1988] to discover the three advantages the datagram network layer provides.

IP routing is done on a hop-by-hop basis. The destination IP address never changes as the datagram proceeds through all the hops, but the encapsulation and destination link-layer address can change at each hop. Most hosts and many routers use a default next-hop router for all nonlocal traffic.

Class A and B addresses are normally subnetted. The number of bits used for the subnet ID is specified by the subnet mask. We gave a detailed example of this, using the [illegible] and introduced variable-length subnets. The use of subnets reduces the size of the Internet routing tables, since many networks can often be accessed through a single point. Information on the interfaces and networks is available through the ifconfig and netstat commands. This includes the IP address of the interface, its subnet mask, broadcast address, and MTU.

We finish the chapter with a discussion of potential changes to the Internet protocol suite, the next generation of IP.

Exercises

3.1 Must the loopback address be 127.0.0.1?

3.2 Identify the routers in Figure 3.5 with more than two network interfaces.

3.3 What's the difference in the subnet mask for a class A address with 16 bits for the subnet ID and a class B address with 8 bits for the subnet ID?

3.4 Read RFC 1219 [Tsuchiya 1991] for a recommended technique for assigning subnet IDs and host IDs.

3.5 Is the subnet mask 255.255.0.255 valid for a class A address?

3.6 Why do you think the MTU of the loopback interface printed in Section 3.9 is set to 1536?

3.7 The TCP/IP protocol suite is built around a datagram network technology, the IP layer, and other protocol suites are built around a connection-oriented network technology. [illegible] the services the datagram network layer provides.

4

ARP: Address Resolution Protocol

4.1 Introduction

The problem that we deal with in this chapter is that IP addresses only make sense to the TCP/IP protocol suite. A data link such as an Ethernet or a token ring has its own addressing scheme (often 48-bit addresses) to which any network layer using the data link must conform. A network such as an Ethernet can be used by different network layers at the same time. For example, a collection of hosts using TCP/IP and another collection of hosts using some PC network software can share the same physical cable.

When an Ethernet frame is sent from one host on a LAN to another, it is the 48-bit Ethernet address that determines for which interface the frame is destined. The device driver software never looks at the destination IP address in the IP datagram.

Address resolution provides a mapping between the two different forms of addresses: 32-bit IP addresses and whatever type of address the data link uses. RFC 826 [Plummer 1982] is the specification of ARP.

Figure 4.1 shows the two protocols we talk about in this chapter and the next: ARP (address resolution protocol) and RARP (reverse address resolution protocol).

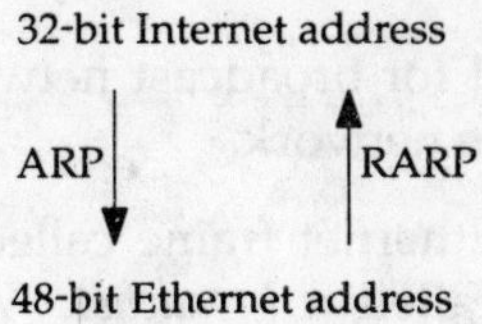

Figure 4.1 Address resolution protocols: ARP and RARP.

ARP provides a dynamic mapping from an IP address to the corresponding hardware address. We use the term *dynamic* since it happens automatically and is normally not a concern of either the application user or the system administrator.

RARP is used by systems without a disk drive (normally diskless workstations or X terminals) but requires manual configuration by the system administrator. We describe it in Chapter 5.

4.2 An Example

Whenever we type a command of the form

```
% ftp bsdi
```

the following steps take place. These numbered steps are shown in Figure 4.2.

1. The application, the FTP client, calls the function `gethostbyname(3)` to convert the hostname (`bsdi`) into its 32-bit IP address. This function is called a *resolver* in the DNS (Domain Name System), which we describe in Chapter 14. This conversion is done using the DNS, or on smaller networks, a static hosts file (`/etc/hosts`).
2. The FTP client asks its TCP to establish a connection with that IP address.
3. TCP sends a connection request segment to the remote host by sending an IP datagram to its IP address. (We'll see the details of how this is done in Chapter 18.)
4. If the destination host is on a locally attached network (e.g., Ethernet, token ring, or the other end of a point-to-point link), the IP datagram can be sent directly to that host. If the destination host is on a remote network, the IP routing function determines the Internet address of a locally attached next-hop router to send the IP datagram to. In either case the IP datagram is sent to a host or router on a locally attached network.
5. Assuming an Ethernet, the sending host must convert the 32-bit IP address into a 48-bit Ethernet address. A translation is required from the *logical* Internet address to its corresponding *physical* hardware address. This is the function of ARP.

   ARP is intended for broadcast networks where many hosts or routers are connected to a single network.
6. ARP sends an Ethernet frame called an *ARP request* to every host on the network. This is called a *broadcast*. We show the broadcast in Figure 4.2 with dashed lines. The ARP request contains the IP address of the destination host (whose name is `bsdi`) and is the request "if you are the owner of this IP address, please respond to me with your hardware address."

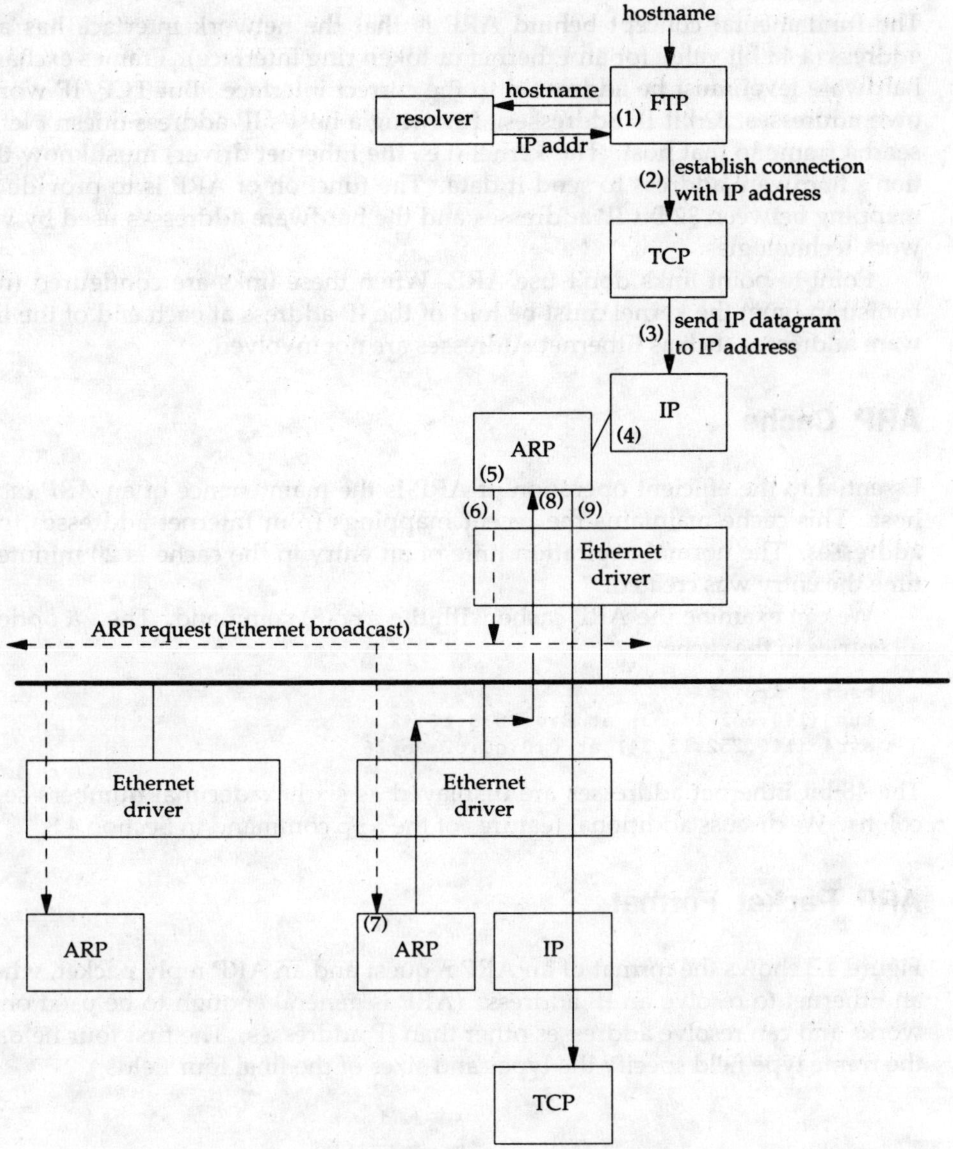

Figure 4.2 Operation of ARP when user types "`ftp` hostname".

7. The destination host's ARP layer receives this broadcast, recognizes that the sender is asking for its hardware address, and replies with an *ARP reply*. This reply contains the IP address and the corresponding hardware address.
8. The ARP reply is received and the IP datagram that forced the ARP request–reply to be exchanged can now be sent.
9. The IP datagram is sent to the destination host.

The fundamental concept behind ARP is that the network interface has a hardware address (a 48-bit value for an Ethernet or token ring interface). Frames exchanged at the hardware level must be addressed to the correct interface. But TCP/IP works with its own addresses: 32-bit IP addresses. Knowing a host's IP address doesn't let the kernel send a frame to that host. The kernel (i.e., the Ethernet driver) must know the destination's hardware address to send it data. The function of ARP is to provide a dynamic mapping between 32-bit IP addresses and the hardware addresses used by various network technologies.

Point-to-point links don't use ARP. When these links are configured (normally at bootstrap time) the kernel must be told of the IP address at each end of the link. Hardware addresses such as Ethernet addresses are not involved.

ARP Cache

Essential to the efficient operation of ARP is the maintenance of an *ARP cache* on each host. This cache maintains the recent mappings from Internet addresses to hardware addresses. The normal expiration time of an entry in the cache is 20 minutes from the time the entry was created.

We can examine the ARP cache with the `arp(8)` command. The `-a` option displays all entries in the cache:

```
bsdi % arp -a
sun (140.252.13.33) at 8:0:20:3:f6:42
svr4 (140.252.13.34) at 0:0:c0:c2:9b:26
```

The 48-bit Ethernet addresses are displayed as six hexadecimal numbers separated by colons. We discuss additional features of the `arp` command in Section 4.8.

ARP Packet Format

Figure 4.3 shows the format of an ARP request and an ARP reply packet, when used on an Ethernet to resolve an IP address. (ARP is general enough to be used on other networks and can resolve addresses other than IP addresses. The first four fields following the frame type field specify the types and sizes of the final four fields.)

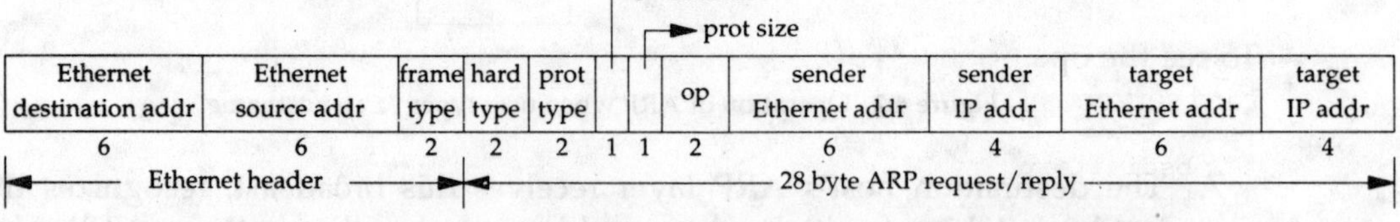

Figure 4.3 Format of ARP request or reply packet when used on an Ethernet.

The first two fields in the Ethernet header are the source and destination Ethernet addresses. The special Ethernet destination address of all one bits means the broadcast address. All Ethernet interfaces on the cable receive these frames.

The 2-byte Ethernet *frame type* specifies the type of data that follows. For an ARP request or an ARP reply, this field is `0x0806`.

The adjectives *hardware* and *protocol* are used to describe the fields in the ARP packets. For example, an ARP request asks for the hardware address (an Ethernet address in this case) corresponding to a protocol address (an IP address in this case).

The *hard type* field specifies the type of hardware address. Its value is 1 for an Ethernet. *Prot type* specifies the type of protocol address being mapped. Its value is `0x0800` for IP addresses. This is purposely the same value as the type field of an Ethernet frame containing an IP datagram. (See Figure 2.1, p. 23.)

The next two 1-byte fields, *hard size* and *prot size*, specify the sizes in bytes of the hardware addresses and the protocol addresses. For an ARP request or reply for an IP address on an Ethernet they are 6 and 4, respectively.

The *op* field specifies whether the operation is an ARP request (a value of 1), ARP reply (2), RARP request (3), or RARP reply (4). (We talk about RARP in Chapter 5.) This field is required since the *frame type* field is the same for an ARP request and an ARP reply.

The next four fields that follow are the sender's hardware address (an Ethernet address in this example), the sender's protocol address (an IP address), the target hardware address, and the target protocol address. Notice there is some duplication of information: the sender's hardware address is available both in the Ethernet header and in the ARP request.

For an ARP request all the fields are filled in except the target hardware address. When a system receives an ARP request directed to it, it fills in its hardware address, swaps the two sender addresses with the two target addresses, sets the *op* field to 2, and sends the reply.

4.5 ARP Examples

In this section we'll use the `tcpdump` command to see what really happens with ARP when we execute normal TCP utilities such as Telnet. Appendix A contains additional details on the `tcpdump` program.

Normal Example

To see the operation of ARP we'll execute the `telnet` command, connecting to the discard server.

```
bsdi % arp -a                          verify ARP cache is empty
bsdi % telnet svr4 discard             connect to the discard server
Trying 140.252.13.34...
Connected to svr4.
Escape character is '^]'.
^]                                     type Control, right bracket to get Telnet client prompt
telnet> quit                           and terminate
Connection closed.
```

While this is happening we run the tcpdump command on another system (sun) with the -e option. This displays the hardware addresses (which in our examples are 48-bit Ethernet addresses).

```
1  0.0                  0:0:c0:6f:2d:40 ff:ff:ff:ff:ff:ff arp 60:
                        arp who-has svr4 tell bsdi
2  0.002174 (0.0022)    0:0:c0:c2:9b:26 0:0:c0:6f:2d:40 arp 60:
                        arp reply svr4 is-at 0:0:c0:c2:9b:26
3  0.002831 (0.0007)    0:0:c0:6f:2d:40 0:0:c0:c2:9b:26 ip 60:
                        bsdi.1030 > svr4.discard: S 596459521:596459521(0)
                        win 4096 <mss 1024> [tos 0x10]
4  0.007834 (0.0050)    0:0:c0:c2:9b:26 0:0:c0:6f:2d:40 ip 60:
                        svr4.discard > bsdi.1030: S 3562228225:3562228225(0)
                        ack 596459522 win 4096 <mss 1024>
5  0.009615 (0.0018)    0:0:c0:6f:2d:40 0:0:c0:c2:9b:26 ip 60:
                        bsdi.1030 > svr4.discard: . ack 1 win 4096 [tos 0x10]
```

Figure 4.4 ARP request and ARP reply generated by TCP connection request.

Figure A.3 in Appendix A contains the raw output from tcpdump used for Figure 4.4. Since this is the first example of tcpdump output in the text, you should review that appendix to see how we've beautified the output.

We have deleted the final four lines of the tcpdump output that correspond to the termination of the connection (which we cover in Chapter 18), since they're not relevant to the discussion here.

In line 1 the hardware address of the source (bsdi) is 0:0:c0:6f:2d:40. The destination hardware address is ff:ff:ff:ff:ff:ff, which is the Ethernet broadcast address. Every Ethernet interface on the cable will receive the frame and process it, as shown in Figure 4.2.

The next output field on line 1, arp, means the *frame type* field is 0x0806, specifying either an ARP request or an ARP reply.

The value 60 printed after the words arp and ip on each of the five lines is the length of the Ethernet frame. Since the size of an ARP request and ARP reply is 42 bytes (28 bytes for the ARP message, 14 bytes for the Ethernet header), each frame has been padded to the Ethernet minimum: 60 bytes.

Referring to Figure 1.7, this minimum of 60 bytes starts with and includes the 14-byte Ethernet header, but does not include the 4-byte Ethernet trailer. Some books state the minimum as 64 bytes, which includes the Ethernet trailer. We purposely did not include the 14-byte Ethernet header in the minimum of 46 bytes shown in Figure 1.7, since the corresponding maximum (1500 bytes) is what's referred to as the MTU—maximum transmission unit (Figure 2.5). We use the MTU often, because it limits the size of an IP datagram, but are normally not concerned with the minimum. Most device drivers or interface cards automatically pad an Ethernet frame to the minimum size. The IP datagrams on lines 3, 4, and 5 (containing the TCP segments) are all smaller than the minimum, and have also been padded to 60 bytes.

The next field on line 1, arp who-has, identifies the frame as an ARP request with the IP address of svr4 as the target IP address and the IP address of bsdi as the sender

IP address. tcpdump prints the hostnames corresponding to the IP address by default. (We'll use the -n option in Section 4.7 to see the actual IP addresses in an ARP request.)

From line 2 we see that while the ARP request is broadcast, the destination address of the ARP reply is bsdi (0:0:c0:6f:2d:40). The ARP reply is sent directly to the requesting host; it is not broadcast.

tcpdump prints arp reply for this frame, along with the hostname and hardware address of the responder.

Line 3 is the first TCP segment requesting that a connection be established. Its destination hardware address is the destination host (svr4). We'll cover the details of this segment in Chapter 18.

The number printed after the line number on each line is the time (in seconds) when the packet was received by tcpdump. Each line other than the first also contains the time difference (in seconds) from the previous line, in parentheses. We can see in this figure that the time between sending the ARP request and receiving the ARP reply is 2.2 ms. The first TCP segment is sent 0.7 ms after this. The overhead involved in using ARP for dynamic address resolution in this example is less than 3 ms.

A final point from the tcpdump output is that we don't see an ARP request from svr4 before it sends its first TCP segment (line 4). While it's possible that svr4 already had an entry for bsdi in its ARP cache, normally when a system receives an ARP request addressed to it, in addition to sending the ARP reply it also saves the requestor's hardware address and IP address in its own ARP cache. This is on the logical assumption that if the requestor is about to send it an IP datagram, the receiver of the datagram will probably send a reply.

ARP Request to a Nonexistent Host

What happens if the host being queried for is down or nonexistent? To see this we specify a nonexistent Internet address—the network ID and subnet ID are that of the local Ethernet, but there is no host with the specified host ID. From Figure 3.10 we see the host IDs 36 through 62 are nonexistent (the host ID of 63 is the broadcast address). We'll use the host ID 36 in this example.

```
                                        telnet to an address this time, not a hostname
bsdi % date ; telnet 140.252.13.36 ; date
Sat Jan 30 06:46:33 MST 1993
Trying 140.252.13.36...
telnet: Unable to connect to remote host: Connection timed out
Sat Jan 30 06:47:49 MST 1993            76 seconds after previous date output

bsdi % arp -a                           check the ARP cache
? (140.252.13.36) at (incomplete)
```

Figure 4.5 shows the tcpdump output.

```
1   0.0                   arp who-has 140.252.13.36 tell bsdi
2   5.509069 ( 5.5091)    arp who-has 140.252.13.36 tell bsdi
3  29.509745 (24.0007)    arp who-has 140.252.13.36 tell bsdi
```

Figure 4.5 ARP requests to a nonexistent host.

This time we didn't specify the `-e` option since we already know that the ARP requests are broadcast.

What's interesting here is to see the frequency of the ARP requests: 5.5 seconds after the first request, then again 24 seconds later. (We examine TCP's timeout and retransmission algorithms in more detail in Chapter 21.) The total time shown in the `tcpdump` output is 29.5 seconds. But the output from the `date` commands before and after the `telnet` command shows that the connection request from the Telnet client appears to have given up after about 75 seconds. Indeed, we'll see later that most BSD implementations set a limit of 75 seconds for a TCP connection request to complete.

In Chapter 18 when we see the sequence of TCP segments that is sent to establish the connection, we'll see that these ARP requests correspond one-to-one with the initial TCP SYN (synchronize) segment that TCP is trying to send.

Note that on the wire we never see the TCP segments. All we can see are the ARP requests. Until an ARP reply comes back, the TCP segments can't be sent, since the destination hardware address isn't known. If we ran `tcpdump` in a filtering mode, looking only for TCP data, there would have been no output at all.

ARP Cache Timeout

A timeout is normally provided for entries in the ARP cache. (In Section 4.8 we'll see that the `arp` command allows an entry to be placed into the cache by the administrator that will never time out.) Berkeley-derived implementations normally have a timeout of 20 minutes for a completed entry and 3 minutes for an incomplete entry. (We saw an incomplete entry in our previous example where we forced an ARP to a nonexistent host on the Ethernet.) These implementations normally restart the 20-minute timeout for an entry each time the entry is used.

> The Host Requirements RFC says that this timeout should occur even if the entry is in use, but most Berkeley-derived implementations do not do this—they restart the timeout each time the entry is referenced.

4.6 Proxy ARP

Proxy ARP lets a router answer ARP requests on one of its networks for a host on another of its networks. This fools the sender of the ARP request into thinking that the router is the destination host, when in fact the destination host is "on the other side" of the router. The router is acting as a proxy agent for the destination host, relaying packets to it from other hosts.

An example is the best way to describe proxy ARP. In Figure 3.10 we showed that the system `sun` was connected to two Ethernets. But we also noted that this wasn't really true, if you compare that figure with the one on the inside front cover. There is in fact a router between `sun` and the subnet 140.252.1, and this router performs proxy ARP to make it appear as though `sun` is actually on the subnet 140.252.1. Figure 4.6 shows the arrangement, with a Telebit NetBlazer, named `netb`, between the subnet and the host `sun`.

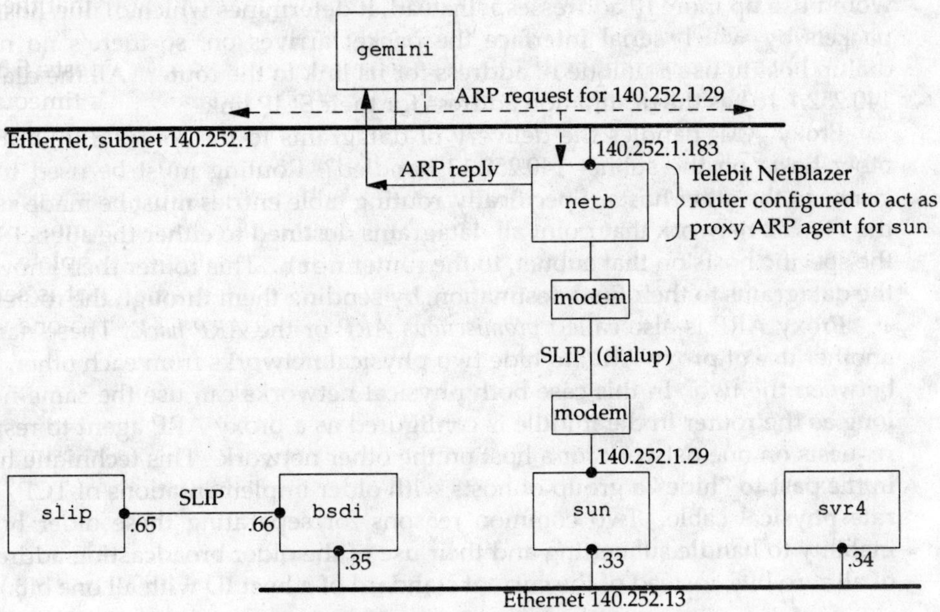

Figure 4.6 Example of proxy ARP.

When some other host on the subnet 140.252.1 (say, `gemini`) has an IP datagram to send to `sun` at address 140.252.1.29, `gemini` compares the network ID (140.252) and subnet ID (1) and since they are equal, issues an ARP request on the top Ethernet in Figure 4.6 for IP address 140.252.1.29. The router `netb` recognizes this IP address as one belonging to one of its dialup hosts, and responds with the hardware address of its Ethernet interface on the cable 140.252.1. The host `gemini` sends the IP datagram to `netb` across the Ethernet, and `netb` forwards the datagram to `sun` across the dialup SLIP link. This makes it transparent to all the hosts on the 140.252.1 subnet that host `sun` is really configured "behind" the router `netb`.

If we execute the `arp` command on the host `gemini`, after communicating with the host `sun`, we see that both IP addresses on the 140.252.1 subnet, `netb` and `sun`, map to the same hardware address. This is often a clue that proxy ARP is being used.

```
gemini % arp -a
                                   many lines for other hosts on the 140.252.1 subnet
netb (140.252.1.183) at 0:80:ad:3:6a:80
sun (140.252.1.29) at 0:80:ad:3:6a:80
```

Another detail in Figure 4.6 that we need to explain is the apparent lack of an IP address at the bottom of the router `netb` (the SLIP link). That is, why don't both ends of the dialup SLIP link have an IP address, as do both ends of the hardwired SLIP link between `bsdi` and `slip`? We noted in Section 3.8 that the destination address of the dialup SLIP link, as shown by the `ifconfig` command, was 140.252.1.183. The NetBlazer doesn't require an IP address for its end of each dialup SLIP link. (Doing so would use up more IP addresses.) Instead, it determines which dialup host is sending it packets by which serial interface the packet arrives on, so there's no need for each dialup host to use a unique IP address for its link to the router. All the dialup hosts use 140.252.1.183 as the destination address for their SLIP link.

Proxy ARP handles the delivery of datagrams to the router `sun`, but how are the other hosts on the subnet 140.252.13 handled? Routing must be used to direct datagrams to the other hosts. Specifically, routing table entries must be made somewhere on the 140.252 network that point all datagrams destined to either the subnet 140.252.13, or the specific hosts on that subnet, to the router `netb`. This router then knows how to get the datagrams to their final destination, by sending them through the router `sun`.

Proxy ARP is also called *promiscuous ARP* or the *ARP hack*. These names are from another use of proxy ARP: to hide two physical networks from each other, with a router between the two. In this case both physical networks can use the same network ID as long as the router in the middle is configured as a proxy ARP agent to respond to ARP requests on one network for a host on the other network. This technique has been used in the past to "hide" a group of hosts with older implementations of TCP/IP on a separate physical cable. Two common reasons for separating these older hosts are their inability to handle subnetting and their use of the older broadcasting address (a host ID of all zero bits, instead of the current standard of a host ID with all one bits).

4.7 Gratuitous ARP

Another feature of ARP that we can watch is called *gratuitous ARP*. It occurs when a host sends an ARP request looking for its own IP address. This is usually done when the interface is configured at bootstrap time.

In our internet, if we bootstrap the host `bsdi` and run `tcpdump` on the host `sun`, we see the packet shown in Figure 4.7.

```
1  0.0                    0:0:c0:6f:2d:40 ff:ff:ff:ff:ff:ff arp 60:
                          arp who-has 140.252.13.35 tell 140.252.13.35
```

Figure 4.7 Example of gratuitous ARP.

(We specified the `-n` flag for `tcpdump` to print numeric dotted-decimal addresses, instead of hostnames.) In terms of the fields in the ARP request, the sender's protocol address and the target's protocol address are identical: 140.252.13.35 for host `bsdi`. Also, the source address in the Ethernet header, `0:0:c0:6f:2d:40` as shown by `tcpdump`, equals the sender's hardware address (from Figure 4.4).

Gratuitous ARP provides two features.

1. It lets a host determine if another host is already configured with the same IP address. The host `bsdi` is not expecting a reply to this request. But if a reply is received, the error message "duplicate IP address sent from Ethernet address: a:b:c:d:e:f" is logged on the console. This is a warning to the system administrator that one of the systems is misconfigured.

2. If the host sending the gratuitous ARP has just changed its hardware address (perhaps the host was shut down, the interface card replaced, and then the host was rebooted), this packet causes any other host on the cable that has an entry in its cache for the old hardware address to update its ARP cache entry accordingly. A little known fact of the ARP protocol [Plummer 1982] is that if a host receives an ARP request from an IP address that is already in the receiver's cache, then that cache entry is updated with the sender's hardware address (e.g., Ethernet address) from the ARP request. This is done for any ARP request received by the host. (Recall that ARP requests are broadcast, so this is done by all hosts on the network each time an ARP request is sent.)

   [Bhide, Elnozahy, and Morgan 1991] describe an application that can use this feature of ARP to allow a backup file server to take over from a failed server by issuing a gratuitous ARP request with the backup's hardware address and the failed server's IP address. This causes all packets destined for the failed server to be sent to the backup instead, without the client applications being aware that the original server has failed.

   Unfortunately the authors then decided against this approach, since it depends on the correct implementation of ARP on all types of clients. They obviously encountered client implementations that did not implement ARP according to its specification.

   Monitoring all the systems on the author's subnet shows that SunOS 4.1.3 and 4.4BSD both issue gratuitous ARPs when bootstrapping, but SVR4 does not.

4.8 `arp` Command

We've used this command with the `-a` flag to display all the entries in the ARP cache. Other options are provided.

The superuser can specify the `-d` option to delete an entry from the ARP cache. (This was used before running a few of the examples, to let us see the ARP exchange.)

Entries can also be added using the `-s` option. It requires a *hostname* and an Ethernet *address*: the IP address corresponding to the *hostname*, and the Ethernet *address* are added to the cache. This entry is made permanent (i.e., it won't time out from the cache) unless the keyword `temp` appears at the end of the command line.

The keyword `pub` at the end of a command line with the `-s` option causes the system to act as an ARP agent for that host. The system will answer ARP requests for the IP address corresponding to the *hostname*, replying with the specified Ethernet *address*. If the advertised *address* is the system's own, then this system is acting as a proxy ARP agent for the specified *hostname*.

4.9 Summary

ARP is a basic protocol in almost every TCP/IP implementation, but it normally does its work without the application or the system administrator being aware. The ARP cache is fundamental to its operation, and we've used the `arp` command to examine and manipulate the cache. Each entry in the cache has a timer that is used to remove both incomplete and completed entries. The `arp` command displays and modifies entries in the ARP cache.

We followed through the normal operation of ARP along with specialized versions: proxy ARP (when a router answers ARP requests for hosts accessible on another of the router's interfaces) and gratuitous ARP (sending an ARP request for your own IP address, normally when bootstrapping).

Exercises

4.1 In the commands we typed to generate the output shown in Figure 4.4 (p. 58), what would happen if, after verifying that the local ARP cache was empty, we type the command

```
bsdi % rsh svr4 arp -a
```

to verify that the ARP cache is also empty on the destination host? (This command causes the `arp -a` command to be executed on the host `svr4`.)

4.2 Describe a test to determine if a given host handles a received gratuitous ARP request correctly.

4.3 Step 7 in Section 4.2 can take a while (milliseconds) because a packet is sent and ARP then waits for the response. How do you think ARP handles multiple datagrams that arrive from IP for the same destination address during this period?

4.4 At the end of Section 4.5 we mentioned that the Host Requirements RFC and Berkeley-derived implementations differ in their handling of the timeout of an active ARP entry. What happens if we're on a Berkeley-derived client and keep trying to contact a server host that's been taken down to replace its Ethernet board? Does this change if the server issues a gratuitous ARP when it bootstraps?

5

RARP: Reverse Address Resolution Protocol

5.1 Introduction

When a system with a local disk is bootstrapped it normally obtains its IP address from a configuration file that's read from a disk file. But a system without a disk, such as an X terminal or a diskless workstation, needs some other way to obtain its IP address.

Each system on a network has a unique hardware address, assigned by the manufacturer of the network interface. The principle of RARP is for the diskless system to read its unique hardware address from the interface card and send an RARP request (a broadcast frame on the network) asking for someone to reply with the diskless system's IP address (in an RARP reply).

While the concept is simple, the implementation is often harder than ARP for reasons described later in this chapter. The official specification of RARP is RFC 903 [Finlayson et al. 1984].

5.2 RARP Packet Format

The format of an RARP packet is almost identical to an ARP packet (Figure 4.3, p. 56). The only differences are that the *frame type* is `0x8035` for an RARP request or reply, and the *op* field has a value of 3 for an RARP request and 4 for an RARP reply.

As with ARP, the RARP request is broadcast and the RARP reply is normally unicast.

5.3 RARP Examples

In our internet we can force the host sun to bootstrap from the network, instead of its local disk. If we run an RARP server and tcpdump on the host bsdi we get the output shown in Figure 5.1. We use the -e flag to have tcpdump print the hardware addresses:

```
1  0.0               8:0:20:3:f6:42 ff:ff:ff:ff:ff:ff rarp 60:
                     rarp who-is 8:0:20:3:f6:42 tell 8:0:20:3:f6:42

2  0.13 (0.13)       0:0:c0:6f:2d:40 8:0:20:3:f6:42 rarp 42:
                     rarp reply 8:0:20:3:f6:42 at sun

3  0.14 (0.01)       8:0:20:3:f6:42 0:0:c0:6f:2d:40 ip 65:
                     sun.26999 > bsdi.tftp: 23 RRQ "8CFC0D21.SUN4C"
```

Figure 5.1 RARP request and reply.

The RARP request is broadcast (line 1) and the RARP reply on line 2 is unicast. The output on line 2, at sun, means the RARP reply contains the IP address for the host sun (140.252.13.33).

On line 3 we see that once sun receives its IP address, it issues a TFTP read-request (RRQ) for the file 8CFC0D21.SUN4C. (TFTP is the Trivial File Transfer Protocol. We describe it in more detail in Chapter 15.) The eight hexadecimal digits in the filename are the hex representation of the IP address 140.252.13.33 for the host sun. This is the IP address that was returned in the RARP reply. The remainder of the filename, SUN4C, indicates the type of system being bootstrapped.

tcpdump says that line 3 is an IP datagram of length 65, and not a UDP datagram (which it really is), because we are running tcpdump with the -e flag, to see the hardware-level addresses. Another point to notice in Figure 5.1 is that the length of the Ethernet frame on line 2 appears to be shorter than the minimum (which we said was 60 bytes in Section 4.5.) The reason is that we are running tcpdump on the system that is sending this Ethernet frame (bsdi). The application, rarpd, writes 42 bytes to the BSD Packet Filter device (14 bytes for the Ethernet header and 28 bytes for the RARP reply) and this is what tcpdump receives a copy of. But the Ethernet device driver pads this short frame to the minimum size for transmission (60). Had we been running tcpdump on another system, the length would have been 60.

We can see in this example that when this diskless system receives its IP address in an RARP reply, it issues a TFTP request to read a bootstrap image. At this point we won't go into additional detail about how diskless systems bootstrap themselves. (Chapter 16 describes the bootstrap sequence of a diskless X terminal using RARP, BOOTP, and TFTP.)

Figure 5.2 shows the resulting packets if there is no RARP server on the network. The destination address of each packet is the Ethernet broadcast address. The Ethernet address following who-is is the target hardware address, and the Ethernet address following tell is the sender's hardware address.

Note the frequency of the retransmissions. The first retransmission occurs after 6.55 seconds and then increases to 42.80 seconds, then goes down to 5.34 seconds, then 6.55, and then works its way back to 42.79 seconds. This continues indefinitely. If we

```
 1    0.0           8:0:20:3:f6:42 ff:ff:ff:ff:ff:ff rarp 60:
                    rarp who-is 8:0:20:3:f6:42 tell 8:0:20:3:f6:42
 2    6.55 ( 6.55)  8:0:20:3:f6:42 ff:ff:ff:ff:ff:ff rarp 60:
                    rarp who-is 8:0:20:3:f6:42 tell 8:0:20:3:f6:42
 3   15.52 ( 8.97)  8:0:20:3:f6:42 ff:ff:ff:ff:ff:ff rarp 60:
                    rarp who-is 8:0:20:3:f6:42 tell 8:0:20:3:f6:42
 4   29.32 (13.80)  8:0:20:3:f6:42 ff:ff:ff:ff:ff:ff rarp 60:
                    rarp who-is 8:0:20:3:f6:42 tell 8:0:20:3:f6:42
 5   52.78 (23.46)  8:0:20:3:f6:42 ff:ff:ff:ff:ff:ff rarp 60:
                    rarp who-is 8:0:20:3:f6:42 tell 8:0:20:3:f6:42
 6   95.58 (42.80)  8:0:20:3:f6:42 ff:ff:ff:ff:ff:ff rarp 60:
                    rarp who-is 8:0:20:3:f6:42 tell 8:0:20:3:f6:42
 7  100.92 ( 5.34)  8:0:20:3:f6:42 ff:ff:ff:ff:ff:ff rarp 60:
                    rarp who-is 8:0:20:3:f6:42 tell 8:0:20:3:f6:42
 8  107.47 ( 6.55)  8:0:20:3:f6:42 ff:ff:ff:ff:ff:ff rarp 60:
                    rarp who-is 8:0:20:3:f6:42 tell 8:0:20:3:f6:42
 9  116.44 ( 8.97)  8:0:20:3:f6:42 ff:ff:ff:ff:ff:ff rarp 60:
                    rarp who-is 8:0:20:3:f6:42 tell 8:0:20:3:f6:42
10  130.24 (13.80)  8:0:20:3:f6:42 ff:ff:ff:ff:ff:ff rarp 60:
                    rarp who-is 8:0:20:3:f6:42 tell 8:0:20:3:f6:42
11  153.70 (23.46)  8:0:20:3:f6:42 ff:ff:ff:ff:ff:ff rarp 60:
                    rarp who-is 8:0:20:3:f6:42 tell 8:0:20:3:f6:42
12  196.49 (42.79)  8:0:20:3:f6:42 ff:ff:ff:ff:ff:ff rarp 60:
                    rarp who-is 8:0:20:3:f6:42 tell 8:0:20:3:f6:42
```

Figure 5.2 RARP requests with no RARP server on the network.

calculate the differences between each timeout interval we see a doubling effect: from 5.34 to 6.55 is 1.21 seconds, from 6.55 to 8.97 is 2.42 seconds, from 8.97 to 13.80 is 4.83 seconds, and so on. When the timeout interval reaches some limit (greater than 42.80 seconds) it's reset to 5.34 seconds.

Increasing the timeout value like this is a better approach than using the same value each time. In Figure 6.8 we'll see one wrong way to perform timeout and retransmission, and in Chapter 21 we'll see TCP's method.

5.4 RARP Server Design

While the concept of RARP is simple, the design of an RARP server is system dependent and complex. Conversely, providing an ARP server is simple, and is normally part of the TCP/IP implementation in the kernel. Since the kernel knows its IP addresses and hardware addresses, when it receives an ARP request for one of its IP addresses, it just replies with the corresponding hardware address.

RARP Servers as User Processes

The complication with an RARP server is that the server normally provides the mapping from a hardware address to an IP address for many hosts (all the diskless systems on the network). This mapping is contained in a disk file (normally `/etc/ethers` on

Unix systems). Since kernels normally don't read and parse disk files, the function of an RARP server is provided as a user process, not as part of the kernel's TCP/IP implementation.

To further complicate matters, RARP requests are transmitted as Ethernet frames with a specific Ethernet frame type field (0x8035 from Figure 2.1.) This means an RARP server must have some way of sending and receiving Ethernet frames of this type. In Appendix A we describe how the BSD Packet Filter, Sun's Network Interface Tap, and the SVR4 Data Link Provider Interface can be used to receive these frames. Since the sending and receiving of these frames is system dependent, the implementation of an RARP server is tied to the system.

Multiple RARP Servers per Network

Another complication is that RARP requests are sent as hardware-level broadcasts, as shown in Figure 5.2. This means they are not forwarded by routers. To allow diskless systems to bootstrap even when the RARP server host is down, multiple RARP servers are normally provided on a single network (e.g., a single cable).

As the number of servers increases (to provide redundancy), the network traffic increases, since every server sends an RARP reply for every RARP request. The diskless system that sent the RARP request normally uses the first RARP reply that it receives. (We never had this problem with ARP, because only a single host sends an ARP reply.) Furthermore, there is a chance that each RARP server can try to respond at about the same time, increasing the probability of collisions on an Ethernet.

5.5 Summary

RARP is used by many diskless systems to obtain their IP address when bootstrapped. The RARP packet format is nearly identical to the ARP packet. An RARP request is broadcast, identifying the sender's hardware address, asking for anyone to respond with the sender's IP address. The reply is normally unicast.

Problems with RARP include its use of a link-layer broadcast, preventing most routers from forwarding an RARP request, and the minimal information returned: just the system's IP address. In Chapter 16 we'll see that BOOTP returns more information for the diskless system that is bootstrapping: its IP address, the name of a host to bootstrap from, and so on.

While the RARP concept is simple, the implementation of an RARP server is system dependent. Hence not all TCP/IP implementations provide an RARP server.

Exercises

5.1 Is a separate *frame type* field required for RARP? Could the same value be used for ARP and RARP 0x0806?

5.2 With multiple RARP servers on a network, how can they prevent their responses from colliding with each on the network?

6

ICMP: Internet Control Message Protocol

6.1 Introduction

ICMP is often considered part of the IP layer. It communicates error messages and other conditions that require attention. ICMP messages are usually acted on by either the IP layer or the higher layer protocol (TCP or UDP). Some ICMP messages cause errors to be returned to user processes.

ICMP messages are transmitted within IP datagrams, as shown in Figure 6.1.

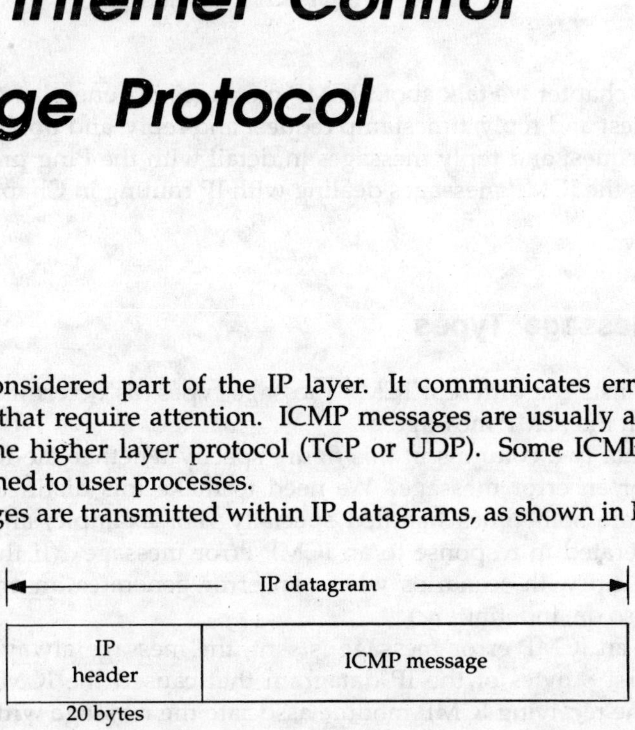

Figure 6.1 ICMP messages encapsulated within an IP datagram.

RFC 792 [Postel 1981b] contains the official specification of ICMP.

Figure 6.2 shows the format of an ICMP message. The first 4 bytes have the same format for all messages, but the remainder differs from one message to the next. We'll show the exact format of each message when we describe it.

There are 15 different values for the *type* field, which identify the particular ICMP message. Some types of ICMP messages then use different values of the *code* field to further specify the condition.

The *checksum* field covers the entire ICMP message. The algorithm used is the same as we described for the IP header checksum in Section 3.2. The ICMP checksum is required.

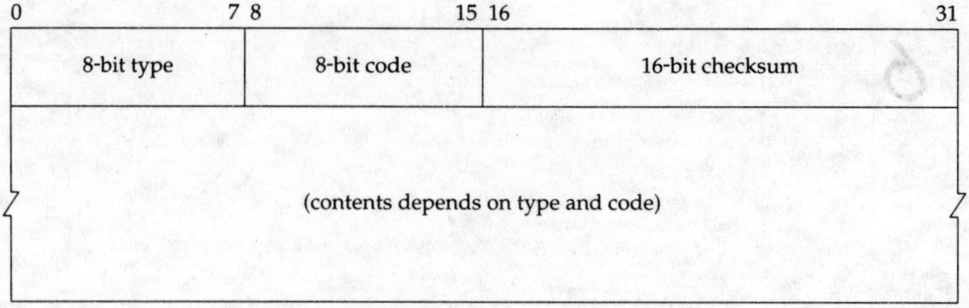

Figure 6.2 ICMP message.

In this chapter we talk about ICMP messages in general and a few in detail: address mask request and reply, timestamp request and reply, and port unreachable. We discuss the echo request and reply messages in detail with the Ping program in Chapter 7, and we discuss the ICMP messages dealing with IP routing in Chapter 9.

6.2 ICMP Message Types

Figure 6.3 lists the different ICMP message types, as determined by the *type* field and *code* field in the ICMP message.

The final two columns in this figure specify whether the ICMP message is a query message or an error message. We need to make this distinction because ICMP error messages are sometimes handled specially. For example, an ICMP error message is never generated in response to an ICMP error message. (If this were not the rule, we could end up with scenarios where an error generates an error, which generates an error, and so on, indefinitely.)

When an ICMP error message is sent, the message always contains the IP header and the first 8 bytes of the IP datagram that caused the ICMP error to be generated. This lets the receiving ICMP module associate the message with one particular protocol (TCP or UDP from the protocol field in the IP header) and one particular user process (from the TCP or UDP port numbers that are in the TCP or UDP header contained in the first 8 bytes of the IP datagram). We'll show an example of this in Section 6.5.

An ICMP error message is never generated in response to

1. An ICMP error message. (An ICMP error message may, however, be generated in response to an ICMP query message.)
2. A datagram destined to an IP broadcast address (Figure 3.9) or an IP multicast address (a class D address, Figure 1.5).
3. A datagram sent as a link-layer broadcast.
4. A fragment other than the first. (We describe fragmentation in Section 11.5.)

type	code	Description	Query	Error
0	0	echo reply (Ping reply, Chapter 7)	•	
3		destination unreachable:		
	0	network unreachable (Section 9.3)		•
	1	host unreachable (Section 9.3)		•
	2	protocol unreachable		•
	3	port unreachable (Section 6.5)		•
	4	fragmentation needed but don't-fragment bit set (Section 11.6)		•
	5	source route failed (Section 8.5)		•
	6	destination network unknown		•
	7	destination host unknown		•
	8	source host isolated (obsolete)		•
	9	destination network administratively prohibited		•
	10	destination host administratively prohibited		•
	11	network unreachable for TOS (Section 9.3)		•
	12	host unreachable for TOS (Section 9.3)		•
	13	communication administratively prohibited by filtering		•
	14	host precedence violation		•
	15	precedence cutoff in effect		•
4	0	source quench (elementary flow control, Section 11.11)		•
5		redirect (Section 9.5):		
	0	redirect for network		•
	1	redirect for host		•
	2	redirect for type-of-service and network		•
	3	redirect for type-of-service and host		•
8	0	echo request (Ping request, Chapter 7)	•	
9	0	router advertisement (Section 9.6)	•	
10	0	router solicitation (Section 9.6)	•	
11		time exceeded:		
	0	time-to-live equals 0 during transit (Traceroute, Chapter 8)		•
	1	time-to-live equals 0 during reassembly (Section 11.5)		•
12		parameter problem:		
	0	IP header bad (catchall error)		•
	1	required option missing		•
13	0	timestamp request (Section 6.4)	•	
14	0	timestamp reply (Section 6.4)	•	
15	0	information request (obsolete)	•	
16	0	information reply (obsolete)	•	
17	0	address mask request (Section 6.3)	•	
18	0	address mask reply (Section 6.3)	•	

Figure 6.3 ICMP message types.

5. A datagram whose source address does not define a single host. This means the source address cannot be a zero address, a loopback address, a broadcast address, or a multicast address.

These rules are meant to prevent the *broadcast storms* that have occurred in the past when ICMP errors were sent in response to broadcast packets.

6.3 ICMP Address Mask Request and Reply

The ICMP address mask request is intended for a diskless system to obtain its subnet mask (Section 3.5) at bootstrap time. The requesting system broadcasts its ICMP request. (This is similar to a diskless system using RARP to obtain its IP address at bootstrap time.) An alternative method for a diskless system to obtain its subnet mask is the BOOTP protocol, which we describe in Chapter 16. Figure 6.4 shows the format of the ICMP address mask request and reply messages.

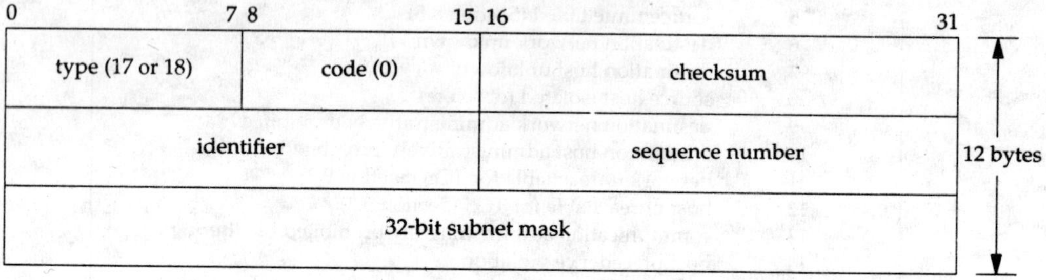

Figure 6.4 ICMP address mask request and reply messages.

The identifier and sequence number fields in the ICMP message can be set to anything the sender chooses, and these values are returned in the reply. This allows the sender to match replies with requests.

We can write a simple program (named `icmpaddrmask`) that issues an ICMP address mask request and prints all replies. Since normal usage is to send the request to the broadcast address, that's what we'll do. The destination address (140.252.13.63) is the broadcast address for the subnet 140.252.13.32 (Figure 3.12).

```
sun % icmpaddrmask 140.252.13.63
received mask = ffffffe0, from 140.252.13.33          from ourself
received mask = ffffffe0, from 140.252.13.35          from bsdi
received mask = ffff0000, from 140.252.13.34          from svr4
```

The first thing we note in this output is that the returned value from `svr4` is wrong. It appears that SVR4 is returning the general class B address mask, assuming no subnets, even though the interface on `svr4` has been configured with the correct subnet mask:

```
svr4 % ifconfig emd0
emd0: flags=23<UP,BROADCAST,NOTRAILERS>
        inet 140.252.13.34 netmask ffffffe0 broadcast 140.252.13.63
```

There is a bug in the SVR4 handling of the ICMP address mask request.

We'll watch this exchange on the host `bsdi` using `tcpdump`. The output is shown in Figure 6.5. We specify the `-e` option to see the hardware addresses.

```
1  0.0             8:0:20:3:f6:42 ff:ff:ff:ff:ff:ff ip 60:
                   sun > 140.252.13.63: icmp: address mask request
2  0.00 (0.00)     0:0:c0:6f:2d:40 ff:ff:ff:ff:ff:ff ip 46:
                   bsdi > sun: icmp: address mask is 0xfffffe0
3  0.01 (0.01)     0:0:c0:c2:9b:26 8:0:20:3:f6:42 ip 60:
                   svr4 > sun: icmp: address mask is 0xffff0000
```

Figure 6.5 ICMP address mask request sent to broadcast address.

Note that the sending host, sun, receives an ICMP reply (the output line with the comment *from ourself* shown earlier), even though nothing is seen on the wire. This is a general characteristic of broadcasting: the sending host receives a copy of the broadcast packet through some internal loopback mechanism. Since by definition the term "broadcast" means *all* the hosts on the local network, it should include the sending host. (Referring to Figure 2.4 [p. 28] what is happening is that when the Ethernet driver recognizes that the destination address is the broadcast address, the packet is sent onto the network *and* a copy is made and passed to the loopback interface.)

Next, bsdi broadcasts the reply, while svr4 sends the reply only to the requestor. Normally the reply should be unicast unless the source IP address of the request is 0.0.0.0, which it isn't in this example. Therefore, sending the reply to the broadcast address is a BSD/386 bug.

> The Host Requirements RFC says that a system must not send an address mask reply unless it is an authoritative agent for address masks. (To be an authoritative agent it must be specifically configured to send these replies. See Appendix E.) As we can see from this example, however, most host implementations send a reply if they get a request. Some hosts even send the wrong reply!

The final point is shown by the following example. We send an address mask request to our own IP address and to the loopback address:

```
sun % icmpaddrmask sun
received mask = ff000000, from 140.252.13.33

sun % icmpaddrmask localhost
received mask = ff000000, from 127.0.0.1
```

In both cases the returned address mask corresponds to the loopback address, the class A address 127.0.0.1. Again, referring to Figure 2.4 we see that IP datagrams sent to the host's own IP address (140.252.13.33 in this example) are actually sent to the loopback interface. The ICMP address mask reply must correspond to the subnet mask of the interface on which the request was received (since a multihomed host can have different subnet masks for each interface), and in both cases the request is received from the loopback interface.

6.4 ICMP Timestamp Request and Reply

The ICMP timestamp request allows a system to query another for the current time. The recommended value to be returned is the number of milliseconds since midnight, Coordinated Universal Time (UTC). (Older manuals refer to UTC as Greenwich Mean Time.) The nice feature of this ICMP message is that it provides millisecond resolution, whereas some other methods for obtaining the time from another host (such as the `rdate` command provided by some Unix systems) provide a resolution of seconds. The drawback is that only the time since midnight is returned—the caller must know the date from some other means.

Figure 6.6 shows the format of the ICMP timestamp request and reply messages.

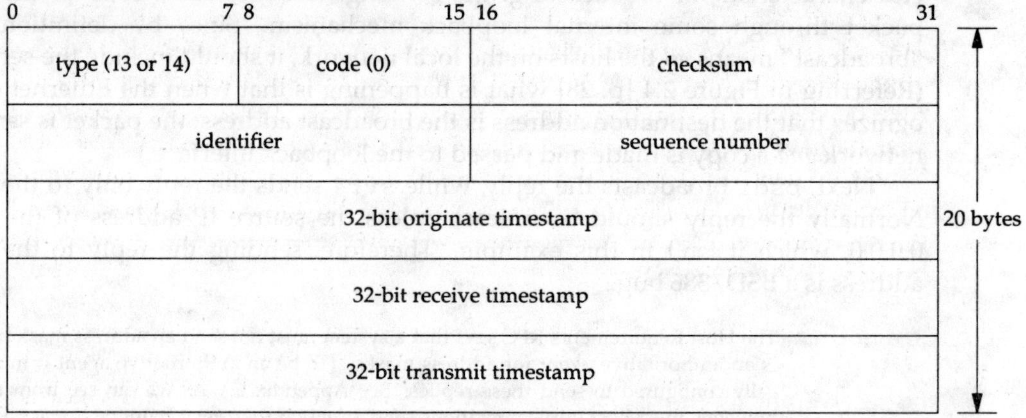

Figure 6.6 ICMP timestamp request and reply messages.

The requestor fills in the *originate* timestamp and sends the request. The replying system fills in the *receive* timestamp when it receives the request, and the *transmit* timestamp when it sends the reply. In actuality, however, most implementations set the latter two fields to the same value. (The reason for providing the three fields is to let the sender compute the time for the request to be sent, and separately compute the time for the reply to be sent.)

Examples

We can write a simple program (named `icmptime`) that sends an ICMP timestamp request to a host and prints the returned reply. We try it first on our small internet:

```
sun % icmptime bsdi
orig = 83573336, recv = 83573330, xmit = 83573330, rtt = 2 ms
difference = -6 ms

sun % icmptime bsdi
orig = 83577987, recv = 83577980, xmit = 83577980, rtt = 2 ms
difference = -7 ms
```

The program prints the three timestamps in the ICMP message: the originate (`orig`), receive (`recv`), and transmit (`xmit`) timestamps. As we can see in this and the following examples, all the hosts set the receive and transmit timestamps to the same value.

We also calculate the round-trip time (`rtt`), which is the time the reply is received minus the time the request was sent. The `difference` is the received timestamp minus the originate timestamp. Figure 6.7 shows the relationship between these values.

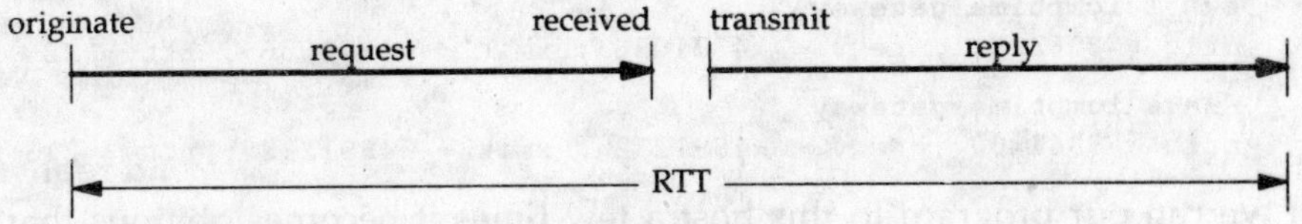

Figure 6.7 Relationship between values printed by our `icmptime` program.

If we believe the RTT and assume that one-half of the RTT is for the request, and the other half for the reply, then the sender's clock needs to be adjusted by `difference` minus one-half the RTT, to have the same time as the host being queried. In the preceding example, the clock on `bsdi` was 7 and 8 ms behind the clock on `sun`.

Since the timestamp values are the number of milliseconds past midnight, UTC, they should always be less than 86,400,000 ($24 \times 60 \times 60 \times 1000$). These examples were run just before 4:00 P.M. in a time zone that is 7 hours behind UTC, so the values being greater than 82,800,000 (2300 hours) makes sense.

If we run this program several times to the host `bsdi` we see that the final digit in the receive and transmit timestamp is always 0. This is because the software release (Version 0.9.4) only provides a 10-ms clock. (We describe this in Appendix B.)

If we run the program twice to the host `svr4` we see that the low-order three digits of the SVR4 timestamp are always 0:

```
sun % icmptime svr4
orig = 83588210, recv = 83588000, xmit = 83588000, rtt = 4 ms
difference = -210 ms

sun % icmptime svr4
orig = 83591547, recv = 83591000, xmit = 83591000, rtt = 4 ms
difference = -547 ms
```

For some reason SVR4 doesn't provide any millisecond resolution using the ICMP timestamp. This imprecision makes the calculated differences useless for subsecond adjustments.

If we try two other hosts on the 140.252.1 subnet, the results show that one clock differs from `sun`'s by 3.7 seconds, and the other by nearly 75 seconds:

```
sun % icmptime gemini
orig = 83601883, recv = 83598140, xmit = 83598140, rtt = 247 ms
difference = -3743 ms

sun % icmptime aix
orig = 83606768, recv = 83532183, xmit = 83532183, rtt = 253 ms
difference = -74585 ms
```

Another interesting example is to the router `gateway` (a Cisco router). It shows that when a system returns a nonstandard timestamp value (something other than milliseconds past midnight, UTC), it is supposed to turn on the high-order bit of the 32-bit timestamp. Our program detects this, and prints the receive and transmit timestamps in angle brackets (after turning off the high-order bit). Also, we can't calculate the difference between the originate and receive timestamps, since they're not the same units.

```
sun % icmptime gateway
orig = 83620811, recv = <4871036>, xmit = <4871036>, rtt = 220 ms
sun % icmptime gateway
orig = 83641007, recv = <4891232>, xmit = <4891232>, rtt = 213 ms
```

If we run our program to this host a few times it becomes obvious that the values do contain millisecond resolution and do count the number of milliseconds past some starting point, but the starting point is not midnight, UTC. (It could be a counter that's incremented every millisecond since the router was bootstrapped, for example.)

As a final example we'll compare `sun`'s clock with a system whose clock is known to be accurate—an NTP stratum 1 server. (We say more about NTP, the Network Time Protocol, below.)

```
sun % icmptime clock.llnl.gov
orig = 83662791, recv = 83662919, xmit = 83662919, rtt = 359 ms
difference = 128 ms
sun % icmptime clock.llnl.gov
orig = 83670425, recv = 83670559, xmit = 83670559, rtt = 345 ms
difference = 134 ms
```

If we calculate the difference minus one-half the RTT, this output indicates that the clock on `sun` is between 38.5 and 51.5 ms fast.

Alternatives

There are other ways to obtain the time and date.

1. We described the daytime service and time service in Section 1.12. The former returns the current time and date in a human readable form, a line of ASCII characters. We can test this service using the `telnet` command:

```
sun % telnet bsdi daytime
Trying 140.252.13.35 ...
Connected to bsdi.
Escape character is '^]'.                first three lines output are from the Telnet client
Wed Feb  3 16:38:33 1993                 here's the daytime service output
Connection closed by foreign host.       this is also from the Telnet client
```

The time server, on the other hand, returns a 32-bit binary value with the number of seconds since midnight January 1, 1900, UTC. While this provides the date, the time value is in units of a second. (The `rdate` command that we mentioned earlier uses the TCP time service.)

2. Serious timekeepers use the Network Time Protocol (NTP) described in RFC 1305 [Mills 1992]. This protocol uses sophisticated techniques to maintain the clocks for a group of systems on a LAN or WAN to within millisecond accuracy. Anyone interested in precise timekeeping on computers should read this RFC.
3. The Open Software Foundation's (OSF) Distributed Computing Environment (DCE) defines a Distributed Time Service (DTS) that also provides clock synchronization between computers. [Rosenberg, Kenney, and Fisher 1992] provide additional details on this service.
4. Berkeley Unix systems provide the daemon `timed(8)` to synchronize the clocks of systems on a local area network. Unlike NTP and DTS, `timed` does not work across wide area networks.

6.5 ICMP Port Unreachable Error

The last two sections looked at ICMP query messages—the address mask and timestamp queries and replies. We'll now examine an ICMP error message, the port unreachable message, a subcode of the ICMP destination unreachable message, to see the additional information returned in an ICMP error message. We'll watch this using UDP (Chapter 11).

One rule of UDP is that if it receives a UDP datagram and the destination port does not correspond to a port that some process has in use, UDP responds with an ICMP port unreachable. We can force a port unreachable using the TFTP client. (We describe TFTP in Chapter 15.)

The well-known UDP port for the TFTP server to be reading from is 69. But most TFTP client programs allow us to specify a different port using the `connect` command. We use this to specify a port of 8888:

```
bsdi % tftp
tftp> connect svr4 8888          specify the hostname and port number
tftp> get temp.foo               try to fetch a file
Transfer timed out.              about 25 seconds later
tftp> quit
```

The `connect` command saves the name of the host to contact and the port number on that host, for when we later issue the `get` command. After typing the `get` command a UDP datagram is sent to port 8888 on host `svr4`. Figure 6.8 shows the `tcpdump` output for the exchange of packets that takes place.

Before the UDP datagram can be sent to `svr4` an ARP request is sent to determine its hardware address (line 1). The ARP reply (line 2) is returned and then the UDP datagram is sent (line 3). (We have left the ARP request–reply in this `tcpdump` output to remind us that this exchange may be required before the first IP datagram is sent from one host to the other. In future output we'll delete this exchange if it's not relevant to the topic being discussed.)

```
 1  0.0                      arp who-has svr4 tell bsdi
 2  0.002050  (0.0020)       arp reply svr4 is-at 0:0:c0:c2:9b:26

 3  0.002723  (0.0007)       bsdi.2924 > svr4.8888: udp 20
 4  0.006399  (0.0037)       svr4 > bsdi: icmp: svr4 udp port 8888 unreachable

 5  5.000776  (4.9944)       bsdi.2924 > svr4.8888: udp 20
 6  5.004304  (0.0035)       svr4 > bsdi: icmp: svr4 udp port 8888 unreachable

 7  10.000887 (4.9966)       bsdi.2924 > svr4.8888: udp 20
 8  10.004416 (0.0035)       svr4 > bsdi: icmp: svr4 udp port 8888 unreachable

 9  15.001014 (4.9966)       bsdi.2924 > svr4.8888: udp 20
10  15.004574 (0.0036)       svr4 > bsdi: icmp: svr4 udp port 8888 unreachable

11  20.001177 (4.9966)       bsdi.2924 > svr4.8888: udp 20
12  20.004759 (0.0036)       svr4 > bsdi: icmp: svr4 udp port 8888 unreachable
```

Figure 6.8 ICMP port unreachable generated by TFTP request.

An ICMP port unreachable is immediately returned (line 4). But the TFTP client appears to ignore the ICMP message, sending another UDP datagram about 5 seconds later (line 5). This continues three more times before the client gives up.

Notice that the ICMP messages are exchanged between hosts, without a port number designation, while each 20-byte UDP datagram is from a specific port (2924) and to a specific port (8888).

The number 20 at the end of each UDP line is the length of the data in the UDP datagram. In this example 20 is the sum of the TFTP's 2-byte opcode, the 9-byte null terminated name `temp.foo`, and the 9-byte null terminated string `netascii`. (See Figure 15.1 for the details of the TFTP packet layout.)

If we run this same example using the `-e` option of `tcpdump` we see the exact length of each ICMP port unreachable message that's returned to the sender. This length is 70 bytes, and is allocated as shown in Figure 6.9.

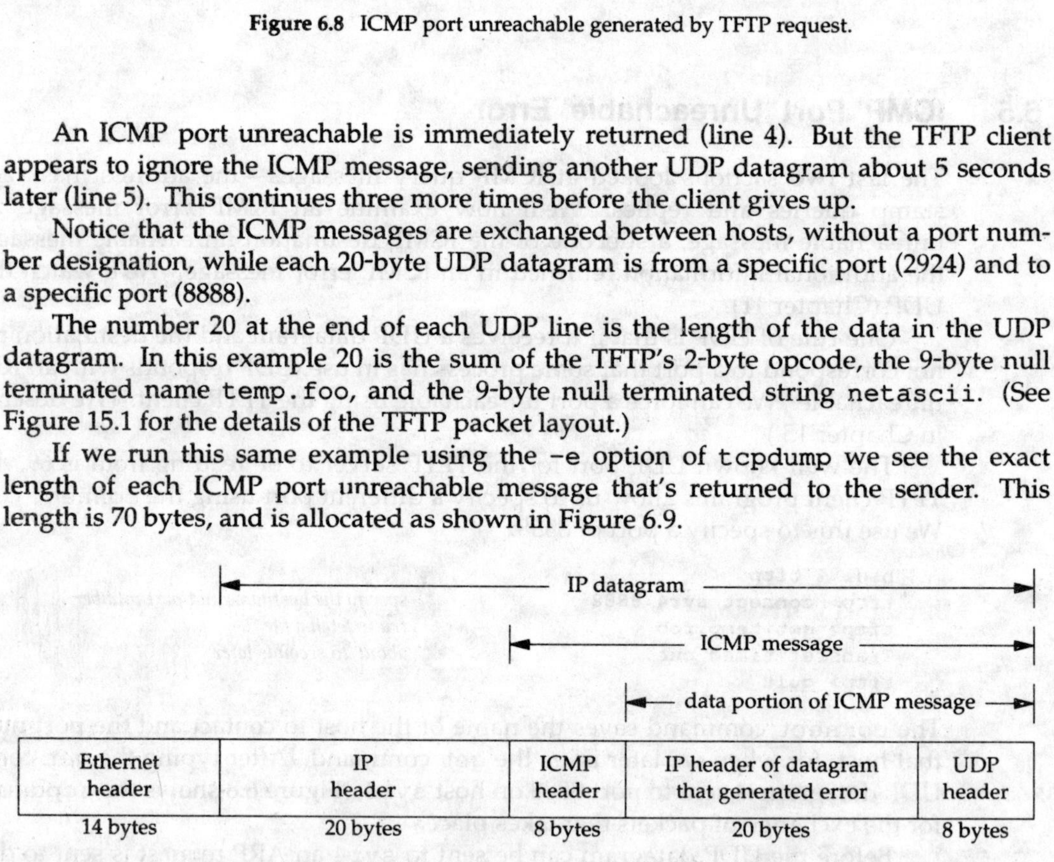

Figure 6.9 ICMP message returned for our "UDP port unreachable" example.

One rule of ICMP is that the ICMP error messages (see the final column of Figure 6.3, p. 71) must include the IP header (including any options) of the datagram that generated the error along with at least the first 8 bytes that followed this IP header. In our example, the first 8 bytes following the IP header contain the UDP header (Figure 11.2).

The important fact is that contained in the UDP header are the source and destination port numbers. It is this destination port number (8888) that caused the ICMP port unreachable to be generated. The source port number (2924) can be used by the system receiving the ICMP error to associate the error with a particular user process (the TFTP client in this example).

One reason the IP header of the datagram that caused the error is sent back is because in this IP header is the protocol field that lets ICMP know how to interpret the 8 bytes that follow (the UDP header in this example). When we look at the TCP header (Figure 17.2) we'll see that the source and destination port numbers are contained in the first 8 bytes of the TCP header.

The general format of the ICMP unreachable messages is shown in Figure 6.10.

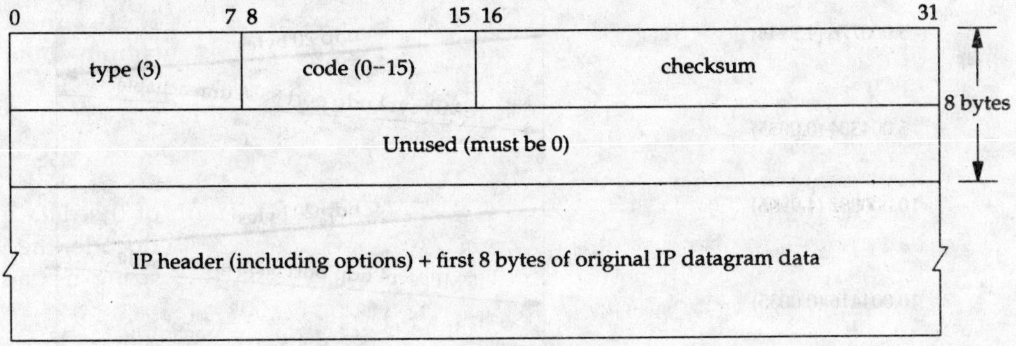

Figure 6.10 ICMP unreachable message.

In Figure 6.3 we noted that there are 16 different ICMP unreachable messages, *codes* 0 through 15. The ICMP port unreachable is *code* 3. Also, although Figure 6.10 indicates that the second 32-bit word in the ICMP message must be 0, the Path MTU Discovery mechanism (Section 2.9) allows a router to place the MTU of the outgoing interface in the low-order 16 bits of this 32-bit value, when *code* equals 4 ("fragmentation needed but the don't fragment bit is set"). We show an example of this error in Section 11.6.

> Although the rules of ICMP allow a system to return more than the first 8 bytes of the data portion of the IP datagram that caused the ICMP error, most Berkeley-derived implementations return exactly 8 bytes. The Solaris 2.2 `ip_icmp_return_data_bytes` option returns the first 64 bytes of data by default (Section E.4).

`tcpdump` Time Line

Throughout the text we'll also display the `tcpdump` output in a time line diagram as shown in Figure 6.11.

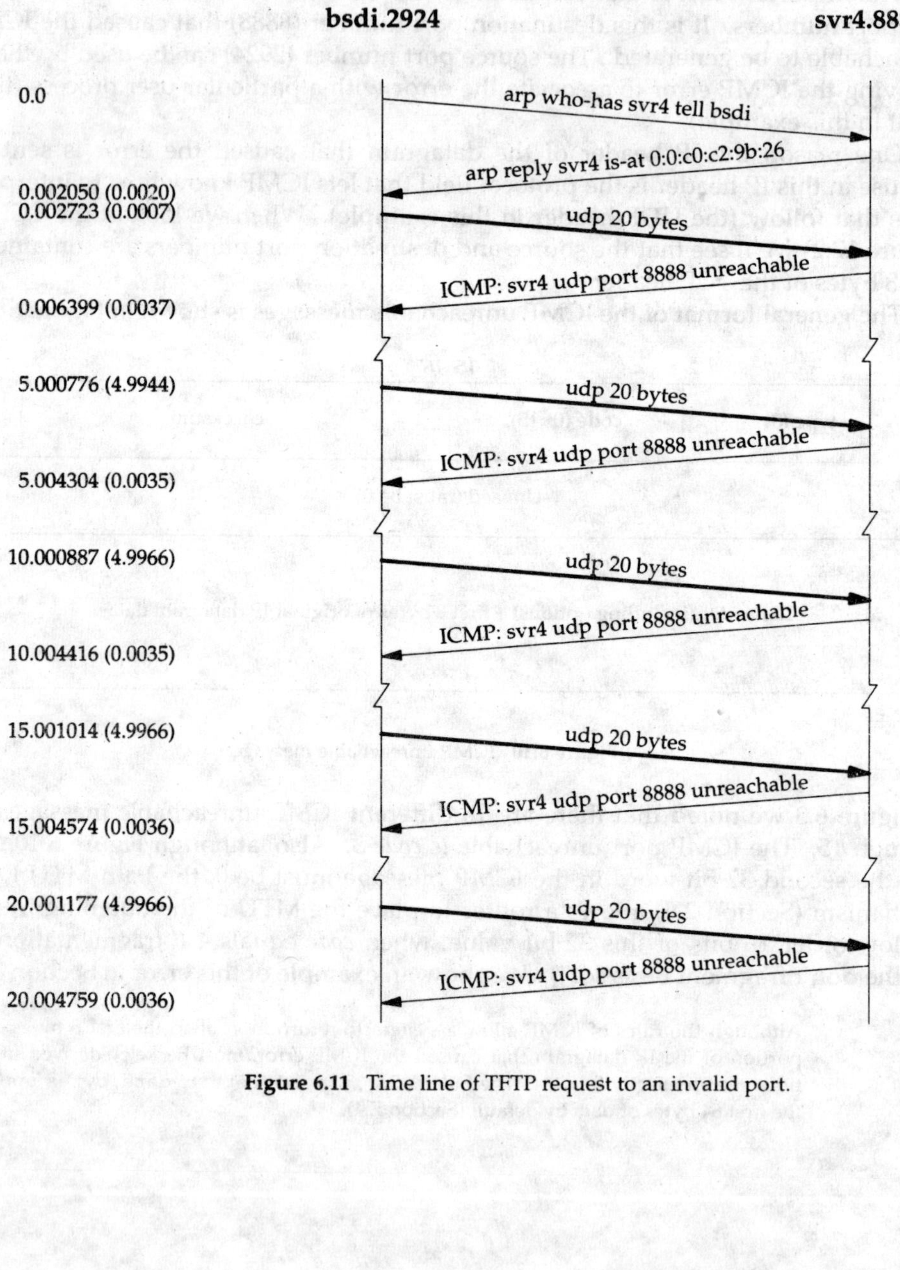

Figure 6.11 Time line of TFTP request to an invalid port.

Time increases down the page and the labels on the far left of the figure are the same time values as in our `tcpdump` output (Figure 6.8). The labels at the top are the hostnames and port numbers for each side of the time line. Be aware that the y-axis down the page is *not* exactly proportional to the time value. When there is a significant time lag, as between each 5-second retransmission in this example, we'll designate that with a squiggle on both sides of the time line. When UDP or TCP data is being transmitted, we show that packet with a thicker line.

Why does the TFTP client keep retransmitting its request when the ICMP messages are being returned? An element of network programming is occurring in which BSD systems don't notify user processes using UDP of ICMP messages that are received for that socket unless the process has issued a `connect` on that socket. The standard BSD TFTP client does not issue the `connect`, so it never receives the ICMP error notification.

Another point to notice here is the poor retransmission timeout algorithm used by this TFTP client. It just assumes that 5 seconds is adequate and retransmits every 5 seconds, for a total of 25 seconds. We'll see later that TCP has a much better algorithm.

> This old-fashioned timeout and retransmission algorithm used by the TFTP client is forbidden by the Host Requirements RFC. Nevertheless, all three systems on the author's subnet, and Solaris 2.2 still use it. AIX 3.2.2 applies an exponential backoff to its timeout, sending packets at 0, 5, 15, and 35 seconds, which is the recommended way. We talk much more about timeouts in Chapter 21.

Finally note that the ICMP messages are returned about 3.5 ms after the UDP datagram is sent, which we'll see in Chapter 7 is similar to the round-trip times for Ping replies.

6.6 4.4BSD Processing of ICMP Messages

Since ICMP covers such a wide range of conditions, from fatal errors to informational messages, each ICMP message is handled differently, even within a given implementation. Figure 6.12 is a redo of Figure 6.3, showing the handling performed by 4.4BSD for each of the possible ICMP messages.

If the final column specifies the kernel, that ICMP message is handled by the kernel. If the final column specifies "user process", then that message is passed to all user processes that have registered with the kernel to read received ICMP messages. If there are none of these user processes, the message is silently discarded. (These user processes also receive a copy of all the other ICMP messages, even those handled by the kernel, but only after the kernel has processed the message.) Some messages are completely ignored. Finally, if the final column is a string in quotes, that is the Unix error message corresponding to that condition. Some of these errors, such as TCP's handling of a source quench, we'll cover in later chapters.

type	*code*	Description	Handled by
0	0	echo reply	user process
3		destination unreachable:	
	0	network unreachable	"No route to host"
	1	host unreachable	"No route to host"
	2	protocol unreachable	"Connection refused"
	3	port unreachable	"Connection refused"
	4	fragmentation needed but DF bit set	"Message too long"
	5	source route failed	"No route to host"
	6	destination network unknown	"No route to host"
	7	destination host unknown	"No route to host"
	8	source host isolated (obsolete)	"No route to host"
	9	dest. network administratively prohibited	"No route to host"
	10	dest. host administratively prohibited	"No route to host"
	11	network unreachable for TOS	"No route to host"
	12	host unreachable for TOS	"No route to host"
	13	communication administratively prohibited	(ignored)
	14	host precedence violation	(ignored)
	15	precedence cutoff in effect	(ignored)
4	0	source quench	kernel for TCP, ignored by UDP
5		redirect:	
	0	redirect for network	kernel updates routing table
	1	redirect for host	kernel updates routing table
	2	redirect for type-of-service and network	kernel updates routing table
	3	redirect for type-of-service and host	kernel updates routing table
8	0	echo request	kernel generates reply
9	0	router advertisement	user process
10	0	router solicitation	user process
11		time exceeded:	
	0	TTL equals 0 during transit	user process
	1	TTL equals 0 during reassembly	user process
12		parameter problem:	
	0	IP header bad (catchall error)	"Protocol not available"
	1	required option missing	"Protocol not available"
13	0	timestamp request	kernel generates reply
14	0	timestamp reply	user process
15	0	information request (obsolete)	(ignored)
16	0	information reply (obsolete)	user process
17	0	address mask request	kernel generates reply
18	0	address mask reply	user process

Figure 6.12 Handling of the ICMP message types by 4.4BSD.

6.7 Summary

This chapter has been a look at the Internet Control Message Protocol, a required part of every implementation. Figure 6.3 lists all the ICMP message types, most of which we'll discuss later in the text.

We looked at the ICMP address mask request and reply and the timestamp request and reply in detail. These are typical of the request–reply messages. Both have an identifier and sequence number in the ICMP message. The sending application stores a unique value in the identifier field, to distinguish between replies for itself and replies for other processes. The sequence number field lets the client match replies with requests.

We also saw the ICMP port unreachable error, a common ICMP error. This let us examine the information returned in an ICMP error: the IP header and the next 8 bytes of the IP datagram that caused the error. This information is required by the receiver of the ICMP error, to know more about the cause of the error. Both TCP and UDP store the source and destination port numbers in the first 8 bytes of their headers for this reason.

Finally, we presented our first time line of `tcpdump` output, a presentation format we'll use in later chapters.

Exercises

6.1 At the end of Section 6.2 we listed five special conditions under which an ICMP error message is not sent. What would happen if these five conditions weren't followed and we sent a broadcast UDP datagram to an unlikely port on the local cable?

6.2 Read the Host Requirements RFC [Braden 1989a] to see if the generation of an ICMP port unreachable is a "must," "should," or "may." What section and page is this found on?

6.3 Read RFC 1349 [Almquist 1992] to see how the IP type-of-service field (Figure 3.2) should be set by ICMP.

6.4 If your system provides the `netstat` command, use it to see what types of ICMP messages are received and sent.

7

Ping Program

7.1 Introduction

The name "ping" is taken from the sonar operation to locate objects. The Ping program was written by Mike Muuss and it tests whether another host is reachable. The program sends an ICMP echo request message to a host, expecting an ICMP echo reply to be returned. (Figure 6.3 lists all the ICMP message types.)

Normally if you can't Ping a host, you won't be able to Telnet or FTP to that host. Conversely, if you can't Telnet to a host, Ping is often the starting point to determine what the problem is. Ping also measures the round-trip time to the host, giving us some indication of how "far away" that host is.

In this chapter we'll use Ping as a diagnostic tool and to further explore ICMP. Ping also gives us an opportunity to examine the IP record route and timestamp options. Chapter 11 of [Stevens 1990] provides the source code for the Ping program.

> Years ago we could make the unqualified statement that if we can't Ping a host, we can't Telnet or FTP to that host. With the increased awareness of security on the Internet, routers that provide access control lists, and firewall gateways, unqualified statements like this are no longer true. Reachability of a given host may depend not only on reachability at the IP layer, but also on what protocol is being used, and the port numbers involved. Ping may show a host as being unreachable, yet we might be able to Telnet to port 25 (the mail server).

7.2 Ping Program

We call the `ping` program that sends the echo requests the *client*, and the host being pinged the *server*. Most TCP/IP implementations support the Ping server directly in the kernel—the server is not a user process. (The two ICMP query services that we described in Chapter 6, the address mask and timestamp requests, are also handled directly by the kernel.)

Figure 7.1 shows the ICMP echo request and echo reply messages.

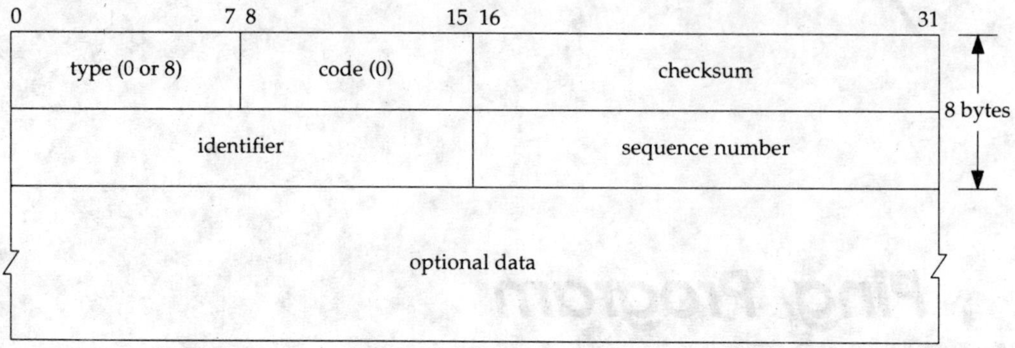

Figure 7.1 Format of ICMP message for echo request and echo reply.

As with other ICMP query messages, the server must echo the *identifier* and *sequence number* fields. Also, any optional data sent by the client must be echoed. These are presumably of interest to the client.

Unix implementations of `ping` set the *identifier* field in the ICMP message to the process ID of the sending process. This allows `ping` to identify the returned responses if there are multiple instances of `ping` running at the same time on the same host.

The *sequence number* starts at 0 and is incremented every time a new echo request is sent. `ping` prints the sequence number of each returned packet, allowing us to see if packets are missing, reordered, or duplicated. IP is a best effort datagram delivery service, so any of these three conditions can occur.

Historically the `ping` program has operated in a mode where it sends an echo request once a second, printing each echo reply that is returned. Newer implementations, however, require the `-s` option to operate this way. By default, these newer implementations send only a single echo request and output "*host* is alive" if an echo reply is received, or "no answer" if no reply is received within 20 seconds.

LAN Output

`ping` output on a LAN normally looks like the following:

```
bsdi % ping svr4
PING svr4 (140.252.13.34): 56 data bytes
64 bytes from 140.252.13.34: icmp_seq=0 ttl=255 time=0 ms
64 bytes from 140.252.13.34: icmp_seq=1 ttl=255 time=0 ms
64 bytes from 140.252.13.34: icmp_seq=2 ttl=255 time=0 ms
64 bytes from 140.252.13.34: icmp_seq=3 ttl=255 time=0 ms
64 bytes from 140.252.13.34: icmp_seq=4 ttl=255 time=0 ms
64 bytes from 140.252.13.34: icmp_seq=5 ttl=255 time=0 ms
64 bytes from 140.252.13.34: icmp_seq=6 ttl=255 time=0 ms
64 bytes from 140.252.13.34: icmp_seq=7 ttl=255 time=0 ms
^?                                               type interrupt key to stop
--- svr4 ping statistics ---
8 packets transmitted, 8 packets received, 0% packet loss
round-trip min/avg/max = 0/0/0 ms
```

When the ICMP echo reply is returned, the sequence number is printed, followed by the TTL, and the round-trip time is calculated. (TTL is the time-to-live field in the IP header. The current BSD `ping` program prints the received TTL each time an echo reply is received—some implementations don't do this. We examine the usage of the TTL in Chapter 8 with the `traceroute` program.)

As we can see from the output above, the echo replies were returned in the order sent (0, 1, 2, and so on).

`ping` is able to calculate the round-trip time by storing the time at which it sends the echo request in the data portion of the ICMP message. When the reply is returned it subtracts this value from the current time. Notice that on the sending system, `bsdi`, the round-trip times are all calculated as 0 ms. This is because of the low-resolution timer available to the program. The BSD/386 Version 0.9.4 system only provides a 10-ms timer. (We talk more about this in Appendix B.) We'll see later that when looking at the `tcpdump` output from this `ping` example on a system with a finer resolution clock (the Sun) the time difference between the ICMP echo request and its echo reply is just under 4 ms.

The first line of output contains the IP address of the destination host, even though we specified its name (`svr4`). This implies that the name has been converted to the IP address by a resolver. We examine resolvers and the DNS in Chapter 14. For now realize that if we type a `ping` command, and a few seconds pass before the first line of output with the IP address is printed, this is the time required for the DNS to determine the IP address corresponding to the hostname.

Figure 7.2 shows the `tcpdump` output for this example.

```
 1  0.0                  bsdi > svr4: icmp: echo request
 2  0.003733 (0.0037)    svr4 > bsdi: icmp: echo reply

 3  0.998045 (0.9943)    bsdi > svr4: icmp: echo request
 4  1.001747 (0.0037)    svr4 > bsdi: icmp: echo reply

 5  1.997818 (0.9961)    bsdi > svr4: icmp: echo request
 6  2.001542 (0.0037)    svr4 > bsdi: icmp: echo reply

 7  2.997610 (0.9961)    bsdi > svr4: icmp: echo request
 8  3.001311 (0.0037)    svr4 > bsdi: icmp: echo reply

 9  3.997390 (0.9961)    bsdi > svr4: icmp: echo request
10  4.001115 (0.0037)    svr4 > bsdi: icmp: echo reply

11  4.997201 (0.9961)    bsdi > svr4: icmp: echo request
12  5.000904 (0.0037)    svr4 > bsdi: icmp: echo reply

13  5.996977 (0.9961)    bsdi > svr4: icmp: echo request
14  6.000708 (0.0037)    svr4 > bsdi: icmp: echo reply

15  6.996764 (0.9961)    bsdi > svr4: icmp: echo request
16  7.000479 (0.0037)    svr4 > bsdi: icmp: echo reply
```

Figure 7.2 `ping` output across a LAN.

The time between sending the echo request and receiving the echo reply is always 3.7 ms. We can also see that echo requests are sent approximately 1 second apart.

Often the first round-trip time is larger than the rest. This occurs if the destination's hardware address isn't in the ARP cache of the sender. As we saw in Chapter 4, sending an ARP request and getting the ARP reply can take a few milliseconds before the first echo request can be sent. The following example shows this:

```
sun % arp -a                                    make sure ARP cache is empty
sun % ping svr4
PING svr4: 56 data bytes
64 bytes from svr4 (140.252 13.34): icmp_seq=0. time=7. ms
64 bytes from svr4 (140.252.13.34): icmp_seq=1. time=4. ms
64 bytes from svr4 (140.252.13.34): icmp_seq=2. time=4. ms
64 bytes from svr4 (140.252.13.34): icmp_seq=3. time=4. ms
?                                               type interrupt key to stop
----svr4 PING Statistics----
4 packets transmitted, 4 packets received, 0% packet loss
round-trip (ms)  min/avg/max = 4/4/7
```

The additional 3 ms in the first RTT is probably for the ARP request and reply.

This example was run on the host sun, which provides a timer with microsecond resolution, but the ping program prints the round-trip times with only millisecond resolution. The earlier example, run under BSD/386 Version 0.9.4, printed the round-trip times as 0 ms, since the available timer provided only 10-ms accuracy. The following output is from BSD/386 Version 1.0 which provides a timer with microsecond resolution and a version of ping that prints the higher resolution.

```
bsdi % ping svr4
PING svr4 (140.252.13.34): 56 data bytes
64 bytes from 140.252.13.34: icmp_seq=0 ttl=255 time=9.304 ms
64 bytes from 140.252.13.34: icmp_seq=1 ttl=255 time=6.089 ms
64 bytes from 140.252.13.34: icmp_seq=2 ttl=255 time=6.079 ms
64 bytes from 140.252.13.34: icmp_seq=3 ttl=255 time=6.096 ms
^?                                               type interrupt key to stop
--- svr4 ping statistics ---
4 packets transmitted, 4 packets received, 0% packet loss
round-trip min/avg/max = 6.079/6.880/9.304 ms
```

WAN Output

On a wide area network the results can be quite different. The following example was captured on a weekday afternoon, a time when the Internet is normally busy:

```
gemini % ping vangogh.cs.berkeley.edu
PING vangogh.cs.berkeley.edu: 56 data bytes
64 bytes from (128.32.130.2): icmp_seq=0. time=660. ms
64 bytes from (128.32.130.2): icmp_seq=5. time=1780. ms
64 bytes from (128.32.130.2): icmp_seq=7. time=380. ms
64 bytes from (128.32.130.2): icmp_seq=8. time=420. ms
64 bytes from (128.32.130.2): icmp_seq=9. time=390. ms
64 bytes from (128.32.130.2): icmp_seq=14. time=110. ms
64 bytes from (128.32.130.2): icmp_seq=15. time=170. ms
64 bytes from (128.32.130.2): icmp_seq=16. time=100. ms
^?                                               type interrupt key to stop
```

```
----vangogh.CS.Berkeley.EDU PING Statistics----
17 packets transmitted, 8 packets received, 52% packet loss
round-trip (ms)  min/avg/max = 100/501/1780
```

Either the echo requests or the echo replies for sequence numbers 1, 2, 3, 4, 6, 10, 11, 12, and 13 were lost somewhere. Note also the large variance in the round-trip times. (This high packet loss rate of 52% is an anomaly. This is not normal for the Internet, even on a weekday afternoon.)

It is also possible across WANs to see packets duplicated (the same sequence number printed two or more times), and to see packets reordered (sequence number $N+1$ printed before sequence number N).

Hardwired SLIP Links

Let's look at the round-trip times encountered over SLIP links, since they often run at slow asynchronous speeds, such as 9600 bits/sec or less. Recall our serial line throughput calculations in Section 2.10. For this example we'll set the speed of the hardwired SLIP link between hosts `bsdi` and `slip` to 1200 bits/sec.

We can estimate the round-trip time as follows. First, notice from the example Ping output shown earlier that by default it sends 56 bytes of data in the ICMP message. With a 20-byte IP header and an 8-byte ICMP header this gives a total IP datagram size of 84 bytes. (We can verify this by running `tcpdump -e` and seeing the Ethernet frame sizes.) Also, from Section 2.4 we know that at least two additional bytes are added: the END byte at the beginning and end of the datagram. It's also possible for additional bytes to be added by the SLIP framing, but that depends on the value of each byte in the datagram. At 1200 bits/sec with 8 bits per byte, 1 start bit, and 1 stop bit, the rate is 120 bytes per second, or 8.33 ms per byte. Our estimate is then $(86 \times 8.33 \times 2)$, or 1433 ms. (The multiplier of 2 is because we are calculating the round-trip time.)

The following output verifies our calculation:

```
svr4 % ping -s slip
PING slip: 56 data bytes
64 bytes from slip (140.252.13.65): icmp_seq=0. time=1480. ms
64 bytes from slip (140.252.13.65): icmp_seq=1. time=1480. ms
64 bytes from slip (140.252.13.65): icmp_seq=2. time=1480. ms
64 bytes from slip (140.252.13.65): icmp_seq=3. time=1480. ms
^?
----slip PING Statistics----
5 packets transmitted, 4 packets received, 20% packet loss
round-trip (ms)  min/avg/max = 1480/1480/1480
```

(The `-s` option is required for SVR4 to send one request every second.) The round-trip time is almost 1.5 seconds but the program is still sending out each ICMP echo request at 1-second intervals. This means there are two outstanding echo requests (sent at time 0 and time 1) before the first reply comes back (at time 1.480). That's also why the summary line says one packet has been lost. It really hasn't been lost, it's probably still on its way back.

We'll return to this slow SLIP link in Chapter 8 when we examine the `traceroute` program.

Dialup SLIP Links

The conditions change with a dialup SLIP link since we now have modems on each end of the link. The modems being used between the systems sun and netb provide what is called V.32 modulation (9600 bits/sec), V.42 error control (also called LAP-M), and V.42bis data compression. This means that our simple calculations, which were fairly accurate for a hardwired link where we knew all the parameters, become less accurate.

Numerous factors are at work. The modems introduce some latency. The size of the packets may decrease with the data compression, but the size may then increase to a multiple of the packet size used by the error control protocol. Also the receiving modem can't release received data bytes until the cyclic redundancy character (the checksum) has been verified. Finally, we're dealing with a computer's asynchronous serial interface on each end, and many operating systems read these interfaces only at fixed intervals, or when a certain number of characters have been received.

As an example, we ping the host gemini from the host sun:

```
sun % ping gemini
PING gemini: 56 data bytes
64 bytes from gemini (140.252.1.11): icmp_seq=0. time=373. ms
64 bytes from gemini (140.252.1.11): icmp_seq=1. time=360. ms
64 bytes from gemini (140.252.1.11): icmp_seq=2. time=340. ms
64 bytes from gemini (140.252.1.11): icmp_seq=3. time=320. ms
64 bytes from gemini (140.252.1.11): icmp_seq=4. time=330. ms
64 bytes from gemini (140.252.1.11): icmp_seq=5. time=310. ms
64 bytes from gemini (140.252.1.11): icmp_seq=6. time=290. ms
64 bytes from gemini (140.252.1.11): icmp_seq=7. time=300. ms
64 bytes from gemini (140.252.1.11): icmp_seq=8. time=280. ms
64 bytes from gemini (140.252.1.11): icmp_seq=9. time=290. ms
64 bytes from gemini (140.252.1.11): icmp_seq=10. time=300. ms
64 bytes from gemini (140.252.1.11): icmp_seq=11. time=280. ms
----gemini PING Statistics----
12 packets transmitted, 12 packets received, 0% packet loss
round-trip (ms)  min/avg/max = 280/314/373
```

Note that the first RTT is not a multiple of 10 ms, but every other line is. If we run this numerous times, we see this property every time. (This is not caused by the resolution of the clock on the host sun, because we know that its clock provides millisecond resolution from the tests we run in Appendix B.)

Also note that the first RTT is larger than the next, and they keep decreasing, and then they range between 280 and 300 ms. If we let it run for a minute or two, the RTTs stay in this range, never going below 260 ms. If we calculate the expected RTT at 9600 bits/sec (Exercise 7.2) we get 180 ms, so our observed values are about 1.5 times the expected value.

If we run ping for 60 seconds and look at the average RTT it calculates, we find that with V.42 and V.42bis our average is 277 ms. (This is better than the average printed for our preceding example, because we ran it longer to amortize the longer RTTs at the beginning.) If we turn off just the V.42bis data compression our average is 330 ms. If we turn off the V.42 error control (which also turns off the V.42bis data compression) our average is 300 ms. These modem parameters do affect the RTTs, and using the error control and data compression appears to be the best.

7.3 IP Record Route Option

The ping program gives us an opportunity to look at the IP record route (RR) option. Most versions of ping provide the -R option that enables the record route feature. It causes ping to set the IP RR option in the outgoing IP datagram (which contains the ICMP echo request message). This causes every router that handles the datagram to add its IP address to a list in the options field. When the datagram reaches the final destination, the list of IP addresses should be copied into the outgoing ICMP echo reply, and all the routers on the return path also add their IP addresses to the list. When ping receives the echo reply it prints the list of IP addresses.

As simple as this sounds, there are pitfalls. Generation of the RR option by the source host, processing of the RR option by the intermediate routers, and reflection of the incoming RR list in an ICMP echo request into the outgoing ICMP echo reply are all optional features. Fortunately, most systems today do support these optional features, but some systems don't reflect the IP list.

The biggest problem, however, is the limited room in the IP header for the list of IP addresses. We saw in Figure 3.1 (p. 34) that the *header length* in the IP header is a 4-bit field, limiting the entire IP header to 15 32-bit words (60 bytes). Since the fixed size of the IP header is 20 bytes, and the RR option uses 3 bytes for overhead (which we describe below), this leaves 37 bytes (60 – 20 – 3) for the list, allowing up to nine IP addresses. In the early days of the ARPANET, nine IP addresses seemed like a lot, but since this is a round-trip list (in the case of the -R option for ping), it's of limited use today. (In Chapter 8 we'll look at the Traceroute tool for determining the route followed by a datagram.) Despite these shortcomings, the record route option works and provides an opportunity to look in detail at the handling of IP options.

Figure 7.3 shows the general format of the RR option in the IP datagram.

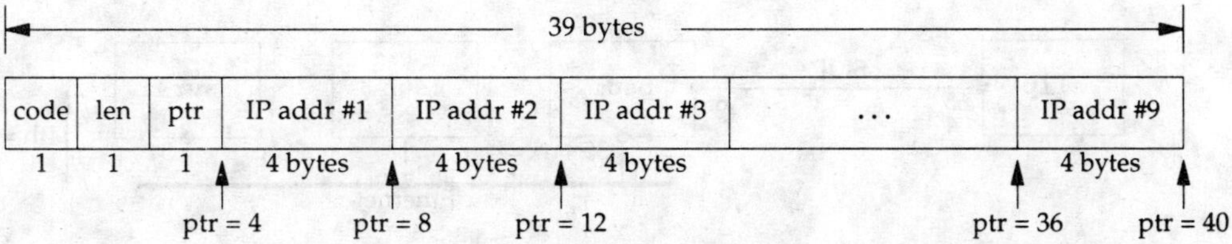

Figure 7.3 General format of record route option in IP header.

Code is a 1-byte field specifying the type of IP option. For the RR option its value is 7. *Len* is the total number of bytes of the RR option, which in this case is 39. (Although it's possible to specify an RR option with less than the maximum size, ping always provides a 39-byte option field, to record up to nine IP addresses. Given the limited room in the IP header for options, it doesn't make sense to specify a size less than the maximum.)

Ptr is called the pointer field. It is a 1-based index into the 39-byte option of where to store the next IP address. Its minimum value is 4, which is the pointer to the first IP address. As each IP address is recorded into the list, the value of *ptr* becomes 8, 12, 16, up to 36. After the ninth address is recorded *ptr* becomes 40, indicating the list is full.

When a router (which by definition is multihomed) records its IP address in the list, which IP address is recorded? It could be the address of the incoming interface or the outgoing interface. RFC 791 [Postel 1981a] specifies that the router records the outgoing IP address. We'll see that when the originating host (the host running `ping`) receives the ICMP echo reply with the RR option enabled, it also records its incoming IP address in the list.

Normal Example

Let's run an example of the RR option with the `ping` program. We'll run `ping` on the host `svr4` to the host `slip`. One intermediate router (`bsdi`) will handle the datagram. The following output is from `svr4`:

```
svr4 % ping -R slip
PING slip (140.252.13.65): 56 data bytes
64 bytes from 140.252.13.65: icmp_seq=0 ttl=254 time=280 ms
RR:    bsdi (140.252.13.66)
       slip (140.252.13.65)
       bsdi (140.252.13.35)
       svr4 (140.252.13.34)
64 bytes from 140.252.13.65: icmp_seq=1 ttl=254 time=280 ms (same route)
64 bytes from 140.252.13.65: icmp_seq=2 ttl=254 time=270 ms (same route)
^?
--- slip ping statistics ---
3 packets transmitted, 3 packets received, 0% packet loss
round-trip min/avg/max = 270/276/280 ms
```

Figure 7.4 shows the four hops that the packets take (two in each direction), and which hop adds which IP address to the RR list.

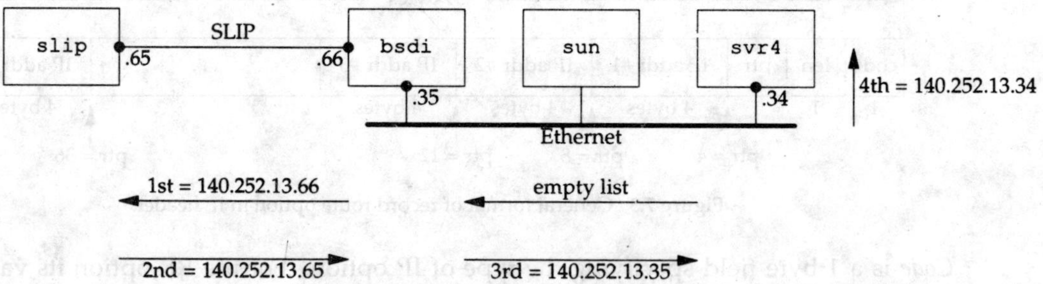

Figure 7.4 `ping` with record route option.

The router `bsdi` adds a different IP address to the list in each direction. It always adds the IP address of the outgoing interface. We can also see that when the ICMP echo reply reaches the originating system (`svr4`) it adds the IP address of the incoming interface to the list.

We can also watch this exchange of packets from the host sun, running tcpdump with its -v option (to see the IP options). Figure 7.5 shows the output.

```
1  0.0                  svr4 > slip: icmp: echo request (ttl 32, id 35835,
                        optlen=40 RR{39}= RR{#0.0.0.0/0.0.0.0/0.0.0.0/
                        0.0.0.0/ 0.0.0.0/0.0.0.0/0.0.0.0/0.0.0.0/0.0.0.0} EOL)

2  0.267746 (0.2677)    slip > svr4: icmp: echo reply (ttl 254, id 1976,
                        optlen=40 RR{39}= RR{140.252.13.66/140.252.13.65/
                        140.252.13.35/#0.0.0.0/0.0.0.0/0.0.0.0/0.0.0.0/
                        0.0.0.0/0.0.0.0} EOL)
```

Figure 7.5 tcpdump output of record route option.

The output optlen=40 indicates there are 40 bytes of option space in the IP header. (Recall that the length of the IP header must be a multiple of 4 bytes.) RR{39} means the record route option is present, and its length field is 39. The list of nine IP addresses is then shown, with a pound sign (#) indicating which IP address is pointed to by the *ptr* field in the RR option header. Since we are watching these packets on the host sun (see Figure 7.4) we only see the ICMP echo request with the empty list, and the ICMP echo reply with three addresses in the list. We have deleted the remaining lines in the tcpdump output, since they are nearly identical to what we show in Figure 7.5.

The notation EOL at the end of the record route information indicates the IP option "end of list" value appeared. The EOL option has a value of 0. What's happening is that 39 bytes of RR data are in the 40 bytes of option space in the IP header. Since the option space is set to 0 before the datagram is sent, this final byte of 0 that follows the 39 bytes of RR data is interpreted as an EOL. That is what we want to have happen. If there are multiple options in the option field of the IP header, and pad bytes are needed before the next option starts, the other special character NOP ("no operation"), with a value of 1, can be used.

In Figure 7.5, SVR4 sets the TTL field of the echo request to 32, and BSD/386 sets it to 255. (It prints as 254 since the router bsdi has already decremented it by one.) Newer systems are setting the TTL of ICMP messages to the maximum (255).

It turns out that of the three TCP/IP implementations used by the author, both BSD/386 and SVR4 support the record route option. That is, they correctly update the RR list when forwarding a datagram, and they correctly reflect the RR list from an incoming ICMP echo request to the outgoing ICMP echo reply. SunOS 4.1.3, however, updates the RR list when forwarding a datagram, but does not reflect the RR list. Solaris 2.x corrects this problem.

Abnormal Output

The following example was seen by the author and provides a starting point for our description of the ICMP redirect message in Chapter 9. We ping the host aix on the 140.252.1 subnet (accessible through the dialup SLIP connection on the host sun) with the record route option. We get the following output, when run on the host slip:

```
slip % ping -R aix
PING aix (140.252.1.92): 56 data bytes
64 bytes from 140.252.1.92: icmp_seq=0 ttl=251 time=650 ms
RR:     bsdi (140.252.13.35)
        sun (140.252.1.29)
        netb (140.252.1.183)
        aix (140.252.1.92)
        gateway (140.252.1.4)          why is this router used?
        netb (140.252.1.183)
        sun (140.252.13.33)
        bsdi (140.252.13.66)
        slip (140.252.13.65)
64 bytes from aix: icmp_seq=1 ttl=251 time=610 ms (same route)
64 bytes from aix: icmp_seq=2 ttl=251 time=600 ms (same route)
^?
--- aix ping statistics ---
4 packets transmitted, 3 packets received, 25% packet loss
round-trip min/avg/max = 600/620/650 ms
```

We could have run this example from the host `bsdi`. We chose to run it from `slip` to see all nine IP addresses in the RR list used.

The puzzle in this output is why the outgoing datagram (the ICMP echo request) went directly from `netb` to `aix`, but the return (the ICMP echo reply) went from `aix`, through the router `gateway`, before going to `netb`. What we're seeing here is a feature of IP routing that we describe below. Figure 7.6 shows the path of the datagrams.

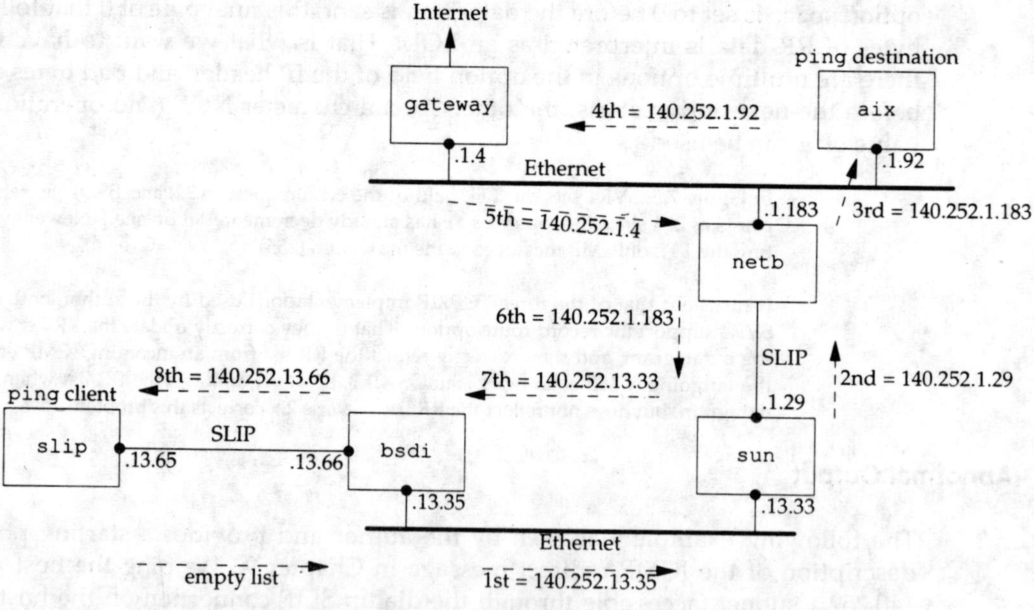

Figure 7.6 `ping` with record route, showing IP routing feature.

The problem is that `aix` does not know to send IP datagrams destined for the subnet 140.252.13 to `netb`. Instead, `aix` has a default entry in its routing table that tells it to send all datagrams to the router `gateway` if it doesn't have a particular route for the destination. The router `gateway` has more routing knowledge than any of the hosts on the 140.252.1 subnet. (There are more than 150 hosts on this Ethernet and instead of running a routing daemon on every one, each has a "default" entry that points to the router `gateway`.)

An unanswered question here is why doesn't `gateway` send an ICMP redirect (Section 9.5) to `aix` to update its routing table? For some reason (perhaps that the datagram generating the redirect is an ICMP echo request message) the redirect is not generated. But if we use Telnet and connect to the daytime server on `aix`, the ICMP redirect is generated, and the routing table on `aix` is updated. If we then execute `ping` with the record route option enabled, the route shows that the datagrams go from `netb` to `aix` and back to `netb`, without the extra hop to the router `gateway`. We'll look at these ICMP redirects in more detail in Section 9.5.

7.4 IP Timestamp Option

The IP timestamp option is similar to the record route option. Figure 7.7 shows the format of the IP timestamp option (compare with Figure 7.3).

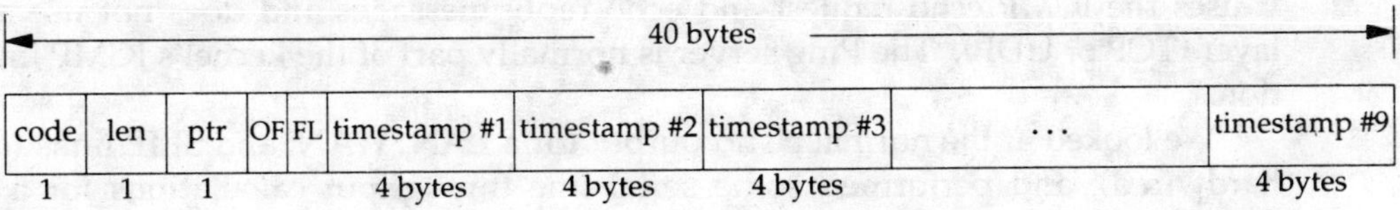

Figure 7.7 General format of timestamp option in IP header.

The *code* field is `0x44` for the timestamp option. The two fields *len* and *ptr* are the same as for the record route option: the total length of the option (normally 36 or 40) and a pointer to the next available entry (5, 9, 13, etc.).

The next two fields are 4-bit values: *OF* is the *overflow* field and *FL* is a *flags* field. The operation of the timestamp option is driven by the *flags* field, as shown in Figure 7.8.

flags	Description
0	Record only timestamps. This is what we show in Figure 7.7.
1	Each router records its IP address and its timestamp. There is room for only four of these pairs in the options list.
3	The sender initializes the options list with up to four pairs of IP addresses and a 0 timestamp. A router records its timestamp only if the next IP address in the list matches the router's.

Figure 7.8 Meaning of the *flags* value for timestamp option.

If a router can't add a timestamp because there's no room left, it just increments the *overflow* field.

The preferred value for the timestamps is the number of milliseconds past midnight, UTC, similar to the ICMP timestamp request and reply (Section 6.4). If this format is not available to a router, it can insert whatever time representation that it uses, but must then turn on the high-order bit of the timestamp to indicate the nonstandard value.

Given the limitations that we encountered with the record route option, things get worse with the timestamp option. If we record both IP addresses and timestamps (a *flags* of 1), we can store only four of these pairs. Recording only timestamps is next to useless because we have no indication regarding which timestamp corresponds to which router (unless we have a fixed topology that never changes). A *flags* of 3 is better, as we can then select which routers insert their timestamp. A more fundamental problem is that you probably have no control over how accurate the timestamp is at any given router. This makes it fruitless to try to measure hop times between routers using this IP option. We'll see that the traceroute program (Chapter 8) provides a better way of measuring hop times between routers.

7.5 Summary

The `ping` program is the basic connectivity test between two systems running TCP/IP. It uses the ICMP echo request and echo reply messages and does not use a transport layer (TCP or UDP). The Ping server is normally part of the kernel's ICMP implementation.

We looked at the normal `ping` output for a LAN, WAN, and SLIP links (dialup and hardwired), and performed some serial line throughput calculations for a dedicated SLIP link. `ping` also let us examine and use the IP record route option. We used this IP option to see how default routes are often used, and will return to this topic in Chapter 9. We also looked at the IP timestamp option, but it is of limited practical use.

Exercises

7.1 Draw a time line for the `ping` output for the SLIP link in Section 7.2.

7.2 Calculate the RTT if the SLIP link between `bsdi` and `slip` is set to 9600 bits/sec. Assume the default of 56 bytes of data.

7.3 The current BSD `ping` program allows us to specify a pattern for the data portion of the ICMP message. (The first 8 bytes of the data portion are not filled with the pattern, since the time at which the packet is sent is stored here.) If we specify a pattern of `0xc0`, recalculate the answer to the previous exercise. (*Hint*: Reread Section 2.4.)

7.4 Does the use of compressed SLIP (CSLIP, Section 2.5) affect the `ping` times that we observed in Section 7.2?

7.5 Examine Figure 2.4 (p. 28). Do you expect any difference between a ping of the loopback address, versus a ping of the host's Ethernet address?

8

Traceroute Program

8.1 Introduction

The Traceroute program, written by Van Jacobson, is a handy debugging tool that allows us to further explore the TCP/IP protocols. Although there are no guarantees that two consecutive IP datagrams from the same source to the same destination follow the same route, most of the time they do. Traceroute lets us see the route that IP datagrams follow from one host to another. Traceroute also lets us use the IP source route option.

The manual page states: "Implemented by Van Jacobson from a suggestion by Steve Deering. Debugged by a cast of thousands with particularly cogent suggestions or fixes from C. Philip Wood, Tim Seaver, and Ken Adelman."

8.2 Traceroute Program Operation

In Section 7.3 we described the IP record route option (RR). Why wasn't this used instead of developing a new application? There are three reasons. First, historically not all routers have supported the record route option, making it unusable on certain paths. (Traceroute doesn't require any special or optional features at any intermediate routers.)

Second, record route is normally a one-way option. The sender enables the option and the receiver has to fetch all the values from the received IP header and somehow return them to the sender. In Section 7.3 we saw that most implementations of the Ping server (the ICMP echo reply function within the kernel) reflect an incoming RR list, but this doubles the number of IP addresses recorded (the outgoing path and the return path), which runs into the limit described in the next paragraph. (Traceroute requires only a working UDP module at the destination—no special server application is required.)

The third and major reason is that the room allocated for options in the IP header isn't large enough today to handle most routes. There is room for only nine IP addresses in the IP header options field. In the old days of the ARPANET this was adequate, but it is far too small nowadays.

Traceroute uses ICMP and the TTL field in the IP header. The TTL field (time-to-live) is an 8-bit field that the sender initializes to some value. The recommended initial value is specified in the Assigned Numbers RFC and is currently 64. Older systems would often initialize it to 15 or 32. We saw in some of the Ping examples in Chapter 7 that ICMP echo replies are often sent with the TTL set to its maximum value of 255.

Each router that handles the datagram is required to decrement the TTL by either one or the number of seconds that the router holds onto the datagram. Since most routers hold a datagram for less than a second, the TTL field has effectively become a hop counter, decremented by one by each router.

> RFC 1009 [Braden and Postel 1987] required a router that held a datagram for more than 1 second to decrement the TTL by the number of seconds. Few routers implemented this requirement. The new Router Requirements RFC [Almquist 1993] makes this optional, allowing a router to treat the TTL as just a hop count.

The purpose of the TTL field is to prevent datagrams from ending up in infinite loops, which can occur during routing transients. For example, when a router crashes or when the connection between two routers is lost, it can take the routing protocols some time (from seconds to a few minutes) to detect the lost route and work around it. During this time period it is possible for the datagram to end up in routing loops. The TTL field puts an upper limit on these looping datagrams.

When a router gets an IP datagram whose TTL is either 0 or 1 it must not forward the datagram. (A destination host that receives a datagram like this can deliver it to the application, since the datagram does not have to be routed. Normally, however, no system should receive a datagram with a TTL of 0.) Instead the router throws away the datagram *and* sends back to the originating host an ICMP "time exceeded" message. The key to Traceroute is that the IP datagram containing this ICMP message has the router's IP address as the source address.

We can now guess the operation of Traceroute. It sends an IP datagram with a TTL of 1 to the destination host. The first router to handle the datagram decrements the TTL, discards the datagram, and sends back the ICMP time exceeded. This identifies the first router in the path. Traceroute then sends a datagram with a TTL of 2, and we find the IP address of the second router. This continues until the datagram reaches the destination host. But even though the arriving IP datagram has a TTL of 1, the destination host won't throw it away and generate the ICMP time exceeded, since the datagram has reached its final destination. How can we determine when we've reached the destination?

Traceroute sends UDP datagrams to the destination host, but it chooses the destination UDP port number to be an unlikely value (larger than 30,000), making it improbable that an application at the destination is using that port. This causes the destination host's UDP module to generate an ICMP "port unreachable" error (Section 6.5) when the datagram arrives. All Traceroute needs to do is differentiate between the received ICMP messages—time exceeded versus port unreachable—to know when it's done.

The Traceroute program must be able to set the TTL field in the outgoing datagram. Not all programming interfaces to TCP/IP support this, and not all implementations support the capability, but most current systems do, and are able to run Traceroute. This programming interface normally requires the user to have superuser privilege, meaning it may take special privilege to run it on your host.

8.3 LAN Output

We're now ready to run traceroute and see the output. We'll use our simple internet (see the figure on the inside front cover) going from svr4 to slip, through the router bsdi. The hardwired SLIP link between bsdi and slip is 9600 bits/sec.

```
svr4 % traceroute slip
traceroute to slip (140.252.13.65), 30 hops max, 40 byte packets
 1  bsdi (140.252.13.35)   20 ms  10 ms  10 ms
 2  slip (140.252.13.65)  120 ms  120 ms  120 ms
```

The first unnumbered line of output gives the name and IP address of the destination and indicates that traceroute won't increase the TTL beyond 30. The datagram size of 40 bytes allows for the 20-byte IP header, the 8-byte UDP header, and 12 bytes of user data. (The 12 bytes of user data contain a sequence number that is incremented each time a datagram is sent, a copy of the outgoing TTL, and the time at which the datagram was sent.)

The next two lines in the output begin with the TTL, followed by the name of the host or router, and its IP address. For each TTL value three datagrams are sent. For each returned ICMP message the round-trip time is calculated and printed. If no response is received within 5 seconds for any of the three datagrams, an asterisk is printed instead and the next datagram is sent. In this output the first three datagrams had a TTL of 1 and the ICMP messages were returned in 20, 10, and 10 ms. The next three datagrams were sent with a TTL of 2 and the ICMP messages were returned 120 ms later. Since the TTL of 2 reached the final destination, the program then stopped.

The round-trip times are calculated by the traceroute program on the sending host. They are the total RTTs from the traceroute program to that router. If we're interested in the per-hop time we have to subtract the value printed for TTL N from the value printed for TTL $N+1$.

Figure 8.1 shows the tcpdump output for this run. As we might have guessed, the reason that the first probe packet to bsdi had an RTT of 20 ms and the next two had an RTT of 10 ms was because of an ARP exchange. tcpdump shows this is indeed the case.

The destination UDP port starts at 33435 and is incremented by one each time a datagram is sent. This starting port number can be changed with a command-line option. The UDP datagram contains 12 bytes of user data, which we calculated earlier when traceroute output that it was sending 40-byte datagrams.

Next, tcpdump prints the comment [ttl 1] when the IP datagram has a TTL of 1. It prints a message like this when the TTL is 0 or 1, to warn us that something looks funny in the datagram. Here we expect to see the TTL of 1, but with some other application it could be a warning that the datagram might not get to its final destination. We should never see a datagram passing by with a TTL of 0, unless the router that put it on the wire is broken.

```
 1  0.0                      arp who-has bsdi tell svr4
 2  0.000586 (0.0006)        arp reply bsdi is-at 0:0:c0:6f:2d:40

 3  0.003067 (0.0025)        svr4.42804 > slip.33435: udp 12 [ttl 1]
 4  0.004325 (0.0013)        bsdi > svr4: icmp: time exceeded in-transit

 5  0.069810 (0.0655)        svr4.42804 > slip.33436: udp 12 [ttl 1]
 6  0.071149 (0.0013)        bsdi > svr4: icmp: time exceeded in-transit

 7  0.085162 (0.0140)        svr4.42804 > slip.33437: udp 12 [ttl 1]
 8  0.086375 (0.0012)        bsdi > svr4: icmp: time exceeded in-transit

 9  0.118608 (0.0322)        svr4.42804 > slip.33438: udp 12
10  0.226464 (0.1079)        slip > svr4: icmp: slip udp port 33438 unreachable

11  0.287296 (0.0608)        svr4.42804 > slip 33439: udp 12
12  0.395230 (0.1079)        slip > svr4: icmp: slip udp port 33439 unreachable

13  0.409504 (0.0143)        svr4.42804 > slip.33440: udp 12
14  0.517430 (0.1079)        slip > svr4: icmp: slip udp port 33440 unreachable
```

Figure 8.1 `tcpdump` output for `traceroute` example from `svr4` to `slip`.

The ICMP message "time exceeded in transit" is what we expect to see from the router `bsdi`, since it will decrement the TTL to 0. The ICMP message comes from the router even though the IP datagram that was thrown away was going to `slip`.

There are two different ICMP "time exceeded" messages (Figure 6.3, p. 71), each with a different *code* field in the ICMP message. Figure 8.2 shows the format of this ICMP error message.

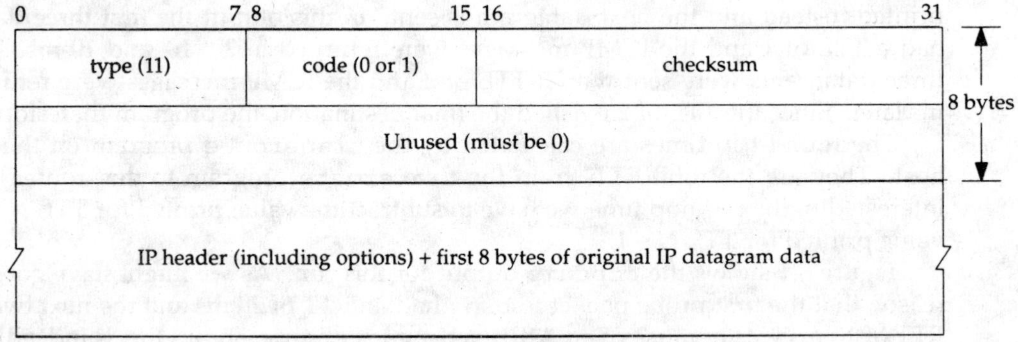

Figure 8.2 ICMP time exceeded message.

The one we've been describing is generated when the TTL reaches 0, and is specified by a *code* of 0.

It's also possible for a host to send an ICMP "time exceeded during reassembly" when it times out during the reassembly of a fragmented datagram. (We talk about fragmentation and reassembly in Section 11.5.) This error is specified by a *code* of 1.

Lines 9–14 in Figure 8.1 correspond to the three datagrams sent with a TTL of 2. These reach the final destination and generate an ICMP port unreachable message.

It is worthwhile to calculate what the round-trip times should be for the SLIP link, similar to what we did in Section 7.2 when we set the link to 1200 bits/sec for the Ping example. The outgoing UDP datagram contains 12 bytes of data, 8 bytes of UDP header, 20 bytes of IP header, and 2 bytes (at least) of SLIP framing (Section 2.4) for a total of 42 bytes. Unlike Ping, however, the size of the return datagrams changes. Recall from Figure 6.9 (p. 78) that the returned ICMP message contains the IP header of the datagram that caused the error and the first 8 bytes of data that followed that IP header (which is a UDP header in the case of `traceroute`). This gives us a total of 20 + 8 + 20 + 8 + 2, or 58 bytes. With a data rate of 960 bytes/sec the expected RTT is (42 + 58)/960 or 104 ms. This corresponds to the 110-ms value measured on `svr4`.

The source port number in Figure 8.1 (42804) seems high. `traceroute` sets the source port number of the UDP datagrams that it sends to the logical-OR of its Unix process ID with 32768. In case `traceroute` is being run multiple times on the same host, each process looks at the source port number in the UDP header that's returned by ICMP, and only handles those messages that are replies to probes that it sent.

There are several points to note with `traceroute`. First, there is no guarantee that the route today will be in use tomorrow, or even that two consecutive IP datagrams follow the same route. If a route changes while the program is running you'll see it occur because `traceroute` prints the new IP address for the given TTL if it changes.

Second, there is no guarantee that the path taken by the returned ICMP message retraces the path of the UDP datagram sent by `traceroute`. This implies that the round-trip times printed may not be a true indication of the outgoing and returning datagram times. (If it takes 1 second for the UDP datagram to travel from the source to a router, but 3 seconds for the ICMP message to travel a different path back to the source, the printed round-trip time is 4 seconds.)

Third, the source IP address in the returned ICMP message is the IP address of the interface on the router on which the UDP datagram *arrived*. This differs from the IP record route option (Section 7.3), where the IP address recorded was the outgoing interface's address. Since every router by definition has two or more interfaces, running `traceroute` from host A to host B can generate different output than from host B to host A. Indeed, if we run `traceroute` from host `slip` to `svr4` the output becomes:

```
slip % traceroute svr4
traceroute to svr4 (140.252.13.34), 30 hops max, 40 byte packets
 1  bsdi (140.252.13.66)  110 ms  110 ms  110 ms
 2  svr4 (140.252.13.34)  110 ms  120 ms  110 ms
```

This time the IP address printed for host `bsdi` is 140.252.13.66, the SLIP interface, while previously it was 140.252.13.35, the Ethernet interface. Since `traceroute` also tries to print the name associated with an IP address, the names can change. (In our example both interfaces on `bsdi` have the same name.)

Consider Figure 8.3. It shows two local area networks with a router connected to each LAN. The two routers are connected with a point-to-point link. If we run `traceroute` from a host on the left LAN to a host on the right LAN, the IP addresses found for the routers will be *if1* and *if3*. But going the other way will print the IP addresses *if4* and *if2*. The two interfaces *if2* and *if3* share the same network ID, while the other two interfaces have different network IDs.

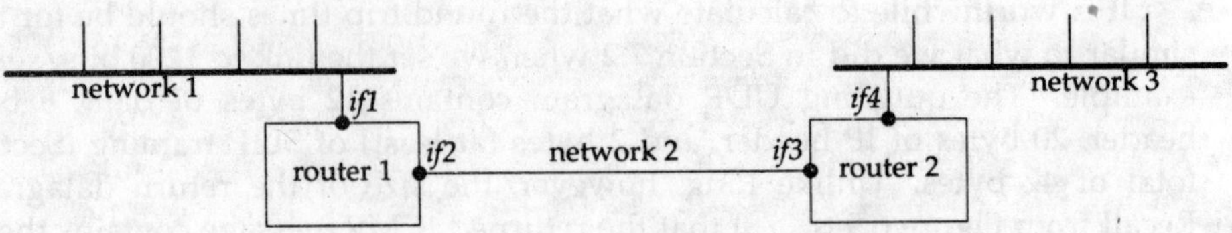

Figure 8.3 Identification of interfaces printed by `traceroute`.

Finally, across wide area networks the `traceroute` output is much easier to comprehend if the IP addresses are printed as readable domain names, instead of as IP addresses. But since the only piece of information `traceroute` has when it receives the ICMP message is an IP address, it does a "reverse name lookup" to find the name, given the IP address. This requires the administrator responsible for that router or host to configure their reverse name lookup function correctly (which isn't always the case). We describe how an IP address is converted to a name using the DNS in Section 14.5.

8.4 WAN Output

The output shown earlier for our small internet is adequate for examining the protocols in action, but more a realistic use of `traceroute` involves larger internets such as the worldwide Internet.

Figure 8.4 is from the host sun to the Network Information Center, the NIC.

```
sun % traceroute nic.ddn.mil
traceroute to nic.ddn.mil (192.112.36.5), 30 hops max, 40 byte packets
 1  netb.tuc.noao.edu (140.252.1.183)  218 ms  227 ms  233 ms
 2  gateway.tuc.noao.edu (140.252.1.4)  233 ms  229 ms  204 ms

 3  butch.telcom.arizona.edu (140.252.104.2)  204 ms  228 ms  234 ms
 4  Gabby.Telcom.Arizona.EDU (128.196.128.1)  234 ms  228 ms  204 ms
 5  NSIgate.Telcom.Arizona.EDU (192.80.43.3)  233 ms  228 ms  234 ms

 6  JPL1.NSN.NASA.GOV (128.161.88.2)  234 ms  590 ms  262 ms
 7  JPL3.NSN.NASA.GOV (192.100.15.3)  238 ms  223 ms  234 ms
 8  GSFC3.NSN.NASA.GOV (128.161.3.33)  293 ms  318 ms  324 ms
 9  GSFC8.NSN.NASA.GOV (192.100.13.8)  294 ms  318 ms  294 ms
10  SURA2.NSN.NASA.GOV (128.161.166.2)  323 ms  319 ms  294 ms
11  nsn-FIX-pe.sura.net (192.80.214.253)  294 ms  318 ms  294 ms
12  GSI.NSN.NASA.GOV (128.161.252.2)  293 ms  318 ms  324 ms

13  NIC.DDN.MIL (192.112.36.5)  324 ms  321 ms  324 ms
```

Figure 8.4 `traceroute` from host sun to `nic.ddn.mil`.

Since running this example for inclusion in the text, the NIC for non-DDN sites (i.e., non-military) has moved from `nic.ddn.mil` to `rs.internic.net`, the new "InterNIC."

Once the datagrams leave the tuc.noao.edu network they enter the telcom.arizona.edu network. They then enter the NASA Science Internet, nsn.nasa.gov. The routers for TTLs 6 and 7 are at the Jet Propulsion Laboratory (JPL). The network sura.net in the output for TTL 11 is the Southeastern Universities Research Association Network. The name GSI at TTL 12 is Government Systems, Inc., the operator of the NIC.

The second RTT for the TTL of 6 (590) is more than double the other two RTTs (234 and 262). This illustrates the dynamics of IP routing. Something happened somewhere between the sending host and this router that slowed down this datagram. Also, we can't tell if it was the outbound datagram that got held up or the return ICMP error.

The RTT for the first probe with a TTL of 3 (204) is less than the RTT for the first probe with a TTL of 2 (233). Since each printed RTT is the total time from the sending host to that router, this can (and does) happen.

The example in Figure 8.5 is from the host sun to the author's publisher.

```
sun % traceroute aw.com
traceroute to aw.com (192.207.117.2), 30 hops max, 40 byte packets
 1  netb.tuc.noao.edu (140.252.1.183)  227 ms  227 ms  234 ms
 2  gateway.tuc.noao.edu (140.252.1.4)  233 ms  229 ms  234 ms

 3  butch.telcom.arizona.edu (140.252.104.2)  233 ms  229 ms  234 ms
 4  Gabby.Telcom.Arizona.EDU (128.196.128.1)  264 ms  228 ms  234 ms
 5  Westgate.Telcom.Arizona.EDU (192.80.43.2)  234 ms  228 ms  234 ms

 6  uu-ua.AZ.westnet.net (192.31.39.233)  263 ms  258 ms  264 ms
 7  enss142.UT.westnet.net (192.31.39.21)  263 ms  258 ms  264 ms

 8  t3-2.Denver-cnss97.t3.ans.net (140.222.97.3)  293 ms  288 ms  275 ms
 9  t3-3.Denver-cnss96.t3.ans.net (140.222.96.4)  283 ms  263 ms  261 ms
10  t3-1.St-Louis-cnss80.t3.ans.net (140.222.80.2)  282 ms  288 ms  294 ms
11  t3-1.Chicago-cnss24.t3.ans.net (140.222.24.2)  293 ms  288 ms  294 ms
12  t3-2.Cleveland-cnss40.t3.ans.net (140.222.40.3)  294 ms  288 ms  294 ms
13  t3-1.New-York-cnss32.t3.ans.net (140.222.32.2)  323 ms  318 ms  324 ms
14  t3-1.Washington-DC-cnss56.t3.ans.net (140.222.56.2)  323 ms  318 ms  324 ms
15  t3-0.Washington-DC-cnss58.t3.ans.net (140.222.58.1)  324 ms  318 ms  324 ms
16  t3-0.enss136.t3.ans.net (140.222.136.1)  323 ms  318 ms  324 ms

17  Washington.DC.ALTER.NET (192.41.177.248)  323 ms  377 ms  324 ms
18  Boston.MA.ALTER.NET (137.39.12.2)  324 ms  347 ms  324 ms
19  AW-gw.ALTER.NET (137.39.62.2)  353 ms  378 ms  354 ms

20  aw.com (192.207.117.2)  354 ms  349 ms  354 ms
```

Figure 8.5 traceroute from host sun.tuc.noao.edu to aw.com.

This time the datagrams enter the regional network westnet.net (TTLs 6 and 7) after leaving the telcom.arizona.edu network. They then enter the NSFNET backbone, t3.ans.net, which is run by Advanced Network & Services. (T3 is the common abbreviation for the 45 Mbits/sec phone lines used by the backbone.) The final network is alter.net, the connection point to the Internet for aw.com.

8.5 IP Source Routing Option

Normally IP routing is dynamic with each router making a decision about which next-hop router to send the datagram to. Applications have no control of this, and are normally not concerned with it. It takes tools such as Traceroute to figure out what the route really is.

The idea behind source routing is that the sender specifies the route. Two forms are provided:

- *Strict* source routing. The sender specifies the *exact* path that the IP datagram must follow. If a router encounters a next hop in the source route that isn't on a directly connected network, an ICMP "source route failed" error is returned.
- *Loose* source routing. The sender specifies a list of IP address that the datagram must traverse, but the datagram can also pass through other routers between any two addresses in the list.

Traceroute provides a way to look at source routing, as we can specify an option allowing us to force a source route, and see what happens.

> Some of the publicly available Traceroute source code packages contain patches to specify loose source routing. But the standard versions normally don't include this option. A comment in the patches is that "Van Jacobson's original traceroute (spring 1988) supported this feature, but he removed it due to pressure from people with broken gateways." For the examples shown in this section, the author installed these patches and modified them to allow both loose and strict source routing.

Figure 8.6 shows the format of the source route option.

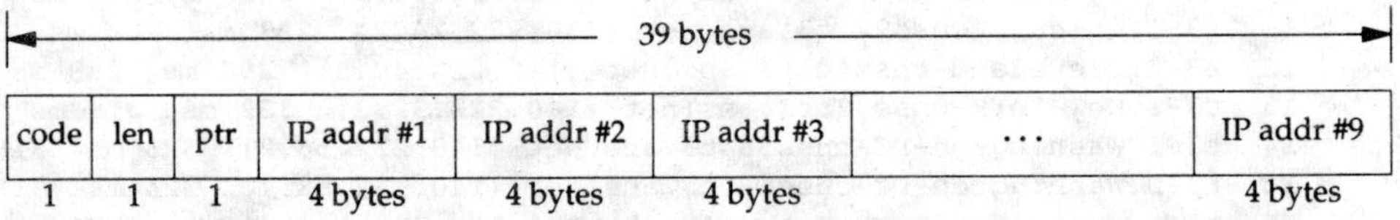

Figure 8.6 General format of the source route option in the IP header.

This format is nearly identical to the format of the record route option that we showed in Figure 7.3. But with source routing we have to fill in the list of IP addresses before sending the IP datagram, while with the record route option we allocate room and zero out the list of IP addresses, letting the routers fill in the next entry in the list. Also, with source routing we only allocate room for and initialize the number of IP addresses required, normally fewer than nine. With the record route option we allocated as much room as we could, for up to nine addresses.

The *code* is `0x83` for loose source routing, and `0x89` for strict source routing. The *len* and *ptr* fields are identical to what we described in Section 7.3.

The source route options are actually called "source and record route" (LSRR and SSRR, for loose and strict) since the list of IP addresses is updated as the datagram passes along the path. What happens is as follows:

- The sending host takes the source route list from the application, removes the first entry (it becomes the destination address of the datagram), moves all the remaining entries left by one entry (where left is as in Figure 8.6), and places the original destination address as the final entry in the list. The pointer still points to the first entry in the list (e.g., the value of the pointer is 4).
- Each router that handles the datagram checks whether it is the destination address of the datagram. If not, the datagram is forwarded as normal. (In this case loose source routing must have been specified, or we wouldn't have received the datagram.)
- If the router is the destination, and the pointer is not greater than the length, then (1) the next address in the list (where *ptr* points) becomes the destination address of the datagram, (2) the IP address corresponding to the outgoing interface replaces the source address just used, and (3) the pointer is incremented by 4.

This is best explained with an example. In Figure 8.7 we assume that the sending application on host *S* sends a datagram to *D*, specifying a source route of *R1*, *R2*, and *R3*.

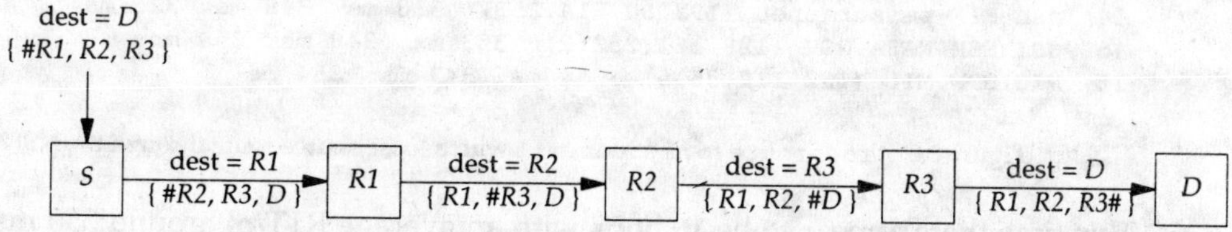

Figure 8.7 Example of IP source routing.

In this figure the pound sign (#) denotes the pointer field, which assumes the values of 4, 8, 12, and 16. The length field will always be 15 (three IP addresses plus 3 bytes of overhead). Notice how the destination address of the IP datagram changes on every hop.

When an application receives data that was source routed, it should fetch the value of the received route and supply a reversed route for sending replies.

> The Host Requirements RFC specifies that a TCP client must be able to specify a source route, and that a TCP server must be able to receive a source route, and use the reverse route for all segments on that TCP connection. If the TCP server later receives a different source route, that newer source route overrides the earlier one.

`traceroute` Examples with Loose Source Routing

The `-g` option to `traceroute` lets us specify intermediate routers to be used with loose source routing. This option can be specified up to eight times. (The reason this is eight and not nine is that the programming interface being used requires that the final entry be the destination.)

Recall from Figure 8.4 that the route to the NIC, `nic.ddn.mil`, was through the NASA Science Internet. In Figure 8.8 we force the datagrams to pass through the NSFNET instead by specifying the router `enss142.UT.westnet.net` (192.31.39.21) as an intermediate router:

```
sun % traceroute -g 192.31.39.21  nic.ddn.mil
traceroute to nic.ddn.mil (192.112.36.5), 30 hops max, 40 byte packets
 1  netb.tuc.noao.edu (140.252.1.183)  259 ms  256 ms  235 ms
 2  butch.telcom.arizona.edu (140.252.104.2)  234 ms  228 ms  234 ms
 3  Gabby.Telcom.Arizona.EDU (128.196.128.1)  234 ms  257 ms  233 ms
 4  enss142.UT.westnet.net (192.31.39.21)  294 ms  288 ms  295 ms
 5  t3-2.Denver-cnss97.t3.ans.net (140.222.97.3)  294 ms  286 ms  293 ms
 6  t3-3.Denver-cnss96.t3.ans.net (140.222.96.4)  293 ms  288 ms  294 ms
 7  t3-1.St-Louis-cnss80.t3.ans.net (140.222.80.2)  294 ms  318 ms  294 ms
 8  * t3-1.Chicago-cnss24.t3.ans.net (140.222.24.2)  318 ms  295 ms
 9  t3-2.Cleveland-cnss40.t3.ans.net (140.222.40.3)  319 ms  318 ms  324 ms
10  t3-1.New-York-cnss32.t3.ans.net (140.222.32.2)  324 ms  318 ms  324 ms
11  t3-1.Washington-DC-cnss56.t3.ans.net (140.222.56.2)  353 ms  348 ms  325 ms
12  t3-0.Washington-DC-cnss58.t3.ans.net (140.222.58.1)  348 ms  347 ms  325 ms
13  t3-0.enss145.t3.ans.net (140.222.145.1)  353 ms  348 ms  325 ms
14  nsn-FIX-pe.sura.net (192.80.214.253)  353 ms  348 ms  325 ms
15  GSI.NSN.NASA.GOV (128.161.252.2)  353 ms  348 ms  354 ms
16  NIC.DDN.MIL (192.112.36.5)  354 ms  347 ms  354 ms
```

Figure 8.8 `traceroute` to `nic.ddn.mil` with a loose source route through the NSFNET.

This time there appear to be 16 hops with an average RTT of around 350 ms, while the normal route shown in Figure 8.4 had only 13 hops and an average RTT of around 322 ms. The default route appears better. (There are also other decisions made when routes are established. Some are made on the basis of the organizational and political boundaries of the networks involved.)

But we said there *appear to be* 16 hops, because a comparison of this output with our previous example through the NSFNET (Figure 8.5) shows three missing routers in this example using loose source routing. (These are probably caused by bugs in the router's generation of ICMP time exceeded errors in response to source routed datagrams.) The router `gateway.tuc.noao.edu` is missing between `netb` and `butch`, and the routers `Westgate.Telcom.Arizona.edu` and `uu-ua.AZ.westnet.net` are also missing between `Gabby` and `enss142.UT.westnet.net`. There is probably a software problem in these missing routers related to incoming datagrams with the loose source routing option. There are really 19 hops between the source and the NIC, when using the NSFNET. Exercise 8.5 continues the discussion of these missing routers.

This example also illustrates another problem. On the command line we have to specify the dotted-decimal IP address of the router `enss142.UT.westnet.net` instead of its name. This is because the reverse name lookup (return the name, given the IP address, Section 14.5), associates the name with the IP address, but the forward lookup (given the name, return the IP address) fails. The forward mapping and reverse mapping are two separate files in the DNS (Domain Name System) and not all administrators keep the two synchronized with each other. It's not uncommon to have one direction work and the other direction fail.

Something that we haven't seen before is the asterisk (`*`) printed for the first RTT for the TTL of 8. This indicates that a timeout occurred and no response was received within 5 seconds for this probe.

Another point that we can infer from a comparison of this figure and Figure 8.4 is that the router `nsn-FIX-pe.sura.net` is connected to both the NSFNET and the NASA Science Internet.

`traceroute` Examples with Strict Source Routing

The `-G` option in the author's version of `traceroute` is identical to the `-g` option described earlier, but the source route is strict instead of loose. We can use this to see what happens when an invalid strict source route is specified. Recall from Figure 8.5 that the normal sequence of routers for datagrams from the author's subnet to the NSFNET is through `netb`, `gateway`, `butch`, and `gabby`. (We've omitted the domain suffixes, `.tuc.noao.edu` and `.telcom.arizona.edu`, in all the output below to make it easier to read.) We specify a strict source route that omits `butch`, trying to go directly from `gateway` to `gabby`. We expect this to fail, as shown in Figure 8.9.

```
sun % traceroute -G netb -G gateway -G gabby westgate
traceroute to westgate (192.80.43.2), 30 hops max, 40 byte packets
 1  netb (140.252.1.183)  272 ms  257 ms  261 ms
 2  gateway (140.252.1.4)  263 ms  259 ms  234 ms
 3  gateway (140.252.1.4)  263 ms !S *  235 ms !S
```

Figure 8.9 `traceroute` with a strict source route that fails.

The key here is the notation `!S` following the RTTs for the TTL of 3. This indicates that `traceroute` received an ICMP "source route failed" error message: a *type* of 3 and a *code* of 5 from Figure 6.3. The asterisk for the second RTT for the TTL of 3 indicates no response was received for that probe. This is what we expect, since it's impossible for `gateway` to send the datagram directly to `gabby`, because they're not directly connected.

The reason that both TTLs 2 and 3 are from `gateway` is that the values for the TTL of 2 are from `gateway` when it receives the datagram with an incoming TTL of 1. It discovers that the TTL has expired before it looks at the (invalid) strict source route, and sends back the ICMP time exceeded. The line with a TTL of 3 is received by `gateway` with an incoming TTL of 2, so it looks at the strict source route, discovers that it's invalid, and sends back the ICMP source route failed error.

Figure 8.10 shows the `tcpdump` output corresponding to this example. This output was collected on the SLIP link between `sun` and `netb`. We had to specify the `-v` option for `tcpdump` to display the source route information. This produces other output that we don't need, such as the datagram ID, which we've deleted. Also, the notation `SSRR` stands for "strict source and record route."

```
 1  0.0                    sun.33593 > netb.33435: udp 12 [ttl 1]
                           (optlen=16 SSRR{#gateway gabby westgate} EOL)
 2  0.270278 (0.2703)      netb > sun: icmp: time exceeded in-transit
 3  0.284784 (0.0145)      sun.33593 > netb.33436: udp 12 [ttl 1]
                           (optlen=16 SSRR{#gateway gabby westgate} EOL)
 4  0.540338 (0.2556)      netb > sun: icmp: time exceeded in-transit
 5  0.550062 (0.0097)      sun.33593 > netb.33437: udp 12 [ttl 1]
                           (optlen=16 SSRR{#gateway gabby westgate} EOL)
 6  0.810310 (0.2602)      netb > sun: icmp: time exceeded in-transit
 7  0.818030 (0.0077)      sun.33593 > netb.33438: udp 12 (ttl 2,
                           optlen=16 SSRR{#gateway gabby westgate} EOL)
 8  1.080337 (0.2623)      gateway > sun: icmp: time exceeded in-transit
 9  1.092564 (0.0122)      sun.33593 > netb.33439: udp 12 (ttl 2,
                           optlen=16 SSRR{#gateway gabby westgate} EOL)
10  1.350322 (0.2578)      gateway > sun: icmp: time exceeded in-transit
11  1.357382 (0.0071)      sun.33593 > netb.33440: udp 12 (ttl 2,
                           optlen=16 SSRR{#gateway gabby westgate} EOL)
12  1.590586 (0.2332)      gateway > sun: icmp: time exceeded in-transit
13  1.598926 (0.0083)      sun.33593 > netb.33441: udp 12 (ttl 3,
                           optlen=16 SSRR{#gateway gabby westgate} EOL)
14  1.860341 (0.2614)      gateway > sun:
                           icmp: gateway unreachable - source route failed
15  1.875230 (0.0149)      sun.33593 > netb.33442: udp 12 (ttl 3,
                           optlen=16 SSRR{#gateway gabby westgate} EOL)
16  6.876579 (5.0013)      sun.33593 > netb.33443: udp 12 (ttl 3,
                           optlen=16 SSRR{#gateway gabby westgate} EOL)
17  7.110518 (0.2339)      gateway > sun:
                           icmp: gateway unreachable - source route failed
```

Figure 8.10 `tcpdump` **output of** `traceroute` **with failed strict source route.**

First note that each UDP datagram sent by `sun` has a destination of `netb`, not the destination host (`westgate`). We described this with the example shown in Figure 8.7. Similarly, the other two routers specified with the `-G` option (`gateway` and `gabby`) and the final destination (`westgate`) become the SSRR option list on the first hop.

We can also see from this output that the timeout used by `traceroute` (the time difference between lines 15 and 16) is 5 seconds.

`traceroute` Round Trips with Loose Source Routing

Earlier we said that there is no guarantee that the route from A to B is the same as the route from B to A. Other than having a login on both systems and running `traceroute` on each end, it's hard to find out if there is a difference in the two paths. Using loose source routing, however, we can determine the route in both directions.

The trick is to specify loose source routing with the destination as the loose route, and the sending host as the final destination. For example, on the host `sun` we can find the paths to and from the host `bruno.cs.colorado.edu` (Figure 8.11).

```
sun % traceroute -g bruno.cs.colorado.edu sun
traceroute to sun (140.252.13.33), 30 hops max, 40 byte packets
 1  netb.tuc.noao.edu (140.252.1.183)  230 ms  227 ms  233 ms
 2  gateway.tuc.noao.edu (140.252.1.4)  233 ms  229 ms  234 ms
 3  butch.telcom.arizona.edu (140.252.104.2)  234 ms  229 ms  234 ms
 4  Gabby.Telcom.Arizona.EDU (128.196.128.1)  233 ms  231 ms  234 ms
 5  NSIgate.Telcom.Arizona.EDU (192.80.43.3)  294 ms  258 ms  234 ms
 6  JPL1.NSN.NASA.GOV (128.161.88.2)  264 ms  258 ms  264 ms
 7  JPL2.NSN.NASA.GOV (192.100.15.2)  264 ms  258 ms  264 ms
 8  NCAR.NSN.NASA.GOV (128.161.97.2)  324 ms *  295 ms
 9  cu-gw.ucar.edu (192.43.244.4)  294 ms  318 ms  294 ms
10  engr-gw.Colorado.EDU (128.138.1.3)  294 ms  288 ms  294 ms
11  bruno.cs.colorado.edu (128.138.243.151)  293 ms  317 ms  294 ms
12  engr-gw-ot.cs.colorado.edu (128.138.204.1)  323 ms  317 ms  384 ms
13  cu-gw.Colorado.EDU (128.138.1.1)  294 ms  318 ms  294 ms
14  enss.ucar.edu (192.43.244.10)  323 ms  318 ms  294 ms
15  t3-1.Denver-cnss97.t3.ans.net (140.222.97.2)  294 ms  288 ms  384 ms
16  t3-0.enss142.t3.ans.net (140.222.142.1)  293 ms  288 ms  294 ms
17  Gabby.Telcom.Arizona.EDU (192.80.43.1)  294 ms  288 ms  294 ms
18  Butch.Telcom.Arizona.EDU (128.196.128.88)  293 ms  317 ms  294 ms
19  gateway.tuc.noao.edu (140.252.104.1)  294 ms  289 ms  294 ms
20  netb.tuc.noao.edu (140.252.1.183)  324 ms  321 ms  294 ms
21  sun.tuc.noao.edu (140.252.13.33)  534 ms  529 ms  564 ms
```

Figure 8.11 `traceroute` example showing unsymmetrical routing path.

The outbound path (TTLs 1–11) differs from the return path (TTLs 11–21), a good illustration that Internet routing need not be symmetrical.

This output also illustrates the point we discussed with Figure 8.3. Compare the output for TTLs 2 and 19: both are for the router `gateway.tuc.noao.edu`, but the two IP addresses are different. Since `traceroute` identifies the incoming interface, and since we're passing through the router in two different directions, once on the outbound path (TTL 2) and then on the return path (TTL 19), we expect this. We see the same effect comparing TTLs 3 and 18, and TTLs 4 and 17.

8.6 Summary

Traceroute is an indispensable tool when working with a TCP/IP network. Its operation is simple: send UDP datagrams starting with a TTL of 1, increasing the TTL by 1, to locate each router in the path. An ICMP time exceeded is returned by each router when it discards the UDP datagram, and an ICMP port unreachable is generated by the final destination.

We ran examples of `traceroute` on both LANs and WANs, and used it to examine IP source routing. We used loose source routing to see if the route to a destination is the same as the return route from that destination.

Exercises

8.1 What can happen if an IP implementation decrements the incoming TTL and then tests for equal to 0?

8.2 How does `traceroute` calculate the RTT? Compare this to the RTT calculation done by `ping`.

8.3 (This exercise and the next one are based on actual problems determined when `traceroute` was being developed, and are from comments in the `traceroute` source code.) Assume there are three routers (R1, R2, and R3) between the source and destination and that the middle router (R2) decrements the TTL but incorrectly forwards the IP datagram when the incoming TTL was 1. Describe what happens. How can you see this occur when running `traceroute`?

8.4 Again assume there are three routers between the source and destination. This time the destination host has a bug whereby it always uses the incoming TTL as the outgoing TTL of an ICMP message. Describe what happens and how you would see this.

8.5 We can run `tcpdump` on the SLIP link between `sun` and `netb` when running the example from Figure 8.8. If we specify the `-v` option we can see the TTL value of the returned ICMP messages. Doing this shows the incoming TTL from `netb` to be 255, from `butch` it's 253, from `Gabby` it's 252, and from `enss142.UT.westnet.net` it's 249. Does this give any additional information about whether there really are some missing routers?

8.6 Both SunOS and SVR4 provide a version of `ping` with a `-l` option that provides a loose source route. The manual pages state that it's intended to be used with the `-R` option (which specifies the record route option). If you have access to either of these systems, try these two options together. What's happening? If you can watch the datagrams with `tcpdump`, describe what's going on.

8.7 Compare the ways `ping` and `traceroute` handle multiple instances of the client on the same host.

8.8 Compare the ways `ping` and `traceroute` measure the round-trip time.

8.9 We said `traceroute` picks the starting UDP destination port number at 33435 and increments this by one for each packet sent. In Section 1.9 we said ephemeral port numbers are normally between 1024 and 5000, making it unlikely that Traceroute's destination port is in use on the destination host. Is this still true under Solaris 2.2? (*Hint*: Read Section E.4.)

8.10 Read RFC 1393 [Malkin 1993b] for a proposed alternative way of determining the path to a destination. What are its advantages and disadvantages?

9

IP Routing

9.1 Introduction

Routing is one of the most important functions of IP. Figure 9.1 shows a simplified view of the processing done at the IP layer. Datagrams to be routed can be generated either on the local host or on some other host. In the latter case this host must be configured to act as a router, or datagrams received through the network interfaces that are not ours are dropped (i.e., silently discarded).

In Figure 9.1 we also show a routing daemon, which is normally a user process. The most common daemons used on Unix systems are the programs `routed` and `gated`. (The term *daemon* means the process is running "in the background," carrying out operations on behalf of the whole system. Daemons are normally started when the system is bootstrapped and run as long as the system is up.) The topics of which routing protocol to use on a given host, how to exchange routing information with adjacent routers, and how the routing protocols work are complex and can fill an entire book of their own. (Interested readers are referred to [Perlman 1992] for many of the details.) We'll look briefly at dynamic routing and the Routing Information Protocol (RIP) in Chapter 10. Our main interest in the current chapter is how a single IP layer makes its routing decisions.

The routing table that we show in Figure 9.1 is accessed frequently by IP (on a busy host this could mean hundreds of times a second) but is updated much less frequently by a routing daemon (possibly about once every 30 seconds). The routing table can also be updated when ICMP "redirect" messages are received, something we'll look at in Section 9.5, and by the `route` command. This command is often executed when the system is bootstrapped, to install some initial routes. We'll also use the `netstat` command in this chapter to display the routing table.

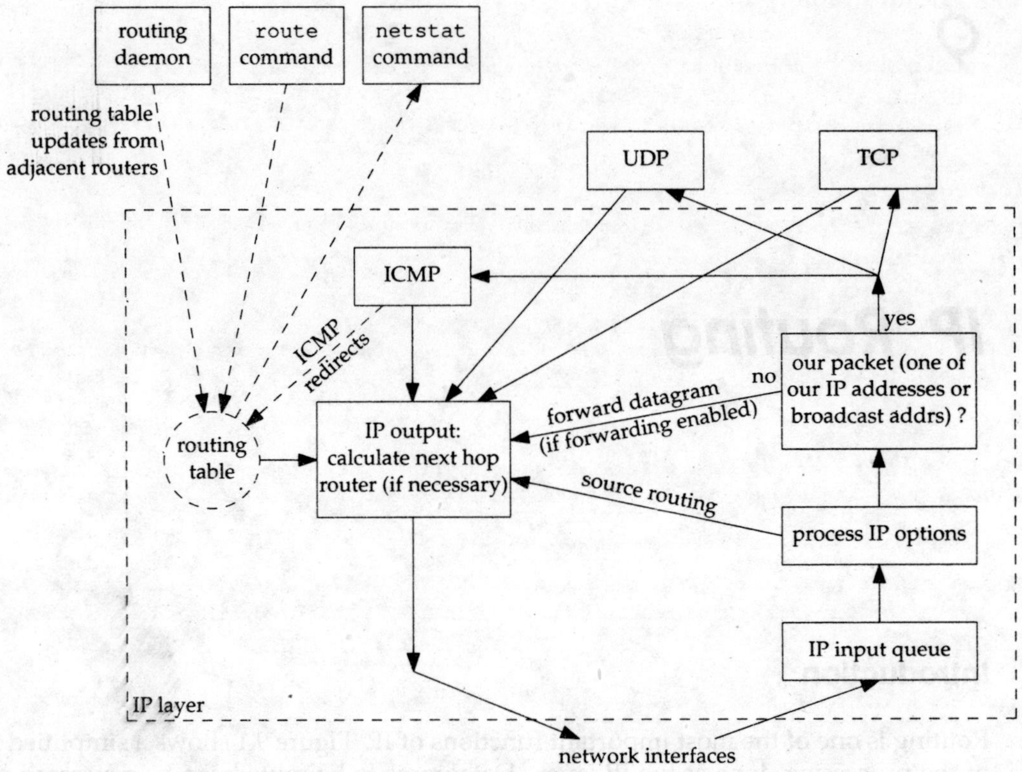

Figure 9.1 Processing done at the IP layer.

9.2 Routing Principles

The place to start our discussion of IP routing is to understand what is maintained by the kernel in its routing table. The information contained in the routing table drives all the routing decisions made by IP.

In Section 3.3 we listed the steps that IP performs when it searches its routing table.

1. Search for a matching host address.
2. Search for a matching network address.
3. Search for a default entry. (The default entry is normally specified in the routing table as a network entry, with a network ID of 0.)

A matching host address is always used before a matching network address.

The routing done by IP, when it searches the routing table and decides which interface to send a packet out, is a *routing mechanism*. This differs from a *routing policy*, which is a set of rules that decides which routes go into the routing table. IP performs the routing mechanism while a routing daemon normally provides the routing policy.

Simple Routing Table

Let s start by looking at some typical host routing tables. On the host svr4 we execute the netstat command with the -r option to list the routing table and the -n option, which prints IP addresses in numeric format, rather than as names. (We do this because some of the entries in the routing table are for networks, not hosts. Without the -n option, the netstat command searches the file /etc/networks for the network names. This confuses the discussion by adding another set of names—network names in addition to hostnames.)

```
svr4 % netstat -rn
Routing tables
Destination          Gateway              Flags    Refcnt Use       Interface
140.252.13.65        140.252.13.35        UGH      0      0         emd0
127.0.0.1            127.0.0.1            UH       1      0         lo0
default              140.252.13.33        UG       0      0         emd0
140.252.13.32        140.252.13.34        U        4      25043     emd0
```

The first line says for destination 140.252.13.65 (host slip) the gateway (router) to send the packet to is 140.252.13.35 (bsdi). This is what we expect, since the host slip is connected to bsdi with a SLIP link, and bsdi is on the same Ethernet as this host.

There are five different flags that can be printed for a given route.

- U The route is up.
- G The route is to a gateway (router). If this flag is not set, the destination is directly connected.
- H The route is to a host, that is, the destination is a complete host address. If this flag is not set, the route is to a network, and the destination is a network address: a net ID, or a combination of a net ID and a subnet ID.
- D The route was created by a redirect (Section 9.5).
- M The route was modified by a redirect (Section 9.5).

The G flag is important because it differentiates between an *indirect route* and a *direct route.* (The G flag is not set for a direct route.) The difference is that a packet going out a direct route has both the IP address and the link-layer address specifying the destination (Figure 3.3, p. 40). When a packet is sent out an indirect route, the IP address specifies the final destination but the link-layer address specifies the gateway (that is, the next-hop router). We saw an example of this in Figure 3.4 (p. 41). In this routing table example we have an indirect route (the G flag is set) so the IP address of a packet using this route is the final destination (140.252.13.65), but the link-layer address must correspond to the router 140.252.13.35.

It's important to understand the difference between the G and H flags. The G flag differentiates between a direct and an indirect route, as described above. The H flag, however, specifies that the destination address (the first column of netstat output) is a complete host address. The absence of the H flag means the destination address is a network address (the host ID portion will be 0). When the routing table is searched for a route to a destination IP address, a host address entry must match the destination address completely, while a network address only needs to match the network ID and any subnet ID of the destination address. Also, some versions of the `netstat` command print all the host entries first, followed by the network entries.

The reference count column gives the number of active uses for each route. A connection-oriented protocol such as TCP holds on to a route while the connection is established. If we established a Telnet connection between the two hosts `svr4` and `slip`, we would see the reference count go to 1. With another Telnet connection the reference count would go to 2, and so on.

The next column ("use") displays the number of packets sent through that route. If we are the only users of the route and we run the `ping` program to send 5 packets, the count goes up by 5. The final column, the interface, is the name of the local interface.

The second line of output is for the loopback interface (Section 2.7), always named `lo0`. The `G` flag is not set, since the route is not to a gateway. The `H` flag indicates that the destination address (127.0.0.1) is a host address, and not a network address. When the `G` field is not set, indicating a direct route, the gateway column gives the IP address of the outgoing interface.

The third line of output is for the default route. Every host can have one or more default routes. This entry says to send packets to the router 140.252.13.33 (`sun`) if a more specific route can't be found. This means the current host (`svr4`) can access other systems across the Internet through the router `sun` (and its SLIP link), using this single routing table entry. Being able to establish a default route is a powerful concept. The flags for this route (`UG`) indicate that it's a route to a gateway, as we expect.

> Here we purposely call `sun` a router and not a host because when it's used as a default router, its IP forwarding function is being used, not its host functionality.
>
> The Host Requirements RFC specifically states that the IP layer must support multiple default routes. Many implementations, however, don't support this. When multiple default routes exist, a common technique is to round robin among them. This is what Solaris 2.2 does, for example.

The final line of output is for the attached Ethernet. The `H` flag is not set, indicating that the destination address (140.252.13.32) is a network address with the host portion set to 0. Indeed, the low-order 5 bits are 0 (Figure 3.11, p. 47). Since this is a direct route (the `G` flag is not set) the gateway column specifies the IP address of the outgoing interface.

Implied in this final entry, but not shown by the `netstat` output, is the mask associated with this destination address (140.252.13.32). If this destination is being compared against the IP address 140.252.13.33, the address is first logically ANDed with the mask associated with the destination (the subnet mask of the interface, `0xffffffe0`, from Section 3.7) before the comparison. For a network route to a directly connected network, the routing table mask defaults to the subnet mask of the interface. But in general the routing table mask can assume any 32-bit value. A value other than the default can be specified as an option to the `route` command.

The complexity of a host's routing table depends on the topology of the networks to which the host has access.

1. The simplest (but least interesting) case is a host that is not connected to any networks at all. The TCP/IP protocols can still be used on the host, but only to communicate with itself! The routing table in this case consists of a single entry for the loopback interface.

2. Next is a host connected to a single LAN, only able to access hosts on that LAN. The routing table consists of two entries: one for the loopback interface and one for the LAN (such as an Ethernet).

3. The next step occurs when other networks (such as the Internet) are reachable through a single router. This is normally handled with a default entry pointing to that router.

4. The final step is when other host-specific or network-specific routes are added. In our example the route to the host `slip`, through the router `bsdi`, is an example of this.

Let's follow through the steps IP performs when using this routing table to route some example packets on the host `svr4`.

1. Assume the destination address is the host `sun`, 140.252.13.33. A search is first made for a matching host entry. The two host entries in the table (`slip` and `localhost`) don't match, so a search is made through the routing table again for a matching network address. A match is found with the entry 140.252.13.32 (the network IDs and subnet IDs match), so the `emd0` interface is used. This is a direct route, so the link-layer address will be the destination address.

2. Assume the destination address is the host `slip`, 140.252.13.65. The first search through the table, for a matching host address, finds a match. This is an indirect route so the destination IP address remains 140.252.13.65, but the link-layer address must be the link-layer address of the gateway 140.252.13.35, and the interface is `emd0`.

3. This time we're sending a datagram across the Internet to the host `aw.com` (192.207.117.2). The first search of the routing table for a matching host address fails, as does the second search for a matching network address. The final step is a search for a default entry, and this succeeds. The route is an indirect route through the gateway 140.252.13.33 using the interface `emd0`.

4. In our final example we send a datagram to our own host. There are four ways to do this, using either the hostname, the host IP address, the loopback name, or the loopback IP address:

```
ftp svr4
ftp 140.252.13.34

ftp localhost
ftp 127.0.0.1
```

In the first two cases, the second search of the routing table yields a network match with 140.252.13.32, and the packet is sent down to the Ethernet driver. As we showed in Figure 2.4 (p. 28) it will be seen that this packet is destined for the host's own IP address, and the packet is sent to the loopback driver, which sends it to the IP input queue.

In the latter two cases, specifying the name of the loopback interface or its IP address, the first search of the routing table finds the matching host address entry, and the packet is sent to the loopback driver, which sends it to the IP input queue.

In all four cases the packet is sent to the loopback driver, but two different routing decisions are made.

Initializing a Routing Table

We never said how these routing table entries are created. Whenever an interface is initialized (normally when the interface's address is set by the `ifconfig` command) a direct route is automatically created for that interface. For point-to-point links and the loopback interface, the route is to a host (i.e., the `H` flag is set). For broadcast interfaces such as an Ethernet, the route is to that network.

Routes to hosts or networks that are not directly connected must be entered into the routing table somehow. One common way is to execute the `route` command explicitly from the initialization files when the system is bootstrapped. On the host `svr4` the following two commands were executed to add the entries that we showed earlier:

```
route add default sun 1
route add slip bsdi 1
```

The third arguments (`default` and `slip`) are the destinations, the fourth argument is the gateway (router), and the final argument is a routing metric. All that the `route` command does with this metric is install the route with the `G` flag set if the metric is greater than 0, or without the `G` flag if the metric is 0.

> Unfortunately, few systems agree on which start-up file contains the `route` commands. Under 4.4BSD and BSD/386 it is `/etc/netstart`, under SVR4 it is `/etc/inet/rc.inet`, under Solaris 2.x it is `/etc/rc2.d/S69inet`, SunOS 4.1.x uses `/etc/rc.local`, and AIX 3.2.2 uses `/etc/rc.net`.

Some systems allow a default router to be specified in a file such as `/etc/defaultrouter`, and this default is added to the routing table on every reboot.

Other ways to initialize a routing table are to run a routing daemon (Chapter 10) or to use the newer router discovery protocol (Section 9.6).

A More Complex Routing Table

The host `sun` is the default router for all the hosts on our subnet, since it has the dialup SLIP link that connects to the Internet (see the figure on the inside front cover).

```
sun % netstat -rn
Routing tables
Destination        Gateway            Flags    Refcnt Use     Interface
140.252.13.65      140.252.13.35      UGH      0      171     le0
127.0.0.1          127.0.0.1          UH       1      766     lo0
140.252.1.183      140.252.1.29       UH       0      0       sl0
default            140.252.1.183      UG       1      2955    sl0
140.252.13.32      140.252.13.33      U        8      99551   le0
```

The first two entries are identical to the first two for the host `svr4`: a host-specific route to `slip` through the router `bsdi`, and the loopback route.

The third line is new. It is a direct route (the `G` flag is not set) to a host (the `H` flag is set) and corresponds to our point-to-point link, the SLIP interface. If we compare it to the output from the `ifconfig` command,

```
sun % ifconfig sl0
sl0: flags=1051<UP,POINTOPOINT,RUNNING>
        inet 140.252.1.29 --> 140.252.1.183 netmask ffffff00
```

we see that the destination address in the routing table is the other end of the point-to-point link (the router `netb`) and the gateway address is really the local IP address of the outgoing interface (140.252.1.29). (We said earlier that the gateway address printed by `netstat` for a direct route is the local IP address of the interface to use.)

The default entry is an indirect route (`G` flag) to a network (no `H` flag), as we expect. The gateway address is the address of the router (140.252.1.183, the other end of the SLIP link) and not the local IP address of the SLIP link (140.252.1.29). Again, this is because it is an indirect route, not a direct route.

We should also note that the third and fourth lines output by `netstat` (the ones with an interface of `sl0`) are created by the SLIP software being used when the SLIP line is brought up, and deleted when the SLIP link is brought down.

No Route to Destination

All our examples so far have assumed that the search of the routing table finds a match, even if the match is the default route. What if there is no default route, and a match isn't found for a given destination?

The answer depends on whether the IP datagram being routed was generated on the host or is being forwarded (e.g., we're acting as a router). If the datagram was generated on this host, an error is returned to the application that sent the datagram, either "host unreachable" or "network unreachable." If the datagram was being forwarded, an ICMP host unreachable error is sent back to original sender. We examine this error in the following section.

9.3 ICMP Host and Network Unreachable Errors

The ICMP "host unreachable" error message is sent by a router when it receives an IP datagram that it cannot deliver or forward. (Figure 6.10 shows the format of the ICMP unreachable messages.) We can see this easily on our network by taking down the dialup SLIP link on the router sun, and trying to send a packet through the SLIP link from any of the other hosts that specify sun as the default router.

> Older implementations of the BSD TCP/IP software generated either a host unreachable, or a network unreachable, depending on whether the destination was on a local subnet or not. 4.4BSD generates only the host unreachable.

Recall from the `netstat` output for the router sun shown in the previous section that the routing table entries that use the SLIP link are added when the SLIP link is brought up, and deleted when the SLIP link is brought down. This means that when the SLIP link is down, there is no default route on sun. But we don't try to change all the other host's routing tables on our small network, having them also remove their default route. Instead we count on the ICMP host unreachable generated by sun for any packets that it gets that it cannot forward.

We can see this by running `ping` on `svr4`, for a host on the other side of the dialup SLIP link (which is down):

```
svr4 % ping gemini
ICMP Host Unreachable from gateway sun (140.252.13.33)
ICMP Host Unreachable from gateway sun (140.252.13.33)
^?                                   type interrupt key to stop
```

Figure 9.2 shows the `tcpdump` output for this example, run on the host `bsdi`.

```
1  0.0                svr4 > gemini: icmp: echo request
2  0.00 (0.00)        sun > svr4: icmp: host gemini unreachable

3  0.99 (0.99)        svr4 > gemini: icmp: echo request
4  0.99 (0.00)        sun > svr4: icmp: host gemini unreachable
```

Figure 9.2 ICMP host unreachable in response to `ping`.

When the router sun finds no route to the host `gemini`, it responds to the echo request with a host unreachable.

If we bring the SLIP link to the Internet up, and try to ping an IP address that is not connected to the Internet, we expect an error. What is interesting is to see how far the packet gets into the Internet, before the error is returned:

```
sun % ping 192.82.148.1              this IP address is not connected to the Internet
PING 192.82.148.1: 56 data bytes
ICMP Host Unreachable from gateway enss142.UT.westnet.net (192.31.39.21)
 for icmp from sun (140.252.1.29) to 192.82.148.1
```

Looking at Figure 8.5 (p. 103) we see that the packet made it through six routers before detecting that the IP address was invalid. Only when it got to the border of the NSFNET backbone was the error detected. This implies that the six routers that forwarded the packet were doing so because of default entries, and only when it reached the NSFNET backbone did a router have complete knowledge of every network connected to the Internet. This illustrates that many routers can operate with just partial knowledge of the big picture.

[Ford, Rekhter, and Braun 1993] define a *top-level routing domain* as one that maintains routing information to most Internet sites and does not use default routes. They note that five of these top-level routing domains exist on the Internet: the NSFNET backbone, the Commercial Internet Exchange (CIX), the NASA Science Internet (NSI), SprintLink, and the European IP Backbone (EBONE).

9.4 To Forward or Not to Forward

We've mentioned a few times that hosts are not supposed to forward IP datagrams unless they have been specifically configured as a router. How is this configuration done?

Most Berkeley-derived implementations have a kernel variable named `ipforwarding`, or some similar name. (See Appendix E.) Some systems (BSD/386 and SVR4, for example) only forward datagrams if this variable is nonzero. SunOS 4.1.x allows three values for the variable: –1 means never forward and never change the value of the variable, 0 means don't forward by default but set this variable to 1 when two or more interfaces are up, and 1 means always forward. Solaris 2.x changes the three values to be 0 (never forward), 1 (always forward), and 2 (only forward when two or more interfaces are up).

Older 4.2BSD hosts forwarded datagrams by default, which caused lots of problems for systems configured improperly. That's why this kernel option must always default to "never forward" unless the system administrator specifically enables forwarding.

9.5 ICMP Redirect Errors

The ICMP redirect error is sent by a router to the sender of an IP datagram when the datagram should have been sent to a different router. The concept is simple, as we show in the three steps in Figure 9.3. The only time we'll see an ICMP redirect is when the host has a choice of routers to send the packet to. (Recall the earlier example of this we saw in Figure 7.6, p. 94.)

1. We assume that the host sends an IP datagram to R1. This routing decision is often made because R1 is the default router for the host.
2. R1 receives the datagram and performs a lookup in its routing table and determines that R2 is the correct next-hop router to send the datagram to. When it sends the datagram to R2, R1 detects that it is sending it out the same interface on which the datagram arrived (the LAN to which the host and the two routers are attached). This is the clue to a router that a redirect can be sent to the original sender.
3. R1 sends an ICMP redirect to the host, telling it to send future datagrams to that destination to R2, instead of R1.

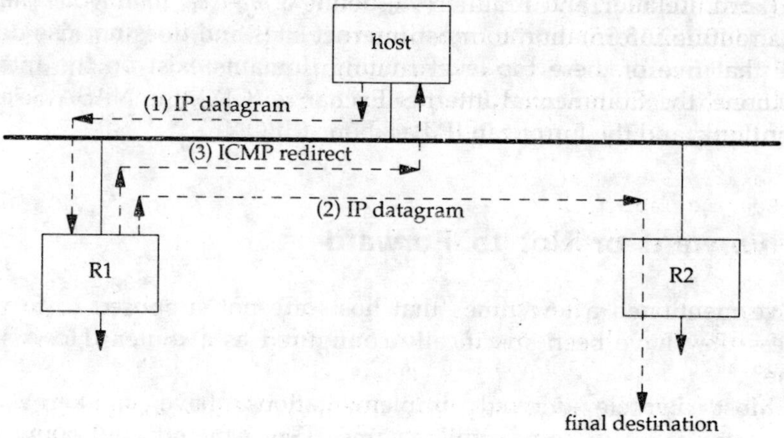

Figure 9.3 Example of an ICMP redirect.

A common use for redirects is to let a host with minimal routing knowledge build up a better routing table over time. The host can start with only a default route (either R1 or R2 from our example in Figure 9.3) and anytime this default turns out to be wrong, it'll be informed by that default router with a redirect, allowing the host to update its routing table accordingly. ICMP redirects allow TCP/IP hosts to be dumb when it comes to routing, with all the intelligence in the routers. Obviously R1 and R2 in our example have to know more about the topology of the attached networks, but all the hosts attached to the LAN can start with a default route and learn more as they receive redirects.

An Example

We can see ICMP redirects in action on our network (inside front cover). Although we show only three hosts (`aix`, `solaris`, and `gemini`) and two routers (`gateway` and `netb`) on the top network, there are more than 150 hosts and 10 other routers on this network. Most of the hosts specify `gateway` as the default router, since it provides access to the Internet.

How is the author's subnet (the bottom four hosts in the figure) accessed from the hosts on the 140.252.1 subnet? First recall that if only a single host is at the end of the SLIP link, proxy ARP is used (Section 4.6). This means nothing special is required for hosts on the top network (140.252.1) to access the host `sun` (140.252.1.29). The proxy ARP software in `netb` handles this.

When a network is at the other end of the SLIP link, however, routing becomes involved. One solution is for every host and router to know that the router `netb` is the gateway for the network 140.252.13. This could be done by either a static route in each host's routing table, or by running a routing daemon in each host. A simpler way (and the method actually used) is to utilize ICMP redirects.

Let's run the ping program from the host solaris on the top network to the host bsdi (140.252.13.35) on the bottom network. Since the subnet IDs are different, proxy ARP can't be used. Assuming a static route has not been installed, the first packet sent will use the default route to the router gateway. Here is the routing table before we run ping:

```
solaris % netstat -rn
Routing Table:
  Destination           Gateway           Flags  Ref   Use   Interface
-----------------  -----------------  -----  -----  ------  ---------
127.0.0.1          127.0.0.1           UH        0     848  lo0
140.252.1.0        140.252.1.32        U         3   15042  le0
224.0.0.0          140.252.1.32        U         3       0  le0
default            140.252.1.4         UG        0    5747
```

(The entry for 224.0.0.0 is for IP multicasting. We describe it in Chapter 12.) If we specify the -v option to ping, we'll see any ICMP messages received by the host. We need to specify this to see the redirect message that's sent.

```
solaris % ping -sv bsdi
PING bsdi: 56 data bytes
ICMP Host redirect from gateway gateway (140.252.1.4)
 to netb (140.252.1.183) for bsdi (140.252.13.35)
64 bytes from bsdi (140.252.13.35): icmp_seq=0. time=383. ms
64 bytes from bsdi (140.252.13.35): icmp_seq=1. time=364. ms
64 bytes from bsdi (140.252.13.35): icmp_seq=2. time=353. ms
^?                                           type interrupt key to stop
----bsdi PING Statistics----
4 packets transmitted, 3 packets received, 25% packet loss
round-trip (ms)  min/avg/max = 353/366/383
```

Before we receive the first ping response, the host receives an ICMP redirect from the default router gateway. If we then look at the routing table, we'll see that the new route to the host bsdi has been inserted. (This new entry is shown in a bolder font.)

```
solaris % netstat -rn
Routing Table:
  Destination           Gateway           Flags  Ref   Use   Interface
-----------------  -----------------  -----  -----  ------  ---------
127.0.0.1          127.0.0.1           UH        0     848  lo0
140.252.13.35      140.252.1.183       UGHD      0       2
140.252.1.0        140.252.1.32        U         3   15045  le0
224.0.0.0          140.252.1.32        U         3       0  le0
default            140.252.1.4         UG        0    5749
```

This is the first time we've seen the D flag, which means the route was installed by an ICMP redirect. The G flag means it's an indirect route to a gateway (netb), and the H flag means it's a host route (as we expect), not a network route.

Since this is a host route, added by a host redirect, it handles only the host bsdi. If we then access the host svr4, another redirect is generated, creating another host route. Similarly, accessing the host slip creates another host route. The point here is that each redirect is for a single host, causing a host route to be added. All three hosts on the author's subnet (bsdi, svr4, and slip) could also be handled by a single network route pointing to the router sun. But ICMP redirects create host routes, not network routes, because the router generating the redirect in this example (gateway) has no knowledge of the subnet structure on the 140.252.13 network.

More Details

Figure 9.4 shows the format of the ICMP redirect message.

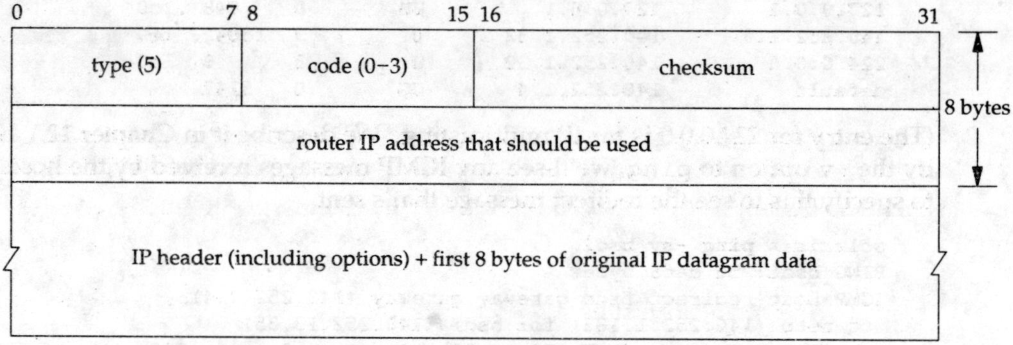

Figure 9.4 ICMP redirect message.

There are four different redirect messages, with different *code* values, as shown in Figure 9.5.

code	Description
0	redirect for network
1	redirect for host
2	redirect for type-of-service and network
3	redirect for type-of-service and host

Figure 9.5 Different *code* values for ICMP redirect.

There are three IP addresses that the receiver of an ICMP redirect must look at: (1) the IP address that caused the redirect (which is in the IP header returned as the data portion of the ICMP redirect), (2) the IP address of the router that sent the redirect (which is the source IP address of the IP datagram containing the redirect), and (3) the IP address of the router that should be used (which is in bytes 4–7 of the ICMP message).

There are numerous rules about ICMP redirects. First, redirects are generated only by routers, not by hosts. Also, redirects are intended to be used by hosts, not routers. It is assumed that routers participate in a routing protocol with other routers, and the routing protocol should obviate the need for redirects. (This means that in Figure 9.1 the routing table should be updated by either a routing daemon or redirects, but not by both.)

4.4BSD, when acting as a router, performs the following checks, all of which must be true before an ICMP redirect is generated.

1. The outgoing interface must equal the incoming interface.
2. The route being used for the outgoing datagram must not have been created or modified by an ICMP redirect, and must not be the router's default route.
3. The datagram must not be source routed.
4. The kernel must be configured to send redirects.

The kernel variable is named `ip_sendredirects`, or something similar. (See Appendix E.) Most current systems (4.4BSD, SunOS 4.1.x, Solaris 2.x, and AIX 3.2.2, for example) enable this variable by default. Other systems such as SVR4 disable it by default.

Additionally, a 4.4BSD host that receives an ICMP redirect performs some checks before modifying its routing table. These are to prevent a misbehaving router or host, or a malicious user, from incorrectly modifying a system's routing table.

1. The new router must be on a directly connected network.
2. The redirect must be from the current router for that destination.
3. The redirect cannot tell the host to use itself as the router.
4. The route that's being modified must be an indirect route.

Our final point about redirects is that routers should send only host redirects (*codes* 1 or 3 from Figure 9.5) and not network redirects. Subnetting makes it hard to specify exactly when a network redirect can be sent instead of a host redirect. Some hosts treat a received network redirect as a host redirect, in case a router sends the wrong type.

9.6 ICMP Router Discovery Messages

We mentioned earlier in this chapter that one way to initialize a routing table is with static routes specified in configuration files. This is often used to set a default entry. A newer way is to use the ICMP router advertisement and solicitation messages.

The general concept is that after bootstrapping, a host broadcasts or multicasts a router solicitation message. One or more routers respond with a router advertisement message. Additionally, the routers periodically broadcast or multicast their router advertisements, allowing any hosts that are listening to update their routing table accordingly.

RFC 1256 [Deering 1991] specifies the format of these two ICMP messages. Figure 9.6 shows the format of the ICMP router solicitation message. Figure 9.7 shows the format of the ICMP router advertisement message sent by routers.

Multiple addresses can be advertised by a router in a single message. *Number of addresses* is the number. *Address entry size* is the number of 32-bit words for each router address, and is always 2. *Lifetime* is the number of seconds that the advertised addresses can be considered valid.

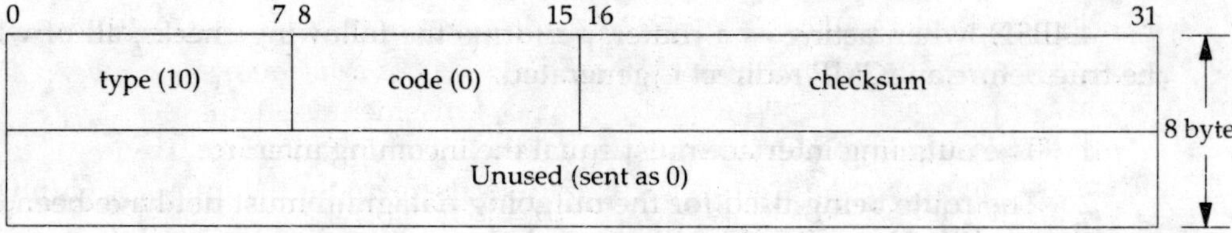

Figure 9.6 Format of ICMP router solicitation message.

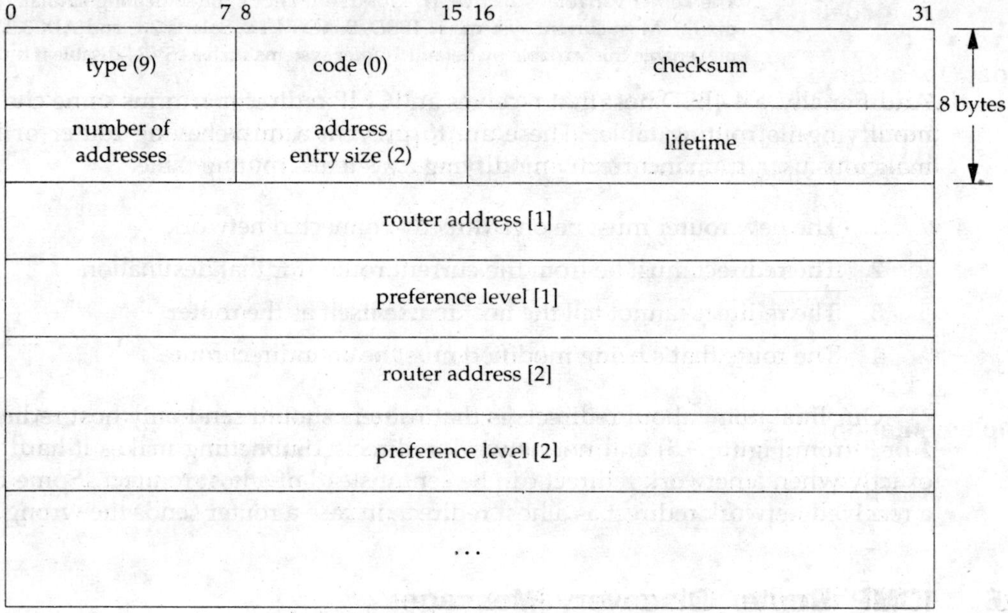

Figure 9.7 Format of ICMP router advertisement message.

One or more pairs of an IP address and a preference then follow. The IP address must be one of the sending router's IP addresses. The *preference level* is a signed 32-bit integer indicating the preference of this address as a default router address, relative to other router addresses on the same subnet. Larger values imply more preferable addresses. The preference level 0x80000000 means the corresponding address, although advertised, is not to be used by the receiver as a default router address. The default value of the preference is normally 0.

Router Operation

When a router starts up it transmits periodic advertisements on all interfaces capable of broadcasting or multicasting. These advertisements are not exactly periodic, but are randomized, to reduce the probability of synchronization with other routers on the same subnet. The normal time interval between advertisements is between 450 and 600 seconds. The default lifetime for a given advertisement is 30 minutes.

Another use of the lifetime field occurs when an interface on a router is disabled. In that case the router can transmit a final advertisement on the interface with the lifetime set to 0.

In addition to the periodic, unsolicited advertisements, a router also listens for solicitations from hosts. It responds to these solicitations with a router advertisement.

If there are multiple routers on a given subnet, it is up to the system administrator to configure the preference level for each router as appropriate. For example, the primary default router would have a higher preference than a backup.

Host Operation

Upon bootstrap a host normally transmits three router solicitations, 3 seconds apart. As soon as a valid advertisement is received, the solicitations stop.

A host also listens for advertisements from adjacent routers. These advertisements can cause the host's default router to change. Also, if an advertisement is not received for the current default, that default can time out.

As long as the normal default router stays up, that router will send advertisements every 10 minutes, with a lifetime of 30 minutes. This means the host's default entry won't time out, even if one or two advertisements are lost.

Implementation

The router discovery messages are normally generated by and processed by a user process (a daemon). This adds yet another program updating the routing table in Figure 9.1, although it would only add or delete a default entry. The daemon would have to be configured to act as a router or a host.

> These two ICMP messages are new and not supported by all systems. Solaris 2.x is the only system in our network that supports these messages (the `in.rdisc` daemon). Although the RFC recommends using IP multicasting whenever possible, router discovery can work using broadcast messages also.

9.7 Summary

The operation of IP routing is fundamental to a system running TCP/IP, be it a host or router. The routing table entries are simple: up to 5 flag bits, a destination IP address (host, network, or default), a next-hop router IP address (for an indirect route) or a local interface IP address (for a direct route), and a pointer to a local interface to use. Host entries have priority over network entries, which have priority over default entries.

A search of this routing table is made for every IP datagram that the system generates or forwards, and can be updated by either a routing daemon or ICMP redirects. By default a system should never forward a datagram unless it has specifically been configured to do so. Static routes can be entered using the `route` command, and the newer ICMP router discovery messages can be used to initialize and dynamically update default entries. Hosts can start with a simple routing table that is updated dynamically by ICMP redirects from its default router.

Our discussion in this chapter has focused on how a single system uses its routing table. In the next chapter we examine how routers exchange routing information with each other.

Exercises

9.1 Why do you think both types of ICMP redirects—network and host—exist?

9.2 In the routing table for `svr4` shown at the beginning of Section 9.2, is a specific route to the host `slip` (140.252.13.65) necessary? What would change if this entry were removed from the routing table?

9.3 Consider a cable with both 4.2BSD hosts and 4.3BSD hosts. Assume the network ID is 140.1. The 4.2BSD hosts only recognize a host ID of all zero bits as the broadcast address (140.1.0.0), while the 4.3BSD hosts normally send a broadcast using a host ID of all one bits (140.1.255.255). Also, the 4.2BSD hosts by default will try to forward incoming datagrams, even if they have only a single interface.

Describe the events that happen when the 4.2BSD hosts receive an IP datagram with the destination address of 140.1.255.255.

9.4 Continue the previous exercise, assuming someone corrects this problem by adding an entry to the ARP cache on one system on the 140.1 subnet (using the `arp` command) saying that the IP address 140.1.255.255 has a corresponding Ethernet address of all one bits (the Ethernet broadcast). Describe what happens now.

9.5 Examine your system's routing table and describe each entry.

10

Dynamic Routing Protocols

10.1 Introduction

Our discussion in the previous chapter dealt with *static routing*. The routing table entries were created by default when an interface was configured (for directly connected interfaces), added by the `route` command (normally from a system bootstrap file), or created by an ICMP redirect (usually when the wrong default was used).

This is fine if the network is small, there is a single connection point to other networks, and there are no redundant routes (where a backup route can be used if a primary route fails). If any of these three conditions is false, dynamic routing is normally used.

This chapter looks at the dynamic routing protocols used by routers to communicate with each other. We concentrate on RIP, the Routing Information Protocol, a widely used protocol that is provided with almost every TCP/IP implementation. We then look at two newer routing protocols, OSPF and BGP. The chapter finishes with an examination of a new routing technique, called classless interdomain routing, that is starting to be implemented across the Internet to conserve class B network numbers.

10.2 Dynamic Routing

Dynamic routing occurs when routers talk to adjacent routers, informing each other of what networks each router is currently connected to. The routers must communicate using a *routing protocol*, of which there are many to choose from. The process on the router that is running the routing protocol, communicating with its neighbor routers, is usually called a *routing daemon*. As shown in Figure 9.1, the routing daemon updates the kernel's routing table with information it receives from neighbor routers.

The use of dynamic routing does *not* change the way the kernel performs routing at the IP layer, as we described in Section 9.2. We called this the *routing mechanism*. The kernel still searches its routing table in the same way, looking for host routes, network routes, and default routes. What changes is the information placed into the routing table—instead of coming from `route` commands in bootstrap files, the routes are added and deleted dynamically by a routing daemon, as routes change over time.

As we mentioned earlier, the routing daemon adds a *routing policy* to the system, choosing which routes to place into the kernel's routing table. If the daemon finds multiple routes to a destination, the daemon chooses (somehow) which route is best, and which one to insert into the kernel's table. If the daemon finds that a link has gone down (perhaps a router crashed or a phone line is out of order), it can delete the affected routes or add alternate routes that bypass the problem.

In a system such as the Internet, many different routing protocols are currently used. The Internet is organized into a collection of *autonomous systems* (ASs), each of which is normally administered by a single entity. A corporation or university campus often defines an autonomous system. The NSFNET backbone of the Internet forms an autonomous system, because all the routers in the backbone are under a single administrative control.

Each autonomous system can select its own routing protocol to communicate between the routers in that autonomous system. This is called an *interior gateway protocol* (IGP) or *intradomain routing protocol*. The most popular IGP has been the *Routing Information Protocol* (RIP). A newer IGP is the *Open Shortest Path First* protocol (OSPF). It is intended as a replacement for RIP. An older IGP that has fallen out of use is HELLO—the IGP used on the original NSFNET backbone in 1986.

> The new Router Requirements RFC [Almquist 1993] states that a router that implements any dynamic routing protocol must support both OSPF and RIP, and may support other IGPs.

Separate routing protocols called *exterior gateway protocols* (EGPs) or *interdomain routing protocols* are used between the routers in different autonomous systems. Historically (and confusingly) the predominant EGP has been a protocol of the same name: EGP. A newer EGP is the Border Gateway Protocol (BGP) that is currently used between the NSFNET backbone and some of the regional networks that attach to the backbone. BGP is intended to replace EGP.

10.3 Unix Routing Daemons

Unix systems often run the routing daemon named `routed`. It is provided with almost every implementation of TCP/IP. This program communicates using only RIP, which we describe in the next section. It is intended for small to medium-size networks.

An alternative program is `gated`. It supports both IGPs and EGPs. [Fedor 1988] describes the early development of `gated`. Figure 10.1 compares the various routing protocols supported by `routed` and two different versions of `gated`. Most systems that run a routing daemon run `routed`, unless they need support for the other protocols supported by `gated`.

Daemon	Interior Gateway Protocol			Exterior Gateway Protocol	
	HELLO	RIP	OSPF	EGP	BGP
`routed`		V1			
`gated`, Version 2	•	V1		•	V1
`gated`, Version 3	•	V1, V2	V2	•	V2, V3

Figure 10.1 Routing protocols supported by `routed` and `gated`.

We describe RIP Version 1 in the next section, the differences with RIP Version 2 in Section 10.5, OSPF in Section 10.6, and BGP in Section 10.7.

10.4 RIP: Routing Information Protocol

This section provides an overview of RIP, because it is the most widely used (and most often maligned) routing protocol. The official specification for RIP is RFC 1058 [Hedrick 1988a], but this RFC was written years after the protocol was widely implemented.

Message Format

RIP messages are carried in UDP datagrams, as shown in Figure 10.2. (We talk more about UDP in Chapter 11.)

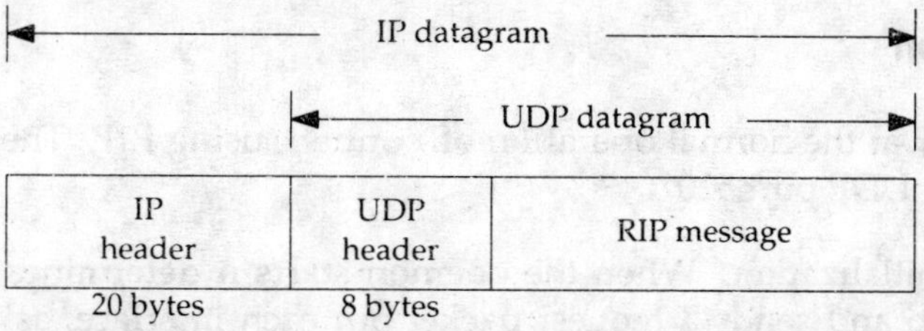

Figure 10.2 RIP message encapsulated within a UDP datagram.

Figure 10.3 shows the format of the RIP message, when used with IP addresses.

A *command* of 1 is a request, and 2 is a reply. There are two other obsolete commands (3 and 4), and two undocumented ones: poll (5) and poll-entry (6). A request asks the other system to send all or part of its routing table. A reply contains all or part of the sender's routing table.

The *version* is normally 1, although RIP Version 2 (Section 10.5) sets this to 2.

The next 20 bytes specify the *address family* (which is always 2 for IP addresses), an *IP address*, and an associated *metric*. We'll see later in this section that RIP metrics are hop counts.

Up to 25 routes can be advertised in a RIP message using this 20-byte format. The limit of 25 is to keep the total size of the RIP message, $20 \times 25 + 4 = 504$, less than 512 bytes. With this limit of 25 routes per message, multiple messages are often required to send an entire routing table.

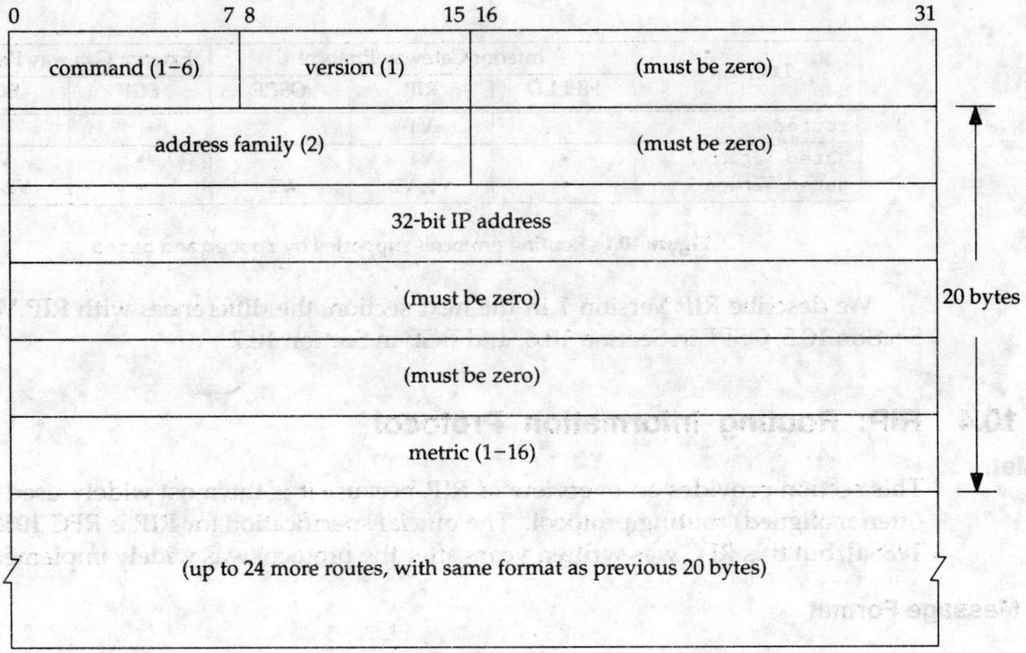

Figure 10.3 Format of a RIP message.

Normal Operation

Let's look at the normal operation of `routed`, using RIP. The well-known port number for RIP is UDP port 520.

- Initialization. When the daemon starts it determines all the interfaces that are up and sends a request packet out each interface, asking for the other router's complete routing table. On a point-to-point link this request is sent to the other end. The request is broadcast if the network supports it. The destination UDP port is 520 (the routing daemon on the other router).

  This request packet has a *command* of 1 but the *address family* is set to 0 and the *metric* is set to 16. This is a special request that asks for a complete routing table from the other end.

- Request received. If the request is the special case we just mentioned, then the entire routing table is sent to the requestor. Otherwise each entry in the request is processed: if we have a route to the specified address, set the metric to our value, else set the metric to 16. (A metric of 16 is a special value called "infinity" and means we don't have a route to that destination.) The response is returned.
- Response received. The response is validated and may update the routing table. New entries can be added, existing entries can be modified, or existing entries can be deleted.

- Regular routing updates. Every 30 seconds, all or part of the router's entire routing table is sent to every neighbor router. The routing table is either broadcast (e.g., on an Ethernet) or sent to the other end of a point-to-point link.
- Triggered updates. These occur whenever the metric for a route changes. The entire routing table need not be sent—only those entries that have changed must be transmitted.

Each route has a timeout associated with it. If a system running RIP finds a route that has not been updated for 3 minutes, that route's metric is set to infinity (16) and marked for deletion. This means we have missed six of the 30-second updates from the router that advertised that route. The deletion of the route from the local routing table is delayed for another 60 seconds to ensure the invalidation is propagated.

Metrics

The metrics used by RIP are hop counts. The hop count for all directly connected interfaces is 1. Consider the routers and networks shown in Figure 10.4. The four dashed lines we show are broadcast RIP messages.

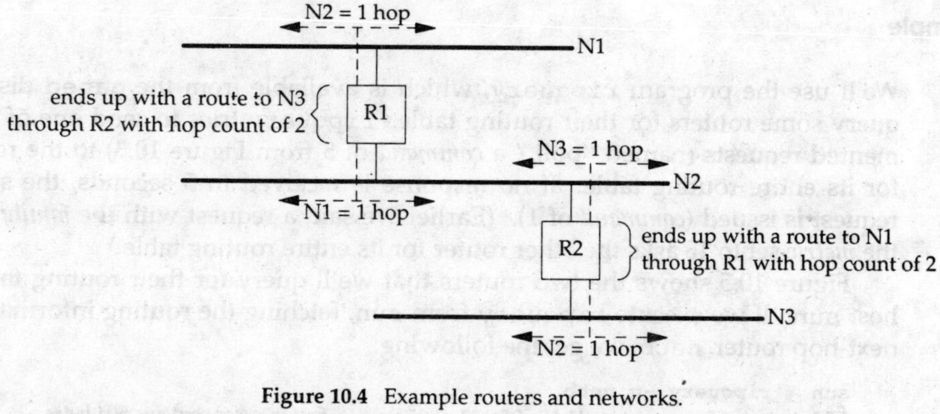

Figure 10.4 Example routers and networks.

Router R1 advertises a route to N2 with a hop count of 1 by sending a broadcast on N1. (It makes no sense to advertise a route to N1 in the broadcast sent on N1.) It also advertises a route to N1 with a hop count of 1 by sending a broadcast on N2. Similarly, R2 advertises a route to N2 with a metric of 1, and a route to N3 with a metric of 1.

If an adjacent router advertises a route to another network with a hop count of 1, then our metric for that network is 2, since we have to send a packet to that router to get to the network. In our example, the metric to N1 for R2 is 2, as is the metric to N3 for R1.

As each router sends its routing tables to its neighbors, a route can be determined to each network within the AS. If there are multiple paths within the AS from a router to a network, the router selects the path with the smallest hop count and ignores the other paths.

The hop count is limited to 15, meaning RIP can be used only within an AS where the maximum number of hops between hosts is 15. The special metric of 16 indicates that no route exists to the IP address.

Problems

As simple as this sounds, there are pitfalls. First, RIP has no knowledge of subnet addressing. If the normal 16-bit host ID of a class B address is nonzero, for example, RIP can't tell if the nonzero portion is a subnet ID or if the IP address is a complete host address. Some implementations use the subnet mask of the interface through which the RIP information arrived, which isn't always correct.

Next, RIP takes a long time to stabilize after the failure of a router or a link. The time is usually measured in minutes. During this settling time routing loops can occur. There are many subtle details in the implementation of RIP that must be followed to help prevent routing loops and to speed convergence. RFC 1058 [Hedrick 1988a] contains many details on how RIP should be implemented.

The use of the hop count as the routing metric omits other variables that should be taken into consideration. Also, a maximum of 15 for the metric limits the sizes of networks on which RIP can be used.

Example

We'll use the program `ripquery`, which is available from the `gated` distribution, to query some routers for their routing table. `ripquery` tries to send one of the undocumented requests (named "poll," a *command* of 5 from Figure 10.3) to the router, asking for its entire routing table. If no response is received in 5 seconds, the standard RIP request is issued (*command* of 1). (Earlier we said a request with the *family* set to 0 and the *metric* set to 16 asks the other router for its entire routing table.)

Figure 10.5 shows the two routers that we'll query for their routing table from the host `sun`. If we execute `ripquery` from `sun`, fetching the routing information from its next-hop router, `netb`, we get the following:

```
sun % ripquery -n netb
504 bytes from netb (140.252.1.183):        first message contains 504 bytes
                                            lots of other lines deleted
        140.252.1.0, metric 1               the top Ethernet in Figure 10.5
        140.252.13.0, metric 1              the bottom Ethernet in Figure 10.5
244 bytes from netb (140.252.1.183):        second message with remaining 244 bytes
                                            lots of other lines deleted
```

As we expect, the metric for our subnet that is announced by `netb` is 1. Additionally, the top Ethernet that `netb` is also attached to (140.252.1.0) has a metric of 1. (The `-n` flag says to print the IP addresses numerically instead of trying to look up the names.) In this example `netb` has been configured to consider all the hosts on the subnet 140.252.13 as directly connected to it—that is, `netb` knows nothing about which hosts are actually on the 140.252.13 subnet. Since there is only one connection point to the 140.252.13 subnet, advertising different metrics for each host makes little practical sense.

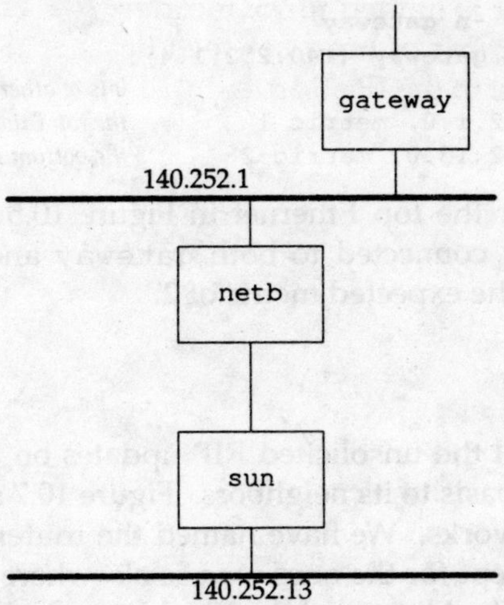

Figure 10.5 Two routers `netb` and `gateway` that we'll query for their routing tables.

Figure 10.6 shows the packet exchange using `tcpdump`. We specify the SLIP interface with the `-i sl0` option.

```
  sun % tcpdump -s600 -i sl0
1 0.0                  sun.2879 > netb.route: rip-poll 24
2 5.014702 (5.0147)    sun.2879 > netb.route: rip-req 24
3 5.560427 (0.5457)    netb.route > sun.2879: rip-resp 25:
4 5.710251 (0.1498)    netb.route > sun.2879: rip-resp 12:
```

Figure 10.6 `tcpdump` output while running `ripquery` program.

The first request issued is the RIP poll command (line 1). This times out after 5 seconds and a normal RIP request is issued (line 2). The number 24 at the end of lines 1 and 2 is the size of the request packets in bytes: the 4-byte RIP header (with the command and version) followed by a single 20-byte address and metric.

Line 3 is the first reply message. The number 25 at the end indicates that 25 address and metric pairs are in the message, which we calculated earlier to be 504 bytes. This is what `ripquery` printed above. We specified the `-s600` option to `tcpdump` telling it to read 600 bytes from the network. This allows it to receive the entire UDP datagram (instead of just the first portion of it) and it then prints the contents of the RIP response. We've omitted that output.

Line 4 is the second response message from the router, with the next 12 address and metric pairs. We can calculate the size of this message to be $12 \times 20 + 4 = 244$, which is what `ripquery` printed earlier.

If we go one router beyond `netb`, to `gateway`, we expect the metric to our subnet (140.252.13.0) to be 2. We can check this by executing:

```
sun % ripquery -n gateway
504 bytes from gateway (140.252.1.4):
                                          lots of other lines deleted
        140.252.1.0, metric 1             the top Ethernet in Figure 10.5
        140.252.13.0, metric 2            the bottom Ethernet in Figure 10.5
```

Here the metric for the top Ethernet in Figure 10.5 (140.252.1.0) stays at 1, since that Ethernet is directly connected to both `gateway` and `netb`. Our subnet 140.252.13.0, however, now has the expected metric of 2.

Another Example

We'll now watch all the unsolicited RIP updates on an Ethernet and see just what RIP sends on a regular basis to its neighbors. Figure 10.7 shows the arrangement of many of the `noao.edu` networks. We have named the routers R*n* for simplicity, where *n* is the subnet number, except for the ones we use elsewhere in the text. We show the point-to-point links with dashed lines and the IP address at each end of these links.

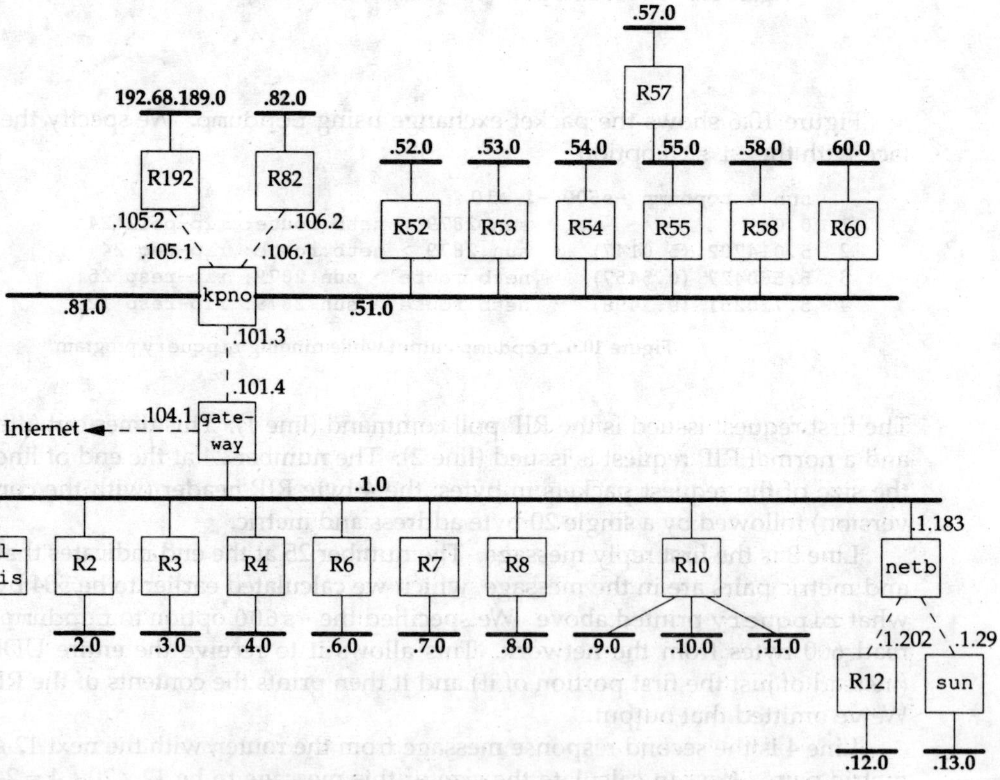

Figure 10.7 Many of the `noao.edu` 140.252 networks.

We'll run the Solaris 2.x program `snoop`, which is similar to `tcpdump`, on the host `solaris`. We can run this program without superuser privileges, but only to capture broadcast packets, multicast packets, or packets sent to the host. Figure 10.8 shows the packets captured during a 60-second period. We have replaced most of the official hostnames with our notation R*n*.

```
solaris % snoop -P -tr udp port 520
  0.00000 R6.tuc.noao.edu -> 140.252.1.255 RIP R (1 destinations)
  4.49708 R4.tuc.noao.edu -> 140.252.1.255 RIP R (1 destinations)
  6.30506 R2.tuc.noao.edu -> 140.252.1.255 RIP R (1 destinations)
 11.68317 R7.tuc.noao.edu -> 140.252.1.255 RIP R (1 destinations)
 16.19790 R8.tuc.noao.edu -> 140.252.1.255 RIP R (1 destinations)
 16.87131 R3.tuc.noao.edu -> 140.252.1.255 RIP R (1 destinations)
 17.02187 gateway.tuc.noao.edu -> 140.252.1.255 RIP R (15 destinations)
 20.68009 R10.tuc.noao.edu -> BROADCAST     RIP R (4 destinations)

 29.87848 R6.tuc.noao.edu -> 140.252.1.255 RIP R (1 destinations)
 34.50209 R4.tuc.noao.edu -> 140.252.1.255 RIP R (1 destinations)
 36.32385 R2.tuc.noao.edu -> 140.252.1.255 RIP R (1 destinations)
 41.34565 R7.tuc.noao.edu -> 140.252.1.255 RIP R (1 destinations)
 46.19257 R8.tuc.noao.edu -> 140.252.1.255 RIP R (1 destinations)
 46.52199 R3.tuc.noao.edu -> 140.252.1.255 RIP R (1 destinations)
 47.01870 gateway.tuc.noao.edu -> 140.252.1.255 RIP R (15 destinations)
 50.66453 R10.tuc.noao.edu -> BROADCAST     RIP R (4 destinations)
```

Figure 10.8 RIP broadcasts captured at `solaris` over a 60-second period.

The `-P` flag captures packets in nonpromiscuous mode, `-tr` prints the relative timestamps, and `udp port 520` captures only UDP datagrams with a source or destination port of 520.

The first six packets, from R6, R4, R2, R7, R8, and R3, each advertise just one network. If we looked at the packets we would see that R6 advertises a route to 140.252.6.0 with a hop count of 1, R4 advertises a route to 140.252.4.0 with a hop count of 1, and so on.

The router `gateway`, however, advertises 15 routes. We can run `snoop` with the `-v` flag and see the entire contents of the RIP message. (This flag outputs the entire contents of the entire packet: the Ethernet header, the IP header, the UDP header, and the RIP message. We've deleted everything except the RIP information.) Figure 10.9 shows the output.

Compare these advertised hop counts on the 140.252.1 network with the topology shown in Figure 10.7.

A puzzle in the output in Figure 10.8 is why R10 is advertising four networks when Figure 10.7 shows only three. If we look at the RIP packet with `snoop` we see the following advertised routes:

```
RIP:  Address          Metric
RIP:  140.251.0.0      16 (not reachable)
RIP:  140.252.9.0      1
RIP:  140.252.10.0     1
RIP:  140.252.11.0     1
```

The route to the class B network 140.251 is bogus and should not be advertised. (It belongs to another institution, not `noao.edu`.)

```
solaris % snoop -P -v -tr udp port 520 host gateway
                                         many lines deleted
RIP:  Opcode = 2 (route response)
RIP:  Version = 1

RIP:  Address          Metric

RIP:  140.252.101.0    1
RIP:  140.252.104.0    1

RIP:  140.252.51.0     2
RIP:  140.252.81.0     2
RIP:  140.252.105.0    2
RIP:  140.252.106.0    2

RIP:  140.252.52.0     3
RIP:  140.252.53.0     3
RIP:  140.252.54.0     3
RIP:  140.252.55.0     3
RIP:  140.252.58.0     3
RIP:  140.252.60.0     3
RIP:  140.252.82.0     3
RIP:  192.68.189.0     3

RIP:  140.252.57.0     4
```

Figure 10.9 RIP response from gateway.

The notation "BROADCAST" output by snoop in Figure 10.8 for the RIP packet sent by R10 means the destination IP address is the limited broadcast address 255.255.255.255 (Section 12.2), instead of the subnet-directed broadcast address (140.252.1.255) that the other routers use.

10.5 RIP Version 2

RFC 1388 [Malkin 1993a] defines newer extensions to RIP, and the result is normally called RIP-2. These extensions don't change the protocol, but pass additional information in the fields labeled "must be zero" in Figure 10.3. RIP and RIP-2 can interoperate if RIP ignores the fields that must be zero.

Figure 10.10 is a redo of that figure, as defined by RIP-2. The *version* is 2 for RIP-2.

The *routing domain* is an identifier of the routing daemon to which this packet belongs. In a Unix implementation this could be the daemon's process ID. This field allows an administrator to run multiple instances of RIP on a single router, each operating within one routing domain.

The *route tag* exists to support exterior gateway protocols. It carries an autonomous system number for EGP and BGP.

The *subnet mask* for each entry applies to the corresponding *IP address*. The *next-hop IP address* is where packets to the corresponding destination IP address should be sent. A value of 0 in this field means packets to the destination should be sent to the system sending the RIP message.

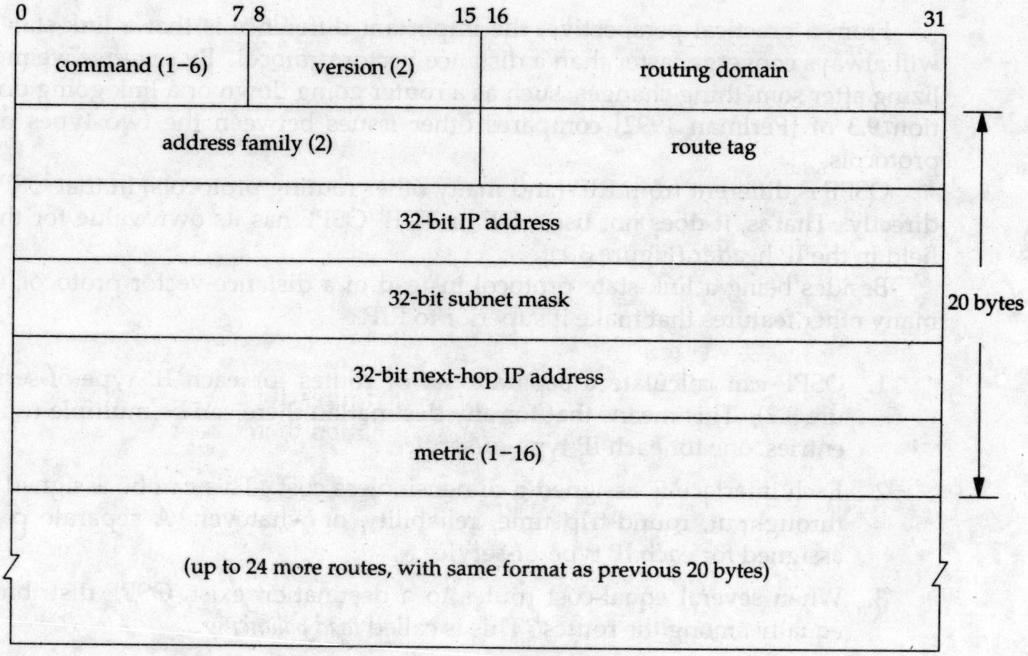

Figure 10.10 Format of a RIP-2 message.

A simple authentication scheme is provided with RIP-2. The first 20-byte entry in a RIP message can specify an *address family* of `0xffff`, with a *route tag* value of 2. The remaining 16 bytes of the entry contain a cleartext password.

Finally, RIP-2 supports multicasting in addition to broadcasting (Chapter 12). This can reduce the load on hosts that are not listening for RIP-2 messages.

10.6 OSPF: Open Shortest Path First

OSPF is a newer alternative to RIP as an interior gateway protocol. It overcomes all the limitations of RIP. OSPF Version 2 is described in RFC 1247 [Moy 1991].

OSPF is a *link-state* protocol, as opposed to RIP, which is a *distance-vector* protocol. The term distance-vector means the messages sent by RIP contain a vector of distances (hop counts). Each router updates its routing table based on the vector of these distances that it receives from its neighbors.

In a link-state protocol a router does not exchange distances with its neighbors. Instead each router actively tests the status of its link to each of its neighbors, sends this information to its other neighbors, which then propagate it throughout the autonomous system. Each router takes this link-state information and builds a complete routing table.

From a practical perspective, the important difference is that a link-state protocol will always converge faster than a distance-vector protocol. By *converge* we mean stabilizing after something changes, such as a router going down or a link going down. Section 9.3 of [Perlman 1992] compares other issues between the two types of routing protocols.

OSPF is different from RIP (and many other routing protocols) in that OSPF uses IP directly. That is, it does not use UDP or TCP. OSPF has its own value for the *protocol* field in the IP header (Figure 3.1).

Besides being a link-state protocol instead of a distance-vector protocol, OSPF has many other features that make it superior to RIP.

1. OSPF can calculate a separate set of routes for each IP type-of-service (Figure 3.2). This means that for any destination there can be multiple routing table entries, one for each IP type-of-service.
2. Each interface is assigned a dimensionless cost. This can be assigned based on throughput, round-trip time, reliability, or whatever. A separate cost can be assigned for each IP type-of-service.
3. When several equal-cost routes to a destination exist, OSPF distributes traffic equally among the routes. This is called *load balancing*.
4. OSPF supports subnets: a subnet mask is associated with each advertised route. This allows a single IP address of any class to be broken into multiple subnets of various sizes. (We showed an example of this in Section 3.7 and called it *variable-length subnets*.) Routes to a host are advertised with a subnet mask of all one bits. A default route is advertised as an IP address of 0.0.0.0 with a mask of all zero bits.
5. Point-to-point links between routers do not need an IP address at each end. These are called *unnumbered* networks. This can save IP addresses—a scarce resource these days!
6. A simple authentication scheme can be used. A cleartext password can be specified, similar to the RIP-2 scheme (Section 10.5).
7. OSPF uses multicasting (Chapter 12), instead of broadcasting, to reduce the load on systems not participating in OSPF.

With most router vendors supporting OSPF, it will start replacing RIP in many networks.

10.7 BGP: Border Gateway Protocol

BGP is an exterior gateway protocol for communication between routers in different autonomous systems. BGP is a replacement for the older EGP that was used on the ARPANET. BGP Version 3 is defined in RFC 1267 [Lougheed and Rekhter 1991].

RFC 1268 [Rekhter and Gross 1991] describes the use of BGP in the Internet. Much of the following description comes from these two RFCs. Also, during 1993 BGP Version 4 was under development (see RFC 1467 [Topolcic 1993]) to support CIDR, which we describe in Section 10.8.

A BGP system exchanges network reachability information with other BGP systems. This information includes the full path of autonomous systems that traffic must transit to reach these networks. This information is adequate to construct a graph of AS connectivity. Routing loops can then be pruned from this graph and routing policy decisions can be enforced.

We first categorize an IP datagram in an AS as either *local traffic* or *transit traffic*. Local traffic in an AS either originates or terminates in that AS. That is, either the source IP address or the destination IP address identifies a host in that AS. Anything else is called transit traffic. A major goal of BGP usage in the Internet is to reduce transit traffic.

An AS can be categorized as one of the following:

1. A *stub AS* has only a single connection to one other AS. A stub AS carries only local traffic.
2. A *multihomed AS* has connections to more than one other AS, but refuses to carry transit traffic.
3. A *transit AS* has connections to more than one other AS and is designed, under certain policy restrictions, to carry both local and transit traffic.

The overall topology of the Internet is then viewed as an arbitrary interconnection of transit, multihomed, and stub ASs. Stub and multihomed ASs need not use BGP—they can run EGP to exchange reachability information with transit ASs.

BGP allows for *policy-based routing*. Policies are determined by the AS administrator and specified to BGP in configuration files. Policy decisions are not part of the protocol, but policy specifications allow a BGP implementation to choose between paths when multiple alternatives exist and to control the redistribution of information. Routing policies are related to political, security, or economic considerations.

BGP is different from RIP and OSPF in that BGP uses TCP as its transport protocol. Two systems running BGP establish a TCP connection between themselves and then exchange the entire BGP routing table. From that point on, incremental updates are sent as the routing table changes.

BGP is a distance vector protocol, but unlike RIP (which announces hops to a destination), BGP enumerates the route to each destination (the sequence of AS numbers to the destination). This removes some of the problems associated with distance-vector protocols. An AS is identified by a 16-bit number.

BGP detects the failure of either the link or the host on the other end of the TCP connection by sending a *keepalive* message to its neighbor on a regular basis. The recommended time between these messages is 30 seconds. This application-level keepalive message is independent of the TCP keepalive option (Chapter 23).

10.8 CIDR: Classless Interdomain Routing

In Chapter 3 we said there is a shortage of class B addresses, requiring sites with multiple networks to now obtain multiple class C network IDs, instead of a single class B network ID. Although the allocation of these class C addresses solves one problem (running out of class B addresses) it introduces another problem: every class C network requires a routing table entry. *Classless Interdomain Routing* (CIDR) is a way to prevent this explosion in the size of the Internet routing tables. It is also called *supernetting* and is described in RFC 1518 [Rekhter and Li 1993] and RFC 1519 [Fuller et al. 1993], with a overview in [Ford, Rekhter, and Braun 1993]. CIDR has the Internet Architecture Board's blessing [Huitema 1993]. RFC 1467 [Topolcic 1993] summarizes the state of deployment of CIDR in the Internet.

The basic concept in CIDR is to allocate multiple IP addresses in a way that allows *summarization* into a smaller number of routing table entries. For example, if a single site is allocated 16 class C addresses, and those 16 are allocated so that they can be summarized, then all 16 can be referenced through a single routing table entry on the Internet. Also, if eight different sites are connected to the same Internet service provider through the same connection point into the Internet, and if the eight sites are allocated eight different IP addresses that can be summarized, then only a single routing table entry need be used on the Internet for all eight sites.

Three features are needed to allow this summarization to take place.

1. Multiple IP addresses to be summarized together for routing must share the same high-order bits of their addresses.
2. The routing tables and routing algorithms must be extended to base their routing decisions on a 32-bit IP address and a 32-bit mask.
3. The routing protocols being used must be extended to carry the 32-bit mask in addition to the 32-bit address. OSPF (Section 10.6) and RIP-2 (Section 10.5) are both capable of carrying the 32-bit mask, as is the proposed BGP Version 4.

As an example, RFC 1466 [Gerich 1993] recommends that new class C addresses in Europe be in the range 194.0.0.0 through 195.255.255.255. In hexadecimal these addresses are from `0xc2000000` through `0xc3ffffff`. This represents 131,072 different class C network IDs, but they all share the same high-order 7 bits. In countries other than Europe a single routing table entry with an IP address of `0xc2000000` and a 32-bit mask of `0xfe000000` (254.0.0.0) could be used to route all of these 65536 class C network IDs to a single point. Subsequent bits of the class C address (that is, the bits following 194 or 195) can also be allocated hierarchically, perhaps by country or by service provider, to allow additional summarization within the European routers using additional bits beyond the 7 high-order bits of the 32-bit mask.

CIDR also uses a technique whereby the best match is always the one with the *longest match*: the one with the greatest number of one bits in the 32-bit mask. Continuing the example from the previous paragraph, perhaps one service provider in Europe needs to use a different entry point router than the rest of Europe. If that provider has been allocated the block of addresses 194.0.16.0 through 194.0.31.255 (16 class C network

IDs), routing table entries for just those networks would have an IP address of 194.0.16.0 and a mask of 255.255.240.0 (`0xfffff000`). A datagram being routed to the address 194.0.22.1 would match both this routing table entry and the one for the rest of the European class C networks. But since the mask 255.255.240 is "longer" than the mask 254.0.0.0, the routing table entry with the longer mask is used.

The term "classless" is because routing decisions are now made based on masking operations of the entire 32-bit IP address. Whether the IP address is class A, B, or C makes no difference.

The initial deployment of CIDR is proposed for new class C addresses. Making just this change will slow down the growth of the Internet routing tables, but does nothing for all the existing routes. This is the short-term solution. As a long-term solution, if CIDR were applied to all IP addresses, and if existing IP addresses were reallocated (and all existing hosts renumbered!) according to continental boundaries and service providers, [Ford, Rekhter, and Braun 1993] claim that the current routing table consisting of 10,000 network entries could be reduced to 200 entries.

10.9 Summary

There are two basic types of routing protocols: interior gateway protocols (IGPs), for routers within an autonomous system, and exterior gateway protocols (EGPs), for routers to communicate with routers in other autonomous systems.

The most popular IGP is the Routing Information Protocol (RIP) with OSPF being a newer IGP that is gaining widespread use. A new and popular EGP is the Border Gateway Protocol (BGP). In this chapter we looked at RIP and the types of messages that it exchanges. RIP Version 2 is a recent enhancement that supports subnetting and other minor improvements. We also described OSPF, BGP, and classless interdomain routing (CIDR), a newer technique being deployed to reduce the size of the Internet routing tables.

There are a two other OSI routing protocols that you may encounter. *Interdomain Routing Protocol* (IDRP) started out as a version of BGP modified for use with OSI addresses instead of IP. *Intermediate System to Intermediate System Protocol* (IS–IS) is the OSI standard IGP. It is used for routing CLNP (Connectionless Network Protocol), an OSI protocol similar to IP. IS–IS and OSPF are similar.

Dynamic routing is still a fertile area of internetworking research. The choice of which routing protocol to use, and which routing daemon to run, is complex. [Perlman 1992] provides many of the details.

Exercises

10.1 In Figure 10.9 which of the routes came to `gateway` from the router `kpno`?

10.2 Assume a router has 30 routes to advertise using RIP, requiring one datagram with 25 routes and another with the remaining 5. What happens if once an hour the first datagram with 25 routes is lost?

10.3 The OSPF packet format has a checksum field, but the RIP packet does not. Why?

10.4 What effect does load balancing, as done by OSPF, have on a transport layer?

10.5 Read RFC 1058 for additional details on the implementation of RIP. In Figure 10.8 each router advertises only the routes that it provides, and none of the other routes that it learned about through the other router's broadcasts on the 140.252.1 network. What is this technique called?

10.6 In Section 3.4 we said there are more than 100 hosts on the 140.252.1 subnet in addition to the eight routers we show in Figure 10.7. What do these 100 hosts do with the eight broadcasts that arrive every 30 seconds (Figure 10.8)?

11

UDP: User Datagram Protocol

11.1 Introduction

UDP is a simple, datagram-oriented, transport layer protocol: each output operation by a process produces exactly one UDP datagram, which causes one IP datagram to be sent. This is different from a stream-oriented protocol such as TCP where the amount of data written by an application may have little relationship to what actually gets sent in a single IP datagram.

Figure 11.1 shows the encapsulation of a UDP datagram as an IP datagram.

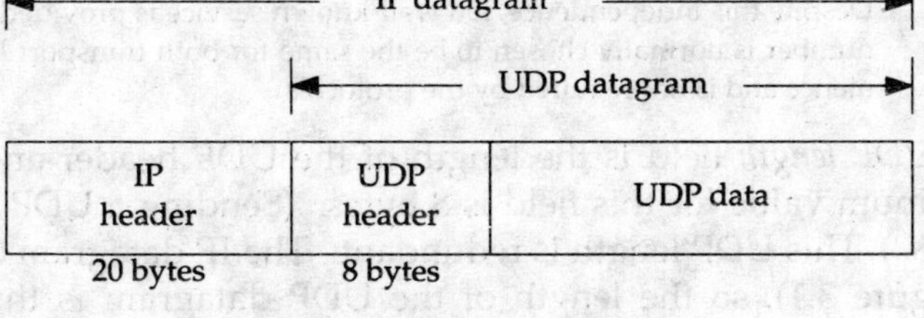

Figure 11.1 UDP encapsulation.

RFC 768 [Postel 1980] is the official specification of UDP.

UDP provides no reliability: it sends the datagrams that the application writes to the IP layer, but there is no guarantee that they ever reach their destination. Given this lack of reliability, we are tempted to think we should avoid UDP and always use a reliable protocol such as TCP. After we describe TCP in Chapter 17 we'll return to this topic and see what types of applications can utilize UDP.

The application needs to worry about the size of the resulting IP datagram. If it exceeds the network's MTU (Section 2.8), the IP datagram is fragmented. This applies to each network that the datagram traverses from the source to the destination, not just the first network connected to the sending host. (We defined this as the *path MTU* in Section 2.9.) We examine IP fragmentation in Section 11.5.

11.2 UDP Header

Figure 11.2 shows the fields in the UDP header.

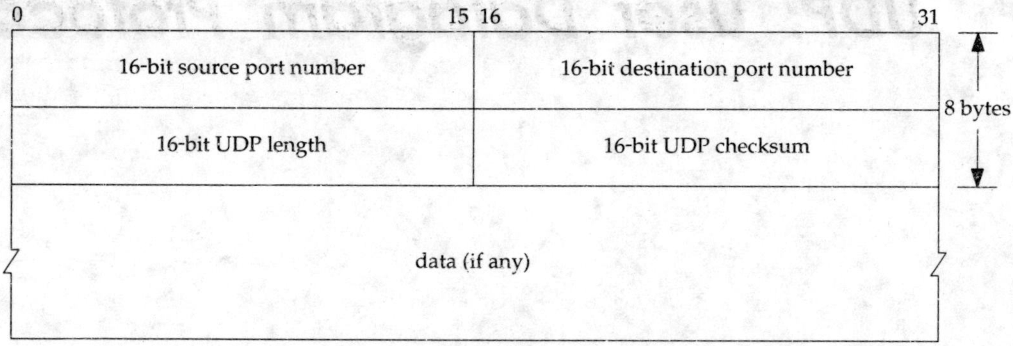

Figure 11.2 UDP header.

The *port numbers* identify the sending process and the receiving process. In Figure 1.8 we showed that TCP and UDP use the destination port number to demultiplex incoming data from IP. Since IP has already demultiplexed the incoming IP datagram to either TCP or UDP (based on the protocol value in the IP header), this means the TCP port numbers are looked at by TCP, and the UDP port numbers by UDP. The TCP port numbers are independent of the UDP port numbers.

Despite this independence, if a well-known service is provided by both TCP and UDP, the port number is normally chosen to be the same for both transport layers. This is purely for convenience and is not required by the protocols.

The *UDP length* field is the length of the UDP header and the UDP data in bytes. The minimum value for this field is 8 bytes. (Sending a UDP datagram with 0 bytes of data is OK.) This UDP length is redundant. The IP datagram contains its total length in bytes (Figure 3.1), so the length of the UDP datagram is this total length minus the length of the IP header (which is specified by the header length field in Figure 3.1).

11.3 UDP Checksum

The *UDP checksum* covers the UDP header and the UDP data. Recall that the checksum in the IP header only covers the IP header—it does not cover any data in the IP datagram. Both UDP and TCP have checksums in their headers to cover their header and their data. With UDP the checksum is optional, while with TCP it is mandatory.

Although the basics for calculating the UDP checksum are similar to what we described in Section 3.2 for the IP header checksum (the ones complement sum of 16-bit words), there are differences. First, the length of the UDP datagram can be an odd number of bytes, while the checksum algorithm adds 16-bit words. The solution is to append a pad byte of 0 to the end, if necessary, just for the checksum computation. (That is, this possible pad byte is not transmitted.)

Next, both UDP and TCP include a 12-byte pseudo-header with the UDP datagram (or TCP segment) just for the checksum computation. This pseudo-header includes certain fields from the IP header. The purpose is to let UDP double-check that the data has arrived at the correct destination (i.e., that IP has not accepted a datagram that is not addressed to this host, and that IP has not given UDP a datagram that is for another upper layer). Figure 11.3 shows the pseudo-header along with a UDP datagram.

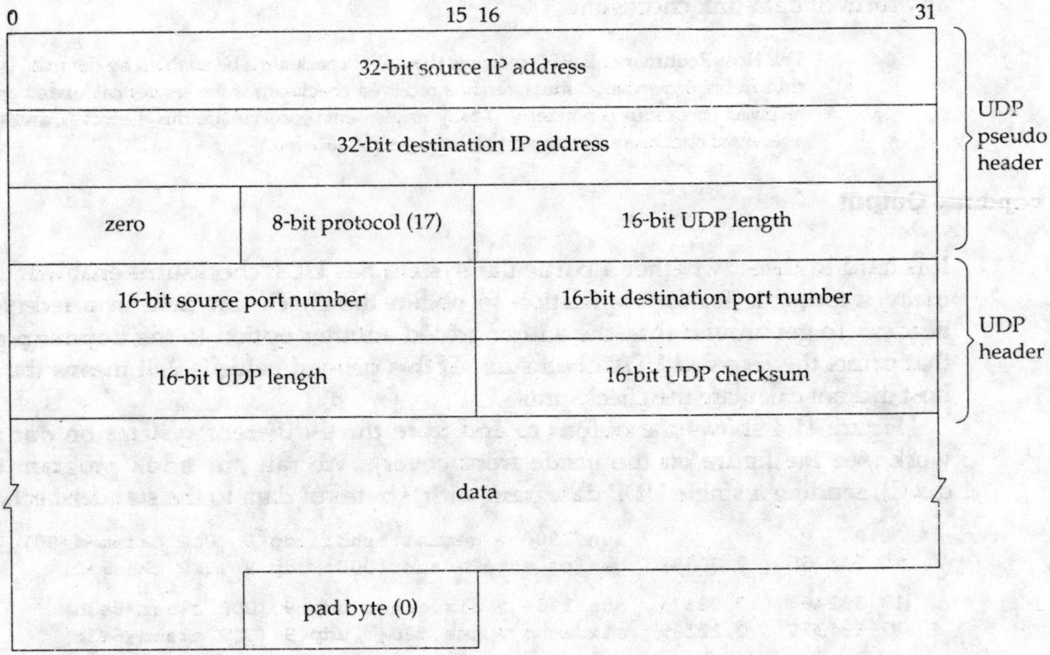

Figure 11.3 Fields used for computation of UDP checksum.

In this figure we explicitly show a datagram with an odd length, requiring a pad byte for the checksum computation. Notice that the length of the UDP datagram appears twice in the checksum computation.

If the calculated checksum is 0, it is stored as all one bits (65535), which is equivalent in ones-complement arithmetic. If the transmitted checksum is 0, it indicates that the sender did not compute the checksum.

If the sender did compute a checksum and the receiver detects a checksum error, the UDP datagram is silently discarded. No error message is generated. (This is what happens if an IP header checksum error is detected by IP.)

This UDP checksum is an end-to-end checksum. It is calculated by the sender, and then verified by the receiver. It is designed to catch any modification of the UDP header or data anywhere between the sender and receiver.

Despite UDP checksums being optional, they should *always* be enabled. During the 1980s some computer vendors turned off UDP checksums by default, to speed up their implementation of Sun's Network File System (NFS), which uses UDP. While this *might* be acceptable on a single LAN, where the cyclic redundancy check on the data-link frame (e.g., Ethernet or token ring frame) can detect most corruption of the frame, when the datagrams pass through routers, all bets are off. Believe it or not, there have been routers with software and hardware bugs that have modified bits in the datagrams being routed. These errors are undetectable in a UDP datagram if the end-to-end UDP checksum is disabled. Also realize that some data-link protocols (e.g., SLIP) don't have any form of data-link checksum.

> The Host Requirements RFC requires that UDP checksums be enabled by default. It also states that an implementation must verify a received checksum if the sender calculated one (i.e., the received checksum is nonzero). Many implementations violate this, however, and only verify a received checksum if outgoing checksums are enabled.

`tcpdump` Output

It is hard to detect whether a particular system has UDP checksums enabled. It is normally impossible for an application to obtain the checksum field in a received UDP header. To get around this, the author added another option to the `tcpdump` program that prints the received UDP checksum. If this printed value is 0, it means the sending host did not calculate the checksum.

Figure 11.4 shows the output to and from three different systems on our test network (see the figure on the inside front cover). We ran our `sock` program (Appendix C), sending a single UDP datagram with 9 bytes of data to the standard echo server.

```
1   0.0                        sun.1900 > gemini.echo: udp 9 (UDP cksum=6e90)
2   0.303755 ( 0.3038)         gemini.echo > sun.1900: udp 9 (UDP cksum=0)

3  17.392480 (17.0887)         sun.1904 > aix.echo: udp 9 (UDP cksum=6e3b)
4  17.614371 ( 0.2219)         aix.echo > sun.1904: udp 9 (UDP cksum=6e3b)

5  32.092454 (14.4781)         sun.1907 > solaris.echo: udp 9 (UDP cksum=6e74)
6  32.314378 ( 0.2219)         solaris.echo > sun.1907: udp 9 (UDP cksum=6e74)
```

Figure 11.4 `tcpdump` output to see whether other hosts enable UDP checksum.

We can see from this that two of the three systems have UDP checksums enabled.

Also notice that for this simple example the outgoing datagram has the same checksum as the incoming datagram (lines 3 and 4, 5 and 6). Looking at Figure 11.3 we see that the two IP addresses are swapped, as are the two port numbers. The other fields in the pseudo-header and the UDP header are the same, as is the data being echoed. This reiterates that the UDP checksums (indeed, all the checksums in the TCP/IP protocol suite) are simple 16-bit sums. They cannot detect an error that swaps two of the 16-bit values.

The author also directed a DNS query at each of the eight root name servers described in Section 14.2. The DNS uses UDP primarily, and only two of the eight had UDP checksums enabled!

Some Statistics

[Mogul 1992] provides counts of various checksum errors on a busy NFS (Network File System) server that had been up for 40 days. Figure 11.5 summarizes these numbers.

Layer	Number of checksum errors	Approximate total number of packets
Ethernet	446	170,000,000
IP	14	170,000,000
UDP	5	140,000,000
TCP	350	30,000,000

Figure 11.5 Counts of corrupted packets detected by various checksums.

The final column is only the approximate total for each row, since other protocols are in use at the Ethernet and IP layers. For example, not all the Ethernet frames are IP datagrams, since minimally ARP is also used on an Ethernet. Not all IP datagrams are UDP or TCP, since ICMP also uses IP.

Note the much higher percentage of TCP checksum errors compared to UDP checksum errors. This is probably because the TCP connections on this system tended to be "long distance" (traversing many routers, bridges, etc.) while the UDP traffic was local.

The bottom line is not to trust the data-link (e.g., Ethernet, token ring, etc.) CRC completely. You should enable the end-to-end checksums all the time. Also, if your data is valuable, you might not want to trust either the UDP or the TCP checksum completely, since these are simple checksums and were not meant to catch all possible errors.

11.4 A Simple Example

We'll use our sock program to generate some UDP datagrams that we can watch with tcpdump:

```
bsdi % sock -v -u -i -n4 svr4 discard
connected on 140.252.13.35.1108 to 140.252.13.34.9
bsdi % sock -v -u -i -n4 -w0 svr4 discard
connected on 140.252.13.35.1110 to 140.252.13.34.9
```

The first time we execute the program we specify the verbose mode (-v) to see the ephemeral port numbers, specify UDP (-u) instead of the default TCP, and use the source mode (`-i`) to send data instead of trying to read and write standard input and output. The `-n4` option says to output 4 datagrams (instead of the default 1024) and the destination host is `svr4`. We described the discard service in Section 1.12. We use the default output size of 1024 bytes per write.

The second time we run the program we specify `-w0`, causing 0-length datagrams to be written. Figure 11.6 shows the `tcpdump` output for both commands.

```
1   0.0                       bsdi.1108 > svr4.discard: udp 1024
2   0.002424 ( 0.0024)        bsdi.1108 > svr4.discard: udp 1024
3   0.006210 ( 0.0038)        bsdi.1108 > svr4.discard: udp 1024
4   0.010276 ( 0.0041)        bsdi.1108 > svr4.discard: udp 1024

5   41.720114 (41.7098)       bsdi.1110 > svr4.discard: udp 0
6   41.721072 ( 0.0010)       bsdi.1110 > svr4.discard: udp 0
7   41.722094 ( 0.0010)       bsdi.1110 > svr4.discard: udp 0
8   41.723070 ( 0.0010)       bsdi.1110 > svr4.discard: udp 0
```

Figure 11.6 `tcpdump` output when UDP datagrams are sent in one direction.

This output shows the four 1024-byte datagrams, followed by the four 0-length datagrams. Each datagram followed the previous by a few milliseconds. (It took 41 seconds to type in the second command.)

There is no communication between the sender and receiver before the first datagram is sent. (We'll see in Chapter 17 that TCP must establish a connection with the other end before the first byte of data can be sent.) Also, there are no acknowledgments by the receiver when the data is received. The sender, in this example, has no idea whether the other end receives the datagrams.

Finally note that the source UDP port number changes each time the program is run. First it is 1108 and then it is 1110. We mentioned in Section 1.9 that the ephemeral port numbers used by clients are typically in the range 1024 through 5000, as we see here.

11.5 IP Fragmentation

As we described in Section 2.8, the physical network layer normally imposes an upper limit on the size of the frame that can be transmitted. Whenever the IP layer receives an IP datagram to send, it determines which local interface the datagram is being sent on (routing), and queries that interface to obtain its MTU. IP compares the MTU with the datagram size and performs fragmentation, if necessary. Fragmentation can take place either at the original sending host or at an intermediate router.

When an IP datagram is fragmented, it is not reassembled until it reaches its final destination. (This handling of reassembly differs from some other networking protocols that require reassembly to take place at the next hop, not at the final destination.) The IP layer at the destination performs the reassembly. The goal is to make fragmentation and reassembly transparent to the transport layer (TCP and UDP), which it is, except for possible performance degradation. It is also possible for the fragment of a datagram to again be fragmented (possibly more than once). The information maintained in the IP header for fragmentation and reassembly provides enough information to do this.

Recalling the IP header (Figure 3.1, p. 34), the following fields are used in fragmentation. The *identification* field contains a unique value for each IP datagram that the sender transmits. This number is copied into each fragment of a particular datagram. (We now see the use for this field.) The *flags* field uses one bit as the "more fragments" bit. This bit is turned on for each fragment comprising a datagram except the final fragment. The *fragment offset* field contains the offset (in 8-byte units) of this fragment from the beginning of the original datagram. Also, when a datagram is fragmented the *total length* field of each fragment is changed to be the size of that fragment.

Finally, one of the bits in the flags field is called the "don't fragment" bit. If this is turned on, IP will not fragment the datagram. Instead the datagram is thrown away and an ICMP error ("fragmentation needed but don't fragment bit set," Figure 6.3) is sent to the originator. We'll see an example of this error in the next section.

When an IP datagram is fragmented, each fragment becomes its own packet, with its own IP header, and is routed independently of any other packets. This makes it possible for the fragments of a datagram to arrive at the final destination out of order, but there is enough information in the IP header to allow the receiver to reassemble the fragments correctly.

Although IP fragmentation looks transparent, there is one feature that makes it less than desirable: if one fragment is lost the entire datagram must be retransmitted. To understand why this happens, realize that IP itself has no timeout and retransmission—that is the responsibility of the higher layers. (TCP performs timeout and retransmission, UDP doesn't. Some UDP applications perform timeout and retransmission themselves.) When a fragment is lost that came from a TCP segment, TCP will time out and retransmit the entire TCP segment, which corresponds to an IP datagram. There is no way to resend only one fragment of a datagram. Indeed, if the fragmentation was done by an intermediate router, and not the originating system, there is no way for the originating system to know how the datagram was fragmented. For this reason alone, fragmentation is often avoided. [Kent and Mogul 1987] provide arguments for avoiding fragmentation.

Using UDP it is easy to generate IP fragmentation. (We'll see later that TCP tries to avoid fragmentation and that it is nearly impossible for an application to force TCP to send segments large enough to require fragmentation.) We can use our `sock` program and increase the size of the datagram until fragmentation occurs. On an Ethernet the maximum amount of data in a frame is 1500 bytes (Figure 2.1), which leaves 1472 bytes for our data, assuming 20 bytes for the IP header and 8 bytes for the UDP header. We'll run our `sock` program, with data sizes of 1471, 1472, 1473, and 1474 bytes. We expect the last two to cause fragmentation:

```
bsdi % sock -u -i -n1 -w1471 svr4 discard
bsdi % sock -u -i -n1 -w1472 svr4 discard
bsdi % sock -u -i -n1 -w1473 svr4 discard
bsdi % sock -u -i -n1 -w1474 svr4 discard
```

Figure 11.7 shows the corresponding `tcpdump` output.

```
1  0.0                    bsdi.1112 > svr4.discard: udp 1471
2  21.008303 (21.0083)    bsdi.1114 > svr4.discard: udp 1472
3  50.449704 (29.4414)    bsdi.1116 > svr4.discard: udp 1473 (frag 26304:1480@0+)
4  50.450040 ( 0.0003)    bsdi > svr4: (frag 26304:1@1480)
5  75.328650 (24.8786)    bsdi.1118 > svr4.discard: udp 1474 (frag 26313:1480@0+)
6  75.328982 ( 0.0003)    bsdi > svr4: (frag 26313:2@1480)
```

Figure 11.7 Watching fragmentation of UDP datagrams.

The first two UDP datagrams (lines 1 and 2) fit into Ethernet frames, and are not fragmented. But the length of the IP datagram corresponding to the write of 1473 bytes is 1501, which must be fragmented (lines 3 and 4). Similarly the datagram generated by the write of 1474 bytes is 1502, and is also fragmented (lines 5 and 6).

When the IP datagram is fragmented, `tcpdump` prints additional information. First, the output `frag 26304` (lines 3 and 4) and `frag 26313` (lines 5 and 6) specify the value of the identification field in the IP header.

The next number in the fragmentation information, the 1480 between the colon and the at sign in line 3, is the size, excluding the IP header. The first fragment of both datagrams contains 1480 bytes of data: 8 bytes for the UDP header and 1472 bytes of user data. (The 20-byte IP header makes the packet exactly 1500 bytes.) The second fragment of the first datagram (line 4) contains 1 byte of data—the remaining byte of user data. The second fragment of the second datagram (line 6) contains the remaining 2 bytes of user data.

Fragmentation requires that the data portion of the generated fragments (that is, everything excluding the IP header) be a multiple of 8 bytes for all fragments other than the final one. In this example, 1480 is a multiple of 8.

The number following the at sign is the offset of the data in the fragment, from the start of the datagram. The first fragment of both datagrams starts at 0 (lines 3 and 5) and the second fragment of both datagrams starts at byte offset 1480 (lines 4 and 6). The plus sign following this offset that is printed for the first fragment of both datagrams means there are more fragments comprising this datagram. This plus sign corresponds to the "more fragments" bit in the 3-bit flags in the IP header. The purpose of this bit is to let the receiver know when it has completed the reassembly of all the fragments for a datagram.

Finally, notice that lines 4 and 6 (fragments other than the first) omit the protocol (UDP) and the source and destination ports. The protocol could be printed, since it's in the IP header that's copied into the fragments. The port numbers, however, are in the UDP header, which only occurs in the first fragment.

Figure 11.8 shows what's happening with the third datagram that is sent (with 1473 bytes of user data). It reiterates that any transport layer header appears only in the first fragment.

Also note the terminology: an *IP datagram* is the unit of end-to-end transmission at the IP layer (before fragmentation and after reassembly), and a *packet* is the unit of data passed between the IP layer and the link layer. A packet can be a complete IP datagram or a fragment of an IP datagram.

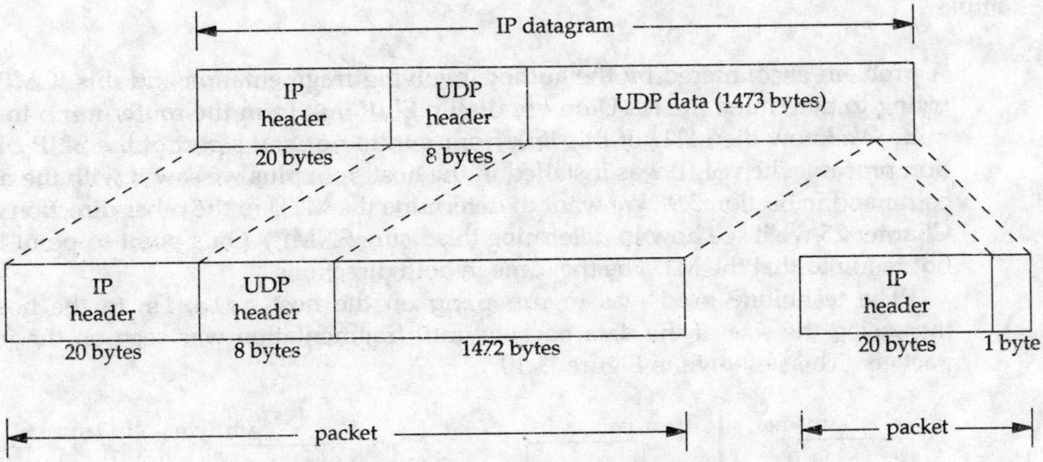

Figure 11.8 Example of UDP fragmentation.

11.6 ICMP Unreachable Error (Fragmentation Required)

Another variation of the ICMP unreachable error occurs when a router receives a datagram that requires fragmentation, but the don't fragment (DF) flag is turned on in the IP header. This error can be used by a program that needs to determine the smallest MTU in the path to a destination—called the *path MTU discovery* mechanism (Section 2.9).

Figure 11.9 shows the format of the ICMP unreachable error for this case. This differs from Figure 6.10 because bits 16–31 of the second 32-bit word can provide the MTU of the next hop, instead of being 0.

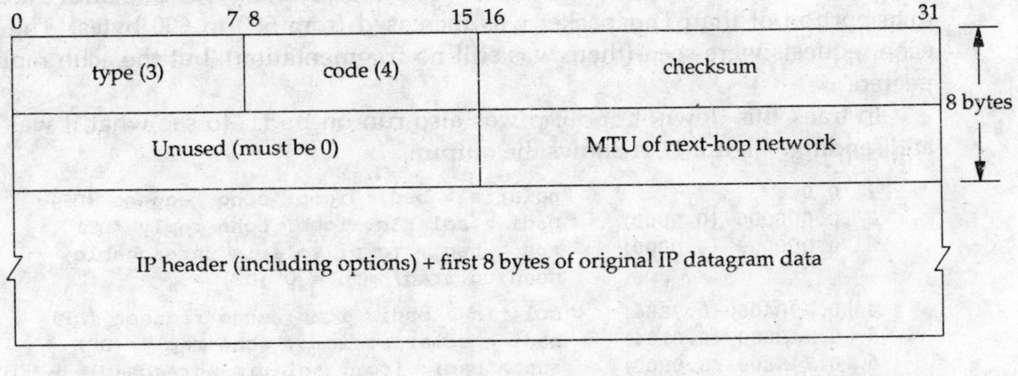

Figure 11.9 ICMP unreachable error when fragmentation required but don't fragment bit set.

If a router doesn't provide this newer format ICMP error, the next-hop MTU is set to 0.

The new Router Requirements RFC [Almquist 1993] states that a router must generate this newer form when originating this ICMP unreachable error.

Example

A problem encountered by the author involving fragmentation and this ICMP error is trying to determine the MTU on the dialup SLIP link from the router netb to the host sun. We know the MTU of this link from sun to netb: it s part of the SLIP configuration process when SLIP was installed in the host sun, plus we saw it with the netstat command in Section 3.9. We want to determine the MTU in the other direction also. (In Chapter 25 we'll see how to determine this using SNMP.) On a point-to-point link, it is not required that the MTU be the same in both directions.

The technique used was to run ping on the host solaris, to the host bsdi, increasing the size of the data packets until fragmentation was seen on the incoming packets. This is shown in Figure 11.10.

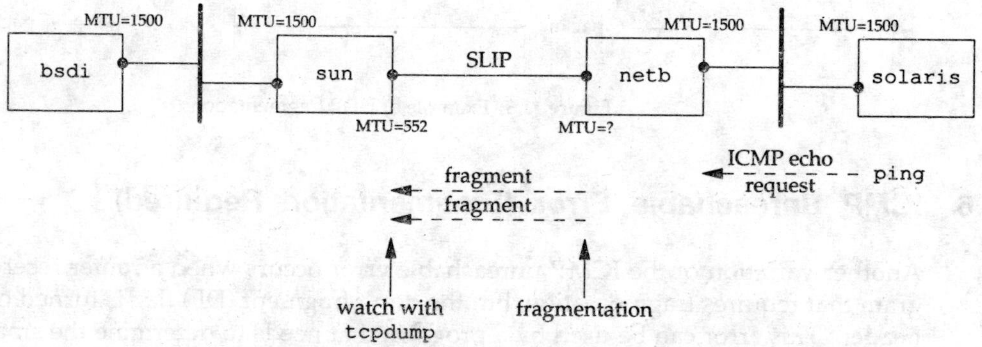

Figure 11.10 Systems being used to determine MTU of SLIP link from netb to sun.

tcpdump was run on the host sun, watching the SLIP link, to see when fragmentation occurred. No fragmentation was observed and everything was fine until the size of the data portion of the ping packet was increased from 500 to 600 bytes. The incoming echo requests were seen (there was still no fragmentation), but the echo replies disappeared.

To track this down, tcpdump was also run on bsdi, to see what it was receiving and sending. Figure 11.11 shows the output.

```
1  0.0                  solaris > bsdi: icmp: echo request (DF)
2  0.000000 (0.0000)    bsdi > solaris: icmp: echo reply (DF)
3  0.000000 (0.0000)    sun > bsdi: icmp: solaris unreachable -
                        need to frag, mtu = 0 (DF)

4  0.738400 (0.7384)    solaris > bsdi: icmp: echo request (DF)
5  0.748800 (0.0104)    bsdi > solaris: icmp: echo reply (DF)
6  0.748800 (0.0000)    sun > bsdi: icmp: solaris unreachable -
                        need to frag, mtu = 0 (DF)
```

Figure 11.11 tcpdump output for ping of bsdi from solaris with 600-byte IP datagram.

First, the notation (DF) in each line means the don't fragment bit is turned on in the IP header. It turns out that Solaris 2.2 normally turns this bit on, as part of its implementation of the path MTU discovery mechanism.

Line 1 shows that the echo request got through the router `netb` to `sun` without being fragmented, and with the DF bit set, so we know that the SLIP MTU of `netb` has not been reached yet.

Next, notice in line 2 that the DF flag is copied into the echo reply. This is what causes the problem. The echo reply is the same size as the echo request (just over 600 bytes), but the MTU on `sun`'s outgoing SLIP interface is 552. The echo reply needs to be fragmented, but the DF flag is set. This causes `sun` to generate the ICMP unreachable error back to `bsdi` (where it's discarded).

This is why we never saw any echo replies on `solaris`. The replies never got past `sun`. Figure 11.12 shows the path of the packets.

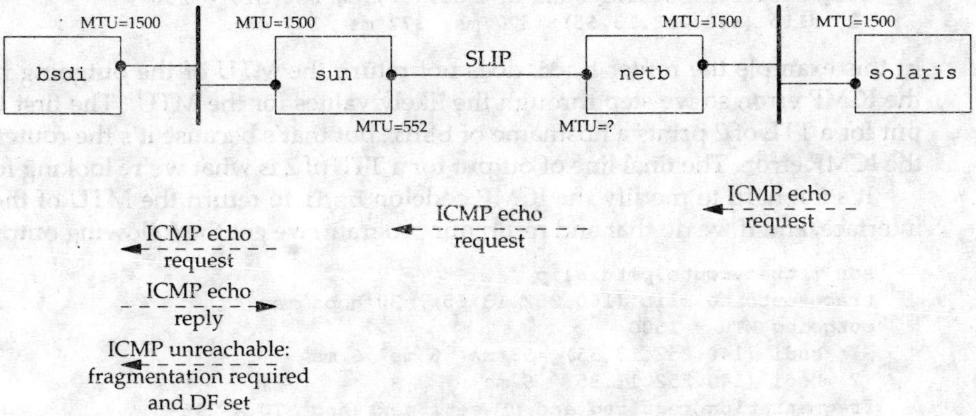

Figure 11.12 Packets exchanged in example.

Finally, the notation `mtu=0` in lines 3 and 6 of Figure 11.11 indicates that `sun` does not return the MTU of the outgoing interface in the ICMP unreachable message, as shown in Figure 11.9. (In Section 25.9 we return to this problem and use SNMP to determine that the MTU of the SLIP interface on `netb` is 1500.)

11.7 Determining the Path MTU Using Traceroute

Although most systems don't support the path MTU discovery feature, we can easily modify a version of `traceroute` (Chapter 8) to let us determine the path MTU. What we'll do is send packets with the "don't fragment" bit set. The size of the first packet we send will equal the MTU of the outgoing interface, and whenever we receive an ICMP "can't fragment" error (which we described in the previous section) we'll reduce the size of the packet. If the router sending the ICMP error sends the newer version that includes the MTU of the outgoing interface, we'll use that value; otherwise we'll try the next smallest MTU. As RFC 1191 [Mogul and Deering 1990] states, there are a limited number of MTUs, so our program has a table of the likely values and moves to the next smallest value.

Let's first try it from our host `sun` to the host `slip`, knowing that the SLIP link has an MTU of 296:

```
sun % traceroute.pmtu slip
traceroute to slip (140.252.13.65), 30 hops max
outgoing MTU = 1500
 1  bsdi (140.252.13.35)  15 ms  6 ms  6 ms
 2  bsdi (140.252.13.35)  6 ms
fragmentation required and DF set, trying new MTU = 1492
fragmentation required and DF set, trying new MTU = 1006
fragmentation required and DF set, trying new MTU = 576
fragmentation required and DF set, trying new MTU = 552
fragmentation required and DF set, trying new MTU = 544
fragmentation required and DF set, trying new MTU = 512
fragmentation required and DF set, trying new MTU = 508
fragmentation required and DF set, trying new MTU = 296
 2  slip (140.252.13.65)  377 ms  377 ms  377 ms
```

In this example the router bsdi does not return the MTU of the outgoing interface in the ICMP error, so we step through the likely values for the MTU. The first line of output for a TTL of 2 prints a hostname of bsdi, but that's because it's the router returning the ICMP error. The final line of output for a TTL of 2 is what we're looking for.

It's not hard to modify the ICMP code on bsdi to return the MTU of the outgoing interface, and if we do that and rerun our program, we get the following output:

```
sun % traceroute.pmtu slip
traceroute to slip (140.252.13.65), 30 hops max
outgoing MTU = 1500
 1  bsdi (140.252.13.35)  53 ms  6 ms  6 ms
 2  bsdi (140.252.13.35)  6 ms
fragmentation required and DF set, next hop MTU = 296
 2  slip (140.252.13.65)  377 ms  378 ms  377 ms
```

Here we don't have to try eight different values for the MTU before finding the right one—the router returns the correct value.

The Worldwide Internet

As an experiment, this modified version of traceroute was run numerous times to various hosts around the world. Fifteen countries (including Antartica) were reached and various transatlantic and transpacific links were used. Before doing this, however, the MTU of the dialup SLIP link between the author's subnet and the router netb (Figure 11.12) was increased to 1500, the same as an Ethernet.

Out of 18 runs, only 2 had a path MTU of less than 1500. One of the transatlantic links had an MTU of 572 (a value not even listed as a likely value in RFC 1191) and the router did return the newer format ICMP error. Another link, between two routers in Japan, wouldn't handle a 1500-byte frame, and the router did not return the newer format ICMP error. Setting the MTU down to 1006 did work.

The conclusion we can make from this experiment is that many, but not all, WANs today can handle packets larger than 512 bytes. Using the path MTU discovery feature will allow applications to take advantage of these larger MTUs.

11.8 Path MTU Discovery with UDP

Let's examine the interaction between an application using UDP and the path MTU discovery mechanism. We want to see what happens when the application writes datagrams that are too big for some intermediate link.

Example

Since the only system that we've been using that supports the path MTU discovery mechanism is Solaris 2.x, we'll use it as the source host to send 650-byte datagrams to `slip`. Since our host `slip` sits behind a SLIP link with an MTU of 296, any UDP datagram greater than 268 bytes (296 – 20 – 8) with the "don't fragment" bit set should cause the router `bsdi` to generate the ICMP "can't fragment" error. Figure 11.13 shows the topology and the MTUs.

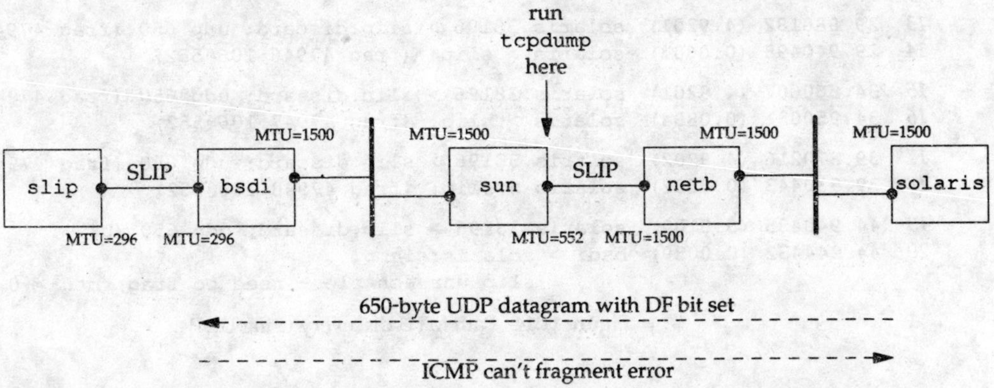

Figure 11.13 Systems used for path MTU discovery using UDP.

The following command generates ten 650-byte UDP datagrams, with a 5-second pause between each datagram:

```
solaris % sock -u -i -n10 -w650 -p5 slip discard
```

Figure 11.14 shows the `tcpdump` output. When this example was run, the router `bsdi` was set to not return the next-hop MTU as part of the ICMP "can't fragment" error.

The first datagram is sent with the DF bit set (line 1) and generates the expected error from the router `bsdi` (line 2). What's puzzling is that the next datagram is also sent with the DF bit set (line 3) and generates the same ICMP error (line 4). We would expect this datagram to be sent with the DF bit off.

On line 5 it appears IP has finally learned that datagrams to this destination should not be sent with the DF bit set, so IP goes ahead and fragments the datagrams at the source host. This is different from earlier examples where IP sends the datagram that is passed to it by UDP and allows the router with the smaller MTU (`bsdi` in this case) to

```
 1  0.0                  solaris.38196 > slip.discard: udp 650 (DF)
 2  0.004218 (0.0042)    bsdi > solaris: icmp:
                             slip unreachable - need to frag, mtu = 0 (DF)

 3  4.980528 (4.9763)    solaris.38196 > slip.discard: udp 650 (DF)
 4  4.984503 (0.0040)    bsdi > solaris: icmp:
                             slip unreachable - need to frag, mtu = 0 (DF)

 5  9.870407 (4.8859)    solaris.38196 > slip.discard: udp 650 (frag 47942:552@0+)
 6  9.960056 (0.0896)    solaris > slip: (frag 47942:106@552)

 7 14.940338 (4.9803)    solaris.38196 > slip.discard: udp 650 (DF)
 8 14.944466 (0.0041)    bsdi > solaris: icmp:
                             slip unreachable - need to frag, mtu = 0 (DF)

 9 19.890015 (4.9455)    solaris.38196 > slip.discard: udp 650 (frag 47944:552@0+)
10 19.950463 (0.0604)    solaris > slip: (frag 47944:106@552)

11 24.870401 (4.9199)    solaris.38196 > slip.discard: udp 650 (frag 47945:552@0+)
12 24.960038 (0.0896)    solaris > slip: (frag 47945:106@552)

13 29.880182 (4.9201)    solaris.38196 > slip.discard: udp 650 (frag 47946:552@0+)
14 29.940498 (0.0603)    solaris > slip: (frag 47946:106@552)

15 34.860607 (4.9201)    solaris.38196 > slip.discard: udp 650 (frag 47947:552@0+)
16 34.950051 (0.0894)    solaris > slip: (frag 47947:106@552)

17 39.870216 (4.9202)    solaris.38196 > slip.discard: udp 650 (frag 47948:552@0+)
18 39.930443 (0.0602)    solaris > slip: (frag 47948:106@552)

19 44.940485 (5.0100)    solaris.38196 > slip.discard: udp 650 (DF)
20 44.944432 (0.0039)    bsdi > solaris: icmp:
                             slip unreachable - need to frag, mtu = 0 (DF)
```

Figure 11.14 Path MTU discovery using UDP.

do the fragmentation. Since the ICMP "can't fragment" message didn't specify the next-hop MTU, it appears that IP guesses that an MTU of 576 is OK. The first fragment (line 5) contains 544 bytes of UDP data, the 8-byte UDP header, and the 20-byte IP header, for a total IP datagram size of 572 bytes. The second fragment (line 6) contains the remaining 106 bytes of UDP data and a 20-byte IP header.

Unfortunately the next datagram, line 7, has its DF bit set, so it's discarded by `bsdi` and the ICMP error returned. What has happened here is that an IP timer has expired telling IP to see if the path MTU has increased by setting the DF bit again. We see this happen again on lines 19 and 20. Comparing the times on lines 7 and 19 it appears that IP turns on the DF bit, to see if the path MTU has increased, every 30 seconds.

> This 30-second timer value is way too small. RFC 1191 recommends a value of 10 minutes. It can be changed by modifying the parameter `ip_ire_pathmtu_interval` (Section E.4). Also there is no way in Solaris 2.2 to turn off this path MTU discovery for a single UDP application or for all UDP applications. It can only be enabled or disabled on a systemwide basis by changing the parameter `ip_path_mtu_discovery`. As we can see from this example, enabling path MTU discovery when UDP applications write datagrams that will probably be fragmented can cause datagrams to be discarded.

The maximum datagram size assumed by the IP layer on `solaris` (576 bytes) is not right. In Figure 11.13 we see that the real MTU is 296 bytes. This means the fragments generated by `solaris` will be fragmented again by `bsdi`. Figure 11.15 shows the `tcpdump` output collected on the destination host (`slip`) for the first datagram that arrives (lines 5 and 6 from Figure 11.14).

```
1  0.0                   solaris.38196 > slip.discard: udp 650 (frag 47942:272@0+)
2  0.304513 (0.3045)     solaris > slip: (frag 47942:272@272+)
3  0.334651 (0.0301)     solaris > slip: (frag 47942:8@544+)
4  0.466642 (0.1320)     solaris > slip: (frag 47942:106@552)
```

Figure 11.15 First datagram arriving at host `slip` from `solaris`.

In this example the host `solaris` should not fragment the outgoing datagrams but should turn off the DF bit and let the router with the smaller MTU do the fragmentation.

Now we'll run the same example but modify the router `bsdi` to return the next-hop MTU in the ICMP "can't fragment" error. Figure 11.16 shows the first six lines of the `tcpdump` output.

```
1  0.0                   solaris.37974 > slip.discard: udp 650 (DF)
2  0.004199 (0.0042)     bsdi > solaris: icmp:
                              slip unreachable - need to frag, mtu = 296 (DF)
3  4.950193 (4.9460)     solaris.37974 > slip.discard: udp 650 (DF)
4  4.954325 (0.0041)     bsdi > solaris: icmp:
                              slip unreachable - need to frag, mtu = 296 (DF)
5  9.779855 (4.8255)     solaris.37974 > slip.discard: udp 650 (frag 35278:272@0+)
6  9.930018 (0.1502)     solaris > slip: (frag 35278:272@272+)
7  9.990170 (0.0602)     solaris > slip: (frag 35278:114@544)
```

Figure 11.16 Path MTU discovery using UDP.

Again, the first two datagrams are sent with the DF bit set, and both elicit the ICMP error. The ICMP error now specifies the next-hop MTU of 296.

In lines 5, 6, and 7 we see the source host perform fragmentation, similar to Figure 11.14. But knowing the next-hop MTU, only three fragments are generated, compared to the four fragments generated by the router `bsdi` in Figure 11.15.

11.9 Interaction Between UDP and ARP

Using UDP we can see an interesting (and often unmentioned) interaction with UDP and typical implementations of ARP.

We use our `sock` program to generate a single UDP datagram with 8192 bytes of data. We expect this to generate six fragments on an Ethernet (see Exercise 11.3). We also assure that the ARP cache is empty before running the program, so that an ARP request and reply must be exchanged before the first fragment is sent.

```
bsdi % arp -a                              verify ARP cache is empty
bsdi % sock -u -i -nl -w8192 svr4 discard
```

We expect the first fragment to cause an ARP request to be sent. Five more fragments are generated by IP and this presents two timing questions that we'll need to use `tcpdump` to answer: are the remaining fragments ready to be sent before the ARP reply is received, and if so, what does ARP do with multiple packets to a given destination when it's waiting for an ARP reply? Figure 11.17 shows the `tcpdump` output.

```
1   0.0                      arp who-has svr4 tell bsdi
2   0.001234 (0.0012)        arp who-has svr4 tell bsdi
3   0.001941 (0.0007)        arp who-has svr4 tell bsdi
4   0.002775 (0.0008)        arp who-has svr4 tell bsdi
5   0.003495 (0.0007)        arp who-has svr4 tell bsdi
6   0.004319 (0.0008)        arp who-has svr4 tell bsdi
7   0.008772 (0.0045)        arp reply svr4 is-at 0:0:c0:c2:9b:26
8   0.009911 (0.0011)        arp reply svr4 is-at 0:0:c0:c2:9b:26
9   0.011127 (0.0012)        bsdi > svr4: (frag 10863:800@7400)
10  0.011255 (0.0001)        arp reply svr4 is-at 0:0:c0:c2:9b:26
11  0.012562 (0.0013)        arp reply svr4 is-at 0:0:c0:c2:9b:26
12  0.013458 (0.0009)        arp reply svr4 is-at 0:0:c0:c2:9b:26
13  0.014526 (0.0011)        arp reply svr4 is-at 0:0:c0:c2:9b:26
14  0.015583 (0.0011)        arp reply svr4 is-at 0:0:c0:c2:9b:26
```

Figure 11.17 Packet exchange when an 8192-byte UDP datagram is sent on an Ethernet.

There are a few surprises in this output. First, six ARP requests are generated before the first ARP reply is returned. What we guess is happening is that IP generates the six fragments rapidly, and each one causes an ARP request.

Next, when the first ARP reply is received (line 7) only the last fragment is sent (line 9)! It appears that the first five fragments have been discarded. Indeed, this is the normal operation of ARP. Most implementations keep only the *last* packet sent to a given destination while waiting for an ARP reply.

> The Host Requirements RFC requires an implementation to prevent this type of *ARP flooding* (repeatedly sending an ARP request for the same IP address at a high rate). The recommended maximum rate is one per second. Here we see six ARP requests in 4.3 ms.
>
> The Host Requirements RFC states that ARP should save at least one packet, and this should be the latest packet. That's what we see here.

Another unexplained anomaly in this output is that `svr4` sends back seven ARP replies, not six.

The final point worth mentioning is that `tcpdump` was left to run for 5 minutes after the final ARP reply was returned, waiting to see if `svr4` sent back an ICMP "time exceeded during reassembly" error. The ICMP error was never sent. (We showed the format of this message in Figure 8.2. A *code* of 1 indicates that the time was exceeded during the reassembly of a datagram.)

The IP layer must start a timer when the first fragment of a datagram appears. Here "first" means the first arrival of any fragment for a given datagram, not the first fragment (with a fragment offset of 0). A normal timeout value is 30 or 60 seconds. If all the fragments for this datagram have not arrived when the timer expires, all these fragments are discarded. If this were not done, fragments that never arrive (as we see in this example) could eventually cause the receiver to run out of buffers.

There are two reasons we don't see the ICMP message here. First, most Berkeley-derived implementations never generate this error! These implementations do set a timer, and do discard all fragments when the timer expires, but the ICMP error is never generated. Second, the first fragment—the one with an offset of 0 containing the UDP header—was never received. (It was the first of the five packets discarded by ARP.) An implementation is not required to generate the ICMP error unless this first fragment has been received. The reason is that the receiver of the ICMP error couldn't tell which user process sent the datagram that was discarded, because the transport layer header is not available. It's assumed that the upper layer (either TCP or the application using UDP) will eventually time out and retransmit.

In this section we've used IP fragmentation to see this interaction between UDP and ARP. We can also see this interaction if the sender quickly transmits multiple UDP datagrams. We chose to use fragmentation because the packets get generated quickly by IP, faster than multiple datagrams can be generated by a user process.

As unlikely as this example might seem, it occurs regularly. NFS sends UDP datagrams whose length just exceeds 8192 bytes. On an Ethernet these are fragmented as we've indicated, and if the appropriate ARP cache entry times out, you can see what we've shown here. NFS will time out and retransmit, but the first IP datagram can still be discarded because of ARP's limited queue.

11.10 Maximum UDP Datagram Size

Theoretically, the maximum size of an IP datagram is 65535 bytes, imposed by the 16-bit total length field in the IP header (Figure 3.1). With an IP header of 20 bytes and a UDP header of 8 bytes, this leaves a maximum of 65507 bytes of user data in a UDP datagram. Most implementations, however, provide less than this maximum.

There are two limits we can encounter. First the application program may be limited by its programming interface. The sockets API (Section 1.15) provides a function that the application can call to set the size of the receive buffer and the send buffer. For a UDP socket, this size is directly related to the maximum size UDP datagram the application can read or write. Most systems today provide a default of just over 8192 bytes for the maximum size of a UDP datagram that can be read or written. (This default is because 8192 is the amount of user data that NFS reads and writes by default.)

The next limitation comes from the kernel's implementation of TCP/IP. There may be implementation features (or bugs) that limit the size of an IP datagram to less than 65535 bytes.

> The author experimented with various UDP datagram sizes, using the sock program. Using the loopback interface under SunOS 4.1.3, the maximum size IP datagram was 32767 bytes. All higher values failed. But going across an Ethernet from BSD/386 to SunOS 4.1.3, the maximum size IP datagram the Sun could accept was 32786 (that is, 32758 bytes of user data). Using the loopback interface under Solaris 2.2, the maximum 65535-byte IP datagram could be sent and received. From Solaris 2.2 to AIX 3.2.2, the maximum 65535-byte IP datagram could be transferred. Obviously this limit depends on the source and destination implementations.

We mentioned in Section 3.2 that a host is required to receive at least a 576-byte IP datagram. Many UDP applications are designed to restrict their application data to 512 bytes or less, to stay below this limit. We saw this in Section 10.4, for example, where the Routing Information Protocol always sent less than 512 bytes of data per datagram. We'll encounter this same limit with other UDP applications: the DNS (Chapter 14), TFTP (Chapter 15), BOOTP (Chapter 16), and SNMP (Chapter 25).

Datagram Truncation

Just because IP is capable of sending and receiving a datagram of a given size doesn't mean the receiving application is prepared to read that size. UDP programming interfaces allow the application to specify the maximum number of bytes to return each time. What happens if the received datagram exceeds the size the application is prepared to deal with?

Unfortunately the answer depends on the programming interface and the implementation.

The traditional Berkeley version of the sockets API truncates the datagram, discarding any excess data. Whether the application is notified depends on the version. (4.3BSD Reno and later can notify the application that the datagram was truncated.)

The sockets API under SVR4 (including Solaris 2.x) does not truncate the datagram. Any excess data is returned in subsequent reads. The application is not notified that multiple reads are being fulfilled from a single UDP datagram.

The TLI API does not discard the data. Instead a flag is returned indicating that more data is available, and subsequent reads by the application return the rest of the datagram.

When we discuss TCP we'll see that it provides a continuous stream of bytes to the application, without any message boundaries. TCP passes the data to the application in whatever size reads the application asks for—there is never any data loss across this interface.

11.11 ICMP Source Quench Error

Using UDP we are also able to generate the ICMP "source quench" error. This is an error that may be generated by a system (router or host) when it receives datagrams at a rate that is too fast to be processed. Note the qualifier "may." A system is not required to send a source quench, even if it runs out of buffers and throws datagrams away.

Figure 11.18 shows the format of the ICMP source quench error. We have a perfect scenario with our test network for generating this error. We can send datagrams from `bsdi` to the router `sun` across the Ethernet that must be routed across the dialup SLIP link. Since the SLIP link is about 1000 times slower than the Ethernet, we should easily be able to overrun its buffer space. The following command sends 100 1024-byte datagrams from the host `bsdi` through the router `sun` to `solaris`. We send the datagrams to the standard discard service, where they'll be ignored:

```
bsdi % sock -u -i -w1024 -n100 solaris discard
```

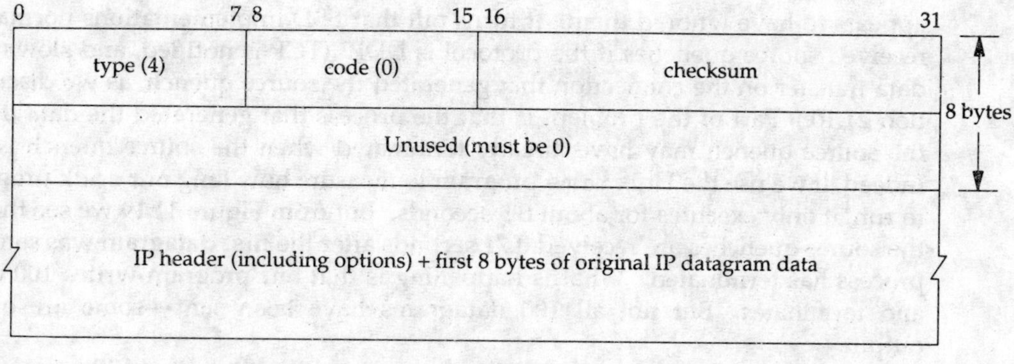

Figure 11.18 ICMP source quench error.

Figure 11.19 shows the `tcpdump` output corresponding to this command.

```
  1 0.0                bsdi.1403 > solaris.discard: udp 1024
                                   26 lines that we don't show
 27 0.10 (0.00)        bsdi.1403 > solaris.discard: udp 1024
 28 0.11 (0.01)        sun > bsdi: icmp: source quench

 29 0.11 (0.00)        bsdi.1403 > solaris.discard: udp 1024
 30 0.11 (0.00)        sun > bsdi: icmp: source quench
                                   142 lines that we don't show
173 0.71 (0.06)        bsdi.1403 > solaris.discard: udp 1024
174 0.71 (0.00)        sun > bsdi: icmp: source quench
```

Figure 11.19 ICMP source quench from the router sun.

We have removed lots of lines from this output; there is a pattern. The first 26 datagrams are received without an error; we show the output only for the first. Starting with our 27th datagram, however, every time we send a datagram, we receive a source quench in return. There are a total of $26 + (74 \times 2) = 174$ lines of output.

From our serial line throughput calculations in Section 2.10, it takes just over 1 second to transfer a 1024-byte datagram at 9600 bits/sec. (In our example it should take longer than this since the $20 + 8 + 1024$ byte datagram will be fragmented because the MTU of the SLIP link from `sun` to `netb` is 552 bytes.) But we can see from the timing in Figure 11.19 that the router `sun` receives all 100 datagrams in less than 1 second, before the first one is through the SLIP link. It's not surprising that we used up many of its buffers.

> Although RFC 1009 [Braden and Postel 1987] requires a router to generate source quenches when it runs out of buffers, the new Router Requirements RFC [Almquist 1993] changes this and says that a router must not originate source quench errors. The current feeling is to deprecate the source quench error, since it consumes network bandwidth and is an ineffective and unfair fix for congestion.

Another point to make regarding this example is that our `sock` program either never received a notification that the source quenches were being received, or if it did, it appears to have ignored them. It turns out that BSD implementations normally ignore received source quenches if the protocol is UDP. (TCP is notified, and slows down the data transfer on the connection that generated the source quench, as we discuss in Section 21.10.) Part of the problem is that the process that generated the data that caused the source quench may have already terminated when the source quench is received. Indeed, if we use the Unix `time` program to measure how long our `sock` program takes to run, it only executes for about 0.5 seconds. But from Figure 11.19 we see that some of the source quenches are received 0.71 seconds after the first datagram was sent, after the process has terminated. What is happening is that our program writes 100 datagrams and terminates. But not all 100 datagrams have been sent—some are queued for output.

This example reiterates that UDP is an unreliable protocol and illustrates the value of end-to-end flow control. Even though our `sock` program successfully wrote 100 datagrams to its network, only 26 were really sent to the destination. The other 74 were probably discarded by the intermediate router. Unless we build some form of acknowledgment into the application, the sender has no idea whether the receiver really got the data.

11.12 UDP Server Design

There are some implications in using UDP that affect the design and implementation of a server. The design and implementation of clients is usually easier than that of servers, which is why we talk about server design and not client design. Servers typically interact with the operating system and most servers need a way to handle multiple clients at the same time.

Normally a client starts, immediately communicates with a single server, and is done. Servers, on the other hand, start and then go to sleep, waiting for a client's request to arrive. In the case of UDP, the server wakes up when a client's datagram arrives, probably containing a request message of some form from the client.

Our interest here is not in the programming aspects of clients and servers ([Stevens 1990] covers all those details), but in the protocol features of UDP that affect the design and implementation of a server using UDP. (We examine the details of TCP server design in Section 18.11.) Although some of the features we describe depend on the implementation of UDP being used, the features are common to most implementations.

Client IP Address and Port Number

What arrives from the client is a UDP datagram. The IP header contains the source and destination IP addresses, and the UDP header contains the source and destination UDP port numbers. When an application receives a UDP datagram, it must be told by the operating system who sent the message—the source IP address and port number.

This feature allows an iterative UDP server to handle multiple clients. Each reply is sent back to the client that sent the request.

Destination IP Address

Some applications need to know who the datagram was sent to, that is, the destination IP address. For example, the Host Requirements RFC states that a TFTP server should ignore received datagrams that are sent to a broadcast address. (We describe broadcasting in Chapter 12 and TFTP in Chapter 15.)

This requires the operating system to pass the destination IP address from the received UDP datagram to the application. Unfortunately, not all implementations provide this capability.

The sockets API provides this capability with the `IP_RECVDSTADDR` socket option. Of the systems used in the text, only BSD/386, 4.4BSD, and AIX 3.2.2 support this option. SVR4, SunOS 4.x, and Solaris 2.x don't support it.

UDP Input Queue

We said in Section 1.8 that most UDP servers are iterative servers. This means a single server process handles all the client requests on a single UDP port (the server's well-known port).

Normally there is a limited size input queue associated with each UDP port that an application is using. This means that requests that arrive at about the same time from different clients are automatically queued by UDP. The received UDP datagrams are passed to the application (when it asks for the next one) in the order they were received.

It is possible, however, for this queue to overflow, causing the kernel's UDP module to discard incoming datagrams. We can see this with the following experiment. We start our `sock` program on the host `bsdi` running as a UDP server:

```
bsdi % sock -s -u -v -E -R256 -r256 -P30 6666
from 140.252.13.33, to 140.252.13.63: 1111111111      from sun, to broadcast address
from 140.252.13.34, to 140.252.13.35: 4444444444444   from svr4, to unicast address
```

We specify the following flags: `-s` to run as a server, `-u` for UDP, `-v` to print the client's IP address, and `-E` to print the destination IP address (which is supported by this system). Additionally we set the UDP receive buffer for this port to 256 bytes (`-R`), along with the size of each application read (`-r`). The flag `-P30` tells it to pause for 30 seconds after creating the UDP port, before reading the first datagram. This gives us time to start the clients on two other hosts, send some datagrams, and see how the receive queueing works.

Once the server is started, and is in its 30-second pause, we start one client on the host `sun` and send three datagrams:

```
sun % sock -u -v 140.252.13.63 6666        to Ethernet broadcast address
connected on 140.252.13.33.1252 to 140.252.13.63.6666
1111111111                                  11 bytes of data (with newline)
222222222                                   10 bytes of data (with newline)
33333333333                                 12 bytes of data (with newline)
```

The destination address is the broadcast address (140.252.13.63). We also start a second client on the host `svr4` and send another three datagrams:

```
svr4 % sock -u -v bsdi 6666
connected on 0.0.0.0.1042 to 140.252.13.35.6666
4444444444444               14 bytes of data (with newline)
555555555555555             16 bytes of data (with newline)
66666666                    9 bytes of data (with newline)
```

The first thing we notice in the interactive output shown earlier on bsdi is that only two datagrams were received by the application: the first one from sun with all 1s, and the first one from svr4 with all 4s. The other four datagrams appear to have been thrown away.

The tcpdump output in Figure 11.20 shows that all six datagrams were delivered to the destination host. The datagrams were typed on the two clients in alternating order: first from sun, then from svr4, and so on. We can also see that all six were delivered in about 12 seconds, within the 30-second period while the server was sleeping.

```
1   0.0                    sun.1252 > 140.252.13.63.6666: udp 11
2   2.499184 (2.4992)      svr4.1042 > bsdi.6666: udp 14
3   4.959166 (2.4600)      sun.1252 > 140.252.13.63.6666: udp 10
4   7.607149 (2.6480)      svr4.1042 > bsdi.6666: udp 16
5  10.079059 (2.4719)      sun.1252 > 140.252.13.63.6666: udp 12
6  12.415943 (2.3369)      svr4.1042 > bsdi.6666: udp 9
```

Figure 11.20 tcpdump for UDP datagrams sent by two clients.

We can also see the server's -E option lets it know the destination IP address of each datagram. If it wanted to, it could choose what to do with the first datagram it receives, which was sent to a broadcast address.

We can see several points in this example. First, the application is not told when its input queue overflows. The excess datagrams are just discarded by UDP. Also, from the tcpdump output we see that nothing is sent back to the client to tell it that its datagram was discarded. There is nothing like an ICMP source quench sent back to the sender. Finally, it appears that the UDP input queue is FIFO (first-in, first-out), whereas we saw that the ARP input queue in Section 11.9 was LIFO (last-in, first-out).

Restricting Local IP Address

Most UDP servers *wildcard* their local IP address when they create a UDP end point. This means that an incoming UDP datagram destined for the server's port will be accepted on any local interface. For example, we can start a UDP server on port 7777:

```
sun % sock -u -s 7777
```

We then use the netstat command to see the state of the end point:

```
sun % netstat -a -n -f inet
Active Internet connections (including servers)
Proto Recv-Q Send-Q  Local Address          Foreign Address        (state)
udp        0      0  *.7777                 *.*
```

We have deleted many lines of output other than the one in which we're interested. The -a flag reports on all network end points. The -n flag prints IP addresses as dotted-decimal numbers, instead of trying to use the DNS to convert the address to a name, and prints numeric port numbers instead of service names. The `-f inet` option reports only TCP and UDP end points.

The local address is printed as `*.7777` where the asterisk means the local IP address has been wildcarded.

When the server creates its end point it can specify one of the host's local IP addresses, including one of its broadcast addresses, as the local IP address for the end point. Incoming UDP datagrams will then be passed to this end point only if the destination IP address matches the specified local address. With our `sock` program, if we specify an IP address before the port number, that IP address becomes the local IP address for the end point. For example,

```
sun % sock -u -s 140.252.1.29 7777
```

restricts the server to datagrams arriving on the SLIP interface (140.252.1.29). The `netstat` output shows this:

```
Proto Recv-Q Send-Q  Local Address          Foreign Address        (state)
udp        0      0  140.252.1.29.7777      *.*
```

If we try to send this server a datagram from a host on the Ethernet, `bsdi` at address 140.252.13.35, an ICMP port unreachable is returned. The server never sees the datagram. Figure 11.21 shows this scenario.

```
1  0.0                        bsdi.1723 > sun.7777: udp 13
2  0.000822 (0.0008)          sun > bsdi: icmp: sun udp port 7777 unreachable
```

Figure 11.21 Rejection of UDP datagram caused by server's local address binding.

It is possible to start different servers at the same port, each with a different local IP address. Normally, however, the system must be told by the application that it is OK to reuse the same port number.

> With the sockets API the `SO_REUSEADDR` socket option must be specified. This is done by our `sock` program by specifying the `-A` option.

On our host `sun` we can start five different servers on the same UDP port (8888):

```
sun % sock -u -s 140.252.1.29 8888           for SLIP link
sun % sock -u -s -A 140.252.13.33 8888       for Ethernet
sun % sock -u -s -A 127.0.0.1 8888           for loopback interface
sun % sock -u -s -A 140.252.13.63 8888       for Ethernet broadcasts
sun % sock -u -s -A 8888                     everything else (wildcard IP address)
```

All except the first of the servers must be started with the `-A` flag, telling the system that it's OK to reuse the same port number. The `netstat` output shows the five servers:

```
Proto Recv-Q Send-Q  Local Address          Foreign Address        (state)
udp        0      0  *.8888                 *.*
udp        0      0  140.252.13.63.8888     *.*
udp        0      0  127.0.0.1.8888         *.*
udp        0      0  140.252.13.33.8888     *.*
udp        0      0  140.252.1.29.8888      *.*
```

In this scenario, the only datagrams that will go to the server with the wildcarded local IP address are those destined to 140.252.1.255, because the other four servers cover all other possibilities.

There is a priority implied when an end point with a wildcard address exists. An end point with a specific IP address that matches the destination IP address is always chosen over a wildcard. The wildcard end point is used only when a specific match is not found.

Restricting Foreign IP Address

In all the `netstat` output that we showed earlier, the foreign IP address and foreign port number are shown as `*.*` meaning the end point will accept an incoming UDP datagram from any IP address and any port number. Most implementations allow a UDP end point to restrict the foreign address.

This means the end point will only receive UDP datagrams from that specific IP address and port number. Our `sock` program uses the `-f` option to specify the foreign IP address and port number:

```
sun % sock -u -s -f 140.252.13.35.4444 5555
```

This sets the foreign IP address to 140.252.13.35 (our host `bsdi`) and the foreign port number to 4444. The server's well-known port is 5555. If we run `netstat` we see that the local IP address has also been set, even though we didn't specify it:

```
Proto Recv-Q Send-Q  Local Address          Foreign Address         (state)
udp        0      0  140.252.13.33.5555     140.252.13.35.4444
```

This is a side effect of specifying the foreign IP address and foreign port on Berkeley-derived systems: if the local address has not been chosen when the foreign address is specified, the local address is chosen automatically. Its value becomes the IP address of the interface chosen by IP routing to reach the specified foreign IP address. Indeed, in this example the IP address on `sun` for the Ethernet that is connected to the foreign address is 140.252.13.33.

Figure 11.22 summarizes the three types of address bindings that a UDP server can establish for itself.

Local Address	Foreign Address	Description
localIP.lport	*foreignIP.fport*	restricted to one client
localIP.lport	*.*	restricted to datagrams arriving on one local interface: *localIP*
*.*lport*	*.*	receives all datagrams sent to *lport*

Figure 11.22 Specification of local and foreign IP addresses and port number for UDP server.

In all cases, *lport* is the server's well-known port and *localIP* must be the IP address of a local interface. The ordering of the three rows in the table is the order that the UDP module applies when trying to determine which local end point receives an incoming datagram. The most specific binding (the first row) is tried first, and the least specific (the last row with both IP addresses wildcarded) is tried last.

Multiple Recipients per Port

Although it's not specified in the RFCs, most implementations allow only one application end point at a time to be associated with any one local IP address and UDP port number. When a UDP datagram arrives at a host destined for that IP address and port number, one copy is delivered to that single end point. The IP address of the end point can be the wildcard, as shown earlier.

For example, under SunOS 4.1.3 we start one server on port 9999 with a wildcarded local IP address:

```
sun % sock -u -s 9999
```

If we then try to start another server with the same wildcarded local address and the same port, it doesn't work, even if we specify the -A option:

```
sun % sock -u -s 9999                    we expect this to fail
can't bind local address: Address already in use
sun % sock -u -s -A 9999                 so we try -A flag this time
can't bind local address: Address already in use
```

On systems that support multicasting (Chapter 12), this changes. Multiple end points can use the same local IP address and UDP port number, although the application normally must tell the API that this is OK (i.e., our -A flag to specify the SO_REUSEADDR socket option).

> 4.4BSD, which supports multicasting, requires the application to set a different socket option (SO_REUSEPORT) to allow multiple end points to share the same port. Furthermore each end point must specify this option, including the first one to use the port.

When a UDP datagram arrives whose destination IP address is a broadcast or multicast address, and there are multiple end points at the destination IP address and port number, one copy of the incoming datagram is passed to *each* end point. (The end point's local IP address can be the wildcard, which matches any destination IP address.) But if a UDP datagram arrives whose destination IP address is a unicast address, only a single copy of the datagram is delivered to *one* of the end points. Which end point gets the unicast datagram is implementation dependent.

11.13 Summary

UDP is a simple protocol. Its official specification, RFC 768 [Postel 1980], requires only three pages. The services it provides to a user process, above and beyond IP, are port numbers and an optional checksum. We used UDP to examine this checksum and to see how fragmentation is performed.

We then examined the ICMP unreachable error that is part of the new path MTU discovery feature (Section 2.9). We watched path MTU discovery using Traceroute and UDP. We also looked at the interaction between UDP and ARP whereby most ARP implementations only retain the most recently transmitted datagram to a given destination, while waiting for an ARP reply.

The ICMP source quench error can be sent by a system that is receiving IP datagrams faster than they can be processed. It is easy to generate these ICMP errors using UDP.

Exercises

11.1 In Section 11.5 we caused fragmentation on an Ethernet by writing a UDP datagram with 1473 bytes of user data. What is the smallest amount of user data that causes fragmentation on an Ethernet if IEEE 802 encapsulation (Section 2.2) is used instead?

11.2 Read RFC 791 [Postel 1981a] to determine why all fragments other than the last must have a length that is a multiple of 8 bytes.

11.3 Assume an Ethernet and a UDP datagram with 8192 bytes of user data. How many fragments are transmitted and what is the offset and length of each fragment?

11.4 Continue the previous exercise, assuming these fragments then traverse a SLIP link with an MTU of 552. You also need to remember that the amount of data in each fragment (i.e., everything other than the IP header) must be a multiple of 8 bytes. How many fragments are transmitted and what is the offset and length of each fragment?

11.5 An application using UDP sends a datagram that gets fragmented into four pieces. Assume that fragments 1 and 2 make it to the destination, with fragments 3 and 4 being lost. The application then times out and retransmits the UDP datagram 10 seconds later and this datagram is fragmented identically to the first transmission (i.e., same offsets and lengths). Assume that this time fragments 1 and 2 are lost but fragments 3 and 4 make it to the destination. Also assume that the reassembly timer on the receiving host is 60 seconds, so when fragments 3 and 4 of the retransmission make it to the destination, fragments 1 and 2 from the first transmission have not been discarded. Can the receiver reassemble the IP datagram from the four fragments it now has?

11.6 How do you know that the fragments in Figure 11.15 really correspond to lines 5 and 6 in Figure 11.14?

11.7 After the host `gemini` had been up for 33 days, the `netstat` program showed that 129 IP datagrams out of 48 million had been dropped because of a bad header checksum, and 20 TCP segments out of 30 million had been dropped because of a bad TCP checksum. Not a single UDP datagram was dropped, however, because of a UDP checksum error, out of the approximately 18 million UDP datagrams. Give two reasons why. (*Hint*: See Figure 11.4.)

11.8 In our discussion of fragmentation we never said what happens to IP options in the IP header—are they copied as part of the IP header in each fragment, or left in the first fragment only? We've described the following IP options: record route (Section 7.3), timestamp (Section 7.4), strict and loose source routing (Section 8.5). How would you expect fragmentation to handle these options? Check your answer with RFC 791.

11.9 In Figure 1.8 (p. 11) we said that incoming UDP datagrams are demultiplexed based on the destination UDP port number. Is that correct?

12

Broadcasting and Multicasting

12.1 Introduction

We mentioned in Chapter 1 that there are three kinds of IP addresses: *unicast*, *broadcast*, and *multicast*. In this chapter we discuss broadcasting and multicasting in more detail.

Broadcasting and multicasting only apply to UDP, where it makes sense for an application to send a single message to multiple recipients. TCP is a connection-oriented protocol that implies a connection between two hosts (specified by IP addresses) and one process on each host (specified by port numbers).

Consider a set of hosts on a shared network such as an Ethernet. Each Ethernet frame contains the source and destination Ethernet addresses (48-bit values). Normally each Ethernet frame is destined for a single host. The destination address specifies a single interface—called a *unicast*. In this way communication between any two hosts doesn't bother any of the remaining hosts on the cable (except for possible contention for the shared media).

There are times, however, when a host wants to send a frame to every other host on the cable—called a *broadcast*. We saw this with ARP and RARP. Multicasting fits between unicasting and broadcasting: the frame should be delivered to a set of hosts that belong to a multicast group.

To understand broadcasting and multicasting we need to understand that filtering takes place on each host, each time a frame passes by on the cable. Figure 12.1 shows a picture of this.

First, the interface card sees every frame that passes by on the cable and makes a decision whether to receive the frame and deliver it to the device driver. Normally the interface card receives only those frames whose destination address is either the hardware address of the interface or the broadcast address. Additionally, most interfaces can be placed into a promiscuous mode whereby they receive a copy of every frame. This mode is used by `tcpdump`, for example.

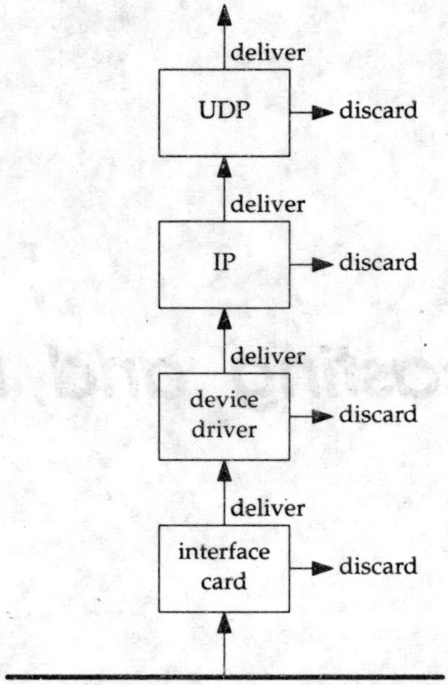

Figure 12.1 Filtering that takes place up the protocol stack when a frame is received.

Today most interfaces can also be configured to receive frames whose destination address is a multicast address, or some subset of multicast addresses. On an Ethernet, a multicast address has the low-order bit of the high-order byte turned on. In hexadecimal this bit looks like `01:00:00:00:00:00`. (We can consider the Ethernet broadcast address, `ff:ff:ff:ff:ff:ff` as a special case of the Ethernet multicast address.)

If the interface card receives the frame, it is passed to the device driver. (One reason the interface card might discard the frame is if the Ethernet checksum is incorrect.) Additional filtering is performed by the device driver. First, the frame type must specify a protocol that is supported (IP, ARP, etc.). Second, additional multicast filtering may be performed, to check whether the host belongs to the addressed multicast group.

The device driver then passes the frame to the next layer, such as IP, if the frame type specifies an IP datagram. IP performs more filtering, based on the source and destination IP addresses, and passes the datagram up to the next layer (such as TCP or UDP) if all is well.

Each time UDP receives a datagram from IP, it performs filtering based on the destination port number, and sometimes the source port number too. If no process is currently using the destination port number, the datagram is discarded and an ICMP port unreachable message is normally generated. (TCP performs similar filtering based on its port numbers.) If the UDP datagram has a checksum error, UDP silently discards it.

The problem with broadcasting is the processing load that it places on hosts that aren't interested in the broadcasts. Consider an application that is designed to use UDP broadcasts. If there are 50 hosts on the cable, but only 20 are participating in the application, every time one of the 20 sends a UDP broadcast, the other 30 hosts have to process the broadcast, all the way up through the UDP layer, before the UDP datagram is discarded. The UDP datagram is discarded by these 30 hosts because the destination port number is not in use.

The intent of multicasting is to reduce this load on hosts with no interest in the application. With multicasting a host specifically joins one or more multicast groups. If possible, the interface card is told which multicast groups the host belongs to, and only those multicast frames are received.

12.2 Broadcasting

In Figure 3.9 we showed four different forms of IP broadcast addresses. We now describe them in more detail.

Limited Broadcast

The *limited broadcast address* is 255.255.255.255. This can be used as the destination address of an IP datagram during the host configuration process, when the host might not know its subnet mask or even its IP address.

A datagram destined for the limited broadcast address is *never* forwarded by a router under any circumstance. It only appears on the local cable.

An unanswered question is: if a host is multihomed and a process sends a datagram to the limited broadcast address, should the datagram be sent out each connected interface that supports broadcasting? If not, an application that wants to broadcast out all interfaces must determine all the interfaces on the host that support broadcasting, and send a copy out each interface.

Most BSD systems treat 255.255.255.255 as an alias for the broadcast address of the first interface that was configured, and don't provide any way to send a datagram out all attached, broadcast-capable interfaces. Indeed, two applications that send UDP datagrams out every interface are `routed` (Section 10.3) and `rwhod` (the server for the BSD `rwho` client). Both of these applications go through a similar start-up procedure to determine all the interfaces on the host, and which ones are capable of broadcasting. The net-directed broadcast address corresponding to that interface is then used as the destination address for datagrams sent out the interface.

> The Host Requirements RFC takes no stand on the issue of whether a multihomed host should send a limited broadcast out all its interfaces.

Net-directed Broadcast

The *net-directed broadcast address* has a host ID of all one bits. A class A net-directed broadcast address is *netid*.255.255.255, where *netid* is the class A network ID.

A router must forward a net-directed broadcast by default, but it must also have an option to disable this forwarding.

Subnet-directed Broadcast

The *subnet-directed broadcast address* has a host ID of all one bits but a specific subnet ID. Classification of an IP address as a subnet-directed broadcast address requires knowledge of the subnet mask. For example, if a router receives a datagram destined for 128.1.2.255, this is a subnet-directed broadcast if the class B network 128.1 has a subnet mask of 255.255.255.0, but it is not a broadcast if the subnet mask is 255.255.254.0 (`0xfffffe00`).

All-subnets-directed Broadcast

An *all-subnets-directed broadcast address* also requires knowledge of the destination network's subnet mask, to differentiate this broadcast address from a net-directed broadcast address. Both the subnet ID and the host ID are all one bits. For example, if the destination's subnet mask is 255.255.255.0, then the class B IP address 128.1.255.255 is an all-subnets-directed broadcast. But if the network is not subnetted, then this is a net-directed broadcast.

Current feeling [Almquist 1993] is that this type of broadcast is obsolete. It is better to use multicasting than an all-subnets-directed broadcast.

[Almquist 1993] notes that RFC 922 requires that an all-subnets-directed broadcast be sent to all subnets, but no current routers do so. This is fortunate since a host that has been misconfigured without its subnet mask sends all its "local" broadcasts to all subnets. For example, if the host with IP address 128.1.2.3 doesn't set a subnet mask, then its broadcast address normally defaults to 128.1.255.255. But if the subnet mask should have been set to 255.255.255.0, then broadcasts from this misconfigured host appear directed to all subnets.

The first widespread implementation of TCP/IP, the 4.2BSD system in 1983, used a host ID of all zero bits for the broadcast address. One of the earliest references to the broadcast IP address is IEN 212 [Gurwitz and Hinden 1982], and it *proposed* to define the IP broadcast address as a host ID of one bits. (IENs are the *Internet Experiment Notes*, basically predecessors to the RFCs.) RFC 894 [Hornig 1984] commented that 4.2BSD used a nonstandard broadcast address, but RFC 906 [Finlayson 1984] noted that there was no Internet standard for the broadcast address. The RFC editor added a footnote to RFC 906 acknowledging the lack of a standard broadcast address, but strongly recommended that a host ID of all one bits be used as the broadcast address. Although Berkeley adopted the use of all one bits for the broadcast address with 4.3BSD in 1986, some operating systems (notably SunOS 4.x) continued to use the nonstandard broadcast address through the early 1990s.

12.3 Broadcasting Examples

How are broadcasts sent and what do routers and hosts do with broadcasts? Unfortunately this is a hard question to answer because it depends on the type of broadcast address, the application, the TCP/IP implementation, and possible configuration switches.

First, the application must support broadcasting. If we execute

```
sun % ping 255.255.255.255
/usr/etc/ping: unknown host 255.255.255.255
```

intending to send a broadcast on the local cable, it doesn't work. But the problem here is a programming problem in the application (`ping`). Most applications that accept either a dotted-decimal IP address or a hostname call the function `inet_addr`(3) to convert the dotted-decimal character string to its 32-bit binary IP address, and if this fails, assume the character string is a hostname. Unfortunately this library function returns –1 to indicate an error (such as a character other than a digit or decimal point in the string), but the limited broadcast address (255.255.255.255) also converts into –1. Most programs then assume that the character string is a hostname, look it up using the DNS (Chapter 14), and end up printing an error such as "unknown host."

If we fix this programming shortfall in the `ping` program, however, the results are often not what we expect. On six different systems tested by the author, only one handled this as expected and generated a broadcast packet on the local cable. Most looked up the IP address 255.255.255.255 in the routing table, applied the default route, and sent a unicast packet to the default router. Eventually the packet was thrown away.

A subnet-directed broadcast is what we should be using. Indeed, in Section 6.3 we sent datagrams to the IP address 140.252.13.63 for the bottom Ethernet in our test network (inside front cover), and got replies from all the hosts on the Ethernet. The subnet-directed broadcast address associated with each interface is the value used with the `ifconfig` command (Section 3.8). If we ping that address, the result is what we expect:

```
sun % arp -a                                    ARP cache is empty

sun % ping 140.252.13.63
PING 140.252.13.63: 56 data bytes
64 bytes from sun (140.252.13.33): icmp_seq=0. time=4. ms
64 bytes from bsdi (140.252.13.35): icmp_seq=0. time=172. ms
64 bytes from svr4 (140.252.13.34): icmp_seq=0. time=192. ms

64 bytes from sun (140.252.13.33): icmp_seq=1. time=1. ms
64 bytes from bsdi (140.252.13.35): icmp_seq=1. time=52. ms
64 bytes from svr4 (140.252.13.34): icmp_seq=1. time=90. ms
^?                                              type interrupt key to stop
----140.252.13.63 PING Statistics----
2 packets transmitted, 6 packets received, -200% packet loss
round-trip (ms)  min/avg/max = 1/85/192

sun % arp -a                                    check ARP cache again
svr4 (140.252.13.34) at 0:0:c0:c2:9b:26
bsdi (140.252.13.35) at 0:0:c0:6f:2d:40
```

IP looks at the destination address (140.252.13.63), determines that it is the subnet-directed broadcast address, and sends the datagram to the link-layer broadcast address.

We mentioned in Section 6.3 that this type of broadcast means all the hosts on the local network, including the sender. We see here that we do get a reply from the sending host (`sun`) in addition to the other hosts on the cable.

In this example we've also shown the ARP cache before and after the `ping` of the broadcast address. This is to show the interaction between broadcasting and ARP. The ARP cache is empty before we execute `ping`, but full afterward. (That is, there is one entry for every other host on the cable that responded to the echo request.) How did this happen when we said that the Ethernet frame is sent to the link-layer broadcast address (0xffffffff)? The sending of these frames by sun does not require ARP.

If we watch ping using tcpdump, we see that it is the recipients of the broadcast frames that generate an ARP request to sun, before they can send their reply. This is because the reply is unicast. We said in Section 4.5 that the receiver of an ARP request (sun in this example) normally adds the requestor's IP address and hardware address to its ARP cache, in addition to sending an ARP reply. This is on the assumption that if the requestor is about to send us a packet, we'll probably want to send something back.

Our use of ping is somewhat special because the type of programming interface that it uses (called "raw sockets" on most Unix implementations) always allows a datagram to be sent to the broadcast address. What if we use an application that was not designed to support broadcasting, such as TFTP? (We cover TFTP in more detail in Chapter 15.)

```
bsdi % tftp                              start the client
tftp> connect 140.252.13.63              specify the IP address of the server
tftp> get temp.foo                       and try to fetch a file from the server
tftp: sendto: Permission denied
tftp> quit                               terminate the client
```

Here we get an error immediately, and nothing is sent on the cable. What's happening here is that the sockets API doesn't allow a process to send a UDP datagram to the broadcast address unless the process specifically states that it plans to broadcast. This is intended to prevent users from mistakenly specifying a broadcast address (as we did here) when the application was never intended to broadcast.

> With the sockets API the application must set the SO_BROADCAST socket option before sending a UDP datagram to a broadcast address.
>
> Not all systems enforce this restriction. Some implementations allow any process to broadcast UDP datagrams, without requiring the process to say so. Others are more restrictive and require a process to have superuser privileges to broadcast.

The next question is whether directed broadcasts are forwarded or not. Some kernels and routers have an option to enable or disable this feature. (See Appendix E.)

If we enable this feature on our router bsdi and run ping from the host slip, we can see if the subnet-directed broadcasts are forwarded by bsdi. Forwarding a directed broadcast means the router takes the incoming unicast datagram, determines that the destination address is the directed broadcast for one of its interfaces, and then forwards the datagram onto the appropriate network using a link-layer broadcast.

```
slip % ping 140.252.13.63
PING 140.252.13.63 (140.252.13.63): 56 data bytes
64 bytes from 140.252.13.35: icmp_seq=0 ttl=255 time=190 ms
64 bytes from 140.252.13.33: icmp_seq=0 ttl=254 time=280 ms (DUP!)
64 bytes from 140.252.13.34: icmp_seq=0 ttl=254 time=360 ms (DUP!)

64 bytes from 140.252.13.35: icmp_seq=1 ttl=255 time=180 ms
64 bytes from 140.252.13.33: icmp_seq=1 ttl=254 time=270 ms (DUP!)
64 bytes from 140.252.13.34: icmp_seq=1 ttl=254 time=360 ms (DUP!)
^?                                       type interrupt key to stop
```

```
--- 140.252.13.63 ping statistics ---
3 packets transmitted, 2 packets received, +4 duplicates, 33% packet loss
round-trip min/avg/max = 180/273/360 ms
```

We see that this does indeed work. We also see that the BSD `ping` program checks for duplicate sequence numbers and prints `DUP!` when this occurs. It normally means a packet was duplicated somewhere, but here we expect to see this, since we sent the requests to a broadcast address.

We can also run this test from a host much farther away from the network to which the broadcast is directed. If we run `ping` from the host `vangogh.cs.berkeley.edu` (14 hops away from our network), it still works if the router `sun` is configured to forward directed broadcasts. In this case the IP datagrams (carrying the ICMP echo requests) are forwarded by every router in the path as a normal datagram. None of them knows that it's really a directed broadcast. The next to last router, `netb`, thinks it's for the host with an ID of 63, and forwards it to `sun`. It is the router `sun` that detects that the destination IP address is really the broadcast address of an attached interface, and turns the datagram into a link-layer broadcast on that network.

Broadcasting is a feature that should be used with great care. In many cases IP multicasting will prove to be a better solution.

12.4 Multicasting

IP multicasting provides two services for an application.

1. Delivery to multiple destinations. There are many applications that deliver information to multiple recipients: interactive conferencing and dissemination of mail or news to multiple recipients, for example. Without multicasting these types of services tend to use TCP today (delivering a separate copy to each destination). Even with multicasting, some of these applications might continue to use TCP for its reliability.

2. Solicitation of servers by clients. A diskless workstation, for example, needs to locate a bootstrap server. Today this is provided using a broadcast (as we'll see with BOOTP in Chapter 16), but a multicast solution would impose less overhead on the hosts that don't provide the service.

In this section we'll take a look at multicast addresses, and the next chapter looks at the protocol used by multicasting hosts and routers (IGMP).

Multicast Group Addresses

Figure 12.2 shows the format of a class D IP address.

					28 bits
Class D	1	1	1	0	multicast group ID

Figure 12.2 Format of a class D IP address.

Unlike the other three classes of IP addresses (A, B, and C), which we showed in Figure 1.5, the 28 bits allocated for the multicast group ID have no further structure.

A *multicast group address* is the combination of the high-order 4 bits of 1110 and the multicast group ID. These are normally written as dotted-decimal numbers and are in the range 224.0.0.0 through 239.255.255.255.

The set of hosts listening to a particular IP multicast address is called a *host group*. A host group can span multiple networks. Membership in a host group is dynamic—hosts may join and leave host groups at will. There is no restriction on the number of hosts in a group, and a host does not have to belong to a group to send a message to that group.

Some multicast group addresses are assigned as well-known addresses by the IANA (Internet Assigned Numbers Authority). These are called *permanent host groups*. This is similar to the well-known TCP and UDP port numbers. Similarly, these well-known multicast addresses are listed in the latest Assigned Numbers RFC. Notice that it is the multicast address of the group that is permanent, not the membership of the group.

For example, 224.0.0.1 means "all systems on this subnet," and 224.0.0.2 means "all routers on this subnet." The multicast address 224.0.1.1 is for NTP, the Network Time Protocol, 224.0.0.9 is for RIP-2 (Section 10.5), and 224.0.1.2 is for SGI's (Silicon Graphics) dogfight application.

Converting Multicast Group Addresses to Ethernet Addresses

The IANA owns an Ethernet address block, which in hexadecimal is `00:00:5e`. This is the high-order 24 bits of the Ethernet address, meaning that this block includes addresses in the range `00:00:5e:00:00:00` through `00:00:5e:ff:ff:ff`. The IANA allocates half of this block for multicast addresses. Given that the first byte of any Ethernet address must be `01` to specify a multicast address, this means the Ethernet addresses corresponding to IP multicasting are in the range `01:00:5e:00:00:00` through `01:00:5e:7f:ff:ff`.

> Our notation here uses the Internet standard bit order, for a CSMA/CD or token bus network, as the bits appear in memory. This is what most programmers and system administrators deal with. The IEEE documentation uses the transmission order of the bits. The Assigned Numbers RFC gives additional details on the differences between these representations.

This allocation allows for 23 bits in the Ethernet address to correspond to the IP multicast group ID. The mapping places the low-order 23 bits of the multicast group ID into these 23 bits of the Ethernet address. This is shown in Figure 12.3.

Since the upper 5 bits of the multicast group ID are ignored in this mapping, it is not unique. Thirty-two different multicast group IDs map to each Ethernet address. For example, the multicast addresses 224.128.64.32 (hex `e0.80.40.20`) and 224.0.64.32 (hex `e0.00.40.20`) both map into the Ethernet address `01:00:5e:00:40:20`.

Since the mapping is not unique, it implies that the device driver or the IP module in Figure 12.1 must perform filtering, since the interface card may receive multicast frames in which the host is really not interested. Also, if the interface card doesn't

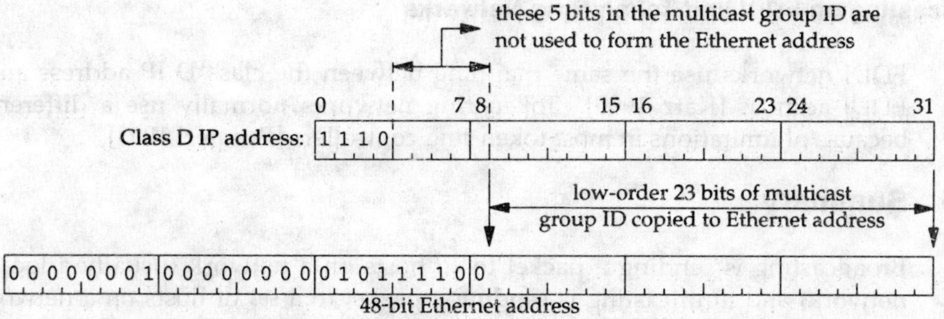

Figure 12.3 Mapping of a class D IP address into Ethernet multicast address.

provide adequate filtering of multicast frames, the device driver may have to receive all multicast frames, and perform the filtering itself.

> LAN interface cards tend to come in two varieties. One type performs multicast filtering based on the hash value of the multicast hardware address, which means some unwanted frames can always get through. The other type has a small, fixed number of multicast addresses to listen for, meaning that when the host needs to receive more multicast addresses than are supported, the interface must be put into a "multicast promiscuous" mode. Hence, both types of interfaces still require that the device driver perform checking that the received frame is really wanted.
>
> Even if the interface performs perfect multicast filtering (based on the 48-bit hardware address), since the mapping from a class D IP address to a 48-bit hardware address is not one-to-one, filtering is still required.
>
> Despite this imperfect address mapping and hardware filtering, multicasting is still better than broadcasting.

Multicasting on a single physical network is simple. The sending process specifies a destination IP address that is a multicast address, the device driver converts this to the corresponding Ethernet address, and sends it. The receiving processes must notify their IP layers that they want to receive datagrams destined for a given multicast address, and the device driver must somehow enable reception of these multicast frames. This is called "joining a multicast group." (The reason we use the plural "receiving processes" is because there are normally multiple receivers for a given multicast message, either on the same host or on multiple hosts, which is why we're using multicasting in the first place.) When a multicast datagram is received by a host, it must deliver a copy to all the processes that belong to that multicast group. This is different from UDP where a single process receives an incoming unicast UDP datagram. With multicasting it is possible for multiple processes on a given host to belong to the same multicast group.

But complications arise when we extend multicasting beyond a single physical network and pass multicast packets through routers. A protocol is needed for multicast routers to know if any hosts on a given physical network belong to a given multicast group. This protocol is called the *Internet Group Management Protocol* (IGMP) and is the topic of the next chapter.

Multicasting on FDDI and Token Ring Networks

FDDI networks use the same mapping between the class D IP address and the 48-bit FDDI address [Katz 1990]. Token ring networks normally use a different mapping, because of limitations in most token ring controllers [Pusateri 1993].

12.5 Summary

Broadcasting is sending a packet to *all* hosts on a network (usually a locally attached network) and multicasting is sending a packet to a *set* of hosts on a network. Basic to these two concepts is an understanding of the different types of filtering that occur when a received frame passes up a protocol stack. Each layer can discard a received packet for different reasons.

There are four types of broadcast addresses: limited, net-directed, subnet-directed, and all-subnets-directed. The most common is subnet-directed. The limited broadcast address is normally seen only when a system is bootstrapping.

Problems occur when trying to broadcast through routers, often because the router may not know the subnet mask of the destination network. The results depend on many factors: which type of broadcast address, configuration parameters, and so on.

A class D IP address is called a multicast group address. It is converted to an Ethernet address by placing its lower 23 bits into a fixed Ethernet address. The mapping is not unique, requiring additional filtering by one of the protocol modules.

Exercises

12.1 Does broadcasting increase the amount of network traffic?

12.2 Consider 50 hosts on an Ethernet: 20 running TCP/IP and 30 running some other protocol suite. How are broadcasts from one protocol suite handled by hosts running the other protocol suite?

12.3 You login to a Unix system that you've never used before and want to find the subnet-directed broadcast address for all attached interfaces that support broadcasting. How can you do this?

12.4 If we `ping` the broadcast address with a large packet size, as in

```
sun % ping 140.252.13.63 1472
PING 140.252.13.63: 1472 data bytes
1480 bytes from sun (140.252.13.33): icmp_seq=0. time=6. ms
1480 bytes from svr4 (140.252.13.34): icmp_seq=0. time=84. ms
1480 bytes from bsdi (140.252.13.35): icmp_seq=0. time=128. ms
```

it works, but increasing the packet size by 1 byte gives us the following error:

```
sun % ping 140.252.13.63 1473
PING 140.252.13.63: 1473 data bytes
sendto: Message too long
```

What's going on?

12.5 Redo Exercise 10.6 assuming the eight RIP messages are multicast instead of broadcast (assume RIP Version 2 is being used). What changes?

13

IGMP: Internet Group Management Protocol

13.1 Introduction

Section 12.4 provided an overview of IP multicasting and described how class D IP addresses are mapped into Ethernet addresses. We briefly mentioned how multicasting occurs on a single physical network, but said complications occur when multiple networks are involved and the multicast datagrams must pass through routers.

In this chapter we'll look at the *Internet Group Management Protocol* (IGMP), which is used by hosts and routers that support multicasting. It lets all the systems on a physical network know which hosts currently belong to which multicast groups. This information is required by the multicast routers, so they know which multicast datagrams to forward onto which interfaces. IGMP is defined in RFC 1112 [Deering 1989].

Like ICMP, IGMP is considered part of the IP layer. Also like ICMP, IGMP messages are transmitted in IP datagrams. Unlike other protocols that we've seen, IGMP has a fixed-size message, with no optional data. Figure 13.1 shows the encapsulation of an IGMP message within an IP datagram.

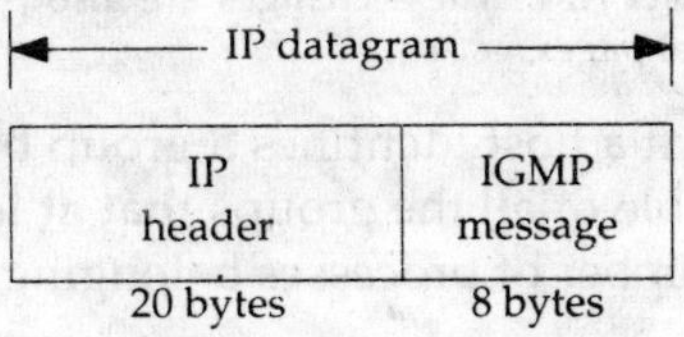

Figure 13.1 Encapsulation of an IGMP message within an IP datagram.

IGMP messages are specified in the IP datagram with a protocol value of 2.

13.2 IGMP Message

Figure 13.2 shows the format of the 8-byte IGMP message.

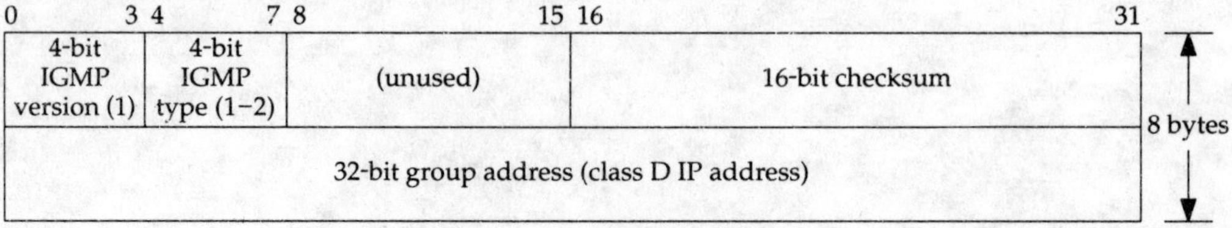

Figure 13.2 Format of fields in IGMP message.

The *IGMP version* is 1. An *IGMP type* of 1 is a query sent by a multicast router, and 2 is a response sent by a host. The *checksum* is calculated in the same manner as the ICMP checksum.

The *group address* is a class D IP address. In a query the group address is set to 0, and in a report it contains the group address being reported. We'll say more about it in the next section when we see how IGMP operates.

13.3 IGMP Protocol

Joining a Multicast Group

Fundamental to multicasting is the concept of a process joining a multicast group on a given interface on a host. (We use the term *process* to mean a program being executed by the operating system.) Membership in a multicast group on a given interface is dynamic—it changes over time as processes join and leave the group.

We imply here that a process must have a way of joining a multicast group on a given interface. A process can also leave a multicast group that it previously joined. These are required parts of any API on a host that supports multicasting. We use the qualifier "interface" because membership in a group is associated with an interface. A process can join the same group on multiple interfaces.

> The release of IP multicasting for Berkeley Unix from Stanford University details these changes for the sockets API. These changes are also provided in Solaris 2.x and documented in the `ip(7)` manual pages.

Implied here is that a host identifies a group by the group address *and* the interface. A host must keep a table of all the groups that at least one process belongs to, and a reference count of the number of processes belonging to the group.

IGMP Reports and Queries

IGMP messages are used by multicast routers to keep track of group membership on each of the router's physically attached networks. The following rules apply.

1. A host sends an IGMP report when the first process joins a group. If multiple processes on a given host join the same group, only one report is sent, the first time a process joins that group. This report is sent out the same interface on which the process joined the group.
2. A host does not send a report when processes leave a group, even when the last process leaves a group. The host knows that there are no members in a given group, so when it receives the next query (next step), it won't report the group.
3. A multicast router sends an IGMP query at regular intervals to see if any hosts still have processes belonging to any groups. The router must send one query out each interface. The group address in the query is 0 since the router expects one response from a host for every group that contains one or more members on that host.
4. A host responds to an IGMP query by sending one IGMP report for each group that still contains at least one process.

Using these queries and reports, a multicast router keeps a table of which of its interfaces have one or more hosts in a multicast group. When the router receives a multicast datagram to forward, it forwards the datagram (using the corresponding multicast link-layer address) only out the interfaces that still have hosts with processes belonging to that group.

Figure 13.3 shows these two IGMP messages, reports sent by hosts, and queries sent by routers. The router is asking each host to identify each group on that interface.

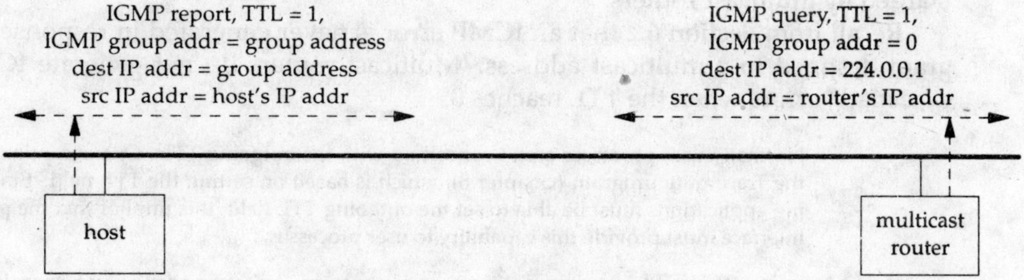

Figure 13.3 IGMP reports and queries.

We talk about the TTL field later in this section.

Implementation Details

There are many implementation details in this protocol that improve its efficiency. First, when a host sends an initial IGMP report (when the first process joins a group), there's no guarantee that the report is delivered (since IP is used as the delivery service). Another report is sent at a later time. This later time is chosen by the host to be a random value between 0 and 10 seconds.

Next, when a host receives a query from a router it doesn't respond immediately, but schedules the responses for later times. (We use the plural "responses" because the host must send one report for each group that contains one or more members.) Since multiple hosts can be sending a report for the same group, each schedules its response using random delays. Also realize that all the hosts on a physical network receive all the reports from other hosts in the same group, because the destination address of the report in Figure 13.3 is the group's address. This means that, if a host is scheduled to send a report, but receives a copy of the same report from another host, the response can be canceled. This is because a multicast router doesn't care how many hosts belong to the group—only whether at least one host belongs to the group. Indeed, a multicast router doesn't even care which host belongs to a group. It only needs to know that at least one host belongs to a group on a given interface.

On a single physical network without any multicast routers, the only IGMP traffic is the reports issued by the hosts that support IP multicasting, when the host joins a new group.

Time-to-Live Field

In Figure 13.3 we noted that the TTL field of the reports and queries is set to 1. This refers to the normal TTL field in the IP header. A multicast datagram with an initial TTL of 0 is restricted to the same host. By default, multicast datagrams are sent with a TTL of 1. This restricts the datagram to the same subnet. Higher TTLs can be forwarded by multicast routers.

Recall from Section 6.2 that an ICMP error is never generated in response to a datagram destined to a multicast address. Multicast routers do not generate ICMP "time exceeded" errors when the TTL reaches 0.

> Normally user processes aren't concerned with the outgoing TTL. One exception, however, is the Traceroute program (Chapter 8), which is based on setting the TTL field. Since multicasting applications must be able to set the outgoing TTL field, this implies that the programming interface must provide this capability to user processes.

By increasing the TTL an application can perform an *expanding ring search* for a particular server. The first multicast datagram is sent with a TTL of 1. If no response is received, a TTL of 2 is tried, then 3, and so on. In this way the application locates the closest server, in terms of hops.

The special range of addresses 224.0.0.0 through 224.0.0.255 is intended for applications that never need to multicast further than one hop. A multicast router should never forward a datagram with one of these addresses as the destination, regardless of the TTL.

All-Hosts Group

In Figure 13.3 we also indicated that the router's IGMP query is sent to the destination IP address of 224.0.0.1. This is called the *all-hosts* group address. It refers to all the multicast-capable hosts and routers on a physical network. Each host automatically joins this multicast group on all multicast-capable interfaces, when the interface is initialized. Membership in this group is never reported.

13.4 An Example

Now that we've gone through some of the details of IP multicasting, let's take a look at the messages involved. We've added IP multicasting support to the host sun and will use some test programs provided with the multicasting software to see what happens.

First we'll use a modified version of the `netstat` command that reports multicast group membership for each interface. (We showed the standard `netstat -ni` output for this host in Section 3.9.) In the following output we show the lines corresponding to multicast groups in a bold font:

```
sun % netstat -nia
Name  Mtu   Network       Address            Ipkts Ierrs    Opkts Oerrs  Coll
le0   1500  140.252.13.  140.252.13.33        4370     0     4924     0     0
                          224.0.0.1
                          08:00:20:03:f6:42
                          01:00:5e:00:00:01
sl0   552   140.252.1    140.252.1.29        13587     0    15615     0     0
                          224.0.0.1
lo0   1536  127           127.0.0.1           1351     0     1351     0     0
                          224.0.0.1
```

The `-n` option prints IP addresses in numeric format (instead of trying to print them as names), `-i` prints the interface statistics, and `-a` reports on all configured interfaces.

The second line of output for `le0` (the Ethernet) shows that this interface belongs to the multicast group 224.0.0.1 ("all hosts"), and two lines later the corresponding Ethernet address is shown: `01:00:5e:00:00:01`. This is what we expect for the Ethernet address, given the mapping we described in Section 12.4. We also see that the other two interfaces that support multicasting, the SLIP link `sl0` and the loopback interface `lo0`, also belong to the all-hosts group.

We must also show the IP routing table, as the normal routing table is used for multicast datagrams. The bold entry shows that all datagrams for 224.0.0.0 are sent to the Ethernet:

```
sun % netstat -rn
Routing tables
Destination          Gateway              Flags   Refcnt Use    Interface
140.252.13.65        140.252.13.35        UGH     0      32     le0
127.0.0.1            127.0.0.1            UH      1      381    lo0
140.252.1.183        140.252.1.29         UH      0      6      sl0
default              140.252.1.183        UG      0      328    sl0
224.0.0.0            140.252.13.33        U       0      66     le0
140.252.13.32        140.252.13.33        U       8      5581   le0
```

If you compare this routing table to the one shown in Section 9.2 for the router sun, you'll see that the multicast entry is the only change.

We now run a test program that lets us join a multicast group on an interface. (We don't show any output for our use of this test program.) We join the group 224.1.2.3 on the Ethernet interface (140.252.13.33). Executing netstat shows that the kernel has joined the group, and again the Ethernet address is what we expect. We show the changes from the previous netstat output in a bold font:

```
sun % netstat -nia
Name  Mtu   Network       Address              Ipkts Ierrs  Opkts Oerrs  Coll
le0   1500  140.252.13.   140.252.13.33        4374     0    4929     0     0
                          224.1.2.3
                          224.0.0.1
                          08:00:20:03:f6:42
                          01:00:5e:01:02:03
                          01:00:5e:00:00:01
sl0   552   140.252.1     140.252.1.29        13862     0   15943     0     0
                          224.0.0.1
lo0   1536  127           127.0.0.1            1360     0    1360     0     0
                          224.0.0.1
```

We have shown the output again for the other two interfaces, sl0 and lo0, to reiterate that the multicast group is joined only on one interface.

Figure 13.4 shows the tcpdump output corresponding to the process joining the multicast group.

```
1  0.0              8:0:20:3:f6:42 1:0:5e:1:2:3 ip 60:
                    sun > 224.1.2.3: igmp report 224.1.2.3 [ttl 1]

2  6.94 (6.94)      8:0:20:3:f6:42 1:0:5e:1:2:3 ip 60:
                    sun > 224.1.2.3: igmp report 224.1.2.3 [ttl 1]
```

Figure 13.4 tcpdump output when a host joins a multicast group.

Line 1 occurs when the host joins the group. The next line is the delayed report that we said is sent at some random time up to 10 seconds afterward.

We have shown the hardware addresses in these two lines, to verify that the Ethernet destination address is the correct multicast address. We can also see that the source IP address is the one corresponding to sun, and the destination IP address is the multicast group address. We can also see that the reported address is that same multicast group address.

Finally, we note that the TTL is 1, as specified. tcpdump prints the TTL in square brackets when its value is 0 or 1. This is because the TTL is normally greater than this. With multicasting, however, we expect to see lots of IP datagrams with a TTL of 1.

Implied in this output is that a multicast router must receive *all* multicast datagrams on all its interfaces. The router has no idea which multicast groups the hosts might join.

Multicast Router Example

Let's continue the previous example, but we'll also start a multicast routing daemon on the host sun. Our interest here is not the details of multicast routing protocols, but to see the IGMP queries and reports that are exchanged. Even though the multicast routing daemon is running on the only host that supports multicasting (sun), all the queries and reports are multicast on the Ethernet, so we can see them on any other system on the Ethernet.

Before starting the routing daemon we joined another multicast group: 224.9.9.9. Figure 13.5 shows the output.

```
 1    0.0                   sun > 224.0.0.4: igmp report 224.0.0.4

 2    0.00 (   0.00)        sun > 224.0.0.1: igmp query
 3    5.10 (   5.10)        sun > 224.9.9.9: igmp report 224.9.9.9

 4    5.22 (   0.12)        sun > 224.0.0.1: igmp query
 5    7.90 (   2.68)        sun > 224.1.2.3: igmp report 224.1.2.3
 6    8.50 (   0.60)        sun > 224.0.0.4: igmp report 224.0.0.4
 7   11.70 (   3.20)        sun > 224.9.9.9: igmp report 224.9.9.9

 8  125.51 (113.81)         sun > 224.0.0.1: igmp query
 9  125.70 (   0.19)        sun > 224.9.9.9: igmp report 224.9.9.9
10  128.50 (   2.80)        sun > 224.1.2.3: igmp report 224.1.2.3
11  129.10 (   0.60)        sun > 224.0.0.4: igmp report 224.0.0.4

12  247.82 (118.72)         sun > 224.0.0.1: igmp query
13  248.09 (   0.27)        sun > 224.1.2.3: igmp report 224.1.2.3
14  248.69 (   0.60)        sun > 224.0.0.4: igmp report 224.0.0.4
15  255.29 (   6.60)        sun > 224.9.9.9: igmp report 224.9.9.9
```

Figure 13.5 tcpdump output while multicast routing daemon is running.

We have not included the Ethernet addresses in this output, because we've already verified that they are what we expect. We've also deleted the notation that the TTL equals 1, because again that's what we expect.

Line 1 is output when the routing daemon starts. It sends a report that it has joined the group 224.0.0.4. Multicast address 224.0.0.4 is a well-known address used by DVMRP (Distance Vector Multicast Routing Protocol), the protocol currently used for multicast routing. (DVMRP is defined in RFC 1075 [Waitzman, Partridge, and Deering 1988].)

When the daemon starts it also sends out a query (line 2). The destination IP address of the query is 224.0.0.1 (all-hosts), as shown in Figure 13.3.

The first report (line 3) is received about 5 seconds later, for group 224.9.9.9. This is the only report received before another query is sent (line 4). These two queries (lines 2 and 4) occur rapidly when the daemon starts up, as it tries to build its multicast routing table.

Lines 5, 6, and 7 are what we expect: one report from the host sun for each group to which it belongs. Notice that the group 224.0.0.4 is reported, in addition to the two groups that we explicitly joined, because as long as the routing daemon is running, it belongs to this group.

The next query on line 8 occurs about 2 minutes after the previous query. Again it elicits the three reports we expect (lines 9, 10, and 11). The reports are in a different order this time, as expected, since the time between receiving the query and sending the report should be randomized.

The final query that we show occurs about 2 minutes after the previous query, and again we have the expected responses.

13.5 Summary

Multicasting is a way to send a message to multiple recipients. In many applications it is better than broadcasting, since multicasting imposes less overhead on hosts that are not participating in the communication. The simple host membership reporting protocol (IGMP) is the basic building block for multicasting.

Multicasting on a LAN or across closely connected LANs uses the techniques we've described in this chapter. Since broadcasting is often restricted to a single LAN, multicasting could be used instead of broadcasting for many applications that use broadcasting today.

A problem that has not been completely solved, however, is multicasting across wide area networks. [Deering and Cheriton 1990] propose extensions to common routing protocols to support multicasting. Section 9.13 of [Perlman 1992] discusses some of the problems with multicasting across WANs.

[Casner and Deering 1992] describe the delivery of audio for an IETF meeting across the Internet using multicasting and a virtual network called the *MBONE* (multicasting backbone).

Exercises

13.1 We said that hosts schedule IGMP reports with random delays. How can the hosts on a LAN try to ensure that no two hosts generate the same random delay?

13.2 In [Casner and Deering 1992] they mention that UDP lacks two features needed for sending audio samples across the MBONE: detection of packet reordering and detection of duplicate packets. How could you add these capabilities above UDP?

14

DNS: The Domain Name System

14.1 Introduction

The *Domain Name System*, or *DNS*, is a distributed database that is used by TCP/IP applications to map between hostnames and IP addresses, and to provide electronic mail routing information. We use the term *distributed* because no single site on the Internet knows all the information. Each site (university department, campus, company, or department within a company, for example) maintains its own database of information and runs a server program that other systems across the Internet (clients) can query. The DNS provides the protocol that allows clients and servers to communicate with each other.

From an application's point of view, access to the DNS is through a *resolver*. On Unix hosts the resolver is accessed primarily through two library functions, `gethostbyname`(3) and `gethostbyaddr`(3), which are linked with the application when the application is built. The first takes a hostname and returns an IP address, and the second takes an IP address and looks up a hostname. The resolver contacts one or more *name servers* to do the mapping.

In Figure 4.2 (p. 55) we showed that the resolver is normally part of the application. It is not part of the operating system kernel as are the TCP/IP protocols. Another fundamental point from this figure is that an application must convert a hostname to an IP address before it can ask TCP to open a connection or send a datagram using UDP. The TCP/IP protocols within the kernel know nothing about the DNS.

In this chapter we'll take a look at how resolvers communicate with name servers using the TCP/IP protocols (mainly UDP). We do not cover all the administrative details of running a name server or all the options available with resolvers and servers. These details can fill an entire book. (See [Albitz and Liu 1992] for all the details on the care and feeding of the standard Unix resolver and name server.)

RFC 1034 [Mockapetris 1987a] specifies the concepts and facilities provided by the DNS, and RFC 1035 [Mockapetris 1987b] details the implementation and specification. The most commonly used implementation of the DNS, both resolver and name server, is called BIND—the Berkeley Internet Name Domain server. The server is called named. An analysis of the wide-area network traffic generated by the DNS is given in [Danzig, Obraczka, and Kumar 1992].

14.2 DNS Basics

The DNS name space is hierarchical, similar to the Unix filesystem. Figure 14.1 shows this hierarchical organization.

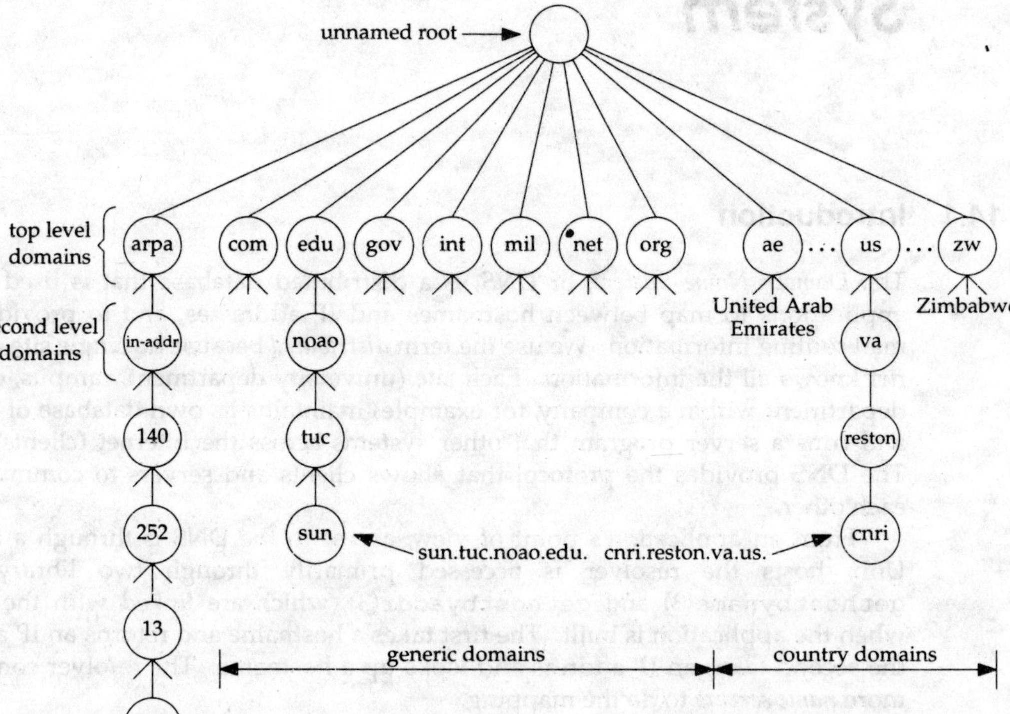

Figure 14.1 Hierarchical organization of the DNS.

Every node (circles in Figure 14.1) has a *label* of up to 63 characters. The root of the tree is a special node with a null label. Any comparison of labels considers uppercase and lowercase characters the same. The *domain name* of any node in the tree is the list of labels, starting at that node, working up to the root, using a period ("dot") to separate the labels. (Note that this is different from the Unix filesystem, which forms a pathname by starting at the top and going down the tree.) Every node in the tree must have a unique domain name, but the same label can be used at different points in the tree.

A domain name that ends with a period is called an *absolute domain name* or a *fully qualified domain name* (FQDN). An example is `sun.tuc.noao.edu.`. If the domain name does not end with a period, it is assumed that the name needs to be completed. How the name is completed depends on the DNS software being used. If the uncompleted name consists of two or more labels, it might be considered to be complete; otherwise a local addition might be added to the right of the name. For example, the name `sun` might be completed by adding the local suffix `.tuc.noao.edu.`.

The top-level domains are divided into three areas:

1. `arpa` is a special domain used for address-to-name mappings. (We describe this in Section 14.5.)
2. The seven 3-character domains are called the *generic* domains. Some texts call these the *organizational* domains.
3. All the 2-character domains are based on the country codes found in ISO 3166. These are called the *country* domains, or the *geographical* domains.

Figure 14.2 lists the normal classification of the seven generic domains.

Domain	Description
com	commercial organizations
edu	educational institutions
gov	other U.S. governmental organizations
int	international organizations
mil	U.S. military
net	networks
org	other organizations

Figure 14.2 The 3-character generic domains.

DNS folklore says that the 3-character generic domains are only for U.S. organizations, and the 2-character country domains for everyone else, but this is false. There are many non-U.S. organizations in the generic domains, and many U.S. organizations in the `.us` country domain. (RFC 1480 [Cooper and Postel 1993] describes the `.us` domain in more detail.) The only generic domains that are restricted to the United States are `.gov` and `.mil`.

Many countries form second-level domains beneath their 2-character country code similar to the generic domains: `.ac.uk`, for example, is for academic institutions in the United Kingdom and `.co.uk` is for commercial organizations in the United Kingdom.

One important feature of the DNS that isn't shown in figures such as Figure 14.1 is the delegation of responsibility within the DNS. No single entity manages every label in the tree. Instead, one entity (the NIC) maintains a portion of the tree (the top-level domains) and delegates responsibility to others for specific zones.

A *zone* is a subtree of the DNS tree that is administered separately. A common zone is a second-level domain, noao.edu, for example. Many second-level domains then divide their zone into smaller zones. For example, a university might divide itself into zones based on departments, and a company might divide itself into zones based on branch offices or internal divisions.

If you are familiar with the Unix filesystem, notice that the division of the DNS tree into zones is similar to the division of a logical Unix filesystem into physical disk partitions. Just as we can't tell from Figure 14.1 where the zones of authority lie, we can't tell from a similar picture of a Unix filesystem which directories are on which disk partitions.

Once the authority for a zone is delegated, it is up to the person responsible for the zone to provide multiple *name servers* for that zone. Whenever a new system is installed in a zone, the DNS administrator for the zone allocates a name and an IP address for the new system and enters these into the name server's database. This is where the need for delegation becomes obvious. At a small university, for example, one person could do this each time a new system was added, but in a large university the responsibility would have to be delegated (probably by departments), since one person couldn't keep up with the work.

A name server is said to have authority for one zone or multiple zones. The person responsible for a zone must provide a *primary name server* for that zone and one or more *secondary name servers*. The primary and secondaries must be independent and redundant servers so that availability of name service for the zone isn't affected by a single point of failure.

The main difference between a primary and secondary is that the primary loads all the information for the zone from disk files, while the secondaries obtain all the information from the primary. When a secondary obtains the information from its primary we call this a *zone transfer*.

When a new host is added to a zone, the administrator adds the appropriate information (name and IP address minimally) to a disk file on the system running the primary. The primary name server is then notified to reread its configuration files. The secondaries query the primary on a regular basis (normally every 3 hours) and if the primary contains newer data, the secondary obtains the new data using a zone transfer.

What does a name server do when it doesn't contain the information requested? It must contact another name server. (This is the *distributed* nature of the DNS.) Not every name server, however, knows how to contact every other name server. Instead every name server must know how to contact the *root name servers*. As of April 1993 there were eight root servers and all the primary servers must know the IP address of each root server. (These IP addresses are contained in the primary's configuration files. The primary servers must know the IP addresses of the root servers, not their DNS names.) The root servers then know the name and location (i.e., the IP address) of each authoritative name server for all the second-level domains. This implies an iterative process: the requesting name server must contact a root server. The root server tells the requesting server to contact another server, and so on. We'll look into this procedure with some examples later in this chapter.

You can fetch the current list of root servers using anonymous FTP. Obtain the file `netinfo/root-servers.txt` from either `ftp.rs.internic.net` or `nic.ddn.mil`.

A fundamental property of the DNS is *caching*. That is, when a name server receives information about a mapping (say, the IP address of a hostname) it caches that information so that a later query for the same mapping can use the cached result and not result in additional queries to other servers. Section 14.7 shows an example of caching.

14.3 DNS Message Format

There is one DNS message defined for both queries and responses. Figure 14.3 shows the overall format of the message.

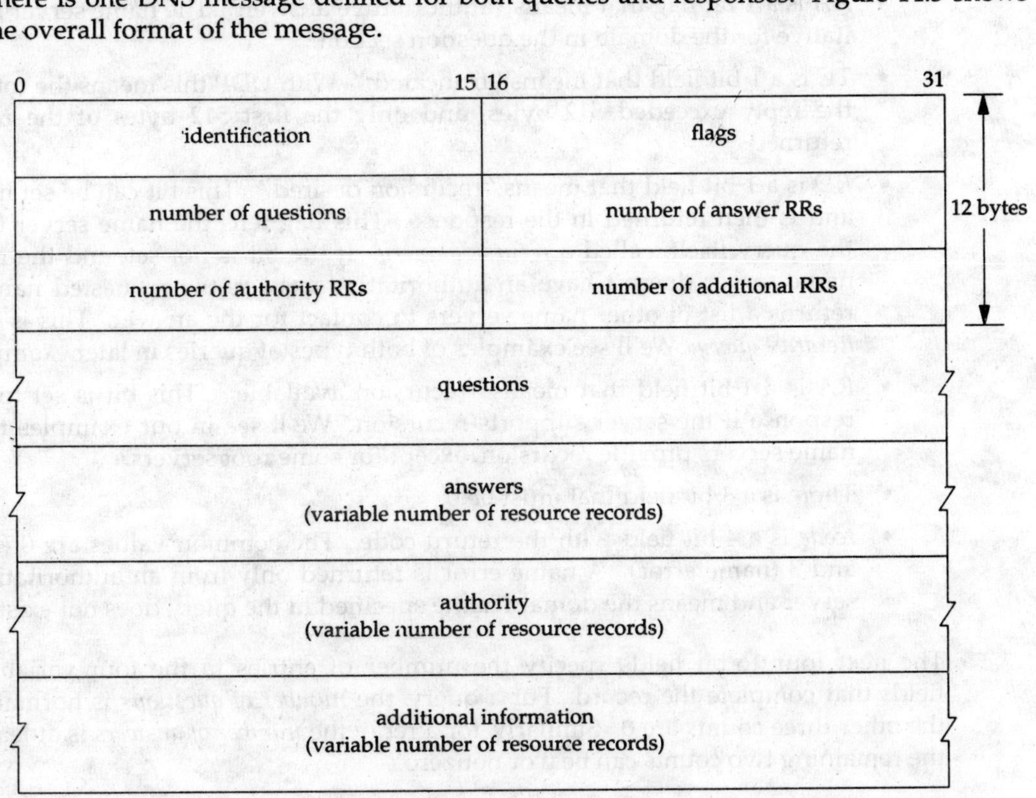

Figure 14.3 General format of DNS queries and responses.

The message has a fixed 12-byte header followed by four variable-length fields.

The *identification* is set by the client and returned by the server. It lets the client match responses to requests.

The 16-bit *flags* field is divided into numerous pieces, as shown in Figure 14.4.

QR	opcode	AA	TC	RD	RA	(zero)	rcode
1	4	1	1	1	1	3	4

Figure 14.4 *flags* field in the DNS header.

We'll start at the leftmost bit and describe each field.

- *QR* is a 1-bit field: 0 means the message is a query, 1 means it's a response.
- *opcode* is a 4-bit field. The normal value is 0 (a standard query). Other values are 1 (an inverse query) and 2 (server status request).
- *AA* is a 1-bit flag that means "authoritative answer." The name server is authoritative for the domain in the question section.
- *TC* is a 1-bit field that means "truncated." With UDP this means the total size of the reply exceeded 512 bytes, and only the first 512 bytes of the reply was returned.
- *RD* is a 1-bit field that means "recursion desired." This bit can be set in a query and is then returned in the response. This flag tells the name server to handle the query itself, called a *recursive query*. If the bit is not set, and the requested name server doesn't have an authoritative answer, the requested name server returns a list of other name servers to contact for the answer. This is called an *iterative query*. We'll see examples of both types of queries in later examples.
- *RA* is a 1-bit field that means "recursion available." This bit is set to 1 in the response if the server supports recursion. We'll see in our examples that most name servers provide recursion, except for some root servers.
- There is a 3-bit field that must be 0.
- *rcode* is a 4-bit field with the return code. The common values are 0 (no error) and 3 (name error). A name error is returned only from an authoritative name server and means the domain name specified in the query does not exist.

The next four 16-bit fields specify the number of entries in the four variable-length fields that complete the record. For a query, the *number of questions* is normally 1 and the other three counts are 0. Similarly, for a reply the *number of answers* is at least 1, and the remaining two counts can be 0 or nonzero.

Question Portion of DNS Query Message

The format of each question in the *question* section is shown in Figure 14.5. There is normally just one question.

The *query name* is the name being looked up. It is a sequence of one or more labels. Each *label* begins with a 1-byte count that specifies the number of bytes that follow. The name is terminated with a byte of 0, which is a label with a length of 0, which is the label of the root. Each count byte must be in the range of 0 to 63, since labels are limited

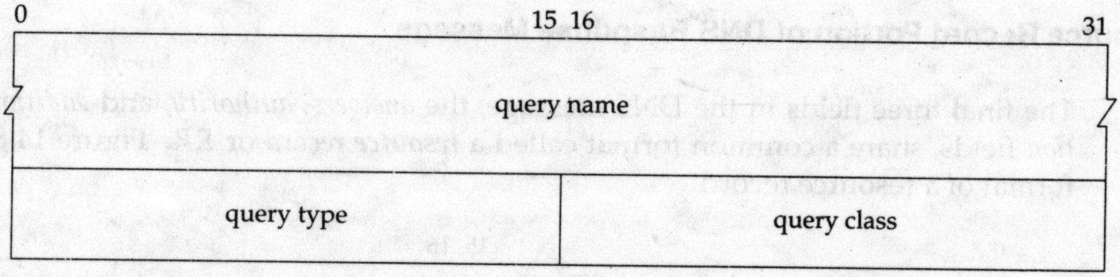

Figure 14.5 Format of *question* portion of DNS query message.

to 63 bytes. (We'll see later in this section that a count byte with the two high-order bits turned on, values 192 to 255, is used with a compression scheme.) Unlike many other message formats that we've encountered, this field is allowed to end on a boundary other than a 32-bit boundary. No padding is used.

Figure 14.6 shows how the domain name `gemini.tuc.noao.edu` is stored.

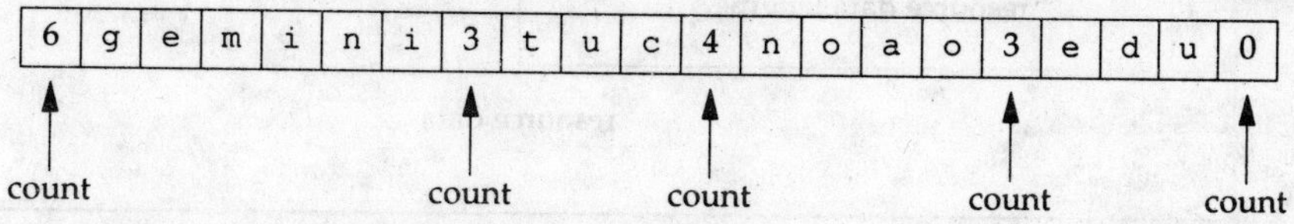

Figure 14.6 Representation of the domain name `gemini.tuc.noao.edu`.

Each question has a *query type* and each response (called a resource record, which we talk about below) has a *type*. There are about 20 different values, some of which are now obsolete. Figure 14.7 shows some of these values. The query type is a superset of the type: two of the values we show can be used only in questions.

Name	Numeric value	Description	*type?*	*query type?*
A	1	IP address	•	•
NS	2	name server	•	•
CNAME	5	canonical name	•	•
PTR	12	pointer record	•	•
HINFO	13	host info	•	•
MX	15	mail exchange record	•	•
AXFR	252	request for zone transfer		•
* or ANY	255	request for all records		•

Figure 14.7 *type* and *query type* values for DNS questions and responses.

The most common query type is an A type, which means an IP address is desired for the *query name*. A PTR query requests the names corresponding to an IP address. This is a pointer query that we describe in Section 14.5. We describe the other query types in Section 14.6.

The *query class* is normally 1, meaning Internet address. (Some other non-IP values are also supported at some locations.)

Resource Record Portion of DNS Response Message

The final three fields in the DNS message, the *answers, authority,* and *additional information* fields, share a common format called a *resource record* or *RR*. Figure 14.8 shows the format of a resource record.

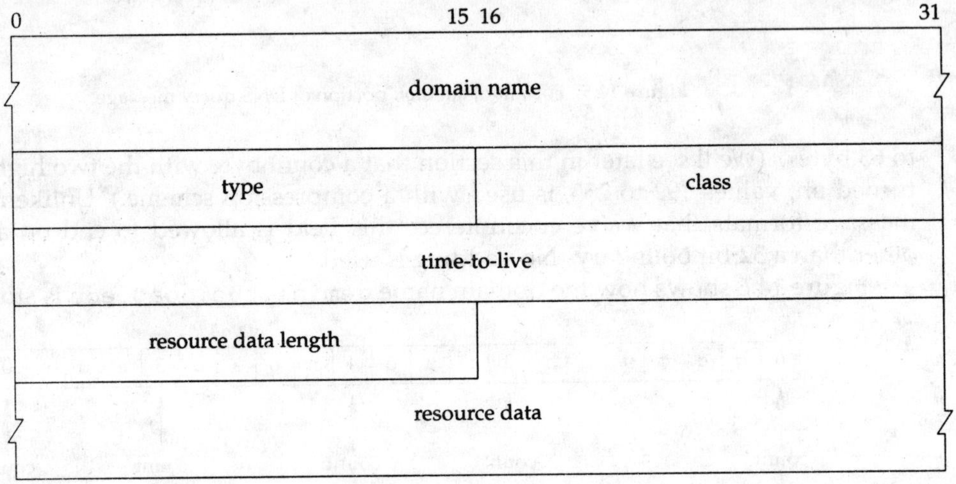

Figure 14.8 Format of DNS resource record.

The *domain name* is the name to which the following resource data corresponds. It is in the same format as we described earlier for the *query name* field (Figure 14.6).

The *type* specifies one of the RR type codes. These are the same as the *query type* values that we described earlier. The *class* is normally 1 for Internet data.

The *time-to-live* field is the number of seconds that the RR can be cached by the client. RRs often have a TTL of 2 days.

The *resource data length* specifies the amount of *resource data*. The format of this data depends on the *type*. For a type of 1 (an A record) the resource data is a 4-byte IP address.

Now that we've described the basic format of the DNS queries and responses, we'll see what is passed in the packets by watching some exchanges using `tcpdump`.

14.4 A Simple Example

Let's start with a simple example to see the communication between a resolver and a name server. We'll run the Telnet client on the host `sun` to the host `gemini`, connecting to the daytime server:

```
sun % telnet gemini daytime
Trying 140.252.1.11 ...                  first three lines of output are from Telnet client
Connected to gemini.tuc.noao.edu.
Escape character is '^]'.
Wed Mar 24 10:44:17 1993                 this is the output from the daytime server
Connection closed by foreign host.       and this is from the Telnet client
```

For this example we direct the resolver on the host sun (where the Telnet client is run) to use the name server on the host noao.edu (140.252.1.54). Figure 14.9 shows the arrangement of the three systems.

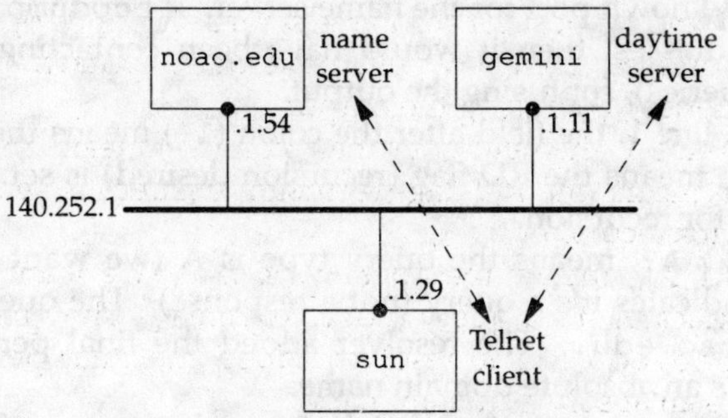

Figure 14.9 Systems being used for simple DNS example.

As we've mentioned before, the resolver is part of the client, and the resolver contacts a name server to obtain the IP address before the TCP connection can be established between Telnet and the daytime server.

In this figure we've omitted the detail that the connection between sun and the 140.252.1 Ethernet is really a SLIP link (see the figure on the inside front cover) because that doesn't affect the discussion. We will, however, run tcpdump on the SLIP link to see the packets exchanged between the resolver and name server.

The file /etc/resolv.conf on the host sun tells the resolver what to do:

```
sun % cat /etc/resolv.conf
nameserver 140.252.1.54
domain tuc.noao.edu
```

The first line gives the IP address of the name server—the host noao.edu. Up to three nameserver lines can be specified, to provide backup in case one is down or unreachable. The domain line specifies the default domain. If the name being looked up is not a fully qualified domain name (it doesn't end with a period) then the default domain .tuc.noao.edu is appended to the name. This is why we can type telnet gemini instead of telnet gemini.tuc.noao.edu.

Figure 14.10 shows the packet exchange between the resolver and name server.

```
1  0.0                      140.252.1.29.1447 > 140.252.1.54.53: 1+ A?
                            gemini.tuc.noao.edu. (37)

2  0.290820 (0.2908)        140.252.1.54.53 > 140.252.1.29.1447: 1* 2/0/0 A
                            140.252.1.11 (69)
```

Figure 14.10 tcpdump output for name server query of the hostname gemini.tuc.noao.edu.

We've instructed tcpdump not to print domain names for the source and destination IP addresses of each IP datagram. Instead it prints 140.252.1.29 for the client (the resolver) and 140.252.1.54 for the name server. Port 1447 is the ephemeral port used by the client and 53 is the well-known port for the name server. If tcpdump had tried to print names instead of IP addresses, then it would have been contacting the same name server (doing pointer queries), confusing the output.

Starting with line 1, the field after the colon (1+) means the identification field is 1, and the plus sign means the RD flag (recursion desired) is set. We see that by default, the resolver asks for recursion.

The next field, A?, means the query type is A (we want an IP address), and the question mark indicates it's a query (not a response). The query name is printed next: gemini.tuc.noao.edu.. The resolver added the final period to the query name, indicating that it's an absolute domain name.

The length of user data in the UDP datagram is shown as 37 bytes: 12 bytes are the fixed-size header (Figure 14.3); 21 bytes for the query name (Figure 14.6), and 4 bytes for the query type and query class. The odd-length UDP datagram reiterates that there is no padding in the DNS messages.

Line 2 in the tcpdump output is the response from the name server and 1* is the identification field with the asterisk meaning the AA flag (authoritative answer) is set. (We expect this server, the primary server for the noao.edu domain, to be authoritative for names within its domain.)

The output 2/0/0 shows the number of resource records in the final three variable-length fields in the response: 2 answer RRs, 0 authority RRs, and 0 additional RRs. tcpdump only prints the first answer, which in this case has a type of A (IP address) with a value of 140.252.1.11.

Why do we get two answers to our query? Because the host gemini is multihomed. Two IP addresses are returned. Indeed, another useful tool with the DNS is a publicly available program named host. It lets us issue queries to a name server and see what comes back. If we run this program we'll see the two IP addresses for this host:

```
sun % host gemini
gemini.tuc.noao.edu      A        140.252.1.11
gemini.tuc.noao.edu      A        140.252.3.54
```

The first answer in Figure 14.10 and the first line of output from the host command are the IP address that shares the same subnet (140.252.1) as the requesting host. This is not an accident. If the name server and the host issuing the query are on the same network (or subnet), then BIND sorts the results so that addresses on common networks appear first.

We can still access the host `gemini` using the other address, but it might be less efficient. Using `traceroute` in this instance shows that the normal route from subnet 140.252.1 to 140.252.3 is not through the host `gemini`, but through another router that's connected to both networks. So in this case if we accessed `gemini` through the other IP address (140.252.3.54) all the packets would require an additional hop. We return to this example and explore the reason for the alternative route in Section 25.9, when we can use SNMP to look at a router's routing table.

There are other programs that provide easy interactive access to the DNS. `nslookup` is supplied with most implementations of the DNS. Chapter 10 of [Albitz and Liu 1992] provides a detailed description of how to use this program. The `dig` program ("Domain Internet Groper") is another publicly available tool that queries DNS servers. `doc` ("Domain Obscenity Control") is a shell script that uses `dig` and diagnoses misbehaving domains by sending queries to the appropriate DNS name servers, and performing simple analysis of the responses. See Appendix F for details on how to obtain these programs.

The final detail to account for in this example is the size of the UDP data in the reply: 69 bytes. We need to know two points to account for these bytes.

1. The question is returned in the reply.
2. There can be many repetitions of domain names in a reply, so a compression scheme is used. Indeed, in our example, there are three occurrences of the domain name `gemini.tuc.noao.edu`.

   The compression scheme is simple. Anywhere the label portion of a domain name can occur, the single count byte (which is between 0 and 63) has its two high-order bits turned on instead. This means it is a 16-bit *pointer* and not an 8-bit count byte. The 14 bits that follow in the pointer specify an offset in the DNS message of a label to continue with. (The offset of the first byte in the identification field is 0.) We purposely said that this pointer can occur wherever a label can occur, not just where a complete domain name can occur, since it's possible for a pointer to form either a complete domain name or just the ending portion of a name. (This is because the ending labels in the names from a given domain tend to be identical.)

Figure 14.11 shows the format of the DNS reply, line 2 from Figure 14.10. We also show the IP and UDP headers to reiterate that DNS messages are normally encapsulated in UDP datagrams. We explicitly show the count bytes in the labels of the domain name in the question. The two answers returned are the same, except for the different IP addresses returned in each answer. In this example the pointer in each answer would have a value of 12, the offset from the start of the DNS header of the complete domain name.

The final point to note from this example is from the second line of output from the Telnet command, which we repeat here:

```
sun % telnet gemini daytime                we only type gemini
Trying 140.252.1.11 ...
Connected to gemini.tuc.noao.edu.          but the Telnet client outputs FQDN
```

We typed just the hostname (`gemini`), not the FQDN, but the Telnet client output the FQDN. What's happening is that the Telnet client looks up the name we type by calling

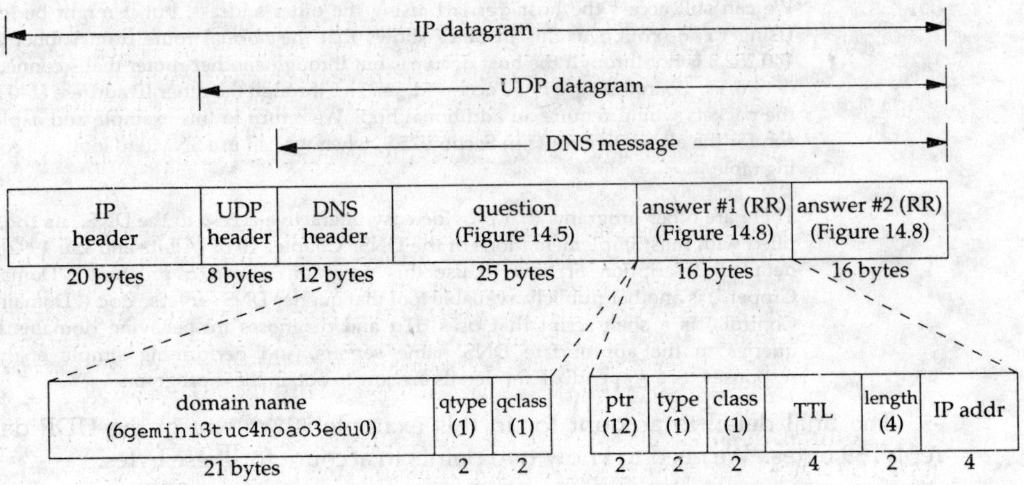

Figure 14.11 Format of DNS reply corresponding to line 2 of Figure 14.10.

the resolver (`gethostbyname`), which returns the IP addresses and the FQDN. Telnet then prints the IP address that it's trying to establish a TCP connection with, and when the connection is established, it outputs the FQDN.

If there is a significant pause between typing the Telnet command and printing the IP address, this delay is caused by the resolver contacting a name server to resolve the name into an IP address. A pause between printing `Trying` and `Connected to`, however, is a delay caused by the establishment of the TCP connection between the client and server, not the DNS.

14.5 Pointer Queries

A perpetual stumbling block in understanding the DNS is how pointer queries are handled—given an IP address, return the name (or names) corresponding to that address.

First return to Figure 14.1 (p. 188) and examine the `arpa` top-level domain, and the `in-addr` domain beneath it. When an organization joins the Internet and obtains authority for a portion of the DNS name space, such as `noao.edu`, they also obtain authority for a portion of the `in-addr.arpa` name space corresponding to their IP address on the Internet. In the case of `noao.edu` it is the class B network ID 140.252. The level of the DNS tree beneath `in-addr.arpa` must be the first byte of the IP address (140 in this example), the next level is the next byte of the IP address (252), and so on. But remember that names are written starting at the bottom of the DNS tree, working upward. This means the DNS name for the host `sun`, with an IP address of 140.252.13.33, is `33.13.252.140.in-addr.arpa`.

We have to write the 4 bytes of the IP address backward because authority is delegated based on network IDs: the first byte of a class A address, the first and second bytes of a class B address, and the first, second, and third bytes of a class C address. The first byte of the IP address must be immediately below the in-addr label, but FQDNs are written from the bottom of the tree up. If FQDNs were written from the top down, then the DNS name for the IP address would be arpa.in-addr.140.252.13.33, but the FQDN for the host would be edu.noao.tuc.sun.

If there was not a separate branch of the DNS tree for handling this address-to-name translation, there would be no way to do the reverse translation other than starting at the root of the tree and trying *every* top-level domain. This could literally take days or weeks, given the current size of the Internet. The in-addr.arpa solution is a clever one, although the reversed bytes of the IP address and the special domain are confusing.

Having to worry about the in-addr.arpa domain and reversing the bytes of the IP address affects us only if we're dealing directly with the DNS, using a program such as host, or watching the packets with tcpdump. From an application's point of view, the normal resolver function (gethostbyaddr) takes an IP address and returns information about the host. The reversal of the bytes and appending the domain in-addr.arpa are done automatically by this resolver function.

Example

Let's use the host program to do a pointer lookup and watch the packets with tcpdump. We'll use the same setup as in Figure 14.9, running the host program on the host sun, and the name server on the host noao.edu. We specify the IP address of our host svr4:

```
sun % host 140.252.13.34
Name: svr4.tuc.noao.edu
Address: 140.252.13.34
```

Since the only command-line argument is an IP address, the host program automatically generates the pointer query. Figure 14.12 shows the tcpdump output.

```
1  0.0                  140.252.1.29.1610 > 140.252.1.54.53: 1+ PTR?
                        34.13.252.140.in-addr.arpa. (44)

2  0.332288 (0.3323)    140.252.1.54.53 > 140.252.1.29.1610: 1* 1/0/0 PTR
                        svr4.tuc.noao.edu. (75)
```

Figure 14.12 tcpdump output for a pointer query.

Line 1 shows that the identifier is 1, the recursion-desired flag is set (the plus sign), and the query type is PTR. (Recall that the question mark means this is a query and not a response.) The data size of 44 bytes is from the 12-byte DNS header, 28 bytes for the 7 labels in the domain name, and 4 bytes for the query type and query class.

The reply has the authoritative-answer bit set (the asterisk) and contains one answer RR. The RR type is PTR and the resource data contains the domain name.

What is passed from the resolver to the name server for a pointer query is not a 32-bit IP address, but the domain name 34.13.252.140.in-addr.arpa.

Hostname Spoofing Check

When an IP datagram arrives at a host for a server, be it a UDP datagram or a TCP connection request segment, all that's available to the server process is the client's IP address and port number (UDP or TCP). Some servers require the client's IP address to have a pointer record in the DNS. We'll see an example of this, using anonymous FTP from an unknown IP address, in Section 27.3.

Other servers, such as the Rlogin server (Chapter 26), not only require that the client's IP address have a pointer record, but then ask the DNS for the IP addresses corresponding to the name returned in the PTR response, and require that one of the returned addresses match the source IP address in the received datagram. This check is because entries in the `.rhosts` file (Section 26.2) contain the hostname, not an IP address, so the server wants to verify that the hostname really corresponds to the incoming IP address.

Some vendors automatically put this check into their resolver routines, specifically the function `gethostbyaddr`. This makes the check available to any program using the resolver, instead of manually placing the check in each application.

We can see an example of this using the SunOS 4.1.3 resolver library. We have written a simple program that performs a pointer query by calling the function `gethostbyaddr`. We have also set our `/etc/resolv.conf` file to use the name server on the host `noao.edu`, which is across the SLIP link from the host `sun`. Figure 14.13 shows the `tcpdump` output collected on the SLIP link when the function `gethostbyaddr` is called to fetch the name corresponding to the IP address 140.252.1.29 (our host `sun`).

```
1  0.0                       sun.1812 > noao.edu.domain:  1+ PTR?
                             29.1.252.140.in-addr.arpa. (43)
2  0.339091 (0.3391)         noao.edu.domain > sun.1812: 1* 1/0/0 PTR
                             sun.tuc.noao.edu. (73)

3  0.344348 (0.0053)         sun.1813 > noao.edu.domain: 2+ A?
                             sun.tuc.noao.edu. (33)
4  0.669022 (0.3247)         noao.edu.domain > sun.1813: 2* 2/0/0 A
                             140.252.1.29 (69)
```

Figure 14.13 Calling resolver function to perform pointer query.

Line 1 is the expected pointer query, and line 2 is the expected response. But the resolver function automatically sends an IP address query in line 3 for the name returned in line 2. The response in line 4 contains two answer records, since the host `sun` has two IP addresses. If one of the addresses does not match the argument to `gethostbyaddr`, a message is sent to the system logging facility, and the function returns an error to the application.

14.6 Resource Records

We've seen a few different types of resource records (RRs) so far: an IP address has a type of A, and PTR means a pointer query. We've also seen that RRs are what a name server returns: answer RRs, authority RRs, and additional information RRs. There are about 20 different types of resource records, some of which we'll now describe. Also, more RR types are being added over time.

A
: An A record defines an IP address. It is stored as a 32-bit binary value.

PTR
: This is the pointer record used for pointer queries. The IP address is represented as a domain name (a sequence of labels) in the `in-addr.arpa` domain.

CNAME
: This stands for "canonical name." It is represented as a domain name (a sequence of labels). The domain name that has a canonical name is often called an *alias*. These are used by some FTP sites to provide an easy to remember alias for some other system.

For example, the `gated` server (mentioned in Section 10.3) is available through anonymous FTP from the server `gated.cornell.edu`. But there is no system named `gated`, this is an alias for some other system. That other system is the canonical name for `gated.cornell.edu`:

```
sun % host -t cname gated.cornell.edu
gated.cornell.edu          CNAME   COMET.CIT.CORNELL.EDU
```

Here we use the `-t` option to specify one particular query type.

HINFO
: Host information: two arbitrary character strings specifying the CPU and operating system. Not all sites provide HINFO records for all their systems, and the information provided may not be up to date.

```
sun % host -t hinfo sun
sun.tuc.noao.edu          HINFO   Sun-4/25          Sun4.1.3
```

MX
: Mail exchange records, which are used in the following scenarios: (1) A site that is not connected to the Internet can get an Internet-connected site to be its mail exchanger. The two sites then work out an alternative way to exchange any mail that arrives, often using the UUCP protocol. (2) MX records provide a way to deliver mail to an alternative host when the destination host is not available. (3) MX records allow organizations to provide virtual hosts that one can send mail to, such as `cs.university.edu`, even if a host with that name doesn't exist. (4) Organizations with firewall gateways can use MX records to limit connectivity to internal systems.

Many sites that are not connected to the Internet have a UUCP link with an Internet connected site such as UUNET. MX records are then provided so that electronic mail can be sent to the site using the standard `user@host` notation. For example, a fictitious domain `foo.com` might have the following MX records:

```
sun % host -t mx foo.com
foo.com                MX        relay1.UU.NET
foo.com                MX        relay2.UU.NET
```

MX records are used by mailers on hosts connected to the Internet. In this example the other mailers are told "if you have mail to send to `user@foo.com`, send the mail to `relay1.uu.net` or `relay2.uu.net`."

MX records have 16-bit integers assigned to them, called *preference values*. If multiple MX records exist for a destination, they're used in order, starting with the smallest preference value.

Another example of MX records handles the case when a host is down or unavailable. In that case the mailer uses the MX records only if it can't connect to the destination using TCP. In the case of the author's primary system, which is connected to the Internet by a SLIP connection, which is down most of the time, we have:

```
sun % host -tv mx sun
Query about sun for record types MX
Trying sun within tuc.noao.edu ...
Query done, 2 answers, authoritative status: no error
sun.tuc.noao.edu       86400  IN     MX     0  sun.tuc.noao.edu
sun.tuc.noao.edu       86400  IN     MX     10 noao.edu
```

We also specified the -v option, to see the preference values. (This option also causes other fields to be output.) The second field, 86400, is the time-to-live value in seconds. This TTL is 24 hours ($24 \times 60 \times 60$). The third column, IN, is the class (Internet). We see that direct delivery to the host itself, the first MX record, has the lowest preference value of 0. If that doesn't work (i.e., the SLIP link is down), the next higher preference is used (10) and delivery is attempted to the host `noao.edu`. If that doesn't work, the sender will time out and retry at a later time.

In Section 28.3 we show examples of SMTP mail delivery using MX records.

NS Name server record. These specify the authoritative name server for a domain. They are represented as domain names (a sequence of labels). We'll see examples of these records in the next section.

These are the common types of RRs. We'll encounter many of them in later examples.

14.7 Caching

To reduce the DNS traffic on the Internet, all name servers employ a cache. With the standard Unix implementation, the cache is maintained in the server, not the resolver. Since the resolver is part of each application, and applications come and go, putting the cache into the program that lives the entire time the system is up (the name server) makes sense. This makes the cache available to any applications that use the server. Any other hosts at the site that use this name server also share the server's cache.

In the scenario that we've used for our examples so far (Figure 14.9), we've run the clients on the host `sun` accessing the name server across the SLIP link on the host `noao.edu`. We'll change that now and run the name server on the host `sun`. In this way if we monitor the DNS traffic on the SLIP link using `tcpdump`, we'll only see queries that can't be handled by the server out of its cache.

By default, the resolver looks for a name server on the local host (UDP port 53 or TCP port 53). We delete the `nameserver` directive from our resolver file, leaving only the `domain` directive:

```
sun % cat /etc/resolv.conf
domain tuc.noao.edu
```

The absence of a `nameserver` directive in this file causes the resolver to use the name server on the local host.

We then use the `host` command to execute the following query:

```
sun % host ftp.uu.net
ftp.uu.net                    A       192.48.96.9
```

Figure 14.14 shows the `tcpdump` output for this query.

```
1  0.0                     sun.tuc.noao.edu.domain > NS.NIC.DDN.MIL.domain:
                           2 A? ftp.uu.net. (28)
2  0.559285 ( 0.5593)      NS.NIC.DDN.MIL.domain > sun.tuc.noao.edu.domain:
                           2- 0/5/5 (229)
3  0.564449 ( 0.0052)      sun.tuc.noao.edu.domain > ns.UU.NET.domain:
                           3+ A? ftp.uu.net. (28)
4  1.009476 ( 0.4450)      ns.UU.NET.domain > sun.tuc.noao.edu.domain:
                           3* 1/0/0 A ftp.UU.NET (44)
```

Figure 14.14 `tcpdump` output for: `host ftp.uu.net`.

This time we've used a new option for `tcpdump`. We collected all the data to or from UDP or TCP ports 53 with the `-w` option. This saves the raw output in a file for later processing. This prevents `tcpdump` from trying to call the resolver itself, to print all the names corresponding to the IP addresses. After we ran our queries, we terminated `tcpdump` and reran it with the `-r` option. This causes it to read the raw output file and generate its normal printed output (which we show in Figure 14.14). This takes a few seconds, since `tcpdump` calls the resolver itself.

The first thing to notice in our tcpdump output is that the identifiers are small integers (2 and 3). This is because we terminated the name server, and then restarted it, to force the cache to be empty. When the name server starts up, it initializes the identifier to 1.

When we type our query, looking for the IP address of the host ftp.uu.net, the name server contacts one of the eight root servers, ns.nic.ddn.mil (line 1). This is the normal A type query that we've seen before, but notice that the recursion-desired flag is *not* specified. (A plus sign would have been printed after the identifier 2 if the flag was set.) In our earlier examples we always saw the resolver set the recursion-desired flag, but here we see that our name server doesn't set the flag when it's contacting one of the root servers. This is because the root servers shouldn't be asked to recursively answer queries—they should be used only to find the addresses of other, authoritative servers.

Line 2 shows that the response comes back with no answer RRs, five authority RRs, and five additional information RRs. The minus sign following the identifier 2 means the recursion-available (RA) flag was not set—this root server wouldn't answer a recursive query even if we asked it to.

Although tcpdump doesn't print the 10 RRs that are returned, we can execute the host command to see what's in the cache:

```
sun % host -v ftp.uu.net
Query about ftp.uu.net for record types A
Trying ftp.uu.net ...
Query done, 1 answer, status: no error
The following answer is not authoritative:
ftp.uu.net                19109    IN    A     192.48.96.9
Authoritative nameservers:
UU.NET                    170308   IN    NS    NS.UU.NET
UU.NET                    170308   IN    NS    UUNET.UU.NET
UU.NET                    170308   IN    NS    UUCP-GW-1.PA.DEC.COM
UU.NET                    170308   IN    NS    UUCP-GW-2.PA.DEC.COM
UU.NET                    170308   IN    NS    NS.EU.NET
Additional information:
NS.UU.NET                 170347   IN    A     137.39.1.3
UUNET.UU.NET              170347   IN    A     192.48.96.2
UUCP-GW-1.PA.DEC.COM      170347   IN    A     16.1.0.18
UUCP-GW-2.PA.DEC.COM      170347   IN    A     16.1.0.19
NS.EU.NET                 170347   IN    A     192.16.202.11
```

This time we specified the -v option to see more than just the A record. This shows that there are five authoritative name servers for the domain uu.net. The five RRs with additional information that are returned by the root server contain the IP addresses of these five name servers. This saves us from having to contact the root server again, to look up the address of one of the servers. This is another implementation optimization in the DNS.

The host command states that the answer is not authoritative. This is because the answer was obtained from our name server's cache, not by contacting an authoritative server.

Returning to line 3 of Figure 14.14, our name server contacts the first of the authoritative servers (ns.uu.net) with the same question: What is the IP address of ftp.uu.net? This time our server sets the recursion-desired flag. The answer is returned on line 4 as a response with one answer RR.

We then execute the host command again, asking for the same name:

```
sun % host ftp.uu.net
ftp.uu.net                A          192.48.96.9
```

This time there is no tcpdump output. This is what we expect, since the answer output by host is returned from the server's cache.

We execute the host command again, looking for the address of ftp.ee.lbl.gov:

```
sun % host ftp.ee.lbl.gov
ftp.ee.lbl.gov            CNAME      ee.lbl.gov
ee.lbl.gov                A          128.3.112.20
```

Figure 14.15 shows the tcpdump output.

```
1  18.664971 (17.6555)   sun.tuc.noao.edu.domain > c.nyser.net.domain:
                         4 A? ftp.ee.lbl.gov. (32)
2  19.429412 ( 0.7644)   c.nyser.net.domain > sun.tuc.noao.edu.domain:
                         4 0/4/4 (188)
3  19.432271 ( 0.0029)   sun.tuc.noao.edu.domain > ns1.lbl.gov.domain:
                         5+ A? ftp.ee.lbl.gov. (32)
4  19.909242 ( 0.4770)   ns1.lbl.gov.domain > sun.tuc.noao.edu.domain:
                         5* 2/0/0 CNAME ee.lbl.gov. (72)
```

Figure 14.15 tcpdump output for: host ftp.ee.lbl.gov.

Line 1 shows that this time our server contacts another of the root servers (c.nyser.net). A name server normally cycles through the various servers for a zone until round-trip estimates are accumulated. The server with the smallest round-trip time is then used.

Since our server is contacting a root server, the recursion-desired flag is not set. This root server does not clear the recursion-available flag, as we saw in line 2 in Figure 14.14. (Even so, a name server still should not ask a root server for a recursive query.)

In line 2 the response comes back with no answers, but four authority RRs and four additional information RRs. As we can guess, the four authority RRs are the names of the name servers for ftp.ee.lbl.gov, and the four other RRs contain the IP addresses of these four servers.

Line 3 is the query of the name server ns1.lbl.gov (the first of the four name servers returned in line 2). The recursion-desired flag is set.

The response in line 4 is different from previous responses. Two answer RRs are returned and tcpdump says that the first one is a CNAME RR. The canonical name of ftp.ee.lbl.gov is ee.lbl.gov.

This is a common usage of CNAME records. The FTP site for LBL always has a name beginning with ftp, but it may move from one host to another over time. Users need only know the name ftp.ee.lbl.gov and the DNS will replace this with its canonical name when referenced.

Remember that when we ran `host`, it printed both the CNAME and the IP address of the canonical name. This is because the response (line 4 in Figure 14.15) contained two answer RRs. The first one is the CNAME and the second is the A record. If the A record had not been returned with the CNAME, our server would have issued another query, asking for the IP address of `ee.lbl.gov`. This is another implementation optimization—both the CNAME and the A record of the canonical name are returned in one response.

14.8 UDP or TCP

We've mentioned that the well-known port numbers for DNS name servers are UDP port 53 and TCP port 53. This implies that the DNS supports both UDP and TCP. But all the examples that we've watched with `tcpdump` have used UDP. When is each protocol used and why?

When the resolver issues a query and the response comes back with the TC bit set ("truncated") it means the size of the response exceeded 512 bytes, so only the first 512 bytes were returned by the server. The resolver normally issues the request again, using TCP. This allows more than 512 bytes to be returned. (Recall our discussion of the maximum UDP datagram size in Section 11.10.) Since TCP breaks up a stream of user data into what it calls *segments*, it can transfer any amount of user data, using multiple segments.

Also, when a secondary name server for a domain starts up it performs a zone transfer from the primary name server for the domain. We also said that the secondary queries the primary on a regular basis (often every 3 hours) to see if the primary has had its tables updated, and if so, a zone transfer is performed. Zone transfers are done using TCP, since there is much more data to transfer than a single query or response.

Since the DNS primarily uses UDP, both the resolver and the name server must perform their own timeout and retransmission. Also, unlike many other Internet applications that use UDP (TFTP, BOOTP, and SNMP), which operate mostly on local area networks, DNS queries and responses often traverse wide area networks. The packet loss rate and variability in round-trip times are normally higher on a WAN than a LAN, increasing the importance of a good retransmission and timeout algorithm for DNS clients.

14.9 Another Example

Let's look at another example that ties together many of the DNS features that we've described. We start an Rlogin client, connecting to an Rlogin server in some other domain. Figure 14.16 shows the exchange of packets that takes place. The following 11 steps take place, assuming none of the information is already cached by the client or server:

1. The client starts and calls its resolver function to convert the hostname that we typed into an IP address. A query of type A is sent to a root server.

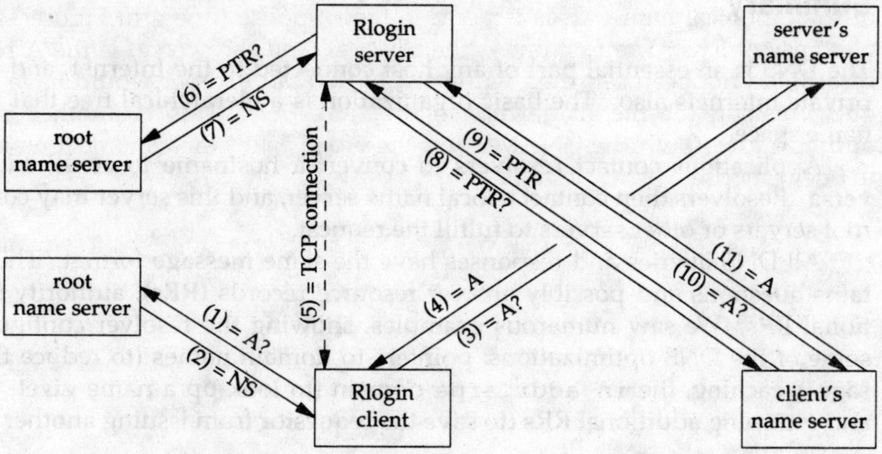

Figure 14.16 Summary of packets exchanged to start up Rlogin client and server.

2. The root server's response contains the name servers for the server's domain.
3. The client's resolver reissues the query of type A to the server's name server. This query normally has the recursion-desired flag set.
4. The response comes back with the IP address of the server host.
5. The Rlogin client establishes a TCP connection with the Rlogin server. (Chapter 18 provides all the details of this step.) Three packets are exchanged between the client and server TCP modules.
6. The Rlogin server receives the connection from the client and calls its resolver to obtain the name of the client host, given the IP address that the server receives from its TCP. This is a PTR query issued to a root name server. This root server can be different from the root server used by the client in step 1.
7. The root server's response contains the name servers for the client's `in-addr.arpa` domain.
8. The server's resolver reissues the PTR query to the client's name server.
9. The PTR response contains the FQDN of the client host.
10. The server's resolver issues a query of type A to the client's name server, asking for the IP addresses corresponding to the name returned in the previous step. This may be done automatically by the server's `gethostbyaddr` function, as we described in Section 14.5, otherwise the Rlogin server does this step explicitly. Also, the client's name server is often the same as the client's `in-addr.arpa` name server, but this isn't required.
11. The response from the client's name server contains the A records for the client host. The Rlogin server compares the A records with the IP address from the client's TCP connection request.

Caching can reduce the number of packets exchanged in this figure.

14.10 Summary

The DNS is an essential part of any host connected to the Internet, and widely used in private internets also. The basic organization is a hierarchical tree that forms the DNS name space.

Applications contact resolvers to convert a hostname to an IP address, and vice versa. Resolvers then contact a local name server, and this server may contact one of the root servers or other servers to fulfill the request.

All DNS queries and responses have the same message format. This message contains questions and possibly answer resource records (RRs), authority RRs, and additional RRs. We saw numerous examples, showing the resolver configuration file and some of the DNS optimizations: pointers to domain names (to reduce the size of messages), caching, the `in-addr.arpa` domain (to look up a name given an IP address), and returning additional RRs (to save the requestor from issuing another query).

Exercises

14.1 Classify a DNS resolver and a DNS name server as either client, server, or both.

14.2 Account for all 75 bytes in the response in Figure 14.12.

14.3 In Section 12.3 we said that an application that accepts either a dotted-decimal IP address or a hostname should assume the former, and if that fails, then assume a hostname. What happens if the order of the tests is reversed?

14.4 Every UDP datagram has an associated length. A process that receives a UDP datagram is told what its length is. When a resolver issues a query using TCP instead of UDP, since TCP is a stream of bytes without any record markers, how does the application know how much data is returned? Notice that there is no length field in the DNS header (Figure 14.3). (*Hint*: Look at RFC 1035.)

14.5 We said that a name server must know the IP addresses of the root servers and that this information is available via anonymous FTP. Unfortunately not all system administrators update their DNS files whenever changes are made to the list of root servers. (Changes do occur to the list of root servers, but not frequently.) How do you think the DNS handles this?

14.6 Fetch the file specified in Exercise 1.8 and determine who is responsible for maintaining the root name servers. How frequently are the root servers updated?

14.7 What is a problem with maintaining the cache in the name server, and having a stateless resolver?

14.8 In the discussion of Figure 14.10 we said that the name server sorts the A records so that addresses on common networks appear first. Who should sort the A records, the name server or the resolver?

15

TFTP: Trivial File Transfer Protocol

15.1 Introduction

TFTP is the Trivial File Transfer Protocol. It is intended to be used when bootstrapping diskless systems (normally workstations or X terminals). Unlike the File Transfer Protocol (FTP), which we describe in Chapter 27 and which uses TCP, TFTP was designed to use UDP, to make it simple and small. Implementations of TFTP (and its required UDP, IP, and a device driver) can fit in read-only memory.

This chapter provides an overview of TFTP because we'll encounter it in the next chapter with the Bootstrap Protocol. We also encountered TFTP in Figure 5.1 when we bootstrapped the host sun from the network. It issued a TFTP request after obtaining its IP address using RARP.

RFC 1350 [Sollins 1992] is the official specification of version 2 of TFTP. Chapter 12 of [Stevens 1990] provides a complete source code implementation of a TFTP client and server, and describes some of the programming techniques used with TFTP.

15.2 Protocol

Each exchange between a client and server starts with the client asking the server to either read a file for the client or write a file for the client. In the normal case of bootstrapping a diskless system, the first request is a read request (RRQ). Figure 15.1 shows the format of the five TFTP messages. (Opcodes 1 and 2 share the same format.)

The first 2 bytes of the TFTP message are an *opcode*. For a read request (RRQ) and write request (WRQ) the *filename* specifies the file on the server that the client wants to read from or write to. We specifically show that this filename is terminated by a byte of 0 in Figure 15.1. The *mode* is one of the ASCII strings `netascii` or `octet` (in any

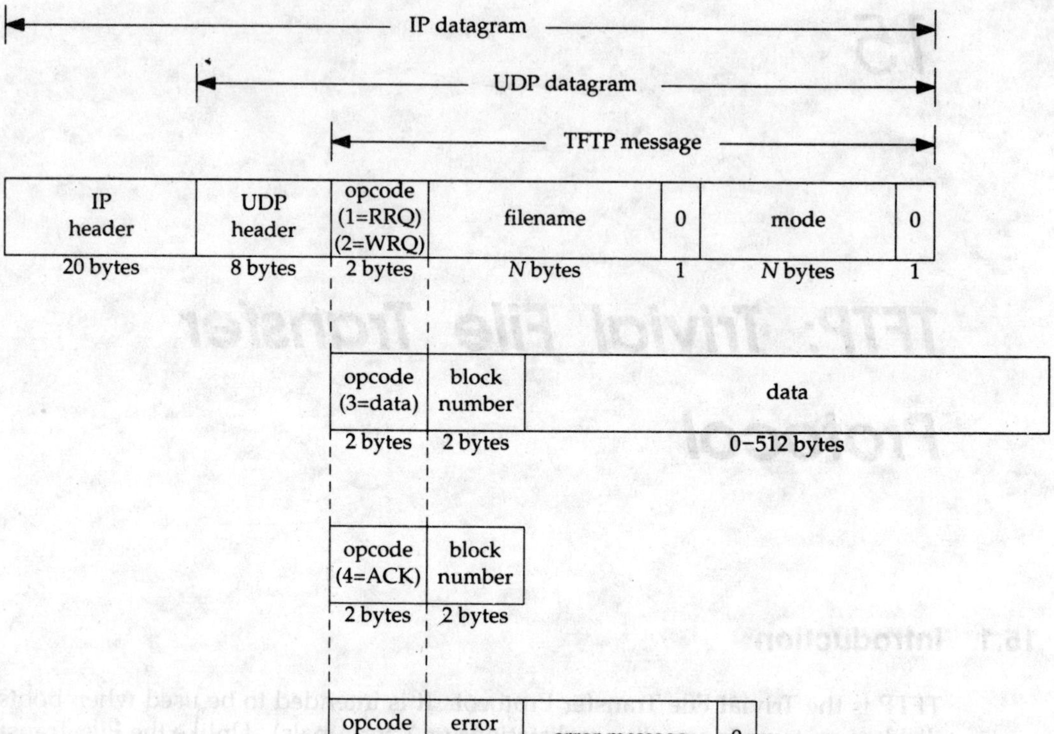

Figure 15.1 Format of the five TFTP messages.

combination of uppercase or lowercase), again terminated by a byte of 0. `netascii` means the data are lines of ASCII text with each line terminated by the 2-character sequence of a carriage return followed by a linefeed (called CR/LF). Both ends must convert between this format and whatever the local host uses as a line delimiter. An `octet` transfer treats the data as 8-bit bytes with no interpretation.

Each data packet contains a *block number* that is later used in an acknowledgment packet. As an example, when reading a file the client sends a read request (RRQ) specifying the filename and mode. If the file can be read by the client, the server responds with a data packet with a block number of 1. The client sends an ACK of block number 1. The server responds with the next data packet, with a block number of 2. The client sends an ACK of block number 2. This continues until the file is transferred. Each data packet contains 512 bytes of data, except for the final packet, which contains 0–511 bytes of data. When the client receives a data packet with less than 512 bytes of data, it knows it has received the final packet.

In the case of a write request (WRQ), the client sends the WRQ specifying the filename and mode. If the file can be written by the client, the server responds with an ACK of block number 0. The client then sends the first 512 bytes of file with a block number of 1. The server responds with an ACK of block number 1.

This type of data transmission is called a *stop-and-wait* protocol. It is found only in simple protocols such as TFTP. We'll see in Section 20.3 that TCP provides a different form of acknowledgment, which can provide higher throughput. TFTP is designed for simplicity of implementation, not high throughput.

The final TFTP message type is the error message, with an *opcode* of 5. This is what the server responds with if a read request or write request can't be processed. Read and write errors during file transmission also cause this message to be sent, and transmission is then terminated. The *error number* gives a numeric error code, followed by an ASCII error message that might contain additional, operating system specific information.

Since TFTP uses the unreliable UDP, it is up to TFTP to handle lost and duplicated packets. Lost packets are detected with a timeout and retransmission implemented by the sender. (Be aware of a potential problem called the "sorcerer's apprentice syndrome" that can occur if both sides time out and retransmit. Section 12.2 of [Stevens 1990] shows how the problem can occur.) As with most UDP applications, there is no checksum in the TFTP messages, which assumes any corruption of the data will be caught by the UDP checksum (Section 11.3).

15.3 An Example

Let's examine TFTP by watching the protocol in action. We'll run the TFTP client on the host `bsdi` and fetch a text file from the host `svr4`:

```
bsdi % tftp svr4                            start the TFTP client
tftp> get test1.c                           fetch a file from the server
Received 962 bytes in 0.3 seconds
tftp> quit                                  and terminate

bsdi % ls -l test1.c                        how many bytes in the file we fetched?
-rw-r--r--  1 rstevens  staff  914 Mar 20 11:41 test1.c

bsdi % wc -l test1.c                        and how many lines?
      48 test1.c
```

The first point that catches our eye is that the file contains 914 bytes under Unix, but TFTP transfers 962 bytes. Using the `wc` program we see that there are 48 lines in the file, so the 48 Unix newline characters are expanded into 48 CR/LF pairs, since the TFTP default is a `netascii` transfer.

Figure 15.2 shows the packet exchange that takes place.

```
1  0.0                      bsdi.1106 > svr4.tftp: 19 RRQ "test1.c"

2  0.287080 (0.2871)        svr4.1077 > bsdi.1106: udp 516
3  0.291178 (0.0041)        bsdi.1106 > svr4.1077: udp 4

4  0.299446 (0.0083)        svr4.1077 > bsdi.1106: udp 454
5  0.312320 (0.0129)        bsdi.1106 > svr4.1077: udp 4
```

Figure 15.2 Packet exchange for TFTP of a file.

Line 1 shows the read request from the client to the server. Since the destination UDP port is the TFTP well-known port (69), `tcpdump` interprets the TFTP packet and prints RRQ and the name of the file. The length of the UDP data is printed as 19 bytes and is accounted for as follows: 2 bytes for the opcode, 7 bytes for the filename, 1 byte of 0, 8 bytes for `netascii`, and another byte of 0.

The next packet is from the server (line 2) and contains 516 bytes: 2 bytes for the opcode, 2 bytes for the block number, and 512 bytes of data. Line 3 is the acknowledgment for this data: 2 bytes for the opcode and 2 bytes for the block number.

The final data packet (line 4) contains 450 bytes of data. The 512 bytes of data in line 2 and this 450 bytes of data account for the 962 bytes of data output by the client.

Note that `tcpdump` doesn't output any additional TFTP protocol information for lines 2–5, whereas it interpreted the TFTP message in line 1. This is because the server's port number changes between lines 1 and 2. The TFTP protocol requires that the client send the first packet (the RRQ or WRQ) to the server's well-known UDP port (69). The server then allocates some other unused ephemeral port on the server's host (1077 in Figure 15.2), which is then used by the server for all further packet exchange between this client and server. The client's port number (1106 in this example) doesn't change. `tcpdump` has no idea that port 1077 on host `svr4` is really a TFTP server.

The reason the server's port number changes is so the server doesn't tie up the well-known port for the amount of time required to transfer the file (which could be many seconds or even minutes). Instead, the well-known port is left available for other TFTP clients to send their requests to, while the current transfer is under way.

Recall from Figure 10.6 (p. 133) that when the RIP server had more than 512 bytes to send to the client, both UDP datagrams came from the server's well-known port. In that example, even though the server had to write multiple datagrams to send all the data back, the server did one write, followed by the next, both from its well-known port. Here, with TFTP, the protocol is different since there is a longer term relationship between the client and server (which we said could be seconds or minutes). If one server process used the well-known port for the duration of the file transfer, it would either have to refuse any further requests that arrived from other clients, or that one server process would have to multiplex file transfers with multiple clients at the same time, on the same port (69). The simplest solution is to have the server obtain a new port after it receives the RRQ or WRQ. Naturally the client must detect this new port when it receives the first data packet (line 2 in Figure 15.2) and then send all further acknowledgments (lines 3 and 5) to that new port.

In Section 16.3 we'll see TFTP used when an X terminal is bootstrapped.

15.4 Security

Notice in the TFTP packets (Figure 15.1) that there is no provision for a username or password. This is a feature (i.e., "security hole") of TFTP. Since TFTP was designed for use during the bootstrap process it could be impossible to provide a username and password.

This feature of TFTP was used by many crackers to obtain copies of a Unix password file and then try to guess passwords. To prevent this type of access, most TFTP servers nowadays provide an option whereby only files in a specific directory (often `/tftpboot` on Unix systems) can be accessed. This directory then contains only the bootstrap files required by the diskless systems.

For additional security, the TFTP server on a Unix system normally sets its user ID and group ID to values that should not be assigned to any real user. This allows access only to files that have world-read or world-write permissions.

15.5 Summary

TFTP is a simple protocol designed to fit into read-only memory and be used only during the bootstrap process of diskless systems. It uses only a few message formats and a stop-and-wait protocol.

To allow multiple clients to bootstrap at the same time, a TFTP server needs to provide some form of concurrency. Because UDP does not provide a unique connection between a client and server (as does TCP), the TFTP server provides concurrency by creating a new UDP port for each client. This allows different client input datagrams to be demultiplexed by the server's UDP module, based on destination port numbers, instead of doing this in the server itself.

The TFTP protocol provides no security features. Most implementations count on the system administrator of the TFTP server to restrict any client's access to the files necessary for bootstrapping only.

Chapter 27 covers the File Transfer Protocol (FTP), which is designed for general purpose, high-throughput file transfer.

Exercises

15.1 Read the Host Requirements RFC to see what a TFTP server should do if it receives a request and the destination IP address of the request is a broadcast address.

15.2 What do you think happens when the TFTP block number wraps around from 65535 to 0? Does RFC 1350 say anything about this?

15.3 We said that the TFTP sender performs the timeout and retransmission to handle lost packets. How does this affect the use of TFTP when it's being used as part of the bootstrap process?

15.4 What is the limiting factor in the time required to transfer a file using TFTP?

16

BOOTP: Bootstrap Protocol

16.1 Introduction

In Chapter 5 we described how a diskless system, with no knowledge of its IP address, can determine its IP address using RARP when it is bootstrapped. There are two problems with RARP: (1) the only thing returned is the IP address, and (2) since RARP uses a link-layer broadcast, RARP requests are not forwarded by routers (necessitating an RARP server on every physical network). This chapter describes an alternative method for a diskless system to bootstrap itself, called the Bootstrap Protocol, or BOOTP.

BOOTP uses UDP and normally works in conjunction with TFTP (Chapter 15). RFC 951 [Croft and Gilmore 1985] is the official specification for BOOTP with clarifications given in RFC 1542 [Wimer 1993].

16.2 BOOTP Packet Format

BOOTP requests and replies are encapsulated in UDP datagrams, as shown in Figure 16.1.

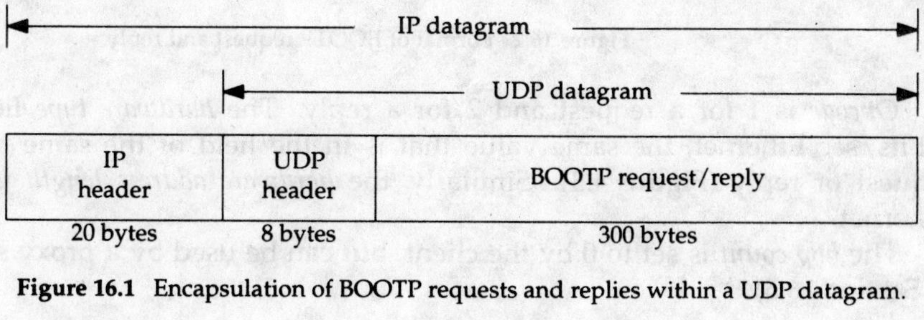

Figure 16.1 Encapsulation of BOOTP requests and replies within a UDP datagram.

Figure 16.2 shows the format of the 300-byte BOOTP request and reply.

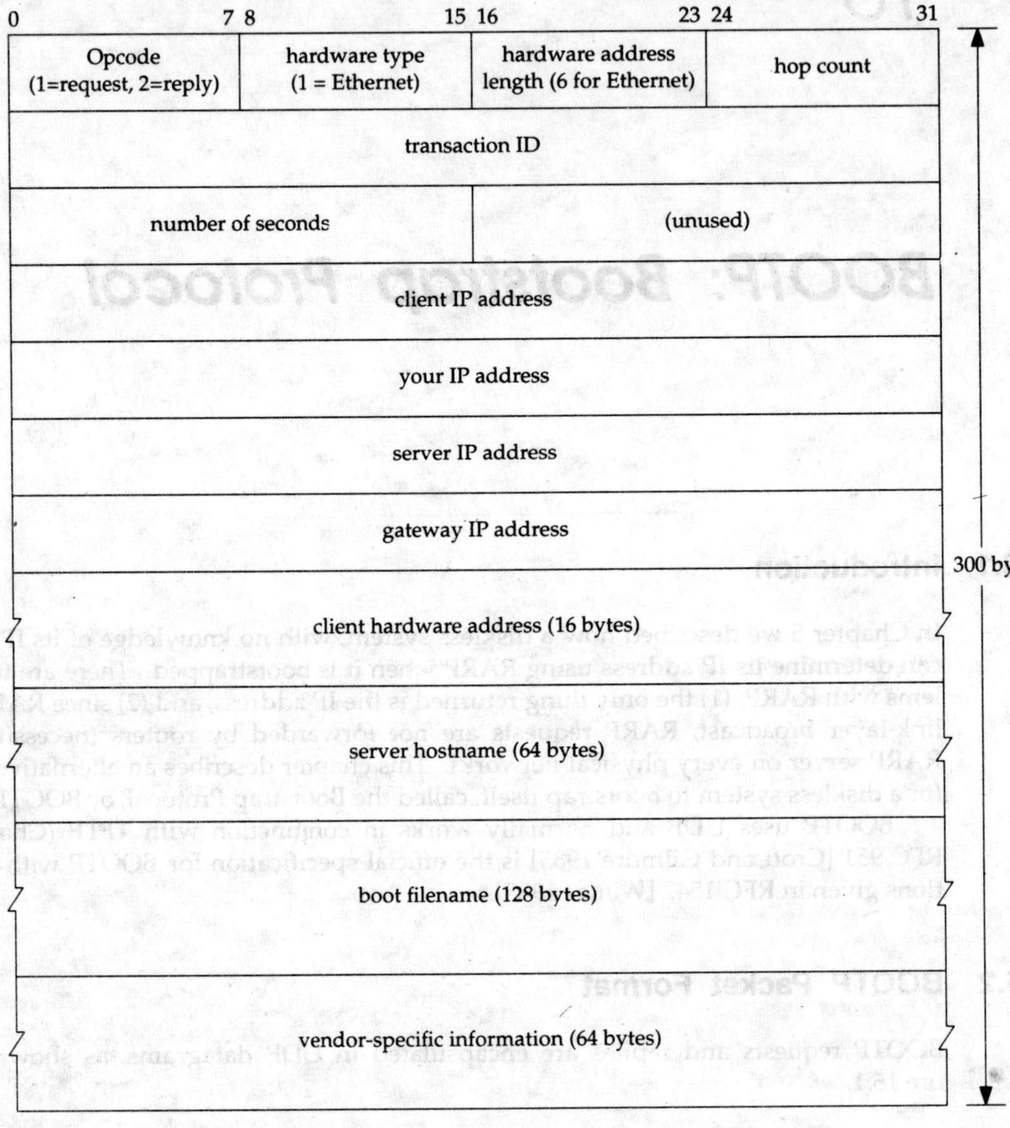

Figure 16.2 Format of BOOTP request and reply.

Opcode is 1 for a request and 2 for a reply. The *hardware type* field is 1 for a 10 Mbits/sec Ethernet, the same value that is in the field of the same name in an ARP request or reply (Figure 4.3). Similarly, the *hardware address length* is 6 bytes for an Ethernet.

The *hop count* is set to 0 by the client, but can be used by a proxy server (described in Section 16.5).

The *transaction ID* is a 32-bit integer set by the client and returned by the server. This lets the client match a response with a request. The client should set this to a random number for each request.

Number of seconds can be set by the client to the time since it started trying to bootstrap. The servers can look at this value, and perhaps a secondary server for a client won't respond until the number of seconds has exceeded some value, implying that the client's primary server is down.

If the client already knows its IP address, it fills in the *client IP address*. Otherwise, the client sets this to 0. In the latter case the server fills in *your IP address* with the client's IP address. The *server IP address* is filled in by the server. If a proxy server is used (Section 16.5), that proxy server fills in its *gateway IP address*.

The client must set its *client hardware address*. Although this is the same value as in the Ethernet header, by placing the field in the UDP datagram also, it is easily available to any user process (e.g., a BOOTP server) that receives the datagram. It is normally much harder (or impossible) for a process reading UDP datagrams to determine the fields in the Ethernet header that carried the UDP datagram.

The *server hostname* is a null terminated string that is optionally filled in by the server. The server can also fill in the *boot filename* with the fully qualified, null terminated pathname of a file to bootstrap from.

The *vendor-specific area* is used for various extensions to BOOTP. Section 16.6 describes some of these extensions.

When a client is bootstrapping using BOOTP (an opcode of 1) the request is normally a link-layer broadcast and the destination IP address in the IP header is normally 255.255.255.255 (the limited broadcast, Section 12.2). The source IP address is often 0.0.0.0 since the client does not know its own IP address yet. Recall from Figure 3.9 that 0.0.0.0 is a valid source IP address when a system is bootstrapping itself.

Port Numbers

There are two well-known ports for BOOTP: 67 for the server and 68 for the client. This means the client does not choose an unused ephemeral port, but uses 68 instead. The reason two port numbers were chosen, instead of just one for the server, is that a server's reply can be (but normally isn't) broadcast.

If the server's reply were broadcast, and if the client were to choose an ephemeral port number, these broadcasts would also be received by other applications on other hosts that happen to be using the same ephemeral port number. Hence, it is considered bad form to broadcast to a random (i.e., ephemeral) port number.

If the client also used the server's well-known port (67) as its port, then all servers on the network are awakened to look at each broadcast reply. (If all the servers were awakened, they would examine the opcode, see that it's a reply and not a request, and go back to sleep.) Therefore the choice was made to have all clients use a single well-known port that differs from the server's well-known port.

If multiple clients are bootstrapping at the same time, and if the server broadcasts the replies, each client sees the replies intended for the other clients. The clients can use the transaction ID field in the BOOTP header to match replies with requests, or the client can examine the returned client hardware address.

16.3 An Example

Let's look at an example of BOOTP when an X terminal is bootstrapped. Figure 16.3 shows the `tcpdump` output. (The client's name is `proteus` and the server's name is `mercury`. This `tcpdump` output was obtained on a different network from the one we've been using for all the other examples in the text.)

```
 1  0.0                     0.0.0.0.68 > 255.255.255.255.bootp:
                            secs:100 ether 0:0:a7:0:62:7c
 2  0.355446 (0.3554)       mercury.bootp > proteus.68: secs:100 Y:proteus
                            S:mercury G:mercury ether 0:0:a7:0:62:7c
                            file "/local/var/bootfiles/Xncd19r"
 3  0.355447 (0.0000)       arp who-has proteus tell 0.0.0.0
 4  0.851508 (0.4961)       arp who-has proteus tell 0.0.0.0
 5  1.371070 (0.5196)       arp who-has proteus tell proteus
 6  1.863226 (0.4922)       proteus.68 > 255.255.255.255.bootp:
                            secs:100 ether 0:0:a7:0:62:7c
 7  1.871038 (0.0078)       mercury.bootp > proteus.68: secs:100 Y:proteus
                            S:mercury G:mercury ether 0:0:a7:0:62:7c
                            file "/local/var/bootfiles/Xncd19r"
 8  3.871038 (2.0000)       proteus.68 > 255.255.255.255.bootp:
                            secs:100 ether 0:0:a7:0:62:7c
 9  3.878850 (0.0078)       mercury.bootp > proteus.68: secs:100 Y:proteus
                            S:mercury G:mercury ether 0:0:a7:0:62:7c
                            file "/local/var/bootfiles/Xncd19r"
10  5.925786 (2.0469)       arp who-has mercury tell proteus
11  5.929692 (0.0039)       arp reply mercury is-at 8:0:2b:28:eb:1d
12  5.929694 (0.0000)       proteus.tftp > mercury.tftp: 37 RRQ
                            "/local/var/bootfiles/Xncd19r"
13  5.996094 (0.0664)       mercury.2352 > proteus.tftp: 516 DATA block 1
14  6.000000 (0.0039)       proteus.tftp > mercury.2352: 4 ACK

                                many lines deleted here

15  14.980472 (8.9805)      mercury.2352 > proteus.tftp: 516 DATA block 2463
16  14.984376 (0.0039)      proteus.tftp > mercury.2352: 4 ACK
17  14.984377 (0.0000)      mercury.2352 > proteus.tftp: 228 DATA block 2464
18  14.984378 (0.0000)      proteus.tftp > mercury.2352: 4 ACK
```

Figure 16.3 Example of BOOTP being used to bootstrap an X terminal.

In line 1 we see the client's request from 0.0.0.0.68, destined for 255.255.255.255.67. The only fields the client has filled in are the number of seconds and its Ethernet address. We'll see that this client always sets the number of seconds to 100. The hop count and transaction ID are both 0 since they are not output by `tcpdump`. (A transaction ID of 0 means the client ignores the field, since it would set this field to a random number if it was going to verify the returned value in the response.)

Line 2 is the reply from the server. The fields filled in by the server are the client's IP address (which `tcpdump` prints as the name `proteus`), the server's IP address (printed as the name `mercury`), the IP address of a gateway (printed as the name `mercury`), and the name of a boot file.

After receiving the BOOTP reply, the client immediately issues an ARP request to see if anyone else on the network has its IP address. The name `proteus` following `who-has` corresponds to the target IP address (Figure 4.3), and the sender's IP address is set to 0.0.0.0. It sends another identical ARP request 0.5 second later, and another one 0.5 second after that. In the third ARP request (line 5) it changes the sender's IP address to be its own IP address. This is a gratuitous ARP request (Section 4.7).

Line 6 shows that the client waits another 0.5 second and broadcasts another BOOTP request. The only difference between this request and line 1 is that now the client puts its own IP address in the IP header. It receives the same reply from the same server (line 7). The client waits another 2 seconds and broadcasts yet another BOOTP request (line 8) and receives the same reply from the same server.

The client then waits another 2 seconds and sends an ARP request for its server `mercury` (line 10). The ARP reply is received and the client immediately issues a TFTP read request for its boot file (line 12). What follows are 2464 TFTP data packets and acknowledgments. The amount of data transferred is $512 \times 2463 + 224 = 1,261,280$ bytes. This loads the operating system into the X terminal. We have deleted most of the TFTP lines from Figure 16.3.

One thing to notice, when comparing this TFTP exchange with Figure 15.2, is that here the client uses the TFTP well-known port (69) for the entire transfer. Since one of the two partners is using port 69, `tcpdump` knows that the packets are TFTP messages, so it is able to interpret each packet using the TFTP protocol. This is why Figure 16.3 indicates which packets contain data, which contain acknowledgments, and what the block number is for each packet. We didn't get this additional information in Figure 15.2 because neither end was using TFTP's well-known port for the data transfer. Normally the TFTP client cannot use TFTP's well-known port, since that port is used by the server on a multiuser system. But here the system is being bootstrapped, so a TFTP server is not provided, allowing the client to use the port for the duration of the transfer. This also implies that the TFTP server on `mercury` doesn't care what the client's port number is—it sends the data to the client's port, whatever that happens to be.

From Figure 16.3 we see that 1,261,280 bytes are transferred in 9 seconds. This is a rate of about 140,000 bytes per second. While this is slower than most FTP file transfers across an Ethernet, it is not that bad for a simple stop-and-wait protocol such as TFTP.

What follows as this X terminal is bootstrapped are additional TFTP transfers of the terminal's font files, some DNS name server queries, and then the initialization of the X protocol. The total time in Figure 16.3 was almost 15 seconds, and another 6 seconds is taken for the remaining steps. This gives a total of 21 seconds to bootstrap the diskless X terminal.

16.4 BOOTP Server Design

The BOOTP client is normally provided in read-only memory on the diskless system. It is interesting to see how the server is normally implemented.

First, the server reads UDP datagrams from its well-known port (67). Nothing special is required. This differs from an RARP server (Section 5.4), which we said had to read Ethernet frames with a type field of "RARP request." The BOOTP protocol also made it easy for the server to obtain the client's hardware address, by placing it into the BOOTP packet (Figure 16.2).

An interesting problem arises: how can the server send a response directly back to the client? The response is a UDP datagram, and the server knows the client's IP address (probably read from a configuration file on the server). But if the BOOTP server sends a UDP datagram to that IP address (the normal way UDP output is handled), the server's host will probably issue an ARP request for that IP address. But the client can't respond to the ARP request since it doesn't know its IP address yet! (This is called the "chicken and egg" issue in RFC 951.)

There are two solutions. The first, commonly used by Unix servers, is for the server to issue an `ioctl`(2) request to the kernel, to place an entry into the ARP cache for this client. (This is what the `arp -s` command does, Section 4.8.) The server can do this since it knows the client's hardware address and IP address. This means that when the server sends the UDP datagram (the BOOTP reply), the server's ARP module will find the client's IP address in the ARP cache.

An alternative solution is for the server to broadcast the BOOTP reply, instead of sending it directly to the client. Since reducing the number of broadcasts on a network is always desirable, this solution should be used only if the server cannot make an entry into its ARP cache. Normally it requires superuser permission to make an entry into the ARP cache, requiring a broadcast reply if the server is nonprivileged.

16.5 BOOTP Through a Router

We said in Section 5.4 that one of the drawbacks of RARP is that it uses a link-layer broadcast, which is normally not forwarded by a router. This required an RARP server on each physical network. BOOTP can be used through a router, if supported by the router. (Most major router vendors do support this feature.)

This is mainly intended for diskless routers, because if a multiuser system with a disk is used as a router, it can probably run a BOOTP server itself. Alternatively, the common Unix BOOTP server (Appendix F) supports this relay mode, but again, if you can run a BOOTP server on the physical network, there's normally no need to forward the requests to yet another server on another network.

What happens is that the router (also called the "BOOTP relay agent") listens for BOOTP requests on the server's well-known port (67). When a request is received, the relay agent places its IP address into the *gateway IP address* field in the BOOTP request, and sends the request to the real BOOTP server. (The address placed by the relay agent into the gateway field is the IP address of the interface on which the request was received.) The relay agent also increments the hops field by one. (This is to prevent infinite loops in case the request is reforwarded. RFC 951 mentions that the request should probably be thrown away if the hop count reaches 3.) Since the outgoing request is a unicast datagram (as opposed to the original client request that was broadcast), it can follow any route to the real BOOTP server, passing through other routers. The real server gets the request, forms the BOOTP reply, and sends it back to the relay agent, not the client. The real server knows that the request has been forwarded, since the gateway field in the request is nonzero. The relay agent receives the reply and sends it to the client.

16.6 Vendor-Specific Information

In Figure 16.2 we showed a 64-byte vendor-specific area. RFC 1533 [Alexander and Droms 1993] defines the format of this area. This area contains optional information for the server to return to the client.

If information is provided, the first 4 bytes of this area are set to the IP address 99.130.83.99. This is called the *magic cookie* and means there is information in the area.

The rest of this area is a list of items. Each item begins with a 1-byte tag field. Two of the items consist of just the tag field: a tag of 0 is a pad byte (to force following items to preferred byte boundaries), and a tag of 255 marks the end of the items. Any bytes remaining in this area after the first end byte should be set to this value (255).

Other than these two 1-byte items, the remaining items consist of a single length byte, followed by the information. Figure 16.4 shows the format of some of the items in the vendor-specific area.

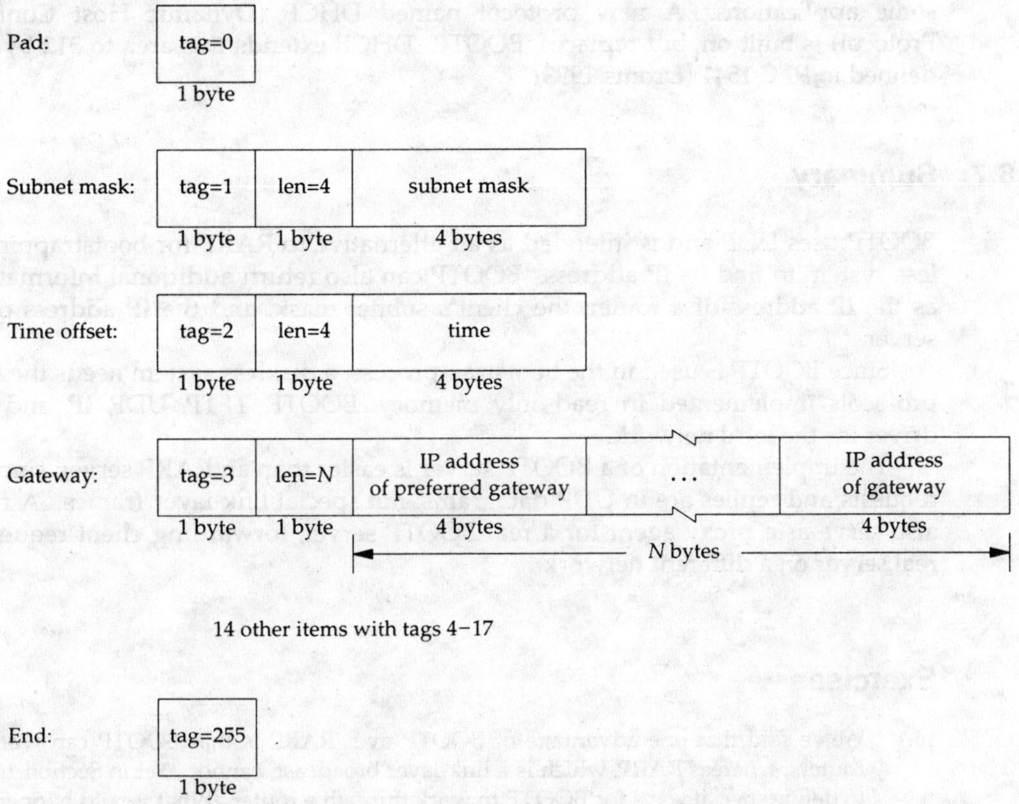

Figure 16.4 Format of some of the items in the vendor-specific area.

The subnet mask and time value are really fixed-length items because their values always occupy 4 bytes. The time offset is the number of seconds since midnight January 1, 1900, UTC.

The gateway item is an example of a variable-length item. The length is always a multiple of 4, and the values are the 32-bit IP addresses of one or more gateways (routers) for the client to use. The first one returned must be the preferred gateway.

There are 14 other items defined in RFC 1533. Probably the most important is the IP address of a DNS name server, with a tag value of 6. Other items return the IP address of a printer server, the IP address of a time server, and so on. Refer to the RFC for all the details.

Returning to our example in Figure 16.3, we never saw an ICMP address mask request (Section 6.3) that would have been broadcast by the client to find its subnet mask. Although it wasn't output by `tcpdump`, we can probably assume that the client's subnet mask was returned in the vendor-specific area of the BOOTP reply.

> The Host Requirements RFC recommends that a system using BOOTP obtain its subnet mask using BOOTP, not ICMP.

The size of the vendor-specific area is limited to 64 bytes. This is a constraint for some applications. A new protocol named DHCP (Dynamic Host Configuration Protocol) is built on, but replaces, BOOTP. DHCP extends this area to 312 bytes and is defined in RFC 1541 [Droms 1993].

16.7 Summary

BOOTP uses UDP and is intended as an alternative to RARP for bootstrapping a diskless system to find its IP address. BOOTP can also return additional information, such as the IP address of a router, the client's subnet mask, and the IP address of a name server.

Since BOOTP is used in the bootstrap process, a diskless system needs the following protocols implemented in read-only memory: BOOTP, TFTP, UDP, IP, and a device driver for the local network.

The implementation of a BOOTP server is easier than an RARP server, since BOOTP requests and replies are in UDP datagrams, not special link-layer frames. A router can also serve as a proxy agent for a real BOOTP server, forwarding client requests to the real server on a different network.

Exercises

16.1 We've said that one advantage of BOOTP over RARP is that BOOTP can work through routers, whereas RARP, which is a link-layer broadcast, cannot. Yet in Section 16.5 we had to define special ways for BOOTP to work through a router. What would happen if a capability were added to routers allowing them to forward RARP requests?

16.2 We said that a BOOTP client must use the transaction ID to match responses with requests, in case there are multiple clients bootstrapping at the same time from a server that broadcasts replies. But in Figure 16.3 the transaction ID is 0, implying that this client ignores the transaction ID. How do you think this client matches the responses with its requests?

17

TCP: Transmission Control Protocol

17.1 Introduction

In this chapter we provide a description of the services provided by TCP for the application layer. We also look at the fields in the TCP header. In the chapters that follow we examine all of these header fields in more detail, as we see how TCP operates.

Our description of TCP starts in this chapter and continues in the next seven chapters. Chapter 18 describes how a TCP connection is established and terminated, and Chapters 19 and 20 look at the normal transfer of data, both for interactive use (remote login) and bulk data (file transfer). Chapter 21 provides the details of TCP's timeout and retransmission, followed by two other TCP timers in Chapters 22 and 23. Finally Chapter 24 takes a look at newer TCP features and TCP performance.

The original specification for TCP is RFC 793 [Postel 1981c], although some errors in that RFC are corrected in the Host Requirements RFC.

17.2 TCP Services

Even though TCP and UDP use the same network layer (IP), TCP provides a totally different service to the application layer than UDP does. TCP provides a connection-oriented, reliable, byte stream service.

The term *connection-oriented* means the two applications using TCP (normally considered a client and a server) must establish a TCP connection with each other before they can exchange data. The typical analogy is dialing a telephone number, waiting for the other party to answer the phone and say "hello," and then saying who's calling. In Chapter 18 we look at how a connection is established, and disconnected some time later when either end is done.

There are exactly two end points communicating with each other on a TCP connection. Concepts that we talked about in Chapter 12, broadcasting and multicasting, aren't applicable to TCP.

TCP provides *reliability* by doing the following:

- The application data is broken into what TCP considers the best sized chunks to send. This is totally different from UDP, where each write by the application generates a UDP datagram of that size. The unit of information passed by TCP to IP is called a *segment*. (See Figure 1.7, p. 10.) In Section 18.4 we'll see how TCP decides what this segment size is.
- When TCP sends a segment it maintains a timer, waiting for the other end to acknowledge reception of the segment. If an acknowledgment isn't received in time, the segment is retransmitted. In Chapter 21 we'll look at TCP's adaptive timeout and retransmission strategy.
- When TCP receives data from the other end of the connection, it sends an acknowledgment. This acknowledgment is not sent immediately, but normally delayed a fraction of a second, as we discuss in Section 19.3.
- TCP maintains a checksum on its header and data. This is an end-to-end checksum whose purpose is to detect any modification of the data in transit. If a segment arrives with an invalid checksum, TCP discards it and doesn't acknowledge receiving it. (It expects the sender to time out and retransmit.)
- Since TCP segments are transmitted as IP datagrams, and since IP datagrams can arrive out of order, TCP segments can arrive out of order. A receiving TCP resequences the data if necessary, passing the received data in the correct order to the application.
- Since IP datagrams can get duplicated, a receiving TCP must discard duplicate data.
- TCP also provides flow control. Each end of a TCP connection has a finite amount of buffer space. A receiving TCP only allows the other end to send as much data as the receiver has buffers for. This prevents a fast host from taking all the buffers on a slower host.

A stream of 8-bit bytes is exchanged across the TCP connection between the two applications. There are no record markers automatically inserted by TCP. This is what we called a *byte stream service*. If the application on one end writes 10 bytes, followed by a write of 20 bytes, followed by a write of 50 bytes, the application at the other end of the connection cannot tell what size the individual writes were. The other end may read the 80 bytes in four reads of 20 bytes at a time. One end puts a stream of bytes into TCP and the same, identical stream of bytes appears at the other end.

Also, TCP does not interpret the contents of the bytes at all. TCP has no idea if the data bytes being exchanged are binary data, ASCII characters, EBCDIC characters, or whatever. The interpretation of this byte stream is up to the applications on each end of the connection.

This treatment of the byte stream by TCP is similar to the treatment of a file by the Unix operating system. The Unix kernel does no interpretation whatsoever of the bytes that an application reads or write—that is up to the applications. There is no distinction to the Unix kernel between a binary file or a file containing lines of text.

17.3 TCP Header

Recall that TCP data is encapsulated in an IP datagram, as shown in Figure 17.1.

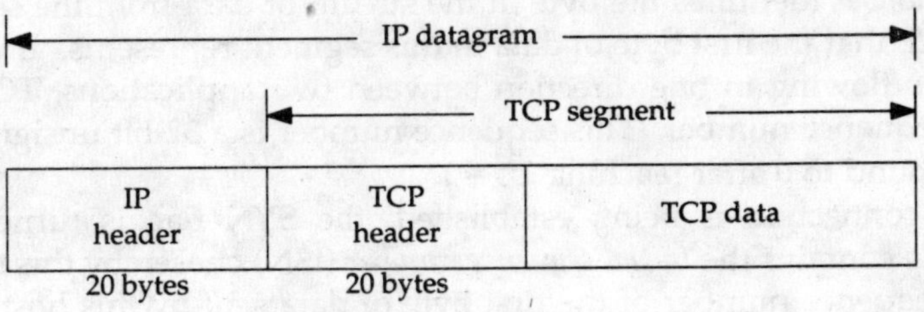

Figure 17.1 Encapsulation of TCP data in an IP datagram.

Figure 17.2 shows the format of the TCP header. Its normal size is 20 bytes, unless options are present.

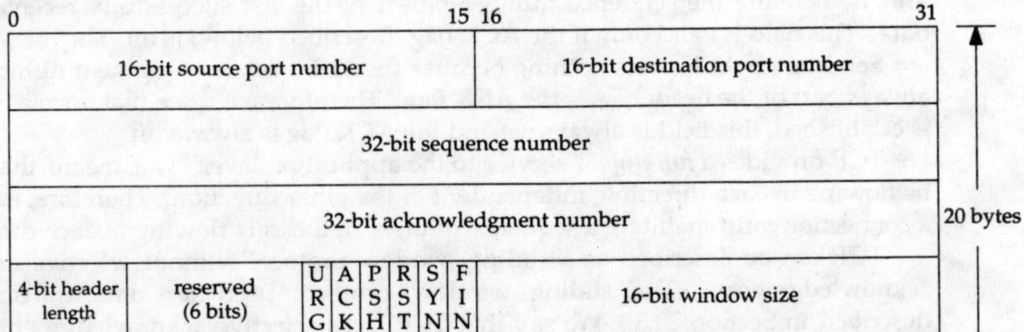

Figure 17.2 TCP header.

Each TCP segment contains the source and destination *port number* to identify the sending and receiving application. These two values, along with the source and destination IP addresses in the IP header, uniquely identify each *connection*.

The combination of an IP address and a port number is sometimes called a *socket*. This term appeared in the original TCP specification (RFC 793), and later it also became used as the name of the Berkeley-derived programming interface (Section 1.15). It is the *socket pair* (the 4-tuple consisting of the client IP address, client port number, server IP address, and server port number) that specifies the two end points that uniquely identifies each TCP connection in an internet.

The *sequence number* identifies the byte in the stream of data from the sending TCP to the receiving TCP that the first byte of data in this segment represents. If we consider the stream of bytes flowing in one direction between two applications, TCP numbers each byte with a sequence number. This sequence number is a 32-bit unsigned number that wraps back around to 0 after reaching $2^{32} - 1$.

When a new connection is being established, the SYN flag is turned on. The *sequence number field* contains the *initial sequence number* (ISN) chosen by this host for this connection. The sequence number of the first byte of data sent by this host will be the ISN plus one because the SYN flag consumes a sequence number. (We describe additional details on exactly how a connection is established and terminated in the next chapter where we'll see that the FIN flag consumes a sequence number also.)

Since every byte that is exchanged is numbered, the *acknowledgment number* contains the next sequence number that the sender of the acknowledgment expects to receive. This is therefore the sequence number plus 1 of the last successfully received byte of data. This field is valid only if the ACK flag (described below) is on.

Sending an ACK costs nothing because the 32-bit acknowledgment number field is always part of the header, as is the ACK flag. Therefore we'll see that once a connection is established, this field is always set and the ACK flag is always on.

TCP provides a *full-duplex* service to the application layer. This means that data can be flowing in each direction, independent of the other direction. Therefore, each end of a connection must maintain a sequence number of the data flowing in each direction.

TCP can be described as a sliding-window protocol without selective or negative acknowledgments. (The sliding window protocol used for data transmission is described in Section 20.3.) We say that TCP lacks selective acknowledgments because the acknowledgment number in the TCP header means that the sender has successfully received up through but not including that byte. There is currently no way to acknowledge selected pieces of the data stream. For example, if bytes 1–1024 are received OK, and the next segment contains bytes 2049–3072, the receiver cannot acknowledge this new segment. All it can send is an ACK with 1025 as the acknowledgment number. There is no means for negatively acknowledging a segment. For example, if the segment with bytes 1025–2048 did arrive, but had a checksum error, all the receiving TCP can send is an ACK with 1025 as the acknowledgment number. In Section 21.7 we'll see how duplicate acknowledgments can help determine that packets have been lost.

The *header length* gives the length of the header in 32-bit words. This is required because the length of the options field is variable. With a 4-bit field, TCP is limited to a 60-byte header. Without options, however, the normal size is 20 bytes.

There are six flag bits in the TCP header. One or more of them can be turned on at the same time. We briefly mention their use here and discuss each flag in more detail in later chapters.

URG The *urgent pointer* is valid (Section 20.8).

ACK The *acknowledgment number* is valid.

PSH The receiver should pass this data to the application as soon as possible (Section 20.5).

RST Reset the connection (Section 18.7).

SYN Synchronize sequence numbers to initiate a connection. This flag and the next are described in Chapter 18.

FIN The sender is finished sending data.

TCP's flow control is provided by each end advertising a *window size*. This is the number of bytes, starting with the one specified by the acknowledgment number field, that the receiver is willing to accept. This is a 16-bit field, limiting the window to 65535 bytes. In Section 24.4 we'll look at the new window scale option that allows this value to be scaled, providing larger windows.

The *checksum* covers the TCP segment: the TCP header and the TCP data. This is a mandatory field that must be calculated and stored by the sender, and then verified by the receiver. The TCP checksum is calculated similar to the UDP checksum, using a pseudo-header as described in Section 11.3.

The *urgent pointer* is valid only if the URG flag is set. This pointer is a positive offset that must be added to the sequence number field of the segment to yield the sequence number of the last byte of urgent data. TCP's urgent mode is a way for the sender to transmit emergency data to the other end. We'll look at this feature in Section 20.8.

The most common *option* field is the maximum segment size option, called the *MSS*. Each end of a connection normally specifies this option on the first segment exchanged (the one with the SYN flag set to establish the connection). It specifies the maximum sized segment that the sender wants to receive. We describe the MSS option in more detail in Section 18.4, and some of the other TCP options in Chapter 24.

In Figure 17.2 we note that the data portion of the TCP segment is optional. We'll see in Chapter 18 that when a connection is established, and when a connection is terminated, segments are exchanged that contain only the TCP header with possible options. A header without any data is also used to acknowledge received data, if there is no data to be transmitted in that direction. There are also some cases dealing with timeouts when a segment can be sent without any data.

17.4 Summary

TCP provides a reliable, connection-oriented, byte stream, transport layer service. We looked briefly at all the fields in the TCP header and will examine them in detail in the following chapters.

TCP packetizes the user data into segments, sets a timeout any time it sends data, acknowledges data received by the other end, reorders out-of-order data, discards duplicate data, provides end-to-end flow control, and calculates and verifies a mandatory end-to-end checksum.

TCP is used by many of the popular applications, such as Telnet, Rlogin, FTP, and electronic mail (SMTP).

Exercises

17.1 We've covered the following packet formats, each of which has a checksum in its corresponding header: IP, ICMP, IGMP, UDP, and TCP. For each one, describe what portion of an IP datagram the checksum covers and whether the checksum is mandatory or optional.

17.2 Why do all the Internet protocols that we've discussed (IP, ICMP, IGMP, UDP, TCP) quietly discard a packet that arrives with a checksum error?

17.3 TCP provides a byte-stream service where record boundaries are not maintained between the sender and receiver. How can applications provide their own record markers?

17.4 Why are the source and destination port numbers at the beginning of the TCP header?

17.5 Why does the TCP header have a header length field while the UDP header (Figure 11.2, p. 144) does not?

18

TCP Connection Establishment and Termination

18.1 Introduction

TCP is a *connection-oriented* protocol. Before either end can send data to the other, a *connection* must be established between them. In this chapter we take a detailed look at how a TCP connection is established and later terminated.

This establishment of a connection between the two ends differs from a *connectionless* protocol such as UDP. We saw in Chapter 11 that with UDP one end just sends a datagram to the other end, without any preliminary handshaking.

18.2 Connection Establishment and Termination

To see what happens when a TCP connection is established and then terminated, we type the following command on the system `svr4`:

```
svr4 % telnet bsdi discard
Trying 140.252.13.35 ...
Connected to bsdi.
Escape character is '^]'
^]                              type Control, right bracket to talk to the Telnet client
telnet> quit                    terminate the connection
Connection closed.
```

The `telnet` command establishes a TCP connection with the host `bsdi` on the port corresponding to the discard service (Section 1.12). This is exactly the type of service we need to see what happens when a connection is established and terminated, without having the server initiate any data exchange.

`tcpdump` Output

Figure 18.1 shows the `tcpdump` output for the segments generated by this command.

```
1  0.0                  svr4.1037 > bsdi.discard: S 1415531521:1415531521(0)
                                                     win 4096 <mss 1024>
2  0.002402 (0.0024)    bsdi.discard > svr4.1037: S 1823083521:1823083521(0)
                                                     ack 1415531522 win 4096
                                                     <mss 1024>
3  0.007224 (0.0048)    svr4.1037 > bsdi.discard: . ack 1823083522 win 4096
4  4.155441 (4.1482)    svr4.1037 > bsdi.discard: F 1415531522:1415531522(0)
                                                     ack 1823083522 win 4096
5  4.156747 (0.0013)    bsdi.discard > svr4.1037: . ack 1415531523 win 4096
6  4.158144 (0.0014)    bsdi.discard > svr4.1037: F 1823083522:1823083522(0)
                                                     ack 1415531523 win 4096
7  4.180662 (0.0225)    svr4.1037 > bsdi.discard:   ack 1823083523 win 4096
```

Figure 18.1 `tcpdump` output for TCP connection establishment and termination.

These seven TCP segments contain TCP headers only. No data is exchanged.

For TCP segments, each output line begins with

source > *destination: flags*

where *flags* represents four of the six flag bits in the TCP header (Figure 17.2). Figure 18.2 shows the five different characters that can appear in the *flags* output.

flag	3-character abbreviation	Description
S	SYN	synchronize sequence numbers
F	FIN	sender is finished sending data
R	RST	reset connection
P	PSH	push data to receiving process as soon as possible
.		none of above four flags is on

Figure 18.2 *flag* characters output by `tcpdump` for flag bits in TCP header.

In this example we see the `S`, `F`, and period. We'll see the other two *flags* (`R` and `P`) later. The other two TCP header flag bits—ACK and URG—are printed specially by `tcpdump`.

It's possible for more than one of the four flag bits in Figure 18.2 to be on in a single segment, but we normally see only one on at a time.

RFC 1025 [Postel 1987], the *TCP and IP Bake Off*, calls a segment with the maximum combination of allowable flag bits turned on at once (SYN, URG, PSH, FIN, and 1 byte of data) a Kamikaze packet. It's also known as a nastygram, Christmas tree packet, and lamp test segment.

In line 1, the field `1415531521:1415531521(0)` means the sequence number of the packet was 1415531521 and the number of data bytes in the segment was 0. `tcpdump` displays this by printing the starting sequence number, a colon, the implied ending sequence number, and the number of data bytes in parentheses. The advantage of displaying both the sequence number and the implied ending sequence number is to see what the implied ending sequence number is, when the number of bytes is greater than 0. This field is output only if (1) the segment contains one or more bytes of data or (2) the SYN, FIN, or RST flag was on. Lines 1, 2, 4, and 6 in Figure 18.1 display this field because of the flag bits—we never exchange any data in this example.

In line 2 the field `ack 1415531522` shows the acknowledgment number. This is printed only if the ACK flag in the header is on.

The field `win 4096` in every line of output shows the window size being advertised by the sender. In these examples, where we are not exchanging any data, the window size never changes from its default of 4096. (We examine TCP's window size in Section 20.4.)

The final field that is output in Figure 18.1, `<mss 1024>` shows the *maximum segment size* (MSS) option specified by the sender. The sender does not want to receive TCP segments larger than this value. This is normally to avoid fragmentation (Section 11.5). We discuss the maximum segment size in Section 18.4, and show the format of the various TCP options in Section 18.10.

Time Line

Figure 18.3 shows the time line for this sequence of packets. (We described some general features of these time lines when we showed the first one in Figure 6.11, p. 80.) This figure shows which end is sending packets. We also expand some of the `tcpdump` output (e.g., printing SYN instead of `S`). In this time line we have also removed the window size values, since they add nothing to the discussion.

Connection Establishment Protocol

Now let's return to the details of the TCP protocol that are shown in Figure 18.3. To establish a TCP connection:

1. The requesting end (normally called the *client*) sends a SYN segment specifying the port number of the *server* that the client wants to connect to, and the client's *initial sequence number* (ISN, 1415531521 in this example). This is segment 1.
2. The server responds with its own SYN segment containing the server's initial sequence number (segment 2). The server also acknowledges the client's SYN by ACKing the client's ISN plus one. A SYN consumes one sequence number.
3. The client must acknowledge this SYN from the server by ACKing the server's ISN plus one (segment 3).

These three segments complete the connection establishment. This is often called the *three-way handshake*.

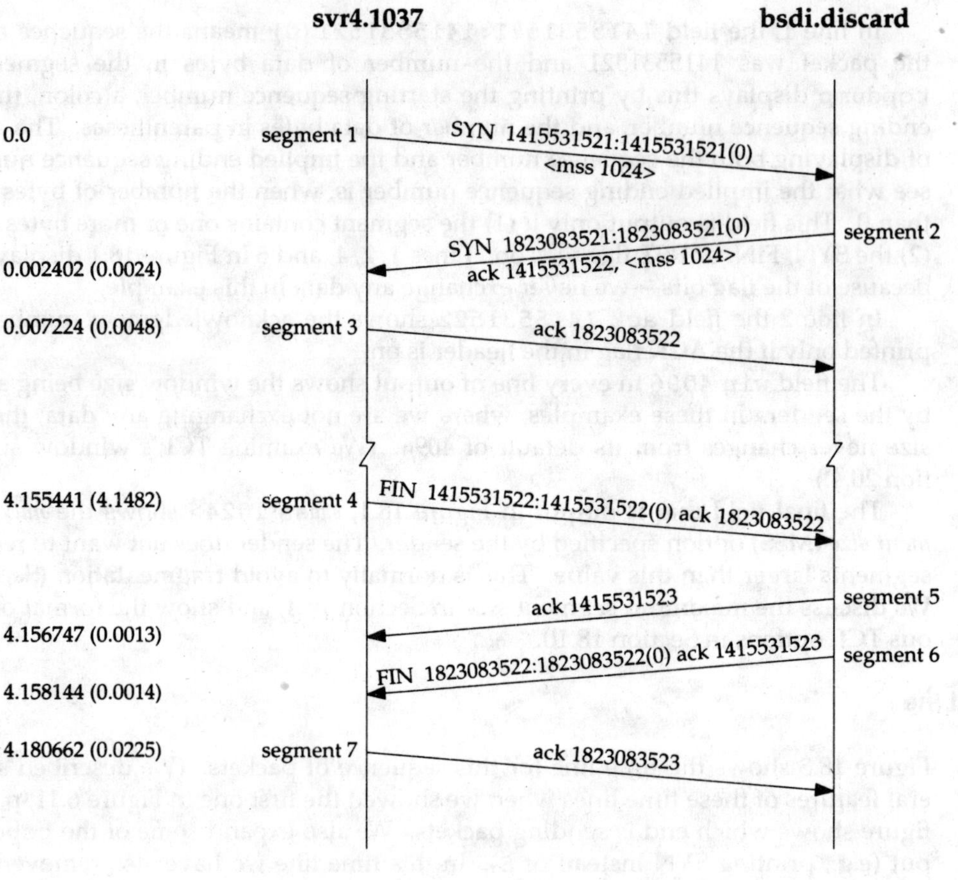

Figure 18.3 Time line of connection establishment and connection termination.

The side that sends the first SYN is said to perform an *active open*. The other side, which receives this SYN and sends the next SYN, performs a *passive open*. (In Section 18.8 we describe a simultaneous open where both sides can do an active open.)

When each end sends its SYN to establish the connection, it chooses an initial sequence number for that connection. The ISN should change over time, so that each connection has a different ISN. RFC 793 [Postel 1981c] specifies that the ISN should be viewed as a 32-bit counter that increments by one every 4 microseconds. The purpose in these sequence numbers is to prevent packets that get delayed in the network from being delivered later and then misinterpreted as part of an existing connection.

How are the sequence numbers chosen? In 4.4BSD (and most Berkeley-derived implementations) when the system is initialized the initial send sequence number is initialized to 1. This practice violates the Host Requirements RFC. (A comment in the code acknowledges that this is wrong.) This variable is then incremented by 64,000 every half-second, and will cycle back to 0 about every 9.5 hours. (This corresponds to a counter that is incremented every 8 microseconds, not every 4 microseconds.) Additionally, each time a connection is established, this variable is incremented by 64,000.

The 4.1-second gap between segments 3 and 4 is the time between establishing the connection and typing the `quit` command to `telnet` to terminate the connection.

Connection Termination Protocol

While it takes three segments to establish a connection, it takes four to terminate a connection. This is caused by TCP's *half-close*. Since a TCP connection is full-duplex (that is, data can be flowing in each direction independently of the other direction), each direction must be shut down independently. The rule is that either end can send a FIN when it is done sending data. When a TCP receives a FIN, it must notify the application that the other end has terminated that direction of data flow. The sending of a FIN is normally the result of the application issuing a close.

The receipt of a FIN only means there will be no more data flowing in that direction. A TCP can still send data after receiving a FIN. While it's possible for an application to take advantage of this half-close, in practice few TCP applications use it. The normal scenario is what we show in Figure 18.3. We describe the half-close in more detail in Section 18.5.

We say that the end that first issues the close (e.g., sends the first FIN) performs the *active close* and the other end (that receives this FIN) performs the *passive close*. Normally one end does the active close and the other does the passive close, but we'll see in Section 18.9 how both ends can do an active close.

Segment 4 in Figure 18.3 initiates the termination of the connection and is sent when the Telnet client closes its connection. This happens when we type `quit`. This causes the client TCP to send a FIN, closing the flow of data from the client to the server.

When the server receives the FIN it sends back an ACK of the received sequence number plus one (segment 5). A FIN consumes a sequence number, just like a SYN. At this point the server's TCP also delivers an end-of-file to the application (the discard server). The server then closes its connection, causing its TCP to send a FIN (segment 6), which the client TCP must ACK by incrementing the received sequence number by one (segment 7).

Figure 18.4 shows the typical sequence of segments that we've described for the termination of a connection. We omit the sequence numbers. In this figure sending the FINs is caused by the applications closing their end of the connection, whereas the ACKs of these FINs are automatically generated by the TCP software.

Connections are normally initiated by the client, with the first SYN going from the client to the server. Either end can actively close the connection (i.e., send the first FIN). Often, however, it is the client that determines when the connection should be terminated, since client processes are often driven by an interactive user, who enters something like "quit" to terminate. In Figure 18.4 we can switch the labels at the top, calling the left side the server and the right side the client, and everything still works fine as shown. (The first example in Section 14.4, for example, shows the daytime server closing the connection.)

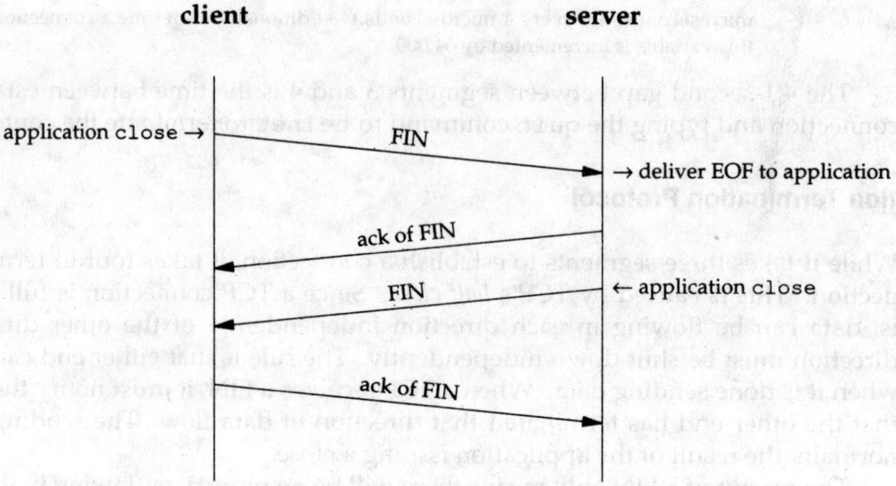

Figure 18.4 Normal exchange of segments during connection termination.

Normal tcpdump Output

Having to sort through all the huge sequence numbers is cumbersome, so the default tcpdump output shows the complete sequence numbers only on the SYN segments, and shows all following sequence numbers as relative offsets from the original sequence numbers. (To generate the output for Figure 18.1 we had to specify the -S option.) The normal tcpdump output corresponding to Figure 18.1 is shown in Figure 18.5.

```
1  0.0                 svr4.1037 > bsdi.discard: S 1415531521:1415531521(0)
                                                   win 4096 <mss 1024>
2  0.002402 (0.0024)   bsdi.discard > svr4.1037: S 1823083521:1823083521(0)
                                                   ack 1415531522
                                                   win 4096 <mss 1024>
3  0.007224 (0.0048)   svr4.1037 > bsdi.discard: . ack 1 win 4096
4  4.155441 (4.1482)   svr4.1037 > bsdi.discard: F 1:1(0) ack 1 win 4096
5  4.156747 (0.0013)   bsdi.discard > svr4.1037: . ack 2 win 4096
6  4.158144 (0.0014)   bsdi.discard > svr4.1037: F 1:1(0) ack 2 win 4096
7  4.180662 (0.0225)   svr4.1037 > bsdi.discard: . ack 2 win 4096
```

Figure 18.5 Normal tcpdump output for connection establishment and termination.

Unless we need to show the complete sequence numbers, we'll use this form of output in all following examples.

18.3 Timeout of Connection Establishment

There are several instances when the connection cannot be established. In one example the server host is down. To simulate this scenario we issue our `telnet` command after disconnecting the Ethernet cable from the server's host. Figure 18.6 shows the `tcpdump` output.

```
1   0.0                   bsdi.1024 > svr4.discard: S 291008001:291008001(0)
                                                     win 4096 <mss 1024>
                                                     [tos 0x10]
2   5.814797 ( 5.8148)    bsdi.1024 > svr4.discard: S 291008001:291008001(0)
                                                     win 4096 <mss 1024>
                                                     [tos 0x10]
3  29.815436 (24.0006)    bsdi.1024 > svr4.discard: S 291008001:291008001(0)
                                                     win 4096 <mss 1024>
                                                     [tos 0x10]
```

Figure 18.6 `tcpdump` output for connection establishment that times out.

The interesting point in this output is how frequently the client's TCP sends a SYN to try to establish the connection. The second segment is sent 5.8 seconds after the first, and the third is sent 24 seconds after the second.

> As a side note, this example was run about 38 minutes after the client was rebooted. This corresponds with the initial sequence number of 291,008,001 (approximately $38 \times 60 \times 64000 \times 2$). Recall earlier in this chapter we said that typical Berkeley-derived systems initialize the initial sequence number to 1 and then increment it by 64,000 every half-second.
>
> Also, this is the first TCP connection since the system was bootstrapped, which is why the client's port number is 1024.

What isn't shown in Figure 18.6 is how long the client's TCP keeps retransmitting before giving up. To see this we have to time the `telnet` command:

```
bsdi % date ; telnet svr4 discard ; date
Thu Sep 24 16:24:11 MST 1992
Trying 140.252.13.34...
telnet: Unable to connect to remote host: Connection timed out
Thu Sep 24 16:25:27 MST 1992
```

The time difference is 76 seconds. Most Berkeley-derived systems set a time limit of 75 seconds on the establishment of a new connection. We'll see in Section 21.4 that the third packet sent by the client would have timed out around 16:25:29, 48 seconds after it was sent, had the client not given up after 75 seconds.

First Timeout Period

One puzzling item in Figure 18.6 is that the first timeout period, 5.8 seconds, is close to 6 seconds, but not exact, while the second period is almost exactly 24 seconds. Ten more of these tests were run and the first timeout period took on various values between 5.59 seconds and 5.93 seconds. The second timeout period, however, was always 24.00 (to two decimal places).

What's happening here is that BSD implementations of TCP run a timer that goes off every 500 ms. This 500-ms timer is used for various TCP timeouts, all of which we cover in later chapters. When we type in the `telnet` command, an initial 6-second timer is established (12 clock ticks), but it may expire anywhere between 5.5 and 6 seconds in the future. Figure 18.7 shows what's happening.

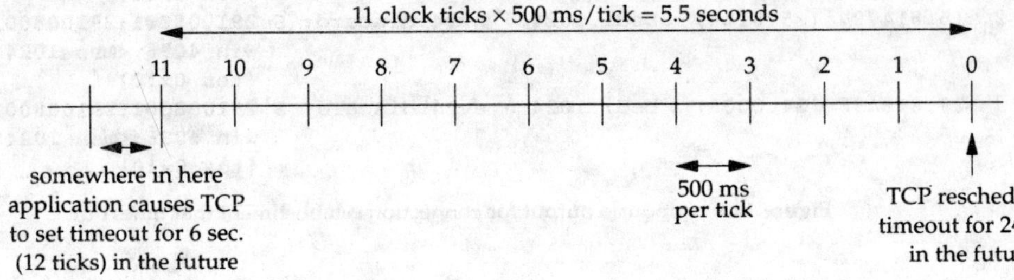

Figure 18.7 TCP 500-ms timer.

Although the timer is initialized to 12 ticks, the first decrement of the timer can occur between 0 and 500 ms after it is set. From that point on the timer is decremented about every 500 ms, but the first period can be variable. (We use the qualifier "about" because the time when TCP gets control every 500 ms can be preempted by other interrupts being handled by the kernel.)

When that 6-second timer expires at the tick labeled 0 in Figure 18.7, the timer is reset for 24 seconds (48 ticks) in the future. This next timer will be close to 24 seconds, since it was set at a time when the TCP's 500-ms timer handler was called by the kernel.

Type-of-Service Field

In Figure 18.6, the notation `[tos 0x10]` appears. This is the type-of-service (TOS) field in the IP datagram (Figure 3.2). The BSD/386 Telnet client sets the field for minimum delay.

18.4 Maximum Segment Size

The maximum segment size (MSS) is the largest "chunk" of data that TCP will send to the other end. When a connection is established, each end can announce its MSS. The values we've seen have all been 1024. The resulting IP datagram is normally 40 bytes larger: 20 bytes for the TCP header and 20 bytes for the IP header.

Some texts refer to this as a "negotiated" option. It is not negotiated in any way. When a connection is established, each end has the option of announcing the MSS it expects to receive. (An MSS option can only appear in a SYN segment.) If one end does not receive an MSS option from the other end, a default of 536 bytes is assumed. (This default allows for a 20-byte IP header and a 20-byte TCP header to fit into a 576-byte IP datagram.)

In general, the larger the MSS the better, until fragmentation occurs. (This may not always be true. See Figures 24.3 and 24.4 for a counterexample.) A larger segment size allows more data to be sent in each segment, amortizing the cost of the IP and TCP headers. When TCP sends a SYN segment, either because a local application wants to initiate a connection, or when a connection request is received from another host, it can send an MSS value up to the outgoing interface's MTU, minus the size of the fixed TCP and IP headers. For an Ethernet this implies an MSS of up to 1460 bytes. Using IEEE 802.3 encapsulation (Section 2.2), the MSS could go up to 1452 bytes.

The values of 1024 that we've seen in this chapter, for connections involving BSD/386 and SVR4, are because many BSD implementations require the MSS to be a multiple of 512. Other systems, such as SunOS 4.1.3, Solaris 2.2, and AIX 3.2.2, all announce an MSS of 1460 when both ends are on a local Ethernet. Measurements in [Mogul 1993] show how an MSS of 1460 provides better performance on an Ethernet than an MSS of 1024.

If the destination IP address is "nonlocal," the MSS normally defaults to 536. While it's easy to say that a destination whose IP address has the same network ID and the same subnet ID as ours is local, and a destination whose IP address has a totally different network ID from ours is nonlocal, a destination with the same network ID but a different subnet ID could be either local or nonlocal. Most implementations provide a configuration option (Appendix E and Figure E.1) that lets the system administrator specify whether different subnets are local or nonlocal. The setting of this option determines whether the announced MSS is as large as possible (up to the outgoing interface's MTU) or the default of 536.

The MSS lets a host limit the size of datagrams that the other end sends it. When combined with the fact that a host can also limit the size of the datagrams that it sends, this lets a host avoid fragmentation when the host is connected to a network with a small MTU.

Consider our host `slip`, which has a SLIP link with an MTU of 296 to the router `bsdi`. Figure 18.8 shows these systems and the host `sun`.

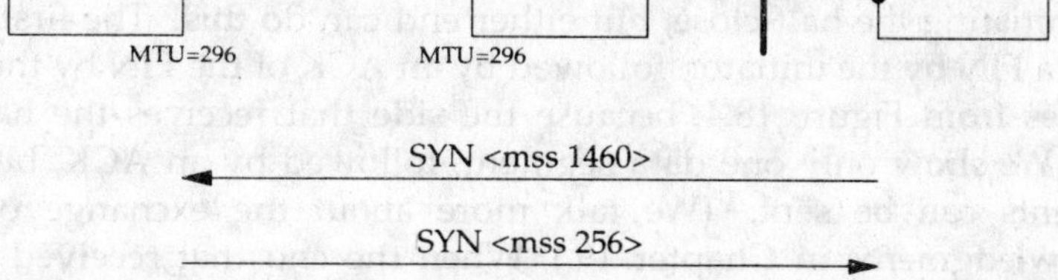

Figure 18.8 TCP connection from `sun` to `slip` showing MSS values.

We initiate a TCP connection from sun to slip and watch the segments using tcpdump. Figure 18.9 shows only the connection establishment (with the window size advertisements removed).

```
1  0.0               sun.1093 > slip.discard: S 517312000:517312000(0)
                                              <mss 1460>

2  0.10 (0.00)       slip.discard > sun.1093: S 509556225:509556225(0)
                                              ack 517312001 <mss 256>

3  0.10 (0.00)       sun.1093 > slip.discard: . ack 1
```

Figure 18.9 tcpdump output for connection establishment from sun to slip.

The important fact here is that sun cannot send a segment with more than 256 bytes of data, since it received an MSS option of 256 (line 2). Furthermore, since slip knows that the outgoing interface's MTU is 296, even though sun announced an MSS of 1460, it will never send more than 256 bytes of data, to avoid fragmentation. It's OK for a system to send *less* than the MSS announced by the other end.

This avoidance of fragmentation works only if either host is directly connected to a network with an MTU of less than 576. If both hosts are connected to Ethernets, and both announce an MSS of 536, but an intermediate network has an MTU of 296, fragmentation will occur. The only way around this is to use the path MTU discovery mechanism (Section 24.2).

18.5 TCP Half-Close

TCP provides the ability for one end of a connection to terminate its output, while still receiving data from the other end. This is called a *half-close*. Few applications take advantage of this capability, as we mentioned earlier.

To use this feature the programming interface must provide a way for the application to say "I am done sending data, so send an end-of-file (FIN) to the other end, but I still want to receive data from the other end, until it sends me an end-of-file (FIN)."

> The sockets API supports the half-close, if the application calls shutdown with a second argument of 1, instead of calling close. Most applications, however, terminate both directions of the connection by calling close.

Figure 18.10 shows a typical scenario for a half-close. We show the client on the left side initiating the half-close, but either end can do this. The first two segments are the same: a FIN by the initiator, followed by an ACK of the FIN by the recipient. But it then changes from Figure 18.4, because the side that receives the half-close can still send data. We show only one data segment, followed by an ACK, but any number of data segments can be sent. (We talk more about the exchange of data segments and acknowledgments in Chapter 19.) When the end that received the half-close is done sending data, it closes its end of the connection, causing a FIN to be sent, and this delivers an end-of-file to the application that initiated the half-close. When this second FIN is acknowledged, the connection is completely closed.

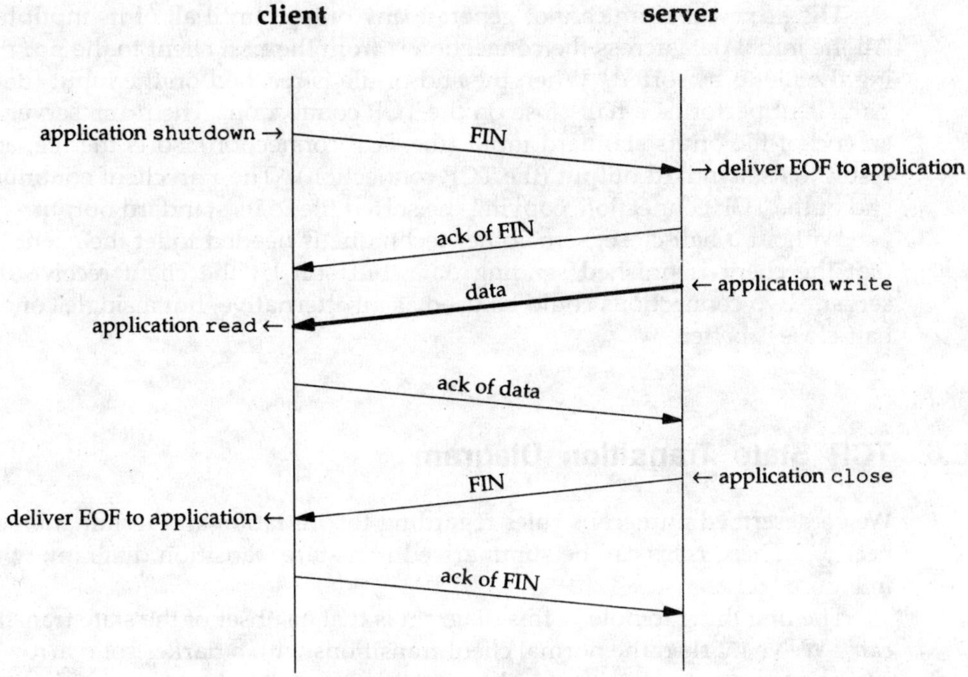

Figure 18.10 Example of TCP's half-close.

Why is there a half-close? One example is the Unix rsh(1) command, which executes a command on another system. The command

```
sun % rsh bsdi sort < datafile
```

executes the sort command on the host bsdi with standard input for the rsh command being read from the file named datafile. A TCP connection is created by rsh between itself and the program being executed on the other host. The operation of rsh is then simple: it copies standard input (datafile) to the connection, and copies from the connection to standard output (our terminal). Figure 18.11 shows the setup. (Remember that a TCP connection is full-duplex.)

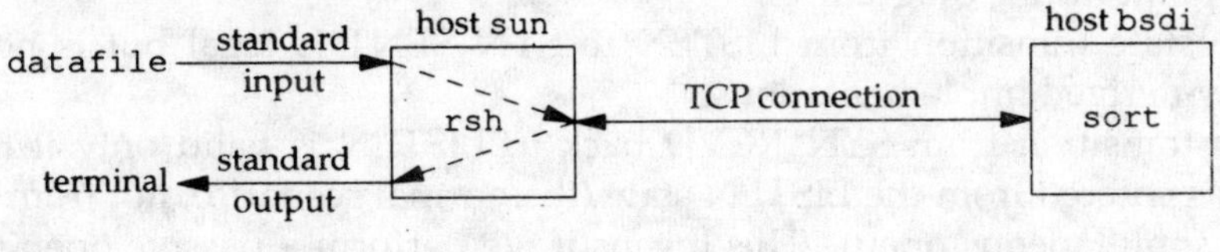

Figure 18.11 The command: rsh bsdi sort < datafile.

On the remote host bsdi the rshd server executes the sort program so that its standard input and standard output are both the TCP connection. Chapter 14 of [Stevens 1990] details the Unix process structure involved, but what concerns us here is the use of the TCP connection and the required use of TCP's half-close.

The sort program cannot generate any output until all of its input has been read. All the initial data across the connection is from the rsh client to the sort server, sending the file to be sorted. When the end-of-file is reached on the input (datafile), the rsh client performs a half-close on the TCP connection. The sort server then receives an end-of-file on its standard input (the TCP connection), sorts the file, and writes the result to its standard output (the TCP connection). The rsh client continues reading its end of the TCP connection, copying the sorted file to its standard output.

Without a half-close, some other technique is needed to let the client tell the server that the client is finished sending data, but still let the client receive data from the server. Two connections could be used as an alternative, but a single connection with a half-close is better.

18.6 TCP State Transition Diagram

We've described numerous rules regarding the initiation and termination of a TCP connection. These rules can be summarized in a state transition diagram, which we show in Figure 18.12.

The first thing to note in this diagram is that a subset of the state transitions is "typical." We've marked the normal client transitions with a darker solid arrow, and the normal server transitions with a darker dashed arrow.

Next, the two transitions leading to the ESTABLISHED state correspond to opening a connection, and the two transitions leading from the ESTABLISHED state are for the termination of a connection. The ESTABLISHED state is where data transfer can occur between the two ends in both directions. Later chapters describe what happens in this state.

We've collected the four boxes in the lower left of this diagram within a dashed box and labeled it "active close." Two other boxes (CLOSE_WAIT and LAST_ACK) are collected in a dashed box with the label "passive close."

The names of the 11 states (CLOSED, LISTEN, SYN_SENT, etc.) in this figure were purposely chosen to be identical to the states output by the netstat command. The netstat names, in turn, are almost identical to the names originally described in RFC 793. The state CLOSED is not really a state, but is the imaginary starting point and ending point for the diagram.

The state transition from LISTEN to SYN_SENT is legal but is not supported in Berkeley-derived implementations.

The transition from SYN_RCVD back to LISTEN is valid only if the SYN_RCVD state was entered from the LISTEN state (the normal scenario), not from the SYN_SENT state (a simultaneous open). This means if we perform a passive open (enter LISTEN), receive a SYN, send a SYN with an ACK (enter SYN_RCVD), and then receive a reset instead of an ACK, the end point returns to the LISTEN state and waits for another connection request to arrive.

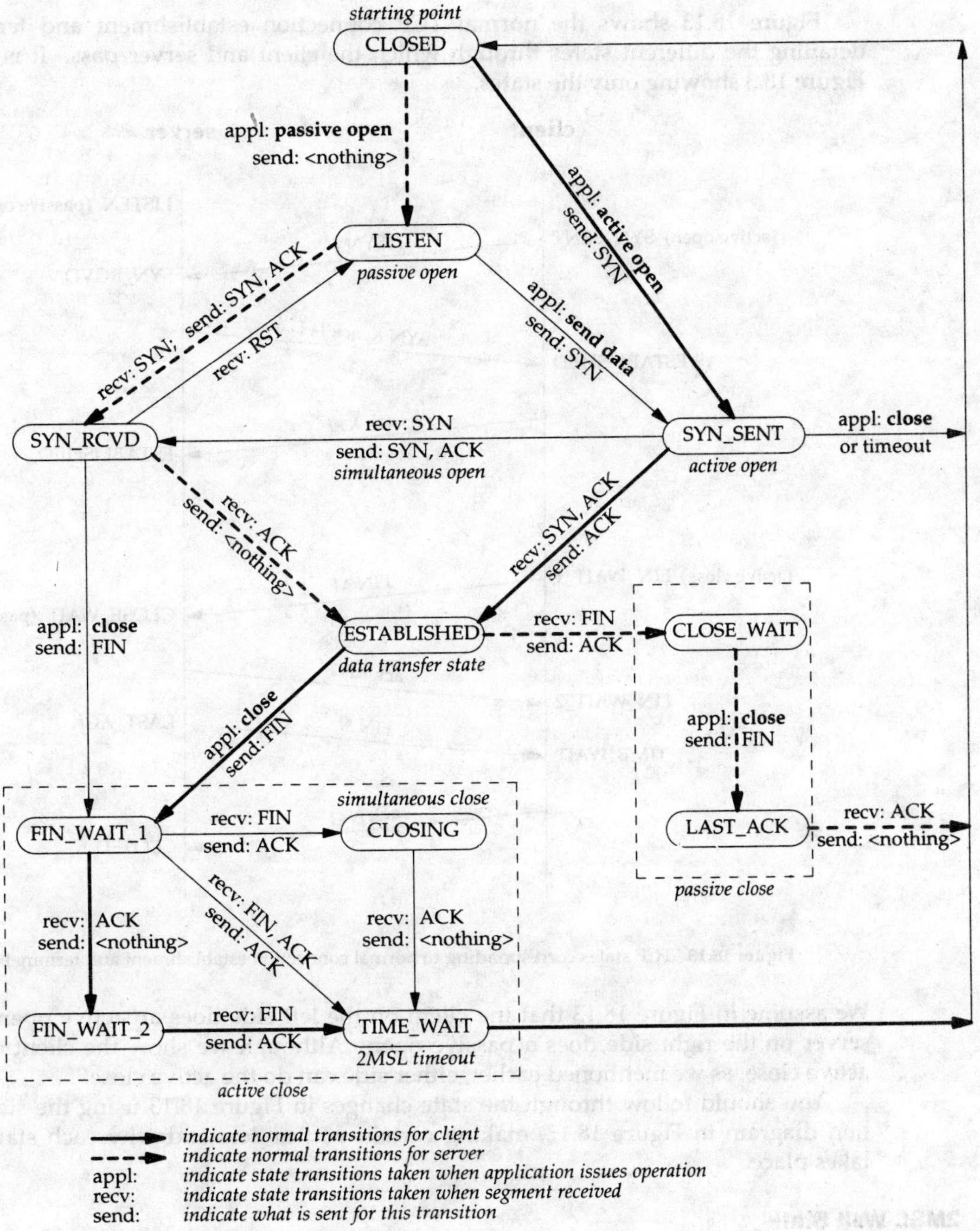

Figure 18.12 TCP state transition diagram.

Figure 18.13 shows the normal TCP connection establishment and termination, detailing the different states through which the client and server pass. It is a redo of Figure 18.3 showing only the states.

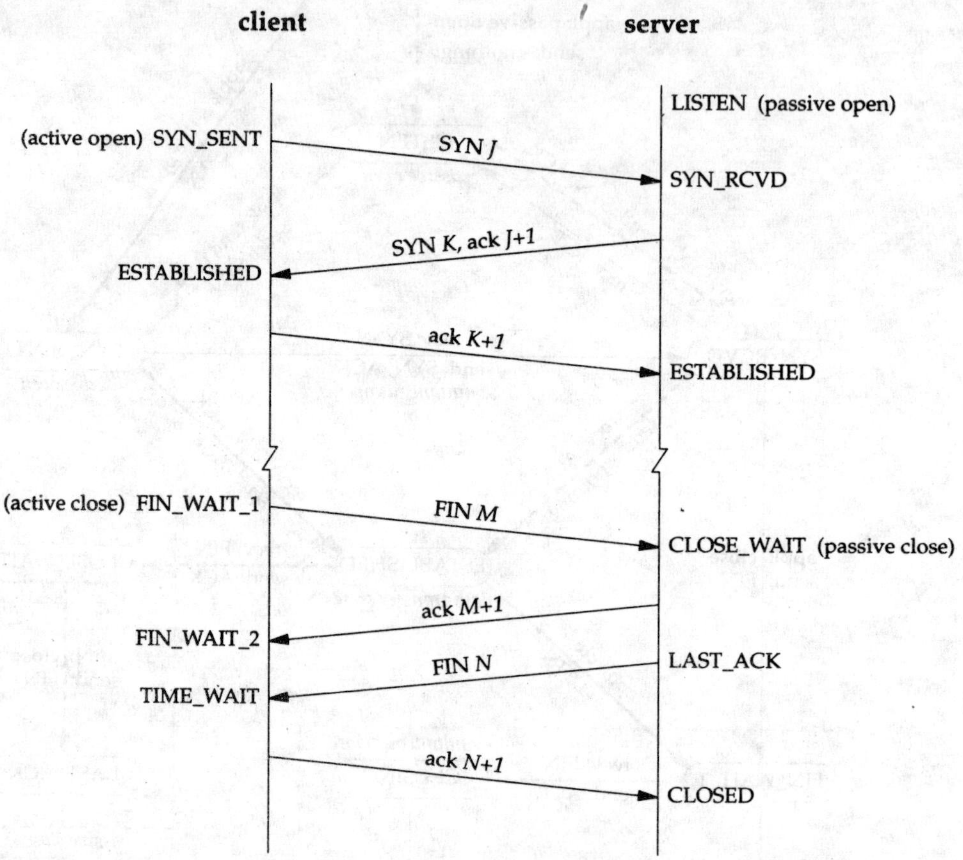

Figure 18.13 TCP states corresponding to normal connection establishment and termination.

We assume in Figure 18.13 that the client on the left side does an active open, and the server on the right side does a passive open. Although we show the client doing the active close, as we mentioned earlier, either side can do the active close.

You should follow through the state changes in Figure 18.13 using the state transition diagram in Figure 18.12, making certain you understand why each state change takes place.

2MSL Wait State

The TIME_WAIT state is also called the 2MSL wait state. Every implementation must choose a value for the *maximum segment lifetime* (MSL). It is the maximum amount of time any segment can exist in the network before being discarded. We know this time limit is bounded, since TCP segments are transmitted as IP datagrams, and the IP datagram has the TTL field that limits its lifetime.

RFC 793 [Postel 1981c] specifies the MSL as 2 minutes. Common implementation values, however, are 30 seconds, 1 minute, or 2 minutes.

Recall from Chapter 8 that the real-world limit on the lifetime of the IP datagram is based on the number of hops, not a timer.

Given the MSL value for an implementation, the rule is: when TCP performs an active close, and sends the final ACK, that connection must stay in the TIME_WAIT state for twice the MSL. This lets TCP resend the final ACK in case this ACK is lost (in which case the other end will time out and retransmit its final FIN).

Another effect of this 2MSL wait is that while the TCP connection is in the 2MSL wait, the socket pair defining that connection (client IP address, client port number, server IP address, and server port number) cannot be reused. That connection can only be reused when the 2MSL wait is over.

Unfortunately most implementations (i.e., the Berkeley-derived ones) impose a more stringent constraint. By default a local port number cannot be reused while that port number is the local port number of a socket pair that is in the 2MSL wait. We'll see examples of this common constraint below.

Some implementations and APIs provide a way to bypass this restriction. With the sockets API, the `SO_REUSEADDR` socket option can be specified. It lets the caller assign itself a local port number that's in the 2MSL wait, but we'll see that the rules of TCP still prevent this port number from being part of a connection that is in the 2MSL wait.

Any delayed segments that arrive for a connection while it is in the 2MSL wait are discarded. Since the connection defined by the socket pair in the 2MSL wait cannot be reused during this time period, when we do establish a valid connection we know that delayed segments from an earlier incarnation of this connection cannot be misinterpreted as being part of the new connection. (A connection is defined by a socket pair. New instances of a connection are called *incarnations* of that connection.)

As we said with Figure 18.13, it is normally the client that does the active close and enters the TIME_WAIT state. The server usually does the passive close, and does not go through the TIME_WAIT state. The implication is that if we terminate a client, and restart the same client immediately, that new client cannot reuse the same local port number. This isn't a problem, since clients normally use ephemeral ports, and don't care what the local ephemeral port number is.

With servers, however, this changes, since servers use well-known ports. If we terminate a server that has a connection established, and immediately try to restart the server, the server cannot assign its well-known port number to its end point, since that port number is part of a connection that is in a 2MSL wait. It may take from 1 to 4 minutes before the server can be restarted.

We can see this scenario using our `sock` program. We start the server, connect to it from a client, and then terminate the server:

```
sun % sock -v -s 6666                      start as server, listening on port 6666
                                           (execute client on bsdi that connects to this port)
connection on 140.252.13.33.6666 from 140.252.13.35.1081
^?                                         then type interrupt key to terminate server
sun % sock -s 6666                         and immediately try to restart server on same port
can't bind local address: Address already in use
sun % netstat                              let's check the state of the connection
Active Internet connections
Proto Recv-Q Send-Q  Local Address         Foreign Address        (state)
tcp        0      0  sun.6666              bsdi.1081              TIME_WAIT
                                           many more lines that are deleted
```

When we try to restart the server, the program outputs an error message indicating it cannot bind its well-known port number, because it's already in use (i.e., it's in a 2MSL wait).

We then immediately execute `netstat` to see the state of the connection, and verify that it is indeed in the TIME_WAIT state.

> If we continually try to restart the server, and measure the time until it succeeds, we can measure the 2MSL value. On SunOS 4.1.3, SVR4, BSD/386, and AIX 3.2.2, it takes 1 minute to restart the server, meaning the MSL is 30 seconds. Under Solaris 2.2 it takes 4 minutes to restart the server, implying an MSL of 2 minutes.

We can see the same error from a client, if the client tries to allocate a port that is part of a connection in the 2MSL wait (something clients normally don't do):

```
sun % sock -v bsdi echo                    start as client, connect to echo server
connected on 140.252.13.33.1162 to 140.252.13.35.7
hello there                                type this line
hello there                                and it's echoed by the server
^D                                         type end-of-file character to terminate client
sun % sock -b1162 bsdi echo
can't bind local address: Address already in use
```

The first time we execute the client we specify the `-v` option to see what the local port number is (1162). The second time we execute the client we specify the `-b` option, telling the client to assign itself 1162 as its local port number. As we expect, the client can't do this, since that port number is part of a connection that is in a 2MSL wait.

We need to reemphasize one effect of the 2MSL wait because we'll encounter it in Chapter 27 with FTP, the File Transfer Protocol. As we said earlier, it is a socket pair (that is, the 4-tuple consisting of a local IP address, local port, remote IP address and remote port) that remains in the 2MSL wait. Although many implementations allow a process to reuse a port number that is part of a connection that is in the 2MSL wait (normally with an option named `SO_REUSEADDR`), TCP *cannot* allow a new connection to be created with the same socket pair. We can see this with the following experiment:

```
sun % sock -v -s 6666                      start as server, listening on port 6666
                                           (execute client on bsdi that connects to this port)
```

```
connection on 140.252.13.33.6666 from 140.252.13.35.1098
^?                                      then type interrupt key to terminate server

sun % sock -b6666 bsdi 1098             try to start as client with local port 6666
can't bind local address: Address already in use

sun % sock -A -b6666 bsdi 1098          try again, this time with -A option
active open error: Address already in use
```

The first time we run our sock program, we run it as a server on port 6666 and connect to it from a client on the host bsdi. The client's ephemeral port number is 1098. We terminate the server so it does the active close. This causes the 4-tuple of 140.252.13.33 (local IP address), 6666 (local port number), 140.252.13.35 (foreign IP address), and 1098 (foreign port number) to enter the 2MSL wait on the server host.

The second time we run the program, we run it as a client and try to specify the local port number as 6666 and connect to host bsdi on port 1098. But the program gets an error when it tries to assign itself the local port number of 6666, because that port number is part of the 4-tuple that is in the 2MSL wait state.

To try and get around this error we run the program again, specifying the -A option, which enables the SO_REUSEADDR option that we mentioned. This lets the program assign itself the port number 6666, but we then get an error when it tries to issue the active open. Even though it can assign itself the port number 6666, it cannot create a connection to port 1098 on the host bsdi, because the socket pair defining that connection is in the 2MSL wait state.

What if we try to establish the connection from the other host? First we must restart the server on sun with the -A flag, since the local port it needs (6666) is part of a connection that is in the 2MSL wait:

```
sun % sock -A -s 6666                   start as server, listening on port 6666
```

Then, before the 2MSL wait is over on sun, we start the client on bsdi:

```
bsdi % sock -b1098 sun 6666
connected on 140.252.13.35.1098 to 140.252.13.33.6666
```

Unfortunately it works! This is a violation of the TCP specification, but is supported by most Berkeley-derived implementations. These implementations allow a new connection request to arrive for a connection that is in the TIME_WAIT state, if the new sequence number is greater than the final sequence number from the previous incarnation of this connection. In this case the ISN for the new incarnation is set to the final sequence number from the previous incarnation plus 128,000. The appendix of RFC 1185 [Jacobson, Braden, and Zhang 1990] shows the pitfalls still possible with this technique.

This implementation feature lets a client and server continually reuse the same port number at each end for successive incarnations of the same connection, but only if the server does the active close. We'll see another example of this 2MSL wait condition in Figure 27.8, with FTP. See Exercise 18.5 also.

Quiet Time Concept

The 2MSL wait provides protection against delayed segments from an earlier incarnation of a connection from being interpreted as part of a new connection that uses the same local and foreign IP addresses and port numbers. But this works only if a host with connections in the 2MSL wait does not crash.

What if a host with ports in the 2MSL wait crashes, reboots within MSL seconds, and immediately establishes new connections using the same local and foreign IP addresses and port numbers corresponding to the local ports that were in the 2MSL wait before the crash? In this scenario, delayed segments from the connections that existed before the crash can be misinterpreted as belonging to the new connections created after the reboot. This can happen regardless of how the initial sequence number is chosen after the reboot.

To protect against this scenario, RFC 793 states that TCP should not create any connections for MSL seconds after rebooting. This is called the *quiet time*.

> Few implementations abide by this since most hosts take longer than MSL seconds to reboot after a crash.

FIN_WAIT_2 State

In the FIN_WAIT_2 state we have sent our FIN and the other end has acknowledged it. Unless we have done a half-close, we are waiting for the application on the other end to recognize that it has received an end-of-file notification and close its end of the connection, which sends us a FIN. Only when the process at the other end does this close will our end move from the FIN_WAIT_2 to the TIME_WAIT state.

This means our end of the connection can remain in this state forever. The other end is still in the CLOSE_WAIT state, and can remain there forever, until the application decides to issue its close.

> Many Berkeley-derived implementations prevent this infinite wait in the FIN_WAIT_2 state as follows. If the application that does the active close does a complete close, not a half-close indicating that it expects to receive data, then a timer is set. If the connection is idle for 10 minutes plus 75 seconds, TCP moves the connection into the CLOSED state. A comment in the code acknowledges that this implementation feature violates the protocol specification.

18.7 Reset Segments

We've mentioned a bit in the TCP header named RST for "reset." In general, a reset is sent by TCP whenever a segment arrives that doesn't appear correct for the referenced connection. (We use the term "referenced connection" to mean the connection specified by the destination IP address and port number, and the source IP address and port number. This is what RFC 793 calls a socket.)

Connection Request to Nonexistent Port

A common case for generating a reset is when a connection request arrives and no process is listening on the destination port. In the case of UDP, we saw in Section 6.5 that an ICMP port unreachable was generated when a datagram arrived for a destination port that was not in use. TCP uses a reset instead.

This example is trivial to generate—we use the Telnet client and specify a port number that's not in use on the destination:

```
bsdi % telnet svr4 20000                    port 20000 should not be in use
Trying 140.252.13.34...
telnet: Unable to connect to remote host: Connection refused
```

This error message is output by the Telnet client immediately. Figure 18.14 shows the packet exchange corresponding to this command.

```
1  0.0                  bsdi.1087 > svr4.20000: S 297416193:297416193(0)
                                                win 4096 <mss 1024>
                                                [tos 0x10]

2  0.003771 (0.0038)    svr4.20000 > bsdi.1087: R 0:0(0) ack 297416194 win 0
```

Figure 18.14 Reset generated by attempt to open connection to nonexistent port.

The values we need to examine in this figure are the sequence number field and acknowledgment number field in the reset. Because the ACK bit was not on in the arriving segment, the sequence number of the reset is set to 0 and the acknowledgment number is set to the incoming ISN plus the number of data bytes in the segment. Although there is no real data in the arriving segment, the SYN bit logically occupies 1 byte of sequence number space; therefore, in this example the acknowledgment number in the reset is set to the ISN, plus the data length (0), plus one for the SYN bit.

Aborting a Connection

We saw in Section 18.2 that the normal way to terminate a connection is for one side to send a FIN. This is sometimes called an *orderly release* since the FIN is sent after all previously queued data has been sent, and there is normally no loss of data. But it's also possible to abort a connection by sending a reset instead of a FIN. This is sometimes called an *abortive release*.

Aborting a connection provides two features to the application: (1) any queued data is thrown away and the reset is sent immediately, and (2) the receiver of the RST can tell that the other end did an abort instead of a normal close. The API being used by the application must provide a way to generate the abort instead of a normal close.

We can watch this abort sequence happen using our sock program. The sockets API provides this capability by using the "linger on close" socket option (SO_LINGER). We specify the -L option with a linger time of 0. This causes the abort to be sent when the connection is closed, instead of the normal FIN. We'll connect to a server version of our sock program on svr4 and type one line of input:

```
bsdi % sock -L0 svr4 8888          this is the client; server shown later
hello, world                       type one line of input that's sent to other end
^D                                 type end-of-file character to terminate client
```

Figure 18.15 shows the `tcpdump` output for this example. (We have deleted all the window advertisements in this figure, since they add nothing to the discussion.)

```
1  0.0                  bsdi.1099 > svr4.8888: S 671112193:671112193(0)
                                               <mss 1024>
2  0.004975 (0.0050)    svr4.8888 > bsdi.1099: S 3224959489:3224959489(0)
                                               ack 671112194 <mss 1024>
3  0.006656 (0.0017)    bsdi.1099 > svr4.8888: . ack 1

4  4.833073 (4.8264)    bsdi.1099 > svr4.8888: P 1:14(13) ack 1
5  5.026224 (0.1932)    svr4.8888 > bsdi.1099: . ack 14

6  9.527634 (4.5014)    bsdi.1099 > svr4.8888: R 14:14(0) ack 1
```

Figure 18.15 Aborting a connection with a reset (RST) instead of a FIN.

Lines 1–3 show the normal connection establishment. Line 4 sends the data line that we typed (12 characters plus the Unix newline character), and line 5 is the acknowledgment of the received data.

Line 6 corresponds to our typing the end-of-file character (Control-D) to terminate the client. Since we specified an abort instead of a normal close (the `-L0` command-line option), the TCP on `bsdi` sends an RST instead of the normal FIN. The RST segment contains a sequence number and acknowledgment number. Also notice that the RST segment elicits no response from the other end—it is not acknowledged at all. The receiver of the reset aborts the connection and advises the application that the connection was reset.

We get the following error on the server for this exchange:

```
svr4 % sock -s 8888                      run as server, listen on port 8888
hello, world                             this is what the client sent over
read error: Connection reset by peer
```

This server reads from the network and copies whatever it receives to standard output. It normally ends by receiving an end-of-file notification from its TCP, but here we see that it receives an error when the RST arrives. The error is what we expect: the connection was reset by the peer.

Detecting Half-Open Connections

A TCP connection is said to be *half-open* if one end has closed or aborted the connection without the knowledge of the other end. This can happen any time one of the two hosts crashes. As long as there is no attempt to transfer data across a half-open connection, the end that's still up won't detect that the other end has crashed.

Another common cause of a half-open connection is when a client host is powered off, instead of terminating the client application and then shutting down the client host. This happens when PCs are being used to run Telnet clients, for example, and the users power off the PC at the end of the day. If there was no data transfer going on when the PC was powered off, the server will never know that the client disappeared. When the user comes in the next morning, powers on the PC, and starts a new Telnet client, a new occurrence of the server is started on the server host. This can lead to many half-open TCP connections on the server host. (In Chapter 23 we'll see a way for one end of a TCP connection to discover that the other end has disappeared using TCP's keepalive option.)

We can easily create a half-open connection. We'll execute the Telnet client on `bsdi`, connecting to the discard server on `svr4`. We type one line of input, and watch it go across with `tcpdump`, and then disconnect the Ethernet cable on the server's host, and reboot the server host. This simulates the server host crashing. (We disconnect the Ethernet cable before rebooting the server to prevent it from sending a FIN out the open connections, which some TCPs do when they are shut down.) After the server has rebooted, we reconnect the cable, and try to send another line from the client to the server. Since the server's TCP has rebooted, and lost all memory of the connections that existed before it was rebooted, it knows nothing about the connection that the data segment references. The rule of TCP is that the receiver responds with a reset.

```
bsdi % telnet svr4 discard                    start the client
Trying 140.252.13.34...
Connected to svr4.
Escape character is '^]'
hi there                                      this line is sent OK
                                              here is where we reboot the server host
another line                                  and this one elicits a reset
Connection closed by foreign host.
```

Figure 18.16 shows the `tcpdump` output for this example. (We have removed from this output the window advertisements, the type-of-service information, and the MSS announcements, since they add nothing to the discussion.)

```
1    0.0                       bsdi.1102 > svr4.discard: S 1591752193:1591752193(0)
2    0.004811 (  0.0048)       svr4.discard > bsdi.1102: S 26368001:26368001(0)
                                                         ack 1591752194
3    0.006516 (  0.0017)       bsdi.1102 > svr4.discard: . ack 1

4    5.167679 (  5.1612)       bsdi.1102 > svr4.discard: P 1:11(10) ack 1
5    5.201662 (  0.0340)       svr4.discard > bsdi.1102: . ack 11

6  194.909929 (189.7083)       bsdi.1102 > svr4.discard: P 11:25(14) ack 1
7  194.914957 (  0.0050)       arp who-has bsdi tell svr4
8  194.915678 (  0.0007)       arp reply bsdi is-at 0:0:c0:6f:2d:40
9  194.918225 (  0.0025)       svr4.discard > bsdi.1102: R 26368002:26368002(0)
```

Figure 18.16 Reset in response to data segment on a half-open connection.

Lines 1–3 are the normal connection establishment. Line 4 sends the line "hi there" to the discard server, and line 5 is the acknowledgment.

At this point we disconnect the Ethernet cable from `svr4`, reboot it, and reconnect the cable. This takes almost 190 seconds. We then type the next line of input to the client ("another line") and when we type the return key the line is sent to the server (line 6 in Figure 18.16). This elicits a response from the server, but note that since the server was rebooted, its ARP cache is empty, so an ARP request and reply are required (lines 7 and 8). Then the reset is sent in line 9. The client receives the reset and outputs that the connection was terminated by the foreign host. (The final message output by the Telnet client is not as informative as it could be.)

18.8 Simultaneous Open

It is possible, although improbable, for two applications to both perform an active open to each other at the same time. Each end must transmit a SYN, and the SYNs must pass each other on the network. It also requires each end to have a local port number that is well known to the other end. This is called a *simultaneous open*.

For example, one application on host A could have a local port of 7777 and perform an active open to port 8888 on host B. The application on host B would have a local port of 8888 and perform an active open to port 7777 on host A.

This is *not* the same as connecting a Telnet client on host A to the Telnet server on host B, at the same time that a Telnet client on host B is connecting to the Telnet server on host A. In this Telnet scenario, both Telnet servers perform passive opens, not active opens, and the Telnet clients assign themselves an ephemeral port number, not a port number that is well known to the other Telnet server.

TCP was purposely designed to handle simultaneous opens and the rule is that only one connection results from this, not two connections. (Other protocol suites, notably the OSI transport layer, create two connections in this scenario, not one.)

When a simultaneous open occurs the state transitions differ from those shown in Figure 18.13. Both ends send a SYN at about the same time, entering the SYN_SENT state. When each end receives the SYN, the state changes to SYN_RCVD (Figure 18.12), and each end resends the SYN and acknowledges the received SYN. When each end receives the SYN plus the ACK, the state changes to ESTABLISHED. These state changes are summarized in Figure 18.17.

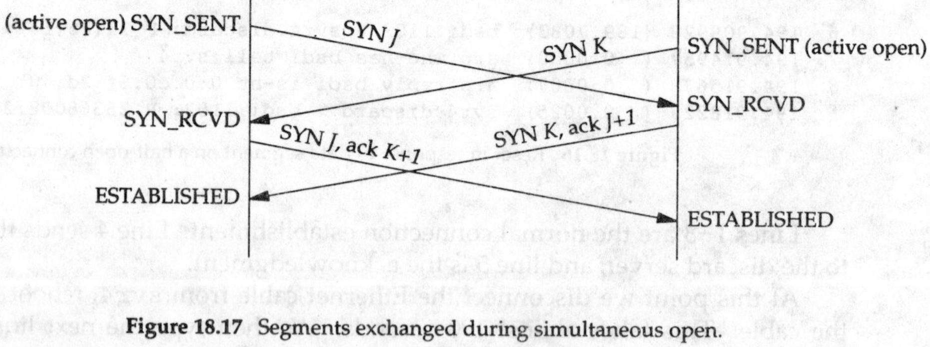

Figure 18.17 Segments exchanged during simultaneous open.

A simultaneous open requires the exchange of four segments, one more than the normal three-way handshake. Also notice that we don't call either end a client or a server, because both ends act as client and server.

An Example

It is possible, though hard, to generate a simultaneous open. The two ends must be started at about the same time, so that the SYNs cross each other. Having a long round-trip time between the two ends helps, to let the SYNs cross. To do this we'll execute one end on our host bsdi, and the other end on the host vangogh.cs.berkeley.edu. Since there is a dialup SLIP link between them, the round-trip time should be long enough (a few hundred milliseconds) to let the SYNs cross.

One end (bsdi) assigns itself a local port of 8888 (the -b command-line option) and performs an active open to port 7777 on the other host:

```
bsdi % sock -v -b8888 vangogh.cs.berkeley.edu 7777
connected on 140.252.13.35.8888 to 128.32.130.2.7777
TCP_MAXSEG = 512
hello, world                                    we type this line
and hi there                                    this line was typed on other end
connection closed by peer                       this is output when FIN received
```

The other end is started at about the same time, assigns itself a local port of 7777, and performs an active open to port 8888:

```
vangogh % sock -v -b7777 bsdi.tuc.noao.edu 8888
connected on 128.32.130.2.7777 to 140.252.13.35.8888
TCP_MAXSEG = 512
hello, world                                    this is typed on the other end
and hi there                                    we type this line
^D                                              and then type our EOF character
```

We specify the -v flag to our sock program to verify the IP address and port numbers on each end of the connection. This flag also prints the MSS used by each end of the connection. We also type in one line on each end, which is sent to the other end and printed, to verify that both ends are indeed talking to each other.

Figure 18.18 shows the exchange of segments across the connection. (We have deleted some new TCP options that appear in the original SYN from vangogh, a 4.4BSD system. We describe these newer options in Section 18.10.) Notice the two SYNs (lines 1 and 2) followed by the two SYNs with ACKs (lines 3 and 4). These perform the simultaneous open.

Line 5 shows the input line "hello, world" going from bsdi to vangogh, with the acknowledgment in line 6. Lines 7 and 8 correspond to the line "and hi there" going in the other direction. Lines 9–12 show the normal connection termination.

> Many Berkeley-derived implementations do not support the simultaneous open correctly. On these systems, if you can get the SYNs to cross, you end up with an infinite exchange of segments, each with a SYN and an ACK, in each direction. The transition from the SYN_SENT state to the SYN_RCVD state in Figure 18.12 is not always tested in many implementations.

```
 1  0.0                  bsdi.8888 > vangogh.7777: S 91904001:91904001(0)
                                                     win 4096 <mss 512>
 2  0.213782 (0.2138)    vangogh.7777 > bsdi.8888: S 1058199041:1058199041(0)
                                                     win 8192 <mss 512>
 3  0.215399 (0.0016)    bsdi.8888 > vangogh.7777: S 91904001:91904001(0)
                                                     ack 1058199042 win 4096
                                                     <mss 512>
 4  0.340405 (0.1250)    vangogh.7777 > bsdi.8888: S 1058199041:1058199041(0)
                                                     ack 91904002 win 8192
                                                     <mss 512>
 5  5.633142 (5.2927)    bsdi.8888 > vangogh.7777: P 1:14(13) ack 1 win 4096
 6  6.100366 (0.4672)    vangogh.7777 > bsdi.8888: . ack 14 win 8192
 7  9.640214 (3.5398)    vangogh.7777 > bsdi.8888: P 1:14(13) ack 14 win 8192
 8  9.796417 (0.1562)    bsdi.8888 > vangogh.7777: . ack 14 win 4096
 9 13.060395 (3.2640)    vangogh.7777 > bsdi.8888: F 14:14(0) ack 14 win 8192
10 13.061828 (0.0014)    bsdi.8888 > vangogh.7777: . ack 15 win 4096
11 13.079769 (0.0179)    bsdi.8888 > vangogh.7777: F 14:14(0) ack 15 win 4096
12 13.299940 (0.2202)    vangogh.7777 > bsdi.8888: . ack 15 win 8192
```

Figure 18.18 Exchange of segments during simultaneous open.

18.9 Simultaneous Close

We said earlier that one side (often, but not always, the client) performs the active close, causing the first FIN to be sent. It's also possible for both sides to perform an active close, and the TCP protocol allows for this *simultaneous close*.

In terms of Figure 18.12, both ends go from ESTABLISHED to FIN_WAIT_1 when the application issues the close. This causes both FINs to be sent, and they probably pass each other somewhere in the network. When the FIN is received, each end transitions from FIN_WAIT_1 to the CLOSING state, and each state sends its final ACK. When each end receives the final ACK, the state changes to TIME_WAIT. Figure 18.19 summarizes these state changes.

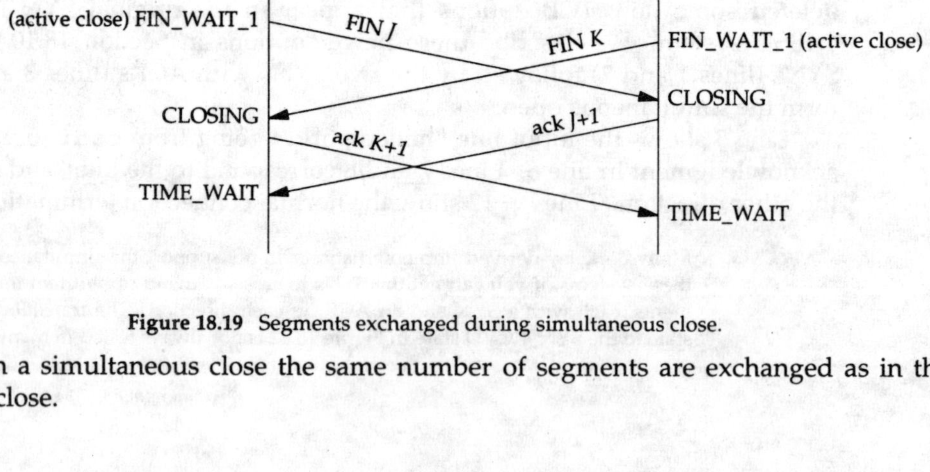

Figure 18.19 Segments exchanged during simultaneous close.

With a simultaneous close the same number of segments are exchanged as in the normal close.

18.10 TCP Options

The TCP header can contain options (Figure 17.2). The only options defined in the original TCP specification are the end of option list, no operation, and the maximum segment size option. We have seen the MSS option in almost every SYN segment in our examples.

Newer RFCs, specifically RFC 1323 [Jacobson, Braden, and Borman 1992], define additional TCP options, most of which are found only in the latest implementations. (We describe these new options in Chapter 24.) Figure 18.20 shows the format of the current TCP options—those from RFC 793 and RFC 1323.

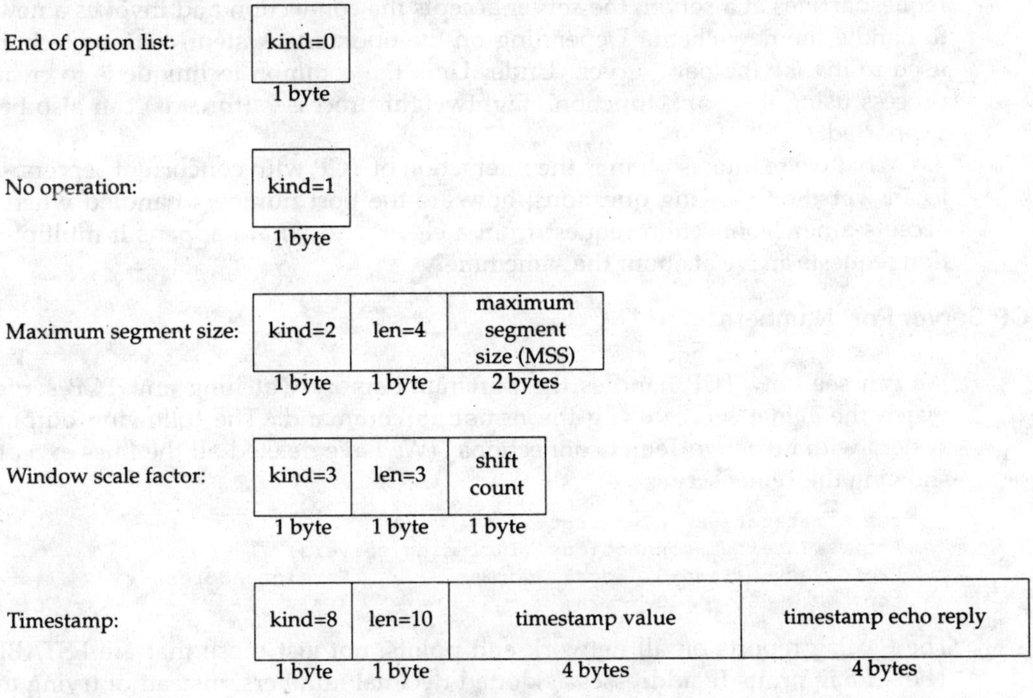

Figure 18.20 TCP options.

Every option begins with a 1-byte *kind* that specifies the type of option. The options with a *kind* of 0 and 1 occupy a single byte. The other options have a *len* byte that follows the *kind* byte. The length is the total length, including the *kind* and *len* bytes.

The reason for the no operation (NOP) option is to allow the sender to pad fields to a multiple of 4 bytes. If we initiate a TCP connection from a 4.4BSD system, the following TCP options are output by `tcpdump` on the initial SYN segment:

```
<mss 512,nop,wscale 0,nop,nop,timestamp 146647 0>
```

The MSS option is set to 512, followed by a NOP, followed by the window scale option. The reason for the first NOP is to pad the 3-byte window scale option to a 4-byte boundary. Similarly, the 10-byte timestamp option is preceded by two NOPs, to occupy 12 bytes, placing the two 4-byte timestamps onto 4-byte boundaries.

> Four other options have been proposed, with *kinds* of 4, 5, 6, and 7 called the selective-ACK and echo options. We don't show them in Figure 18.20 because the echo options have been replaced with the timestamp option, and selective ACKs, as currently defined, are still under discussion and were not included in RFC 1323. Also, the T/TCP proposal for TCP transactions (Section 24.7) specifies three options with *kinds* of 11, 12, and 13.

18.11 TCP Server Design

We said in Section 1.8 that most TCP servers are concurrent. When a new connection request arrives at a server, the server accepts the connection and invokes a new process to handle the new client. Depending on the operating system, various techniques are used to invoke the new server. Under Unix the common technique is to create a new process using the `fork` function. Lightweight processes (threads) can also be used, if supported.

What we're interested in is the interaction of TCP with concurrent servers. We need to answer the following questions: how are the port numbers handled when a server accepts a new connection request from a client, and what happens if multiple connection requests arrive at about the same time?

TCP Server Port Numbers

We can see how TCP handles the port numbers by watching any TCP server. We'll watch the Telnet server using the `netstat` command. The following output is on a system with no active Telnet connections. (We have deleted all the lines except the one showing the Telnet server.)

```
sun % netstat -a -n -f inet
Active Internet connections (including servers)
Proto Recv-Q Send-Q  Local Address          Foreign Address        (state)
tcp        0      0  *.23                   *.*                    LISTEN
```

The `-a` flag reports on all network end points, not just those that are ESTABLISHED. The `-n` flag prints IP addresses as dotted-decimal numbers, instead of trying to use the DNS to convert the address to a name, and prints numeric port numbers (e.g., 23) instead of service names (e.g., Telnet). The `-f inet` option reports only TCP and UDP end points.

The local address is output as `*.23`, where the asterisk is normally called the *wildcard* character. This means that an incoming connection request (i.e., a SYN) will be accepted on any local interface. If the host were multihomed, we could specify a single IP address for the local IP address (one of the host's IP addresses), and only connections received on that interface would be accepted. (We'll see an example of this later in this section.) The local port is 23, the well-known port number for Telnet.

The foreign address is output as `*.*`, which means the foreign IP address and foreign port number are not known yet, because the end point is in the LISTEN state, waiting for a connection to arrive.

We now start a Telnet client on the host `slip` (140.252.13.65) that connects to this server. Here are the relevant lines from the `netstat` output:

```
Proto Recv-Q Send-Q  Local Address        Foreign Address       (state)
tcp        0      0  140.252.13.33.23     140.252.13.65.1029    ESTABLISHED
tcp        0      0  *.23                 *.*                   LISTEN
```

The first line for port 23 is the ESTABLISHED connection. All four elements of the local and foreign address are filled in for this connection: the local IP address and port number, and the foreign IP address and port number. The local IP address corresponds to the interface on which the connection request arrived (the Ethernet interface, 140.252.13.33).

The end point in the LISTEN state is left alone. This is the end point that the concurrent server uses to accept future connection requests. It is the TCP module in the kernel that creates the new end point in the ESTABLISHED state, when the incoming connection request arrives and is accepted. Also notice that the port number for the ESTABLISHED connection doesn't change: it's 23, the same as the LISTEN end point.

We now initiate another Telnet client from the same client (`slip`) to this server. Here is the relevant `netstat` output:

```
Proto Recv-Q Send-Q  Local Address        Foreign Address       (state)
tcp        0      0  140.252.13.33.23     140.252.13.65.1030    ESTABLISHED
tcp        0      0  140.252.13.33.23     140.252.13.65.1029    ESTABLISHED
tcp        0      0  *.23                 *.*                   LISTEN
```

We now have two ESTABLISHED connections from the same host to the same server. Both have a local port number of 23. This is not a problem for TCP since the foreign port numbers are different. They must be different because each of the Telnet clients uses an ephemeral port, and the definition of an ephemeral port is one that is not currently in use on that host (`slip`).

This example reiterates that TCP demultiplexes incoming segments using all four values that comprise the local and foreign addresses: destination IP address, destination port number, source IP address, and source port number. TCP cannot determine which process gets an incoming segment by looking at the destination port number only. Also, the only one of the three end points at port 23 that will receive incoming connection requests is the one in the LISTEN state. The end points in the ESTABLISHED state cannot receive SYN segments, and the end point in the LISTEN state cannot receive data segments.

Next we initiate a third Telnet client, from the host `solaris` that is across the SLIP link from `sun`, and not on its Ethernet.

```
Proto Recv-Q Send-Q  Local Address        Foreign Address       (state)
tcp        0      0  140.252.1.29.23      140.252.1.32.34603    ESTABLISHED
tcp        0      0  140.252.13.33.23     140.252.13.65.1030    ESTABLISHED
tcp        0      0  140.252.13.33.23     140.252.13.65.1029    ESTABLISHED
tcp        0      0  *.23                 *.*                   LISTEN
```

The local IP address of the first ESTABLISHED connection now corresponds to the interface address of SLIP link on the multihomed host `sun` (140.252.1.29).

Restricting Local IP Address

We can see what happens when the server does not wildcard its local IP address, setting it to one particular local interface address instead. If we specify an IP address (or hostname) to our sock program when we invoke it as a server, that IP address becomes the local IP address of the listening end point. For example

```
sun % sock -s 140.252.1.29 8888
```

restricts this server to connections arriving on the SLIP interface (140.252.1.29). The netstat output reflects this:

```
Proto Recv-Q Send-Q  Local Address          Foreign Address        (state)
tcp        0      0  140.252.1.29.8888      *.*                    LISTEN
```

If we connect to this server across the SLIP link, from the host solaris, it works.

```
Proto Recv-Q Send-Q  Local Address          Foreign Address        (state)
tcp        0      0  140.252.1.29.8888      140.252.1.32.34614     ESTABLISHED
tcp        0      0  140.252.1.29.8888      *.*                    LISTEN
```

But if we try to connect to this server from a host on the Ethernet (140.252.13), the connection request is not accepted by the TCP module. If we watch it with tcpdump the SYN is responded to with an RST, as we show in Figure 18.21.

```
1  0.0                    bsdi.1026 > sun.8888: S 3657920001:3657920001(0)
                                                 win 4096 <mss 1024>

2  0.000859 (0.0009)      sun.8888 > bsdi.1026: R 0:0(0) ack 3657920002 win 0
```

Figure 18.21 Rejection of a connection request based on local IP address of server.

The server application never sees the connection request—the rejection is done by the kernel's TCP module, based on the local IP address specified by the application.

Restricting Foreign IP Address

In Section 11.12 we saw that a UDP server can normally specify the foreign IP address and foreign port, in addition to specifying the local IP address and local port. The interface functions shown in RFC 793 allow a server doing a passive open to have either a fully specified foreign socket (to wait for a particular client to issue an active open) or a unspecified foreign socket (to wait for any client).

Unfortunately, most APIs don't provide a way to do this. The server must leave the foreign socket unspecified, wait for the connection to arrive, and then examine the IP address and port number of the client.

Figure 18.22 summarizes the three types of address bindings that a TCP server can establish for itself. In all cases, *lport* is the server's well-known port and *localIP* must be the IP address of a local interface. The ordering of the three rows in the table is the order that the TCP module applies when trying to determine which local end point receives an incoming connection request. The most specific binding (the first row, if supported) is tried first, and the least specific (the last row with both IP addresses wildcarded) is tried last.

Local Address	Foreign Address	Description
localIP.lport	*foreignIP.fport*	restricted to one client (normally not supported)
localIP.lport	*.*	restricted to connections arriving on one local interface: *localIP*
*.*lport*	*.*	receives all connections sent to *lport*

Figure 18.22 Specification of local and foreign IP addresses and port number for TCP server.

Incoming Connection Request Queue

A concurrent server invokes a new process to handle each client, so the listening server should always be ready to handle the next incoming connection request. That's the underlying reason for using concurrent servers. But there is still a chance that multiple connection requests arrive while the listening server is creating a new process, or while the operating system is busy running other higher priority processes. How does TCP handle these incoming connection requests while the listening application is busy?

In Berkeley-derived implementations the following rules apply.

1. Each listening end point has a fixed length queue of connections that have been accepted by TCP (i.e., the three-way handshake is complete), but not yet accepted by the application.

   Be careful to differentiate between TCP accepting a connection and placing it on this queue, and the application taking the accepted connection off this queue.

2. The application specifies a limit to this queue, commonly called the backlog. This backlog must be between 0 and 5, inclusive. (Most applications specify the maximum value of 5.)

3. When a connection request arrives (i.e., the SYN segment), an algorithm is applied by TCP to the current number of connections already queued for this listening end point, to see whether to accept the connection or not. We would expect the backlog value specified by the application to be the maximum number of queued connections allowed for this end point, but it's not that simple. Figure 18.23 shows the relationship between the backlog value and the real maximum number of queued connections allowed by traditional Berkeley systems and Solaris 2.2.

Backlog value	Max # of queued connections	
	Traditional BSD	Solaris 2.2
0	1	0
1	2	1
2	4	2
3	5	3
4	7	4
5	8	5

Figure 18.23 Maximum number of accepted connections allowed for listening end point.

Keep in mind that this backlog value specifies only the maximum number of queued connections for one listening end point, all of which have already been accepted by TCP and are waiting to be accepted by the application. This backlog has no effect whatsoever on the maximum number of established connections allowed by the system, or on the number of clients that a concurrent server can handle concurrently.

The Solaris values in this figure are what we expect. The traditional BSD values are (for some unknown reason) the backlog value times 3, divided by 2, plus 1.

4. If there is room on this listening end point's queue for this new connection (based on Figure 18.23), the TCP module ACKs the SYN and completes the connection. The server application with the listening end point won't see this new connection until the third segment of the three-way handshake is received. Also, the client may think the server is ready to receive data when the client's active open completes successfully, before the server application has been notified of the new connection. (If this happens, the server's TCP just queues the incoming data.)
5. If there is not room on the queue for the new connection, TCP just ignores the received SYN. Nothing is sent back (i.e., no RST segment). If the listening server doesn't get around to accepting some of the already accepted connections that have filled its queue to the limit, the client's active open will eventually time out.

We can see this scenario take place with our `sock` program. We invoke it with a new option (`-O`) that tells it to pause after creating the listening end point, before accepting any connection requests. If we then invoke multiple clients during this pause period, it should cause the server's queue of accepted connections to fill, and we can see what happens with `tcpdump`.

```
bsdi % sock -s -v -q1 -O30 7777
```

The `-q1` option sets the backlog of the listening end point to 1, which for this traditional BSD system should allow two pending connection requests (Figure 18.23). The `-O30` option causes the program to sleep for 30 seconds before accepting any client connections. This gives us 30 seconds to start some clients, to fill the queue. We'll start four clients on the host `sun`.

Figure 18.24 shows the `tcpdump` output, starting with the first SYN from the first client. (We have removed the window size advertisements and MSS announcements. We have also marked the client port numbers in bold when the TCP connection is established—the three-way handshake.)

The first client's connection request from port 1090 is accepted by TCP (segments 1–3). The second client's connection request from port 1091 is also accepted by TCP (segments 4–6). The server application is still asleep, and has not accepted either connection yet. Everything has been done by the TCP module in the kernel. Also, the two clients have returned successfully from their active opens, since the three-way handshakes are complete.

```
 1  0.0                   sun.1090 > bsdi.7777: S 1617152000:1617152000(0)
 2  0.002310 ( 0.0023)    bsdi.7777 > sun.1090: S 4164096001:4164096001(0)
                                                ack 1617152001
 3  0.003098 ( 0.0008)    sun.1090 > bsdi.7777: . ack 1

 4  4.291007 ( 4.2879)    sun.1091 > bsdi.7777: S 1617792000:1617792000(0)
 5  4.293349 ( 0.0023)    bsdi.7777 > sun.1091: S 4164672001:4164672001(0)
                                                ack 1617792001
 6  4.294167 ( 0.0008)    sun.1091 > bsdi.7777: . ack 1

 7  7.131981 ( 2.8378)    sun.1092 > bsdi.7777: S 1618176000:1618176000(0)
 8 10.556787 ( 3.4248)    sun.1093 > bsdi.7777: S 1618688000:1618688000(0)
 9 12.695916 ( 2.1391)    sun.1092 > bsdi.7777: S 1618176000:1618176000(0)
10 16.195772 ( 3.4999)    sun.1093 > bsdi.7777: S 1618688000:1618688000(0)
11 24.695571 ( 8.4998)    sun.1092 > bsdi.7777: S 1618176000:1618176000(0)

12 28.195454 ( 3.4999)    sun.1093 > bsdi.7777: S 1618688000:1618688000(0)
13 28.197810 ( 0.0024)    bsdi.7777 > sun.1093: S 4167808001:4167808001(0)
                                                ack 1618688001
14 28.198639 ( 0.0008)    sun.1093 > bsdi.7777: . ack 1

15 48.694931 (20.4963)    sun.1092 > bsdi.7777: S 1618176000:1618176000(0)
16 48.697292 ( 0.0024)    bsdi.7777 > sun.1092: S 4170496001:4170496001(0)
                                                ack 1618176001
17 48.698145 ( 0.0009)    sun.1092 > bsdi.7777: . ack 1
```

Figure 18.24 tcpdump **output for backlog example.**

We try to start a third client in segment 7 (port 1092), and a fourth in segment 8 (port 1093). TCP ignores both SYNs since the queue for this listening end point is full. Both clients retransmit their SYNs in segments 9, 10, 11, 12, and 15. The fourth client's third retransmission is accepted (segments 12–14) because the server's 30-second pause is over, causing the server to remove the two connections that were accepted, emptying its queue. (The reason it appears this connection was accepted by the server at the time 28.19, and not at a time greater than 30, is because it took a few seconds to start the first client [segment 1, the starting time point in the output] after starting the server.) The third client's fourth retransmission is then accepted (segments 15–17). The fourth client connection (port 1093) is accepted by the server before the third client connection (port 1092) because of the timing interactions between the server's 30-second pause and the client's retransmissions.

We would expect the queue of accepted connections to be passed to the application in FIFO (first-in, first-out) order. That is, after TCP accepts the connections on ports 1090 and 1091, we expect the application to receive the connection on port 1090 first, and then the connection on port 1091. But a bug has existed for years in many Berkeley-derived implementations causing them to be returned in a LIFO (last-in, first-out) order instead. Vendors have recently started fixing this bug, but it still exists in systems such as SunOS 4.1.3.

TCP ignores the incoming SYN when the queue is full, and doesn't respond with an RST, because this is a soft error, not a hard error. Normally the queue is full because the application or the operating system is busy, preventing the application from servicing incoming connections. This condition could change in a short while. But if the server's TCP responded with a reset, the client's active open would abort (which is what we saw happen if the server wasn't started). By ignoring the SYN, the server forces the client TCP to retransmit the SYN later, hoping that the queue will then have room for the new connection.

A subtle point in this example, which is found in most TCP/IP implementations, is that TCP accepts an incoming connection request (i.e., a SYN) if there is room on the listener's queue, without giving the application a chance to see who it's from (the source IP address and source port number). This is not required by TCP, it's just the common implementation technique (i.e., the way the Berkeley sources have always done it). If an API such as TLI (Section 1.15) gives the application a way to learn when a connection request arrives, and then allows the application to choose whether to accept the connection or not, be aware that with TCP, when the application is supposedly told that the connection has just arrived, TCP's three-way handshake is over! Other transport layers may be implemented to provide this separation to the application between arrival and acceptance (i.e., the OSI transport layer) but not TCP.

> Solaris 2.2 provides an option that prevents TCP from accepting an incoming connection request until the application says so (`tcp_eager_listeners` in Section E.4).

This behavior also means that a TCP server has no way to cause a client's active open to fail. When a new client connection is passed to the server application, TCP's three-way handshake is over, and the client's active open has completed successfully. If the server then looks at the client's IP address and port number, and decides it doesn't want to service this client, all the server can do is either close the connection (causing a FIN to be sent) or reset the connection (causing an RST to be sent). In either case the client thought everything was OK when its active open completed, and may have already sent a request to the server.

18.12 Summary

Before two processes can exchange data using TCP, they must establish a connection between themselves. When they're done they terminate the connection. This chapter has provided a detailed look at how connections are established using a three-way handshake, and terminated using four segments.

We used `tcpdump` to show all the fields in the TCP header. We've also seen how a connection establishment can time out, how resets are sent, what happens with a half-open connection, and how TCP provides a half-close, simultaneous opens, and simultaneous closes.

Fundamental to understanding the operation of TCP is its state transition diagram. We've followed through the steps involved in connection establishment and termination, and the state transitions that take place. We also looked at the implications of TCP's connection establishment on the design of concurrent TCP servers.

A TCP connection is uniquely defined by a 4-tuple: the local IP address, local port number, foreign IP address, and foreign port number. Whenever a connection is terminated, one end must maintain knowledge of the connection, and we saw that the TIME_WAIT state handles this. The rule is that the end that does the active open enters this state for twice the implementation's MSL.

Exercises

18.1 In Section 18.2 we said that the initial sequence number (ISN) normally starts at 1 and is incremented by 64,000 every half-second and every time an active open is performed. This would imply that the low-order three digits of the ISN would always be 001. But in Figure 18.3 these low-order three digits are 521 in each direction. What's going on?

18.2 In Figure 18.15 we typed 12 characters and saw 13 bytes sent by TCP. In Figure 18.16 we typed eight characters but TCP sent 10 bytes. Why was 1 byte added in the first case, but 2 bytes in the second case?

18.3 What's the difference between a half-open connection and a half-closed connection?

18.4 If we start our `sock` program as a server, and then terminate it (without having a client connect to it), we can immediately restart the server. This implies that it doesn't go through the 2MSL wait state. Explain this in terms of the state transition diagram.

18.5 In Section 18.6 we showed that a client cannot reuse the same local port number while that port is part of a connection in the 2MSL wait. But if we run our `sock` program twice in a row as a client, connecting to the daytime server, we can reuse the same local port number. Additionally, we're able to create a new incarnation of a connection that should be in the 2MSL wait. What's going on?

```
sun % sock -v bsdi daytime
connected on 140.252.13.33.1163 to 140.252.13.35.13
Wed Jul  7 07:54:51 1993
connection closed by peer
sun % sock -v -b1163 bsdi daytime          reuse same local port number
connected on 140.252.13.33.1163 to 140.252.13.35.13
Wed Jul  7 07:55:01 1993
connection closed by peer
```

18.6 At the end of Section 18.6 when describing the FIN_WAIT_2 state, we mentioned that many implementations move a connection from this state into the CLOSED state if the application did a complete close (not a half-close) after just over 11 minutes. If the other end (in the CLOSE_WAIT state) waited 12 minutes before issuing its close (i.e., sending its FIN), what would its TCP get in response to the FIN?

18.7 Which end of a telephone conversation does the active open, and which does the passive open? Are simultaneous opens allowed? Are simultaneous closes allowed?

18.8 In Figure 18.6 we don't see an ARP request or an ARP reply. Obviously the hardware address for host `svr4` must be in the ARP cache on `bsdi`. What would change in this figure if this ARP cache entry was not present?

18.9 Explain the following `tcpdump` output. Compare it with Figure 18.13.

```
1  0.0                  solaris.32990 > bsdi.discard: S 40140288:40140288(0)
                                                      win 8760 <mss 1460>
2  0.003295 (0.0033)  bsdi.discard > solaris.32990: S 4208081409:4208081409(0)
                                                      ack 40140289 win 4096
                                                      <mss 1024>
3  0.419991 (0.4167)  solaris.32990 > bsdi.discard: P 1:257(256) ack 1 win 9216
4  0.449852 (0.0299)  solaris.32990 > bsdi.discard: F 257:257(0) ack 1 win 9216
5  0.451965 (0.0021)  bsdi.discard > solaris.32990: . ack 258 win 3840
6  0.464569 (0.0126)  bsdi.discard > solaris.32990: F 1:1(0) ack 258 win 4096
7  0.720031 (0.2555)  solaris.32990 > bsdi.discard: . ack 2 win 9216
```

18.10 Why doesn't the server in Figure 18.4 combine the ACK of the client's FIN with its own FIN, reducing the number of segments to three?

18.11 In Figure 18.16 why is the sequence number of the RST 26368002?

18.12 Does TCP's querying the link layer for the MTU violate the spirit of layering?

18.13 Assume in Figure 14.16 that each DNS query is issued using TCP instead of UDP. How many packets are exchanged?

18.14 With an MSL of 120 seconds, what is the maximum at which a system can initiate new connections and then do an active close?

18.15 Read RFC 793 to see what happens when an end point that is in the TIME_WAIT state receives a duplicate of the FIN that placed it into this state.

18.16 Read RFC 793 to see what happens when an end point that is in the TIME_WAIT state receives an RST.

18.17 Read the Host Requirements RFC to obtain the definition of a *half-duplex* TCP close.

18.18 In Figure 1.8 (p. 11) we said that incoming TCP segments are demultiplexed based on the destination TCP port number. Is that correct?

19

TCP Interactive Data Flow

19.1 Introduction

The previous chapter dealt with the establishment and termination of TCP connections. We now examine the transfer of data using TCP.

Studies of TCP traffic, such as [Caceres et al. 1991], usually find that on a packet-count basis about half of all TCP segments contain bulk data (FTP, electronic mail, Usenet news) and the other half contain interactive data (Telnet and Rlogin, for example). On a byte-count basis the ratio is around 90% bulk data and 10% interactive, since bulk data segments tend to be full sized (normally 512 bytes of user data), while interactive data tends to be much smaller. (The above-mentioned study found that 90% of Telnet and Rlogin packets carry less than 10 bytes of user data.)

TCP obviously handles both types of data, but different algorithms come into play for each. In this chapter we'll look at interactive data transfer, using the Rlogin application. We'll see how delayed acknowledgments work and how the Nagle algorithm reduces the number of small packets across wide area networks. The same algorithms apply to Telnet. In the next chapter we'll look at bulk data transfer.

19.2 Interactive Input

Let's look at the flow of data when we type an interactive command on an Rlogin connection. Many newcomers to TCP/IP are surprised to find that each interactive keystroke normally generates a data packet. That is, the keystrokes are sent from the client to the server 1 byte at a time (not one line at a time). Furthermore, Rlogin has the remote system (the server) echo the characters that we (the client) type. This could generate four segments: (1) the interactive keystroke from the client, (2) an acknowledgment of the keystroke from the server, (3) the echo of the keystroke from the server, and (4) an acknowledgment of the echo from the client. Figure 19.1 shows this flow of data.

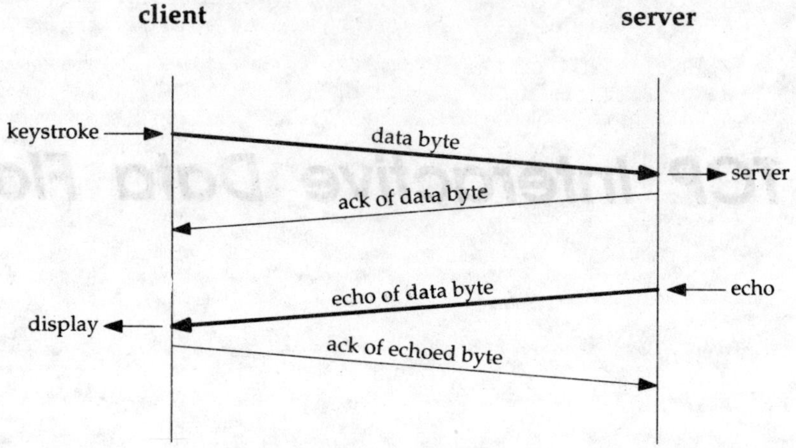

Figure 19.1 One possible way to do remote echo of interactive keystroke.

Normally, however, segments 2 and 3 are combined—the acknowledgment of the keystroke is sent along with the echo. We describe the technique that combines these (called delayed acknowledgments) in the next section.

We purposely use Rlogin for the examples in this chapter because it always sends one character at a time from the client to the server. When we describe Telnet in Chapter 26, we'll see that it has an option that allows lines of input to be sent from the client to the server, which reduces the network load.

Figure 19.2 shows the flow of data when we type the five characters `date\n`. (We do not show the connection establishment and we have removed all the type-of-service output. BSD/386 sets the TOS for an Rlogin connection for minimum delay.) Line 1 sends the character `d` from the client to the server. Line 2 is the acknowledgment of this character and its echo. (This is combining the middle two segments in Figure 19.1.) Line 3 is the acknowledgment of the echoed character. Lines 4–6 correspond to the character `a`, lines 7–9 to the character `t`, and lines 10–12 to the character `e`. The fractional second delays between lines 3–4, 6–7, 9–10, and 12–13 are the human delays between typing each character.

Notice that lines 13–15 are slightly different. One character is sent from the client to the server (the Unix newline character, from our typing the RETURN key) but two characters are echoed. These two characters are a carriage return and linefeed (CR/LF), to move the cursor back to the left and space down one line.

Line 16 is the output of the `date` command from the server. The 30 bytes are composed of the following 28 characters

```
Sat Feb  6 07:52:17 MST 1993
```

```
 1  0.0                   bsdi.1023 > svr4.login: P 0:1(1) ack 1 win 4096
 2  0.016497 (0.0165)     svr4.login > bsdi.1023: P 1:2(1) ack 1 win 4096
 3  0.139955 (0.1235)     bsdi.1023 > svr4.login: . ack 2 win 4096

 4  0.458037 (0.3181)     bsdi.1023 > svr4.login: P 1:2(1) ack 2 win 4096
 5  0.474386 (0.0163)     svr4.login > bsdi.1023: P 2:3(1) ack 2 win 4096
 6  0.539943 (0.0656)     bsdi.1023 > svr4.login: . ack 3 win 4096

 7  0.814582 (0.2746)     bsdi.1023 > svr4.login: P 2:3(1) ack 3 win 4096
 8  0.831108 (0.0165)     svr4.login > bsdi.1023: P 3:4(1) ack 3 win 4096
 9  0.940112 (0.1090)     bsdi.1023 > svr4.login: . ack 4 win 4096

10  1.191287 (0.2512)     bsdi.1023 > svr4.login: P 3:4(1) ack 4 win 4096
11  1.207701 (0.0164)     svr4.login > bsdi.1023: P 4:5(1) ack 4 win 4096
12  1.339994 (0.1323)     bsdi.1023 > svr4.login: . ack 5 win 4096

13  1.680646 (0.3407)     bsdi.1023 > svr4.login: P 4:5(1) ack 5 win 4096
14  1.697977 (0.0173)     svr4.login > bsdi.1023: P 5:7(2) ack 5 win 4096
15  1.739974 (0.0420)     bsdi.1023 > svr4.login: . ack 7 win 4096

16  1.799841 (0.0599)     svr4.login > bsdi.1023: P 7:37(30) ack 5 win 4096
17  1.940176 (0.1403)     bsdi.1023 > svr4.login: . ack 37 win 4096
18  1.944338 (0.0042)     svr4.login > bsdi.1023: P 37:44(7) ack 5 win 4096
19  2.140110 (0.1958)     bsdi.1023 > svr4.login: . ack 44 win 4096
```

Figure 19.2 TCP segments when `date` typed on Rlogin connection.

plus a CR/LF pair at the end. The next 7 bytes sent from the server to the client (line 18) are the client's prompt on the server host: `svr4 % `. Line 19 acknowledges these 7 bytes.

Notice how the TCP acknowledgments operate. Line 1 sends the data byte with the sequence number 0. Line 2 ACKs this by setting the acknowledgment sequence number to 1, the sequence number of the last successfully received byte plus one. (This is also called the sequence number of the next expected byte.) Line 2 also sends the data byte with a sequence number of 1 from the server to the client. This is ACKed by the client in line 3 by setting the acknowledged sequence number to 2.

19.3 Delayed Acknowledgments

There are some subtle points in Figure 19.2 dealing with timing that we'll cover in this section. Figure 19.3 shows the time line for the exchange in Figure 19.2. (We have deleted all the window advertisements from this time line, and have added a notation indicating what data is being transferred.)

We have labeled the seven ACKs sent from `bsdi` to `svr4` as *delayed ACKs*. Normally TCP does not send an ACK the instant it receives data. Instead, it delays the ACK, hoping to have data going in the same direction as the ACK, so the ACK can be sent along with the data. (This is sometimes called having the ACK *piggyback* with the data.) Most implementations use a 200-ms delay—that is, TCP will delay an ACK up to 200 ms to see if there is data to send with the ACK.

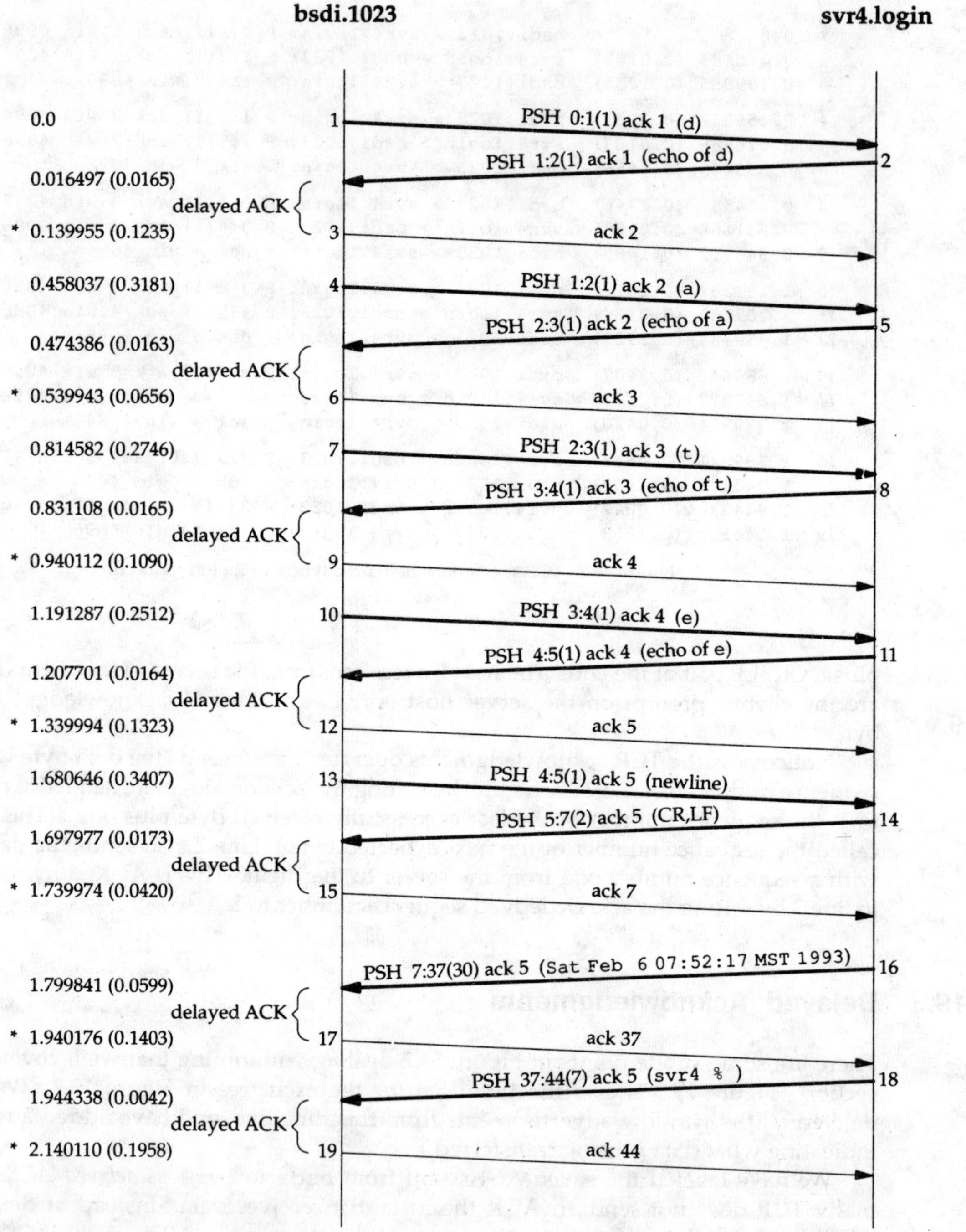

Figure 19.3 Time line of data flow for `date` command typed on an `rlogin` connection.

If we look at the time differences between `bsdi` receiving the data and sending the ACK, they appear to be random: 123.5, 65.6, 109.0, 132.3, 42.0, 140.3, and 195.8 ms. Look instead at the actual times (starting from 0) when the ACKs are sent: 139.9, 539.9, 940.1, 1339.9, 1739.9, 1940.1, and 2140.1 ms. (We have marked these with an asterisk to the left of the time in Figure 19.3.) There is a multiple of 200 ms between these times. What is happening here is that TCP has a timer that goes off every 200 ms, but it goes off at fixed points in time—every 200 ms relative to when the kernel was bootstrapped. Since the data being acknowledged arrives randomly (at times 16.4, 474.3, 831.1, etc.), TCP asks to be notified the next time the kernel's 200-ms timer expires. This can be anywhere from 1 to 200 ms in the future.

If we look at how long it takes `svr4` to generate the echo of each character it receives, the times are 16.5, 16.3, 16.5, 16.4, and 17.3 ms. Since this time is less than 200 ms, we never see a delayed ACK on that side. There is always data ready to be sent before the delayed ACK timer expires. (We could still see a delayed ACK if the wait period, about 16 ms, crosses one of the kernel's 200-ms clock tick boundaries. We just don't see any of these in this example.)

We saw this same scenario in Figure 18.7 with the 500-ms TCP timer used when detecting a timeout. Both TCP timers, the 200- and 500-ms timers, go off at times relative to when the kernel was bootstrapped. Whenever TCP sets a timer, it can go off anywhere between 1–200 or 1–500 ms in the future.

The Host Requirements RFC states that TCP should implement a delayed ACK but the delay must be less than 500 ms.

19.4 Nagle Algorithm

We saw in the previous section that 1 byte at a time normally flows from the client to the server across an Rlogin connection. This generates 41-byte packets: 20 bytes for the IP header, 20 bytes for the TCP header, and 1 byte of data. These small packets (called *tinygrams*) are normally not a problem on LANs, since most LANs are not congested, but these tinygrams can add to congestion on wide area networks. A simple and elegant solution was proposed in RFC 896 [Nagle 1984], called the *Nagle algorithm*.

This algorithm says that when a TCP connection has outstanding data that has not yet been acknowledged, small segments cannot be sent until the outstanding data is acknowledged. Instead, small amounts of data are collected by TCP and sent in a single segment when the acknowledgment arrives. The beauty of this algorithm is that it is self-clocking: the faster the ACKs come back, the faster the data is sent. But on a slow WAN, where it is desired to reduce the number of tinygrams, fewer segments are sent. (We'll see in Section 22.3 that the definition of "small" is less than the segment size.)

We saw in Figure 19.3 that the round-trip time on an Ethernet for a single byte to be sent, acknowledged, and echoed averaged around 16 ms. To generate data faster than this we would have to be typing more than 60 characters per second. This means we rarely encounter this algorithm when sending data between two hosts on a LAN.

Things change, however, when the round-trip time (RTT) increases, typically across a WAN. Let's look at an Rlogin connection between our host `slip` and the host `vangogh.cs.berkeley.edu`. To get out of our network (see inside front cover), two SLIP links must be traversed, and then the Internet is used. We expect much longer round-trip times. Figure 19.4 shows the time line of some data flow while characters were being typed quickly on the client (similar to a fast typist). (We have removed the type-of-service information, but have left in the window size advertisements.)

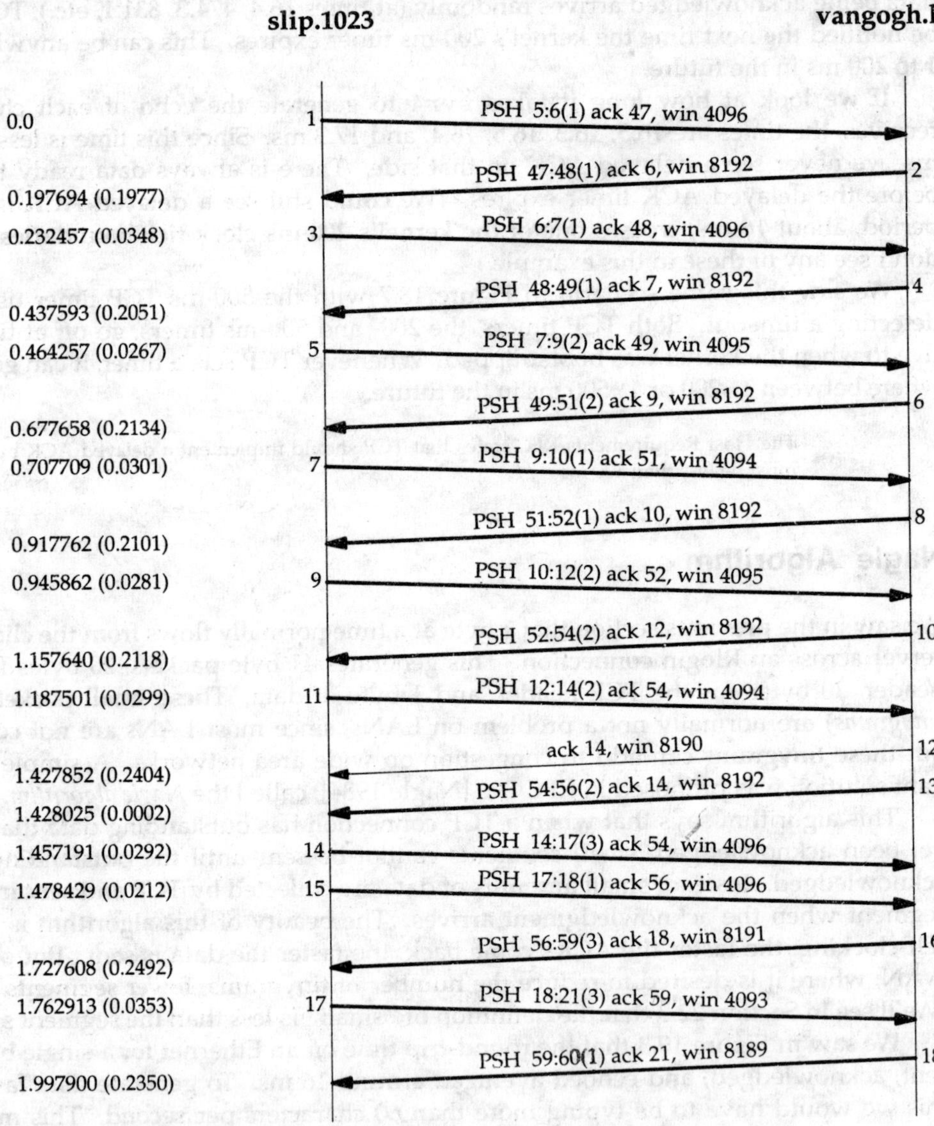

Figure 19.4 Data flow using `rlogin` between `slip` and `vangogh.cs.berkeley.edu`.

The first thing we notice, comparing Figure 19.4 with Figure 19.3, is the lack of delayed ACKs from `slip` to `vangogh`. This is because there is always data ready to send before the delayed ACK timer expires.

Next, notice the various amounts of data being sent from the left to the right: 1, 1, 2, 1, 2, 2, 3, 1, and 3 bytes. This is because the client is collecting the data to send, but doesn't send it until the previously sent data has been acknowledged. By using the Nagle algorithm only nine segments were used to send 16 bytes, instead of 16 segments.

Segments 14 and 15 appear to contradict the Nagle algorithm, but we need to look at the sequence numbers to see what's really happening. Segment 14 is in response to the ACK received in segment 12, since the acknowledged sequence number is 54. But before this data segment is sent by the client, segment 13 arrives from the server. Segment 15 contains the ACK of segment 13, sequence number 56. So the client is obeying the Nagle algorithm, even though we see two back-to-back data segments from the client to the server.

Also notice in Figure 19.4 that one delayed ACK is present, but it's from the server to the client (segment 12). We are assuming this is a delayed ACK since it contains no data. The server must have been busy at this time, so that the Rlogin server was not able to echo the character before the server's delayed ACK timer expired.

Finally, look at the amounts of data and the sequence numbers in the final two segments. The client sends 3 bytes of data (numbered 18, 19, and 20), then the server acknowledges these 3 bytes (the ACK of 21 in the final segment) but sends back only 1 byte (numbered 59). What's happening here is that the server's TCP is acknowledging the 3 bytes of data once it has received them correctly, but it won't have the echo of these 3 bytes ready to send back until the Rlogin server sends them. This shows that TCP can acknowledge received data before the application has read and processed that data. The TCP acknowledgment just means TCP has correctly received the data. We also have an indication that the server process has not read these 3 bytes of data because the advertised window in the final segment is 8189, not 8192.

Disabling the Nagle Algorithm

There are times when the Nagle algorithm needs to be turned off. The classic example is the X Window System server (Section 30.5): small messages (mouse movements) must be delivered without delay to provide real-time feedback for interactive users doing certain operations.

Here we'll show another example that's easier to demonstrate—typing one of the terminal's special function keys during an interactive login. The function keys normally generate multiple bytes of data, often beginning with the ASCII escape character. If TCP gets the data 1 byte at a time, it's possible for it to send the first byte (the ASCII ESC) and then hold the remaining bytes of the sequence waiting for the ACK of this byte. But when the server receives this first byte it doesn't generate an echo until the remaining bytes are received. This often triggers the delayed ACK algorithm on the server, meaning that the remaining bytes aren't sent for up to 200 ms. This can lead to noticeable delays to the interactive user.

The sockets API uses the `TCP_NODELAY` socket option to disable the Nagle algorithm.

The Host Requirements RFC states that TCP should implement the Nagle algorithm but there must be a way for an application to disable it on an individual connection.

An Example

We can see this interaction between the Nagle algorithm and keystrokes that generate multiple bytes. We establish an Rlogin connection from our host `slip` to the host `vangogh.cs.berkeley.edu`. We then type the F1 function key, which generates 3 bytes: an escape, a left bracket, and an M. We then type the F2 function key, which generates another 3 bytes. Figure 19.5 shows the `tcpdump` output. (We have removed the type-of-service information and the window advertisements.)

```
                               type F1 key
 1  0.0                        slip.1023 > vangogh.login: P 1:2(1) ack 2
 2  0.250520 (0.2505)          vangogh.login > slip.1023: P 2:4(2) ack 2
 3  0.251709 (0.0012)          slip.1023 > vangogh.login: P 2:4(2) ack 4
 4  0.490344 (0.2386)          vangogh.login > slip.1023: P 4:6(2) ack 4
 5  0.588694 (0.0984)          slip.1023 > vangogh.login: . ack 6
                               type F2 key
 6  2.836830 (2.2481)          slip.1023 > vangogh.login: P 4:5(1) ack 6
 7  3.132388 (0.2956)          vangogh.login > slip.1023: P 6:8(2) ack 5
 8  3.133573 (0.0012)          slip.1023 > vangogh.login: P 5:7(2) ack 8
 9  3.370346 (0.2368)          vangogh.login > slip.1023: P 8:10(2) ack 7
10  3.388692 (0.0183)          slip.1023 > vangogh.login: . ack 10
```

Figure 19.5 Watching the Nagle algorithm when typing characters that generate multiple bytes of data.

Figure 19.6 shows the time line for this exchange. At the bottom of this figure we show the 6 bytes going from the client to the server with their sequence numbers, and the 8 bytes of echo being returned.

When the first byte of input is read by the `rlogin` client and written to TCP, it is sent by itself as segment 1. This is the first of the 3 bytes generated by the F1 key. Its echo is returned in segment 2, and only then are the next 2 bytes sent (segment 3). The echo of the second 2 bytes is received in segment 4 and acknowledged in segment 5.

The reason the echo of the first byte occupies 2 bytes (segment 2) is because the ASCII escape character is echoed as 2 bytes: a caret and a left bracket. The next 2 bytes of input, a left bracket and an M, are echoed as themselves.

The same exchange occurs when the next special function key is typed (segments 6–10). As we expect, the time difference between segments 5 and 10 (`slip` sending the acknowledgment of the echo) is a multiple of 200 ms, since both ACKs are delayed.

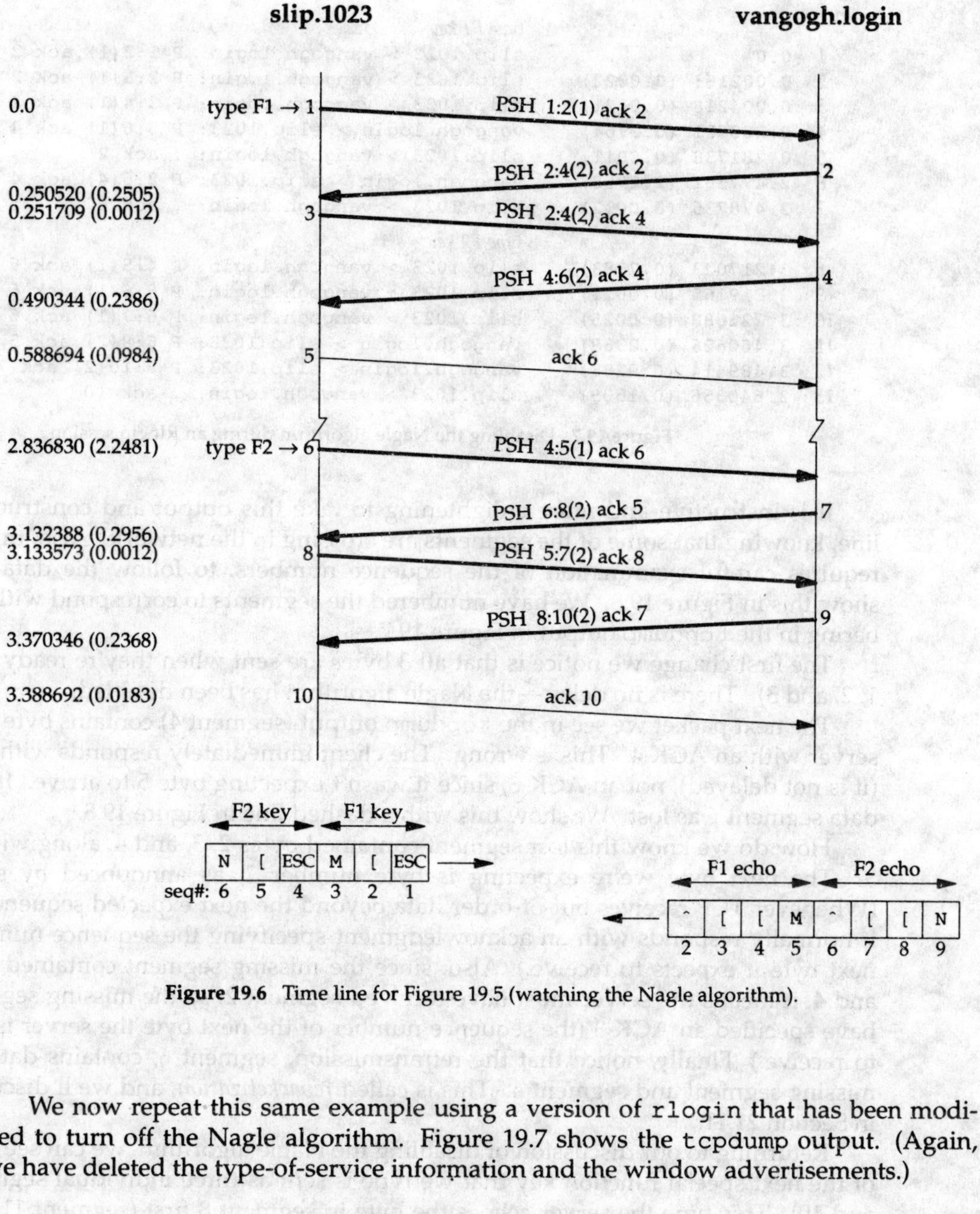

Figure 19.6 Time line for Figure 19.5 (watching the Nagle algorithm).

We now repeat this same example using a version of `rlogin` that has been modified to turn off the Nagle algorithm. Figure 19.7 shows the `tcpdump` output. (Again, we have deleted the type-of-service information and the window advertisements.)

```
                                        type F1 key
 1  0.0                                 slip.1023 > vangogh.login: P 1:2(1) ack 2
 2  0.002163 (0.0022)                   slip.1023 > vangogh.login: P 2:3(1) ack 2
 3  0.004218 (0.0021)                   slip.1023 > vangogh.login: P 3:4(1) ack 2
 4  0.280621 (0.2764)                   vangogh.login > slip.1023: P 5:6(1) ack 4
 5  0.281738 (0.0011)                   slip.1023 > vangogh.login: . ack 2
 6  2.477561 (2.1958)                   vangogh.login > slip.1023: P 2:6(4) ack 4
 7  2.478735 (0.0012)                   slip.1023 > vangogh.login: . ack 6

                                        type F2 key
 8  3.217023 (0.7383)                   slip.1023 > vangogh.login: P 4:5(1) ack 6
 9  3.219165 (0.0021)                   slip.1023 > vangogh.login: P 5:6(1) ack 6
10  3.221688 (0.0025)                   slip.1023 > vangogh.login: P 6:7(1) ack 6
11  3.460626 (0.2389)                   vangogh.login > slip.1023: P 6:8(2) ack 5
12  3.489414 (0.0288)                   vangogh.login > slip.1023: P 8:10(2) ack 7
13  3.640356 (0.1509)                   slip.1023 > vangogh.login: . ack 10
```

Figure 19.7 Disabling the Nagle algorithm during an Rlogin session.

It is instructive and more enlightening to take this output and construct the time line, knowing that some of the segments are crossing in the network. Also, this example requires careful examination of the sequence numbers, to follow the data flow. We show this in Figure 19.8. We have numbered the segments to correspond with the numbering in the `tcpdump` output in Figure 19.7.

The first change we notice is that all 3 bytes are sent when they're ready (segments 1, 2, and 3). There is no delay—the Nagle algorithm has been disabled.

The next packet we see in the `tcpdump` output (segment 4) contains byte 5 from the server with an ACK 4. This is wrong. The client immediately responds with an ACK 2 (it is not delayed), not an ACK 6, since it wasn't expecting byte 5 to arrive. It appears a data segment was lost. We show this with a dashed line in Figure 19.8.

How do we know this lost segment contained bytes 2, 3, and 4, along with an ACK 3? The next byte we're expecting is byte number 2, as announced by segment 5. (Whenever TCP receives out-of-order data beyond the next expected sequence number, it normally responds with an acknowledgment specifying the sequence number of the next byte it expects to receive.) Also, since the missing segment contained bytes 2, 3, and 4, it means the server must have received segment 2, so the missing segment must have specified an ACK 3 (the sequence number of the next byte the server is expecting to receive.) Finally, notice that the retransmission, segment 6, contains data from the missing segment and segment 4. This is called *repacketization*, and we'll discuss it more in Section 21.11.

Returning to our discussion of disabling the Nagle algorithm, we can see the 3 bytes of the next special function key that we type is sent as three individual segments (8, 9, and 10). This time the server echoes the byte in segment 8 first (segment 11), and then echoes the bytes in segments 9 and 10 (segment 12).

What we've seen in this example is that the default use of the Nagle algorithm can cause additional delays when multibyte keystrokes are entered while running an interactive application across a WAN. (See Exercise 19.3.)

We return to the topic of timeout and retransmission in Chapter 21.

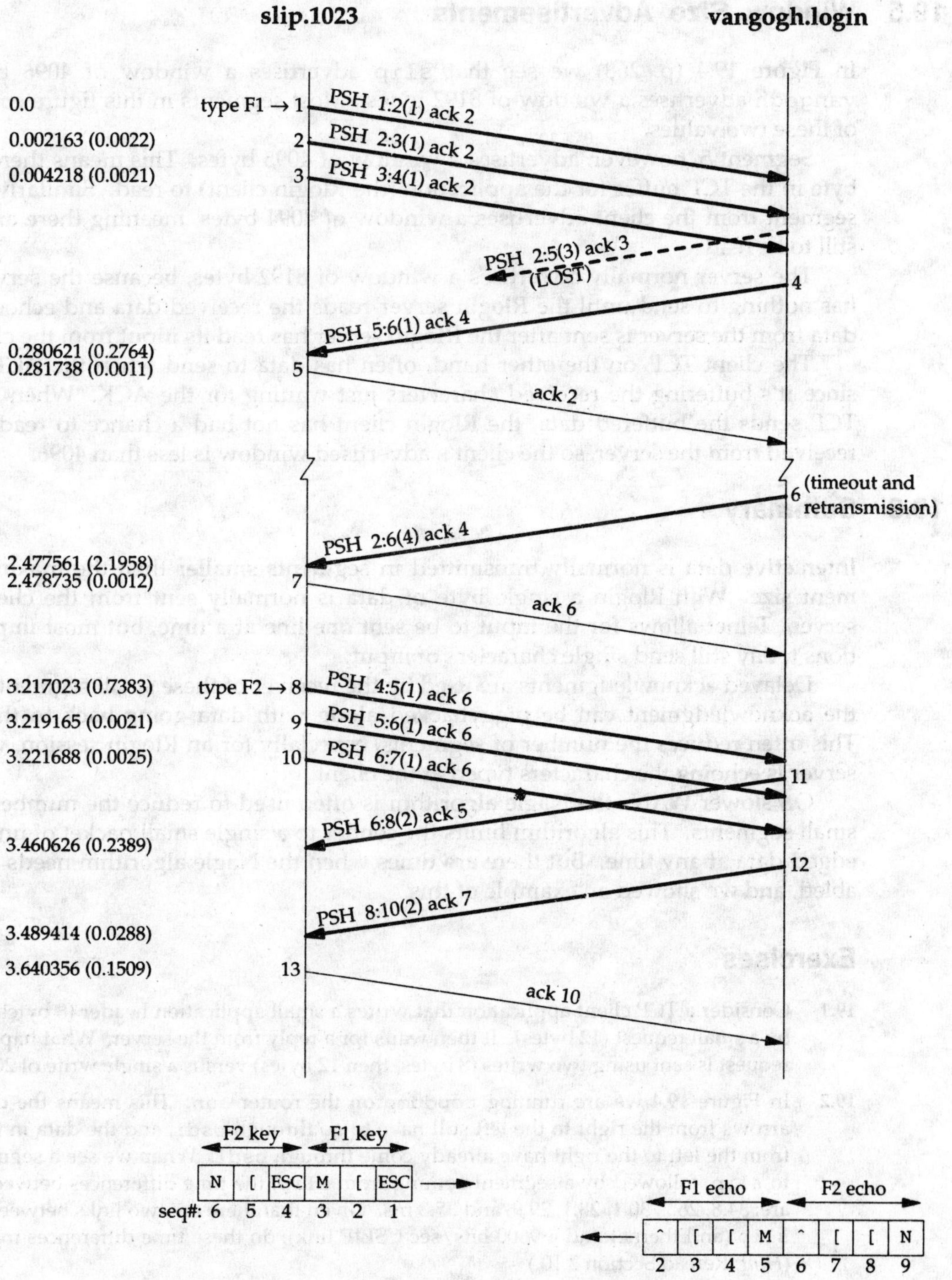

Figure 19.8 Time line for Figure 19.7 (Nagle algorithm disabled).

19.5 Window Size Advertisements

In Figure 19.4 (p. 268) we see that `slip` advertises a window of 4096 bytes and `vangogh` advertises a window of 8192 bytes. Most segments in this figure contain one of these two values.

Segment 5, however, advertises a window of 4095 bytes. This means there is still 1 byte in the TCP buffer for the application (the Rlogin client) to read. Similarly, the next segment from the client advertises a window of 4094 bytes, meaning there are 2 bytes still to be read.

The server normally advertises a window of 8192 bytes, because the server's TCP has nothing to send until the Rlogin server reads the received data and echoes it. The data from the server is sent after the Rlogin server has read its input from the client.

The client TCP, on the other hand, often has data to send when the ACK arrives, since it's buffering the received characters just waiting for the ACK. When the client TCP sends the buffered data, the Rlogin client has not had a chance to read the data received from the server, so the client's advertised window is less than 4096.

19.6 Summary

Interactive data is normally transmitted in segments smaller than the maximum segment size. With Rlogin a single byte of data is normally sent from the client to the server. Telnet allows for the input to be sent one line at a time, but most implementations today still send single characters of input.

Delayed acknowledgments are used by the receiver of these small segments to see if the acknowledgment can be piggybacked along with data going back to the sender. This often reduces the number of segments, especially for an Rlogin session, where the server is echoing the characters typed at the client.

On slower WANs the Nagle algorithm is often used to reduce the number of these small segments. This algorithm limits the sender to a single small packet of unacknowledged data at any time. But there are times when the Nagle algorithm needs to be disabled, and we showed an example of this.

Exercises

19.1 Consider a TCP client application that writes a small application header (8 bytes) followed by a small request (12 bytes). It then waits for a reply from the server. What happens if the request is sent using two writes (8 bytes, then 12 bytes) versus a single write of 20 bytes?

19.2 In Figure 19.4 we are running `tcpdump` on the router `sun`. This means the data in the arrows from the right to the left still have to go through `bsdi`, and the data in the arrows from the left to the right have already come through `bsdi`. When we see a segment going to `slip`, followed by a segment coming from `slip`, the time differences between the two are: 34.8, 26.7, 30.1, 28.1, 29.9, and 35.3 ms. Given that there are two links between `sun` and `slip` (an Ethernet and a 9600 bits/sec CSLIP link), do these time differences make sense? (*Hint*: Reread Section 2.10.)

19.3 Compare the time required to send a special function key and have it acknowledged using the Nagle algorithm (Figure 19.6) and with the algorithm disabled (Figure 19.8).

20

TCP Bulk Data Flow

20.1 Introduction

In Chapter 15 we saw that TFTP uses a stop-and-wait protocol. The sender of a data block required an acknowledgment for that block before the next block was sent. In this chapter we'll see that TCP uses a different form of flow control called a *sliding window* protocol. It allows the sender to transmit multiple packets before it stops and waits for an acknowledgment. This leads to faster data transfer, since the sender doesn't have to stop and wait for an acknowledgment each time a packet is sent.

We also look at TCP's PUSH flag, something we've seen in many of the previous examples. We also look at slow start, the technique used by TCP for getting the flow of data established on a connection, and then we examine bulk data throughput.

20.2 Normal Data Flow

Let's start with a one-way transfer of 8192 bytes from the host `svr4` to the host `bsdi`. We run our `sock` program on `bsdi` as the server:

```
bsdi % sock -i -s 7777
```

The `-i` and `-s` flags tell the program to run as a "sink" server (read from the network and discard the data), and the server's port number is specified as 7777. The corresponding client is then run as:

```
svr4 % sock -i -n8 bsdi 7777
```

This causes the client to perform eight 1024-byte writes to the network. Figure 20.1 shows the time line for this exchange. We have left the first three segments in the output to show the MSS values for each end.

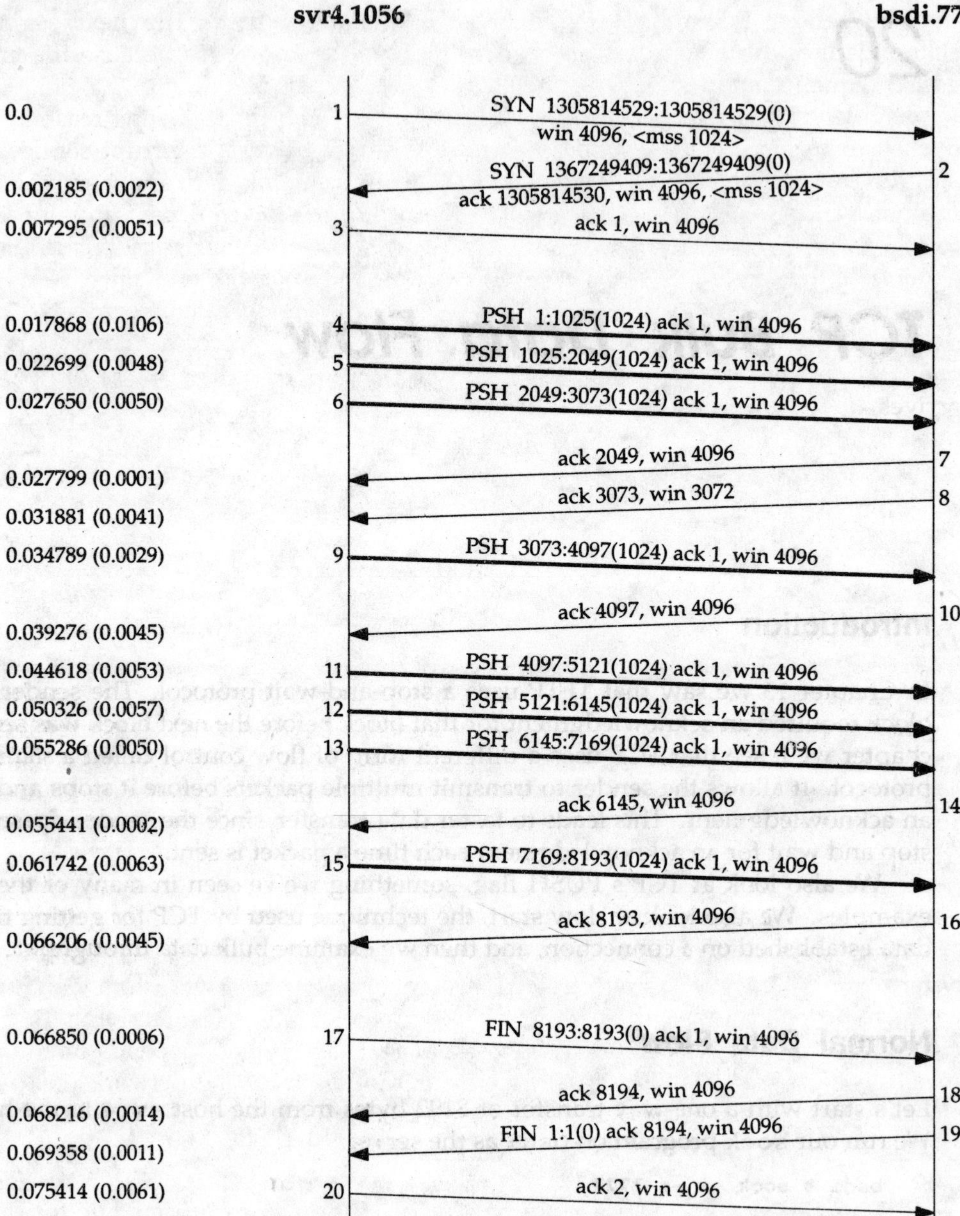

Figure 20.1 Transfer of 8192 bytes from `svr4` to `bsdi`.

The sender transmits three data segments (4–6) first. The next segment (7) acknowledges the first two data segments only. We know this because the acknowledged sequence number is 2049, not 3073.

Segment 7 specifies an ACK of 2049 and not 3073 for the following reason. When a packet arrives it is initially processed by the device driver's interrupt service routine and then placed onto IP's input queue. The three segments 4, 5, and 6 arrive one after the other and are placed onto IP's input queue in the received order. IP will pass them to TCP in the same order. When TCP processes segment 4, the connection is marked to generate a delayed ACK. TCP processes the next segment (5) and since TCP now has two outstanding segments to ACK, the ACK of 2049 is generated (segment 7), and the delayed ACK flag for this connection is turned off. TCP processes the next input segment (6) and the connection is again marked for a delayed ACK. Before segment 9 arrives, however, it appears the delayed ACK timer goes off, and the ACK of 3073 (segment 8) is generated. Segment 8 advertises a window of 3072 bytes, implying that there are still 1024 bytes of data in the TCP receive buffer that the application has not read.

Segments 11–16 show the "ACK every other segment" strategy that is common. Segments 11, 12, and 13 arrive and are placed on IP's input queue. When segment 11 is processed by TCP the connection is marked for a delayed ACK. When segment 12 is processed, an ACK is generated (segment 14) for segments 11 and 12, and the delayed ACK flag for this connection is turned off. Segment 13 causes the connection to be marked again for a delayed ACK but before the timer goes off, segment 15 is processed, causing the ACK (segment 16) to be sent immediately.

It is important to notice that the ACK in segments 7, 14, and 16 acknowledge two received segments. With TCP's sliding-window protocol the receiver does not have to acknowledge every received packet. With TCP, the ACKs are cumulative—they acknowledge that the receiver has correctly received all bytes up through the acknowledged sequence number minus one. In this example three of the ACKs acknowledge 2048 bytes of data and two acknowledge 1024 bytes of data. (This ignores the ACKs in the connection establishment and termination.)

What we are watching with `tcpdump` are the dynamics of TCP in action. The ordering of the packets that we see on the wire depends on many factors, most of which we have no control over: the sending TCP implementation, the receiving TCP implementation, the reading of data by the receiving process (which depends on the process scheduling by the operating system), and the dynamics of the network (i.e., Ethernet collisions and backoffs). There is no single correct way for two TCPs to exchange a given amount of data.

To show how things can change, Figure 20.2 shows another time line for the same exchange of data between the same two hosts, captured a few minutes after the one in Figure 20.1.

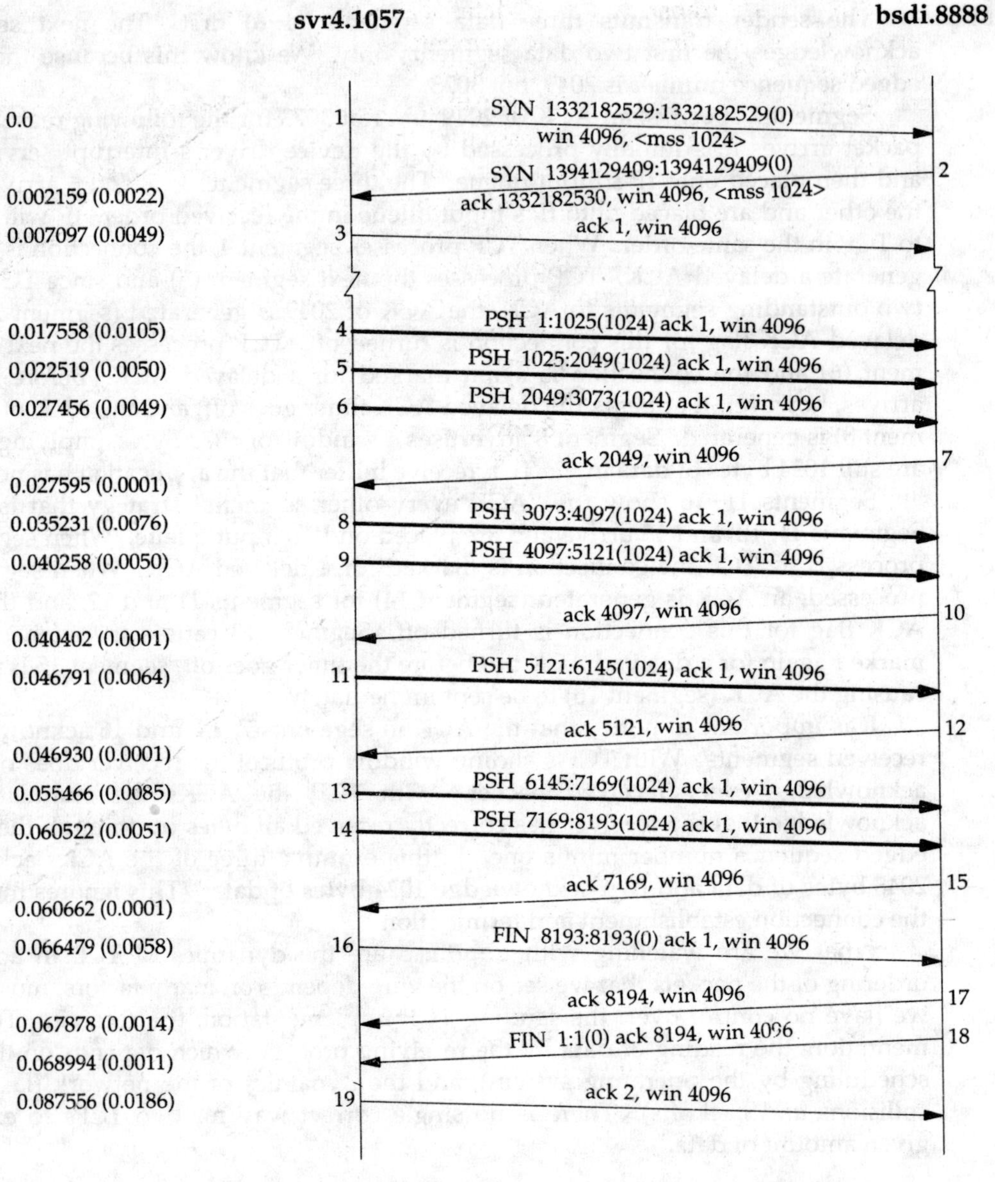

Figure 20.2 Another transfer of 8192 bytes from `svr4` to `bsdi`.

A few things have changed. This time the receiver does not send an ACK of 3073; instead it waits and sends the ACK of 4097. The receiver sends only four ACKs (segments 7, 10, 12, and 15): three of these are for 2048 bytes and one for 1024 bytes. The ACK of the final 1024 bytes of data appears in segment 17, along with the ACK of the FIN. (Compare segment 17 in this figure with segments 16 and 18 in Figure 20.1.)

Fast Sender, Slow Receiver

Figure 20.3 shows another time line, this time from a fast sender (a Sparc) to a slow receiver (an 80386 with a slow Ethernet card). The dynamics are different again.

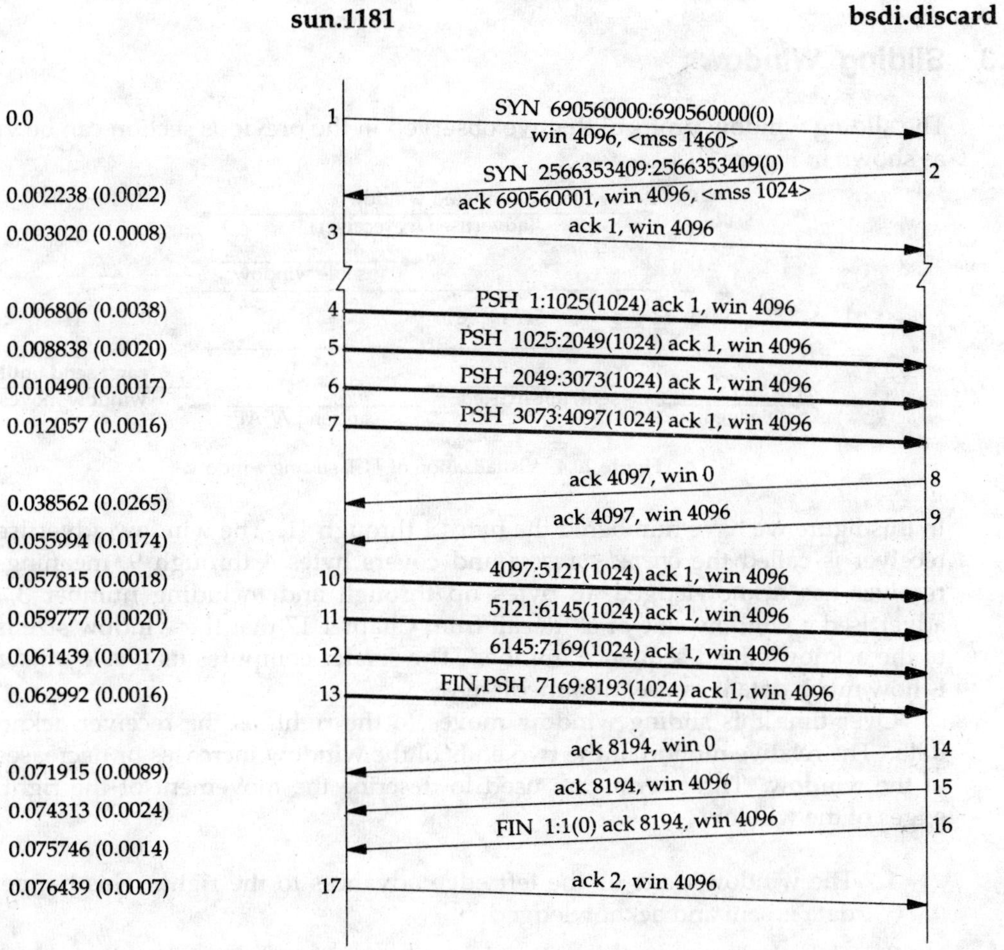

Figure 20.3 Sending 8192 bytes from a fast sender to a slow receiver.

The sender transmits four back-to-back data segments (4–7) to fill the receiver's window. The sender then stops and waits for an ACK. The receiver sends the ACK (segment 8) but the advertised window is 0. This means the receiver has all the data, but it's all in the receiver's TCP buffers, because the application hasn't had a chance to read the data. Another ACK (called a *window update*) is sent 17.4 ms later, announcing that the receiver can now receive another 4096 bytes. Although this looks like an ACK, it is called a window update because it does not acknowledge any new data, it just advances the right edge of the window.

The sender transmits its final four segments (10–13), again filling the receiver's window. Notice that segment 13 contains two flag bits: PUSH and FIN. This is followed by another two ACKs from the receiver. Both of these acknowledge the final 4096 bytes of data (bytes 4097 through 8192) and the FIN (numbered 8193).

20.3 Sliding Windows

The sliding window protocol that we observed in the previous section can be visualized as shown in Figure 20.4.

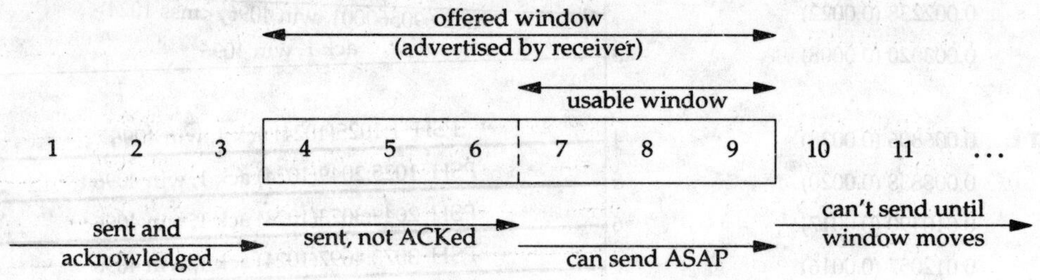

Figure 20.4 Visualization of TCP sliding window.

In this figure we have numbered the bytes 1 through 11. The window advertised by the receiver is called the *offered window* and covers bytes 4 through 9, meaning that the receiver has acknowledged all bytes up through and including number 3, and has advertised a window size of 6. Recall from Chapter 17 that the window size is relative to the acknowledged sequence number. The sender computes its *usable window*, which is how much data it can send immediately.

Over time this sliding window moves to the right, as the receiver acknowledges data. The relative motion of the two ends of the window increases or decreases the size of the window. Three terms are used to describe the movement of the right and left edges of the window.

1. The window *closes* as the left edge advances to the right. This happens when data is sent and acknowledged.
2. The window *opens* when the right edge moves to the right, allowing more data to be sent. This happens when the receiving process on the other end reads acknowledged data, freeing up space in its TCP receive buffer.
3. The window *shrinks* when the right edge moves to the left. The Host Requirements RFC strongly discourages this, but TCP must be able to cope with a peer that does this. Section 22.3 shows an example when one side would like to shrink the window by moving the right edge to the left, but cannot.

Figure 20.5 shows these three terms. The left edge of the window cannot move to the left, because this edge is controlled by the acknowledgment number received from

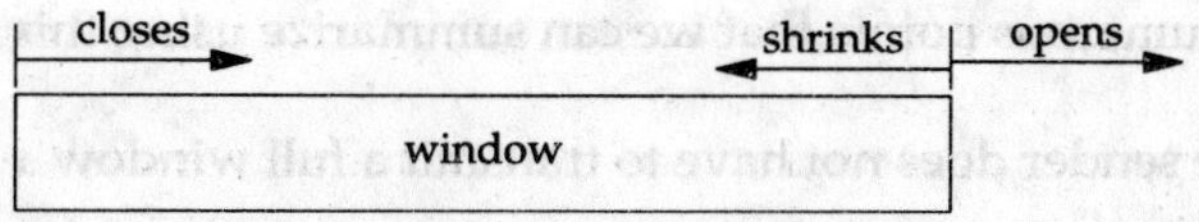

Figure 20.5 Movement of window edges.

the other end. If an ACK were received that implied moving the left edge to the left, it is a duplicate ACK, and discarded.

If the left edge reaches the right edge, it is called a *zero window*. This stops the sender from transmitting any data.

An Example

Figure 20.6 shows the dynamics of TCP's sliding window protocol for the data transfer in Figure 20.1.

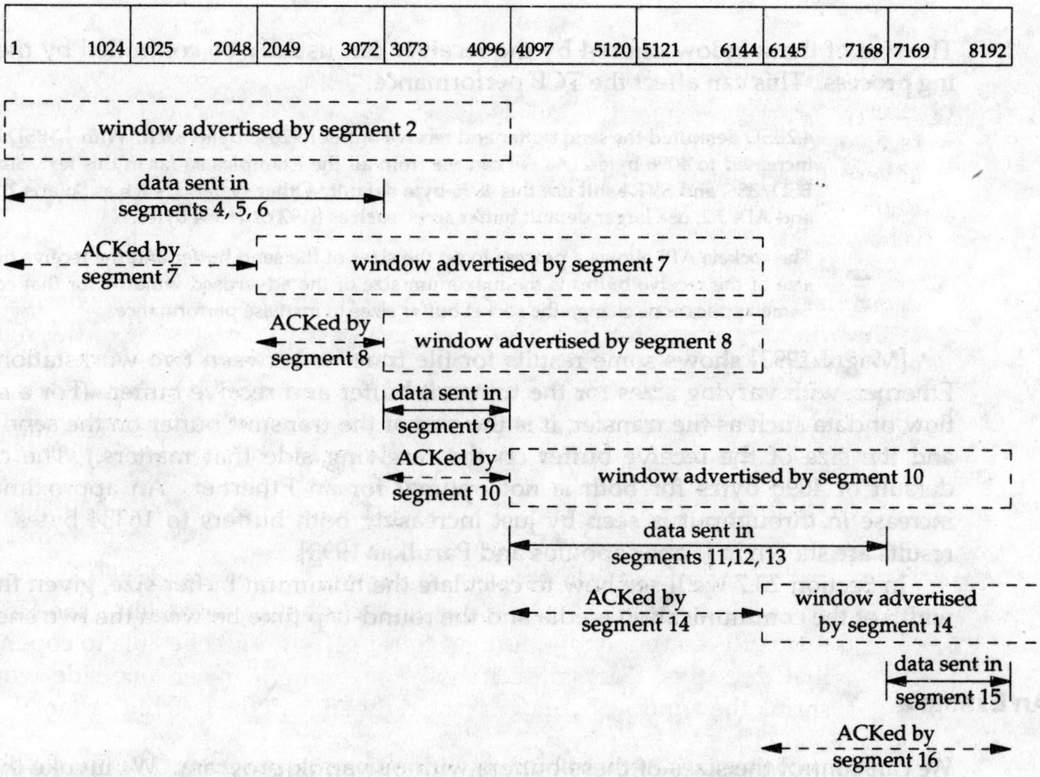

Figure 20.6 Sliding window protocol for Figure 20.1.

There are numerous points that we can summarize using this figure as an example.

1. The sender does not have to transmit a full window's worth of data.
2. One segment from the receiver acknowledges data and slides the window to the right. This is because the window size is relative to the acknowledged sequence number.
3. The size of the window can decrease, as shown by the change from segment 7 to segment 8, but the right edge of the window must not move leftward.
4. The receiver does not have to wait for the window to fill before sending an ACK. We saw earlier that many implementations send an ACK for every two segments that are received.

We'll see more examples of the dynamics of the sliding window protocol in later examples.

20.4 Window Size

The size of the window offered by the receiver can usually be controlled by the receiving process. This can affect the TCP performance.

> 4.2BSD defaulted the send buffer and receive buffer to 2048 bytes each. With 4.3BSD both were increased to 4096 bytes. As we can see from all the examples so far in this text, SunOS 4.1.3, BSD/386, and SVR4 still use this 4096-byte default. Other systems, such as Solaris 2.2, 4.4BSD, and AIX 3.2, use larger default buffer sizes, such as 8192 or 16384 bytes.
>
> The sockets API allows a process to set the sizes of the send buffer and the receive buffer. The size of the receive buffer is the maximum size of the advertised window for that connection. Some applications change the socket buffer sizes to increase performance.

[Mogul 1993] shows some results for file transfer between two workstations on an Ethernet, with varying sizes for the transmit buffer and receive buffer. (For a one-way flow of data such as file transfer, it is the size of the transmit buffer on the sending side and the size of the receive buffer on the receiving side that matters.) The common default of 4096 bytes for both is not optimal for an Ethernet. An approximate 40% increase in throughput is seen by just increasing both buffers to 16384 bytes. Similar results are shown in [Papadopoulos and Parulkar 1993].

In Section 20.7 we'll see how to calculate the minimum buffer size, given the bandwidth of the communication media and the round-trip time between the two ends.

An Example

We can control the sizes of these buffers with our sock program. We invoke the server as:

```
bsdi % sock -i -s -R6144 5555
```

which sets the size of the receive buffer (-R option) to 6144 bytes. We then start the client on the host sun and have it perform one write of 8192 bytes:

```
sun % sock -i -n1 -w8192 bsdi 5555
```

Figure 20.7 shows the results.

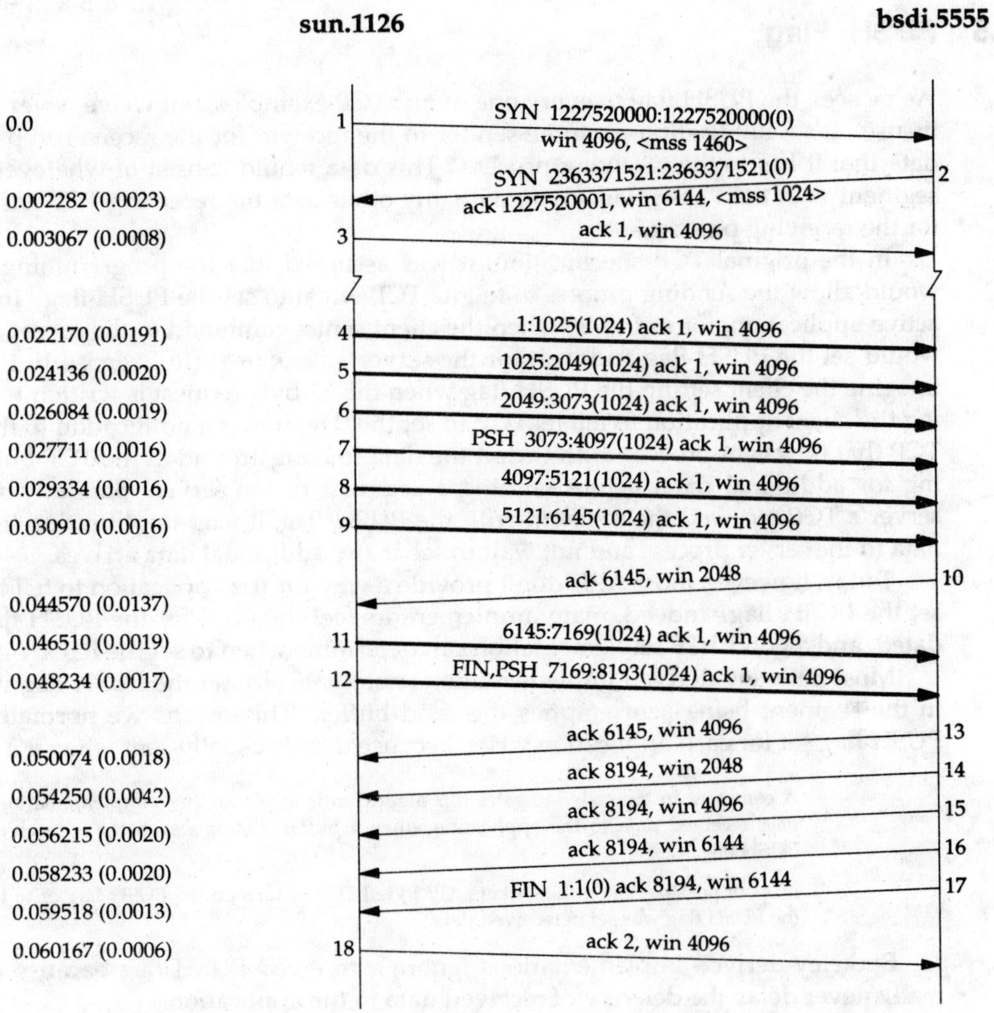

Figure 20.7 Data transfer with receiver offering a window size of 6144 bytes.

First notice that the receiver's window size is offered as 6144 bytes in segment 2. Because of this larger window, the client sends six segments immediately (segments 4–9), and then stops. Segment 10 acknowledges all the data (bytes 1 through 6144) but offers a window of only 2048, probably because the receiving application hasn't had a chance to read more than 2048 bytes. Segments 11 and 12 complete the data transfer from the client, and this final data segment also carries the FIN flag.

Segment 13 contains the same acknowledgment sequence number as segment 10, but advertises a larger window. Segment 14 acknowledges the final 2048 bytes of data and the FIN, and segments 15 and 16 just advertise a larger window. Segments 17 and 18 complete the normal close.

20.5 PUSH Flag

We've seen the PUSH flag in every one of our TCP examples, but we've never described its use. It's a notification from the sender to the receiver for the receiver to pass all the data that it has to the receiving process. This data would consist of whatever is in the segment with the PUSH flag, along with any other data the receiving TCP has collected for the receiving process.

In the original TCP specification, it was assumed that the programming interface would allow the sending process to tell its TCP when to set the PUSH flag. In an interactive application, for example, when the client sent a command to the server, the client would set the PUSH flag and wait for the server's response. (In Exercise 19.1 we could imagine the client setting the PUSH flag when the 12-byte request is written.) By allowing the client application to tell its TCP to set the flag, it was a notification to the client's TCP that the client process didn't want the data to hang around in the TCP buffer, waiting for additional data, before sending a segment to the server. Similarly, when the server's TCP received the segment with the PUSH flag, it was a notification to pass the data to the server process and not wait to see if any additional data arrives.

Today, however, most APIs don't provide a way for the application to tell its TCP to set the PUSH flag. Indeed, many implementors feel the need for the PUSH flag is outdated, and a good TCP implementation can determine when to set the flag by itself.

Most Berkeley-derived implementations automatically set the PUSH flag if the data in the segment being sent empties the send buffer. This means we normally see the PUSH flag set for each application write, because data is usually sent when it's written.

> A comment in the code indicates this algorithm is to please those implementations that only pass received data to the application when a buffer fills or a segment is received with the PUSH flag.
>
> It is not possible using the sockets API to tell TCP to turn on the PUSH flag or to tell whether the PUSH flag was set in received data.

Berkeley-derived implementations ignore a received PUSH flag because they normally never delay the delivery of received data to the application.

Examples

In Figure 20.1 (p. 276) we see the PUSH flag turned on for all eight data segments (4–6, 9, 11–13, and 15). This is because the client did eight writes of 1024 bytes, and each write emptied the send buffer.

Look again at Figure 20.7 (p. 283). We expect the PUSH flag to be set on segment 12, since that is the final data segment. Why was the PUSH flag set on segment 7, when the sender knew there were still more bytes to send? The reason is that the size of the sender's send buffer is 4096 bytes, even though we specified a single write of 8192 bytes.

Another point to note in Figure 20.7 concerns the three consecutive ACKs, segments 14, 15, and 16. We saw two consecutive ACKs in Figure 20.3, but that was because the receiver had advertised a window of 0 (stopping the sender) so when the window opened up, another ACK was required, with the nonzero window, to restart the sender. In Figure 20.7, however, the window never reaches 0. Nevertheless, when the size of the window increases by 2048 bytes, another ACK is sent (segments 15 and 16) to provide this window update to the other end. (These two window updates in segments 15 and 16 are not needed, since the FIN has been received from the other end, meaning it will not send any more data.) Many implementations send this window update if the window increases by either two maximum sized segments (2048 bytes in this example, with an MSS of 1024) or 50% of the maximum possible window (3072 bytes in this example, with a maximum window of 6144). We'll see this again in Section 22.3 when we examine the silly window syndrome in detail.

As another example of the PUSH flag, look again at Figure 20.3 (p. 279). The reason we see the flag on for the first four data segments (4–7) is because each one caused a segment to be generated by TCP and passed to the IP layer. But then TCP had to stop, waiting for an ACK to move the 4096-byte window. While waiting for the ACK, TCP takes the final 4096 bytes of data from the application. When the window opens up (segment 9) the sending TCP knows it has four segments that it can send immediately, so it only turns on the PUSH flag for the final segment (13).

20.6 Slow Start

In all the examples we've seen so far in this chapter, the sender starts off by injecting multiple segments into the network, up to the window size advertised by the receiver. While this is OK when the two hosts are on the same LAN, if there are routers and slower links between the sender and the receiver, problems can arise. Some intermediate router must queue the packets, and it's possible for that router to run out of space. [Jacobson 1988] shows how this naive approach can reduce the throughput of a TCP connection drastically.

TCP is now required to support an algorithm called *slow start*. It operates by observing that the rate at which new packets should be injected into the network is the rate at which the acknowledgments are returned by the other end.

Slow start adds another window to the sender's TCP: the *congestion window*, called *cwnd*. When a new connection is established with a host on another network, the congestion window is initialized to one segment (i.e., the segment size announced by the other end). Each time an ACK is received, the congestion window is increased by one segment. (*cwnd* is maintained in bytes, but slow start always increments it by the segment size.) The sender can transmit up to the minimum of the congestion window and the advertised window. The congestion window is flow control imposed by the sender, while the advertised window is flow control imposed by the receiver.

The sender starts by transmitting one segment and waiting for its ACK. When that ACK is received, the congestion window is incremented from one to two, and two segments can be sent. When each of those two segments is acknowledged, the congestion window is increased to four. This provides an exponential increase.

At some point the capacity of the internet can be reached, and an intermediate router will start discarding packets. This tells the sender that its congestion window has gotten too large. When we talk about TCP's timeout and retransmission algorithms in the next chapter, we'll see how this is handled, and what happens to the congestion window. For now, let's watch slow start in action.

An Example

Figure 20.8 shows data being sent from the host `sun` to the host `vangogh.cs.berkeley.edu`. The data traverses a slow SLIP link, which should be the bottleneck. (We have removed the connection establishment from this time line.)

We see the sender transmit one segment with 512 bytes of data and then wait for its ACK. The ACK is received 716 ms later, which is an indicator of the round-trip time. The congestion window is then increased to two segments, and two segments are sent. When the ACK in segment 5 is received, the congestion window is increased to three segments. Two more segments are sent (not three) because the ACK for segment 4 is still outstanding. When the ACK in segment 8 is received, the congestion window is increased to 4 but only two more segments are sent, because the ACKs for segments 6 and 7 are still outstanding.

We'll return to slow start in Section 21.6 and see how it's normally implemented with another technique called *congestion avoidance.*

20.7 Bulk Data Throughput

Let's look at the interaction of the window size, the windowed flow control, and slow start on the throughput of a TCP connection carrying bulk data.

Figure 20.9 shows the steps over time of a connection between a sender on the left and a receiver on the right. Sixteen units of time are shown. We show only discrete units of time in this figure, for simplicity. We show segments carrying data going from the left to right in the top half of each picture, numbered 1, 2, 3, and so on. The ACKs go in the other direction in the bottom half of each picture. We draw the ACKs smaller, and show the segment number being acknowledged.

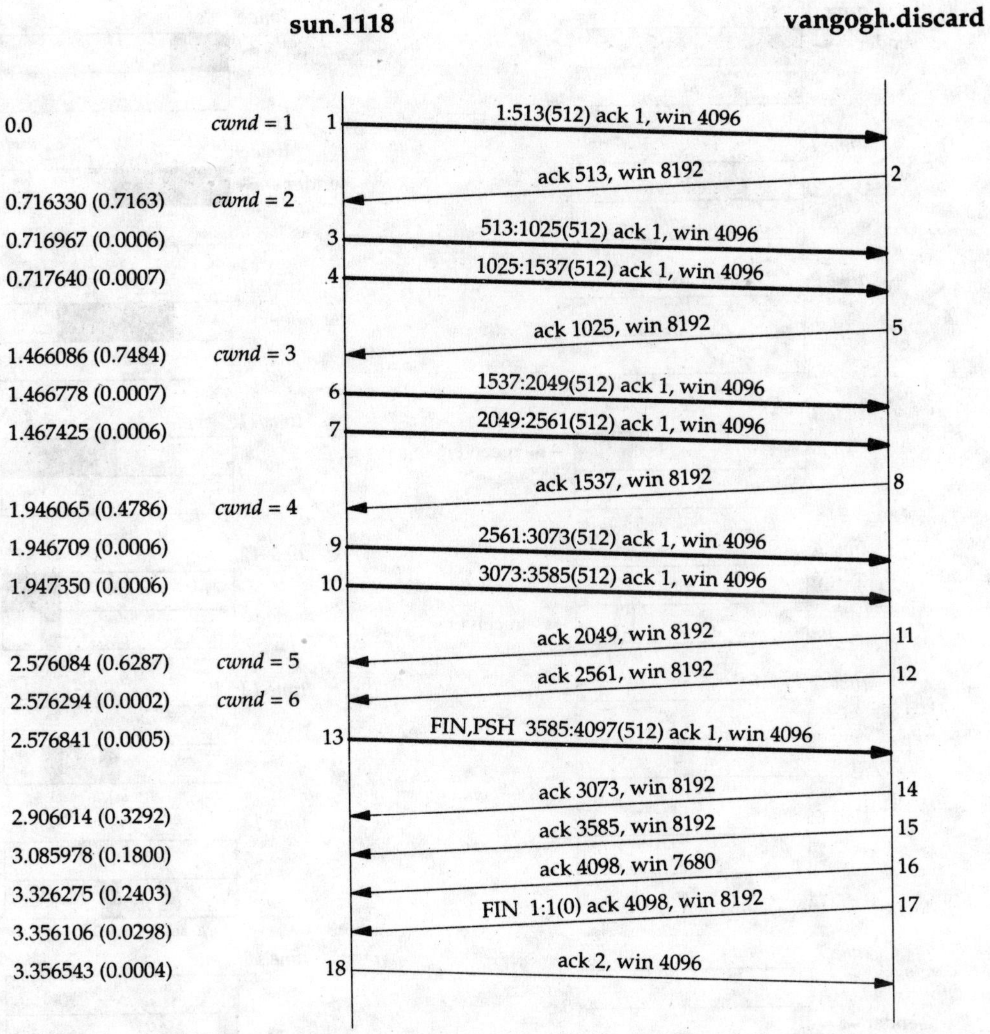

Figure 20.8 Example of slow start.

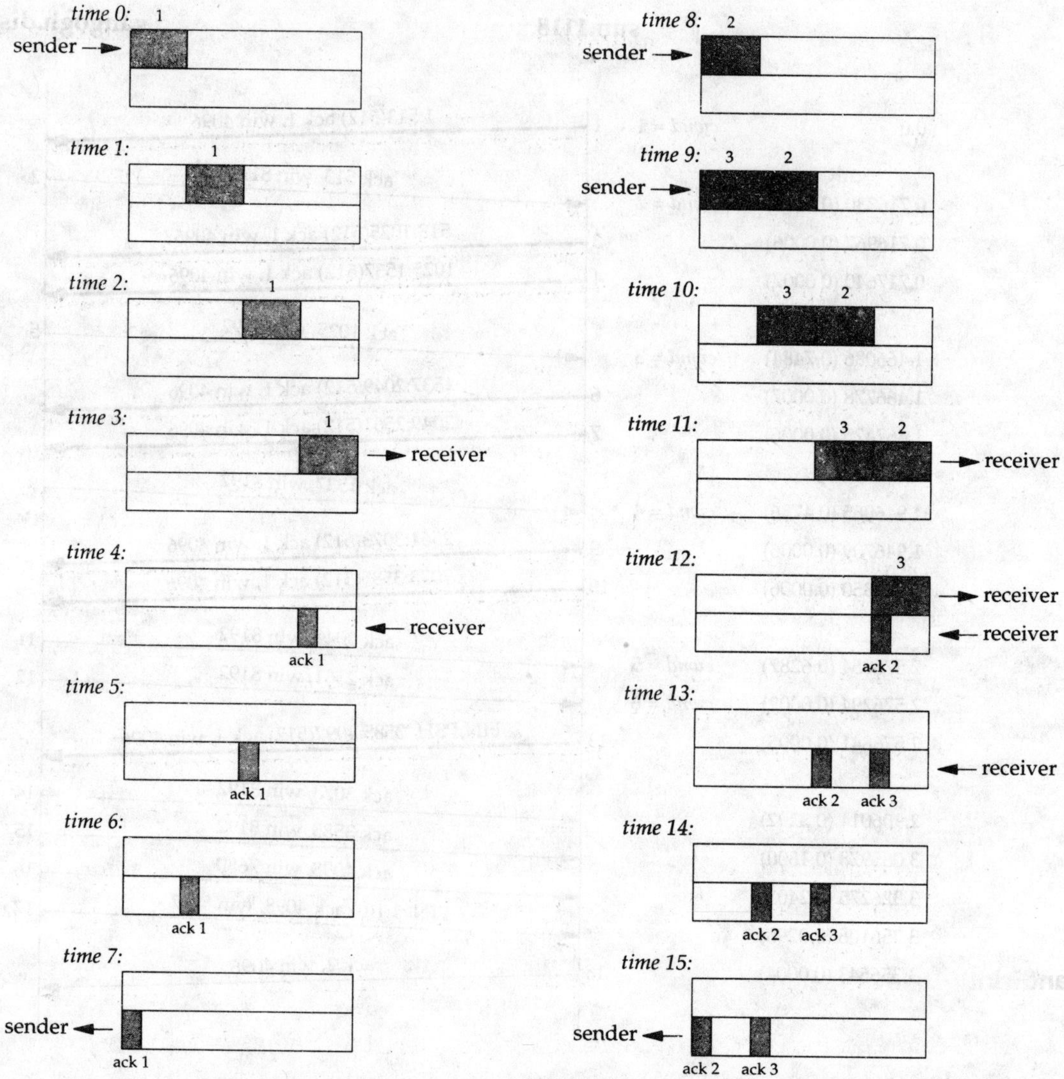

Figure 20.9 Times 0–15 for bulk data throughput example.

At time 0 the sender transmits one segment. Since the sender is in slow start (its congestion window is one segment), it must wait for the acknowledgment of this segment before continuing.

At times 1, 2, and 3 the segment moves one unit of time to the right. At time 4 the receiver reads the segment and generates the acknowledgment. At times 5, 6, and 7 the ACK moves to the left one unit, back to the sender. We have a round-trip time (RTT) of 8 units of time.

We have purposely drawn the ACK segment smaller than the data segment, since it's normally just an IP header and a TCP header. We're showing only a unidirectional flow of data here. Also, we assume that the ACK moves at the same speed as the data segment, which isn't always true.

In general the time to send a packet depends on two factors: a propagation delay (caused by the finite speed of light, latencies in transmission equipment, etc.) and a transmission delay that depends on the speed of the media (how many bits per second the media can transmit). For a given path between two nodes the propagation delay is fixed while the transmission delay depends on the packet size. At lower speeds the transmission delay dominates (e.g., Exercise 7.2 where we didn't even consider the propagation delay), whereas at gigabit speeds the propagation delay dominates (e.g., Figure 24.6).

When the sender receives the ACK it can transmit two more segments (which we've numbered 2 and 3), at times 8 and 9. Its congestion window is now two segments. These two segments move right toward the receiver, where the ACKs are generated at times 12 and 13. The spacing of the ACKs returned to the sender is identical to the spacing of the data segments. This is called the *self-clocking* behavior of TCP. Since the receiver can only generate ACKs when the data arrives, the spacing of the ACKs at the sender identifies the arrival rate of the data at the receiver. (In actuality, however, queueing on the return path can change the arrival rate of the ACKs.)

Figure 20.10 shows the next 16 time units. The arrival of the two ACKs increases the congestion window from two to four segments, and these four segments are sent at times 16–19. The first of the ACKs returns at time 23. The four ACKs increase the congestion window from four to eight segments, and these eight segments are transmitted at times 24–31.

At time 31, and at all successive times, the pipe between the sender and receiver is full. It cannot hold any more data, regardless of the congestion window or the window advertised by the receiver. Each unit of time a segment is removed from the network by the receiver, and another is placed into the network by the sender. However many data segments fill the pipe, there are an equal number of ACKs making the return trip. This is the ideal steady state of the connection.

Bandwidth-Delay Product

We can now answer the question: how big should the window be? In our example, the sender needs to have eight segments outstanding and unacknowledged at any time, for maximum throughput. The receiver's advertised window must be that large, since that limits how much the sender can transmit.

We can calculate the capacity of the pipe as

$$\textit{capacity}\text{ (bits)} = \textit{bandwidth}\text{ (bits/sec)} \times \textit{round-trip time}\text{ (sec)}$$

This is normally called the *bandwidth-delay product*. This value can vary widely, depending on the network speed and the RTT between the two ends. For example, a T1 telephone line (1,544,000 bits/sec) across the United States (about a 60-ms RTT) gives a bandwidth-delay product of 11,580 bytes. This is reasonable in terms of the buffer sizes we talked about in Section 20.4, but a T3 telephone line (45,000,000 bits/sec) across the United States gives a bandwidth-delay product of 337,500 bytes, which is bigger than the maximum allowable TCP window advertisement (65535 bytes). We describe the

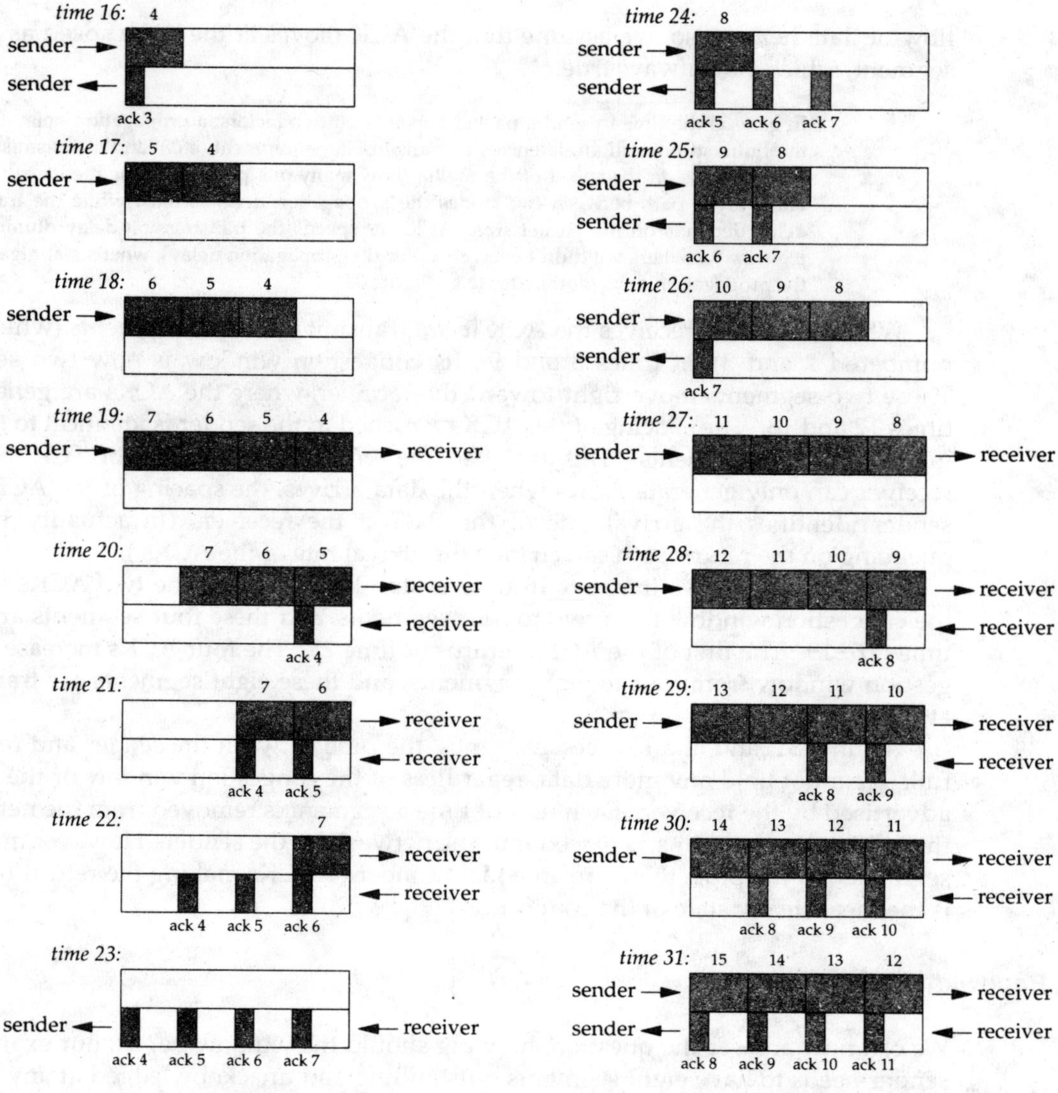

Figure 20.10 Times 16–31 for bulk data throughput example.

new TCP window scale option in Section 24.4 that gets around this current limitation of TCP.

> The value 1,544,000 bits/sec for a T1 phone line is the raw bit rate. The data rate is actually 1,536,000 bits/sec, since 1 bit in 193 is used for framing. The raw bit rate of a T3 phone line is actually 44,736,000 bits/sec, and the data rate can reach 44,210,000 bits/sec. For our discussion we'll use 1.544 Mbits/sec and 45 Mbits/sec.

Either the bandwidth or the delay can affect the capacity of the pipe between the sender and receiver. In Figure 20.11 we show graphically how a doubling of the RTT doubles the capacity of the pipe.

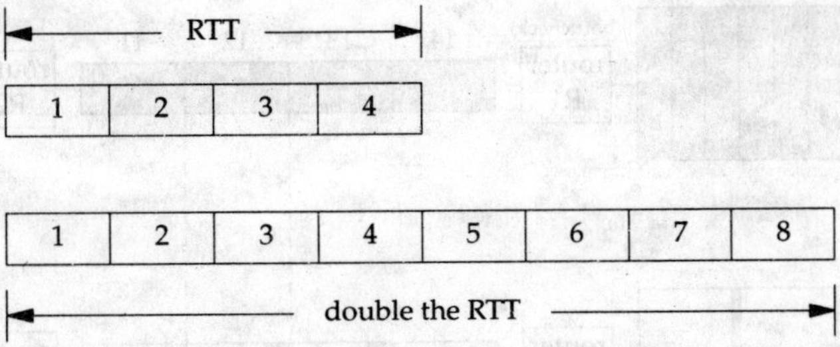

Figure 20.11 Doubling the RTT doubles the capacity of the pipe.

In the lower illustration of Figure 20.11, with the longer RTT, the pipe can hold eight segments, instead of four.

Similarly, Figure 20.12 shows that doubling the bandwidth also doubles the capacity of the pipe.

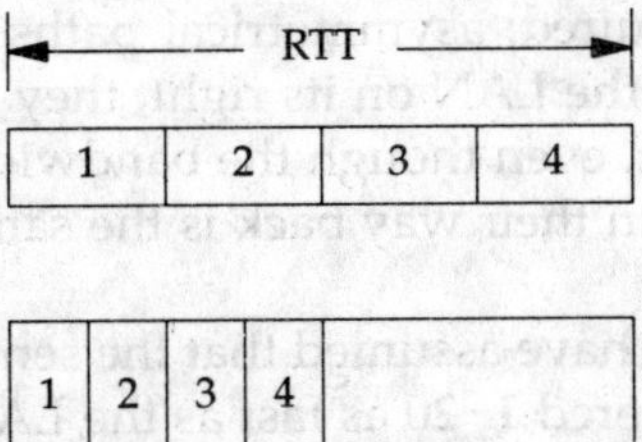

Figure 20.12 Doubling the bandwidth doubles the capacity of the pipe.

In the lower illustration of Figure 20.12, we assume that the network speed has doubled, allowing us to send four segments in half the time as in the top picture. Again, the capacity of the pipe has doubled. (We assume that the segments in the top half of this figure have the same area, that is the same number of bits, as the segments in the bottom half.)

Congestion

Congestion can occur when data arrives on a big pipe (a fast LAN) and gets sent out a smaller pipe (a slower WAN). Congestion can also occur when multiple input streams arrive at a router whose output capacity is less than the sum of the inputs.

Figure 20.13 shows a typical scenario with a big pipe feeding a smaller pipe. We say this is typical because most hosts are connected to LANs, with an attached router that is connected to a slower WAN. (Again, we are assuming the areas of all the data segments (9–20) in the top half of the figure are the same, and the areas of all the acknowledgments in the bottom half are all the same.)

In this figure we have labeled the router R1 as the "bottleneck," because it is the congestion point. It can receive packets from the LAN on its left faster than they can be

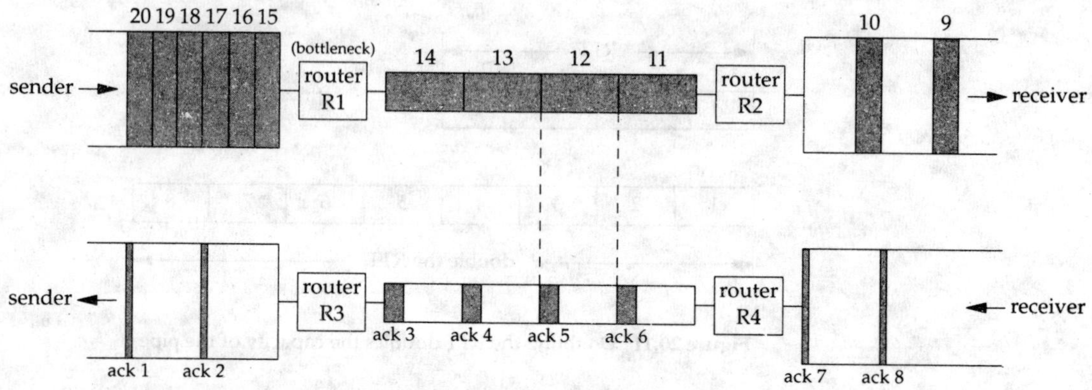

Figure 20.13 Congestion caused by a bigger pipe feeding a smaller pipe.

sent out the WAN on its right. (Commonly R1 and R3 are the same router, as are R2 and R4, but that's not required; asymmetrical paths can occur.) When router R2 puts the received packets onto the LAN on its right, they maintain the same spacing as they did on the WAN on its left, even though the bandwidth of the LAN is higher. Similarly, the spacing of the ACKs on their way back is the same as the spacing of the slowest link in the path.

In Figure 20.13 we have assumed that the sender did not use slow start, and sent the segments we've numbered 1–20 as fast as the LAN could take them. (This assumes the receiving host advertised a window of at least 20 segments.) The spacing of the ACKs will correspond to the bandwidth of the slowest link, as we show. We are assuming the bottleneck router has adequate buffering for all 20 segments. This is not guaranteed, and can lead to that router discarding packets. We'll see how to avoid this when we talk about congestion avoidance in Section 21.6.

20.8 Urgent Mode

TCP provides what it calls *urgent mode*, allowing one end to tell the other end that "urgent data" of some form has been placed into the normal stream of data. The other end is notified that this urgent data has been placed into the data stream, and it's up to the receiving end to decide what to do.

The notification from one end to the other that urgent data exists in the data stream is done by setting two fields in the TCP header (Figure 17.2, p. 225). The URG bit is turned on and the 16-bit *urgent pointer* is set to a positive offset that must be added to the sequence number field in the TCP header to obtain the sequence number of the last byte of urgent data.

There is continuing debate about whether the urgent pointer points to the last byte of urgent data, or to the byte following the last byte of urgent data. The original TCP specification gave both interpretations but the Host Requirements RFC identifies which is correct: the urgent pointer points to the last byte of urgent data.

The problem, however, is that most implementations (i.e., the Berkeley-derived implementations) continue to use the wrong interpretation. An implementation that follows the specification in the Host Requirements RFC might be compliant, but might not communicate correctly with most other hosts.

TCP must inform the receiving process when an urgent pointer is received and one was not already pending on the connection, or if the urgent pointer advances in the data stream. The receiving application can then read the data stream and must be able to tell when the urgent pointer is encountered. As long as data exists from the receiver's current read position until the urgent pointer, the application is considered to be in an "urgent mode." After the urgent pointer is passed, the application returns to its normal mode.

TCP itself says little more about urgent data. There is no way to specify where the urgent data starts in the data stream. The only information sent across the connection by TCP is that urgent mode has begun (the URG bit in the TCP header) and the pointer to the last byte of urgent data. Everything else is left to the application.

Unfortunately many implementations incorrectly call TCP's urgent mode *out-of-band* data. If an application really wants a separate out-of-band channel, a second TCP connection is the easiest way to accomplish this. (Some transport layers do provide what most people consider true out-of-band data: a logically separate data path using the same connection as the normal data path. This is not what TCP provides.)

The confusion between TCP's urgent mode and out-of-band data is also because the predominant programming interface, the sockets API, maps TCP's urgent mode into what sockets calls out-of-band data.

What is urgent mode used for? The two most commonly used applications are Telnet and Rlogin, when the interactive user types the interrupt key, and we show examples of this use of urgent mode in Chapter 26. Another is FTP, when the interactive user aborts a file transfer, and we show an example of this in Chapter 27.

Telnet and Rlogin use urgent mode from the server to the client because it's possible for this direction of data flow to be stopped by the client TCP (i.e., it advertises a window of 0). But if the server process enters urgent mode, the server TCP immediately sends the urgent pointer and the URG flag, even though it can't send any data. When the client TCP receives this notification, it in turn notifies the client process, so the client can read its input from the server, to open the window, and let the data flow.

What happens if the sender enters urgent mode multiple times before the receiver processes all the data up through the first urgent pointer? The urgent pointer just advances in the data stream, and its previous position at the receiver is lost. There is only one urgent pointer at the receiver and its value is overwritten when a new value for the urgent pointer arrives from the other end. This means if the contents of the data stream that are written by the sender when it enters urgent mode are important to the receiver, these data bytes must be specially marked (somehow) by the sender. We'll see that Telnet marks all of its command bytes in the data stream by prefixing them with a byte of 255.

An Example

Let's watch how TCP sends urgent data, even when the receiver's window is closed. We'll start our sock program on the host bsdi and have it pause for 10 seconds after the connection is established (the -P option), before it reads from the network. This lets the other end fill the send window.

```
bsdi % sock -i -s -P10 5555
```

We then start the client on the host sun telling it to use a send buffer of 8192 bytes (-S option) and perform six 1024-byte writes to the network (-n option). We also specify -U5 telling it to write 1 byte of data and enter urgent mode before writing the fifth buffer to the network. We specify the verbose flag to see the order of the writes:

```
sun % sock -v -i -n6 -S8192 -U5 bsdi 5555
connected on 140.252.13.33.1305 to 140.252.13.35.5555
SO_SNDBUF = 8192
TCP_MAXSEG = 1024
wrote 1024 bytes
wrote 1024 bytes
wrote 1024 bytes
wrote 1024 bytes
wrote 1 byte of urgent data
wrote 1024 bytes
wrote 1024 bytes
```

We set the send buffer size to 8192 bytes, to let the sending application immediately write all of its data. Figure 20.14 shows the tcpdump output for this exchange. (We have removed the connection establishment.) Lines 1–5 show the sender filling the receiver's window with four 1024-byte segments. The sender is then stopped because the receiver's window is full. (The ACK on line 4 acknowledges data, but does not move the right edge of the window.)

After the fourth application write of normal data, the application writes 1 byte of data and enters urgent mode. Line 6 is the result of this application write. The urgent pointer is set to 4098. The urgent pointer is sent with the URG flag even though the sender cannot send any data.

Five of these ACKs are sent in about 13 ms (lines 6–10). The first is sent when the application writes 1 byte and enters urgent mode. The next two are sent when the application does the final two writes of 1024 bytes. (Even though TCP can't send these 2048 bytes of data, each time the application performs a write, the TCP output function is called, and when it sees that urgent mode has been entered, sends another urgent notification.) The fourth of these ACKs occurs when the application closes its end of the connection. (The TCP output function is again called.) The sending application terminates milliseconds after it starts—before the receiving application has issued its first read. TCP queues all the data and sends it when it can. (This is why we specified a send buffer size of 8192—so all the data can fit in the buffer.) The fifth of these ACKs is probably generated by the reception of the ACK on line 4. The sending TCP has probably already queued its fourth segment for output (line 5) before this ACK arrives. The receipt of this ACK from the other end also causes the TCP output routine to be called.

```
 1  0.0                  sun.1305 > bsdi.5555: P 1:1025(1024) ack 1 win 4096
 2  0.073743 (0.0737)    sun.1305 > bsdi.5555: P 1025:2049(1024) ack 1 win 4096
 3  0.096969 (0.0232)    sun.1305 > bsdi.5555: P 2049:3073(1024) ack 1 win 4096
 4  0.157514 (0.0605)    bsdi.5555 > sun.1305: . ack 3073 win 1024
 5  0.164267 (0.0068)    sun.1305 > bsdi.5555: P 3073:4097(1024) ack 1 win 4096

 6  0.167961 (0.0037)    sun.1305 > bsdi.5555: . ack 1 win 4096 urg 4098
 7  0.171969 (0.0040)    sun.1305 > bsdi.5555: . ack 1 win 4096 urg 4098
 8  0.176196 (0.0042)    sun.1305 > bsdi.5555: . ack 1 win 4096 urg 4098
 9  0.180373 (0.0042)    sun.1305 > bsdi.5555: . ack 1 win 4096 urg 4098
10  0.180768 (0.0004)    sun.1305 > bsdi.5555: . ack 1 win 4096 urg 4098

11  0.367533 (0.1868)    bsdi.5555 > sun.1305: . ack 4097 win 0
12  0.368478 (0.0009)    sun.1305 > bsdi.5555: . ack 1 win 4096 urg 4098

13  9.829712 (9.4612)    bsdi.5555 > sun.1305: . ack 4097 win 2048
14  9.831578 (0.0019)    sun.1305 > bsdi.5555: . 4097:5121(1024) ack 1 win 4096
                                                  urg 4098
15  9.833303 (0.0017)    sun.1305 > bsdi.5555: . 5121:6145(1024) ack 1 win 4096
16  9.835089 (0.0018)    bsdi.5555 > sun.1305: . ack 4097 win 4096
17  9.835913 (0.0008)    sun.1305 > bsdi.5555: FP 6145:6146(1) ack 1 win 4096
18  9.840264 (0.0044)    bsdi.5555 > sun.1305: . ack 6147 win 2048
19  9.842386 (0.0021)    bsdi.5555 > sun.1305: . ack 6147 win 4096
20  9.843622 (0.0012)    bsdi.5555 > sun.1305: F 1:1(0) ack 6147 win 4096
21  9.844320 (0.0007)    sun.1305 > bsdi.5555: . ack 2 win 4096
```

Figure 20.14 tcpdump output for TCP urgent mode.

The receiver then acknowledges the final 1024 bytes of data (line 11) but also advertises a window of 0. The sender responds with another segment containing the urgent notification.

The receiver advertises a window of 2048 bytes in line 13, when the application wakes up and reads some of the data from the receive buffer. The next two 1024-byte segments are sent (lines 14 and 15). The first segment has the urgent notification set, since the urgent pointer is within this segment. The second segment has turned the urgent notification off.

When the receiver opens the window again (line 16) the sender transmits the final byte of data (numbered 6145) and also initiates the normal connection termination.

Figure 20.15 shows the sequence numbers of the 6145 bytes of data that are sent. We see that the sequence number of the byte written when urgent mode was entered is 4097, but the value of the urgent pointer in Figure 20.14 is 4098. This confirms that this implementation (SunOS 4.1.3) sets the urgent pointer to 1 byte beyond the last byte of urgent data.

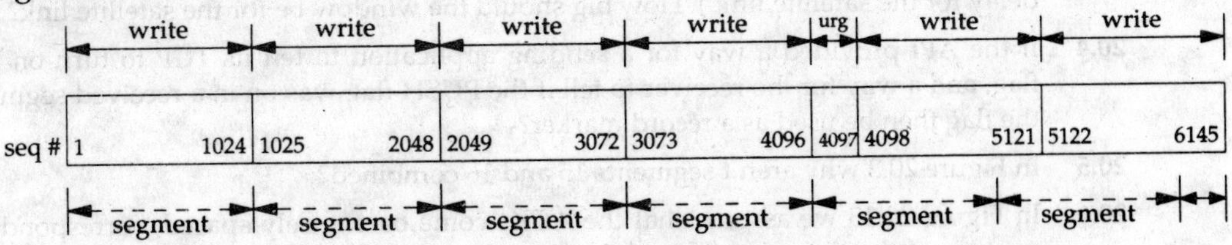

Figure 20.15 Application writes and TCP segments for urgent mode example.

This figure also lets us see how TCP repacketizes the data that the application wrote. The single byte that was output when urgent mode was entered is sent along with the next 1023 bytes of data in the buffer. The next segment also contains 1024 bytes of data, and the final segment contains 1 byte of data.

20.9 Summary

As we said early in the chapter, there is no single way to exchange bulk data using TCP. It is a dynamic process that depends on many factors, some of which we can control (e.g., send and receive buffer sizes) and some of which we have no control over (e.g., network congestion, implementation features). In this chapter we've examined many TCP transfers, explaining all the characteristics and algorithms that we could see.

Fundamental to the efficient transfer of bulk data is TCP's sliding window protocol. We then looked at what it takes for TCP to get the fastest transfer possible by keeping the pipe between the sender and receiver full. We measured the capacity of this pipe as the bandwidth-delay product, and saw the relationship between this and the window size. We return to this concept in Section 24.8 when we look at TCP performance.

We also looked at TCP's PUSH flag, since we'll always see it in trace output, but we have no control over its setting. The final topic was TCP's urgent data, which is often mistakenly called "out-of-band data." TCP's urgent mode is just a notification from the sender to the receiver that urgent data has been sent, along with the sequence number of the final byte of urgent data. The programming interface for the application to use with urgent data is often less than optimal, which leads to much confusion.

Exercises

20.1 In Figure 20.6 (p. 281) we could have shown a byte numbered 0 and a byte numbered 8193. What do these 2 bytes designate?

20.2 Look ahead to Figure 22.1 (p. 324) and explain the setting of the PUSH flag by the host `bsdi`.

20.3 In a Usenet posting someone complained about a throughput of 120,000 bits/sec on a 256,000 bits/sec link with a 128-ms delay between the United States and Japan (47% utilization), and a throughput of 33,000 bits/sec when the link was routed over a satellite (13% utilization). What does the window size appear to be for both cases? (Assume a 500-ms delay for the satellite link.) How big should the window be for the satellite link?

20.4 If the API provided a way for a sending application to tell its TCP to turn on the PUSH flag, and a way for the receiver to tell if the PUSH flag was on in a received segment, could the flag then be used as a record marker?

20.5 In Figure 20.3 why aren't segments 15 and 16 combined?

20.6 In Figure 20.13 we assume that the ACKs come back nicely spaced, corresponding to the spacing of the data segments. What happens if the ACKs are queued somewhere on the return path, causing a bunch of them to arrive at the same time at the sender?

21

TCP Timeout and Retransmission

21.1 Introduction

TCP provides a reliable transport layer. One of the ways it provides reliability is for each end to acknowledge the data it receives from the other end. But data segments and acknowledgments can get lost. TCP handles this by setting a timeout when it sends data, and if the data isn't acknowledged when the timeout expires, it retransmits the data. A critical element of any implementation is the timeout and retransmission strategy. How is the timeout interval determined, and how frequently does a retransmission occur?

We've already seen two examples of timeout and retransmission: (1) In the ICMP port unreachable example in Section 6.5 we saw the TFTP client using UDP employing a simple (and poor) timeout and retransmission strategy: it assumed 5 seconds was an adequate timeout period and retransmitted every 5 seconds. (2) In the ARP example to a nonexistent host (Section 4.5), we saw that when TCP tried to establish the connection it retransmitted its SYN using a longer delay between each retransmission.

TCP manages four different timers for each connection.

1. A *retransmission* timer is used when expecting an acknowledgment from the other end. This chapter looks at this timer in detail, along with related issues such as congestion avoidance.
2. A *persist* timer keeps window size information flowing even if the other end closes its receive window. Chapter 22 describes this timer.
3. A *keepalive* timer detects when the other end on an otherwise idle connection crashes or reboots. Chapter 23 describes this timer.
4. A *2MSL* timer measures the time a connection has been in the TIME_WAIT state. We described this state in Section 18.6.

In this chapter we start with a simple example of TCP's timeout and retransmission and then move to a larger example that lets us look at all the details involved in TCP's timer management. We look at how typical implementations measure the round-trip time of TCP segments and how TCP uses these measurements to estimate the retransmission timeout of the next segment it transmits. We then look at TCP's congestion avoidance—what TCP does when packets are lost—and follow through an actual example where packets are lost. We also look at the newer fast retransmit and fast recovery algorithms, and see how they let TCP detect lost packets faster than waiting for a timer to expire.

21.2 Simple Timeout and Retransmission Example

Let's first look at the retransmission strategy used by TCP. We'll establish a connection, send some data to verify that everything is OK, disconnect the cable, send some more data, and watch what TCP does:

```
bsdi % telnet svr4 discard
Trying 140.252.13.34...
Connected to svr4.
Escape character is '^]'.
hello, world                               send this line normally
and hi                                     disconnect cable before sending this line
Connection closed by foreign host.         output when TCP gives up after 9 minutes
```

Figure 21.1 shows the tcpdump output. (We have removed all the type-of-service information that is set by bsdi.)

```
 1    0.0                 bsdi.1029 > svr4.discard: S 1747921409:1747921409(0)
                                                      win 4096 <mss 1024>
 2    0.004811 ( 0.0048)  svr4.discard > bsdi.1029: S 3416685569:3416685569(0)
                                                      ack 1747921410
                                                      win 4096 <mss 1024>
 3    0.006441 ( 0.0016)  bsdi.1029 > svr4.discard: . ack 1 win 4096

 4    6.102290 ( 6.0958)  bsdi.1029 > svr4.discard: P 1:15(14) ack 1 win 4096
 5    6.259410 ( 0.1571)  svr4.discard > bsdi.1029: . ack 15 win 4096

 6   24.480158 (18.2207)  bsdi.1029 > svr4.discard: P 15:23(8) ack 1 win 4096
 7   25.493733 ( 1.0136)  bsdi.1029 > svr4.discard: P 15:23(8) ack 1 win 4096
 8   28.493795 ( 3.0001)  bsdi.1029 > svr4.discard: P 15:23(8) ack 1 win 4096
 9   34.493971 ( 6.0002)  bsdi.1029 > svr4.discard: P 15:23(8) ack 1 win 4096
10   46.484427 (11.9905)  bsdi.1029 > svr4.discard: P 15:23(8) ack 1 win 4096
11   70.485105 (24.0007)  bsdi.1029 > svr4.discard: P 15:23(8) ack 1 win 4096
12  118.486408 (48.0013)  bsdi.1029 > svr4.discard: P 15:23(8) ack 1 win 4096
13  182.488164 (64.0018)  bsdi.1029 > svr4.discard: P 15:23(8) ack 1 win 4096
14  246.489921 (64.0018)  bsdi.1029 > svr4.discard: P 15:23(8) ack 1 win 4096
15  310.491678 (64.0018)  bsdi.1029 > svr4.discard: P 15:23(8) ack 1 win 4096
16  374.493431 (64.0018)  bsdi.1029 > svr4.discard: P 15:23(8) ack 1 win 4096
17  438.495196 (64.0018)  bsdi.1029 > svr4.discard: P 15:23(8) ack 1 win 4096
18  502.486941 (63.9917)  bsdi.1029 > svr4.discard: P 15:23(8) ack 1 win 4096
19  566.488478 (64.0015)  bsdi.1029 > svr4.discard: R 23:23(0) ack 1 win 4096
```

Figure 21.1 Simple example of TCP's timeout and retransmission.

Lines 1, 2, and 3 correspond to the normal TCP connection establishment. Line 4 is the transmission of "hello, world" (12 characters plus the carriage return and linefeed), and line 5 is its acknowledgment. We then disconnect the Ethernet cable from `svr4`.

Line 6 shows "and hi" being sent. Lines 7–18 are 12 retransmissions of that segment, and line 19 is when the sending TCP finally gives up and sends a reset.

Examine the time difference between successive retransmissions: with rounding they occur 1, 3, 6, 12, 24, 48, and then 64 seconds apart. We'll see later in this chapter that the first timeout is actually set for 1.5 seconds after the first transmission. (The reason it occurs 1.0136 seconds after the first transmission, and not exactly 1.5 seconds, was explained in Figure 18.7.) After this the timeout value is doubled for each retransmission, with an upper limit of 64 seconds.

This doubling is called an *exponential backoff*. Compare this to the TFTP example in Section 6.5, where every retransmission occurred 5 seconds after the previous.

The time difference between the first transmission of the packet (line 6 at time 24.480) and the reset (line 19 at time 566.488) is about 9 minutes. Modern TCP's are persistent when trying to send data!

> On most implementations this total timeout value is not tunable. Solaris 2.2 allows the administrator to change this (the `tcp_ip_abort_interval` variable in Section E.4) and its default is only 2 minutes, not the more common 9 minutes.

21.3 Round-Trip Time Measurement

Fundamental to TCP's timeout and retransmission is the measurement of the round-trip time (RTT) experienced on a given connection. We expect this can change over time, as routes might change and as network traffic changes, and TCP should track these changes and modify its timeout accordingly.

First TCP must measure the RTT between sending a byte with a particular sequence number and receiving an acknowledgment that covers that sequence number. Recall from the previous chapter that normally there is not a one-to-one correspondence between data segments and ACKs. In Figure 20.1 (p. 276) this means that one RTT that can be measured by the sender is the time between the transmission of segment 4 (data bytes 1–1024) and the reception of segment 7 (the ACK of bytes 1–2048), even though this ACK is for an additional 1024 bytes. We'll use M to denote the measured RTT.

The original TCP specification had TCP update a smoothed RTT estimator (called R) using the low-pass filter

$$R \leftarrow \alpha R + (1 - \alpha)M$$

where α is a smoothing factor with a recommended value of 0.9. This smoothed RTT is updated every time a new measurement is made. Ninety percent of each new estimate is from the previous estimate and 10% is from the new measurement.

Given this smoothed estimator, which changes as the RTT changes, RFC 793 recommended the retransmission timeout value (RTO) be set to

$$RTO = R\beta$$

where β is a delay variance factor with a recommended value of 2.

[Jacobson 1988] details the problems with this approach, basically that it can't keep up with wide fluctuations in the RTT, causing unnecessary retransmissions. As Jacobson notes, unnecessary retransmissions add to the network load, when the network is already loaded. It is the network equivalent of pouring gasoline on a fire.

What's needed is to keep track of the variance in the RTT measurements, in addition to the smoothed RTT estimator. Calculating the *RTO* based on both the mean and variance provides much better response to wide fluctuations in the round-trip times, than just calculating the *RTO* as a constant multiple of the mean. Figures 5 and 6 in [Jacobson 1988] show a comparison of the RFC 793 *RTO* values for some actual round-trip times, versus the *RTO* calculations we show below, which take into account the variance of the round-trip times.

As described by Jacobson, the mean deviation is a good approximation to the standard deviation, but easier to compute. (Calculating the standard deviation requires a square root.) This leads to the following equations that are applied to each RTT measurement M.

$$Err = M - A$$

$$A \leftarrow A + gErr$$

$$D \leftarrow D + h(|Err| - D)$$

$$RTO = A + 4D$$

where A is the smoothed RTT (an estimator of the average) and D is the smoothed mean deviation. Err is the difference between the measured value just obtained and the current RTT estimator. Both A and D are used to calculate the next retransmission timeout (*RTO*). The gain g is for the average and is set to 1/8 (0.125). The gain for the deviation is h and is set to 0.25. The larger gain for the deviation makes the *RTO* go up faster when the RTT changes.

[Jacobson 1988] specified $2D$ in the calculation of *RTO*, but after further research, [Jacobson 1990c] changed the value to $4D$, which is what appeared in the BSD Net/1 implementation.

Jacobson specifies a way to do all these calculations using integer arithmetic, and this is the implementation typically used. (That's one reason g, h, and the multiplier 4 are all powers of 2, so the operations can be done using shifts instead of multiplies and divides.)

Comparing the original method with Jacobson's, we see that the calculations of the smoothed average are similar (α is one minus the gain g) but a different gain is used. Also, Jacobson's calculation of the *RTO* depends on both the smoothed RTT and the smoothed mean deviation, whereas the original method used a multiple of the smoothed RTT.

We'll see how these estimators are initialized in the next section, when we go through an example.

Karn's Algorithm

A problem occurs when a packet is retransmitted. Say a packet is transmitted, a timeout occurs, the *RTO* is backed off as shown in Section 21.2, the packet is retransmitted with the longer *RTO*, and an acknowledgment is received. Is the ACK for the first transmission or the second? This is called the *retransmission ambiguity problem.*

[Karn and Partridge 1987] specify that when a timeout and retransmission occur, we cannot update the RTT estimators when the acknowledgment for the retransmitted data finally arrives. This is because we don't know to which transmission the ACK corresponds. (Perhaps the first transmission was delayed and not thrown away, or perhaps the ACK of the first transmission was delayed.)

Also, since the data was retransmitted, and the exponential backoff has been applied to the *RTO*, we reuse this backed off *RTO* for the next transmission. Don't calculate a new *RTO* until an acknowledgment is received for a segment that was not retransmitted.

21.4 An RTT Example

We'll use the following example throughout this chapter to examine various implementation details of TCP's timeout and retransmission, slow start, and congestion avoidance.

Using our `sock` program, 32768 bytes of data are sent from our host `slip` to the discard service on the host `vangogh.cs.berkeley.edu` using the command:

```
slip % sock -D -i -n32 vangogh.cs.berkeley.edu discard
```

From the figure on the inside front cover, `slip` is connected to the 140.252.1 Ethernet by two SLIP links, and from there across the Internet to the destination. With two 9600 bits/sec SLIP links, we expect some measurable delays.

This command performs 32 1024-byte writes, and since the MTU between `slip` and `bsdi` is 296, this becomes 128 segments, each with 256 bytes of user data. The total time for the transfer is about 45 seconds and we see one timeout and three retransmissions.

While this transfer was running we ran `tcpdump` on the host `slip` and captured all the segments sent and received. Additionally we specified the `-D` option to turn on socket debugging (Section A.6). We were then able to run a modified version of the `trpt`(8) program to print numerous variables in the connection control block relating to the round-trip timing, slow start, and congestion avoidance.

Given the volume of trace output, we can't show it all. Instead we'll look at pieces as we proceed through the chapter. Figure 21.2 shows the transfer of data and acknowledgments for the first 5 seconds. We have modified this output slightly from our previous display of `tcpdump` output. Although we only measure the times that the packet is sent or received on the host running `tcpdump`, in this figure we want to show that the packets are crossing in the network (which they are, since this WAN connection is not like a shared Ethernet), and show when the receiving host is probably generating the ACKs. (We have also removed all the window advertisements from this figure. `slip` always advertised a window of 4096, and `vangogh` always advertised a window of 8192.)

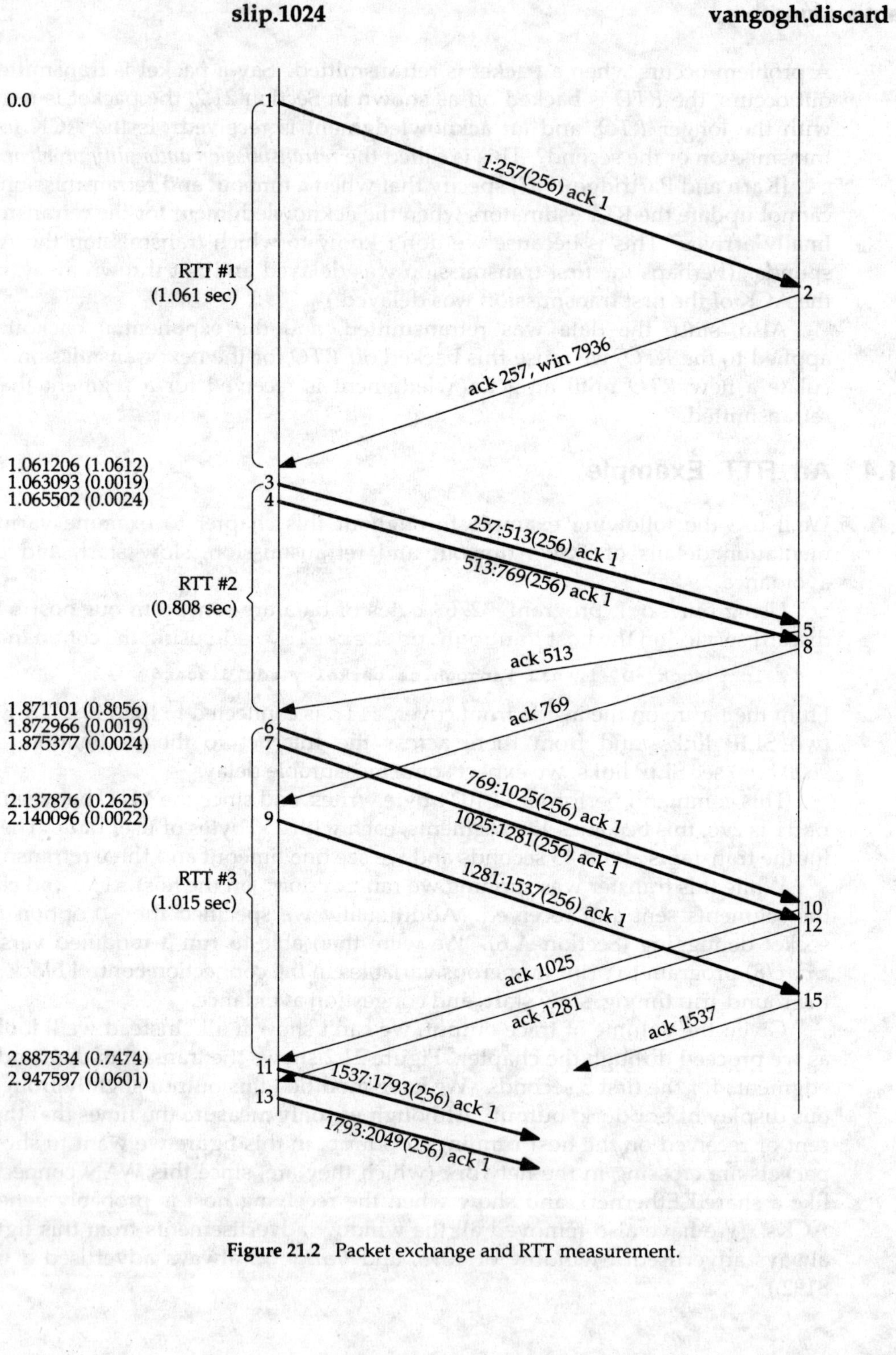

Figure 21.2 Packet exchange and RTT measurement.

Also note in this figure that we have numbered the segments 1–13 and 15, in the order in which they were sent or received on the host `slip`. This correlates with the `tcpdump` output that was collected on this host.

Round-Trip Time Measurements

Three curly braces have been placed on the left side of the time line indicating which segments were timed for RTT calculations. Not all data segments are timed.

Most Berkeley-derived implementations of TCP measure only one RTT value per connection at any time. If the timer for a given connection is already in use when a data segment is transmitted, that segment is not timed.

The timing is done by incrementing a counter every time the 500-ms TCP timer routine is invoked. This means that a segment whose acknowledgment arrives 550 ms after the segment was sent could end up with either a 1 tick RTT (implying 500 ms) or a 2 tick RTT (implying 1000 ms).

In addition to this tick counter for each connection, the starting sequence number of the data in the segment is also remembered. When an acknowledgment that includes this sequence number is received, the timer is turned off. If the data was not retransmitted when the ACK arrives, the smoothed RTT and smoothed mean deviation are updated based on this new measurement.

The timer for the connection in Figure 21.2 is started when segment 1 is transmitted, and turned off when its acknowledgment (segment 2) arrives. Although its RTT is 1.061 seconds (from the `tcpdump` output), examining the socket debug information shows that three of TCP's clock ticks occurred during this period, implying an RTT of 1500 ms.

The next segment timed is number 3. When segment 4 is transmitted 2.4 ms later, it cannot be timed, since the timer for this connection is already in use. When segment 5 arrives, acknowledging the data that was being timed, its RTT is calculated to be 1 tick (500 ms), even though we see that its RTT is 0.808 seconds from the `tcpdump` output.

The timer is started again when segment 6 is transmitted, and turned off when its acknowledgment (segment 10) is received 1.015 seconds later. The measured RTT is 2 clock ticks. Segments 7 and 9 cannot be timed, since the timer is already being used. Also, when segment 8 is received (the ACK of 769), nothing is updated since the acknowledgment was not for bytes being timed.

Figure 21.3 shows the relationship in this example between the actual RTTs that we can determine from the `tcpdump` output, and the counted clock ticks.

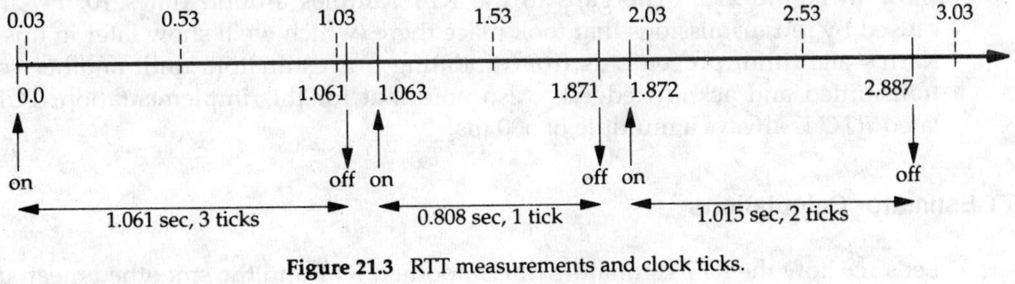

Figure 21.3 RTT measurements and clock ticks.

On the top we show the clock ticks, every 500 ms. On the bottom we show the times output by `tcpdump`, and when the timer for the connection is turned on and off. We know that 3 ticks occur between sending segment 1 and receiving segment 2, 1.061 seconds later, so we assume the first tick occurs at time 0.03. (The first tick must be between 0.00 and 0.061.) The figure then shows how the second measured RTT was counted as 1 tick, and the third as 2 ticks.

In this complete example, 128 segments were transmitted, and 18 RTT samples were collected. Figure 21.4 shows the measured RTT (taken from the `tcpdump` output) along with the *RTO* used by TCP for the timeout (taken from the socket debug output). The x-axis starts at time 0 in Figure 21.2, when the first data segment is transmitted; not when the first SYN is transmitted.

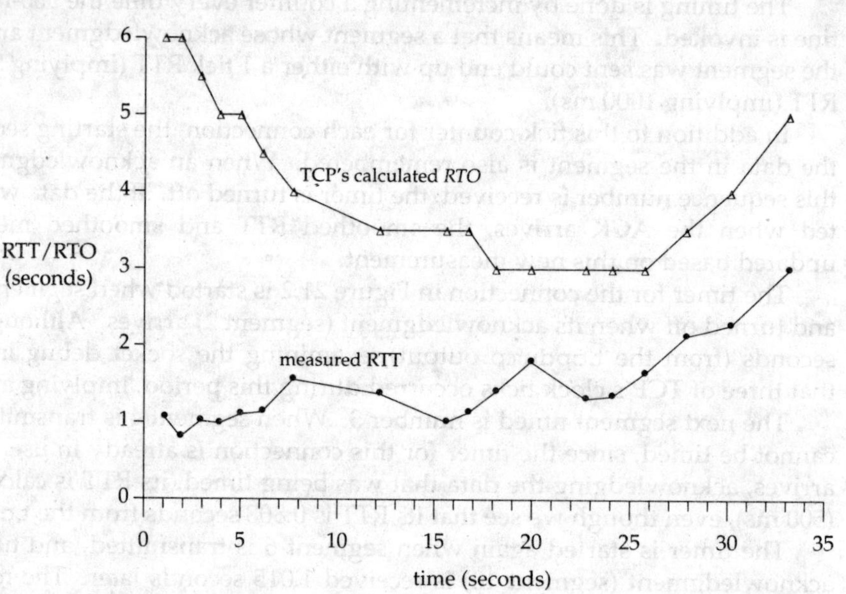

Figure 21.4 Measured RTT and TCP's calculated *RTO* for example.

The first three data points for the measured RTT correspond to the 3 RTTs that we show in Figure 21.2. The gaps in the RTT samples around times 10, 14, and 21 are caused by retransmissions that took place there (which we'll show later in this chapter). Karn's algorithm prevents us from updating our estimators until another segment is transmitted and acknowledged. Also note that for this implementation, TCP's calculated *RTO* is always a multiple of 500 ms.

RTT Estimator Calculations

Let's see how the RTT estimators (the smoothed RTT and the smoothed mean deviation) are initialized and updated, and how each retransmission timeout is calculated.

The variables A and D are initialized to 0 and 3 seconds, respectively. The initial retransmission timeout is calculated using the formula

$$RTO = A + 2D = 0 + 2 \times 3 = 6 \text{ seconds}$$

(The factor $2D$ is used only for this initial calculation. After this $4D$ is added to A to calculate RTO, as shown earlier.) This is the RTO for the transmission of the initial SYN.

It turns out that this initial SYN is lost, and we time out and retransmit. Figure 21.5 shows the first four lines from the tcpdump output file.

```
1  0.0                     slip.1024 > vangogh.discard: S 35648001:35648001(0)
                                                        win 4096 <mss 256>

2  5.802377  (5.8024)      slip.1024 > vangogh.discard: S 35648001:35648001(0)
                                                        win 4096 <mss 256>

3  6.269395  (0.4670)      vangogh.discard > slip.1024: S 1365512705:1365512705(0)
                                                        ack 35648002
                                                        win 8192 <mss 512>

4  6.270796  (0.0014)      slip.1024 > vangogh.discard: . ack 1 win 4096
```

Figure 21.5 Timeout and retransmission of initial SYN.

When the timeout occurs after 5.802 seconds, the current RTO is calculated as

$$RTO = A + 4D = 0 + 4 \times 3 = 12 \text{ seconds}$$

The exponential backoff is then applied to the RTO of 12. Since this is the first timeout we use a multiplier of 2, giving the next timeout value as 24 seconds. The next timeout is calculated using a multiplier of 4, giving a value of 48 seconds: 12×4. (These initial RTOs for the first SYN on a connection, 6 seconds and then 24 seconds, are what we saw in Figure 4.5.)

The ACK arrives 467 ms after the retransmission. The values of A and D are not updated, because of Karn's algorithm dealing with the retransmission ambiguity. The next segment sent is the ACK on line 4, but it is not timed since it is only an ACK. (Only segments containing data are timed.)

When the first data segment is sent (segment 1 in Figure 21.2) the RTO is not changed, again owing to Karn's algorithm. The current value of 24 seconds is reused until an RTT measurement is made. This means the RTO for time 0 in Figure 21.4 is really 24, but we didn't plot that point.

When the ACK for the first data segment arrives (segment 2 in Figure 21.2), three clock ticks were counted and our estimators are initialized as

$$A = M + 0.5 = 1.5 + 0.5 = 2$$

$$D = A/2 = 1$$

(The value 1.5 for M is for 3 clock ticks.) The previous initialization of A and D to 0 and 3 was for the initial RTO calculation. This initialization is for the first calculation of the estimators using the first RTT measurement M. The RTO is calculated as

$$RTO = A + 4D = 2 + 4 \times 1 = 6 \text{ seconds}$$

When the ACK for the second data segment arrives (segment 5 in Figure 21.2), 1 clock tick is counted (0.5 seconds) and our estimators are updated as

$$Err = M - A = 0.5 - 2 = -1.5$$

$$A = A + gErr = 2 - 0.125 \times 1.5 = 1.8125$$

$$D = D + h(|Err| - D) = 1 + 0.25 \times (1.5 - 1) = 1.125$$

$$RTO = A + 4D = 1.8125 + 4 \times 1.125 = 6.3125$$

There are some subtleties in the fixed-point representations of *Err*, *A*, and *D*, and the fixed-point calculations that are actually used (which we've shown in floating-point for simplicity). These differences yield an *RTO* of 6 seconds (not 6.3125), which is what we plot in Figure 21.4 for time 1.871.

Slow Start

We described the slow start algorithm in Section 20.6. We can see it in action again in Figure 21.2 (p. 302).

Only one segment is initially transmitted on the connection, and its acknowledgment must be received before another segment is transmitted. When segment 2 is received, two more segments are transmitted.

21.5 Congestion Example

Now let's look at the transmission of the data segments. Figure 21.6 is a plot of the starting sequence number in a segment versus the time that the segment was sent. This provides a nice way to visualize the data transmission. Normally the data points should move up and to the right, with the slope of the points being the transfer rate. Retransmissions will appear as motion down and to the right.

At the beginning of Section 21.4 we said the total time for the transfer was about 45 seconds, but we show only 35 seconds in this figure. These 35 seconds account for sending the data segments only. The first data segment was not transmitted until 6.3 seconds after the first SYN was sent, because the first SYN appears to have been lost and was retransmitted (Figure 21.5). Also, after the final data segment and the FIN were sent (at time 34.1 in Figure 21.6) it took another 4.0 seconds to receive the final 14 ACKs from the receiver, before the receiver's FIN was received.

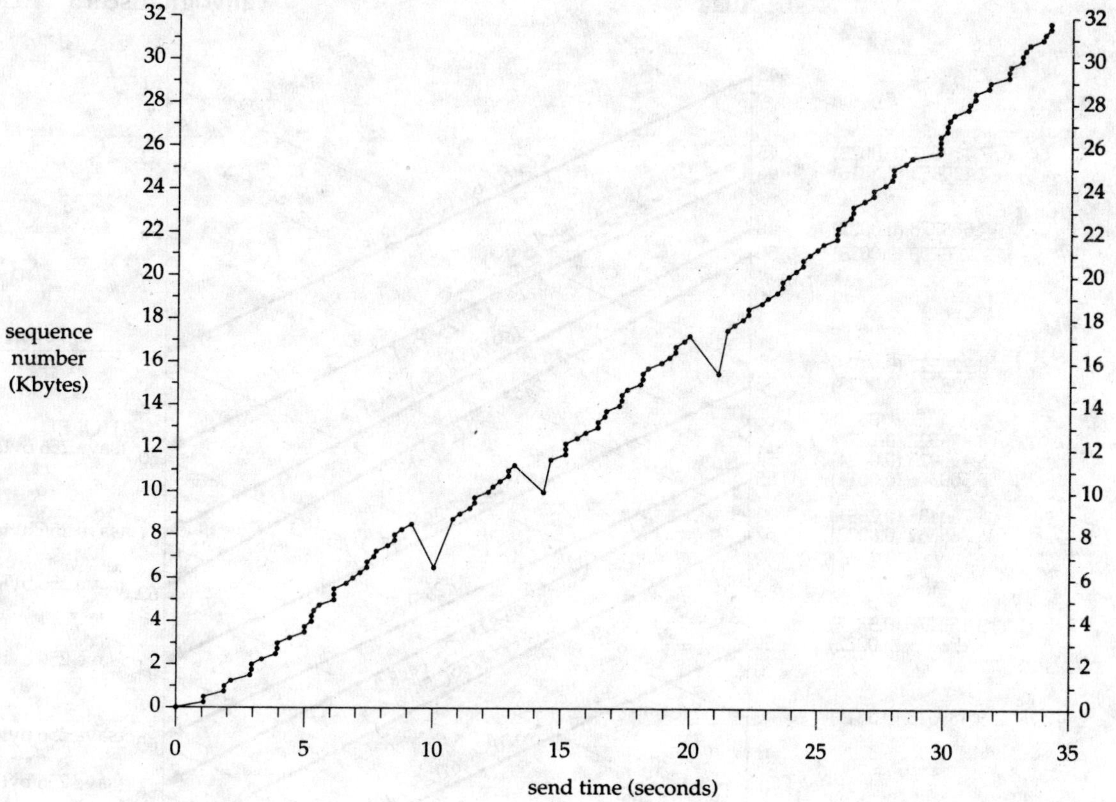

Figure 21.6 Sending of 32768 bytes of data from `slip` to `vangogh`.

We can immediately see the three retransmissions around times 10, 14, and 21 in Figure 21.6. At each of these three points we can also see that only one segment is retransmitted, because only one dot dips below the upward slope.

Let's examine the first of these dips in detail (around the 10-second mark). From the `tcpdump` output we can put together Figure 21.7.

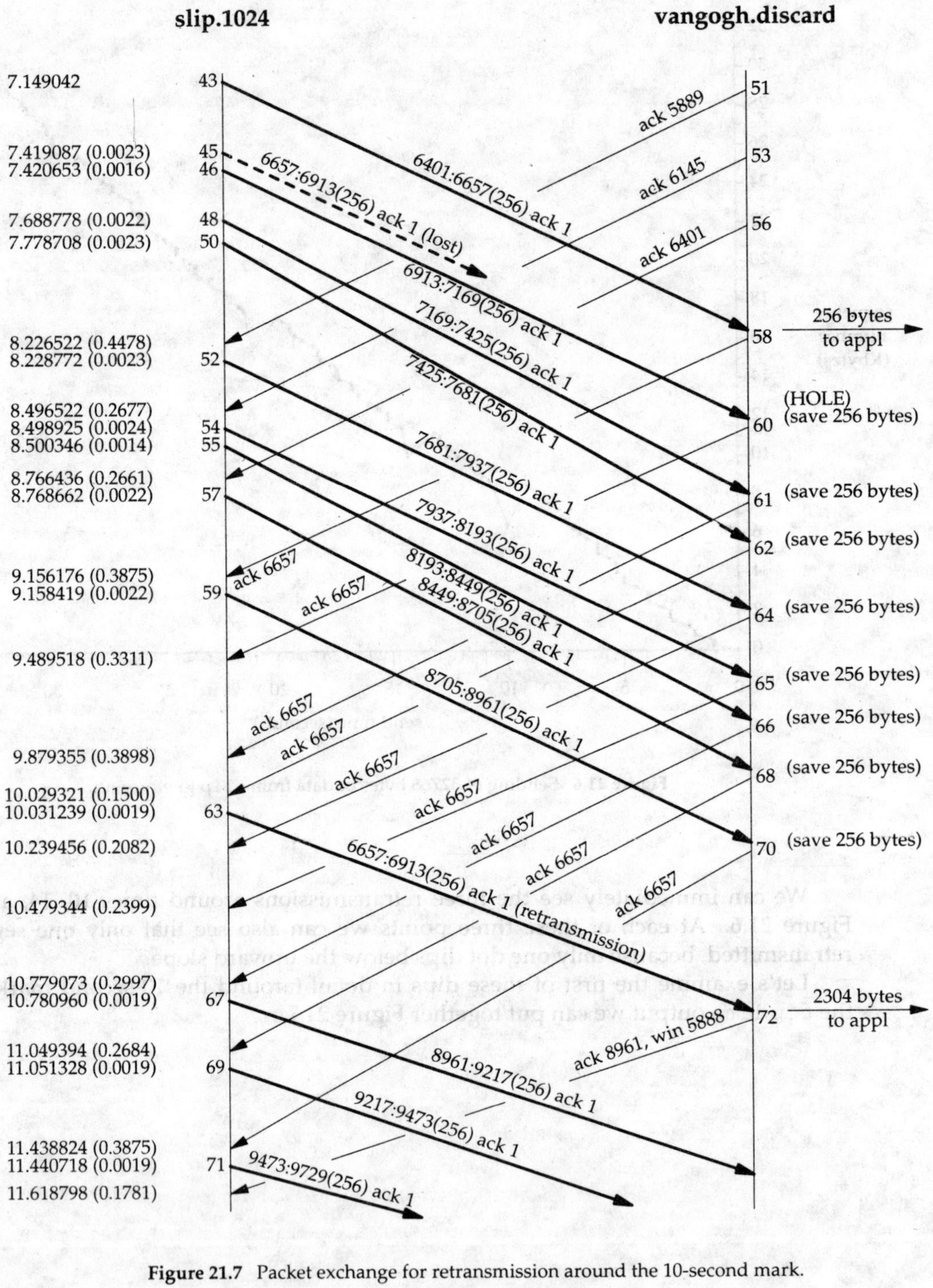

Figure 21.7 Packet exchange for retransmission around the 10-second mark.

We have removed all the window advertisements from this figure, except for segment 72, which we discuss below. `slip` always advertised a window of 4096, and `vangogh` advertised a window of 8192. The segments are numbered in this figure as a continuation of Figure 21.2, where the first data segment across the connection was numbered 1. As in Figure 21.2, the segments are numbered according to their send or receive order on the host `slip`, where `tcpdump` was being run. We have also removed a few segments that have no relevance to the discussion (44, 47, and 49, all ACKs from `vangogh`).

It appears that segment 45 got lost or arrived damaged—we can't tell from this output. What we see on the host `slip` is the acknowledgment for everything up through but not including byte 6657 (segment 58), followed by eight more ACKs of this same sequence number. It is the reception of segment 62, the third of the duplicate ACKs, that forces the retransmission of the data starting at sequence number 6657 (segment 63). Indeed, Berkeley-derived implementations count the number of duplicate ACKs received, and when the third one is received, assume that a segment has been lost and retransmit only one segment, starting with that sequence number. This is Jacobson's *fast retransmit* algorithm, which is followed by his *fast recovery* algorithm. We discuss both algorithms in Section 21.7.

Notice that after the retransmission (segment 63), the sender continues normal data transmission (segments 67, 69, and 71). TCP does not wait for the other end to acknowledge the retransmission.

Let's examine what happens at the receiver. When normal data is received in sequence (segment 43), the receiving TCP passes the 256 bytes of data to the user process. But the next segment received (segment 46) is out of order: the starting sequence number of the data (6913) is not the next expected sequence number (6657). TCP saves the 256 bytes of data and responds with an ACK of the highest sequence number successfully received, plus one (6657). The next seven segments received by `vangogh` (48, 50, 52, 54, 55, 57, and 59) are also out of order. The data is saved by the receiving TCP, and duplicate ACKs are generated.

Currently there is no way for TCP to tell the other end that a segment is missing. Also, TCP cannot acknowledge out-of-order data. All `vangogh` can do at this point is continue sending the ACKs of 6657.

When the missing data arrives (segment 63), the receiving TCP now has data bytes 6657–8960 in its buffer, and passes these 2304 bytes to the user process. All 2304 bytes are acknowledged in segment 72. Also notice that this ACK advertises a window of 5888 (8192 – 2304), since the user process hasn't had a chance to read the 2304 bytes that are ready for it.

If we look in detail at the `tcpdump` output for the dips around times 14 and 21 in Figure 21.6, we see that they too were caused by the receipt of three duplicate ACKs, indicating that a packet had been lost. In each of these cases only a single packet was retransmitted.

We'll continue this example in Section 21.8, after describing more about the congestion avoidance algorithms.

21.6 Congestion Avoidance Algorithm

Slow start, which we described in Section 20.6, is the way to initiate data flow across a connection. But at some point we'll reach the limit of an intervening router, and packets can be dropped. Congestion avoidance is a way to deal with lost packets. It is described in [Jacobson 1988].

The assumption of the algorithm is that packet loss caused by damage is very small (much less than 1%), therefore the loss of a packet signals congestion somewhere in the network between the source and destination. There are two indications of packet loss: a timeout occurring and the receipt of duplicate ACKs. (We saw the latter in Section 21.5. If we are using a timeout as an indication of congestion, we can see the need for a good RTT algorithm, such as that described in Section 21.3.)

Congestion avoidance and slow start are independent algorithms with different objectives. But when congestion occurs we want to slow down the transmission rate of packets into the network, and then invoke slow start to get things going again. In practice they are implemented together.

Congestion avoidance and slow start require that two variables be maintained for each connection: a congestion window, *cwnd*, and a slow start threshold size, *ssthresh*. The combined algorithm operates as follows:

1. Initialization for a given connection sets *cwnd* to one segment and *ssthresh* to 65535 bytes.
2. The TCP output routine never sends more than the minimum of *cwnd* and the receiver's advertised window.

   Congestion avoidance is flow control imposed by the sender, while the advertised window is flow control imposed by the receiver. The former is based on the sender's assessment of perceived network congestion; the latter is related to the amount of available buffer space at the receiver for this connection.
3. When congestion occurs (indicated by a timeout or the reception of duplicate ACKs), one-half of the current window size (the minimum of *cwnd* and the receiver's advertised window, but at least two segments) is saved in *ssthresh*. Additionally, if the congestion is indicated by a timeout, *cwnd* is set to one segment (i.e., slow start).
4. When new data is acknowledged by the other end, we increase *cwnd*, but the way it increases depends on whether we're performing slow start or congestion avoidance.

   If *cwnd* is less than or equal to *ssthresh*, we're doing slow start; otherwise we're doing congestion avoidance. Slow start continues until we're halfway to where we were when congestion occurred (since we recorded half of the window size that got us into trouble in step 2), and then congestion avoidance takes over.

   Slow start has *cwnd* start at one segment, and be incremented by one segment every time an ACK is received. As mentioned in Section 20.6, this opens the window exponentially: send one segment, then two, then four, and so on.

Congestion avoidance dictates that *cwnd* be incremented by 1/*cwnd* each time an ACK is received. This is an additive increase, compared to slow start's exponential increase. We want to increase *cwnd* by at most one segment each round-trip time (regardless how many ACKs are received in that RTT), whereas slow start will increment *cwnd* by the number of ACKs received in a round-trip time.

All 4.3BSD releases and 4.4BSD incorrectly add a small fraction of the segment size (the segment size divided by 8) during congestion avoidance. This is wrong and should not be emulated in future releases [Floyd 1994]. Nevertheless, we show this term in future calculations, to arrive at the same answer as the (incorrect) implementation.

The 4.3BSD Tahoe release, described in [Leffler et al. 1989], performed slow start only if the other end was on a different network. This was changed with the 4.3BSD Reno release so that slow start is always performed.

Figure 21.8 is a visual description of slow start and congestion avoidance. We show *cwnd* and *ssthresh* in units of segments, but they're really maintained in bytes.

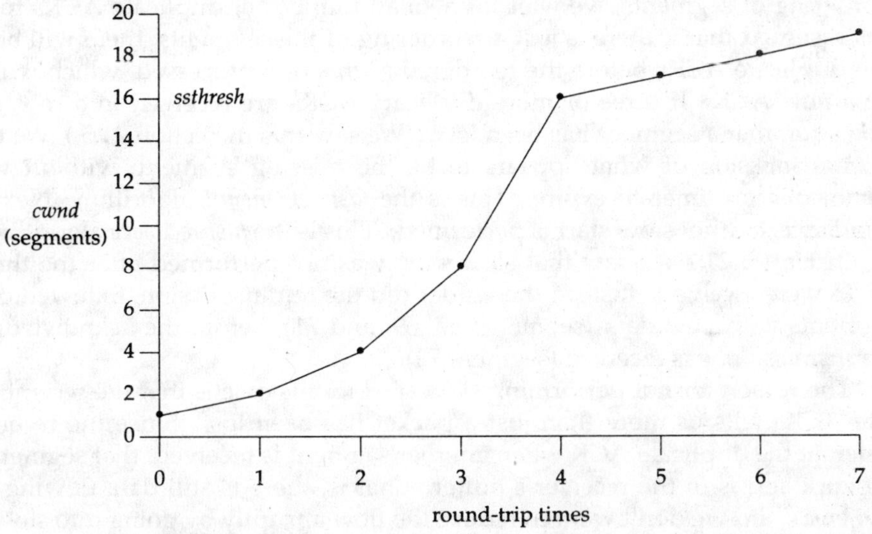

Figure 21.8 Visualization of slow start and congestion avoidance.

In this figure we assume that congestion occurred when *cwnd* had a value of 32 segments. *ssthresh* is then set to 16 segments and *cwnd* is set to 1 segment. One segment is then sent at time 0 and assuming its ACK is returned at time 1, *cwnd* is incremented to 2 segments. Two segments are then sent and assuming their ACKs return by time 2, *cwnd* is incremented to 4 segments (once for each ACK). This exponential increase continues until *cwnd* equals *ssthresh*, after 8 ACKs are received between times 3 and 4. From this point on the increase in *cwnd* is linear, with a maximum increase of one segment per round-trip time.

As we can see in this figure, the term "slow start" is not completely correct. It is a slower transmission of packets than what caused the congestion, but the rate of increase in the number of packets injected into the network increases during slow start. The rate of increase doesn't slow down until *ssthresh* is reached, when congestion avoidance takes over.

21.7 Fast Retransmit and Fast Recovery Algorithms

Modifications to the congestion avoidance algorithm were proposed in 1990 [Jacobson 1990b]. We've already seen these modifications in action in our congestion example (Section 21.5).

Before describing the change, realize that TCP is required to generate an immediate acknowledgment (a duplicate ACK) when an out-of-order segment is received. This duplicate ACK should not be delayed. The purpose of this duplicate ACK is to let the other end know that a segment was received out of order, and to tell it what sequence number is expected.

Since we don't know whether a duplicate ACK is caused by a lost segment or just a reordering of segments, we wait for a small number of duplicate ACKs to be received. It is assumed that if there is just a reordering of the segments, there will be only one or two duplicate ACKs before the reordered segment is processed, which will then generate a new ACK. If three or more duplicate ACKs are received in a row, it is a strong indication that a segment has been lost. (We saw this in Section 21.5.) We then perform a retransmission of what appears to be the missing segment, without waiting for a retransmission timer to expire. This is the *fast retransmit* algorithm. Next, congestion avoidance, but not slow start is performed. This is the *fast recovery* algorithm.

In Figure 21.7 we saw that slow start was not performed after the three duplicate ACKs were received. Instead the sender did the retransmission, followed by three more segments with new data (segments 67, 69, and 71), before the acknowledgment of the retransmission was received (segment 72).

The reason for not performing slow start in this case is that the receipt of the duplicate ACKs tells us more than just a packet has been lost. Since the receiver can only generate the duplicate ACK when another segment is received, that segment has left the network and is in the receiver's buffer. That is, there is still data flowing between the two ends, and we don't want to reduce the flow abruptly by going into slow start.

This algorithms are usually implemented together as follows.

1. When the third duplicate ACK is received, set *ssthresh* to one-half of the minimum of the current congestion window (*cwnd*) and the receiver's advertised window.

   Retransmit the missing segment.

   Set *cwnd* to *ssthresh* plus 3 times the segment size.

2. Each time another duplicate ACK arrives, increment *cwnd* by the segment size and transmit a packet (if allowed by the new value of *cwnd*).

3. When the next ACK arrives that acknowledges new data, set *cwnd* to *ssthresh* (the value set in step 1). This should be the ACK of the retransmission from step 1, one round-trip time after the retransmission. Additionally, this ACK should

acknowledge all the intermediate segments sent between the lost packet and the receipt of the third duplicate ACK. This step is congestion avoidance, since we're slowing down to one-half the rate we were at when the packet was lost.

We'll see what happens to the two variables *cwnd* and *ssthresh* in the calculations in the next section.

The fast retransmit algorithm first appeared in the 4.3BSD Tahoe release, but it was incorrectly followed by slow start. The fast recovery algorithm appeared in the 4.3BSD Reno release.

21.8 Congestion Example (Continued)

Watching a connection using `tcpdump` and the socket debug option (which we described in Section 21.4) we can see the values of *cwnd* and *ssthresh* as each segment is transmitted. If the MSS is 256 bytes, the initial values of *cwnd* and *ssthresh* are 256 and 65535, respectively. Each time an ACK is received we can see *cwnd* incremented by the MSS, taking on the values 512, 768, 1024, 1280, and so on. Assuming congestion doesn't occur, eventually the congestion window will exceed the receiver's advertised window, meaning the advertised window will limit the data flow.

A more interesting example is to see what happens when congestion occurs. We'll use the same example from Section 21.4. There were four occurrences of congestion while this example was being run. There was a timeout on the transmission of the initial SYN to establish the connection (Figure 21.5), followed by three lost packets during the data transfer (Figure 21.6).

Figure 21.9 shows the values of the two variables *cwnd* and *ssthresh* when the initial SYN is retransmitted, followed by the first seven data segments. (We showed the exchange of the initial data segments and their ACKs in Figure 21.2.) We show the data bytes transmitted using the `tcpdump` notation: 1:257(256) means bytes 1 through 256.

When the timeout of the SYN occurs, *ssthresh* is set to its minimum value (512 bytes, which is two segments for this example). *cwnd* is set to one segment (256 bytes, which it was already at) to enter the slow start phase.

When the SYN and ACK are received, nothing happens to the two variables, since new data is not being acknowledged.

When the ACK 257 arrives, we are still in slow start since *cwnd* is less than or equal to *ssthresh*, so *cwnd* in incremented by 256. The same thing happens when the ACK 513 arrives.

When the ACK 769 arrives we are no longer in slow start, but enter congestion avoidance. The new value for *cwnd* is calculated as

$$cwnd \leftarrow cwnd + \frac{segsize \times segsize}{cwnd} + \frac{segsize}{8}$$

This is the $1/cwnd$ increase that we mentioned earlier, taking into account that *cwnd* is really maintained in bytes and not segments. For this example we calculate

$$cwnd \leftarrow 768 + \frac{256 \times 256}{768} + \frac{256}{8}$$

Segment# (Figure 21.2)	Action			Variable	
	Send	Receive	Comment	*cwnd*	*ssthresh*
			initialize	256	65535
	SYN				
			timeout	256	512
	SYN		retransmit		
		SYN, ACK			
	ACK				
1	1:257(256)				
2		ACK 257	slow start	512	512
3	257:513(256)				
4	513:769(256)				
5		ACK 513	slow start	768	512
6	769:1025(256)				
7	1025:1281(256)				
8		ACK 769	cong. avoid	885	512
9	1281:1537(256)				
10		ACK 1025	cong. avoid	991	512
11	1537:1793(256)				
12		ACK 1281	cong. avoid	1089	512

Figure 21.9 Example of congestion avoidance.

which equals 885 (using integer arithmetic). When the next ACK 1025 arrives we calculate

$$cwnd \leftarrow 885 + \frac{256 \times 256}{885} + \frac{256}{8}$$

which equals 991. (In these expressions we include the incorrect 256/8 term to match the values calculated by the implementation, as we noted on p. 311.)

This additive increase in *cwnd* continues until the first retransmission, around the 10-second mark in Figure 21.6. Figure 21.10 is a plot of the same data as in Figure 21.6, with the value of *cwnd* added.

The first six values for *cwnd* in this figure are the values we calculated for Figure 21.9. It is impossible in this figure to tell the difference visually between the exponential increase during slow start and the additive increase during congestion avoidance, because the slow start phase is so quick.

We need to explain what is happening at the three points where a retransmission occurs. Recall that each of the retransmissions took place because three duplicate ACKs were received, indicating a packet had been lost. This is the fast retransmit algorithm from Section 21.7. *ssthresh* is immediately set to one-half the window size that was in effect when the retransmission took place, but *cwnd* is allowed to keep increasing while the duplicate ACKs are received, since each duplicate ACK means that a segment has left the network (the receiving TCP has buffered it, waiting for the missing hole in the data to arrive). This is the fast recovery algorithm.

Figure 21.11 is similar to Figure 21.9, showing the values of *cwnd* and *ssthresh*. The segment numbers in the first column correspond to Figure 21.7.

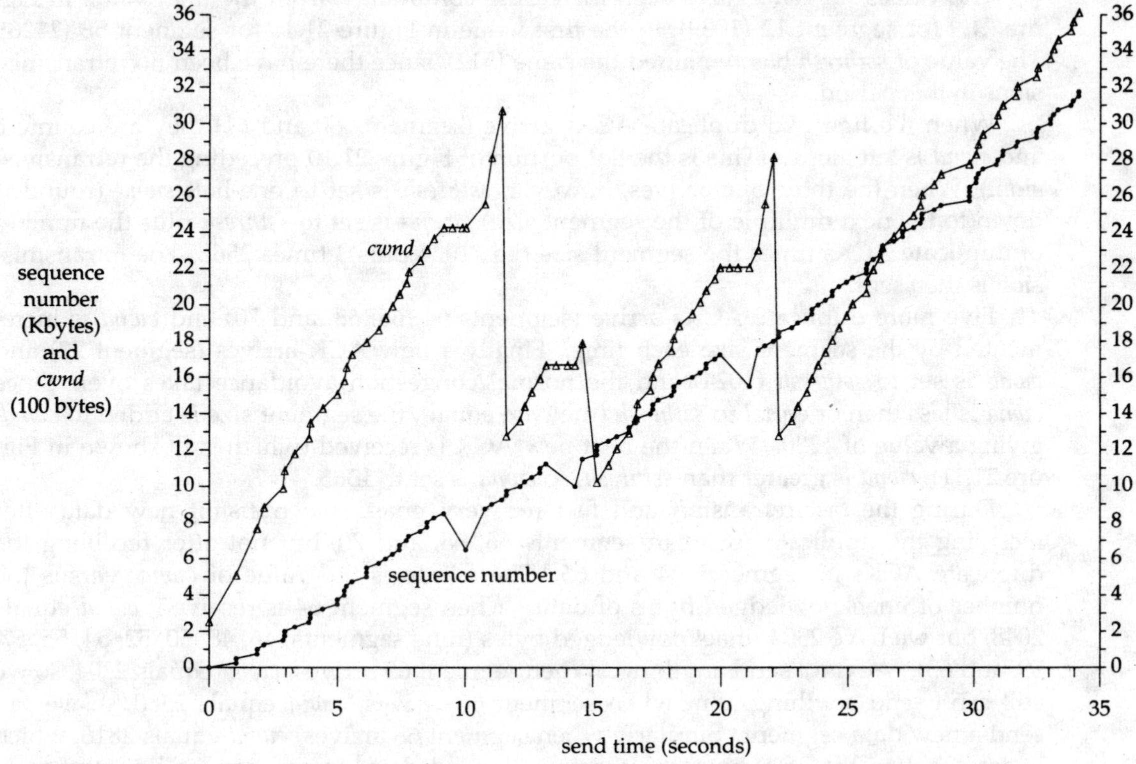

Figure 21.10 Value of *cwnd* and send sequence number while data is being transmitted.

Segment# (Figure 21.7)	Action			Variable	
	Send	Receive	Comment	*cwnd*	*ssthresh*
58		ACK 6657	ACK of new data	2426	512
59	8705:8961(256)				
60		ACK 6657	duplicate ACK #1	2426	512
61		ACK 6657	duplicate ACK #2	2426	512
62		ACK 6657	duplicate ACK #3	1792	1024
63	6657:6913(256)		retransmission		
64		ACK 6657	duplicate ACK #4	2048	1024
65		ACK 6657	duplicate ACK #5	2304	1024
66		ACK 6657	duplicate ACK #6	2560	1024
67	8961:9217(256)				
68		ACK 6657	duplicate ACK #7	2816	1024
69	9217:9473(256)				
70		ACK 6657	duplicate ACK #8	3072	1024
71	9473:9729(256)				
72		ACK 8961	ACK of new data	1280	1024

Figure 21.11 Example of congestion avoidance (continued).

The values for *cwnd* have been increasing continually, from the final value in Figure 21.9 for segment 12 (1089), to the first value in Figure 21.11 for segment 58 (2426). The value of *ssthresh* has remained the same (512), since there have been no retransmissions in this period.

When the first two duplicate ACKs arrive (segments 60 and 61) they are counted, and *cwnd* is left alone. (This is the flat portion of Figure 21.10 preceding the retransmission.) When the third one arrives, however, *ssthresh* is set to one-half *cwnd* (rounded down to the next multiple of the segment size). *cwnd* is set to *ssthresh* plus the number of duplicate ACKs times the segment size (i.e., 1024 plus 3 times 256). The retransmission is then sent.

Five more duplicate ACKs arrive (segments 64–66, 68, and 70) and *cwnd* is incremented by the segment size each time. Finally a new ACK arrives (segment 72) and *cwnd* is set to *ssthresh* (1024) and the normal congestion avoidance takes over. Since *cwnd* is less than or equal to *ssthresh* (they are equal), the segment size is added to *cwnd*, giving a value of 1280. When the next new ACK is received (which isn't shown in Figure 21.11), *cwnd* is greater than *ssthresh*, so *cwnd* is set to 1363.

During the fast retransmit and fast recovery phase, we transmit new data after receiving the duplicate ACKs in segments 66, 68, and 70, but not after receiving the duplicate ACKs in segments 64 and 65. The reason is the value of *cwnd*, versus the number of unacknowledged bytes of data. When segment 64 is received, *cwnd* equals 2048, but we have 2304 unacknowledged bytes (nine segments: 46, 48, 50, 52, 54, 55, 57, 59, and 63). We can't send anything. When segment 65 arrives, *cwnd* equals 2304, so we still can't send anything. But when segment 66 arrives, *cwnd* equals 2560, so we can send a new data segment. Similarly when segment 68 arrives, *cwnd* equals 2816, which is greater than the 2560 bytes of unacknowledged data, so we can send another new data segment. The same scenario happens when segment 70 is received.

When the next retransmission takes place at time 14.3 in Figure 21.10, it is also triggered by the reception of three duplicate ACKs, so we see the same increase in *cwnd* as one more duplicate ACK arrives, followed by a decrease to 1024.

The retransmission at time 21.1 in Figure 21.10 is also triggered by duplicate ACKs. We receive three more duplicates after the retransmission, so we see three additional increases in *cwnd*, followed by a decrease to 1280. For the remainder of the transfer *cwnd* increases linearly to a final value of 3615.

21.9 Per-Route Metrics

Newer TCP implementations maintain many of the metrics that we've described in this chapter in the routing table entry. When a TCP connection is closed, if enough data was sent to obtain meaningful statistics, and if the routing table entry for the destination is not a default route, the following information is saved in the routing table entry, for the next use of the entry: the smoothed RTT, the smoothed mean deviation, and the slow start threshold. The quantity "enough data" is 16 windows of data. This gives 16 RTT samples, which allows the smoothed RTT filter to converge within 5% of the correct value.

Additionally, the `route(8)` command can be used by the administrator to set the metrics for a given route: the three values mentioned in the preceding paragraph, along with the MTU, the outbound bandwidth-delay product (Section 20.7), and the inbound bandwidth-delay product.

When a new TCP connection is established, either actively or passively, if the routing table entry being used for the connection has values for these metrics, the corresponding variable is initialized from the metrics.

21.10 ICMP Errors

Let's see how TCP handles ICMP errors that are returned for a given connection. The most common ICMP errors that TCP can encounter are source quench, host unreachable, and network unreachable.

Current Berkeley-based implementations handle these ICMP errors as follows:

- A received source quench causes the congestion window, *cwnd*, to be set to one segment to initiate slow start, but the slow start threshold, *ssthresh*, is not changed, so the window will open until it's either open all the way (limited by the window size and round-trip time) or until congestion occurs.
- A received host unreachable or network unreachable is effectively ignored, since these two errors are considered transient. It could be that an intermediate router has gone down and it can take the routing protocols a few minutes to stabilize on an alternative route. During this period either of these two ICMP errors can occur, but they must not abort the connection. Instead, TCP keeps trying to send the data that caused the error, although it may eventually time out. (Recall in Figure 21.1 that TCP did not give up for 9 minutes.)

  Current Berkeley-based implementations record that the ICMP error occurred, and if the connection times out, the ICMP error is translated into a more relevant error code than "connection timed out."

  > Earlier BSD implementations incorrectly aborted a connection whenever an ICMP host unreachable or network unreachable was received.

An Example

We can see how an ICMP host unreachable is handled by taking our dialup SLIP link down during the middle of a connection. We establish a connection from the host `slip` to the host `aix`. (From the figure on the inside front cover we see that this connection goes through our dialup SLIP link.) After establishing the connection and transferring some data, the dialup SLIP link between the routers `sun` and `netb` is taken down. This causes the default routing table entry on `sun` (which we showed in Section 9.2) to be removed. We expect `sun` to then respond to IP datagrams destined for the 140.252.1 Ethernet with an ICMP host unreachable. We want to see how TCP handles these ICMP errors.

Here is the interactive session on the host `slip`:

```
slip % sock aix echo                    run our sock program
test line                               type this line
test line                               and it's echoed
                                        SLIP link is brought down here
another line                            then type this line and watch retransmissions
                                        SLIP link is reestablished here
another line                            and the line and its echo are exchanged
line number 3
line number 3
the last line
                                        SLIP link is brought down here, and not reestablished
read error: No route to host            TCP finally gives up
```

Figure 21.12 shows the corresponding `tcpdump` output, captured on the router `bsdi`. (We have removed the connection establishment and all the window advertisements.) We connect to the echo server on the host `aix` and type "test line" (line 1). It is echoed (line 2) and the echo is acknowledged (line 3). We then take down the SLIP link.

We type "another line" (line 3) and expect to see TCP time out and retransmit the message. Indeed, this line is sent six times before a reply is received. Lines 4–13 show the first transmission and the next four retransmissions, each of which generates an ICMP host unreachable from the router `sun`. This is what we expect: the IP datagrams go from `slip` to the router `bsdi` (which has a default route that points to `sun`), and then to `sun`, where the broken link is detected.

While these retransmissions are taking place, the SLIP link is brought back up, and the retransmission on line 14 gets delivered. Line 15 is the echo from `aix`, and line 16 is the acknowledgment of the echo.

This shows that TCP ignores the ICMP host unreachable errors and keeps retransmitting. We can also see the expected exponential backoff in each retransmission timeout: the first appears to be 2.5 seconds, which is then multiplied by 2 (giving 5 seconds), then 4 (10 seconds), then 8 (20 seconds), then 16 (40 seconds).

We then type the third line of input ("line number 3") and see it sent on line 17, echoed on line 18, and the echo acknowledged on line 19.

We now want to see what happens when TCP retransmits and gives up, after receiving the ICMP host unreachable, so we take down the SLIP link again. After taking it down we type "the last line" and see it transmitted 13 times before TCP gives up. (We have deleted lines 30–43 from the output. They are additional retransmissions.)

The thing we notice, however, is the error message printed by our `sock` program when it finally gives up: "No route to host." This corresponds to the Unix error associated with the ICMP host unreachable error (Figure 6.12, p. 82). This shows that TCP saves the ICMP error that it receives on the connection, and when it finally gives up, it prints that error, instead of "Connection timed out."

Finally, notice the different retransmission intervals in lines 22–46, compared to lines 6–14. It appears that TCP updated its estimators when the third line we typed was sent and acknowledged without any retransmissions in lines 17–19. The initial retransmission timeout is now 3 seconds, giving successive values of 6, 12, 24, 48, and then the upper limit of 64.

```
 1      0.0                        slip.1035 > aix.echo: P 1:11(10) ack 1
 2      0.212271 (  0.2123)        aix.echo > slip.1035: P 1:11(10) ack 11
 3      0.310685 (  0.0984)        slip.1035 > aix.echo: . ack 11

                                   SLIP link brought down here

 4    174.758100 (174.4474)        slip.1035 > aix.echo: P 11:24(13) ack 11
 5    174.759017 (  0.0009)        sun > slip: icmp: host aix unreachable

 6    177.150439 (  2.3914)        slip.1035 > aix.echo: P 11:24(13) ack 11
 7    177.151271 (  0.0008)        sun > slip: icmp: host aix unreachable

 8    182.150200 (  4.9989)        slip.1035 > aix.echo: P 11:24(13) ack 11
 9    182.151189 (  0.0010)        sun > slip: icmp: host aix unreachable

10    192.149671 (  9.9985)        slip.1035 > aix.echo: P 11:24(13) ack 11
11    192.150608 (  0.0009)        sun > slip: icmp: host aix unreachable

12    212.148783 ( 19.9982)        slip.1035 > aix.echo: P 11:24(13) ack 11
13    212.149786 (  0.0010)        sun > slip: icmp: host aix unreachable

                                   SLIP link brought up here

14    252.146774 ( 39.9970)        slip.1035 > aix.echo: P 11:24(13) ack 11
15    252.439257 (  0.2925)        aix.echo > slip.1035: P 11:24(13) ack 24
16    252.505331 (  0.0661)        slip.1035 > aix.echo: . ack 24

17    261.977246 (  9.4719)        slip.1035 > aix.echo: P 24:38(14) ack 24
18    262.158758 (  0.1815)        aix.echo > slip.1035: P 24:38(14) ack 38
19    262.305086 (  0.1463)        slip.1035 > aix.echo: . ack 38

                                   SLIP link brought down here

20    458.155330 (195.8502)        slip.1035 > aix.echo: P 38:52(14) ack 38
21    458.156163 (  0.0008)        sun > slip: icmp: host aix unreachable

22    461.136904 (  2.9807)        slip.1035 > aix.echo: P 38:52(14) ack 38
23    461.137826 (  0.0009)        sun > slip: icmp: host aix unreachable

24    467.136461 (  5.9986)        slip.1035 > aix.echo: P 38:52(14) ack 38
25    467.137385 (  0.0009)        sun > slip: icmp: host aix unreachable

26    479.135811 ( 11.9984)        slip.1035 > aix.echo: P 38:52(14) ack 38
27    479.136647 (  0.0008)        sun > slip: icmp: host aix unreachable

28    503.134816 ( 23.9982)        slip.1035 > aix.echo: P 38:52(14) ack 38
29    503.135740 (  0.0009)        sun > slip: icmp: host aix unreachable

                                   14 lines of output deleted here

44   1000.219573 ( 64.0959)        slip.1035 > aix.echo: P 38:52(14) ack 38
45   1000.220503 (  0.0009)        sun > slip: icmp: host aix unreachable

46   1064.201281 ( 63.9808)        slip.1035 > aix.echo: R 52:52(0) ack 38
47   1064.202182 (  0.0009)        sun > slip: icmp: host aix unreachable
```

Figure 21.12 TCP handling of received ICMP host unreachable error.

21.11 Repacketization

When TCP times out and retransmits, it does not have to retransmit the identical segment again. Instead, TCP is allowed to perform *repacketization*, sending a bigger segment, which can increase performance. (Naturally, this bigger segment cannot exceed the MSS announced by the other receiver.) This is allowed in the protocol because TCP identifies the data being sent and acknowledged by its byte number, not its segment number.

We can easily see this in action. We use our `sock` program to connect to the discard server and type one line. We then disconnect the Ethernet cable and type a second line. While this second line is being retransmitted, we type a third line. We expect the next retransmission to contain both the second and third lines.

```
bsdi % sock svr4 discard
hello there                    first line gets sent OK
                               then we disconnect the Ethernet cable
line number 2                  this line gets retransmitted
and 3                          type this line before second line sent OK
                               then reconnect Ethernet cable
```

Figure 21.13 shows the `tcpdump` output. (We have removed the connection establishment, the connection termination, and all the window advertisements.)

```
1   0.0                        bsdi.1032 > svr4.discard: P 1:13(12) ack 1
2   0.140489  ( 0.1405)        svr4.discard > bsdi.1032: . ack 13

                               Ethernet cable disconnected here

3   26.407696 (26.2672)        bsdi.1032 > svr4.discard: P 13:27(14) ack 1
4   27.639390 ( 1.2317)        bsdi.1032 > svr4.discard: P 13:27(14) ack 1
5   30.639453 ( 3.0001)        bsdi.1032 > svr4.discard: P 13:27(14) ack 1

                               third line typed here

6   36.639653 ( 6.0002)        bsdi.1032 > svr4.discard: P 13:33(20) ack 1
7   48.640131 (12.0005)        bsdi.1032 > svr4.discard: P 13:33(20) ack 1

                               Ethernet cable reconnected here

8   72.640768 (24.0006)        bsdi.1032 > svr4.discard: P 13:33(20) ack 1
9   72.719091 ( 0.0783)        svr4.discard > bsdi.1032: . ack 33
```

Figure 21.13 Repacketization of data by TCP.

Lines 1 and 2 show the first line ("hello there") being sent and its acknowledgment. We then disconnect the Ethernet cable and type "line number 2" (14 bytes, including the newline). These bytes are transmitted on line 3, and then retransmitted on lines 4 and 5.

Before the retransmission on line 6 we type "and 3" (6 bytes, including the newline) and see this retransmission contain 20 bytes: both lines that we typed. When the acknowledgment arrives on line 9, it is for all 20 bytes.

21.12 Summary

This chapter has provided a detailed look at TCP's timeout and retransmission strategy. Our first example was a lost SYN to establish a connection and we saw how an exponential backoff is applied to successive retransmission timeout values.

TCP calculates the round-trip time and then uses these measurements to keep track of a smoothed RTT estimator and a smoothed mean deviation estimator. These two estimators are then used to calculate the next retransmission timeout value. Many implementations only measure a single RTT per window. Karn's algorithm removes the retransmission ambiguity problem by preventing us from measuring the RTT when a packet is lost.

Our detailed example, which included three lost packets, let us see many of TCP's algorithms in action: slow start, congestion avoidance, fast retransmit, and fast recovery. We were also able to hand calculate TCP RTT estimators along with the congestion window and slow-start threshold, and verify the values with the actual values from the trace output.

We finished the chapter by looking at the effect various ICMP errors have on a TCP connection and how TCP is allowed to repacketize its data. We saw how the "soft" ICMP errors don't cause a connection to be terminated, but are remembered so that if the connection terminates abnormally, the soft error can be reported.

Exercises

21.1 In Figure 21.5 the first timeout was calculated as 6 seconds and the next as 24 seconds. If the ACK for the initial SYN had not arrived after the 24-second timeout expired, when would the next timeout occur?

21.2 In the discussion following Figure 21.5 we said that the timeout intervals are calculated as 6, 24, and then 48 seconds, as we saw in Figure 4.5. But if we watch a TCP connection to a nonexistent host from an SVR4 system, the timeout intervals are 6, 12, 24, and 48 seconds. What's going on?

21.3 Compare the performance of TCP's sliding window versus TFTP's stop-and-wait protocol as follows. In this chapter we transferred 32768 bytes in about 35 seconds (Figure 21.6) across a link with an RTT that averaged around 1.5 seconds (Figure 21.4). Calculate how long TFTP would take for the same transfer.

21.4 In Section 21.7 we said that the receipt of a duplicate ACK is caused by a segment being lost or reordered. In Section 21.5 we saw the generation of duplicate ACKs caused by a lost segment. Draw a picture showing that a reordering of segments also generates duplicate ACKs.

21.5 There is a noticeable blip in Figure 21.6 between times 28.8 and 29.8. Is this a retransmission?

21.6 In Section 21.6 we said that the 4.3BSD Tahoe release only performed slow start if the destination was on a different network. How do you think "different network" was determined? (*Hint*: Look at Appendix E.)

21.7 In Section 20.2 we said that TCP normally ACKs every other segment. But in Figure 21.2 we see the receiver ACK every segment. Why?

21.8 Are per-route metrics really useful, given the prevalence of default routes?

22

TCP Persist Timer

22.1 Introduction

We've seen that TCP has the receiver perform flow control by specifying the amount of data it is willing to accept from the sender: the window size. What happens when the window size goes to 0? This effectively stops the sender from transmitting data, until the window becomes nonzero.

We saw this scenario in Figure 20.3 (p. 279). When the sender received segment 9, opening the window that was shut down by segment 8, it immediately started sending data. TCP must handle the case of this acknowledgment that opens the window (segment 9) being lost. Acknowledgments are not reliably transmitted—that is, TCP does not ACK acknowledgments, it only ACKs segments containing data.

If an acknowledgment is lost, we could end up with both sides waiting for the other: the receiver waiting to receive data (since it provided the sender with a nonzero window) and the sender waiting to receive the window update allowing it to send. To prevent this form of deadlock from occurring the sender uses a *persist timer* that causes it to query the receiver periodically, to find out if the window has been increased. These segments from the sender are called *window probes*. In this chapter we'll examine window probes and the persist timer. We'll also examine the silly window syndrome, which is tied to the persist timer.

22.2 An Example

To see the persist timer in action we'll start a receiver process that listens for a connection request from a client, accepts the connection request, and then goes to sleep for a long time before reading from the network.

Our `sock` program lets us specify a pause option `-P` that sleeps between the server accepting the connection request and performing the first read. We'll invoke the server as:

```
svr4 % sock -i -s -P100000 5555
```

This has the server sleep for 100,000 seconds (27.8 hours) before reading from the network. The client is run on the host `bsdi` and performs 1024-byte writes to port 5555 on the server. Figure 22.1 shows the `tcpdump` output. (We have removed the connection establishment from the output.)

```
1   0.0                    bsdi.1027 > svr4.5555: P 1:1025(1024) ack 1 win 4096
2   0.191961 ( 0.1920)    svr4.5555 > bsdi.1027: . ack 1025 win 4096
3   0.196950 ( 0.0050)    bsdi.1027 > svr4.5555: . 1025:2049(1024) ack 1 win 4096
4   0.200340 ( 0.0034)    bsdi.1027 > svr4.5555: . 2049:3073(1024) ack 1 win 4096
5   0.207506 ( 0.0072)    svr4.5555 > bsdi.1027: . ack 3073 win 4096
6   0.212676 ( 0.0052)    bsdi.1027 > svr4.5555: . 3073:4097(1024) ack 1 win 4096
7   0.216113 ( 0.0034)    bsdi.1027 > svr4.5555: P 4097:5121(1024) ack 1 win 4096
8   0.219997 ( 0.0039)    bsdi.1027 > svr4.5555: P 5121:6145(1024) ack 1 win 4096
9   0.227882 ( 0.0079)    svr4.5555 > bsdi.1027: . ack 5121 win 4096
10  0.233012 ( 0.0051)    bsdi.1027 > svr4.5555: P 6145:7169(1024) ack 1 win 4096
11  0.237014 ( 0.0040)    bsdi.1027 > svr4.5555: P 7169:8193(1024) ack 1 win 4096
12  0.240961 ( 0.0039)    bsdi.1027 > svr4.5555: P 8193:9217(1024) ack 1 win 4096
13  0.402143 ( 0.1612)    svr4.5555 > bsdi.1027: . ack 9217 win 0

14  5.351561 ( 4.9494)    bsdi.1027 > svr4.5555: . 9217:9218(1) ack 1 win 4096
15  5.355571 ( 0.0040)    svr4.5555 > bsdi.1027: . ack 9217 win 0

16  10.351714 ( 4.9961)   bsdi.1027 > svr4.5555: . 9217:9218(1) ack 1 win 4096
17  10.355670 ( 0.0040)   svr4.5555 > bsdi.1027: . ack 9217 win 0

18  16.351881 ( 5.9962)   bsdi.1027 > svr4.5555: . 9217:9218(1) ack 1 win 4096
19  16.355849 ( 0.0040)   svr4.5555 > bsdi.1027: . ack 9217 win 0

20  28.352213 (11.9964)   bsdi.1027 > svr4.5555: . 9217:9218(1) ack 1 win 4096
21  28.356178 ( 0.0040)   svr4.5555 > bsdi.1027: . ack 9217 win 0

22  52.352874 (23.9967)   bsdi.1027 > svr4.5555: . 9217:9218(1) ack 1 win 4096
23  52.356839 ( 0.0040)   svr4.5555 > bsdi.1027: . ack 9217 win 0

24  100.354224 (47.9974)  bsdi.1027 > svr4.5555: . 9217:9218(1) ack 1 win 4096
25  100.358207 ( 0.0040)  svr4.5555 > bsdi.1027: . ack 9217 win 0

26  160.355914 (59.9977)  bsdi.1027 > svr4.5555: . 9217:9218(1) ack 1 win 4096
27  160.359835 ( 0.0039)  svr4.5555 > bsdi.1027: . ack 9217 win 0

28  220.357575 (59.9977)  bsdi.1027 > svr4.5555: . 9217:9218(1) ack 1 win 4096
29  220.361668 ( 0.0041)  svr4.5555 > bsdi.1027: . ack 9217 win 0

30  280.359254 (59.9976)  bsdi.1027 > svr4.5555: . 9217:9218(1) ack 1 win 4096
31  280.363315 ( 0.0041)  svr4.5555 > bsdi.1027: . ack 9217 win 0
```

Figure 22.1 Example of persist timer probing a zero-sized window.

Segments 1–13 shows the normal data transfer from the client to the server, filling up the window with 9216 bytes of data. The server advertises a window of 4096, and has a default socket buffer size of 4096, but really accepts a total of 9216 bytes. This is some form of interaction between the TCP/IP code and the streams subsystem in SVR4.

In segment 13 the server acknowledges the previous four data segments, but advertises a window of 0, stopping the client from transmitting any more data. This causes the client to set its persist timer. If the client doesn't receive a window update when the timer expires, it probes the empty window, to see if a window update has been lost. Since our server process is asleep, the 9216 bytes of data are buffered by TCP, waiting for the application to issue a read.

Notice the spacing of the window probes by the client. The first (segment 14) is 4.949 seconds after receiving the zero-sized window. The next (segment 16) is 4.996 seconds later. The spacing is then about 6, 12, 24, 48, and 60 seconds after the previous.

Why are the spacings always a fraction of a second less than 5, 6, 12, 24, 48, and 60? These probes are triggered by TCP's 500-ms timer expiring. When the timer expires, the window probe is sent, and a reply is received about 4 ms later. The receipt of the reply causes the timer to be restarted, but the time until the next clock tick is about 500 minus 4 ms.

The normal TCP exponential backoff is used when calculating the persist timer. The first timeout is calculated as 1.5 seconds for a typical LAN connection. This is multiplied by 2 for a second timeout value of 3 seconds. A multiplier of 4 gives the next value of 6, a multiplier of 8 gives a value of 12, and so on. But the persist timer is always bounded between 5 and 60 seconds, which accounts for the values we see in Figure 22.1.

The window probes contain 1 byte of data (sequence number 9217). TCP is always allowed to send 1 byte of data beyond the end of a closed window. Notice, however, that the acknowledgments returned with the window size of 0 do not ACK this byte. (They ACK the receipt of all bytes through and including byte number 9216.) Therefore this byte keeps being retransmitted.

The characteristic of the persist state that is different from the retransmission timeout in Chapter 21 is that TCP *never* gives up sending window probes. These window probes continue to be sent at 60-second intervals until the window opens up or either of the applications using the connection is terminated.

22.3 Silly Window Syndrome

Window-based flow control schemes, such as the one used by TCP, can fall victim to a condition known as the *silly window syndrome* (SWS). When it occurs, small amounts of data are exchanged across the connection, instead of full-sized segments [Clark 1982].

It can be caused by either end: the receiver can advertise small windows (instead of waiting until a larger window could be advertised) and the sender can transmit small amounts of data (instead of waiting for additional data, to send a larger segment). Correct avoidance of the silly window syndrome is performed on both ends.

1. The receiver must not advertise small windows. The normal algorithm is for the receiver not to advertise a larger window than it is currently advertising (which can be 0) until the window can be increased by either one full-sized segment (i.e., the MSS being received) or by one-half the receiver's buffer space, whichever is smaller.

2. Sender avoidance of the silly window syndrome is done by not transmitting unless one of the following conditions is true: (a) a full-sized segment can be sent, (b) we can send at least one-half of the maximum sized window that the other end has ever advertised, or (c) we can send everything we have and either we are not expecting an ACK (i.e., we have no outstanding unacknowledged data) or the Nagle algorithm is disabled for this connection (Section 19.4).

   Condition (b) deals with hosts that always advertise tiny windows, perhaps smaller than the segment size. Condition (c) prevents us from sending small segments when we have unacknowledged data that is waiting to be ACKed and the Nagle algorithm is enabled. If the application is doing small writes (e.g., smaller than the segment size), it is condition (c) that avoids the silly window syndrome.

   These three conditions also let us answer the question: if the Nagle algorithm prevents us from sending small segments while there is outstanding unacknowledged data, how small is small? From condition (a) we see that "small" means the number of bytes is less than the segment size. Condition (b) only comes into play with older, primitive hosts.

Condition (b) in step 2 requires that the sender keep track of the maximum window size advertised by the other end. This is an attempt by the sender to guess the size of the other end's receive buffer. Although the size of the receiver buffer could decrease while the connection is established, in practice this is rare.

An Example

We'll now go through a detailed example to see the silly window syndrome avoidance in action, which also involves the persist timer. We'll use our `sock` program with the sending host, `sun`, doing six 1024-byte writes to the network:

```
sun % sock -i -n6 bsdi 7777
```

But we'll put some pauses in the receiving process on the host `bsdi`, pausing 4 seconds before doing the first read, and then pausing 2 seconds between successive reads. Additionally, the receiver issues 256-byte reads:

```
bsdi % sock -i -s -P4 -p2 -r256 7777
```

The reason for the initial pause is to let the receiver's buffer fill, forcing it to stop the transmitter. Since the receiver then performs small reads from the network, we expect to see the receiver perform silly window syndrome avoidance.

Figure 22.2 is the time line for the transfer of the 6144 bytes of data. (We have deleted the connection establishment.)

We also need to track what happens with the application that's reading the data at each point in time, along with the number of bytes currently in the receive buffer, and the number of bytes of available space in the receive buffer. Figure 22.3 shows everything that's happening.

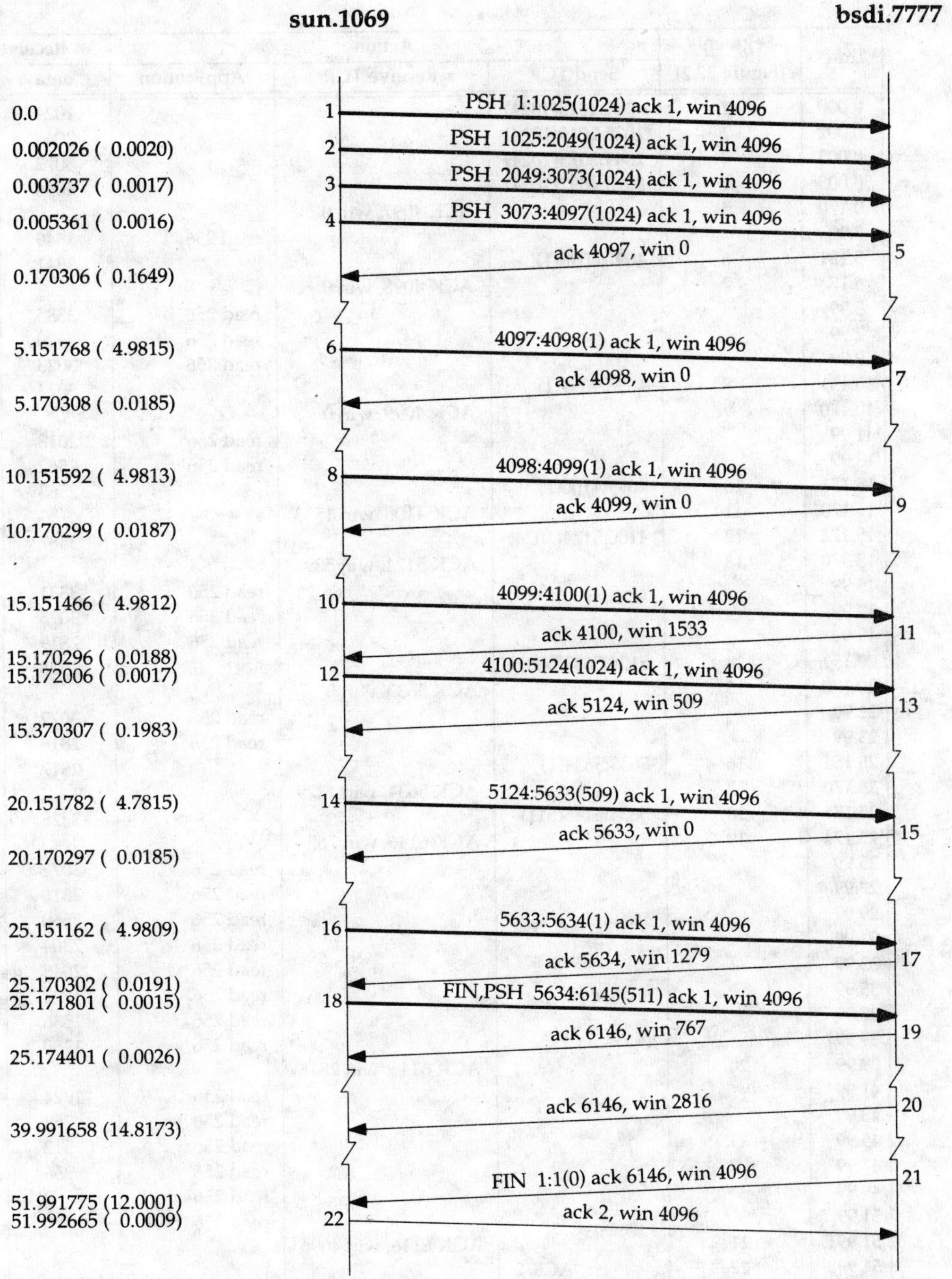

Figure 22.2 Time line showing receiver avoidance of silly window syndrome.

Time	Segment# (Figure 22.2)	Action			Receiver buffer	
		Send TCP	Receive TCP	Application	data	available
0.000	1	1:1025(1024)			1024	3072
0.002	2	1025:2049(1024)			2048	2048
0.003	3	2049:3073(1024)			3072	1024
0.005	4	3073:4097(1024)			4096	0
0.170	5		ACK 4097, win 0			
3.99				read 256	3840	256
5.151	6	4097:4098(1)			3841	255
5.17	7		ACK 4098, win 0			
5.99				read 256	3585	511
7.99				read 256	3329	767
9.99				read 256	3073	1023
10.151	8	4098:4099(1)			3074	1022
10.170	9		ACK 4099, win 0			
11.99				read 256	2818	1278
13.99				read 256	2562	1534
15.151	10	4099:4100(1)			2563	1533
15.170	11		ACK 4100, win 1533			
15.172	12	4100:5124(1024)			3587	509
15.370	13		ACK 5124, win 509			
15.99				read 256	3331	765
17.99				read 256	3075	1021
19.99				read 256	2819	1277
20.151	14	5124:5633(509)			3328	768
20.170	15		ACK 5633, win 0			
21.99				read 256	3072	1024
23.99				read 256	2816	1280
25.151	16	5633:5634(1)			2817	1279
25.170	17		ACK 5634, win 1279			
25.171	18	5634:6145(511)			3328	768
25.174	19		ACK 6146, win 767			
25.99				read 256	3072	1024
27.99				read 256	2816	1280
29.99				read 256	2560	1536
31.99				read 256	2304	1792
33.99				read 256	2048	2048
35.99				read 256	1792	2304
37.99				read 256	1536	2560
39.99				read 256	1280	2816
39.99	20		ACK 6146, win 2816			
41.99				read 256	1024	3072
43.99				read 256	768	3328
45.99				read 256	512	3584
47.99				read 256	256	3840
49.99				read 256	0	4096
51.99				read 256 (EOF)	0	4096
51.991	21		ACK 6146, win 4096			
51.992	22	ACK 2				

Figure 22.3 Sequence of events for receiver avoidance of the silly window syndrome.

In Figure 22.3 the first column is the relative point in time for each action. Those times with three digits to the right of the decimal point are taken from the tcpdump output (Figure 22.2). Those times with 99 to the right of the decimal point are the assumed times of the action on the receiving host. (Having these relative times on the receiver contain 99 for the hundredths of a second correlates them with segments 20 and 22 in Figure 22.2, the only two events on the receiver that we can see with tcpdump that are triggered by a timeout on the receiving host. All the other packets that we see from bsdi are triggered by the reception of a segment from the sender. It also makes sense, because this would place the initial 4-second pause just before time 0 when the sender transmits the first data segment. This is about when the receiver would get control, after receiving the ACK of its SYN in the connection establishment.)

The amount of data in the receiver's buffer increases when it receives data from the sender, and decreases as the application reads data from the buffer. What we want to follow are the window advertisements sent by the receiver to the sender, and what those window advertisements are. This lets us see how the silly window syndrome is avoided by the receiver.

The first four data segments and the corresponding ACK (segments 1–5) show the sender filling the receiver's buffer. At that point the sender is stopped but it still has more data to send. It sets its persist timer for its minimum value of 5 seconds.

When the persist timer expires, 1 byte of data is sent (segment 6). The receiving application has read 256 bytes from the receive buffer (at time 3.99), so the byte is accepted and acknowledged (segment 7). But the advertised window is still 0, since the receiver does not have room for either one full-sized segment or one-half of its buffer. This is silly window avoidance by the receiver.

The sender's persist timer is reset and goes off again 5 seconds later (at time 10.151). One byte is again sent and acknowledged (segments 8 and 9). Again the amount of room in the receiver's buffer (1022 bytes) forces it to advertise a window of 0.

When the sender's persist timer expires next, at time 15.151, another byte is sent and acknowledged (segments 10 and 11). This time the receiver has 1533 bytes available in its buffer, so a nonzero window is advertised. The sender immediately takes advantage of the window and sends 1024 bytes (segment 12). The acknowledgment of these 1024 bytes (segment 13) advertises a window of 509 bytes. This appears to contradict what we've seen earlier with small window advertisements.

What's happening here is that segment 11 advertised a window of 1533 bytes but the sender only transmitted 1024 bytes. If the acknowledgment in segment 13 advertised a window of 0, it would violate the TCP principle that a window cannot shrink by moving the right edge of the window to the left (Section 20.3). That's why the small window of 509 bytes must be advertised.

Next we see that the sender does not immediately transmit into this small window. This is silly window avoidance by the sender. Instead it waits for another persist timer to expire at time 20.151, when it sends 509 bytes. Even though it ends up sending this small segment with 509 bytes of data, it waits 5 seconds before doing so, to see if an ACK arrives that opens up the window more. These 509 bytes of data leave only 768 bytes of available space in the receive buffer, so the acknowledgment (segment 15) advertises a window of 0.

The persist timer goes off again at time 25.151, and the sender transmits 1 byte. The receive buffer then has 1279 bytes of space, which is the window advertised in segment 17.

The sender has only 511 additional bytes of data to transmit, which it sends immediately upon receiving the window advertisement of 1279 (segment 18). This segment also contains the FIN flag. The receiver acknowledges the data and the FIN, advertising a window of 767. (See Exercise 22.2.)

Since the sending application issues a close after performing its six 1024-byte writes, the sender's end of the connection goes from the ESTABLISHED state to the FIN_WAIT_1 state, to the FIN_WAIT_2 state (Figure 18.12). It sits in this state until receiving a FIN from the other end. There is no timer in this state (recall our discussion at the end of Section 18.6), since the FIN that it sent in segment 18 was acknowledged in segment 19. This is why we see no further transmissions by the sender until it receives the FIN (segment 21).

The receiving application continues reading 256 bytes of data every 2 seconds from the receive buffer. Why is the ACK sent at time 39.99 (segment 20)? The amount of room in the receive buffer has gone from its last advertised value of 767 (segment 19) to 2816 when the application reads at time 39.99. This equals 2049 bytes of additional space in the receive buffer. Recalling the first rule at the start of this section, the receiver now sends a window update because the amount of room has increased by one-half the room in the receive buffer. This implies that the receiving TCP checks whether to send a window update every time the application reads data from TCP's receive buffer.

The final application read occurs at time 51.99 and the application receives an end-of-file notification, since the buffer is empty. This causes the final two segments (21 and 22), which complete the termination of the connection.

22.4 Summary

TCP's persist timer is set by one end of a connection when it has data to send, but has been stopped because the other end has advertised a zero-sized window. The sender keeps probing the closed window using a retransmission interval similar to what we saw in Chapter 21. This probing of the closed window continues indefinitely.

When we ran an example to see the persist timer we also encountered TCP's avoidance of the silly window syndrome. This is to prevent TCP from advertising small windows or from sending small segments. In our example we saw avoidance of the silly window syndrome by both the sender and the receiver.

Exercises

22.1 In Figure 22.3 notice the times of all the acknowledgments (segments 5, 7, 9, 11, 13, 15, and 17): 0.170, 5.170, 10.170, 15.170, 15.370, 20.170, and 25.170. Also notice the time differences between sending the data and receiving the ACK: 164.9, 18.5, 18.7, 18.8, 198.3, 18.5, and 19.1 ms. Explain what's probably going on.

22.2 In Figure 22.3 at time 25.174 a window of 767 is advertised, but 768 bytes are available in the receive buffer. Why the difference of 1 byte?

23

TCP Keepalive Timer

23.1 Introduction

Many newcomers to TCP/IP are surprised to learn that no data whatsoever flows across an idle TCP connection. That is, if neither process at the ends of a TCP connection is sending data to the other, nothing is exchanged between the two TCP modules. There is no polling, for example, as you might find with other networking protocols. This means we can start a client process that establishes a TCP connection with a server, and walk away for hours, days, weeks or months, and the connection remains up. Intermediate routers can crash and reboot, phone lines may go down and back up, but as long as neither host at the ends of the connection reboots, the connection remains established.

This assumes that neither application—the client or server—has application-level timers to detect inactivity, causing either application to terminate. Recall at the end of Section 10.7 that BGP sends an application probe to the other end every 30 seconds. This is an application timer that is independent of the TCP keepalive timer.

There are times, however, when a server wants to know if the client's host has either crashed and is down, or crashed and rebooted. The *keepalive timer*, a feature of many implementations, provides this capability.

> Keepalives are not part of the TCP specification. The Host Requirements RFC provides three reasons not to use them: (1) they can cause perfectly good connections to be dropped during transient failures, (2) they consume unnecessary bandwidth, and (3) they cost money on an internet that charges by the packet. Nevertheless, many implementations provide the keepalive timer.

The keepalive timer is a controversial feature. Many feel that this polling of the other end has no place in TCP and should be done by the application, if desired. This is one of the *religious issues*, because of the fervor expressed by some on the topic.

The keepalive option can cause an otherwise good connection between two processes to be terminated because of a temporary loss of connectivity in the network joining the two end systems. For example, if the keepalive probes are sent during the time that an intermediate router has crashed and is rebooting, TCP will think that the client's host has crashed, which is not what has happened.

The keepalive feature is intended for server applications that might tie up resources on behalf of a client, and want to know if the client host crashes. Many versions of the Telnet server and Rlogin server enable the keepalive option by default.

A common example showing the need for the keepalive feature nowadays is when personal computer users use TCP/IP to login to a host using Telnet. If they just power off the computer at the end of the day, without logging off, they leave a half-open connection. In Figure 18.16 we showed how sending data across a half-open connection caused a reset to be returned, but that was from the client end, where the client was sending the data. If the client disappears, leaving the half-open connection on the server's end, and the server is waiting for some data from the client, the server will wait forever. The keepalive feature is intended to detect these half-open connections from the server side.

23.2 Description

In this description we'll call the end that enables the keepalive option the server, and the other end the client. There is nothing to stop a client from setting this option, but normally it's set by servers. It can also be set by both ends of a connection, if it's important for each end to know if the other end disappears. (In Chapter 29 we'll see that when NFS uses TCP, both the client and server set this option. But in Chapter 26 with Rlogin and Telnet, only the servers set the option, not the clients.)

If there is no activity on a given connection for 2 hours, the server sends a probe segment to the client. (We'll see what the probe segment looks like in the examples that follow.) The client host must be in one of four states.

1. The client host is still up and running and reachable from the server. The client's TCP responds normally and the server knows that the other end is still up. The server's TCP will reset the keepalive timer for 2 hours in the future. If there is application traffic across the connection before the next 2-hour timer expires, the timer is reset for 2 hours in the future, following the exchange of data.

2. The client's host has crashed and is either down or in the process of rebooting. In either case, its TCP is not responding. The server will not receive a response to its probe and it times out after 75 seconds. The server sends a total of 10 of these probes, 75 seconds apart, and if it doesn't receive a response, the server considers the client's host as down and terminates the connection.

3. The client's host has crashed and rebooted. Here the server will receive a response to its keepalive probe, but the response will be a reset, causing the server to terminate the connection.

4. The client's host is up and running, but unreachable from the server. This is the same as scenario 2, because TCP can't distinguish between the two. All it can tell is that no replies are received to its probes.

The server does not have to worry about the client's host being shut down and then rebooted. (This refers to an operator shutdown, instead of the host crashing.) When the system is shut down by an operator, all application processes are terminated (i.e., the client process), which causes the client's TCP to send a FIN on the connection. Receiving the FIN would cause the server's TCP to report an end-of-file to the server process, allowing the server to detect this scenario.

In the first scenario the server application has no idea that the keepalive probes are taking place. Everything is handled at the TCP layer. It's transparent to the application until one of scenarios 2, 3, or 4 occurs. In these three scenarios an error is returned to the server application by its TCP. (Normally the server has issued a read from the network, waiting for data from the client. If the keepalive feature returns an error, it is returned to the server as the return value from the read.) In scenario 2 the error is something like "connection timed out," and in scenario 3 we expect "connection reset by peer." The fourth scenario may look like the connection timed out, or may cause another error to be returned, depending on whether an ICMP error related to the connection is received. We look at all four scenarios in the next section.

A perpetual question by people discovering the keepalive option is whether the 2-hour idle time value can be changed. They normally want it much lower, on the order of minutes. As we show in Appendix E, the value can usually be changed, but in all the systems described in this appendix, the keepalive interval is a system-wide value, so changing it affects all users of the option.

The Host Requirements RFC says that an implementation may provide the keepalive feature, but it must not be enabled unless the application specifically says so. Also, the keepalive interval must be configurable, but it must default to no less than 2 hours.

23.3 Keepalive Examples

We'll now go through scenarios 2, 3, and 4 from the previous section, to see the packets exchanged using the keepalive option.

Other End Crashes

Let's see what happens when the server host crashes and does not reboot. To simulate this we'll do the following steps:

- Establish a connection between a client (our `sock` program on the host `bsdi`) and the standard echo server on the host `svr4`. The client enables the keepalive option with the `-K` option.
- Verify that data can go across the connection.
- Watch the client's TCP send keepalive packets every 2 hours, and see them acknowledged by the server's TCP.

- Disconnect the Ethernet cable from the server, and leave it off until the example is complete. This makes the client think the server host has crashed.
- We expect the client to send 10 keepalive probes, 75 seconds apart, before declaring the connection dead.

Here is the interactive output on the client:

```
bsdi % sock -K svr4 echo                  -K for keepalive option
hello, world                              type this at beginning, to verify connection is up
hello, world                              and see this echoed
                                          disconnect Ethernet cable after 4 hours
read error: Connection timed out          this happens about 6 hours and 11 minutes after start
```

Figure 23.1 shows the `tcpdump` output. (We have removed the connection establishment and the window advertisements.)

```
 1        0.0                  bsdi.1055 > svr4.echo: P 1:14(13) ack 1
 2        0.006105 (   0.0061) svr4.echo > bsdi.1055: P 1:14(13) ack 14
 3        0.093140 (   0.0870) bsdi.1055 > svr4.echo: . ack 14

 4     7199.972793 (7199.8797) arp who-has svr4 tell bsdi
 5     7199.974878 (   0.0021) arp reply svr4 is-at 0:0:c0:c2:9b:26
 6     7199.975741 (   0.0009) bsdi.1055 > svr4.echo: . ack 14
 7     7199.979843 (   0.0041) svr4.echo > bsdi.1055: . ack 14

 8    14400.134330 (7200.1545) arp who-has svr4 tell bsdi
 9    14400.136452 (   0.0021) arp reply svr4 is-at 0:0:c0:c2:9b:26
10    14400.137391 (   0.0009) bsdi.1055 > svr4.echo: . ack 14
11    14400.141408 (   0.0040) svr4.echo > bsdi.1055: . ack 14

12    21600.318309 (7200.1769) arp who-has svr4 tell bsdi
13    21675.320373 (  75.0021) arp who-has svr4 tell bsdi
14    21750.322407 (  75.0020) arp who-has svr4 tell bsdi
15    21825.324460 (  75.0021) arp who-has svr4 tell bsdi
16    21900.436749 (  75.1123) arp who-has svr4 tell bsdi
17    21975.438787 (  75.0020) arp who-has svr4 tell bsdi
18    22050.440842 (  75.0021) arp who-has svr4 tell bsdi
19    22125.432883 (  74.9920) arp who-has svr4 tell bsdi
20    22200.434697 (  75.0018) arp who-has svr4 tell bsdi
21    22275.436788 (  75.0021) arp who-has svr4 tell bsdi
```

Figure 23.1 Keepalive packets that determine that a host has crashed.

Lines 1, 2, and 3 send the line "hello, world" from the client to the server and back. The first keepalive probe occurs 2 hours (7200 seconds) later on line 4. The first thing we see is an ARP request and an ARP reply, before the TCP segment on line 6 can be sent. The keepalive probe on line 6 elicits a response from the other end (line 7). The same sequence of packets is exchanged 2 hours later in lines 8–11.

If we could see all the fields in the keepalive probes, lines 6 and 10, we would see that the sequence number field is one less than the next sequence number to be sent (i.e., 13 in this example, when it should be 14), but because there is no data in the segment, `tcpdump` does not print the sequence number field. (It only prints the sequence number for empty segments that contain the SYN, FIN, or RST flags.) It is the receipt of this incorrect sequence number that forces the server's TCP to respond with an ACK to the keepalive probe. The response tells the client the next sequence number that the server is expecting (14).

> Some older implementations based on 4.2BSD do not respond to these keepalive probes unless the segment contains data. Some systems can be configured to send one garbage byte of data in the probe to elicit the response. The garbage byte causes no harm, because it's not the expected byte (it's a byte that the receiver has previously received and acknowledged), so it's thrown away by the receiver. Other systems send the 4.3BSD-style segment (no data) for the first half of the probe period, and if no response is received, switch to the 4.2BSD-style segment for the last half.

We then disconnect the cable and expect the next probe, 2 hours later, to fail. When this next probe takes place, notice that we never see the TCP segments on the cable, because the host is not responding to ARP requests. We can still see that the client sends 10 probes, spaced 75 seconds apart, before giving up. We can see from our interactive script that the error code returned to the client process by TCP gets translated into "Connection timed out," which is what happened.

Other End Crashes and Reboots

In this example we'll see what happens when the client crashes and reboots. The initial scenario is the same as before, but after we verify that the connection is up, we disconnect the server from the Ethernet, reboot it, and then reconnect it to the Ethernet. We expect the next keepalive probe to generate a reset from the server, because the server now knows nothing about this connection. Here is the interactive session:

```
bsdi % sock -K svr4 echo         -K to enable keepalive option
hi there                         type this to verify connection is up
hi there                         and this is echoed back from other end
                                 here server is rebooted while disconnected from Ethernet
read error: Connection reset by peer
```

Figure 23.2 shows the `tcpdump` output. (We have removed the connection establishment and the window advertisements.)

```
1   0.0                           bsdi.1057 > svr4.echo: P 1:10(9) ack 1
2   0.006406 (    0.0064)         svr4.echo > bsdi.1057: P 1:10(9) ack 10
3   0.176922 (    0.1705)         bsdi.1057 > svr4.echo:    ack 10

4   7200.067151 (7199.8902)       arp who-has svr4 tell bsdi
5   7200.069751 (   0.0026)       arp reply svr4 is-at 0:0:c0:c2:9b:26
6   7200.070468 (   0.0007)       bsdi.1057 > svr4.echo: . ack 10
7   7200.075050 (   0.0046)       svr4.echo > bsdi.1057: R 1135563275:1135563275(0)
```

Figure 23.2 Keepalive example when other host has crashed and rebooted.

We establish the connection and send 9 bytes of data from the client to the server (lines 1–3). Two hours later the first keepalive probe is sent by the client, and the response is a reset from the server. The client application prints the error "Connection reset by peer," which makes sense.

Other End Is Unreachable

In this example the client has not crashed, but is not reachable during the 10-minute period when the keepalive probes are sent. An intermediate router may have crashed, a phone line may be temporarily out of order, or something similar.

To simulate this example we'll establish a TCP connection from our host `slip` through our dialup SLIP link to the host `vangogh.cs.berkeley.edu`, and then take the link down. First, here is the interactive output:

```
slip % sock -K vangogh.cs.berkeley.edu echo
testing                                         we type this line
testing                                         and see it echoed
                                                sometime in here the dialup SLIP link is taken down
read error: No route to host
```

Figure 23.3 shows the `tcpdump` output that was collected on the router `bsdi`. (The connection establishment and window advertisements have been removed.)

```
 1        0.0                    slip.1056 > vangogh.echo: P 1:9(8) ack 1
 2        0.277669 (    0.2777)  vangogh.echo > slip.1056: P 1:9(8) ack 9
 3        0.424423 (    0.1468)  slip.1056 > vangogh.echo: . ack 9

 4     7200.818081 (7200.3937)  slip.1056 > vangogh.echo: . ack 9
 5     7201.243046 (    0.4250)  vangogh.echo > slip.1056: . ack 9

 6    14400.688106 (7199.4451)  slip.1056 > vangogh.echo: . ack 9
 7    14400.689261 (    0.0012)  sun > slip: icmp: net vangogh unreachable

 8    14475.684360 (  74.9951)  slip.1056 > vangogh.echo: . ack 9
 9    14475.685504 (    0.0011)  sun > slip: icmp: net vangogh unreachable

                                 14 lines deleted

24    15075.759603 (  75.1008)  slip.1056 > vangogh.echo: R 9:9(0) ack 9
25    15075.760761 (    0.0012)  sun > slip: icmp: net vangogh unreachable
```

Figure 23.3 Keepalive example when other end is unreachable.

We start the example the same as before: lines 1–3 verify that the connection is up. The first keepalive probe 2 hours later is fine (lines 4 and 5), but before the next one occurs in another 2 hours, we bring down the SLIP connection between the routers `sun` and `netb`. (Refer to the inside front cover for the topology.)

The keepalive probe in line 6 elicits an ICMP network unreachable from the router `sun`. As we described in Section 21.10, this is just a soft error to the receiving TCP on the host `slip`. It records that the ICMP error was received, but the receipt of the error does not take down the connection. Eight more keepalive probes are sent, 75 seconds apart, before the sending host gives up. The error returned to the application generates a different message this time: "No route to host." We saw in Figure 6.12 (p. 82) that this corresponds to the ICMP network unreachable error.

23.4 Summary

As we said earlier, the keepalive feature is controversial. Protocol experts continue to debate whether it belongs in the transport layer, or should be handled entirely by the application.

It operates by sending a probe packet across a connection after the connection has been idle for 2 hours. Four different scenarios can occur: the other end is still there, the other end has crashed, the other end has crashed and rebooted, or the other end is currently unreachable. We saw each of these scenarios with an example, and saw different errors returned for the last three conditions.

In the first two examples that we looked at, had this feature not been provided, and without any application-level timer, our client would never have known that the other end had crashed, or crashed and rebooted. In the final example, however, nothing was wrong with the other end, the connection between them was temporarily down. We must be aware of this limitation when using keepalives.

Exercises

23.1 List some advantages of the keepalive feature.

23.2 List some disadvantages of the keepalive feature.

24

TCP Futures and Performance

24.1 Introduction

TCP has operated for many years over data links ranging from 1200 bits/sec dialup SLIP links to Ethernets. Ethernets were the predominant form of data link for TCP/IP in the 1980s and early 1990s. Although TCP operates correctly at speeds higher than an Ethernet (T3 phone lines, FDDI, and gigabit networks, for example), certain TCP limits start to be encountered at these higher speeds.

This chapter looks at some proposed modifications to TCP that allow it to obtain the maximum throughput at these higher speeds. We first look at the path MTU discovery mechanism, which we've seen earlier in the text, focusing this time on how it operates with TCP. This often lets TCP use an MTU greater than 536 for nonlocal connections, increasing its throughput.

We then look at long fat pipes, networks that have a large bandwidth-delay product, and the TCP limits that are encountered on these networks. Two new TCP options are described that deal with long fat pipes: a window scale option (to increase TCP's maximum window above 65535 bytes) and a timestamp option. This latter option lets TCP perform more accurate RTT measurement for data segments, and also provides protection against wrapped sequence numbers, which can occur at high speeds. These two options are defined in RFC 1323 [Jacobson, Braden, and Borman 1992].

We also look at the proposed T/TCP, modifications to TCP for transactions. The transaction mode of communication features a client request responded to by a server reply. It is a common paradigm for client–server computing. The goal of T/TCP is to reduce the number of segments exchanged by the two ends, avoiding the three-way handshake and the four segments to close the connection, so that the client receives the server's reply in one RTT plus the time required to process the request.

What is impressive about these new options—path MTU discovery, the window scale option, the timestamp option, and T/TCP—is that they are backward compatible with existing TCP implementations. Newer systems that include these options can still interoperate with all older systems. With the exception of an additional field in an ICMP message that can be used by path MTU discovery, these newer options need only be implemented on the end systems that want to take advantage of them.

We finish the chapter by looking at recently published figures dealing with TCP performance.

24.2 Path MTU Discovery

In Section 2.9 we described the concept of the *path MTU*. It is the minimum MTU on any network that is currently in the path between two hosts. Path MTU discovery entails setting the "don't fragment" (DF) bit in the IP header to discover if any router on the current path needs to fragment IP datagrams that we send. In Section 11.6 we showed the ICMP unreachable error returned by a router that is asked to forward an IP datagram with the DF bit set when the MTU is less than the datagram size. In Section 11.7 we showed a version of the `traceroute` program that used this mechanism to determine the path MTU to a destination. In Section 11.8 we saw how UDP handled path MTU discovery. In this section we'll examine how this mechanism is used by TCP, as specified by RFC 1191 [Mogul and Deering 1990].

> Of the various systems used in this text (see the Preface) only Solaris 2.x supports path MTU discovery.

TCP's path MTU discovery operates as follows. When a connection is established, TCP uses the minimum of the MTU of the outgoing interface, or the MSS announced by the other end, as the starting segment size. Path MTU discovery does not allow TCP to exceed the MSS announced by the other end. If the other end does not specify an MSS, it defaults to 536. It is also possible for an implementation to save path MTU information on a per-route basis, as we mentioned in Section 21.9.

Once the initial segment size is chosen, all IP datagrams sent by TCP on that connection have the DF bit set. If an intermediate router needs to fragment a datagram that has the DF bit set, it discards the datagram and generates the ICMP "can't fragment" error we described in Section 11.6.

If this ICMP error is received, TCP decreases the segment size and retransmits. If the router generated the newer form of this ICMP error, the segment size can be set to the next-hop MTU minus the sizes of the IP and TCP headers. If the older ICMP error is returned, the probable value of the next smallest MTU (Figure 2.5) must be tried. When a retransmission caused by this ICMP error occurs, the congestion window should not change, but slow start should be initiated.

Since routes can change dynamically, when some time has passed since the last decrease of the path MTU, a larger value (up to the minimum of the MSS announced by the other end, or the outgoing interface MTU) can be tried. RFC 1191 recommends this time interval be about 10 minutes. (We saw in Section 11.8 that Solaris 2.2 uses a 30-second timer for this.)

Given the normal default MSS of 536 for nonlocal destinations, path MTU discovery avoids fragmentation across intermediate links with an MTU of less than 576 (which is rare). It can also avoid fragmentation on local destinations when an intermediate link (e.g., an Ethernet) has a smaller MTU than the end-point networks (e.g., a token ring). But for path MTU discovery to be more useful, and take advantage of wide area networks with MTUs greater than 576, implementations must stop using a default MSS of 536 bytes for nonlocal destinations. A better choice for the MSS is the MTU of the outgoing interface (minus the size of the IP and TCP headers, of course). (In Appendix E we'll see that most implementations allow the system administrator to change this default MSS value.)

An Example

We can see how path MTU discovery operates when an intermediate router has an MTU less than either of the end point's interface MTUs. Figure 24.1 shows the topology for this example.

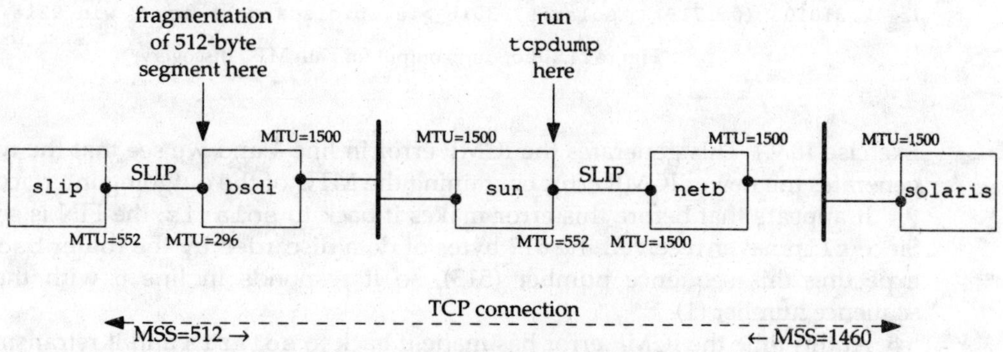

Figure 24.1 Topology for path MTU example.

We'll establish a connection from the host `solaris` (which supports the path MTU discovery mechanism) to the host `slip`. This setup is identical to the one used for our UDP path MTU discovery example (Figure 11.13) but here we have set the MTU of the interface on `slip` to 552, instead of its normal 296. This causes `slip` to announce an MSS of 512. But leaving the MTU of the SLIP link on `bsdi` at 296 will cause TCP segments greater than 256 to be fragmented, and we can see how the path MTU discovery mechanism on `solaris` handles this.

We'll run our `sock` program on `solaris` and perform one 512-byte write to the discard server on `slip`:

```
solaris % sock -i -n1 -w512 slip discard
```

Figure 24.2 shows the `tcpdump` output, collected on the SLIP interface on the host `sun`.

The MSS values in lines 1 and 2 are what we expect. We then see `solaris` send a 512-byte segment (line 3) containing the 512 bytes of data and the ACK of the SYN. (We saw this combination of the ACK of a SYN along with the first segment of data in

```
 1  0.0                  solaris.33016 > slip.discard: S 1171660288:1171660288(0)
                                                       win 8760 <mss 1460> (DF)
 2  0.101597 (0.1016)   slip.discard > solaris.33016: S 137984001:137984001(0)
                                                       ack 1171660289 win 4096
                                                       <mss 512>
 3  0.630609 (0.5290)   solaris.33016 > slip.discard: P 1:513(512)
                                                       ack 1 win 9216 (DF)
 4  0.634433 (0.0038)   bsdi > solaris: icmp:
                             slip unreachable - need to frag, mtu = 296 (DF)
 5  0.660331 (0.0259)   solaris.33016 > slip.discard: F 513:513(0)
                                                       ack 1 win 9216 (DF)
 6  0.752664 (0.0923)   slip.discard > solaris.33016: . ack 1 win 4096
 7  1.110342 (0.3577)   solaris.33016 > slip.discard: P 1:257(256)
                                                       ack 1 win 9216 (DF)
 8  1.439330 (0.3290)   slip.discard > solaris.33016: . ack 257 win 3840
 9  1.770154 (0.3308)   solaris.33016 > slip.discard: FP 257:513(256)
                                                        ack 1 win 9216 (DF)
10  2.095987 (0.3258)   slip.discard > solaris.33016: . ack 514 win 3840
11  2.138193 (0.0422)   slip.discard > solaris.33016: F 1:1(0) ack 514 win 4096
12  2.310103 (0.1719)   solaris.33016 > slip.discard: . ack 2 win 9216 (DF)
```

Figure 24.2 tcpdump output for path MTU discovery.

Exercise 18.9.) This generates the ICMP error in line 4 and we see that the router bsdi generates the newer ICMP error containing the MTU of the outgoing interface.

It appears that before this error makes it back to solaris, the FIN is sent (line 5). Since slip never received the 512 bytes of data discarded by the router bsdi, it is not expecting this sequence number (513), so it responds in line 6 with the expected sequence number (1).

At this time the ICMP error has made it back to solaris and it retransmits the 512 bytes of data in two 256-byte segments (lines 7 and 9). Both are sent with the DF bit set, since there could be another router beyond bsdi with a smaller MTU.

A longer transfer was run (taking about 15 minutes) and after moving from the 512-byte initial segment to 256-byte segments, solaris never tried the higher segment size again.

Big Packets or Small Packets?

Conventional wisdom says that bigger packets are better [Mogul 1993, Sec. 15.2.8] because sending fewer big packets "costs less" than sending more smaller packets. (This assumes the packets are not large enough to cause fragmentation, since that introduces another set of problems.) The reduced cost is that associated with the network (packet header overhead), routers (routing decisions), and hosts (protocol processing and device interrupts). Not everyone agrees with this [Bellovin 1993].

Consider the following example. We send 8192 bytes through four routers, each connected with a T1 telephone line (1,544,000 bits/sec). First we use two 4096-byte packets, as shown in Figure 24.3.

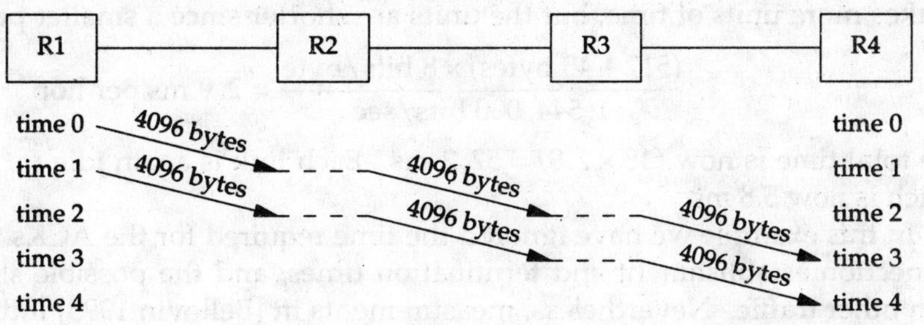

Figure 24.3 Sending two 4096-byte packets through four routers.

The basic problem is that routers are store-and-forward devices. They normally receive the entire input packet, validate the IP header including the IP checksum, make their routing decision, and start sending the output packet. In this figure we're assuming the ideal case where it takes no time for these operations to occur at the router (the horizontal dashed lines). Nevertheless, it takes four units of time to send all 8192 bytes from R1 to R4. The time for each hop is

$$\frac{(4096 + 40 \text{ bytes}) \times 8 \text{ bits/byte}}{1,544,000 \text{ bits/sec}} = 21.4 \text{ ms per hop}$$

(We account for the 40 bytes of IP and TCP header.) The total time to send the data is the number of packets plus the number of hops, minus one, which we can see visually in this example is four units of time, or 85.6 ms. Each link is idle for two units of time, or 42.8 ms.

Figure 24.4 shows what happens if we send sixteen 512-byte packets.

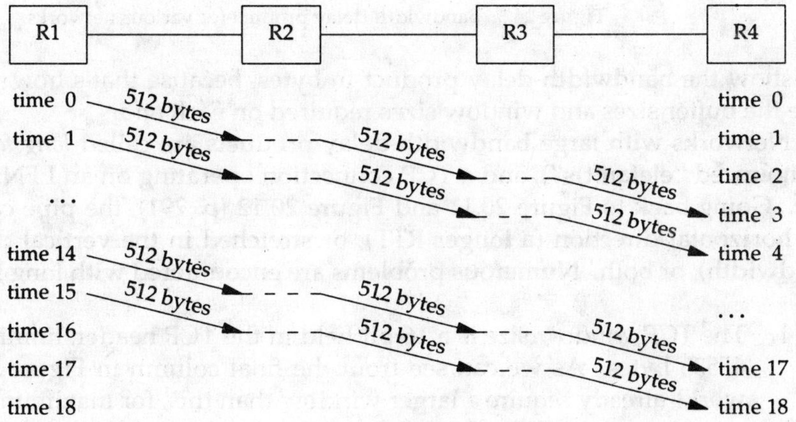

Figure 24.4 Sending sixteen 512-byte packets through four routers.

It takes more units of time, but the units are shorter since a smaller packet is being sent.

$$\frac{(512 + 40 \text{ bytes}) \times 8 \text{ bits/byte}}{1,544,000 \text{ bits/sec}} = 2.9 \text{ ms per hop}$$

The total time is now $(18 \times 2.9) = 52.2$ ms. Each link is again idle for two units of time, which is now 5.8 ms.

In this example we have ignored the time required for the ACKs to be returned, the connection establishment and termination times, and the possible sharing of the links with other traffic. Nevertheless, measurements in [Bellovin 1993] indicate that bigger is not always better. More research is required in this area on various networks.

24.3 Long Fat Pipes

In Section 20.7 we showed the capacity of a connection as

capacity (bits) = *bandwidth* (bits/sec) × *round-trip time* (sec)

and called this the *bandwidth-delay product*. This is also called the size of the pipe between the end points.

Existing limits in TCP are being encountered as this product increases to larger and larger values. Figure 24.5 shows some values for various types of networks.

Network	Bandwidth (bits/sec)	Round-trip time (ms)	Bandwidth-delay product (bytes)
Ethernet LAN	10,000,000	3	3,750
T1 telephone line, transcontinental	1,544,000	60	11,580
T1 telephone line, satellite	1,544,000	500	96,500
T3 telephone line, transcontinental	45,000,000	60	337,500
gigabit, transcontinental	1,000,000,000	60	7,500,000

Figure 24.5 Bandwidth-delay product for various networks.

We show the bandwidth-delay product in bytes, because that's how we typically measure the buffer sizes and window sizes required on each end.

Networks with large bandwidth-delay products are called *long fat networks* (LFNs, pronounced "elefan(t)s"), and a TCP connection operating on an LFN is called a *long fat pipe*. Going back to Figure 20.11 and Figure 20.12 (p. 291), the pipe can be stretched in the horizontal direction (a longer RTT), or stretched in the vertical direction (a higher bandwidth), or both. Numerous problems are encountered with long fat pipes.

1. The TCP window size is a 16-bit field in the TCP header, limiting the window to 65535 bytes. As we can see from the final column in Figure 24.5, existing networks already require a larger window than this, for maximum throughput.

   The window scale option described in Section 24.4 solves this problem.

2. Packet loss in an LFN can reduce throughput drastically. If only a single segment is lost, the fast retransmit and fast recovery algorithm that we described in

Section 21.7 is required to keep the pipe from draining. But even with this algorithm, the loss of more than one packet within a window typically causes the pipeline to drain. (If the pipe drains, slow start gets things going again, but that takes multiple round-trip times to get the pipe filled again.)

Selective acknowledgments (SACKs) were proposed in RFC 1072 [Jacobson and Braden 1988] to handle multiple dropped packets within a window. But this feature was omitted from RFC 1323, because the authors felt several technical problems needed to be worked out before including them in TCP.

3. We saw in Section 21.4 that many TCP implementations only measure one round-trip time per window. They do not measure the RTT of every segment. Better RTT measurements are required for operating on an LFN.

   The timestamp option, which we describe in Section 24.5, allows more segments to be timed, including retransmissions.

4. TCP identifies each byte of data with a 32-bit unsigned sequence number. What's to prevent a segment that gets delayed in the network from reappearing at a later time, after the connection that it was associated with has been terminated, and after a new connection has been established between the same two hosts and port numbers? First recall that the TTL field in the IP header puts an upper bound on the lifetime of any IP datagram—255 hops or 255 seconds, whichever comes first. In Section 18.6 we defined the maximum segment lifetime (MSL) as an implementation parameter used to prevent this scenario from happening. The recommended value of the MSL is 2 minutes (giving a 2MSL of 240 seconds), but we saw in Section 18.6 that many implementations use an MSL value of 30 seconds.

   A different problem with TCP's sequence numbers appears with LFNs. Since the sequence number space is finite, the same sequence number is reused after 4,294,967,296 bytes have been transmitted. What if a segment containing the byte with a sequence number N gets delayed in the network and then reappears later, while the connection is still up? This is only a problem if the same sequence number N is reused within the MSL period, that is, if the network is so fast that sequence number wrap occurs in less than MSL. On an Ethernet it takes almost 60 minutes to send this much data, so there is no chance of this happening, but the time required for the wrap to occur drops as the bandwidth increases: a T3 telephone line (45 Mbits/sec) wraps in 12 minutes, FDDI (100 Mbits/sec) in 5 minutes, and a gigabit network (1000 Mbits/sec) in 34 seconds. The problem here is not the bandwidth-delay product, but the bandwidth itself.

   In Section 24.6 we describe a way to handle this: the PAWS algorithm (protection against wrapped sequence numbers), which uses the TCP timestamp option.

4.4BSD contains all the options and algorithms that we describe in the following sections: the window scale option, the timestamp option, and the protection against wrapped sequence numbers. Numerous vendors are also starting to support these options.

Gigabit Networks

When networks reach gigabit speeds, things change. [Partridge 1994] covers gigabit networks in detail. Here we'll look at the differences between latency and bandwidth [Kleinrock 1992].

Consider sending a one million byte file across the United States, assuming a 30-ms latency. Figure 24.6 shows two scenarios, the top illustration uses a T1 telephone line (1,544,000 bits/sec) and the bottom uses a 1 gigabit/sec network. Time is shown along the x-axis, with the sender on the left and the receiver on the right, and capacity on the y-axis. The shaded area in both pictures is the one million bytes to send.

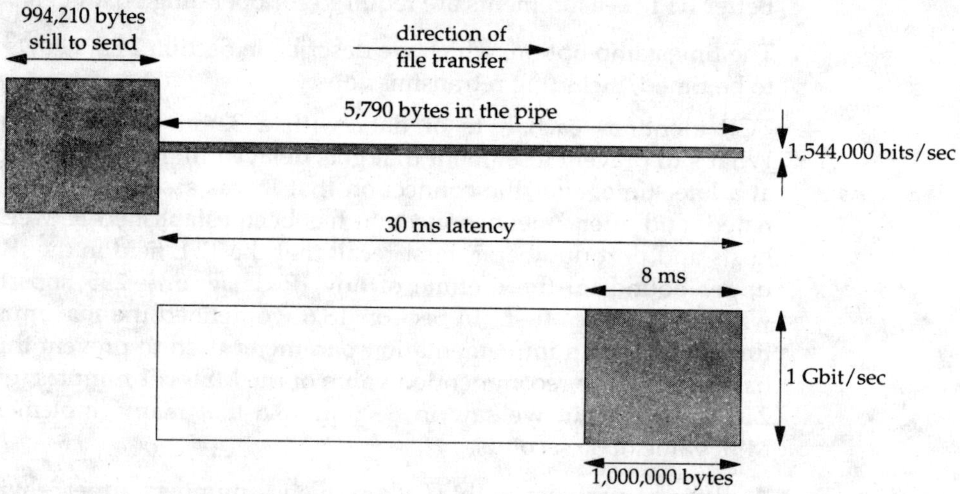

Figure 24.6 Sending a 1-Mbyte file across networks with a 30-ms latency.

Figure 24.6 shows the status of both networks after 30 ms. With both networks the first bit of data reaches the other end after 30 ms (the latency), but with the T1 network the capacity of the pipe is only 5,790 bytes, so 994,210 bytes are still at the sender, waiting to be sent. The capacity of the gigabit network, however, is 3,750,000 bytes, so the entire file uses just over 25% of the pipe. The last bit of the file reaches the receiver 8 ms after the first bit.

The total time to transfer the file across the T1 network is 5.211 seconds. If we throw more bandwidth at the problem, a T3 network (45,000,000 bits/sec), the total time decreases to 0.208 seconds. Increasing the bandwidth by a factor of 29 reduces the total time by a factor of 25.

With the gigabit network the total time to transfer the file is 0.038 seconds: the 30-ms latency plus the 8 ms for the actual file transfer. Assuming we could double the bandwidth to 2 gigabits/sec, we only reduce the total time to 0.034 seconds: the same 30-ms latency plus 4 ms to transfer the file. Doubling the bandwidth now decreases the total time by only 10%. At gigabit speeds we are latency limited, not bandwidth limited.

The latency is caused by the speed of light and can't be decreased (unless Einstein was wrong). The effect of this fixed latency becomes worse when we consider the packets required to establish and terminate a connection. Gigabit networks will cause several networking issues to be looked at differently.

24.4 Window Scale Option

The window scale option increases the definition of the TCP window from 16 to 32 bits. Instead of changing the TCP header to accommodate the larger window, the header still holds a 16-bit value, and an option is defined that applies a scaling operation to the 16-bit value. TCP then maintains the "real" window size internally as a 32-bit value.

We saw an example of this option in Figure 18.20 (p. 253). The 1-byte shift count is between 0 (no scaling performed) and 14. This maximum value of 14 is a window of 1,073,725,440 bytes (65535×2^{14}).

This option can only appear in a SYN segment; therefore the scale factor is fixed in each direction when the connection is established. To enable window scaling, both ends must send the option in their SYN segments. The end doing the active open sends the option in its SYN, but the end doing the passive open can send the option only if the received SYN specifies the option. The scale factor can be different in each direction.

If the end doing the active open sends a nonzero scale factor, but doesn't receive a window scale option from the other end, it sets its send and receive shift count to 0. This lets newer systems interoperate with older systems that don't understand the new option.

> The Host Requirements RFC requires TCP to accept an option in any segment. (The only previously defined option, the maximum segment size, only appeared in SYN segments.) It further requires TCP to ignore any option it doesn't understand. This is made easy since all the new options have a length field (Figure 18.20, p. 253).

Assume we are using the window scale option, with a shift count of *S* for sending and a shift count of *R* for receiving. Then every 16-bit advertised window that we receive from the other end is left shifted by *R* bits to obtain the real advertised window size. Every time we send a window advertisement to the other end, we take our real 32-bit window size and right shift it *S* bits, placing the resulting 16-bit value in the TCP header.

The shift count is automatically chosen by TCP, based on the size of the receive buffer. The size of this buffer is set by the system, but the capability is normally provided for the application to change it. (We discussed this buffer in Section 20.4.)

An Example

If we initiate a connection using our `sock` program from the 4.4BSD host `vangogh.cs.berkeley.edu`, we can see its TCP calculate the window scale factor. The following interactive output shows two consecutive runs of the program, first specifying a receive buffer of 128000 bytes, and then a receive buffer of 220000 bytes:

```
vangogh % sock -v -R128000 bsdi.tuc.noao.edu echo
SO_RCVBUF = 128000
connected on 128.32.130.2.4107 to 140.252.13.35.7
TCP_MAXSEG = 512
hello, world                                    we type this line
hello, world                                    and it's echoed here
^D                                              type end-of-file character to terminate

vangogh % sock -v -R220000 bsdi.tuc.noao.edu echo
SO_RCVBUF = 220000
connected on 128.32.130.2.4108 to 140.252.13.35.7
TCP_MAXSEG = 512
bye, bye                                        type this line
bye, bye                                        and it's echoed here
^D                                              type end-of-file character to terminate
```

Figure 24.7 shows the `tcpdump` output for these two connections. (We have deleted the final 8 lines for the second connection, because nothing new is shown.)

```
 1  0.0                 vangogh.4107 > bsdi.echo: S 462402561:462402561(0)
                          win 65535
                          <mss 512,nop,wscale 1,nop,nop,timestamp 995351 0>
 2  0.003078 ( 0.0031)  bsdi.echo > vangogh.4107: S 177032705:177032705(0)
                          ack 462402562 win 4096 <mss 512>
 3  0.300255 ( 0.2972)  vangogh.4107 > bsdi.echo: . ack 1 win 65535

 4  16.920087 (16.6198) vangogh.4107 > bsdi.echo: P 1:14(13) ack 1 win 65535
 5  16.923063 ( 0.0030) bsdi.echo > vangogh.4107: P 1:14(13) ack 14 win 4096
 6  17.220114 ( 0.2971) vangogh.4107 > bsdi.echo: . ack 14 win 65535

 7  26.640335 ( 9.4202) vangogh.4107 > bsdi.echo: F 14:14(0) ack 14 win 65535
 8  26.642688 ( 0.0024) bsdi.echo > vangogh.4107: . ack 15 win 4096
 9  26.643964 ( 0.0013) bsdi.echo > vangogh.4107: F 14:14(0) ack 15 win 4096
10  26.880274 ( 0.2363) vangogh.4107 > bsdi.echo: . ack 15 win 65535

11  44.400239 (17.5200) vangogh.4108 > bsdi.echo: S 468226561:468226561(0)
                          win 65535
                          <mss 512,nop,wscale 2,nop,nop,timestamp 995440 0>
12  44.403358 ( 0.0031) bsdi.echo > vangogh.4108: S 182792705:182792705(0)
                          ack 468226562 win 4096 <mss 512>
13  44.700027 ( 0.2967) vangogh.4108 > bsdi.echo: . ack 1 win 65535

                        remainder of this connection deleted
```

Figure 24.7 Example of window scale option.

In line 1 vangogh advertises a window of 65535 and specifies the window scale option with a shift count of 1. This advertised window is the largest possible value that is less than the receive buffer size (128000), because the window field in a SYN segment is never scaled.

The scale factor of 1 means vangogh would like to send window advertisements up to 131070 (65535×2^1). This will accommodate our receive buffer size (128000). Since `bsdi` does not send the window scale option in its SYN (line 2), the option is not used.

Notice that vangogh continues to use the largest window possible (65535) for the remainder of the connection.

For the second connection vangogh requests a shift count of 2, meaning it would like to send window advertisements up to 262140 (65535×2^2), which is greater than our receive buffer size (220000).

24.5 Timestamp Option

The timestamp option lets the sender place a timestamp value in every segment. The receiver reflects this value in the acknowledgment, allowing the sender to calculate an RTT for each received ACK. (We must say "each received ACK" and not "each segment" since TCP normally acknowledges multiple segments per ACK.) We said that many current implementations only measure one RTT per window, which is OK for windows containing eight segments. Larger window sizes, however, require better RTT calculations.

> Section 3.1 of RFC 1323 gives the signal processing reasons for requiring better RTT estimates for bigger windows. Basically the RTT is measured by sampling a data signal (the data segments) at a lower frequency (once per window). This introduces *aliasing* into the estimated RTT. When there are eight segments per window, the sample rate is one-eighth the data rate, which is tolerable, but with 100 segments per window, the sample rate is 1/100th the data rate. This can cause the estimated RTT to be inaccurate, resulting in unnecessary retransmissions. If a segment is lost, it only gets worse.

Figure 18.20 showed the format of the timestamp option. The sender places a 32-bit value in the first field, and the receiver echoes this back in the reply field. TCP headers containing this option will increase from the normal 20 bytes to 32 bytes.

The timestamp is a monotonically increasing value. Since the receiver echoes what it receives, the receiver doesn't care what the timestamp units are. This option does not require any form of clock synchronization between the two hosts. RFC 1323 recommends that the timestamp value increment by one between 1 ms and 1 second.

> 4.4BSD increments the timestamp clock once every 500 ms and this timestamp clock is reset to 0 on a reboot.
>
> In Figure 24.7, if we look at the timestamp in segment 1 and the timestamp in segment 11, the difference (89 units) corresponds to 500 ms per unit for the time difference of 44.4 seconds.

The specification of this option during connection establishment is handled the same way as the window scale option in the previous section. The end doing the active open specifies the option in its SYN. Only if it receives the option in the SYN from the other end can the option be sent in future segments.

We've seen that a receiving TCP does not have to acknowledge every data segment that it receives. Many implementations send an ACK for every other data segment. If the receiver sends an ACK that acknowledges two received data segments, which received timestamp is sent back in the timestamp echo reply field?

To minimize the amount of state maintained by either end, only a single timestamp value is kept per connection. The algorithm to choose when to update this value is simple.

1. TCP keeps track of the timestamp value to send in the next ACK (a variable named *tsrecent*) and the acknowledgment sequence number from the last ACK that was sent (a variable named *lastack*). This sequence number is the next sequence number the receiver is expecting.
2. When a segment arrives, if the segment contains the byte numbered *lastack*, then the timestamp value from the segment is saved in *tsrecent*.
3. Whenever a timestamp option is sent, *tsrecent* is sent as the timestamp echo reply field and the sequence number field is saved in *lastack*.

This algorithm handles the following two cases:

1. If ACKs are delayed by the receiver, the timestamp value returned as the echo value will correspond to the earliest segment being acknowledged.

   For example, if two segments containing bytes 1–1024 and 1025–2048 arrive, both with a timestamp option, and the receiver acknowledges them both with an ACK 2049, the timestamp in the ACK will be the value from the first segment containing bytes 1–1024. This is correct because the sender must calculate its retransmission timeout taking the delayed ACKs into consideration.
2. If a received segment is in-window but out-of-sequence, implying that a previous segment has been lost, when that missing segment is received, its timestamp will be echoed, not the timestamp from the out-of-sequence segment.

   For example, assume three segments, each containing 1024 bytes, are received in the following order: segment 1 with bytes 1–1024, segment 3 with bytes 2049–3072, then segment 2 with bytes 1025–2048. The ACKs sent back will be ACK 1025 with the timestamp from segment 1 (a normal ACK for data that was expected), ACK 1025 with the timestamp from segment 1 (a duplicate ACK in response to the in-window but the out-of-sequence segment), then ACK 3073 with the timestamp from segment 2 (not the later timestamp from segment 3). This has the effect of overestimating the RTT when segments are lost, which is better than underestimating it. Also, if the final ACK contained the timestamp from segment 3, it might include the time required for the duplicate ACK to be returned and segment 2 to be retransmitted, or it might include the time for the sender's retransmission timeout for segment 2 to expire. In either case, echoing the timestamp from segment 3 could bias the sender's RTT calculations.

Although the timestamp option allows for better RTT calculations, it also provides a way for the receiver to avoid receiving old segments and considering them part of the existing data segment. The next section describes this.

24.6 PAWS: Protection Against Wrapped Sequence Numbers

Consider a TCP connection using the window scale option with the largest possible window, 1 gigabyte (2^{30}). (The largest window is just smaller than this, 65535×2^{14}, not $2^{16} \times 2^{14}$, but that doesn't affect this discussion.) Also assume the timestamp option is being used and that the timestamp value assigned by the sender increments by one for each window that is sent. (This is conservative. Normally the timestamp increments faster than this.) Figure 24.8 shows the possible data flow between the two hosts, when transferring 6 gigabytes. To avoid lots of 10-digit numbers, we use the notation G to mean a multiple of 1,073,741,824. We also use the notation from `tcpdump` that *J*:*K* means byte *J* through and including byte *K*–1.

Time	Bytes sent	Send sequence#	Send timestamp	Receive
A	0G:1G	0G:1G	1	OK
B	1G:2G	1G:2G	2	OK but one segment lost and retransmitted
C	2G:3G	2G:3G	3	OK
D	3G:4G	3G:4G	4	OK
E	4G:5G	0G:1G	5	OK
F	5G:6G	1G:2G	6	OK but lost segment reappears

Figure 24.8 Transferring 6 gigabytes in six 1-gigabyte windows.

The 32-bit sequence number wraps between times D and E. We assume that one segment gets lost at time B and is retransmitted. We also assume that this lost segment reappears at time F.

This assumes that the time difference between the segment getting lost and reappearing is less than the MSL; otherwise the segment would have been discarded by some router when its TTL expired. As we mentioned earlier, it is only with high-speed connections that this problem appears, where old segments can reappear and contain sequence numbers currently being transmitted.

We can also see from Figure 24.8 that using the timestamp prevents this problem. The receiver considers the timestamp as a 32-bit extension of the sequence number. Since the lost segment that reappears at time F has a timestamp of 2, which is less than the most recent valid timestamp (5 or 6), it is discarded by the PAWS algorithm.

The PAWS algorithm does not require any form of time synchronization between the sender and receiver. All the receiver needs is for the timestamp values to be monotonically increasing, and to increase by at least one per window.

24.7 T/TCP: A TCP Extension for Transactions

TCP provides a *virtual-circuit* transport service. There are three distinct phases in the life of a connection: establishment, data transfer, and termination. Applications such as remote login and file transfer are well suited to a virtual-circuit service.

Other applications, however, are designed to use a transaction service. A *transaction* is a client request followed by a server response with the following characteristics:

1. The overhead of connection establishment and connection termination should be avoided. When possible, send one request packet and receive one reply packet.
2. The latency should be reduced to RTT plus SPT, where RTT is the round-trip time and SPT is the server processing time to handle the request.
3. The server should detect duplicate requests and not replay the transaction when a duplicate request arrives. (Avoiding the replay means the server does not process the request again. The server sends back the saved reply corresponding to that request.)

One application that we've already seen that uses this type of service is the Domain Name System (Chapter 14), although the DNS is not concerned with the server replaying duplicate requests.

Today the choice an application designer has is TCP or UDP. TCP provides too many features for transactions, and UDP doesn't provide enough. Usually the application is built using UDP (to avoid the overhead of TCP connections) but many of the desirable features (dynamic timeout and retransmission, congestion avoidance, etc.) are placed into the application, where they're reinvented over and over again.

A better solution is to provide a transport layer that provides efficient handling of transactions. The transaction protocol we describe in this section is called T/TCP. Our description is from its definition, RFC 1379 [Braden 1992b] and [Braden 1992c].

Most TCPs require 7 segments to open and close a connection (see Figure 18.13, p. 242). Three more segments are then added: one with the request, another with the reply and an ACK of the request, and a third with the ACK of the reply. If additional control bits are added onto the segments—that is, the first segment contains a SYN, the client request, and a FIN—the client still sees a minimal overhead of twice the RTT plus SPT. (Sending a SYN along with data and a FIN is legal; whether current TCPs handle it correctly is another question.)

Another problem with TCP is the TIME_WAIT state and its required 2MSL wait. As shown in Exercise 18.14, this limits the transaction rate between two hosts to about 268 per second.

The two modifications required for TCP to handle transactions are to avoid the three-way handshake and shorten the TIME_WAIT state. T/TCP avoids the three-way handshake by using an accelerated open:

1. It assigns a 32-bit *connection count* (CC) value to connections it opens, either actively or passively. A host's CC value is assigned from a global counter that gets incremented by 1 each time it's used.
2. Every segment between two hosts using T/TCP includes a new TCP option named CC. This option has a length of 6 bytes and contains the sender's 32-bit CC value for the connection.

3. A host maintains a per-host cache of the last CC value received in an acceptable SYN segment from that host.
4. When a CC option is received on an initial SYN, the receiver compares the value with the cached value for the sender. If the received CC is greater than the cached CC, the SYN is new and any data in the segment is passed to the receiving application (the server). The connection is called *half-synchronized*.

   If the received CC is not greater than the cached CC, or if the receiving host doesn't have a cached CC for this client, the normal TCP three-way handshake is performed.
5. The SYN, ACK segment in response to an initial SYN echoes the received CC value in another new option named CCECHO.
6. The CC value in a non-SYN segment detects and rejects any duplicate segments from previous incarnations of the same connection.

The accelerated open avoids the need for a three-way handshake unless either the client or server has crashed and rebooted. The cost is that the server must remember the last CC received from each client.

The TIME_WAIT state is shortened by calculating the TIME_WAIT delay dynamically, based on the measured RTT between the two hosts. The TIME_WAIT delay is set to 8 times *RTO*, the retransmission timeout value (Section 21.3).

Using these features the minimal transaction sequence is an exchange of three segments:

1. Client to server, caused by an active open: client-SYN, client-data (the request), client-FIN, and client-CC.

   When the server TCP with the passive open receives this segment, if the client-CC is greater than the cached CC for this client host, the client-data is passed to the server application, which processes the request.
2. Server to client: server-SYN, server-data (reply), server-FIN, ACK of client-FIN, server-CC, and CCECHO of client-CC. Since TCP acknowledgments are cumulative, this ACK of the client FIN acknowledges the client's SYN, data, and FIN.

   When the client TCP receives this segment it passes the reply to the client application.
3. Client to server: ACK of server-FIN, which acknowledges the server's SYN, data, and FIN.

The client's response time to its request is RTT plus SPT.

There are many fine points to the implementation of this TCP option that are covered in the references. We summarize them here:

- The server's SYN, ACK (the second segment) should be delayed, to allow the reply to piggyback with it. (Normally the ACK of a SYN is not delayed.) It can't delay too long, or the client will time out and retransmit.

- The request can require multiple segments, but the server must handle their possible out-of-order arrival. (Normally when data arrives before the SYN, the data is discarded and a reset is generated. With T/TCP this out-of-order data should be queued instead.)
- The API must allow the server process to send data and close the connection in a single operation to allow the FIN in the second segment to piggyback with the reply. (Normally the application would write the reply, causing a data segment to be sent, and then close the connection, causing the FIN to be sent.)
- The client is sending data in the first segment before receiving an MSS announcement from the server. To avoid restricting the client to an MSS of 536, the MSS for a given host should be cached along with its CC value.
- The client is also sending data to the server without receiving a window advertisement from the server. T/TCP suggests a default window of 4096 bytes and also caching the congestion threshold for the server.
- With the minimal three-segment exchange there is only one RTT that can be measured in each direction. Plus the client's measured RTT includes the server's processing time. This means the smoothed RTT value and its variance also must be cached for the server, similar to what we described in Section 21.9.

The appealing feature of T/TCP is that it is a minimal set of changes to an existing protocol but allows backward compatibility with existing implementations. It also takes advantage of existing engineering features of TCP (dynamic timeout and retransmission, congestion avoidance, etc.) instead of forcing the application to deal with these issues.

An alternative transaction protocol is VMTP, the Versatile Message Transaction Protocol. It is described in RFC 1045 [Cheriton 1988]. Unlike T/TCP, which is a small set of extensions to an existing protocol, VMTP is a complete transport layer that uses IP. VMTP handles error detection, retransmission, and duplicate suppression. It also supports multicast communication.

24.8 TCP Performance

Published numbers in the mid-1980s showed TCP throughput on an Ethernet to be around 100,000 to 200,000 bytes per second. (Section 17.5 of [Stevens 1990] gives these references.) A lot has changed since then. It is now common for off-the-shelf hardware (workstations and faster personal computers) to deliver 800,000 bytes or more per second.

It is a worthwhile exercise to calculate the theoretical maximum throughput we could see with TCP on a 10 Mbits/sec Ethernet [Warnock 1991]. We show the basics for this calculation in Figure 24.9. This figure shows the total number of bytes exchanged for a full-sized data segment and an ACK.

Field	Data #bytes	ACK #bytes
Ethernet preamble	8	8
Ethernet destination address	6	6
Ethernet source address	6	6
Ethernet type field	2	2
IP header	20	20
TCP header	20	20
user data	1460	0
pad (to Ethernet minimum)	0	6
Ethernet CRC	4	4
interpacket gap (9.6 microsec)	12	12
total	1538	84

Figure 24.9 Field sizes for Ethernet theoretical maximum throughput calculation.

We must account for all the overhead: the preamble, the PAD bytes that are added to the acknowledgment, the CRC, and the minimum interpacket gap (9.6 microseconds, which equals 12 bytes at 10 Mbits/sec).

We first assume the sender transmits two back-to-back full-sized data segments, and then the receiver sends an ACK for these two segments. The maximum throughput (user data) is then

$$\textit{throughput} = \frac{2 \times 1460 \text{ bytes}}{2 \times 1538 + 84 \text{ bytes}} \times \frac{10,000,000 \text{ bits/sec}}{8 \text{ bits/byte}} = 1,155,063 \text{ bytes/sec}$$

If the TCP window is opened to its maximum size (65535, not using the window scale option), this allows a window of 44 1460-byte segments. If the receiver sends an ACK every 22nd segment the calculation becomes

$$\textit{throughput} = \frac{22 \times 1460 \text{ bytes}}{22 \times 1538 + 84 \text{ bytes}} \times \frac{10,000,000 \text{ bits/sec}}{8 \text{ bits/byte}} = 1,183,667 \text{ bytes/sec}$$

This is the theoretical limit, and makes certain assumptions: an ACK sent by the receiver doesn't collide on the Ethernet with one of the sender's segments; the sender can transmit two segments with the minimum Ethernet spacing; and the receiver can generate the ACK within the minimum Ethernet spacing. Despite the optimism in these numbers, [Warnock 1991] measured a sustained rate of 1,075,000 bytes/sec on an Ethernet, with a standard multiuser workstation (albeit a fast workstation), which is 90% of the theoretical value.

Moving to faster networks, such as FDDI (100 Mbits/sec), [Schryver 1993] indicates that three commercial vendors have demonstrated TCP over FDDI between 80 and 98 Mbits/sec. When even greater bandwidth is available, [Borman 1992] reports up to 781 Mbits/sec between two Cray Y-MP computers over an 800 Mbits/sec HIPPI channel, and 907 Mbits/sec between two processes using the loopback interface on a Cray Y-MP.

The following practical limits apply for any real-world scenario [Borman 1991].

1. You can't run any faster than the speed of the slowest link.
2. You can't go any faster than the memory bandwidth of the slowest machine. This assumes your implementation makes a single pass over the data. If not (i.e., your implementation makes one pass over the data to copy it from user space into the kernel, then another pass over the data to calculate the TCP checksum), you'll run even slower. [Dalton et al. 1993] describe performance improvements to the standard Berkeley sources that reduce the number of data copies to one. [Partridge and Pink 1993] applied the same "copy-and-checksum" change to UDP, along with other performance improvements, and improved UDP performance by about 30%.
3. You can't go any faster than the window size offered by the receiver, divided by the round-trip time. (This is our bandwidth-delay product equation, using the window size as the bandwidth-delay product, and solving for the bandwidth.) If we use the maximum window scale factor of 14 from Section 24.4, we have a window size of 1 Gbyte, so this divided by the RTT is the bandwidth limit.

The bottom line in all these numbers is that the real upper limit on how fast TCP can run is determined by the size of the TCP window and the speed of light. As concluded by [Partridge and Pink 1993], many protocol performance problems are implementation deficiencies rather than inherent protocol limits.

24.9 Summary

This chapter has looked at five new TCP features: path MTU discovery, window scale option, timestamp option, protection against wrapped sequence numbers, and improved transactional processing using TCP. We saw that the middle three features are required for optimal performance on long fat pipes—networks with a large bandwidth-delay product.

Path MTU discovery allows TCP to use windows larger than the default of 536 for nonlocal connections, when the path MTU is larger. This can improve performance.

The window scale option takes the maximum TCP window size from 65535 bytes to just over 1 gigabyte. The timestamp option lets more segments be accurately timed, and also lets the receiver provide protection against wrapped sequence numbers (PAWS). This is essential for high-speed connections. These new TCP options are negotiated at connection establishment, and ignored by older systems that don't understand them, allowing newer systems to interoperate with older systems.

The TCP extensions for transactions, T/TCP, allow a client–server request–reply sequence to be completed using only three segments in the usual case. It avoids the three-way handshake and shortens the TIME_WAIT state by caching a small amount of information for each host with which it has established a connection. It also overloads the data segments with the SYN and FIN flags.

We finished the chapter with a look at TCP performance, since there is still much inaccurate folklore about how fast TCP can run. For a well-tuned implementation using the newer features described in this chapter, TCP performance is limited only by the maximum 1-gigabyte window and the speed of light (i.e., the round-trip time).

Exercises

24.1 What does it mean when a system sends an initial SYN segment with a window scale factor of 0?

24.2 If the host `bsdi` in Figure 24.7 supported the window scale option, what is the expected value of the 16-bit window size field in the TCP header from `vangogh` in segment 3? Similarly, if the option were in use for the second connection in that figure, what would be the advertised window in segment 13?

24.3 Instead of fixing the window scale factor when the connection is established, could the window scale option have been defined to also appear when the scaling factor changes?

24.4 At what data rate does sequence number wrap become a problem, assuming an MSL of 2 minutes?

24.5 PAWS is defined to operate within a single connection only. What modifications would have to be made to TCP to use PAWS as a replacement for the 2MSL wait (the TIME_WAIT state)?

24.6 In our example at the end of Section 24.4, why did our `sock` program output the size of the receive buffer before the line that followed (with the IP addresses and port numbers)?

24.7 Redo the calculations of the *throughput* in Section 24.8 assuming an MSS of 1024.

24.8 How does the timestamp option affect Karn's algorithm (Section 21.3)?

24.9 If TCP sends data with the SYN segment that's generated by an active open (without using the extensions we described in Section 24.7), what does the receiving TCP do with the data?

24.10 In Section 24.7 we said that without the T/TCP extensions, even if the active open is sent with data and a FIN, the client delay in receiving the server's response is still twice the RTT plus SPT. Show the segments to account for this.

24.11 Redo Exercise 18.14 assuming T/TCP support and the minimum *RTO* supported by Berkeley-derived systems of one-half second.

24.12 If we implement T/TCP and measure the transaction time between two hosts, what can we compare it to, to determine its efficiency?

25

SNMP: Simple Network Management Protocol

25.1 Introduction

As the number of networks within an organization grows, along with the diversity of systems comprising this internet (routers from various vendors, hosts with embedded router functionality, terminal servers, etc.), managing all these systems within a coherent framework becomes important. This chapter looks at the standards used within the Internet protocol suite for network management.

Network management of a TCP/IP internet consists of *network management stations* (managers) communicating with *network elements*. The network elements can be anything that runs the TCP/IP protocol suite: hosts, routers, X terminals, terminal servers, printers, and so on. The software in the network element that runs the management software is called the *agent*. Management stations are normally workstations with color monitors that graphically display relevant facts about the elements being monitored (which links are up and down, volume of traffic across various links over time, etc.).

The communication can be two way: the manager asking the agent for a specific value ("how many ICMP port unreachables have you generated?"), or the agent telling the manager that something important happened ("an attached interface has gone down"). Also, the manager should be able to set variables in the agent ("change the value of the default IP TTL to 64"), in addition to reading variables from the agent.

TCP/IP network management consists of three pieces.

1. A *Management Information Base* (MIB) that specifies what variables the network elements maintain (the information that can be queried and set by the manager). RFC 1213 [McCloghrie and Rose 1991] defines the second version of this, called MIB-II.

2. A set of common structures and an identification scheme used to reference the variables in the MIB. This is called the *Structure of Management Information* (SMI) and is specified in RFC 1155 [Rose and McCloghrie 1990]. For example, the SMI specifies that a `Counter` is a nonnegative integer that counts from 0 through 4,294,967,295 and then wraps around to 0.
3. The protocol between the manager and the element, called the *Simple Network Management Protocol* (SNMP). RFC 1157 [Case et al. 1990] specifies the protocol. This details the format of the packets exchanged. Although a wide variety of transport protocols could be used, UDP is normally used with SNMP.

These RFCs define what is now called SNMPv1, or just SNMP, which is the topic of this chapter. During 1993 additional RFCs were published specifying SNMP Version 2 (SNMPv2), which we describe in Section 25.12.

Our approach to SNMP in this chapter is to describe the protocol between the manager and the agent first, and then look at the data types for the variables maintained by the agent. We describe the database of information maintained by the agent (the MIB), looking at the groups that we've described in this text: IP, UDP, TCP, and so on. We show examples at each point along the way, tying network management back to the protocol concepts from earlier chapters.

25.2 Protocol

SNMP defines only five types of messages that are exchanged between the manager and agent.

1. Fetch the value of one or more variables: the `get-request` operator.
2. Fetch the next variable after one or more specified variables: the `get-next-request` operator. (We describe what we mean by "next" later in this chapter.)
3. Set the value of one or more variables: the `set-request` operator.
4. Return the value of one or more variables: the `get-response` operator. This is the message returned by the agent to the manager in response to the `get-request`, `get-next-request`, and `set-request` operators.
5. Notify the manager when something happens on the agent: the `trap` operator.

The first three messages are sent from the manager to the agent, and the last two are from the agent to the manager. (We'll refer to the first three as the `get`, `get-next`, and `set` operators.) Figure 25.1 summarizes these five operators.

Since four of the five SNMP messages are simple request–reply protocols (the manager sends a request, the agent sends back a reply) SNMP uses UDP. This means that a request from the manager may not arrive at the agent, and the agent's reply may not make it back to the manager. The manager probably wants to implement a timeout and retransmission.

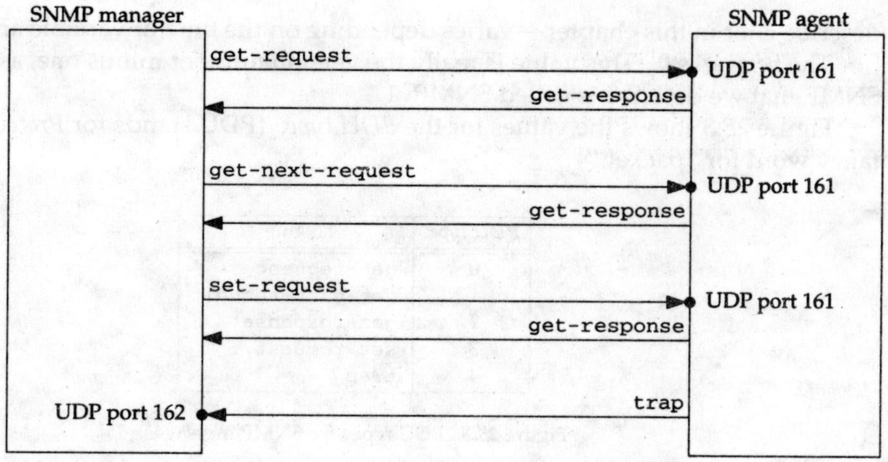

Figure 25.1 Summary of the five SNMP operators.

The manager sends its three requests to UDP port 161. The agent sends traps to UDP port 162. By using two different port numbers, a single system can easily run both a manager and an agent. (See Exercise 25.1.)

Figure 25.2 shows the format of the five SNMP messages, encapsulated in a UDP datagram.

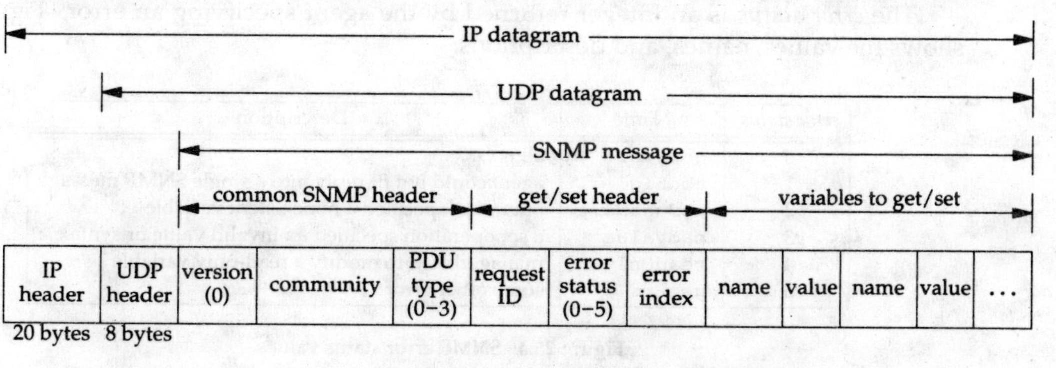

Figure 25.2 Format of the five SNMP messages.

In this figure we specify the size in bytes of the IP and UDP headers only. This is because the encoding used for the SNMP message—called ASN.1 and BER, which we describe later in this chapter—varies depending on the type of variable and its value.

The *version* is 0. This value is really the version number minus one, as the version of SNMP that we describe is called SNMPv1.

Figure 25.3 shows the values for the *PDU type*. (PDU stands for *Protocol Data Unit*, a fancy word for "packet.")

PDU type	Name
0	`get-request`
1	`get-next-request`
2	`get-response`
3	`set-request`
4	`trap`

Figure 25.3 PDU types for SNMP messages.

The *community* is a character string that is a cleartext password between the manager and agent. A common value is the 6-character string `public`.

For the `get`, `get-next`, and `set` operators, the *request ID* is set by the manager, and returned by the agent in the `get-response` message. We've seen this type of variable with other UDP applications. (Recall the DNS *identification* field in Figure 14.3, and the *transaction ID* field in Figure 16.2.) It lets the client (the manager in this case) match the responses from the server (the agent) to the queries that the client issued. This field also allows the manager to issue multiple requests to one or more agents, and then be able to sort out the returned replies.

The *error status* is an integer returned by the agent specifying an error. Figure 25.4 shows the values, names, and descriptions.

error status	Name	Description
0	`noError`	all is OK
1	`tooBig`	agent could not fit reply into a single SNMP message
2	`noSuchName`	operation specified a nonexistent variable
3	`badValue`	a set operation specified an invalid value or syntax
4	`readOnly`	manager tried to modify a read-only variable
5	`genErr`	some other error

Figure 25.4 SNMP error status values.

If an error occurred, the *error index* is an integer offset specifying which variable was in error. It is set by the agent only for the `noSuchName`, `badValue`, and `readOnly` errors.

A list of variable names and values follows in the `get`, `get-next`, and `set` requests. The value portion is ignored for the `get` and `get-next` operators.

For the `trap` operator (a *PDU type* of 4), the format of the SNMP message changes. We describe the fields in the trap header when we describe this operator in Section 25.10.

25.3 Structure of Management Information

SNMP uses only a few different types of data. In this section we'll look at those data types, without worrying about how the data is actually encoded (that is, the bit pattern used to store the data).

- `INTEGER`. Some variables are declared as an integer with no restrictions (e.g., the MTU of an interface), some are defined as taking on specific values (e.g., the IP forwarding flag is 1 if forwarding is enabled or 2 if forwarding is disabled), and others are defined with a minimum and maximum value (e.g., UDP and TCP port numbers are between 0 and 65535).
- `OCTET STRING`. A string of 0 or more 8-bit bytes. Each byte has a value between 0 and 255. In the BER encoding used for this data type and the next, a count of the number of bytes in the string precedes the string. These strings are not null-terminated strings.
- `DisplayString`. A string of 0 or more 8-bit bytes, but each byte must be a character from the NVT ASCII set (Section 26.4). All variables of this type in the MIB-II must contain no more than 255 characters. (A 0-length string is OK.)
- `OBJECT IDENTIFIER`. We describe these in the next section.
- `NULL`. This indicates that the corresponding variable has no value. It is used, for example, as the value of all the variables in a `get` or `get-next` request, since the values are being queried, not set.
- `IpAddress`. An `OCTET STRING` of length 4, with 1 byte for each byte of the IP address.
- `PhysAddress`. An `OCTET STRING` specifying a physical address (e.g., a 6-byte Ethernet address).
- `Counter`. A nonnegative integer whose value increases monotonically from 0 to $2^{32} - 1$ (4,294,967,295), and then wraps back to 0.
- `Gauge`. A nonnegative integer between 0 and $2^{32} - 1$, whose value can increase or decrease, but latches at its maximum value. That is, if the value increments to $2^{32} - 1$, it stays there until reset. The MIB variable `tcpCurrEstab` is an example: it is the number of TCP connections currently in the ESTABLISHED or CLOSE_WAIT state.
- `TimeTicks`. A counter that counts the time in hundredths of a second since some epoch. Different variables can specify this counter from a different epoch, so the epoch used for each variable of this type is specified when the variable is declared in the MIB. For example, the variable `sysUpTime` is the number of hundredths of a second that the agent has been up.
- `SEQUENCE`. This is similar to a structure in the C programming language. For example, we'll see that the MIB defines a `SEQUENCE` named `UdpEntry` containing information about an agent's active UDP end points. (By "active" we mean ports currently in use by an application.) Two entries are in the structure:

1. `udpLocalAddress`, of type `IpAddress`, containing the local IP address.
2. `udpLocalPort`, of type `INTEGER`, in the range 0 through 65535, specifying the local port number.

- `SEQUENCE OF`. This is the definition of a vector, with all elements having the same data type. If each element has a simple data type, such as an integer, then we have a simple vector (a one-dimensional array). But we'll see that SNMP uses this data type with each element of the vector being a `SEQUENCE` (structure). We can then think of it as a two-dimensional array or table.

  For example, the UDP listener table is named `udpTable` and it is a `SEQUENCE OF` the 2-element `SEQUENCE` (structure) `UdpEntry` that we just described. Figure 25.5 shows this two-dimensional array.

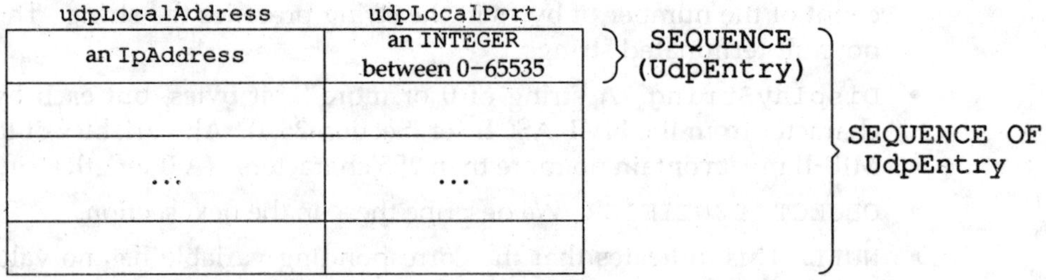

Figure 25.5 UDP listener table (`udpTable`) as a two-dimensional array in SNMP.

The number of rows in these tables is not specified by SNMP, but we'll see that a manager using the `get-next` operator (Section 25.7) can determine when the final row of a table has been returned. Also, in Section 25.6 we'll see how the manager specifies which row of a table it wants to get or set.

25.4 Object Identifiers

An *object identifier* is a data type specifying an authoritatively named object. By "authoritative" we mean that these identifiers are not assigned randomly, but are allocated by some organization that has responsibility for a group of identifiers.

An object identifier is a sequence of integers separated by decimal points. These integers traverse a tree structure, similar to the DNS (Figure 14.1) or a Unix filesystem. There is an unnamed root at the top of the tree where the object identifiers start. (This is the same direction of tree traversal that's used with a Unix filesystem.)

Figure 25.6 shows the structure of this tree when used with SNMP. All variables in the MIB start with the object identifier 1.3.6.1.2.1.

Each node in the tree is also given a textual name. The name corresponding to the object identifier 1.3.6.1.2.1 is `iso.org.dod.internet.mgmt.mib`. These names are for human readability. The *names* of the MIB variables that are in the packets exchanged between the manager and agent (Figure 25.2) are the numeric object identifiers, all of which begin with 1.3.6.1.2.1.

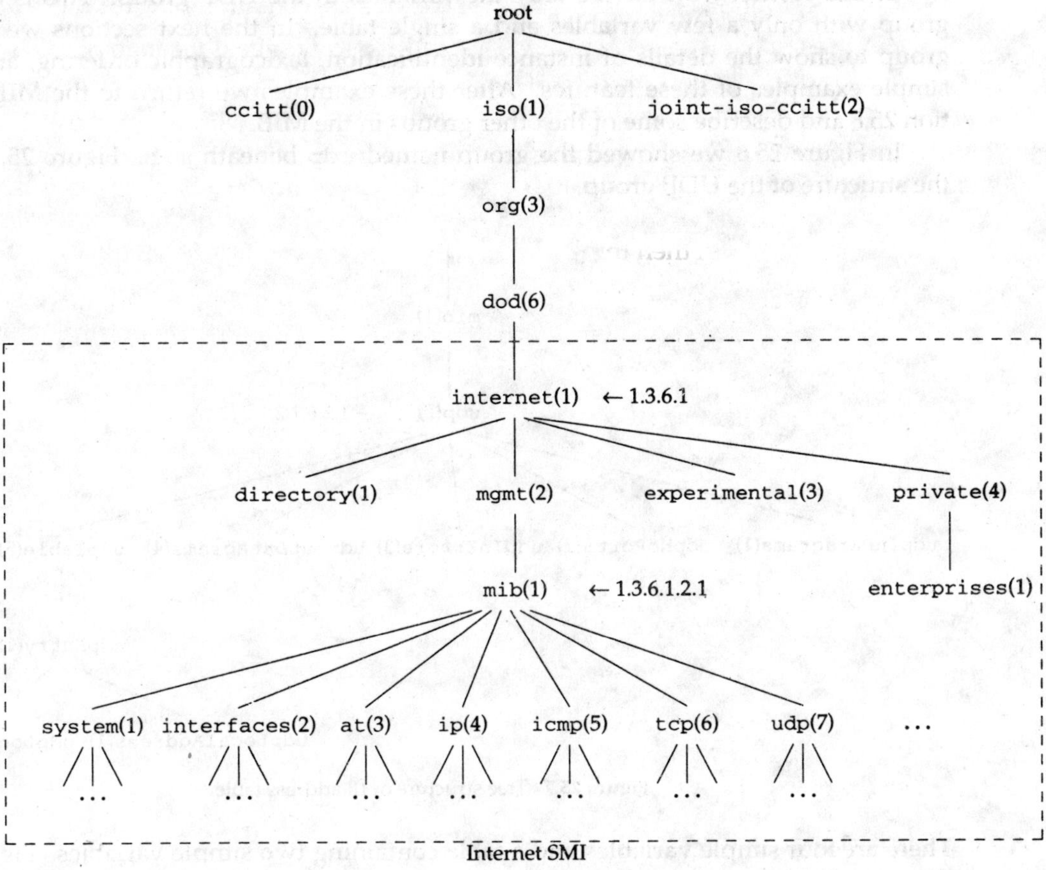

Figure 25.6 Object identifiers in the Management Information Base.

Besides the `mib` object identifiers in Figure 25.6 we also show one named `iso.org.dod.internet.private.enterprises` (1.3.6.1.4.1). This is where vendor-specific MIBs are located. The Assigned Numbers RFC lists around 400 identifiers registered below this node.

25.5 Introduction to the Management Information Base

The *Management Information Base*, or MIB, is the database of information maintained by the agent that the manager can query or set. We describe what's called MIB-II, specified in RFC 1213 [McCloghrie and Rose 1991].

As shown in Figure 25.6, the MIB is divided into groups named `system`, `interfaces`, `at` (address translation), `ip`, and so on.

In this section we describe only the variables in the UDP group. This is a simple group with only a few variables and a single table. In the next sections we use this group to show the details of instance identification, lexicographic ordering, and some simple examples of these features. After these examples we return to the MIB in Section 25.8 and describe some of the other groups in the MIB.

In Figure 25.6 we showed the group named udp beneath mib. Figure 25.7 shows the structure of the UDP group.

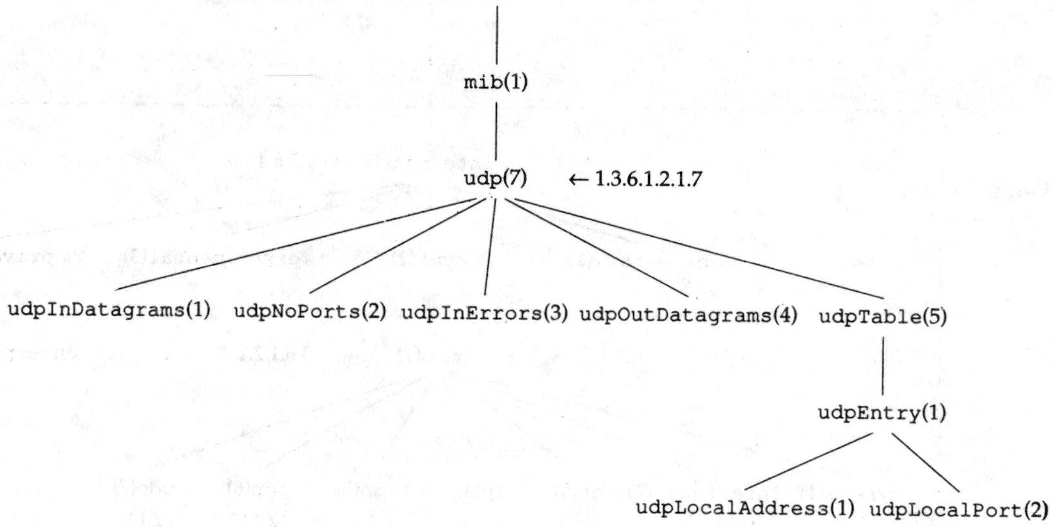

Figure 25.7 Tree structure of IP address table.

There are four simple variables and a table containing two simple variables. Figure 25.8 describes the four simple variables.

Name	Datatype	R/W	Description
`udpInDatagrams`	`Counter`		Number of UDP datagrams delivered to user processes.
`udpNoPorts`	`Counter`		Number of received UDP datagrams for which no application process was at the destination port.
`udpInErrors`	`Counter`		Number of undeliverable UDP datagrams for reasons other than no application at destination port (e.g., UDP checksum error).
`udpOutDatagrams`	`Counter`		Number of UDP datagrams sent.

Figure 25.8 Simple variables in udp group.

We'll use this format to describe all the MIB variables in this chapter. The column labeled "R/W" is empty if the variable is read-only, or contains a bullet (•) if the variable is read–write. We always include this column, even if all the variables in a group are read-only (since they are in the udp group) to reiterate that none of the variables can be set by the manager. Also, when the data type is an INTEGER with bounds, we specify the lower limit and upper limit, as we do for the UDP port number in the next figure.

Figure 25.9 describes the two simple variables in the `udpTable`.

UDP listener table, index = <*udpLocalAddress*>.<*udpLocalPort*>			
Name	Datatype	R/W	Description
`udpLocalAddress`	`IpAddress`		Local IP address for this listener. 0.0.0.0 indicates the listener is willing to receive datagrams on any interface.
`udpLocalPort`	`[0..65535]`		Local port number for this listener.

Figure 25.9 Variables in `udpTable`.

Each time we describe the variables in an SNMP table, the first row of the figure indicates the value of the "index" used to reference each row of the table. We show some examples of this in the next section.

Case Diagrams

There is a relationship between the first three counters in Figure 25.8. Case Diagrams [Case and Partridge 1989] visually illustrate the relationships between the various MIB variables in a given group. Figure 25.10 is a Case Diagram for the UDP group.

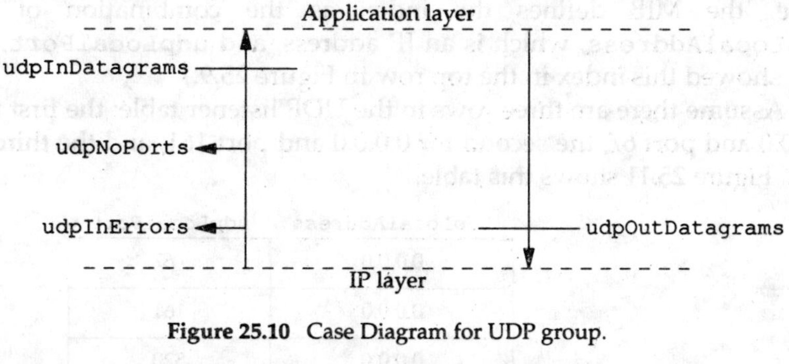

Figure 25.10 Case Diagram for UDP group.

What this diagram shows is that the number of UDP datagrams delivered to applications (`udpInDatagrams`) is the number of UDP datagrams delivered from IP to UDP, minus `udpInErrors`, minus `udpNoPorts`. Also, the number of UDP datagrams delivered to IP (`udpOutDatagrams`) is the number passed to UDP from the applications. This illustrates that `udpInDatagrams` does not include `udpInErrors` or `udpNoPorts`.

These diagrams were used during the development of the MIB to verify that all data paths for a packet were accounted for. [Rose 1994] shows Case Diagrams for all the groups in the MIB.

25.6 Instance Identification

Every variable in the MIB must be identified when SNMP is referencing it, to fetch or set its value. First, only leaf nodes are referenced. SNMP does not manipulate entire rows or columns of tables. Returning to Figure 25.7, the leaf nodes are the four that we described in Figure 25.8 and the two in Figure 25.9. `mib`, `udp`, `udpTable`, and `udpEntry` are not leaf nodes.

Simple Variables

Simple variables are referenced by appending ".0" to the variable's object identifier. For example, the counter `udpInDatagrams` from Figure 25.8, whose object identifier is 1.3.6.1.2.1.7.1, is referenced as 1.3.6.1.2.1.7.1.0. The textual name of this reference is `iso.org.dod.internet.mgmt.mib.udp.udpInDatagrams.0`.

Although references to this variable are normally abbreviated as just `udpInDatagrams.0`, we reiterate that the *name* of the variable that appears in the SNMP message (Figure 25.2) is the object identifier 1.3.6.1.2.1.7.1.0.

Tables

Instance identification of table entries is more detailed. Let's return to the UDP listener table (Figure 25.7).

One or more indexes are specified in the MIB for each table. For the UDP listener table, the MIB defines the index as the combination of the two variables `udpLocalAddress`, which is an IP address, and `udpLocalPort`, which is an integer. (We showed this index in the top row in Figure 25.9.)

Assume there are three rows in the UDP listener table: the first row is for IP address 0.0.0.0 and port 67, the second for 0.0.0.0 and port 161, and the third for 0.0.0.0 and port 520. Figure 25.11 shows this table.

udpLocalAddress	udpLocalPort
0.0.0.0	67
0.0.0.0	161
0.0.0.0	520

Figure 25.11 Sample UDP listener table.

This implies that the system is willing to receive UDP datagrams on any interface for ports 67 (BOOTP server), 161 (SNMP), and 520 (RIP). The three rows in the table are referenced as shown in Figure 25.12.

Lexicographic Ordering

There is an implied ordering in the MIB based on the order of the object identifiers. All the entries in MIB tables are lexicographically ordered by their object identifiers. This means the six variables in Figure 25.12 are ordered in the MIB as shown in Figure 25.13. Two key points result from this lexicographic ordering.

Row	Object identifier	Abbreviated name	Value
1	1.3.6.1.2.1.7.5.1.1.0.0.0.0.67 1.3.6.1.2.1.7.5.1.2.0.0.0.0.67	`udpLocalAddress.0.0.0.0.67` `udpLocalPort.0.0.0.0.67`	0.0.0.0 67
2	1.3.6.1.2.1.7.5.1.1.0.0.0.0.161 1.3.6.1.2.1.7.5.1.2.0.0.0.0.161	`udpLocalAddress.0.0.0.0.161` `udpLocalPort.0.0.0.0.161`	0.0.0.0 161
3	1.3.6.1.2.1.7.5.1.1.0.0.0.0.520 1.3.6.1.2.1.7.5.1.2.0.0.0.0.520	`udpLocalAddress.0.0.0.0.520` `udpLocalPort.0.0.0.0.520`	0.0.0.0 520

Figure 25.12 Instance identification for rows in UDP listener table.

Column	Object identifier (lexicographically ordered)	Abbreviated name	Value

1	1.3.6.1.2.1.7.5.1.1.0.0.0.0.67
	1.3.6.1.2.1.7.5.1.1.0.0.0.0.161
	1.3.6.1.2.1.7.5.1.1.0.0.0.0.520
		`udpLocalAddress.0.0.0.0.67`
		`udpLocalAddress.0.0.0.0.161`
		`udpLocalAddress.0.0.0.0.520`
			0.0.0.0
			0.0.0.0
			0.0.0.0

2	1.3.6.1.2.1.7.5.1.2.0.0.0.0.67
	1.3.6.1.2.1.7.5.1.2.0.0.0.0.161
	1.3.6.1.2.1.7.5.1.2.0.0.0.0.520
		`udpLocalPort.0.0.0.0.67`
		`udpLocalPort.0.0.0.0.161`
		`udpLocalPort.0.0.0.0.520`
			67
			161
			520

Figure 25.13 Lexicographic ordering of UDP listener table.

1. Since all instances for a given variable (`udpLocalAddress`) appear before all instances for the next variable in the table (`udpLocalPort`), this implies that tables are accessed in a column–row order. This results from the lexicographic ordering of the object identifiers, not the human-readable names.

2. The ordering of the rows in a table depends on the values of the indexes for the table. In Figure 25.13, 67 is lexicographically less than 161, which is lexicographically less than 520.

Figure 25.14 shows this column–row order for our sample UDP listener table.

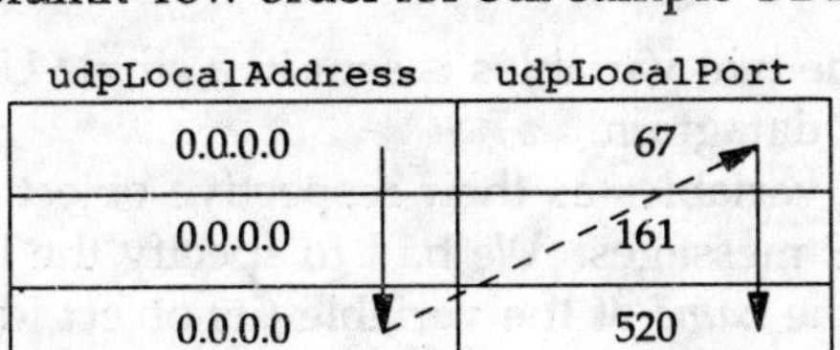

Figure 25.14 UDP listener table, showing column–row ordering.

We'll also see this column–row ordering when we use the `get-next` operator in the next section.

25.7 Simple Examples

In this section we'll show some examples that fetch the values of variables from an SNMP agent. The software used to query the agent is called snmpi and is from the ISODE system. Both are described briefly in [Rose 1994].

Simple Variables

We'll query a router for two simple variables from the UDP group:

```
sun % snmpi -a gateway -c secret

snmpi> get udpInDatagrams.0 udpNoPorts.0
udpInDatagrams.0=616168
udpNoPorts.0=33
snmpi> quit
```

The -a option identifies the agent we want to communicate with, and the -c option specifies the SNMP *community*. It is a password supplied by the client (snmpi in this case) and if the server (the agent in the system gateway) recognizes the community name, it honors the manager's request. An agent could allow clients within one community read-only access to its variables, and clients in another community read–write access.

The program outputs its snmpi> prompt, and we can type commands such as get, which translates into an SNMP get-request message. When we're done, we type quit. (In all further examples we'll remove this final quit command.)

Figure 25.15 shows the two lines of tcpdump output for this example.

```
1  0.0                  sun.1024 > gateway.161: GetRequest(42)
                        1.3.6.1.2.1.7.1.0 1.3.6.1.2.1.7.2.0

2  0.348875 (0.3489)    gateway.161 > sun.1024: GetResponse(46)
                        1.3.6.1.2.1.7.1.0=616168
                        1.3.6.1.2.1.7.2.0=33
```

Figure 25.15 tcpdump output for simple SNMP query.

The request for the two variables is sent in a single UDP datagram, and the response is also a single UDP datagram.

We show the variables as their respective object identifiers, because that is what's sent in the SNMP messages. We had to specify the instance of the two variables as 0. Notice also that the *name* of the variable (its object identifier) is always returned in the response. We'll see below that this is required for the get-next operator to work.

get-next Operator

The operation of the get-next operator is based on the lexicographic ordering of the MIB. We start the following example by asking for the next object identifier after udp (without specifying any instance, since this is not a leaf object). This returns the first object in the UDP group. We then ask for the next entry after this one, and the second entry is returned. We repeat this one more time to get the third entry:

```
sun % snmpi -a gateway -c secret

snmpi> next udp
udpInDatagrams.0=616318

snmpi> next udpInDatagrams.0
udpNoPorts.0=33

snmpi> next udpNoPorts.0
udpInErrors.0=0
```

This example shows why a `get-next` operator must return the name of the variable: we ask the agent for the next variable, and the agent returns its *name* and *value*.

Using the `get-next` operator in this fashion, one could imagine a manager with a loop that starts at the beginning of the MIB and queries the agent for every variable that the agent maintains. Another use of this operator is to iterate through tables.

Table Access

We can reiterate the column–row ordering of tables using our simple query program to step through the entire UDP listener table. We start by asking for the next variable after `udpTable`. Since this is not a leaf object we can't specify an instance, but the `get-next` operator still returns the next object in the table. We then work our way through the table, with the agent returning the next variable, in column–row order:

```
sun % snmpi -a gateway -c secret

snmpi> next udpTable
udpLocalAddress.0.0.0.0.67=0.0.0.0

snmpi> next udpLocalAddress.0.0.0.0.67
udpLocalAddress.0.0.0.0.161=0.0.0.0

snmpi> next udpLocalAddress.0.0.0.0.161
udpLocalAddress.0.0.0.0.520=0.0.0.0

snmpi> next udpLocalAddress.0.0.0.0.520
udpLocalPort.0.0.0.0.67=67

snmpi> next udpLocalPort.0.0.0.0.67
udpLocalPort.0.0.0.0.161=161

snmpi> next udpLocalPort.0.0.0.0.161
udpLocalPort.0.0.0.0.520=520

snmpi> next udpLocalPort.0.0.0.0.520
snmpInPkts.0=59                          we're finished with the UDP listener table
```

We see that the order returned corresponds to Figure 25.14.

How does a manager know when it reaches the end of a table? Since the response to the `get-next` operator contains the name of the next entry in the MIB after the table, the manager can tell when the name changes. In our example the last entry in the UDP listener table is followed by the variable `snmpInPkts`.

25.8 Management Information Base (Continued)

We now return to the description of the MIB. We describe only the following groups: `system` (system identification), `if` (interfaces) , `at` (address translation), `ip`, `icmp`, and `tcp`. Additional groups are defined.

`system` Group

The `system` group is simple; it consists of seven simple variables (i.e.. no tables). Figure 25.16 shows their names, data types, and descriptions.

Name	Datatype	R/W	Description
sysDescr	DisplayString		Textual description of entity.
sysObjectID	ObjectID		Vendor's ID within the subtree 1.3.6.1.4.1.
sysUpTime	TimeTicks		Time in hundredths of a second since network management portion of system was rebooted.
sysContact	DisplayString	•	Name of contact person and how to contact them.
sysName	DisplayString	•	Node's fully qualified domain name (FQDN).
sysLocation	DisplayString	•	Physical location of node.
sysServices	[0..127]		Value indicating services provided by node. It is the sum of the layers in the OSI model supported by the node. The following values are added together, depending on the services provided: 0x01 (physical), 0x02 (datalink), 0x04 (internet), 0x08 (end-to-end), 0x40 (application).

Figure 25.16 Simple variables in `system` group.

We can query the router `netb` for some of these variables:

```
sun % snmpi -a netb -c secret

snmpi> get sysDescr.0 sysObjectID.0 sysUpTime.0 sysServices.0
sysDescr.0="Epilogue Technology SNMP agent for Telebit NetBlazer"
sysObjectID.0=1.3.6.1.4.1.12.42.3.1
sysUpTime.0=22 days, 11 hours, 23 minutes, 2 seconds (194178200 timeticks)
sysServices.0=0xc<internet,transport>
```

The system's object identifier is in the `internet.private.enterprises` group (1.3.6.1.4.1) from Figure 25.6 (p. 365). From the Assigned Numbers RFC we can determine that the next object identifier (12) is assigned to the vendor (Epilogue).

We can also see that the `sysServices` variable is the sum of 4 and 8: this element supports the Internet layer (i.e., routing) and the transport layer (i.e., end-to-end).

`interface` Group

Only one simple variable is defined for this group: the number of interfaces on the system, shown in Figure 25.17.

Name	Datatype	R/W	Description
ifNumber	INTEGER		Number of network interfaces on system.

Figure 25.17 Simple variable in if group.

This group also defines a table with 22 columns. Each row of the table defines the characteristics for each interface, as shown in Figure 25.18.

Interface table, index = < *IfIndex* >			
Name	**Datatype**	**R/W**	**Description**
ifIndex	INTEGER		Index of interface, between one and ifNumber.
ifDescr	DisplayString		Textual description of interface.
ifType	INTEGER		Type, for example: 6 = Ethernet, 7 = 802.3 Ethernet, 9 = 802.5 token ring, 23 = PPP, 28 = SLIP, and many other values.
ifMtu	INTEGER		MTU of interface.
ifSpeed	Gauge		Speed in bits/sec.
ifPhysAddress	PhysAddress		Physical address, or string of 0 length for interfaces without physical addresses (e.g., serial links).
ifAdminStatus	[1..3]	•	Desired state of interface: 1 = up, 2 = down, 3 = testing.
ifOperStatus	[1..3]		Current state of interface: 1 = up, 2 = down, 3 = testing.
ifLastChange	TimeTicks		Value of sysUpTime when interface entered current operational state.
ifInOctets	Counter		Total number of bytes received, including framing characters.
ifInUcastPkts	Counter		Number of unicast packets delivered to higher layers.
ifInNUcastPkts	Counter		Number of nonunicast (i.e., broadcast or multicast) packets delivered to higher layers.
ifInDiscards	Counter		Number of received packets discarded even though no error in packet (i.e., out of buffers).
ifInErrors	Counter		Number of received packets discarded because of errors.
ifInUnknownProtos	Counter		Number of received packets discarded because of unknown protocol.
ifOutOctets	Counter		Number of bytes transmitted, including framing characters.
ifOutUcastPkts	Counter		Number of unicast packets received from higher layers.
ifOutNUcastPkts	Counter		Number of nonunicast (i.e., broadcast or multicast) packets received from higher layers.
ifOutDiscards	Counter		Number of outbound packets discarded even though no error in packet (i.e., out of buffers).
ifOutErrors	Counter		Number of outbound packets discarded because of errors.
ifOutQLen	Gauge		Number of packets in output queue.
ifSpecific	ObjectID		A reference to MIB definitions specific to this particular type of media.

Figure 25.18 Variables in interface table: ifTable.

We can query the host sun for some of these variables for all its interfaces. We expect to find three interfaces, as in Section 3.8, if the SLIP interface is up:

```
sun % snmpi -a sun

snmpi> next ifTable                    first see what index of first interface is
ifIndex.1=1

snmpi> get ifDescr.1 ifType.1 ifMtu.1 ifSpeed.1 ifPhysAddress.1
ifDescr.1="le0"
ifType.1=ethernet-csmacd(6)
ifMtu.1=1500
ifSpeed.1=10000000
ifPhysAddress.1=0x08:00:20:03:f6:42

snmpi> next ifDescr.1 ifType.1 ifMtu.1 ifSpeed.1 ifPhysAddress.1
ifDescr.2="sl0"
ifType.2=propPointToPointSerial(22)
ifMtu.2=552
ifSpeed.2=0
ifPhysAddress.2=0x00:00:00:00:00:00

snmpi> next ifDescr.2 ifType.2 ifMtu.2 ifSpeed.2 ifPhysAddress.2
ifDescr.3="lo0"
ifType.3=softwareLoopback(24)
ifMtu.3=1536
ifSpeed.3=0
ifPhysAddress.3=0x00:00:00:00:00:00
```

We first get five variables for the first interface using the `get` operator, and then get the same five variables for the second interface using the `get-next` operator. The last command gets these same five variables for the third interface, again using the `get-next` command.

The interface type for the SLIP link is reported as proprietary point-to-point serial, not SLIP. Also, the speed of the SLIP link is not reported.

It is critical to understand the relationship between the `get-next` operator and the column–row ordering. When we say `next ifDescr.1` it returns the next row of the table for this variable, not the next variable in the same row. If tables were stored in a row–column order instead, we wouldn't be able to step to the next occurrence of a given variable this way.

at Group

The address translation group is mandatory for all systems, but was deprecated by MIB-II. Starting with MIB-II, each network protocol group (e.g., IP) contains its own address translation tables. For IP it is the `ipNetToMediaTable`.

Only a single table with three columns is defined for the `at` group, shown in Figure 25.19.

We can use a new command within the `snmpi` program to dump an entire table. We'll query the router named `kinetics` (which routes between a TCP/IP network and an AppleTalk network) for its entire ARP cache. This output reiterates the lexicographic ordering of the entries in the table:

Address translation table, index = <*atIfIndex*>.1.<*atNetAddress*>			
Name	Datatype	R/W	Description
atIfIndex	INTEGER	•	Interface number: ifIndex.
atPhysAddress	PhysAddress	•	Physical address. Setting this to a string of 0 length invalidates the entry.
atNetAddress	NetworkAddress	•	IP address.

Figure 25.19 Address translation table: atTable.

```
sun % snmpi -a kinetics -c secret dump at
atIfIndex.1.1.140.252.1.4=1
atIfIndex.1.1.140.252.1.22=1
atIfIndex.1.1.140.252.1.183=1
atIfIndex.2.1.140.252.6.4=2
atIfIndex.2.1.140.252.6.6=2

atPhysAddress.1.1.140.252.1.4=0xaa:00:04:00:f4:14
atPhysAddress.1.1.140.252.1.22=0x08:00:20:0f:2d:38
atPhysAddress.1.1.140.252.1.183=0x00:80:ad:03:6a:80
atPhysAddress.2.1.140.252.6.4=0x00:02:16:48
atPhysAddress.2.1.140.252.6.6=0x00:02:3c:48

atNetAddress.1.1.140.252.1.4=140.252.1.4
atNetAddress.1.1.140.252.1.22=140.252.1.22
atNetAddress.1.1.140.252.1.183=140.252.1.183
atNetAddress.2.1.140.252.6.4=140.252.6.4
atNetAddress.2.1.140.252.6.6=140.252.6.6
```

If we watch the packet exchange using tcpdump, when snmpi dumps an entire table it first issues a get-next for the table name (at in this example) to get the first entry. It prints the first entry and issues another get-next. This continues until the entire table has been dumped.

Figure 25.20 shows the arrangement of this table.

atIfIndex	atPhysAddress	atNetAddress
1	0xaa:00:04:00:f4:14	140.252.1.4
1	0x08:00:20:0f:2d:38	140.252.1.22
1	0x00:80:ad:03:6a:80	140.252.1.183
2	0x00:02:16:48	140.252.6.4
2	0x00:02:3c:48	140.252.6.6

Figure 25.20 Example of at table (ARP cache).

The AppleTalk physical addresses on interface number 2 are 32-bit values, not the 48-bit Ethernet addresses to which we're accustomed. Also note that an entry exists for our router (netb at 140.252.1.183), which we expect, since kinetics and netb are on the same Ethernet (140.252.1) and kinetics must use ARP to send the SNMP responses back to us.

ip Group

The ip group defines numerous variables and three tables. Figure 25.21 defines the simple variables.

Name	Datatype	R/W	Description
ipForwarding	[1..2]	•	1 means the system is forwarding IP datagrams, and 2 means it is not.
ipDefaultTTL	INTEGER	•	Default TTL value when transport layer doesn't provide one.
ipInReceives	Counter		Total number of received IP datagrams from all interfaces.
ipInHdrErrors	Counter		Number of IP datagrams discarded because of header errors (e.g., checksum error, version number mismatch, TTL exceeded, etc.).
ipInAddrErrors	Counter		Number of IP datagrams discarded because of incorrect destination address.
ipForwDatagrams	Counter		Number of IP datagrams for which an attempt was made to forward.
ipInUnknownProtos	Counter		Number of locally addressed IP datagrams with an invalid protocol field.
ipInDiscards	Counter		Number of received IP datagrams discarded because of a lack of buffer space.
ipInDelivers	Counter		Number of IP datagrams delivered to appropriate protocol module.
ipOutRequests	Counter		Total number of IP datagrams passed to IP for transmission. Does not include those counted in ipForwDatagrams.
ipOutDiscards	Counter		Number of output IP datagrams discarded because of a lack of buffer space.
ipOutNoRoutes	Counter		Number of IP datagrams discarded because no route could be found.
ipReasmTimeout	INTEGER		Maximum number of seconds that received fragments are held while awaiting reassembly.
ipReasmReqds	Counter		Number of IP fragments received that needed to be reassembled.
ipReasmOKs	Counter		Number of IP datagrams successfully reassembled.
ipReasmFails	Counter		Number of failures by IP reassembly algorithm.
ipFragOKs	Counter		Number of IP datagrams that have been successfully fragmented.
ipFragFails	Counter		Number of IP datagrams that needed to be fragmented but couldn't because the "don't fragment" flag was set.
ipFragCreates	Counter		Number of IP fragments generated by fragmentation.
ipRoutingDiscards	Counter		Number of routing entries chosen to be discarded even though they were valid.

Figure 25.21 Simple variables in ip group.

The first table in the ip group is the IP address table. It contains one row for each IP address on the system. Each row contains five variables, described in Figure 25.22.

IP address table, index = < *ipAdEntAddr* >			
Name	Datatype	R/W	Description
ipAdEntAddr	IpAddress		IP address for this row.
ipAdEntIfIndex	INTEGER		Corresponding interface number: ifIndex.
ipAdEntNetMask	IpAddress		Subnet mask for this IP address.
ipAdEntBcastAddr	[0..1]		Value of least-significant bit of the IP broadcast address. Normally 1.
ipAdEntReasmMaxSize	[0..65535]		Size of largest IP datagram received on this interface that can be reassembled.

Figure 25.22 IP address table: ipAddrTable.

We can query the host sun for its entire IP address table:

```
sun % snmpi -a sun dump ipAddrTable

ipAdEntAddr.127.0.0.1=127.0.0.1
ipAdEntAddr.140.252.1.29=140.252.1.29
ipAdEntAddr.140.252.13.33=140.252.13.33

ipAdEntIfIndex.127.0.0.1=3                loopback interface, lo0
ipAdEntIfIndex.140.252.1.29=2             SLIP interface, sl0
ipAdEntIfIndex.140.252.13.33=1            Ethernet interface, le0

ipAdEntNetMask.127.0.0.1=255.0.0.0
ipAdEntNetMask.140.252.1.29=255.255.255.0
ipAdEntNetMask.140.252.13.33=255.255.255.224

ipAdEntBcastAddr.127.0.0.1=1              all three use one bits for broadcast
ipAdEntBcastAddr.140.252.1.29=1
ipAdEntBcastAddr.140.252.13.33=1

ipAdEntReasmMaxSize.127.0.0.1=65535
ipAdEntReasmMaxSize.140.252.1.29=65535
ipAdEntReasmMaxSize.140.252.13.33=65535
```

The interface numbers can be compared with the output following Figure 25.18, and the IP addresses and subnet masks can be compared with the values output by the ifconfig command in Section 3.8.

The next table, Figure 25.23, is the IP routing table. (Recall our description of routing tables in Section 9.2.) The index used to access each row of the table is the destination IP address.

Figure 25.24 is the IP routing table on the host sun obtained with the dump ipRouteTable command using snmpi. We have deleted all five of the routing metrics, since they are all –1. In the column headings we've also removed the prefix ipRoute from each variable name.

IP routing table, index = < *ipRouteDest* >			
Name	**Datatype**	**R/W**	**Description**
`ipRouteDest`	`IpAddress`	•	Destination IP address. A value of 0.0.0.0 indicates a default entry.
`ipRouteIfIndex`	`INTEGER`	•	Interface number: `ifIndex`.
`ipRouteMetric1`	`INTEGER`	•	Primary routing metric. The meaning of the metric depends on the routing protocol (`ipRouteProto`). A value of –1 means it's not used.
`ipRouteMetric2`	`INTEGER`	•	Alternative routing metric.
`ipRouteMetric3`	`INTEGER`	•	Alternative routing metric.
`ipRouteMetric4`	`INTEGER`	•	Alternative routing metric.
`ipRouteNextHop`	`IpAddress`	•	IP address of next-hop router.
`ipRouteType`	`INTEGER`	•	Route type: 1 = other, 2 = invalidated route, 3 = direct, 4 = indirect.
`ipRouteProto`	`INTEGER`		Routing protocol: 1 = other, 4 = ICMP redirect, 8 = RIP, 13 = OSPF, 14 = BGP, and others.
`ipRouteAge`	`INTEGER`	•	Number of seconds since route was last updated or determined to be correct.
`ipRouteMask`	`IpAddress`	•	Mask to be logically ANDed with destination IP address before being compared with `ipRouteDest`.
`ipRouteMetric5`	`INTEGER`	•	Alternative routing metric.
`ipRouteInfo`	`ObjectID`		Reference to MIB definitions specific to this particular routing protocol.

Figure 25.23 IP routing table: `ipRouteTable`.

Dest	IfIndex	NextHop	Type	Proto	Mask
0.0.0.0	2	140.252.1.183	indirect(4)	other(1)	0.0.0.0
127.0.0.1	3	127.0.0.1	direct(3)	other(1)	255.255.255.255
140.252.1.183	2	140.252.1.29	direct(3)	other(1)	255.255.255.255
140.252.13.32	1	140.252.13.33	direct(3)	other(1)	255.255.0.0
140.252.13.65	1	140.252.13.35	indirect(4)	other(1)	255.255.255.255

Figure 25.24 IP routing table for the router sun.

For comparison, here is the IP routing table in the format output by `netstat` (which we discussed in Section 9.2). Figure 25.24 is lexicographically ordered, unlike the `netstat` output:

```
sun % netstat -rn
Routing tables
Destination        Gateway            Flags    Refcnt Use     Interface
140.252.13.65      140.252.13.35      UGH      0      115     le0
127.0.0.1          127.0.0.1          UH       1      1107    lo0
140.252.1.183      140.252.1.29       UH       0      86      sl0
default            140.252.1.183      UG       2      1628    sl0
140.252.13.32      140.252.13.33      U        8      68359   le0
```

The final table in the ip group is the address translation table, Figure 25.25. As we said earlier, the at group is now deprecated, and this IP table replaces it.

IP address translation table, index = < *ipNetToMediaIfIndex* >.< *ipNetToMediaNetAddress* >			
Name	Datatype	R/W	Description
ipNetToMediaIfIndex	INTEGER	•	Corresponding interface: ifIndex.
ipNetToMediaPhysAddress	PhysAddress	•	Physical address.
ipNetToMediaNetAddress	IpAddress	•	IP address.
ipNetToMediaType	[1..4]	•	Type of mapping: 1 = other, 2 = invalidated, 3 = dynamic, 4 = static.

Figure 25.25 IP address translation table: ipNetToMediaTable.

Here is the ARP cache on the system sun:

```
sun % arp -a
svr4 (140.252.13.34) at 0:0:c0:c2:9b:26
bsdi (140.252.13.35) at 0:0:c0:6f:2d:40
```

and the corresponding SNMP output:

```
sun % snmpi -a sun dump ipNetToMediaTable
ipNetToMediaIfIndex.1.140.252.13.34=1
ipNetToMediaIfIndex.1.140.252.13.35=1
ipNetToMediaPhysAddress.1.140.252.13.34=0x00:00:c0:c2:9b:26
ipNetToMediaPhysAddress.1.140.252.13.35=0x00:00:c0:6f:2d:40
ipNetToMediaNetAddress.1.140.252.13.34=140.252.13.34
ipNetToMediaNetAddress.1.140.252.13.35=140.252.13.35
ipNetToMediaType.1.140.252.13.34=dynamic(3)
ipNetToMediaType.1.140.252.13.35=dynamic(3)
```

icmp Group

The icmp group consists of four general counters (total number of input and output ICMP messages, and number of input and output ICMP messages with errors) and 22 counters for the different ICMP message types: 11 input counters and 11 output counters. These are shown in Figure 25.26.

For the ICMP messages with additional codes (recall from Figure 6.3 that there are 15 different codes for destination unreachable), a separate counter is not maintained by SNMP for each code.

tcp Group

Figure 25.27 describes the simple variables in the tcp group. Many of these refer to the TCP states that we showed in Figure 18.12.

Name	Datatype	R/W	Description
icmpInMsgs	Counter		Total number of received ICMP messages.
icmpInErrors	Counter		Number of received ICMP messages with errors (e.g., invalid ICMP checksum).
icmpInDestUnreachs	Counter		Number of received ICMP destination unreachable message.
icmpInTimeExcds	Counter		Number of received ICMP time exceeded message.
icmpInParmProbs	Counter		Number of received ICMP parameter problem message.
icmpInSrcQuenchs	Counter		Number of received ICMP source quench messages.
icmpInRedirects	Counter		Number of received ICMP redirect messages.
icmpInEchos	Counter		Number of received ICMP echo request messages.
icmpInEchoReps	Counter		Number of received ICMP echo reply messages.
icmpInTimestamps	Counter		Number of received ICMP timestamp request messages.
icmpInTimestampReps	Counter		Number of received ICMP timestamp reply messages.
icmpInAddrMasks	Counter		Number of received ICMP address mask request messages.
icmpInAddrMaskReps	Counter		Number of received ICMP address mask reply messages.
icmpOutMsgs	Counter		Total number of output ICMP messages.
icmpOutErrors	Counter		Number of ICMP messages not sent because of a problem within ICMP (e.g., lack of buffers).
icmpOutDestUnreachs	Counter		Number of ICMP destination unreachable messages sent.
icmpOutTimeExcds	Counter		Number of ICMP time exceeded messages sent.
icmpOutParmProbs	Counter		Number of ICMP parameter problem messages sent.
icmpOutSrcQuenchs	Counter		Number of ICMP source quench messages sent.
icmpOutRedirects	Counter		Number of ICMP redirect messages sent.
icmpOutEchos	Counter		Number of ICMP echo request messages sent.
icmpOutEchoReps	Counter		Number of ICMP echo reply messages sent.
icmpOutTimestamps	Counter		Number of ICMP timestamp requests sent.
icmpOutTimestampReps	Counter		Number of ICMP timestamp reply messages sent.
icmpOutAddrMasks	Counter		Number of ICMP address mask request messages sent.
icmpOutAddrMaskReps	Counter		Number of ICMP address mask reply messages sent.

Figure 25.26 Simple variables in `icmp` group.

We can query some of these variables on the system sun:

```
sun % snmpi -a sun

snmpi> get tcpRtoAlgorithm.0 tcpRtoMin.0 tcpRtoMax.0 tcpMaxConn.0
tcpRtoAlgorithm.0=vanj(4)
tcpRtoMin.0=200
tcpRtoMax.0=12800
tcpMaxConn.0=-1
```

This system (SunOS 4.1.3) uses the Van Jacobson retransmission timeout algorithm, uses timeouts between 200 ms and 12.8 seconds, and has no fixed limit on the number of TCP connections. (This upper limit of 12.8 seconds appears wrong, since most implementations use an upper limit of 64 seconds, as we saw in Chapter 21.)

The `tcp` group has a single table, the TCP connection table, shown in Figure 25.28. This contains one row for each connection. Each row contains five variables: the state of the connection, local IP address, local port number, remote IP address, and remote port number.

Name	Datatype	R/W	Description
tcpRtoAlgorithm	INTEGER		Algorithm used to calculate retransmission timeout value: 1 = none of the following, 2 = a constant RTO, 3 = MIL-STD-1778 Appendix B, 4 = Van Jacobson's algorithm.
tcpRtoMin	INTEGER		Minimum retransmission timeout value, in milliseconds.
tcpRtoMax	INTEGER		Maximum retransmission timeout value, in milliseconds.
tcpMaxConn	INTEGER		Maximum number of TCP connections. Value is –1 if dynamic.
tcpActiveOpens	Counter		Number of transitions from CLOSED to SYN_SENT states.
tcpPassiveOpens	Counter		Number of transitions from LISTEN to SYN_RCVD states.
tcpAttemptFails	Counter		Number of transitions from SYN_SENT or SYN_RCVD to CLOSED, plus number of transitions from SYN_RCVD to LISTEN.
tcpEstabResets	Counter		Number of transitions from ESTABLISHED or CLOSE_WAIT states to CLOSED.
tcpCurrEstab	Gauge		Number of connections currently in ESTABLISHED or CLOSE_WAIT states.
tcpInSegs	Counter		Total number of segments received.
tcpOutSegs	Counter		Total number of segments sent, excluding those containing only retransmitted bytes.
tcpRetransSegs	Counter		Total number of retransmitted segments.
tcpInErrs	Counter		Total number of segments received with an error (such as invalid checksum).
tcpOutRsts	Counter		Total number of segments sent with RST flag set.

Figure 25.27 Simple variables in `tcp` group.

index = < *tcpConnLocalAddress* >.< *tcpConnLocalPort* >.< *tcpConnRemAddress* >.< *tcpConnRemPort* >			
Name	**Datatype**	**R/W**	**Description**
tcpConnState	[1..12]	•	State of connection: 1 = CLOSED, 2 = LISTEN, 3 = SYN_SENT, 4 = SYN_RCVD, 5 = ESTABLISHED, 6 = FIN_WAIT_1, 7 = FIN_WAIT_2, 8 = CLOSE_WAIT, 9 = LAST_ACK, 10 = CLOSING, 11 = TIME_WAIT, 12 = delete TCB. The only value that the manager can set this variable to is 12 (e.g., immediately terminate the connection).
tcpConnLocalAddress	IpAddress		Local IP address. 0.0.0.0 indicates the listener is willing to accept connections on any interface.
tcpConnLocalPort	[0..65535]		Local port number.
tcpConnRemAddress	IpAddress		Remote IP address.
tcpConnRemPort	[0..65535]		Remote port number.

Figure 25.28 TCP connection table: `tcpConnTable`.

Let's look at this table on the system `sun`. We show only a portion of the table, since there are many servers listening for connections. Before dumping this table two TCP connections were established:

```
sun % rlogin gemini                    IP address of gemini is 140.252.1.11
```

and

```
sun % telnet localhost                 IP address should be 127.0.0.1
```

The only listening server that we show is the FTP server, on port 21:

```
sun % snmpi -a sun dump tcpConnTable

tcpConnState.0.0.0.0.21.0.0.0.0.0=listen(2)
tcpConnState.127.0.0.1.23.127.0.0.1.1415=established(5)
tcpConnState.127.0.0.1.1415.127.0.0.1.23=established(5)
tcpConnState.140.252.1.29.1023.140.252.1.11.513=established(5)
tcpConnLocalAddress.0.0.0.0.21.0.0.0.0.0=0.0.0.0
tcpConnLocalAddress.127.0.0.1.23.127.0.0.1.1415=127.0.0.1
tcpConnLocalAddress.127.0.0.1.1415.127.0.0.1.23=127.0.0.1
tcpConnLocalAddress.140.252.1.29.1023.140.252.1.11.513=140.252.1.29

tcpConnLocalPort.0.0.0.0.21.0.0.0.0.0=21
tcpConnLocalPort.127.0.0.1.23.127.0.0.1.1415=23
tcpConnLocalPort.127.0.0.1.1415.127.0.0.1.23=1415
tcpConnLocalPort.140.252.1.29.1023.140.252.1.11.513=1023

tcpConnRemAddress.0.0.0.0.21.0.0.0.0.0=0.0.0.0
tcpConnRemAddress.127.0.0.1.23.127.0.0.1.1415=127.0.0.1
tcpConnRemAddress.127.0.0.1.1415.127.0.0.1.23=127.0.0.1
tcpConnRemAddress.140.252.1.29.1023.140.252.1.11.513=140.252.1.11

tcpConnRemPort.0.0.0.0.21.0.0.0.0.0=0
tcpConnRemPort.127.0.0.1.23.127.0.0.1.1415=1415
tcpConnRemPort.127.0.0.1.1415.127.0.0.1.23=23
tcpConnRemPort.140.252.1.29.1023.140.252.1.11.513=513
```

For the `rlogin` to `gemini` only one entry appears, since `gemini` is a different host. We only see the client end of the connection (local port 1023), but both ends of the Telnet connection appear (client port 1415 and server port 23), since the connection is through the loopback interface. We can also see that the listening FTP server has a local IP address of 0.0.0.0, indicating it will accept connections on any interface.

25.9 Additional Examples

We now return to some earlier problems we encountered in the text, and use SNMP to understand what's happening.

Interface MTU

Recall our experiment in Section 11.6, in which we tried to determine the MTU of the SLIP link from `netb` to `sun`. We can now use SNMP to obtain this MTU. We first obtain the interface number (`ipRouteIfIndex`) of the SLIP link (140.252.1.29) from the IP routing table. Using this we go into the interface table and fetch the MTU (along with the description and type) of the SLIP link:

```
sun % snmpi -a netb -c secret

snmpi> get ipRouteIfIndex.140.252.1.29
ipRouteIfIndex.140.252.1.29=12
```

```
snmpi> get ifDescr.12 ifType.12 ifMtu.12
ifDescr.12="Telebit NetBlazer dynamic dial virtual interface"
ifType.12=other(1)
ifMtu.12=1500
```

We see that even though the link is a SLIP link, the MTU is set to the Ethernet value of 1500, probably to avoid fragmentation.

Routing Tables

Recall our discussion of address sorting performed by the DNS in Section 14.4 (p. 194). We showed how the first IP address returned by the name server was the one that shared a subnet with the client. We also mentioned that using the other IP address would probably work, but could be less efficient. Let's look at using the alternative IP address and see what happens. We'll use SNMP to look at a routing table entry, and tie together many concepts from earlier chapters dealing with IP routing.

The host `gemini` is multihomed, with two Ethernet interfaces. First let's verify that we can Telnet to both addresses:

```
sun % telnet 140.252.1.11 daytime
Trying 140.252.1.11 ...
Connected to 140.252.1.11.
Escape character is '^]'.
Sat Mar 27 09:37:24 1993
Connection closed by foreign host.

sun % telnet 140.252.3.54 daytime
Trying 140.252.3.54 ...
Connected to 140.252.3.54.
Escape character is '^]'.
Sat Mar 27 09:37:35 1993
Connection closed by foreign host.
```

So there is no connectivity difference between the two addresses. Now we'll use `traceroute` to see if there is a different route for each address:

```
sun % traceroute 140.252.1.11
traceroute to 140.252.1.11 (140.252.1.11), 30 hops max, 40 byte packets
 1  netb (140.252.1.183)  299 ms  234 ms  233 ms
 2  gemini (140.252.1.11)  233 ms  228 ms  234 ms

sun % traceroute 140.252.3.54
traceroute to 140.252.3.54 (140.252.3.54), 30 hops max, 40 byte packets
 1  netb (140.252.1.183)  245 ms  212 ms  234 ms
 2  swnrt (140.252.1.6)  233 ms  229 ms  234 ms
 3  gemini (140.252.3.54)  234 ms  233 ms  234 ms
```

There is an extra hop if we use the address on subnet 140.252.3. Let's find the reason for the extra hop. (The router `swnrt` is R3 from Figure 3.6, p. 43.)

Figure 25.29 shows the arrangement of the systems. We can tell from the `traceroute` output that the host `gemini` and the router `swnrt` are both connected to two networks: 140.252.1 and 140.252.3.

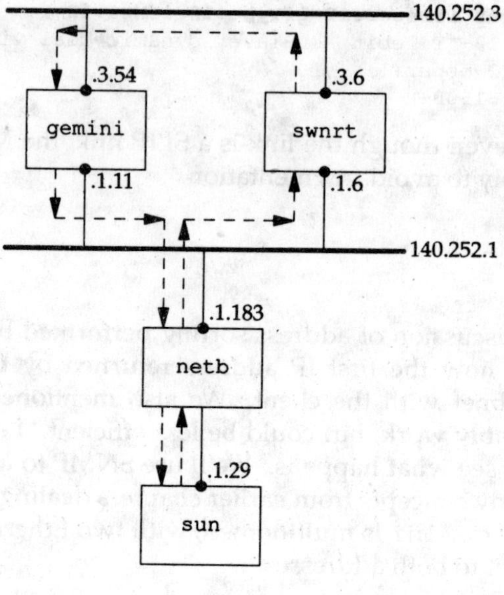

Figure 25.29 Topology of systems being used for example.

Recall in Figure 4.6 that we explained how proxy ARP is used by the router `netb` to make it appear as though `sun` was directly connected to the Ethernet 140.252.1. We've also omitted the modems on the SLIP link between `sun` and `netb`, since they're not relevant to this discussion.

In Figure 25.29 we show the path of the Telnet data using dashed arrows, when the address 140.252.3.54 is specified. How do we know that the return packets go directly from `gemini` to `netb`, and don't go back the way they came? We use our version of `traceroute` with loose source routing from Section 8.5:

```
sun % traceroute -g 140.252.3.54 sun
traceroute to sun (140.252.13.33), 30 hops max, 40 byte packets
 1  netb (140.252.1.183)  244 ms  256 ms  234 ms
 2  * * *
 3  gemini (140.252.3.54)  285 ms  227 ms  234 ms
 4  netb (140.252.1.183)  263 ms  259 ms  294 ms
 5  sun (140.252.13.33)  534 ms  498 ms  504 ms
```

When we specify loose source routing, the router `swnrt` never responds. If we look at the earlier output from `traceroute`, without source routing, we see that `swnrt` is indeed the second hop. The reason for the timeouts must be that the router does not generate the ICMP time exceeded errors when the datagram specifies loose source routing. What we are looking for in this `traceroute` output is that the return path from `gemini` (TTLs 3, 4, and 5) goes directly to `netb`, and not through the router `swnrt`.

The question that we need SNMP to answer is what does the routing table entry on `netb` look like for the destination network 140.252.3? It is `netb` that sends the packets to `swnrt` and not directly to `gemini`. We use the `get` command to fetch the value of the next-hop router for this destination:

```
sun % snmpi -a netb -c secret get ipRouteNextHop.140.252.3.0
ipRouteNextHop.140.252.3.0=140.252.1.6
```

This routing table entry tells `netb` to send the packets to `swnrt`, which is what we see happen.

Why does `gemini` send the packets directly back through `netb`? Because on `gemini` the destination address of the return packets is 140.252.1.29, and that network (140.252.1) is a directly connected interface.

What we're seeing in this example is a policy routing decision. The default route to network 140.252.3 is through the router `swnrt` because `gemini` is intended to be a multihomed host, not a router. This is an example of a multihomed host that does not want to be a router.

25.10 Traps

All the examples we've looked at so far in this chapter have been from the manager to the agent. As shown in Figure 25.1, it's also possible for the agent to send a *trap* to the manager, to indicate that something has happened on the agent that the manager might want to know about. Traps are sent to UDP port 162 on the manager.

In Figure 25.2 we showed the format of the trap PDU. We'll go through all the fields in this message when we look at some `tcpdump` output below.

Six specific traps are defined, with a seventh one allowing a vendor to implement an enterprise-specific trap. Figure 25.30 describes the values for the *trap type* in the trap message (Figure 25.2).

trap type	Name	Description
0	`coldStart`	Agent is initializing itself.
1	`warmStart`	Agent is reinitializing itself.
2	`linkDown`	An interface has changed from the up to the down state (Figure 25.18). The first variable in the message identifies the interface.
3	`linkUp`	An interface has changed from the down to the up state (Figure 25.18). The first variable in the message identifies the interface.
4	`authenticationFailure`	A message was received from an SNMP manager with an invalid community.
5	`egpNeighborLoss`	An EGP peer has changed to the down state. The first variable in the messages contains the IP address of the peer.
6	`enterpriseSpecific`	Look in the *specific code* field for information on the trap.

Figure 25.30 Trap types.

We can see some traps using `tcpdump`. We'll start the SNMP agent on the system `sun` and see it generate a `coldStart` trap. (We tell the agent to send traps to the host `bsdi`. Although we're not running a manager on `bsdi` to handle the traps, we can run tcpdump and see what packets get generated. Recall from Figure 25.1 that a trap is sent from the agent to the manager, but there is no acknowledgment sent by the manager, so we don't need a manager to handle the traps.) We then send a request using the snmpi program, but with an invalid community name. This should generate an authenticationFailure trap. Figure 25.31 shows the output.

```
1  0.0             sun.snmp > bsdi.snmp-trap: C=traps Trap(28)
                    E:unix.1.2.5 [140.252.13.33] coldStart 20

2  18.86 (18.86)    sun.snmp > bsdi.snmp-trap: C=traps Trap(29)
                    E:unix.1.2.5 [140.252.13.33] authenticationFailure 1907
```

Figure 25.31 tcpdump output of traps generated by SNMP agent.

First we notice that both UDP datagrams are from the SNMP agent (port 161, printed as the name snmp) with a destination port of 162 (printed as the name snmp-trap).

The notation C=traps is the community name of the trap message. This is a configuration option with the ISODE SNMP agent being used.

The next notation, Trap(28) in line 1 and Trap(29) in line 2 is the *PDU type* and length.

The next field of output for both lines is E:unix.1.2.5. This is the *enterprise*: the agent's sysObjectID. It falls under the 1.3.6.1.4.1 node of the tree in Figure 25.6 (iso.org.dod.internet.private.enterprises), so this agent's object identifier is 1.3.6.1.4.1.4.1.2.5. Its abbreviated name is unix.agents.fourBSD-isode.5. The final number (5) is the version number of this release of the ISODE agent. This enterprise value identifies the agent software generating the trap.

The next field output by tcpdump is the IP address of the agent (140.252.13.33).

The *trap type* is printed as coldStart on line 1, and authenticationFailure on line 2. These correspond to *trap type* values of 0 and 4, respectively (Figure 25.30). Since these are not enterprise-specific traps, the *specific code* must be 0, and is not printed.

Next comes the *timestamp* field, printed as 20 and 1907. This is a TimeTicks value, representing the number of hundredths of a second since the agent initialized. In the case of the cold start trap, the trap was generated 200 ms after the agent was initialized. The tcpdump output indicates that the second trap occurred 18.86 seconds after the first one, which corresponds to the printed value of 1907 hundredths of a second, minus 200 ms.

Figure 25.2 indicates that a trap message can contain interesting variables that the agents wants to send to the manager, but there aren't any in our examples.

25.11 ASN.1 and BER

The formal specification of SNMP uses *Abstract Syntax Notation 1* (ASN.1) and the actual encoding of the bits in the SNMP messages (Figure 25.2) uses the corresponding *Basic Encoding Rules* (BER). Unlike most texts that describe SNMP, we have purposely left a discussion of ASN.1 and BER until the end. When they're discussed first, it can confuse the reader and obfuscate the real purpose of SNMP—network management. In this section we only give an overview of these two topics. Chapter 8 of [Rose 1990] covers ASN.1 and BER in detail.

ASN.1 is a formal language for describing data and the properties of the data. It says nothing about how the data is stored or encoded. All the fields in the MIB and the SNMP messages are described using ASN.1. For example, the ASN.1 definition of the data type `IpAddress` from the SMI looks like:

```
IpAddress ::=
    [APPLICATION 0]              -- in network-byte order
        IMPLICIT OCTET STRING (SIZE (4))
```

Similarly, from the MIB we find the following definition of a simple variable:

```
udpNoPorts OBJECT-TYPE
    SYNTAX  Counter
    ACCESS  read-only
    STATUS  mandatory
    DESCRIPTION
            "The total number of received UDP datagrams for which
            there was no application at the destination port."
    ::= { udp 2 }
```

The definition of tables using `SEQUENCE` and `SEQUENCE OF` is more complex.

Given these ASN.1 definitions, there are many ways to encode the data into a stream of bits for transmission. SNMP uses BER. The representation of a small integer, such as 64, requires 3 bytes using BER. One byte says the value is an integer, the next byte says how many bytes are used to store the integer (1), and the final byte contains the binary value.

Fortunately the details of ASN.1 and BER are only important to implementors of SNMP. They are not fundamental to the understanding and use of network management.

25.12 SNMP Version 2

During 1993 11 RFCs were published defining revisions to SNMP. The first of these, RFC 1441 [Case et al. 1993], provides an introduction to SNMP Version 2 (SNMPv2). Two books also describe SNMPv2 [Stallings 1993; Rose 1994]. Two publicly available implementations already exist (see Appendix B.3 of [Rose 1994]), but vendor implementations probably won't be widely available until 1994.

In this section we describe the major differences from SNMPv1 to SNMPv2.

1. A new packet type `get-bulk-request` allows the manager to retrieve large blocks of data efficiently.
2. Another new packet type `inform-request` allows one manager to send information to another manager.

3. Two new MIBs are defined: the SNMPv2 MIB and the SNMPv2-M2M MIB (Manager-to-Manager).
4. SNMPv2 provides security enhancements over SNMPv1. In SNMPv1 the community name passed from the manager to the agent is a cleartext password. SNMPv2 can provide authentication and privacy.

As vendors start to provide SNMPv2-capable agents, management stations will also appear that can handle both. [Routhier 1993] describes extending an implementation of SNMPv1 to support SNMPv2.

25.13 Summary

SNMP is a simple request–reply protocol between an SNMP manager and an SNMP agent. The management information base (MIB) defines the variables that are maintained by the agent, for the manager to query or set. Only a limited number of data types are used to define these variables.

All the variables are identified by object identifiers, a hierarchical naming scheme consisting of long strings of numbers that are normally abbreviated into a simple name, for human readability. A specific instance of a variable is identified by appending an instance to the object identifier.

Many SNMP variables are contained in tables, with a fixed number of columns, but a variable number of rows. Fundamental to SNMP is the identification scheme used to identify each row in a table (when we don't know how many rows are in the table), and the lexicographic ordering (column–row order). The end result, SNMP's `get-next` operator, is basic to any SNMP manager.

We then described the following groups of SNMP variables: system, interface, address translation, IP, ICMP, TCP, and UDP. This was followed by two examples, one to determine the MTU of an interface, and the other to look at the routing table of a router.

We completed the chapter by looking at SNMP traps, a way for the agent to notify the manager that something significant has occurred, and a brief mention of ASN.1 and BER. These latter two topics are probably the most confusing aspects of SNMP, but fortunately their details are needed only by implementors.

Exercises

25.1 We said that using two different ports (161 and 162) allows a system to run both a manager and agent. What would happen if the same port number were used for both?

25.2 How would you list an entire routing table using `get-next`?

26

Telnet and Rlogin: Remote Login

26.1 Introduction

Remote login is one of the most popular Internet applications. Instead of having a hard-wired terminal on each host, we can login to one host and then remote login across the network to any other host (that we have an account on, of course).

Two popular applications provide remote login across TCP/IP internets.

1. Telnet is a standard application that almost every TCP/IP implementation provides. It works between hosts that use different operating systems. Telnet uses option negotiation between the client and server to determine what features each end can provide.
2. Rlogin is from Berkeley Unix and was developed to work between Unix systems only, but it has been ported to other operating systems also.

In this chapter we look at both Telnet and Rlogin. We start with Rlogin because it's simpler.

Telnet is one of the oldest of the Internet applications, dating back to 1969 on the ARPANET. Its name is actually an acronym that stands for "telecommunications network protocol."

Remote login uses the client–server paradigm. Figure 26.1 shows the typical arrangement of the Telnet client and server. (We could draw a similar picture for an Rlogin client and server.)

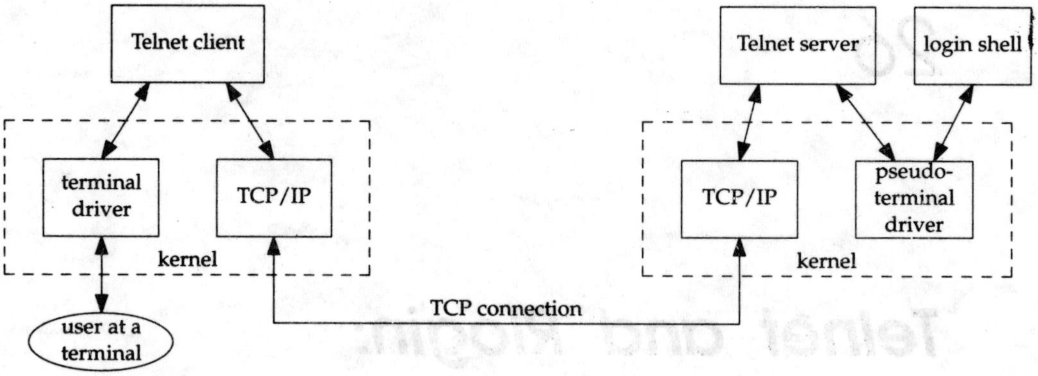

Figure 26.1 Overview of Telnet client–server.

There are numerous points in this figure.

1. The Telnet client interacts with both the user at the terminal and the TCP/IP protocols. Normally everything we type is sent across the TCP connection, and everything received from the connection is output to our terminal.
2. The Telnet server often deals with what's called a *pseudo-terminal* device, at least under Unix systems. This makes it appear to the login shell that's invoked on the server, and to any programs run by the login shell, that they're talking to a terminal device. Some applications, such as full-screen editors, assume they're talking to a terminal device. Indeed, making the login shell on the server think that it's talking to a terminal is often one of the hardest programming aspects involved in writing a remote login server.
3. Only a single TCP connection is used. Since there are times when the Telnet client must talk to the Telnet server (and vice versa) there needs to be some way to delineate commands that are sent across the connection, versus user data. We'll see how both Telnet and Rlogin handle this.
4. We show dashed boxes in Figure 26.1 to note that the terminal and pseudo-terminal drivers, along with the TCP/IP implementation, are normally part of the operating system kernel. The Telnet client and server, however, are often user applications.
5. We show the login shell on the server host to reiterate that we have to login to the server. We must have an account on that system to login to it, using either Telnet or Rlogin.

It is interesting to compare the complexity of Telnet and Rlogin by looking at the number of lines of source code required to implement the client and server for each. Figure 26.2 shows these counts for the standard Telnet and Rlogin client and server, as distributed in different versions from Berkeley (Figure 1.10).

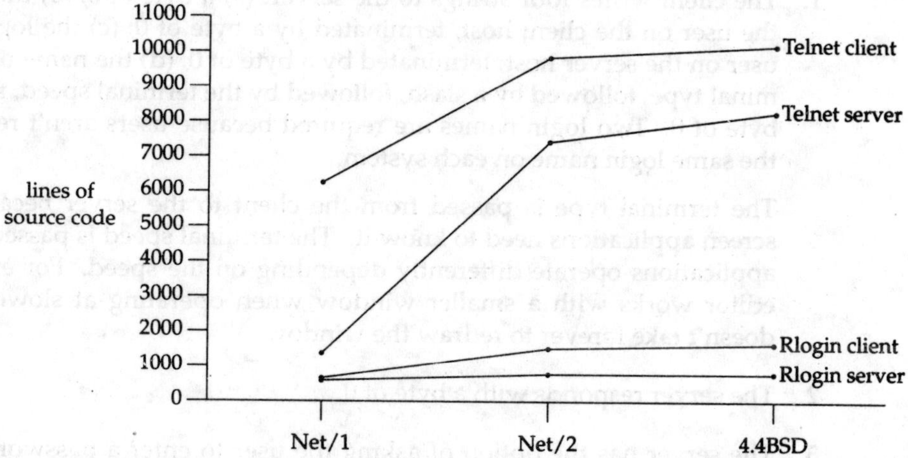

Figure 26.2 Comparison of Telnet/Rlogin/client/server, number of lines of source code.

It is the continuing addition of new options to Telnet that causes its implementation to grow, while Rlogin remains simple and stable.

Remote login is not a high-volume data transfer application. As we've mentioned earlier, lots of small packets are normally exchanged between the two end systems. [Paxson 1993] found that the ratio of bytes sent by the client (the user typing at the terminal) to the number of bytes sent back by the server is about 1:20. This is because we type short commands that often generate lots of output.

26.2 Rlogin Protocol

Rlogin appeared with 4.2BSD and was intended for remote login only between Unix hosts. This makes it a simpler protocol than Telnet, since option negotiation is not required when the operating system on the client and server are known in advance. Over the past few years, Rlogin has also been ported to several non-Unix environments.

RFC 1282 [Kantor 1991] specifies the Rlogin protocol. As with the Routing Information Protocol (RIP) RFC, however, this one was written after Rlogin had been in use for many years. Chapter 15 of [Stevens 1990] describes programming remote login clients and servers, and provides the complete source code for the Rlogin client and server. Chapters 25 and 26 of [Comer and Stevens 1993] provide the implementation details and source code for a Telnet client.

Application Startup

Rlogin uses a single TCP connection between the client and server. After the normal TCP connection establishment is complete, the following application protocol takes place between the client and server.

1. The client writes four strings to the server: (a) a byte of 0, (b) the login name of the user on the client host, terminated by a byte of 0, (c) the login name of the user on the server host, terminated by a byte of 0, (d) the name of the user's terminal type, followed by a slash, followed by the terminal speed, terminated by a byte of 0. Two login names are required because users aren't required to have the same login name on each system.

   The terminal type is passed from the client to the server because many full-screen applications need to know it. The terminal speed is passed because some applications operate differently depending on the speed. For example, the `vi` editor works with a smaller window when operating at slower speeds, so it doesn't take forever to redraw the window.

2. The server responds with a byte of 0.

3. The server has the option of asking the user to enter a password. This is handled as normal data exchange across the Rlogin connection—there is no special protocol. The server sends a string to the client (which the client displays on the terminal), often `Password:`. If the client does not enter a password within some time limit (often 60 seconds), the server closes the connection.

   We can create a file in our home directory on the server (named `.rhosts`) with lines containing a hostname and our username. If we login from the specified host with that username, we are not prompted for a password. Most security texts, such as [Curry 1992], strongly suggest never using this feature because of the security hole it presents.

   If we are prompted by the server for a password, what we type is sent to the server as *cleartext*. Each character of the password that we type is sent as is. Anyone who can read the raw network packets can read the characters of our password. Newer implementations of the Rlogin client, such as 4.4BSD, first try to use Kerberos, which avoids sending cleartext passwords across the network. This requires a compatible server that also supports Kerberos. ([Curry 1992] describes Kerberos in more detail.)

4. The server normally sends a request to the client asking for the terminal's window size (described later).

The client sends 1 byte at a time to the server and all echoing is done by the server. We saw this in Section 19.2. Also, the Nagle algorithm is normally enabled (Section 19.4), causing multiple input bytes to be sent as a single TCP segment across slower networks. The operation is simple: everything typed by the user is sent to the server, and everything sent by the server to the client is displayed on the terminal.

Additional commands exist that can be sent from the client to the server and from the server to the client. Let's first describe the scenarios that require these commands.

Flow Control

By default, flow control is done by the Rlogin client. The client recognizes the ASCII STOP and START characters (Control-S and Control-Q) typed by the user, and stops or starts the terminal output.

If this isn't done, each time we type Control-S to stop the terminal output, the Control-S character is sent across the network to the server, and the server stops writing to the network—but up to a window's worth of output may have been already written by the server and will be displayed before the output is stopped. Hundreds or thousands of bytes of data will scroll down the screen before the output stops. Figure 26.3 shows this scenario.

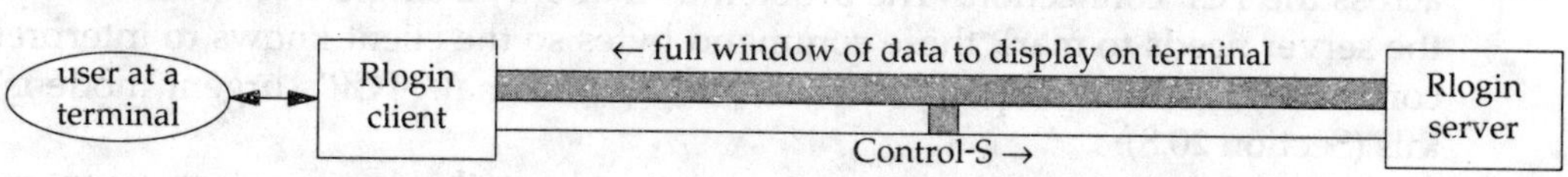

Figure 26.3 Rlogin connection if server performs STOP/START processing.

To an interactive user this delayed response to the Control-S character is bad.

Sometimes, however, the application running on the server needs to interpret each byte of input, and doesn't want the client looking at the input bytes and treating Control-S and Control-Q specially. (The `emacs` editor is an example of an application that uses these two characters for its own commands.) To handle this, the capability is provided for the server to tell the client whether or not to perform flow control.

Client Interrupt

A problem similar to flow control occurs when we type the interrupt key (often DELETE or Control-C), to abort the process currently running on the server. The scenario is similar to what we show in Figure 26.3, with up to one window full of data in the pipe from the server to the client, while the interrupt key makes its way across the connection in the other direction. We want the interrupt key to terminate what's being displayed on the screen as quickly as possible.

In both this case and the flow control scenario, it is rare for the flow of data from the client to the server to be stopped by flow control. This direction contains only characters that we type. Therefore it is not necessary for these special input characters (Control-S or interrupt) to be sent from the client to the server using TCP's urgent mode.

Window Size Changes

With a windowed display we can dynamically change the size of the window while an application is running. Some applications (typically those that manipulate the entire window, such as a full-screen editor) need to know these changes. Most current Unix systems provide the capability for an application to be told of these window size changes.

With remote login, however, the change in the window size occurs on the client, but the application that needs to be told is running on the server. Some form of notification is required for the Rlogin client to tell the server that the window size has changed, and what the new size is.

Server to Client Commands

We can now summarize the four commands that the Rlogin server can send to the client across the TCP connection. The problem is that only a single TCP connection is used, so the server needs to mark these command bytes so the client knows to interpret them as commands, and not display the bytes on the terminal. TCP's urgent mode is used for this (Section 20.8).

When the server sends a command to the client, the server enters urgent mode with the last byte of urgent data being the command byte from the server. When the client receives the urgent mode notification, it reads from the connection, saving the data until the command byte (the last byte of urgent data) is encountered. The data that's saved by the client can be displayed on the terminal, or discarded, depending on the command. Figure 26.4 describes the four command bytes.

Byte	Description
`0x02`	Flush output. The client discards all the data received from the server, up through the command byte (the last byte of urgent data). The client also discards any pending terminal output that may be buffered. The server sends this command when it receives the interrupt key from the client.
`0x10`	The client stops performing flow control.
`0x20`	The client resumes flow control processing.
`0x80`	The client responds immediately by sending the current window size to the server, and notifies the server in the future if the window size changes. This command is normally sent by the server immediately after the connection is established.

Figure 26.4 Rlogin commands from the server to the client.

One reason for sending these commands using TCP's urgent mode is that the first command ("flush output") needs to be sent to the client even if the flow of data from the server to the client is stopped by TCP's windowed flow control. This condition—the server's output to the client being flow control stopped—is likely to occur, since processes running on the server can usually generate output faster than the client's terminal can display it. Conversely, it is rare for the flow of data from the client to the server to be flow control stopped, since this direction of data flow contains the characters that we type.

Recall our example in Figure 20.14 where we saw the urgent notification go across the connection even though the window size was 0. (We'll see another example of this in the next section.) The remaining three commands aren't time critical, but they use the same technique for simplicity.

Client to Server Commands

Only one command from the client to the server is currently defined: sending the current window size to the server. Window size changes from the client are not sent to the server unless the client receives the command `0x80` (Figure 26.4) from the server.

Again, since a single TCP connection is used, the client must have some way of marking the commands that it sends across the connection, so that the server doesn't pass them to the application running on the server. The client does this by sending 2 bytes of `0xff` followed by two special flag bytes.

For the window size command, the two flag bytes are each the ASCII character `s`. Following this are four 16-bit values (in network byte order): the number of rows (e.g., 25), the number of characters per row (e.g., 80), the number of pixels in the X direction, and the number of pixels in the Y direction. Often the final two 16-bit values are 0, because most applications invoked by the Rlogin server deal with the size of the screen in characters, not pixels.

This form of command that we've described from the client to the server is called *in-band signaling* since the command bytes are sent in the normal stream of data. The bytes used to denote these in-band commands, `0xff`, are chosen because we are unlikely to type keys that generate these bytes. But the Rlogin method is not perfect. If we could generate two consecutive bytes of `0xff` from our keyboard, followed by two ASCII `s`'s, the next 8 bytes we type will be interpreted as window sizes.

The Rlogin commands from the server to the client, which we described in Figure 26.4, are termed *out-of-band signaling* since the technique used is called "out-of-band data" by most APIs. But recall our discussion of TCP's urgent mode in Section 20.8 where we said that urgent mode is not out-of-band data, and the command byte is sent in the normal stream of data, pointed to by the urgent pointer.

Since in-band signaling is used from the client to the server, the server must examine every byte that it receives from the client, looking for two consecutive bytes of `0xff`. But with out-of-band signaling used from the server to the client, the client does not need to examine the data that it receives from the server, until the server enters urgent mode. Even in urgent mode, the client only needs to look at the byte pointed to by the urgent pointer. Since the ratio of bytes from the client to server, versus from the server to client, is about 1:20, it makes sense to use in-band signaling for the low-volume data flow (client to server) and out-of-band signaling for the higher volume data flow (server to client).

Client Escapes

Normally everything we type to the Rlogin client is sent to the server. Occasionally, however, we want to talk directly to the Rlogin client program itself, and not have what we type sent to the server. This is done by typing a tilde (~) as the first character of a line, followed by one of the following four characters:

1. A period terminates the client.
2. The end-of-file character (often Control-D) terminates the client.

3. The job control suspend character (often Control-Z) suspends the client.
4. The job-control delayed-suspend character (often Control-Y) suspends only the client input. Everything we type is now interpreted by whatever program we run on the client host, but anything sent to the Rlogin client by the Rlogin server is output to our terminal. This can be used when we start a long running job on the server and we want to know when it outputs something, but we want to continue running other programs on the client.

The last two commands are supported only if the client Unix system supports job control.

26.3 Rlogin Examples

We'll look at two examples: the first shows the client–server protocol at the start of an Rlogin session, and the second shows what happens when we type our interrupt key to abort a running process on the server that is generating lots of output. In Figure 19.2 we showed the normal flow of data across an Rlogin session.

Initial Client–Server Protocol

Figure 26.5 shows the time line for an Rlogin connection from the host `bsdi` to the server on `svr4`. (We have removed the normal TCP connection establishment, the window advertisements, and the type-of-service information.)

The protocol we described in the previous section can be seen in segments 1–9. The client sends a single byte of 0 (segment 1) followed by three strings (segment 3). In this example the three strings are `rstevens` (the login name on the client), `rstevens` (the login name on the server), and `ibmpc3/9600` (the terminal type and speed). The server authenticates this and responds with a byte of 0 (segment 5).

The server then sends the window request command (segment 7). It is sent using TCP's urgent mode and again we see an implementation (SVR4) that uses the older, but more common interpretation, where the urgent pointer specifies the sequence number plus one of the last byte of urgent data. The client responds with 12 bytes of data: 2 bytes of `0xff`, 2 bytes of `s`, and 4 16-bit values.

The next four segments from the server (10, 12, 14, and 16) are the operating system greeting from the server. This is followed by the 7-byte shell prompt on the server: "`svr4 % `" in segment 18.

The data entered by the client is then sent 1 byte at a time, as shown in Figure 19.2. The connection can be closed by either end. If we type a command that causes the shell running on the server to terminate, the server's end does the active close. If we type an escape to the Rlogin client (normally a tilde), followed by a period or our end-of-file character, the client does the active close.

The client port number in Figure 26.5 is 1023, which is within the range controlled by the IANA (Section 1.9). The Rlogin protocol requires the client to have a port number less than 1024, termed a *reserved port*. On Unix systems, a client cannot obtain a reserved port unless the

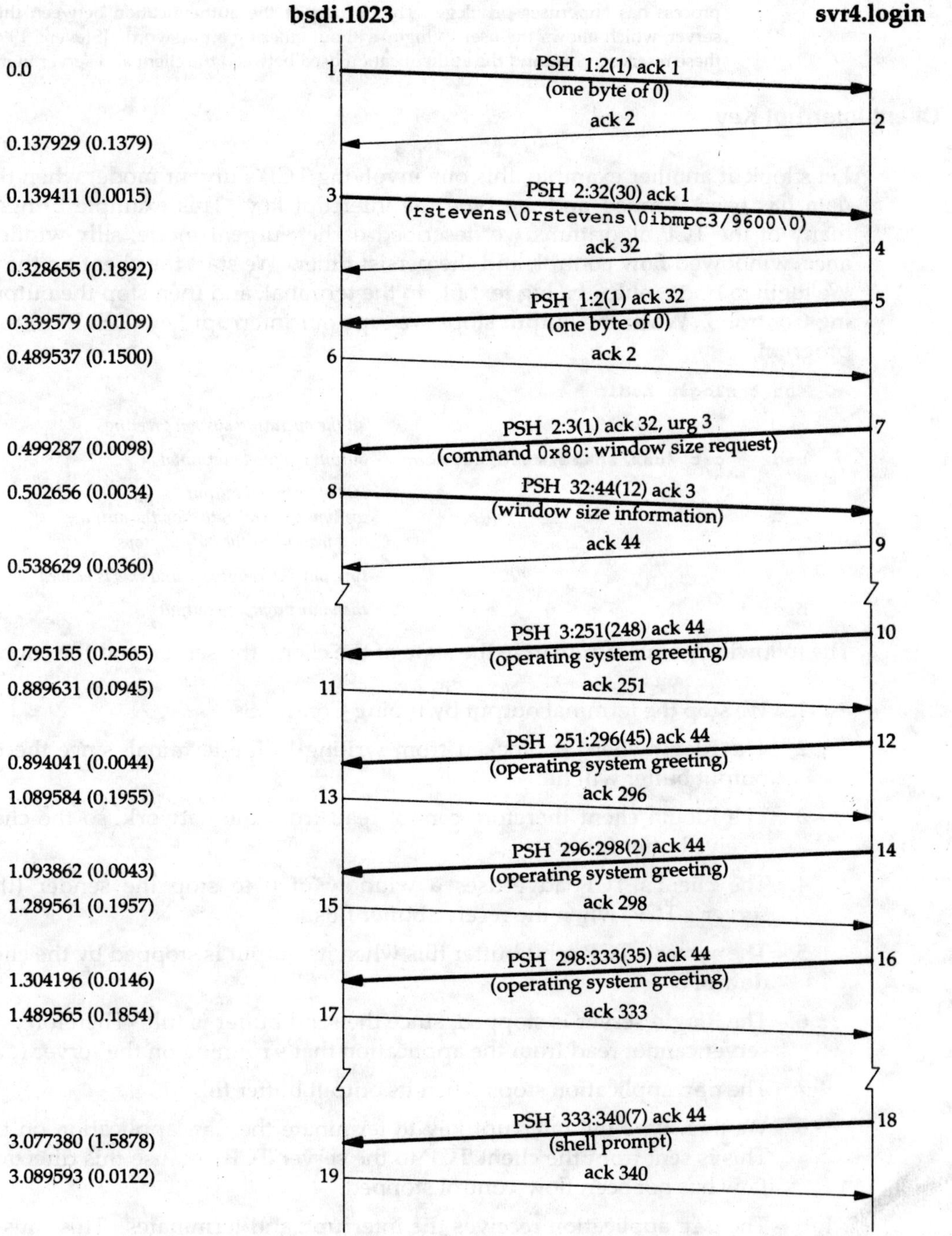

Figure 26.5 Time line for an Rlogin connection.

process has superuser privilege. This is part of the authentication between the client and server, which allows the user to login without entering a password. [Stevens 1990] discusses these reserved ports and the authentication used between the client and server in more detail.

Client Interrupt Key

Let's look at another example, this one involving TCP's urgent mode, when the flow of data has been stopped and we type the interrupt key. This example brings together many of the TCP algorithms we described earlier: urgent mode, silly window avoidance, windowed flow control, and the persist timer. We start the client on the host sun. We login to bsdi, output a big text file to the terminal, and then stop the output by typing Control-S. When the output stops we type our interrupt key (DELETE) to abort the program:

```
sun % rlogin bsdi
                                        all the operating system greetings
bsdi % cat /usr/share/misc/termcap      output big file to terminal
                                        lots of terminal output
                                        we type Control-S to stop the output,
                                        and wait until the output stops
^?                                      type our interrupt key, and this is echoed
bsdi %                                  then our prompt is output
```

The following points summarize the state of the client, the server, and the connection.

1. We stop the terminal output by typing Control-S.
2. The Rlogin client is blocked from writing to the terminal, since the terminal's output buffer will fill.
3. The Rlogin client therefore cannot read from the network, so the client's TCP receive buffer fills.
4. The client's TCP advertises a window of 0 to stop the sender (the Rlogin server's TCP) when the receive buffer fills.
5. The server's TCP send buffer fills when its output is stopped by the client's window of 0.
6. The Rlogin server is stopped, since the send buffer is full. Therefore, the Rlogin server cannot read from the application that's running on the server (`cat`).
7. The `cat` application stops when its output buffer fills.
8. We then type the interrupt key to terminate the `cat` application on the server. This is sent from the client TCP to the server TCP because this direction of data flow has not been flow-control stopped.
9. The `cat` application receives the interrupt, and terminates. This causes its output buffer (which the Rlogin server is reading) to be flushed, which wakes up the Rlogin server. The Rlogin server then enters urgent mode and sends the "flush output" command (`0x02`) to the client.

Figure 26.6 is a summary of the data flow from the server to the client. (The sequence numbers are taken from the time line that we show next.)

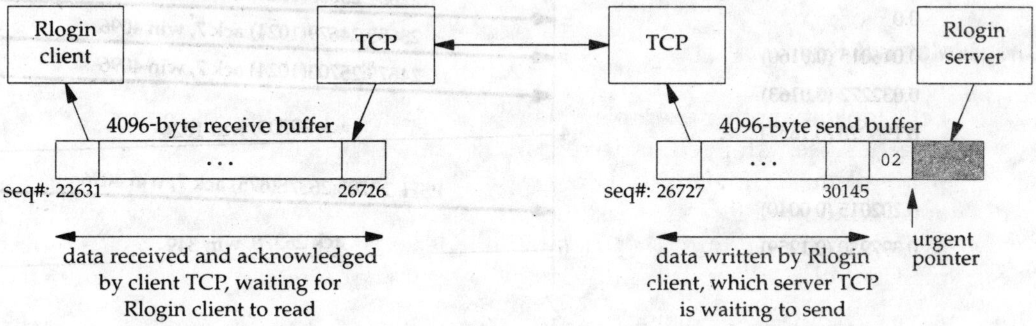

Figure 26.6 Summary of data flow from server to client in Rlogin example.

The shaded portion of the send buffer is the unused portion of the 4096-byte buffer. Figure 26.7 is the time line for this example.

In segments 1–3 the server sends full-sized segments to the client. The ACK in segment 4 only advertises a window of 1024 because the output is stopped: since the client can't write to the terminal, it can't read from the network. Segment 5 is not full sized, and the ACK in segment 6 advertises only the remaining space in the 4096-byte receive buffer. The client must advertise a window of 349 bytes, because if it advertised a window of 0 (which we might expect from silly window avoidance, Section 22.3), it would be moving the right edge of the window to the left, which must not happen (Section 20.3). Since the server can't send a full-sized buffer when it receives segment 6, it performs silly window avoidance, sends nothing, and sets a 5-second persist timer. When the timer expires it sends 349 bytes (segment 7) and since the client's output is still stopped, the acknowledgment in segment 8 advertises a window of 0.

At this point we type our interrupt key and it is transmitted in segment 9. A window of 0 bytes is still advertised. When the Rlogin server receives the interrupt key it passes it to the application (`cat`) and the application terminates. Since the application was terminated by a terminal interrupt, its output is flushed and this is passed to the Rlogin server. This causes the server to send the "flush output" command to the client using TCP's urgent mode. We see this in segment 10. Notice, however, that the command byte of `0x02` is at sequence number 30146 (the urgent pointer minus one). There are 3419 bytes ahead of the command byte (sequence numbers 26727:30145) buffered at the server that the server wants to send.

Segment 10, with the urgent notification, contains the next byte of data from the server to the client (sequence number 26727). It does not contain the "flush output" command byte. The server can send this single byte in segment 10 because we saw in Section 22.2 that a sender with data can always probe a closed window by sending 1 byte of data. The client's TCP responds immediately in segment 11 with a zero window, but the receipt of the urgent notification in segment 10 causes the client's TCP to notify the Rlogin client that the other end of the connection has entered urgent mode.

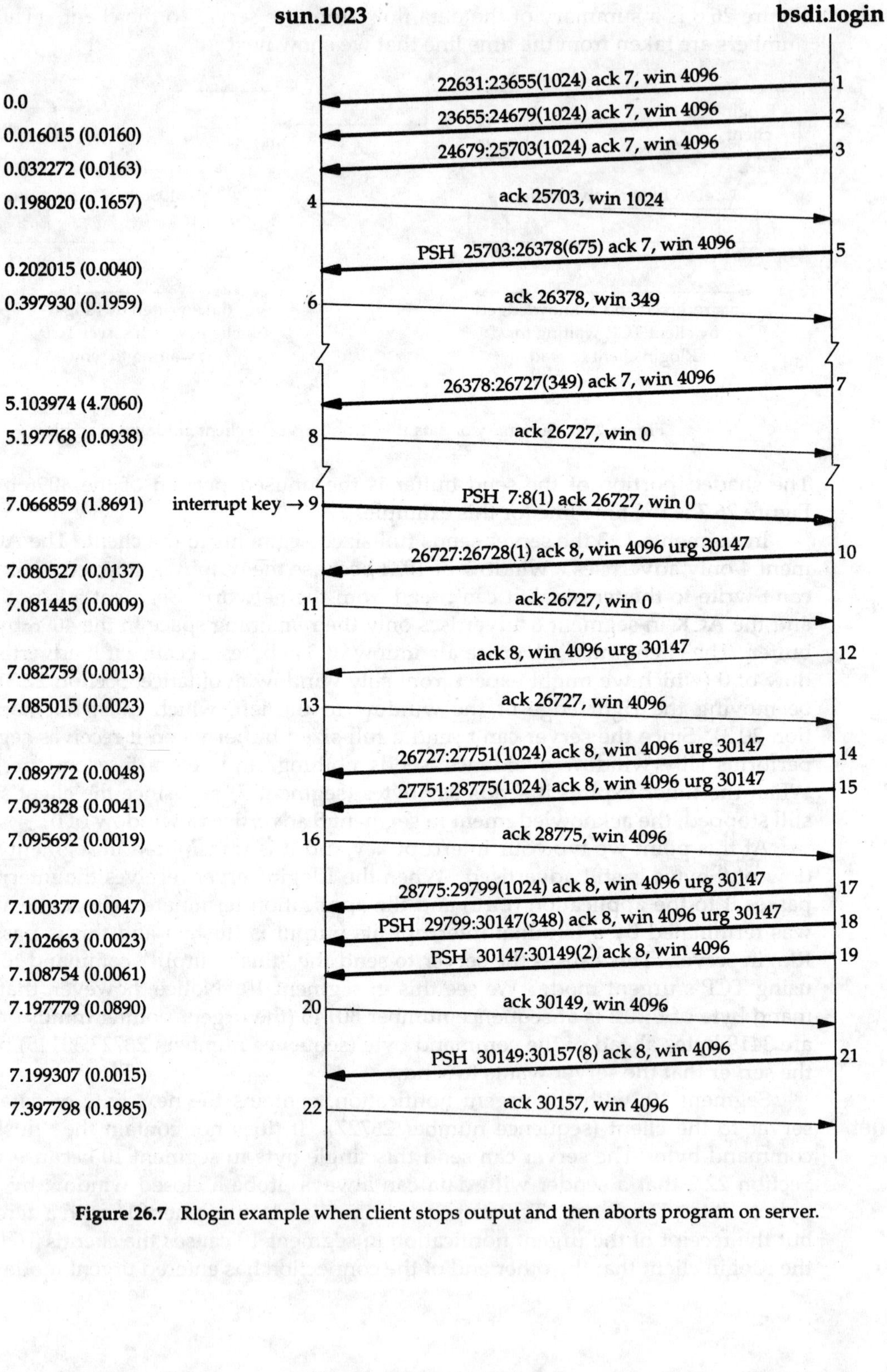

Figure 26.7 Rlogin example when client stops output and then aborts program on server.

Once the Rlogin client receives the urgent notification from its TCP, and starts reading the data that's already waiting for it, the window opens up (segment 13). The data buffered by the server is then sent (segments 14, 15, 17, and 18). The last of these contains the final byte of urgent data (sequence number 30146), which contains the command byte from the server to the client. When the client reads this byte it discards all the data that it read in segments 14, 15, 17, and 18, and flushes its terminal output queue. The next 2 bytes, in segment 19, are the echo of the interrupt key: "^?". The final segment we show (21) contains the shell prompt from the client.

This example shows how data can be buffered at both ends of the connection when the client types the interrupt key. If this action only discarded the 3419 bytes buffered at the server, without discarding the 4096 bytes at the client, these 4096 bytes of data, along with whatever was buffered in the terminal output queue on the client, would be output.

26.4 Telnet Protocol

Telnet was designed to work between any host (i.e., any operating system) and any terminal. Its specification in RFC 854 [Postel and Reynolds 1983a] defines the lowest common denominator terminal, called the *network virtual terminal* (NVT). The NVT is an imaginary device from which both ends of the connection, the client and server, map their real terminal to and from. That is, the client operating system must map whatever type of terminal the user is on to the NVT. The server must then map the NVT into whatever terminal type the server supports.

The NVT is a character device with a keyboard and printer. Data typed by the user on the keyboard is sent to the server, and data received from the server is output to the printer. By default the client echoes what the user types to the printer, but we'll see that options are normally supported to change this.

NVT ASCII

The term *NVT ASCII* refers to the 7-bit U.S. variant of the ASCII character set used throughout the Internet protocol suite. Each 7-bit character is sent as an 8-bit byte, with the high-order bit set to 0.

An end-of-line is transmitted as the 2-character sequence CR (carriage return) followed by an LF (linefeed). We show this as `\r\n`. A carriage return is transmitted as the 2-character sequence CR followed by a NUL (byte of 0). We show this as `\r\0`.

In the following chapters we'll see that FTP, SMTP, Finger, and Whois all use NVT ASCII for client commands and server responses.

Telnet Commands

Telnet uses in-band signaling in both directions. The byte `0xff` (255 decimal) is called IAC, for "interpret as command." The next byte is the command byte. To send the data byte 255, two consecutive bytes of 255 are sent. (In the previous paragraph we said that the data stream is NVT ASCII, which are 7-bit values, implying a data byte of 255 cannot be sent by Telnet. There is a binary option for Telnet, RFC 856 [Postel and Reynolds 1983b], which we don't discuss, that allows 8-bit data transmission.) Figure 26.8 lists all the Telnet commands.

Name	Code (decimal)	Description
EOF	236	end-of-file
SUSP	237	suspend current process (job control)
ABORT	238	abort process
EOR	239	end of record
SE	240	suboption end
NOP	241	no operation
DM	242	data mark
BRK	243	break
IP	244	interrupt process
AO	245	abort output
AYT	246	are you there?
EC	247	escape character
EL	248	erase line
GA	249	go ahead
SB	250	suboption begin
WILL	251	option negotiation (Figure 26.9)
WONT	252	option negotiation
DO	253	option negotiation
DONT	254	option negotiation
IAC	255	data byte 255

Figure 26.8 Telnet commands, when preceded by IAC (255).

Since many of these commands are rarely used, we describe the important commands when we encounter them in the discussion below and in the examples in the next section.

Option Negotiation

Although Telnet starts with both sides assuming an NVT, the first exchange that normally takes place across a Telnet connection is option negotiation. The option negotiation is symmetric—either side can send a request to the other.

Either side can send one of four different requests for any given option.

1. WILL. The sender wants to enable the option itself.
2. DO. The sender wants the receiver to enable the option.
3. WONT. The sender wants to disable the option itself.
4. DONT. The sender wants the receiver to disable the option.

Since the rules of Telnet allow a side to either accept or reject a request to enable an option (cases 1 and 2 above), but require a side to always honor a request to disable an option (cases 3 and 4 above), these four cases lead to the six scenarios shown in Figure 26.9.

	Sender		Receiver	Description
1.	WILL	→		**sender** wants to **enable** option
		←	DO	receiver says OK
2.	WILL	→		**sender** wants to **enable** option
		←	DONT	receiver says NO
3.	DO	→		sender wants **receiver** to **enable** option
		←	WILL	receiver says OK
4.	DO	→		sender wants **receiver** to **enable** option
		←	WONT	receiver says NO
5.	WONT	→		**sender** wants to **disable** option
		←	DONT	receiver must say OK
6.	DONT	→		sender wants **receiver** to **disable** option
		←	WONT	receiver must say OK

Figure 26.9 Six scenarios for Telnet option negotiation.

Option negotiation requires 3 bytes: the IAC byte, followed by the byte for WILL, DO, WONT, or DONT, followed by an ID byte specifying the option to enable or disable. Currently more than 40 different options can be negotiated. The Assigned Numbers RFC specifies the value for the option byte and the relevant RFC that describes the option. Figure 26.10 shows the option codes that we'll see in this chapter.

Option ID (decimal)	Name	RFC
1	echo	857
3	suppress go ahead	858
5	status	859
6	timing mark	860
24	terminal type	1091
31	window size	1073
32	terminal speed	1079
33	remote flow control	1372
34	linemode	1184
36	environment variables	1408

Figure 26.10 Telnet option codes discussed in the text.

Telnet option negotiation, like most of the Telnet protocol, is intended to be symmetrical. Either end can initiate the negotiation of an option. But remote login is not a symmetrical application. The client performs some tasks, and the server performs others. We'll see as we look at some of the Telnet options that some are intended only for the client (asking to enable linemode, for example), and some are only for the server.

Suboption Negotiation

Some options require more information than just "enable" or "disable." Specifying the terminal type is an example: an ASCII string must be sent by the client identifying the type of terminal. To handle these options, suboption negotiation is defined.

RFC 1091 [VanBokkelen 1989] defines the suboption negotiation for the terminal type. First one side (normally the client) asks to enable the option by sending the 3-byte sequence

<IAC, WILL, 24>

where 24 (decimal) is the option ID for the terminal type option. If the receiver (the server) says OK, its response is

<IAC, DO, 24>

The server then sends

<IAC, SB, 24, 1, IAC, SE>

asking the client for its terminal type. SB is the suboption-begin command. The next byte of 24 identifies that this is a suboption for the terminal type option. (SB is always followed by the option number to which the suboption refers.) The next byte of 1 means "send your terminal type." The suboption-end command must be prefixed by an IAC, just like the SB command. The client responds with the command

<IAC, SB, 24, 0, 'I', 'B', 'M', 'P', 'C', IAC, SE>

if its terminal type is the string `ibmpc`. The fourth byte, 0, means "my terminal type is." (The "official" list of acceptable terminal types is in the Assigned Numbers RFC, but on Unix systems at least, any name that is acceptable to the server is OK. This is normally the terminals supported by either the `termcap` or `terminfo` database.) The terminal type is specified in the Telnet suboption as all uppercase, and normally converted to lowercase by the server.

Half-Duplex, Character at a Time, Line at a Time, or Linemode?

There are four modes of operation for most Telnet clients and servers.

1. Half-duplex.

   This is the default mode, but it is rarely used today. The default NVT is a half-duplex device that requires a GO AHEAD command (GA) from the server before accepting user input. The user input is echoed locally from the NVT keyboard to the NVT printer so that only completed lines are sent from the client to the server.

   While this provides the lowest common denominator for terminal support, it doesn't adequately handle full-duplex terminals communicating with hosts that support full-duplex communications, which is the norm today. RFC 857 [Postel and Reynolds 1983c] defines the ECHO option and RFC 858 [Postel and Reynolds 1983d] defines the SUPPRESS GO AHEAD option. The combination of these two options provides support for the next mode, character at a time, with remote echo.

2. Character at a time.

   This is what we saw with Rlogin. Each character we type is sent by itself to the server. The server echoes most characters, unless the application on the server turns echoing off.

   The problems with this mode are perceptible delays in echoing across long delay networks and the high volume of network traffic. Nevertheless, we'll see this is the common default for most implementations today.

   We'll see that the way to enter this mode is for the server to have the SUPPRESS GO AHEAD option enabled. This can be negotiated by having the client send a DO SUPPRESS GO AHEAD (asking to enable the option at the server), or the server sending a WILL SUPPRESS GO AHEAD to the client (asking to enable the option itself). The server normally follows this with a WILL ECHO, asking to do the echoing.

3. Line at a time.

   This is often called "kludge line mode," because its implementation comes from reading between the lines in RFC 858. This RFC states that both the ECHO and SUPPRESS GO AHEAD options must be in effect to have character-at-a-time input with remote echo. Kludge line mode takes this to mean that when either of these options is not enabled, Telnet is in a line-at-a-time mode. In the next section we'll see an example of how this mode is negotiated, and how it is disabled when a program that needs to receive every keystroke is run on the server.

4. Linemode.

   We use this term to refer to the real linemode option, defined in RFC 1184 [Borman 1990]. This option is negotiated between the client and server and corrects all the deficiencies in the kludge line mode. Newer implementations support this option.

Figure 26.11 shows the default operating mode between various Telnet clients and servers. The entry "char" means character at a time, "kludge" means the kludge line mode, and "linemode" means the real RFC 1184 linemode.

Client	Server					
	SunOS 4.1.3	Solaris 2.2	SVR4	AIX 3.2.2	BSD/386	4.4BSD
SunOS 4.1.3	char	char	char	char	kludge	kludge
Solaris 2.2	char	char	char	char	kludge	kludge
SVR4	char	char	char	char	kludge	kludge
AIX 3.2.2	char	char	char	char	kludge	kludge
BSD/386	char	char	char	char	linemode	linemode
4.4BSD	char	char	char	char	linemode	linemode

Figure 26.11 Default modes of operation between various Telnet clients and servers.

The only two implementations in this figure that support real linemode are BSD/386 and 4.4BSD. These two servers are also the only ones that attempt to negotiate kludge line mode if real linemode isn't supported by the client. All the clients and servers shown in this figure do support kludge line mode, but they don't select it by default, unless negotiated by the server.

Synch Signal

Telnet defines its *synch signal* as the Data Mark command (DM in Figure 26.8) sent as TCP urgent data. The DM command is the synchronization mark in the data stream that tells the receiver to return to normal processing. It can be sent in either direction across a Telnet connection.

When one end receives notification that the other end has entered urgent mode, it starts reading the data stream, discarding all data other than Telnet commands. The final byte of urgent data is the DM byte. The reason for using TCP's urgent mode is to allow the Telnet commands to be sent across the connection, even if the TCP data flow has been stopped by TCP's flow control.

We'll see examples of Telnet's synch signal in the next section.

Client Escapes

As with the Rlogin client, the Telnet client also lets us talk to it, instead of sending what we type to the server. The normal client escape character is Control-] (control and the right bracket, commonly printed as "`^]`"). This causes the client to print its prompt, normally "`telnet> `". There are lots of commands that we can type at this point to change characteristics of the session or to print information. A `help` command is provided by most Unix clients that displays the available commands.

We'll see examples of the client escape, and some of the commands we can issue, in the next section.

26.5 Telnet Examples

We'll now look at Telnet option negotiation, along with the three different modes of operation: character at a time, real linemode, and kludge line mode. We also see what happens when an interactive user aborts a running process on the server with the interrupt key.

Character-at-a-Time Mode

We start with the basic character-at-a-time mode, similar to Rlogin. Each character we type on the terminal is sent by itself to the server, and the server echoes the character. But we'll run a newer client (BSD/386) that tries to enable many newer options, and see them refused by the older server (SVR4).

To see what's negotiated between the client and server we'll enable a client option that displays all the option negotiation, and we'll also run `tcpdump` to obtain a time line of the packet exchange. Figure 26.12 shows the interactive session.

```
bsdi % telnet                                invoke client without any command-line options

telnet> toggle options                       tell client to display all the option processing
Will show option processing.

telnet> open svr4                            now establish connection with server
Trying 140.252.13.34...
Connected to svr4.
Escape character is '^]'.

SENT DO SUPPRESS GO AHEAD                    1. (line numbers for discussion that follows)
SENT WILL TERMINAL TYPE                      2.
SENT WILL NAWS                               3.
SENT WILL TSPEED                             4.
SENT WILL LFLOW                              5.
SENT WILL LINEMODE                           6.
SENT WILL ENVIRON                            7.
SENT DO STATUS                               8.
RCVD DO TERMINAL TYPE                        9.
RCVD WILL SUPPRESS GO AHEAD                  10.
RCVD DONT NAWS                               11.
RCVD DONT TSPEED                             12.
RCVD DONT LFLOW                              13.
RCVD DONT LINEMODE                           14.
RCVD DONT ENVIRON                            15.
RCVD WONT STATUS                             16.
RCVD IAC SB TERMINAL-TYPE SEND               17.
SENT IAC SB TERMINAL-TYPE IS "IBMPC3"        18.
RCVD WILL ECHO                               19.
SENT DO ECHO                                 20.
RCVD DO ECHO                                 21.
SENT WONT ECHO                               22.

UNIX(r) System V Release 4.0 (svr4)

RCVD DONT ECHO                               23.
login: rstevens                              we type our login name
Password:                                    and password, which the server does not echo
                                             operating system greeting is then output ...
                                             then shell prompt
```

Figure 26.12 Initial option negotiation by Telnet client and server.

We've numbered the option negotiation lines that begin with SENT or RCVD, for the discussion that follows.

1. The client initiates the negotiation of the SUPPRESS GO AHEAD option. This option starts with a DO since the GO AHEAD command is normally sent by the server to the client, and the client wants the server to enable the option. (This is confusing since enabling the option disables the GA commands from being sent.) The server OKs this option in line 10.

2. The client wants to send its terminal type as specified in RFC 1091 [VanBokkelen 1989]. This is common with Unix clients. This option starts with a WILL since the client wants to enable the option at its end.
3. NAWS stands for "negotiate about window size" and is defined in RFC 1073 [Waitzman 1988]. If the server agrees (which it doesn't, in line 11), the client then sends a suboption with the number of rows and columns in the terminal window. Additionally, the client will send this suboption at any time later if the window size changes. (This is similar to what we saw with the Rlogin `0x80` command in Figure 26.4.)
4. The TSPEED option lets the sender (normally the client) send its terminal speed, as defined in RFC 1079 [Hedrick 1988b]. If the server agrees (which it doesn't, in line 12), the client then sends a suboption with its transmit speed and receive speed.
5. LFLOW stands for "local flow control," and is defined in RFC 1372 [Hedrick and Borman 1992]. The client sends this option to the server stating that it is willing to enable and disable flow control on command. If the server agrees (which it doesn't in line 13), the server would send a suboption to the client whenever the processing of Control-S and Control-Q needs to switch between the client and server. (This is similar to what we saw with the Rlogin `0x10` and `0x20` commands in Figure 26.4.) As we said in our discussion of Rlogin, the interactive user obtains better response to flow control when it's done by the client, not by the server.
6. LINEMODE is the real linemode that we mentioned in Section 26.4. All the terminal character processing is done by the Telnet client (backspace, erase line, etc.) and complete lines are sent to the server. We'll see an example of it later in this section. This option is refused in line 14.
7. The ENVIRON option lets the client send environment variables to the server, as defined in RFC 1408 [Borman 1993a]. This can automatically propagate variables in the user's environment on the client host to the server. The server refuses this option in line 15. (An environment variable in Unix is often an uppercase name, followed by an equals sign, followed by a string value, but this is only a convention.) By default the BSD/386 Telnet client sends only the two variables `DISPLAY` and `PRINTER`, if they're defined and if the option is enabled. The Telnet user can specify additional environment variables to be sent.
8. The STATUS option (RFC 859 [Postel and Reynolds 1983e]) lets one end ask the other for its perception of the current status of the Telnet options. In this example the client is asking the server to enable the option (DO). If the server agreed (which it doesn't in line 16), the client could ask the server in a suboption to send its status.
9. This is the first response from the server. The server agrees to enable the terminal type option. (Almost every Unix server supports this option.) The client, however, cannot send its terminal type until the server asks for it with a suboption (line 17).

10. The server agrees to suppress sending the GO AHEAD command.
11. The server does not agree to let the client send its window size.
12. The server does not agree to let the client send its terminal speed.
13. The server does not agree to let the client perform flow control.
14. The server does not agree to let the client enable the linemode option.
15. The server does not agree to let the client send environment variables.
16. The server will not send status information.
17. This is a suboption with the server asking the client to send its terminal type.
18. The client sends its terminal type as the 6-character string `IBMPC3`.
19. The server asks the client to let the server perform echoing. This is the first time the server has initiated the negotiation of an option.
20. The client agrees to let the server perform echoing.
21. The server asks the client to perform echoing. This command seems superfluous, given the exchange in the previous two lines, and it is. This is yet another kludge in most Unix Telnet servers to determine if the client is a 4.2BSD host or a later BSD release. If the client responds with WILL ECHO, it is probably an older 4.2BSD host and does not support TCP's urgent mode correctly. (In that case urgent mode won't be used.)
22. The client responds with WONT ECHO, implying it is not a 4.2BSD host.
23. The server responds to the received WONT ECHO with a DONT ECHO.

Figure 26.13 shows the time line for this client–server exchange. (We have removed the connection establishment.)

Segment 1 contains lines 1–8 from Figure 26.12. Each option occupies 3 bytes, for a segment containing 24 bytes. It is the client that starts the option negotiation. This segment shows that multiple Telnet options can appear in a single TCP segment.

Segment 3 is line 9 from Figure 26.12, the DO TERMINAL TYPE command. Segment 5 contains the next eight option responses from the server, lines 10–17 from Figure 26.12. The length of this segment is 27 bytes because lines 10–16 are regular options, each requiring 3 bytes, along with the suboption (line 17), which requires 6 bytes. The 12 bytes in segment 6 correspond to line 18, the client sending the suboption with its terminal type.

Segment 8 (53 bytes) is a combination of two Telnet commands with 47 bytes of data to be output on the terminal. The first 6 bytes are the two commands from the server: WILL ECHO and DO ECHO (lines 19 and 21). The next 47 bytes are:

```
\r\n\r\nUNIX(r) System V Release 4.0 (svr4)\r\n\r\0\r\n\r\0
```

The first 4 bytes produce the two blank lines before the string is output. The 2-byte sequence `\r\n` is considered a newline by Telnet. The 2-byte sequence `\r\0` is considered a carriage return. This segment shows that data and commands can appear in the same segment. The Telnet client and Telnet server must scan every byte they receive, looking for the IAC byte and then processing what follows.

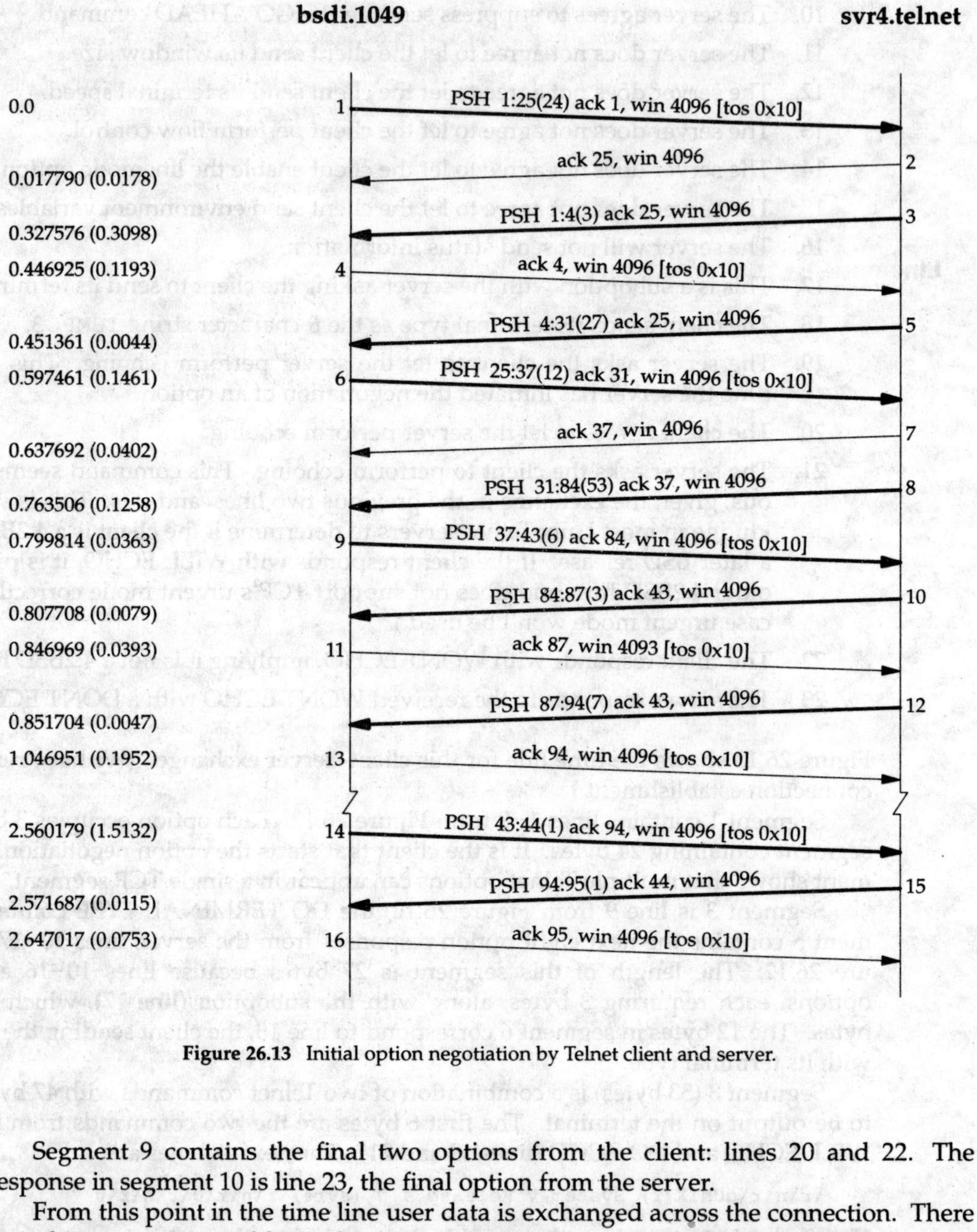

Figure 26.13 Initial option negotiation by Telnet client and server.

Segment 9 contains the final two options from the client: lines 20 and 22. The response in segment 10 is line 23, the final option from the server.

From this point in the time line user data is exchanged across the connection. There is nothing to prevent additional option negotiation, we just don't see any in this example. Segment 12 is the `login:` prompt from the server. Segment 14 is the first character we type of our login name, with its echo returned in segment 15. This is the type of interactive traffic we saw in Section 19.2 with Rlogin: one character at a time sent by the client, with the server performing the echo.

The option negotiation in Figure 26.12 is initiated by the client, but throughout this text we've been using the Telnet client to connect to standard servers such as the daytime server and the echo server, to demonstrate various feature of TCP. When we watched the packet exchange in these examples, such as Figure 18.1, we never saw the client initiate option negotiation. Why? The Unix Telnet client does not initiate any option negotiation if a port number other than the standard Telnet port (23) is specified. This lets the Telnet client, using the standard NVT, exchange data with other, non-Telnet servers. We've used it with the daytime, echo, and discard servers throughout the text, and we'll use it with the FTP and SMTP servers in later chapters.

Linemode

To see Telnet's linemode option in action we'll run the client on our host `bsdi`, connecting to the 4.4BSD server on `vangogh.cs.berkeley.edu`. Both BSD/386 and 4.4BSD support this option.

We won't go through all the packets and option and suboption negotiations, because they're similar to the previous example and the linemode option is quite detailed. Instead we'll note the following differences with the option negotiation.

1. The 4.4BSD server supports more of the options that the BSD/386 tries to negotiate: window size, local flow control, status, accepting environment variables, and terminal speed.
2. The 4.4BSD server tries to negotiate a newer option that the BSD/386 client doesn't support: authentication (to avoid sending the user's password in cleartext across the connection).
3. The client sends the WILL LINEMODE option, as before, but the server responds with DO LINEMODE, since it's supported. This causes the client to send its 16 special characters to the server as a suboption. These are the current values of the special terminal characters in effect at the client: the interrupt character, the end-of-file character, and so on.

   The server sends a suboption to the client telling the client to process all input lines, performing any editing functions (erase character, erase line, etc.). The client sends only completed lines to the server. The server also tells the client to translate any interrupts keys or signal keys into the corresponding Telnet character. For example, if the interrupt key is Control-C, and we type Control-C to interrupt a running process on the server, the client sends the Telnet IP command (<IAC, IP>) to the server.
4. Another difference occurs when we type our password. With Rlogin and character-at-a-time Telnet, the server is responsible for echoing, so when the server reads the password, it doesn't echo the characters. In linemode, however, the client does the echoing. To handle this, the following exchange takes place:
   (a) The server sends WILL ECHO, telling the client that the server will echo.
   (b) The client responds with DO ECHO.
   (c) The server sends the string `Password:` to the client, and the client outputs the string to the terminal.

(d) We type our password and the client sends it to the server when we type the RETURN key. The password is not echoed, since the client thinks the server will echo it.

(e) The server sends the 2-byte sequence CR, LF, to move the cursor, since the RETURN that completed the password was not echoed.

(f) The server sends WONT ECHO.

(g) The client responds with DONT ECHO. The client resumes echoing.

Once we login, the client builds complete lines and sends them to the server. This is the intent of the linemode option. It reduces the number of segments exchanged between the client and server, and provides faster response to client keystrokes (i.e., echoing and editing). Figure 26.14 shows the packet exchange when we type the command

```
vangogh % date
```

across a Telnet connection using linemode. (We have removed the type-of-service information, along with the window advertisements.)

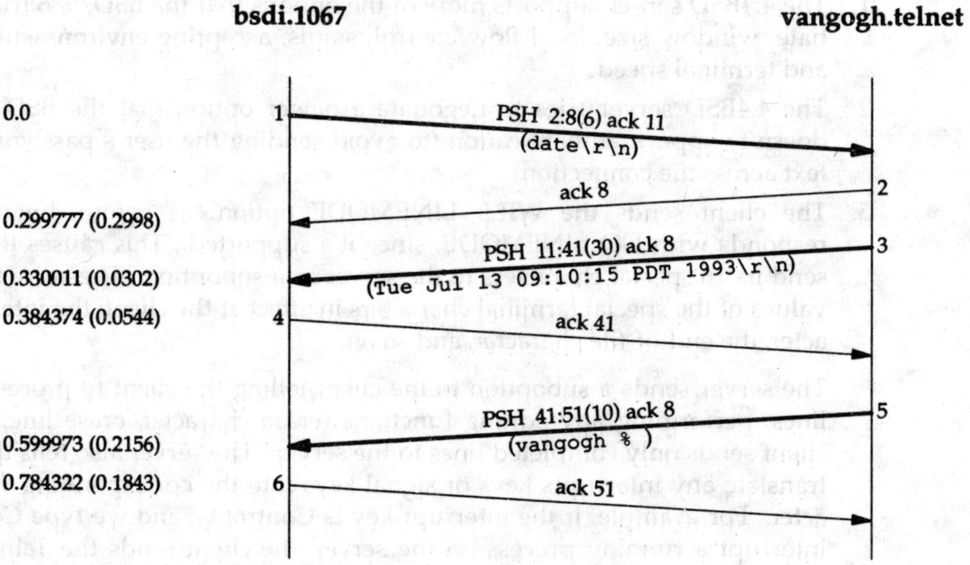

Figure 26.14 Sending a command from client to server using Telnet linemode.

If we compare this with the same command typed to Rlogin (Figure 19.2) we see that Telnet's linemode uses two segments (one with data, one for the ACK, total of 86 bytes including the IP and TCP headers), while 15 segments are used with Rlogin (5 with typed data, 5 with echoed data, 5 ACKs, total of 611 bytes). That is an enormous savings!

What if we run an application on the server that needs to use the single-character mode? (The `vi` editor is an example.) The following steps take place.

1. When the application starts on the server and changes the mode of its pseudo-terminal, the Telnet server is notified that single-character mode is required. The server sends WILL ECHO to the client, along with the linemode suboption that tells the client not to build complete lines, but to send one character at a time.
2. The client responds with DO ECHO and acknowledges the linemode suboption.
3. The application runs on the server. Each character we type is sent to the server by itself (constrained by the Nagle algorithm, of course), and the server does any required echoing.
4. When the application terminates, and restores the mode of its pseudo-terminal, the Telnet server is notified. The server sends WONT ECHO to the client, along with the linemode suboption telling the client to build complete lines.
5. The client responds with DONT ECHO and acknowledges the linemode suboption.

The difference between this scenario and typing our password shows that the echo function and character-at-a-time versus line-at-a-time are independent features. When we type our password, echo must be off but line-at-a-time is OK. For a full-screen application such as an editor, echo is off and character-at-a-time is required.

Figure 26.15 summarizes the different modes we've seen with Telnet and Rlogin.

Application	Client sends: character at-a-time	Client sends: line at-a-time	Client echo?	Example
Rlogin	•		no	
Telnet, character at a time	•		no	
Telnet, linemode		•	yes	normal commands
Telnet, linemode		•	no	typing our password
Telnet, linemode	•		no	`vi` editor

Figure 26.15 Comparison of Rlogin and Telnet modes of operation.

Line-at-a-Time Mode (Kludge Line Mode)

We saw in Figure 26.11 that newer servers that support the linemode option go into kludge line-at-a-time mode, if the client doesn't support linemode. We also mentioned that all the clients and servers in that figure supported the kludge line mode, but it wasn't the default, and must be explicitly enabled by the server or by the user. Let's see how the kludge line mode is enabled, using Telnet options.

We first describe how the BSD/386 server negotiates this mode, when the client doesn't support real linemode.

1. When the client rejects the server's request to enable linemode, the server sends the DO TIMING MARK option. RFC 860 [Postel and Reynolds 1983f] defines

this Telnet option. It is intended for the two ends to synchronize with each other, as we'll see later in this section when we look at user interrupts. This use of the option is just to determine if the client supports the kludge line mode.

2. The client responds with a WILL TIMING MARK, indicating it supports the kludge line mode.
3. The server sends the WONT SUPPRESS GO AHEAD option along with the WONT ECHO option, saying that it wants to disable these two options. We mentioned earlier that character-at-a-time mode assumes that both SUPPRESS GO AHEAD and ECHO are both on, so turning off these options is the kludge that starts line mode.
4. The client responds with DONT SUPPRESS GO AHEAD and DONT ECHO.
5. The `login:` prompt is sent by the server and we type our login name. It is sent to the server as a complete line and echoed locally by the client.
6. The server sends the string `Password:` along with the WILL ECHO option. This turns off echoing of the password we type by the Telnet client, because it thinks the server will echo. The client responds with DO ECHO.
7. We type our password. It is sent by the client to the server as a complete line.
8. Echoing is turned back on by the server sending WONT ECHO, which the client responds to with DONT ECHO.

At this point normal commands are handled similar to the linemode option. The client performs all editing and echoing, sending complete lines to the server.

We mentioned earlier that all the clients and servers in Figure 26.11 with an entry of "char" support the kludge line mode, but start by default in character-at-a-time mode. We can easily watch the negotiation that takes place when we tell the client to enter line mode:

```
                                          client is sun, server is svr4
svr4 %                                    type Control-] to talk to Telnet client (not echoed)
telnet> status                            verify currently in character-at-a-time mode
Connected to svr4.tuc.noao.edu
Operating in character-at-a-time mode.
Escape character is '^]'.
telnet> toggle options                    let's watch the option processing
Will show option processing.
telnet> mode line                         and switch to kludge line mode
SENT dont SUPPRESS GO AHEAD               client sends these two options
SENT dont ECHO
RCVD wont SUPPRESS GO AHEAD               and server responds to both with WONT
RCVD wont ECHO
```

This puts the Telnet session in the kludge line mode, with both the SUPPRESS GO AHEAD and ECHO options disabled.

If we run an application such as the vi editor on the server, we have the same problem we had with the linemode option. The server needs to tell the client to switch from kludge line mode to character-at-a-time mode while the application runs, and then switch back when it's finished. The following technique is used.

1. The Telnet server knows it must change to character-at-a-time mode because the application changes the mode of its pseudo-terminal, which notifies the server. The server sends WILL SUPPRESS GO AHEAD and WILL ECHO. This puts the client into character-at-a-time mode.
2. The client responds with DO SUPPRESS GO AHEAD and DO ECHO.
3. The application runs on the server.
4. When the application terminates and changes the mode of its pseudo-terminal, the Telnet server puts the client back into kludge line mode. It sends WONT SUPPRESS GO AHEAD and WONT ECHO.
5. The client responds with DONT SUPPRESS GO AHEAD and DONT ECHO, indicating that it's back in kludge line mode.

Figure 26.16 summarizes the various settings of the SUPPRESS GO AHEAD and ECHO options for character-at-a-time mode and kludge line mode.

Mode	SUPPRESS GO AHEAD	ECHO	Example
character at a time	on	on	vi editor during kludge line mode
kludge line mode	off	off	normal commands
kludge line mode	off	on	typing our password

Figure 26.16 Settings of Telnet options during kludge line mode.

Linemode: Client Interrupt Key

Let's see what Telnet does when the client types the interrupt key. We establish a session between the client bsdi and the server vangogh.cs.berkeley.edu. Figure 26.17 shows the time line when the interrupt key is typed. (We have removed the window advertisements and the type-of-service.)

In segment 1 the interrupt key (often Control-C or DELETE) is converted into Telnet's IP (interrupt process) command: <IAC, IP>. The next 3 bytes, <IAC, DO, TM>, comprise Telnet's DO TIMING MARK option. This mark is sent by the client and must be responded to with either a WILL or a WONT. In either case, all data received from the server before that response is thrown away (except for Telnet commands). This is a synchronization mark from the client to the server and back. Segment 1 is not sent using TCP's urgent mode.

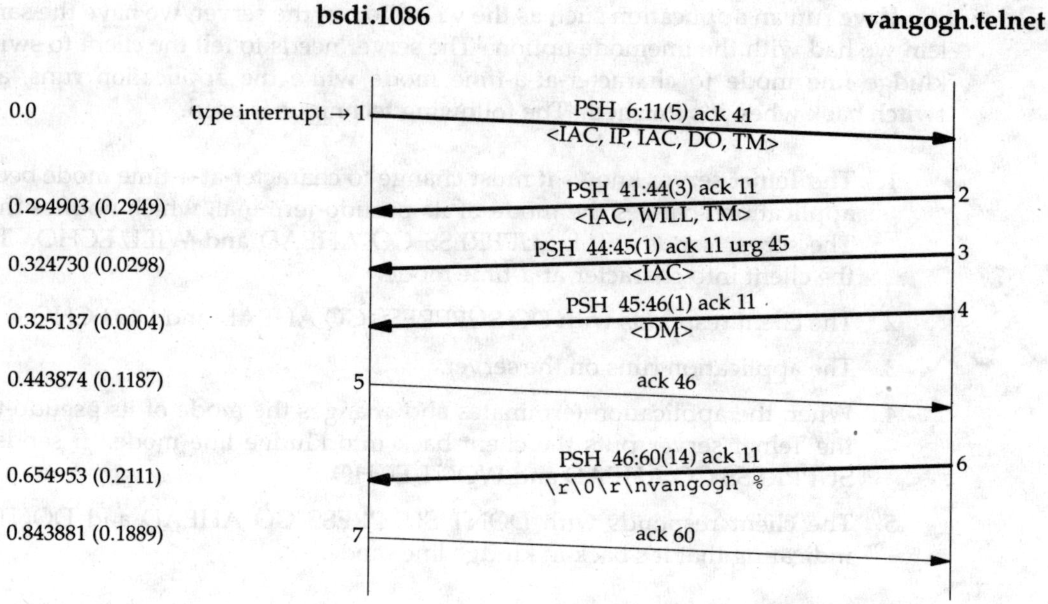

Figure 26.17 Typing interrupt key during linemode operation.

The Host Requirements RFC states that the IP command should be sent using Telnet's synch signal. If it were, the <IAC, IP> would be followed by <IAC, DM>, with the urgent pointer pointing at the DM byte. Most Unix Telnet clients have an option that sends the IP command with the synch signal, but the option defaults off (as we see here).

Segment 2 is the server's reply to the DO TIMING MARK option. It is followed in segments 3 and 4 by a Telnet synch signal: <IAC, DM>. The urgent pointer in segment 3 points to the DM byte, which is sent in segment 4.

If there had been a window full of data queued or in flight from the server to the client, all this data would have been thrown away by the client after sending the IP command in segment 1. Even if the server were stopped by TCP's flow control from sending the data in segments 2, 3, and 4, the urgent pointer is still sent. This is similar to what we saw with Rlogin in Figure 26.7.

Why is the synch signal sent as two segments (3 and 4)? The reason is the problem we detailed in Section 20.8 dealing with TCP's urgent pointer. The Host Requirements RFC says it should point to the last byte of urgent data, while most Berkeley-derived implementations have it point 1 byte beyond the last byte of urgent data. (Recall in Figure 26.6 that the urgent pointer pointed 1 byte beyond the command byte.) The Telnet server purposely writes the first byte of the synch signal as urgent data, knowing the urgent pointer will (incorrectly) point to the next byte that it writes (the data mark, DM), but this first write with the IAC byte is sent immediately, along with the urgent pointer, followed in the next segment by the DM byte.

The final segment of data, segment 6, is just the next shell prompt from the server.

26.6 Summary

This chapter has shown the operation of the Rlogin and Telnet applications. Both provide remote login from a client host to a server host, to let us run programs on the server.

The two applications are different. Rlogin was written assuming both ends of the connection are Unix hosts, so only one option is provided. It is a simple protocol. Telnet, on the other hand, has been around longer and makes no assumptions about the type of host at each end. Telnet is intended to work between different operating systems.

To support a heterogeneous environment, Telnet provides option negotiation between the client and server, to add capabilities if both ends support it. This provides a bare bones implementation for simple clients or servers, but can take advantage of newer features when supported by both ends.

We watched Telnet option negotiation and saw the three types of data transfer: character-at-a-time, kludge line mode, and real linemode. Today the trend is toward line-at-a-time input, when possible, to reduce network traffic and provide better response to the interactive user for line editing and echoing.

Figure 26.18 summarizes and compares the different features provided by Rlogin and Telnet.

Feature	Rlogin	Telnet
transport protocol	One TCP connection. Uses urgent mode.	One TCP connection. Uses urgent mode.
packet mode	Always character-at-a-time, remote echo.	Common default is character-at-a-time, remote echo. Kludge line mode with client echo commonly supported. New option for real linemode with client echo. Always character-at-a-time when application on server requires it.
flow control	Normally done by client, can be disabled by server.	Normally done by server, option allows client to do it.
terminal type	Always provided.	Option, commonly supported.
terminal speed	Always provided.	Option.
window size	Option supported by most servers.	Option.
environment variables	Not supported.	Option.
automatic login	Default. May be prompted for password, which is sent as cleartext. Newer versions support Kerberos login.	Default is to type login name and password. Password is sent as cleartext. Authentication option provided by newer versions.

Figure 26.18 Summary of features provided by Rlogin and Telnet.

Both the Telnet server and the Rlogin server normally set TCP's keepalive option (Chapter 23), if supported by the server's TCP implementation, to detect if the client host crashes. Both applications also use TCP's urgent mode to send server commands to the client even if the flow of data in this direction has been flow control stopped.

Exercises

26.1 Identify all the delayed ACKs in Figure 26.5.

26.2 Why was segment 12 in Figure 26.7 sent?

26.3 We said that the Rlogin client must use a reserved port (Section 1.9). (Normally the Rlogin client only uses reserved ports in the range 512–1023.) What limitation does this present to a host? Is there a way around this?

26.4 Read RFC 1097, describing the Telnet subliminal-message option.

27

FTP: File Transfer Protocol

27.1 Introduction

FTP is another commonly used application. It is the Internet standard for file transfer. We must be careful to differentiate between *file transfer*, which is what FTP provides, and *file access*, which is provided by applications such as NFS (Sun's Network File System, Chapter 29). The file transfer provided by FTP copies a complete file from one system to another system. To use FTP we need an account to login to on the server, or we need to use it with a server that allows *anonymous FTP* (which we show an example of in this chapter).

Like Telnet, FTP was designed from the start to work between different hosts, running different operating systems, using different file structures, and perhaps different character sets. Telnet, however, achieved heterogeneity by forcing both ends to deal with a single standard: the NVT using 7-bit ASCII. FTP handles all the differences between different systems using a different approach. FTP supports a limited number of file types (ASCII, binary, etc.) and file structures (byte stream or record oriented).

RFC 959 [Postel and Reynolds 1985] is the official specification for FTP. This RFC contains a history of the evolution of file transfer over the years.

27.2 FTP Protocol

FTP differs from the other applications that we've described because it uses two TCP connections to transfer a file.

1. The *control connection* is established in the normal client–server fashion. The server does a passive open on the well-known port for FTP (21) and waits for a

client connection. The client does an active open to TCP port 21 to establish the control connection. The control connection stays up for the entire time that the client communicates with this server. This connection is used for commands from the client to the server and for the server's replies.

The IP type-of-service for the control connection should be "minimize delay" since the commands are normally typed by a human user (Figure 3.2).

2. A *data connection* is created each time a file is transferred between the client and server. (It is also created at other times, as we'll see later.)

   The IP type-of-service for the data connection should be "maximize throughput" since this connection is for file transfer.

Figure 27.1 shows the arrangement of the client and server and the two connections between them.

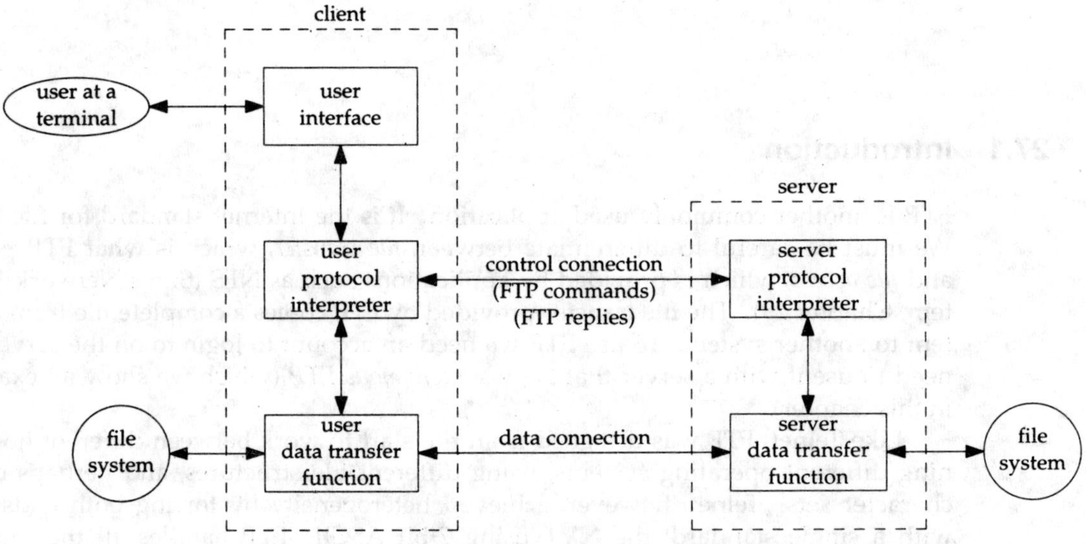

Figure 27.1 Processes involved in file transfer.

This figure shows that the interactive user normally doesn't deal with the commands and replies that are exchanged across the control connection. Those details are left to the two protocol interpreters. The box labeled "user interface" presents whatever type of interface is desired to the interactive user (full-screen menu selection, line-at-a-time commands, etc.) and converts these into FTP commands that are sent across the control connection. Similarly the replies returned by the server across the control connection can be converted to any format to present to the interactive user.

This figure also shows that it is the two protocol interpreters that invoke the two data transfer functions, when necessary.

Data Representation

Numerous choices are provided in the FTP protocol specification to govern the way the file is transferred and stored. A choice must be made in each of four dimensions.

1. File type.
   (a) ASCII file type.
   (Default) The text file is transferred across the data connection in NVT ASCII. This requires the sender to convert the local text file into NVT ASCII, and the receiver to convert NVT ASCII to the local text file type. The end of each line is transferred using the NVT ASCII representation of a carriage return, followed by a linefeed. This means the receiver must scan every byte, looking for the CR, LF pair. (We saw the same scenario with TFTP's ASCII file transfer in Section 15.2.)

   (b) EBCDIC file type.
   An alternative way of transferring text files when both ends are EBCDIC systems.

   (c) Image file type. (Also called binary.)
   The data is sent as a contiguous stream of bits. Normally used to transfer binary files.

   (d) Local file type.
   A way of transferring binary files between hosts with different byte sizes. The number of bits per byte is specified by the sender. For systems using 8-bit bytes, a local file type with a byte size of 8 is equivalent to the image file type.

2. Format control. This choice is available only for ASCII and EBCDIC file types.

   (a) Nonprint.
   (Default) The file contains no vertical format information.

   (b) Telnet format control.
   The file contains Telnet vertical format controls for a printer to interpret.

   (c) Fortran carriage control.
   The first character of each line is the Fortran format control character.

3. Structure.

   (a) File structure.
   (Default) The file is considered as a contiguous stream of bytes. There is no internal file structure.

   (b) Record structure.
   This structure is only used with text files (ASCII or EBCDIC).

(c) Page structure.
Each page is transmitted with a page number to let the receiver store the pages in a random order. Provided by the TOPS-20 operating system. (The Host Requirements RFC recommends against implementing this structure.)

4. Transmission mode. This specifies how the file is transferred across the data connection.
   (a) Stream mode.
   (Default) The file is transferred as a stream of bytes. For a file structure, the end-of-file is indicated by the sender closing the data connection. For a record structure, a special 2-byte sequence indicates the end-of-record and end-of-file.
   (b) Block mode.
   The file is transferred as a series of blocks, each preceded by one or more header bytes.
   (c) Compressed mode.
   A simple run-length encoding compresses consecutive appearances of the same byte. In a text file this would commonly compress strings of blanks, and in a binary file this would commonly compress strings of 0 bytes. (This is rarely used or supported. There are better ways to compress files for FTP.)

If we calculate the number of combinations of all these choices, there could be 72 different ways to transfer and store a file. Fortunately we can ignore many of the options, because they are either antiquated or not supported by most implementations.

Common Unix implementations of the FTP client and server restrict us to the following choices:

- Type: ASCII or image.
- Format control: nonprint only.
- Structure: file structure only.
- Transmission mode: stream mode only.

This limits us to one of two modes: ASCII or image (binary).

This implementation meets the minimum requirements of the Host Requirements RFC. (This RFC also requires support for the record structure, but only if the operating system supports it, which Unix doesn't.)

Many non-Unix implementations provide FTP capabilities to handle their own file formats. The Host Requirements RFC states "The FTP protocol includes many features, some of which are not commonly implemented. However, for every feature in FTP, there exists at least one implementation."

FTP Commands

The commands and replies sent across the control connection between the client and server are in NVT ASCII. This requires a CR, LF pair at the end of each line (i.e., each command or each reply).

The only Telnet commands (those that begin with IAC) that can be sent by the client to the server are interrupt process (<IAC, IP>) and the Telnet synch signal (<IAC, DM> in urgent mode). We'll see that these two Telnet commands are used to abort a file transfer that is in progress, or to query the server while a transfer is in progress. Additionally, if the server receives a Telnet option command from the client (WILL, WONT, DO, or DONT) it responds with either DONT or WONT.

The commands are 3 or 4 bytes of uppercase ASCII characters, some with optional arguments. More than 30 different FTP commands can be sent by the client to the server. Figure 27.2 shows some of the commonly used commands, most of which we'll encounter in this chapter.

Command	Description
ABOR	abort previous FTP command and any data transfer
LIST *filelist*	list files or directories
PASS *password*	password on server
PORT *n1,n2,n3,n4,n5,n6*	client IP address (*n1.n2.n3.n4*) and port ($n5 \times 256 + n6$)
QUIT	logoff from server
RETR *filename*	retrieve (get) a file
STOR *filename*	store (put) a file
SYST	server returns system type
TYPE *type*	specify file type: A for ASCII, I for image
USER *username*	username on server

Figure 27.2 Common FTP commands.

We'll see in the examples in the next section that sometimes there is a one-to-one correspondence between what the interactive user types and the FTP command sent across the control connection, but for some operations a single user command results in multiple FTP commands across the control connection.

FTP Replies

The replies are 3-digit numbers in ASCII, with an optional message following the number. The intent is that the software needs to look only at the number to determine how to process the reply, and the optional string is for human consumption. Since the clients normally output both the numeric reply and the message string, an interactive user can determine what the reply says by just reading the string (and not have to memorize what all the numeric reply codes mean).

Each of the three digits in the reply code has a different meaning. (We'll see in Chapter 28 that the Simple Mail Transfer Protocol, SMTP, uses the same conventions for commands and replies.)

Figure 27.3 shows the meanings of the first and second digits of the reply code.

Reply	Description
1yz	Positive preliminary reply. The action is being started but expect another reply before sending another command.
2yz	Positive completion reply. A new command can be sent.
3yz	Positive intermediate reply. The command has been accepted but another command must be sent.
4yz	Transient negative completion reply. The requested action did not take place, but the error condition is temporary so the command can be reissued later.
5yz	Permanent negative completion reply. The command was not accepted and should not be retried.
x0z	Syntax errors.
x1z	Information.
x2z	Connections. Replies referring to the control or data connections.
x3z	Authentication and accounting. Replies for the login or accounting commands.
x4z	Unspecified.
x5z	Filesystem status.

Figure 27.3 Meanings of first and second digits of 3-digit reply codes.

The third digit gives additional meaning to the error message. For example, here are some typical replies, along with a possible message string.

- 125 Data connection already open; transfer starting.
- 200 Command OK.
- 214 Help message (for human user).
- 331 Username OK, password required.
- 425 Can't open data connection.
- 452 Error writing file.
- 500 Syntax error (unrecognized command).
- 501 Syntax error (invalid arguments).
- 502 Unimplemented MODE type.

Normally each FTP command generates a one-line reply. For example, the QUIT command could generate the reply:

```
221 Goodbye.
```

If a multiline reply is needed, the first line contains a hyphen instead of a space after the 3-digit reply code, and the final line contains the same 3-digit reply code, followed by a space. For example, the HELP command could generate the reply:

```
214- The following commands are recognized (* =>'s unimplemented).
   USER    PORT    STOR    MSAM*   RNTO    NLST    MKD     CDUP
   PASS    PASV    APPE    MRSQ*   ABOR    SITE    XMKD    XCUP
   ACCT*   TYPE    MLFL*   MRCP*   DELE    SYST    RMD     STOU
   SMNT*   STRU    MAIL*   ALLO    CWD     STAT    XRMD    SIZE
   REIN*   MODE    MSND*   REST    XCWD    HELP    PWD     MDTM
   QUIT    RETR    MSOM*   RNFR    LIST    NOOP    XPWD
214 Direct comments to ftp-bugs@bsdi.tuc.noao.edu.
```

Connection Management

There are three uses for the data connection.

1. Sending a file from the client to the server.
2. Sending a file from the server to the client.
3. Sending a listing of files or directories from the server to the client.

The FTP server sends file listings back across the data connection, rather than as multiline replies across the control connection. This avoids any line limits that restrict the size of a directory listing and makes it easier for the client to save the output of a directory listing into a file, instead of printing the listing to the terminal.

We've said that the control connection stays up for the duration of the client–server connection, but the data connection can come and go, as required. How are the port numbers chosen for the data connection, and who does the active open and passive open?

First, we said earlier that the common transmission mode (under Unix the *only* transmission mode) is the stream mode, and that the end-of-file is denoted by closing the data connection. This implies that a brand new data connection is required for every file transfer or directory listing. The normal procedure is as follows:

1. The creation of the data connection is under control of the client, because it's the client that issues the command that requires the data connection (get a file, put a file, or list a directory).
2. The client normally chooses an ephemeral port number on the client host for its end of the data connection. The client issues a passive open from this port.
3. The client sends this port number to the server across the control connection using the PORT command.
4. The server receives the port number on the control connection, and issues an active open to that port on the client host. The server's end of the data connection always uses port 20.

Figure 27.4 shows the state of the connections while step 3 is being performed. We assume the client's ephemeral port for the control connection is 1173, and the client's ephemeral port for the data connection is 1174. The command sent by the client is the PORT command and its arguments are six decimal numbers in ASCII, separated by commas. The first four numbers specify the IP address on the client that the server should issue the active open to (140.252.13.34 in this example), and the next two specify the 16-bit port number. Since the 16-bit port number is formed from two numbers, its value in this example is $4 \times 256 + 150 = 1174$.

Figure 27.5 shows the state of the connection when the server issues the active open to the client's end of the data connection. The server's end point is at port 20.

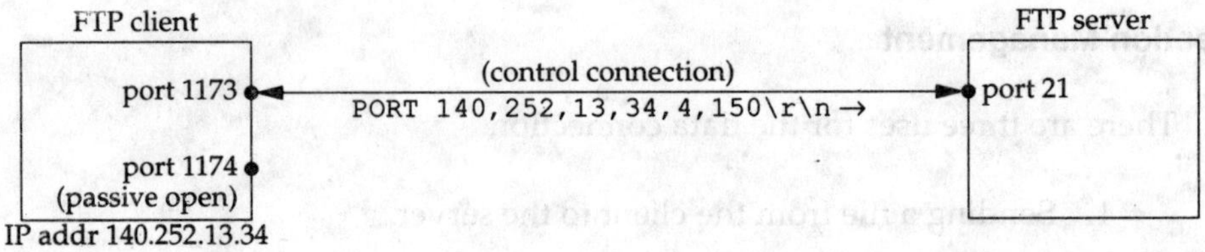

Figure 27.4 PORT command going across FTP control connection.

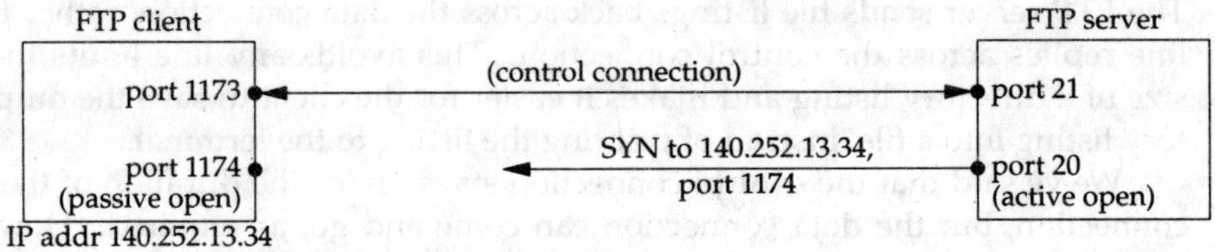

Figure 27.5 FTP server doing active open of data connection.

The server always does the active open of the data connection. Normally the server also does the active close of the data connection, except when the client is sending a file to the server in stream mode, which requires the client to close the connection (which gives the server the end-of-file notification).

It is also possible for the client to not issue the PORT command, in which case the server issues the active open to the same port number being used by the client for its end of the control connection (1173 in this example). This is OK, since the server's port numbers for the two connections are different: one is 20 and the other is 21. Nevertheless, in the next section we'll see why current implementations normally don't do this.

27.3 FTP Examples

We now look at some examples using FTP: its management of the data connection, how text files are sent using NVT ASCII, FTP's use of the Telnet synch signal to abort an in-progress transfer, and finally the popular "anonymous FTP."

Connection Management: Ephemeral Data Port

Let's first look at FTP's connection management with a simple FTP session that just lists a file on the server. We run the client on the host `svr4` with the `-d` flag (debug). This tells it to print the commands and replies that are exchanged across the control connection. All the lines preceded by `--->` are sent by the client to the server, and the lines that begin with a 3-digit number are the server's replies. The client's interactive prompt is `ftp>`.

`svr4 % `**`ftp -d bsdi`**	*-d option for debug output*
`Connected to bsdi.`	*client does active open of control connection*
`220 bsdi FTP server (Version 5.60) ready.`	*server responds it is ready*
`Name (bsdi:rstevens):`	*client prompts us for a login name*
`---> USER rstevens`	*we type RETURN, so client sends default*
`331 Password required for rstevens.`	
`Password:`	*we type our password; it's not echoed*
`---> PASS XXXXXXX`	*client sends it as cleartext*
`230 User rstevens logged in.`	
`ftp> `**`dir hello.c`**	*ask for directory listing of a single file*
`---> PORT 140,252,13,34,4,150`	*see Figure 27.4*
`200 PORT command successful.`	
`---> LIST hello.c`	
`150 Opening ASCII mode data connection for /bin/ls.`	
`-rw-r--r--  1 rstevens  staff  38 Jul 17 12:47 hello.c`	
`226 Transfer complete.`	
`remote: hello.c`	*output by client*
`56 bytes received in 0.03 seconds (1.8 Kbytes/s)`	
`ftp> `**`quit`**	*we're done*
`---> QUIT`	
`221 Goodbye.`	

When the FTP client prompts us for a login name, it prints the default (our login name on the client). When we type the RETURN key, this default is sent.

Asking for a directory listing of a single file causes a data connection to be established and used. This example follows the procedure we showed in Figures 27.4 and 27.5. The client asks its TCP for an ephemeral port number for its end of the data connection, and sends this port number (1174) to the server in a PORT command. We can also see that a single interactive user command (`dir`) becomes two FTP commands (PORT and LIST).

Figure 27.6 is the time line of the packet exchange across the control connection. (We have removed the establishment and termination of the control connection, along with all the window size advertisements.) We note in this figure where the data connection is opened, used, and then closed.

Figure 27.7 is the time line for the data connection. The times in this figure are from the same starting point as Figure 27.6. We have removed all window advertisements, but have left in the type-of-service field, to show that the data connection uses a different type-of-service (maximize throughput) than the control connection (minimize delay). (The TOS values are in Figure 3.2.)

In this time line the FTP server does the active open of the data connection, from port 20 (called `ftp-data`), to the port number from the PORT command (1174). Also in this example, where the server writes to the data connection, the server does the active close of the data connection, which tells the client when the listing is complete.

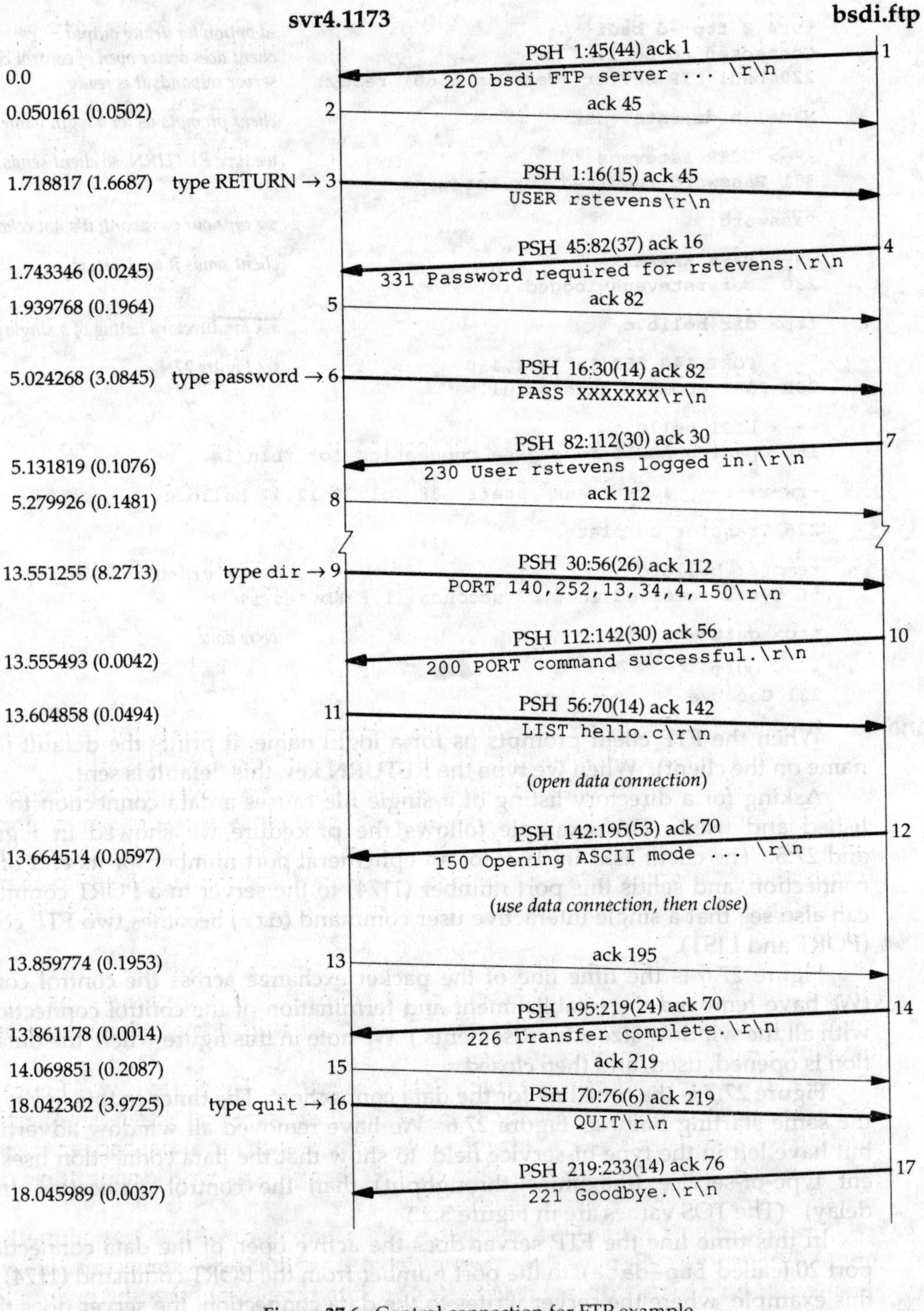

Figure 27.6 Control connection for FTP example.

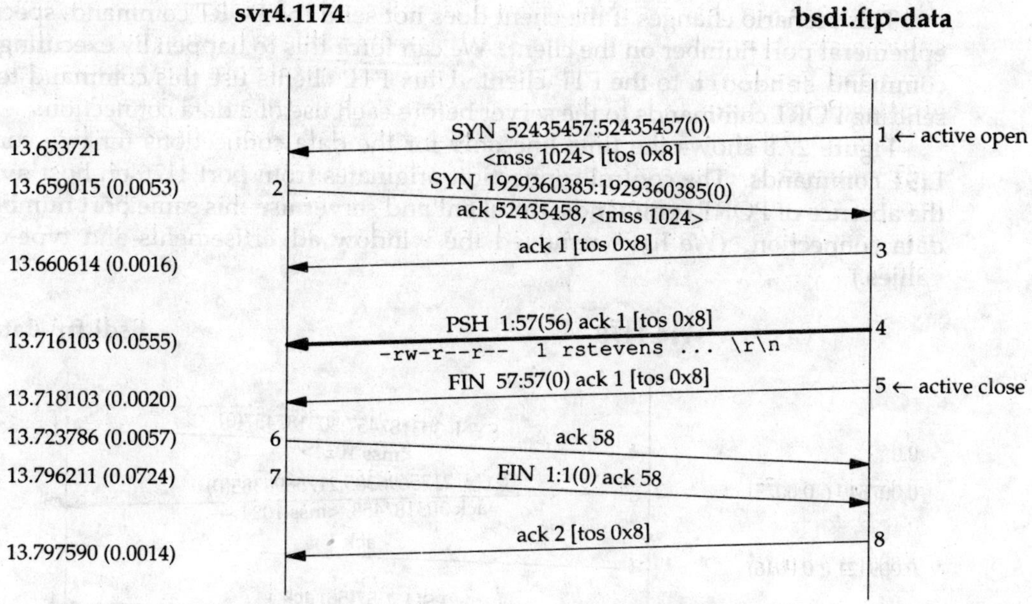

Figure 27.7 Data connection for FTP example.

Connection Management: Default Data Port

If the client does not send a PORT command to the server, to specify the port number for the client's end of the data connection, the server uses the same port number for the data connection that is being used for the control connection. This can cause problems for clients that use the stream mode (which the Unix FTP clients and server always use), as we show below.

> The Host Requirements RFC recommends that an FTP client using the stream mode send a PORT command to use a nondefault port number before each use of the data connection.

Returning to the previous example (Figure 27.6), what if we asked for another directory listing a few seconds after the first? The client would ask its kernel to choose another ephemeral port number (perhaps 1175) and the next data connection would be between `svr4` port 1175 and `bsdi` port 20. But in Figure 27.7 the server did the active close of the data connection, and we showed in Section 18.6 that the server won't be able to assign port 20 to the new data connection, because that local port number was used by an earlier connection that is still in the 2MSL wait state.

The server gets around this by specifying the `SO_REUSEADDR` option that we mentioned in Section 18.6. This lets it assign port 20 to the new connection, and the new connection will have a different foreign port number (1175) from the one that's in the 2MSL wait (1174), so everything is OK.

This scenario changes if the client does not send the PORT command, specifying an ephemeral port number on the client. We can force this to happen by executing the user command `sendport` to the FTP client. Unix FTP clients use this command to turn off sending PORT commands to the server before each use of a data connection.

Figure 27.8 shows the time line only for the data connections for two consecutive LIST commands. The control connection originates from port 1176 on host `svr4`, so in the absence of PORT commands, the client and server use this same port number for the data connection. (We have removed the window advertisements and type-of-service values.)

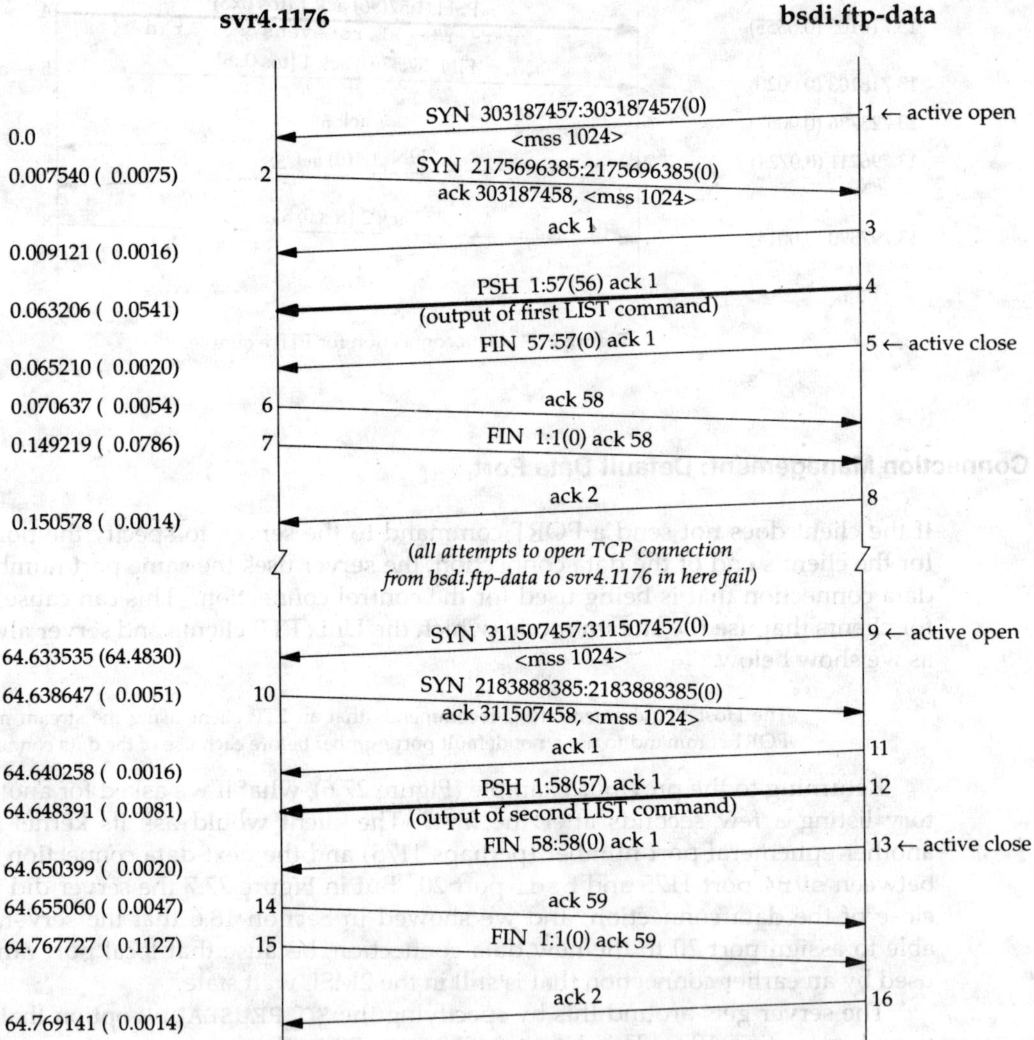

Figure 27.8 Data connection for two consecutive LIST commands.

The sequence of events is as follows.

1. The control connection is established from the client port 1176 to the server port 21. (We don't show this.)
2. When the client does the passive open for the data connection on port 1176, it must specify the SO_REUSEADDR option since that port is already in use by the control connection on the client.
3. The server does the active open of the data connection (segment 1) from port 20 to port 1176. The client accepts this (segment 2), even though port 1176 is already in use on the client, because the two socket pairs

   ```
   <svr4, 1176, bsdi, 21>
   <svr4, 1176, bsdi, 20>
   ```

   are different (the port numbers on `bsdi` are different). TCP demultiplexes incoming segments by looking at the source IP address, source port number, destination IP address, and destination port number, so as long as one of the four elements differs, all is OK.
4. The server does the active close of the data connection (segment 5), which puts the socket pair

   ```
   <svr4, 1176, bsdi, 20>
   ```

   in a 2MSL wait on the server.
5. The client sends another LIST command across the control connection. (We don't show this.) Before doing this the client does a passive open on port 1176 for its end of the data connection. The client must specify the SO_REUSEADDR option again, since the port number 1176 is already in use.
6. The server issues an active open for the data connection from port 20 to port 1176. Before doing this the server must specify SO_REUSEADDR, since the local port (20) is associated with a connection that is in the 2MSL wait, but from what we showed in Section 18.6, the connection won't succeed. The reason is that the socket pair for the connection request equals the socket pair from step 4 that is still in a 2MSL wait. The rules of TCP forbid the server from sending the SYN. There is no way for the server to override this 2MSL wait of the socket pair before reusing the same socket pair.

   At this point the BSD server retries the connection request every 5 seconds, up to 18 times, for a total of 90 seconds. We see that segment 9 succeeds about 1 minute later. (We mentioned in Chapter 18 that SVR4 uses an MSL of 30 seconds, for a 2MSL wait of 1 minute.) We don't see any SYNs from these failures in this time line because the active opens fail and the server's TCP doesn't even send a SYN.

The reason the Host Requirements RFC recommends using the PORT command is to avoid this 2MSL wait between successive uses of a data connection. By continually changing the port number on one end, the problem we just showed disappears.

Text File Transfer: NVT ASCII Representation or Image?

Let's verify that the transmission of a text file uses NVT ASCII by default. This time we don't specify the -d flag, so we don't see the client commands, but notice that the client still prints the server's responses:

```
sun % ftp bsdi
Connected to bsdi.
220 bsdi FTP server (Version 5.60) ready.
Name (bsdi:rstevens):                                          we type RETURN
331 Password required for rstevens.
Password:                                                      we type our password
230 User rstevens logged in.
ftp> get hello.c                                               fetch a file
200 PORT command successful.
150 Opening ASCII mode data connection for hello.c (38 bytes).
226 Transfer complete.                                         server says file contains 38 bytes
local: hello.c remote: hello.c                                 output by client
42 bytes received in 0.0037 seconds (11 Kbytes/s)              42 bytes across data connection
ftp> quit
221 Goodbye.
sun % ls -l hello.c
-rw-rw-r--  1 rstevens       38 Jul 18 08:48 hello.c           but file contains 38 bytes
sun % wc -l hello.c                                            count the lines in the file
       4 hello.c
```

Forty-two bytes are transferred across the data connection because the file contains four lines. Each Unix newline character (\n) is converted into the NVT ASCII 2-byte end-of-line sequence (\r\n) by the server for transmission, and then converted back by the client for storage.

Newer clients attempt to determine if the server is of the same system type, and if so, transfer files in binary (image file type) instead of ASCII. This helps in two ways.

1. The sender and receiver don't have to look at every byte (a big savings).
2. Fewer bytes are transferred if the host operating system uses fewer bytes for the end-of-line than the 2-byte NVT ASCII sequence (a smaller savings).

We can see this optimization using a BSD/386 client and server. We'll enable the debug mode, to see the client FTP commands:

```
bsdi % ftp -d slip                               specify -d to see client commands
Connected to slip.
220 slip FTP server (Version 5.60) ready.
Name (slip:rstevens):                            we type RETURN
---> USER rstevens
331 Password required for rstevens.
Password:                                        we type our password
```

```
---> PASS XXXX
230 User rstevens logged in.
---> SYST                                    this is sent automatically by client
215 UNIX Type: L8 Version: BSD-199103        server's reply
Remote system type is UNIX.                  information output by client
Using binary mode to transfer files.         information output by client
ftp> get hello.c                             fetch a file
---> TYPE I                                  sent automatically by client
200 Type set to I.
---> PORT 140,252,13,66,4,84                 port number = 4 × 256 + 84 = 1108
200 PORT command successful.
---> RETR hello.c
150 Opening BINARY mode data connection for hello.c (38 bytes).
226 Transfer complete.
38 bytes received in 0.035 seconds (1.1 Kbytes/s)   only 38 bytes this time
ftp> quit
---> QUIT
221 Goodbye.
```

After we login to the server, the client FTP automatically sends the SYST command, which the server responds to with its system type. If the reply begins with the string "`215 UNIX Type: L8`", and if the client is running on a Unix system with 8 bits per byte, binary mode (image) is used for all file transfers, unless changed by the user.

When we fetch the file `hello.c` the client automatically sends the command TYPE I to set the file type to image. Only 38 bytes are transferred across the data connection.

> The Host Requirements RFC says an FTP server must support the SYST command (it was an option in RFC 959). But the only systems used in the text (see inside front cover) that support it are BSD/386 and AIX 3.2.2. SunOS 4.1.3 and Solaris 2.x reply with 500 (command not understood). SVR4 has the extremely unsocial behavior of replying with 500 *and* closing the control connection!

Aborting A File Transfer: Telnet Synch Signal

We now look at how the FTP client aborts a file transfer from the server. Aborting a file transfer from the client to the server is easy—the client stops sending data across the data connection and sends an ABOR to the server on the control connection. Aborting a receive, however, is more complicated, because the client wants to tell the server to stop sending data immediately. We mentioned earlier that the Telnet synch signal is used, as we'll see in this example.

We'll initiate a receive and type our interrupt key after it has started. Here is the interactive session, with the initial login deleted:

```
ftp> get a.out                               fetch a large file
---> TYPE I                                  client and server are both 8-bit byte Unix systems
200 Type set to I.
---> PORT 140,252,13,66,4,99
200 PORT command successful.
```

```
---> RETR a.out
150 Opening BINARY mode data connection for a.out (28672 bytes).
^?                                               type our interrupt key
receive aborted                                  output by client
waiting for remote to finish abort               output by client
426 Transfer aborted. Data connection closed.
226 Abort successful
1536 bytes received in 1.7 seconds (0.89 Kbytes/s)
```

After we type our interrupt key, the client immediately tells us it initiated the abort and is waiting for the server to complete. The server sends two replies: 426 and 226. Both replies are sent by the Unix server when it receives the urgent data from the client with the ABOR command.

Figures 27.9 and 27.10 show the time line for this session. We have combined the control connection (solid lines) and the data connection (dashed lines) to show the relationship between the two.

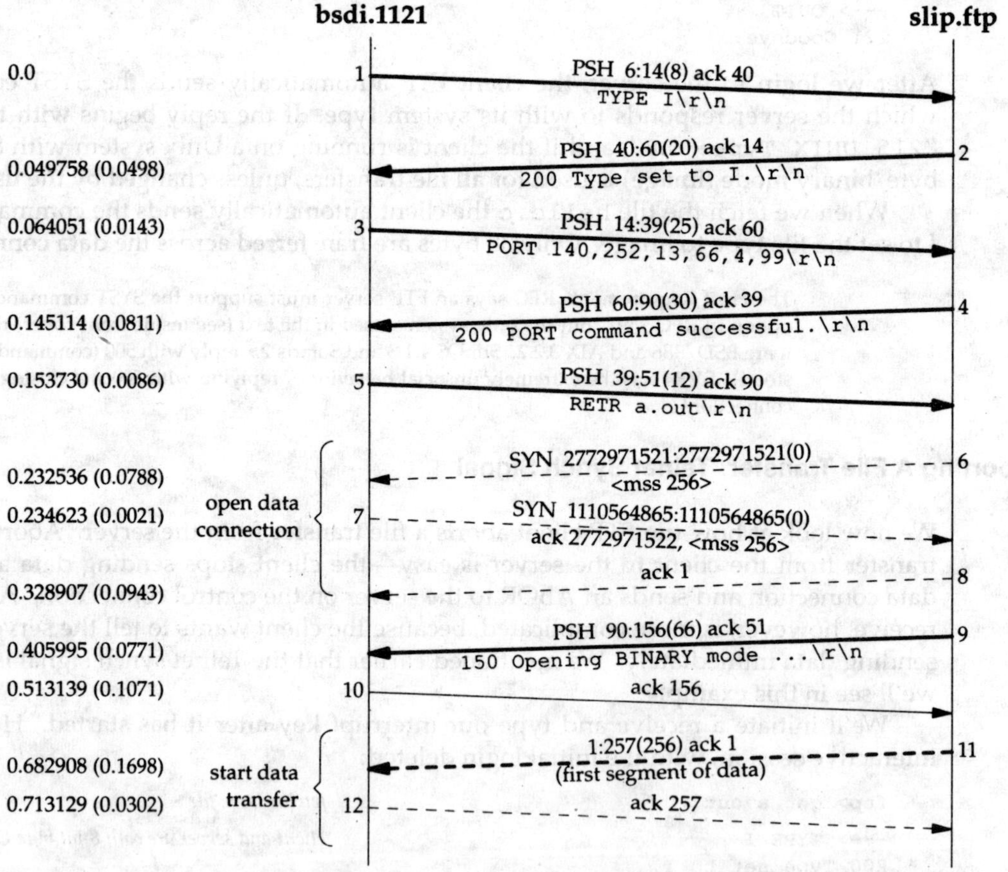

Figure 27.9 Aborting a file transfer (first half).

The first 12 segments in Figure 27.9 are what we expect. The commands and replies across the control connection set up the file transfer, the data connection is opened, and the first segment of data is sent from the server to the client.

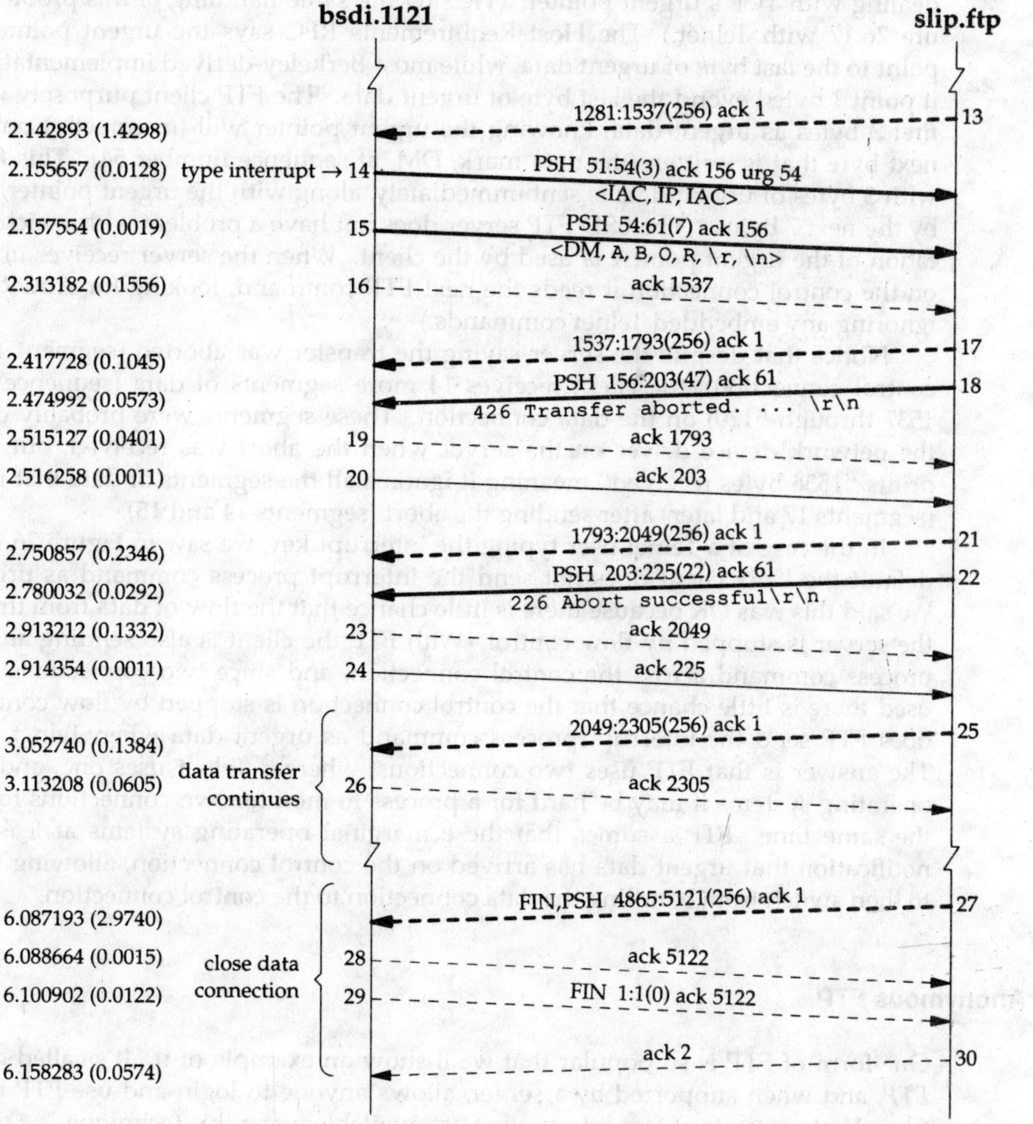

Figure 27.10 Aborting a file transfer (second half).

In Figure 27.10, segment 13 is the receipt of the sixth data segment from the server on the data connection, followed by segment 14, which is generated by our typing the interrupt key. Ten bytes are sent by the client to abort the transfer:

<IAC, IP, IAC, DM, A, B, O, R, \r, \n>

We see two segments (14 and 15) because of the problem we detailed in Section 20.8 dealing with TCP's urgent pointer. (We saw the same handling of this problem in Figure 26.17 with Telnet.) The Host Requirements RFC says the urgent pointer should point to the last byte of urgent data, while most Berkeley-derived implementations have it point 1 byte beyond the last byte of urgent data. The FTP client purposely writes the first 3 bytes as urgent data, knowing the urgent pointer will (incorrectly) point to the next byte that is written (the data mark, DM, at sequence number 54). This first write with 3 bytes of urgent data is sent immediately, along with the urgent pointer, followed by the next 7 bytes. (The BSD FTP server does not have a problem with which interpretation of the urgent pointer is used by the client. When the server receives urgent data on the control connection it reads the next FTP command, looking for ABOR or STAT, ignoring any embedded Telnet commands.)

Notice that despite the server saying the transfer was aborted (segment 18, on the control connection), the client receives 14 more segments of data (sequence numbers 1537 through 5120) on the data connection. These segments were probably queued in the network device driver on the server when the abort was received, but the client prints "1536 bytes received" meaning it ignores all the segments of data that it receives (segments 17 and later) after sending the abort (segments 14 and 15).

In the case of a Telnet user typing the interrupt key, we saw in Figure 26.17 that by default the Unix client does not send the interrupt process command as urgent data. We said this was OK because there is little chance that the flow of data from the client to the server is stopped by flow control. With FTP the client is also sending an interrupt process command across the control connection, and since two connections are being used there is little chance that the control connection is stopped by flow control. Why does FTP send the interrupt process command as urgent data when Telnet does not? The answer is that FTP uses two connections, whereas Telnet uses one, and on some operating systems it may be hard for a process to monitor two connections for input at the same time. FTP assumes that these marginal operating systems at least provide notification that urgent data has arrived on the control connection, allowing the server to then switch from handling the data connection to the control connection.

Anonymous FTP

One form of FTP is so popular that we'll show an example of it. It's called *anonymous FTP*, and when supported by a server, allows anyone to login and use FTP to transfer files. Vast amounts of free information are available using this technique.

How to find which site has what you're looking for is a totally different problem. We mention it briefly in Section 30.4.

We'll use anonymous FTP to the site `ftp.uu.net` (a popular anonymous FTP site) to fetch the errata file for this book. To use anonymous FTP we login with the username of "anonymous" (you learn to spell it correctly after a few times). When prompted for a password we type our electronic mail address.

```
sun % ftp ftp.uu.net
Connected to ftp.uu.net.
220 ftp.UU.NET FTP server (Version 2.0WU(13) Fri Apr 9 20:44:32 EDT 1993) ready.
Name (ftp.uu.net:rstevens): anonymous
331 Guest login ok, send your complete e-mail address as password.
Password:                          we type rstevens@noao.edu; it's not echoed
230-
230-                Welcome to the UUNET archive.
230-   A service of UUNET Technologies Inc, Falls Church, Virginia
230-   For information about UUNET, call +1 703 204 8000, or see the files
230-   in /uunet-info
                                   more greeting lines
230 Guest login ok, access restrictions apply.
ftp> cd published/books            change to the desired directory
250 CWD command successful.
ftp> binary                        we'll transfer a binary file
200 Type set to I.
ftp> get stevens.tcpipiv1.errata.Z fetch the file
200 PORT command successful.
150 Opening BINARY mode data connection for stevens.tcpipiv1.errata.Z (105 bytes).
226 Transfer complete.             (you may get a different file size)
local: stevens.tcpipiv1.errata.Z remote: stevens.tcpipiv1.errata.Z
105 bytes received in 4.1 seconds (0.83 Kbytes/s)
ftp> quit
221 Goodbye.
sun % uncompress stevens.tcpipiv1.errata.Z
sun % more stevens.tcpipiv1.errata
```

The `uncompress` is because many files available for anonymous FTP are compressed using the Unix `compress`(1) program, resulting in a file extension of `.Z`. These files must be transferred using the binary file type, not the ASCII file type.

Anonymous FTP from an Unknown IP Address

We can tie together some features of routing and the Domain Name System using anonymous FTP. In Section 14.5 we talked about pointer queries in the DNS—taking an IP address and returning the hostname. Unfortunately not all system administrators set up their name servers correctly with regard to pointer queries. They often add new hosts to the file required for name-to-address mapping, but forget to add them to the file for address-to-name mapping. We often see this with `traceroute`, when it prints an IP address instead of a hostname.

Some anonymous FTP servers require that the client have a valid domain name. This allows the server to log the domain name of the host that's doing the transfer. Since the only client identification the server receives in the IP datagram from the client is the IP address of the client, the server can call the DNS to do a pointer query, and obtain the domain name of the client. If the name server responsible for the client host is not set up correctly, this pointer query can fail.

To see this error we'll do the following steps.

1. Change the IP address of our host `slip` (see the figure on the inside front cover) to 140.252.13.67. This is a valid IP address for the author's subnet, but not entered into the name server for the `noao.edu` domain.
2. Change the destination IP address of the SLIP link on `bsdi` to 140.252.13.67.
3. Add a routing table entry on `sun` that directs datagrams for 140.252.13.67 to the router `bsdi`. (Recall our discussion of this routing table in Section 9.2.)

Our host `slip` is still reachable across the Internet, because we saw in Section 10.4 that the routers `gateway` and `netb` just sent any datagram destined for the subnet 140.252.13 to the router `sun`. Our router `sun` knows what to do with these datagrams from the routing table entry we made in step 3 above. What we have created is a host with complete Internet connectivity, but without a valid domain name. That is, a pointer query for the IP address 140.252.13.67 will fail.

We now use anonymous FTP to a server that we know requires a valid domain name:

```
slip % ftp ftp.uu.net
Connected to ftp.uu.net.
220 ftp.UU.NET FTP server (Version 2.0WU(13) Fri Apr 9 20:44:32 EDT 1993) ready.
Name (ftp.uu.net:rstevens): anonymous
530- Sorry, we're unable to map your IP address 140.252.13.67 to a hostname
530- in the DNS.  This is probably because your nameserver does not have a
530- PTR record for your address in its tables, or because your reverse
530- nameservers are not registered.  We refuse service to hosts whose
530- names we cannot resolve.  If this is simply because your nameserver is
530- hard to reach or slow to respond then try again in a minute or so, and
530- perhaps our nameserver will have your hostname in its cache by then.
530- If not, try reaching us from a host that is in the DNS or have your
530- system administrator fix your servers.
530 User anonymous access denied..
Login failed.
Remote system type is UNIX.
Using binary mode to transfer files.
ftp> quit
221 Goodbye.
```

The error reply from the server is self-explanatory.

27.4 Summary

FTP is the Internet standard for file transfer. Unlike most other TCP applications, it uses two TCP connections between the client and server—a control connection that is left up for the duration of the client–server session, and a data connection that is created and deleted as necessary.

The connection management used by FTP for the data connection has let us examine in more detail the connection management requirements of TCP. We saw the interaction of TCP's 2MSL wait state on clients that don't issue PORT commands.

FTP uses NVT ASCII from Telnet for all commands and replies across the control connection. The default data transfer mode is often NVT ASCII also. We saw that newer Unix clients automatically send a command to see if the server is an 8-bit byte Unix host, and if so, use binary mode for all file transfers, which is more efficient.

We also showed an example of anonymous FTP, a popular form of software distribution on the Internet.

Exercises

27.1 In Figure 27.8, what would change if the client did the active open of the second data connection instead of the server?

27.2 In the FTP client examples in this chapter we added the notation to lines such as

```
local: hello.c remote: hello.c
42 bytes received in 0.0037 seconds (11 Kbytes/s)
```

that the lines were output by the client. Without looking at the source code, how are we certain these are not from the server?

28

SMTP: Simple Mail Transfer Protocol

28.1 Introduction

Electronic mail (e-mail) is undoubtedly one of the most popular applications. [Caceres et al. 1991] shows that about one-half of all TCP connections are for the *Simple Mail Transfer Protocol*, SMTP. (On a byte count basis, FTP connections carry more data.) [Paxson 1993] found that the average mail message contains around 1500 bytes of data, but some messages contain megabytes of data, because electronic mail is sometimes used to send files.

Figure 28.1 shows an outline of e-mail exchange using TCP/IP.

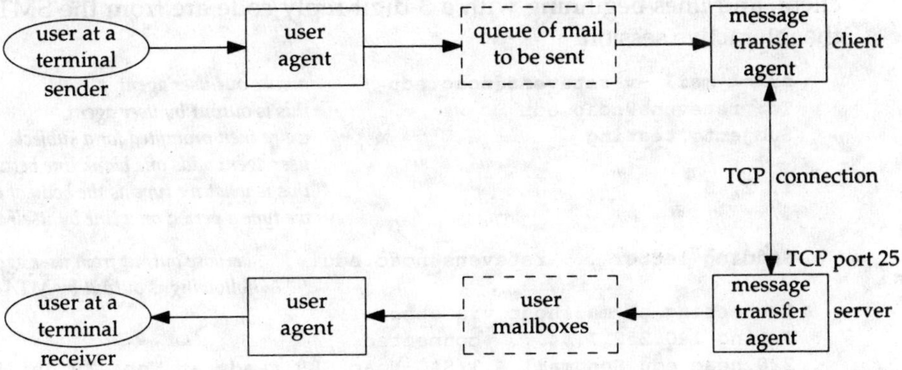

Figure 28.1 Outline of Internet electronic mail.

Users deal with a *user agent*, of which there are a multitude to choose from. Popular user agents for Unix include MH, Berkeley Mail, Elm, and Mush.

The exchange of mail using TCP is performed by a *message transfer agent* (MTA). The most common MTA for Unix systems is Sendmail. Users normally don't deal with the MTA. It is the responsibility of the system administrator to set up the local MTA. Users often have a choice, however, for their user agent.

This chapter examines the exchange of electronic mail between the two MTAs using TCP. We do not look at the operation or design of user agents.

RFC 821 [Postel 1982] specifies the SMTP protocol. This is how two MTAs communicate with each other across a single TCP connection. RFC 822 [Crocker 1982] specifies the format of the electronic mail message that is transmitted using RFC 821 between the two MTAs.

28.2 SMTP Protocol

The communication between the two MTAs uses NVT ASCII. Commands are sent by the client to the server, and the server responds with numeric reply codes and optional human-readable strings. This is similar to what we saw with FTP in the previous chapter.

There are a small number of commands that the client can send to the server: less than a dozen. (By comparison, FTP has more than 40 commands.) Rather than describing each one, we'll start with a simple example to show what happens when we send mail.

Simple Example

We'll send a simple one-line message and watch the SMTP connection. We invoke our user agent with the -v flag, which is passed to the mail transport agent (Sendmail in this case). This MTA displays what is sent and received across the SMTP connection when this flag is specified. Lines beginning with >>> are commands sent by the SMTP client, and lines beginning with a 3-digit reply code are from the SMTP server. Here is the interactive session:

```
sun % mail -v rstevens@noao.edu                invoke our user agent
To: rstevens@noao.edu                          this is output by user agent
Subject: testing                               we're then prompted for a subject
                                               user agent adds one blank line between headers and body
1, 2, 3.                                       this is what we type as the body of the message
.                                              we type a period on a line by itself to say we're done

Sending letter ... rstevens@noao.edu...        verbose output from user agent
                                               following is output by MTA (Sendmail)
Connecting to mailhost via ether...
Trying 140.252.1.54...  connected.
220 noao.edu Sendmail 4.1/SAG-Noao.G89 ready at Mon, 19 Jul 93 12:47:34 MST

>>> HELO sun.tuc.noao.edu.
250 noao.edu Hello sun.tuc.noao.edu., pleased to meet you

>>> MAIL From:<rstevens@sun.tuc.noao.edu>
250 <rstevens@sun.tuc.noao.edu>... Sender ok
```

```
>>> RCPT To:<rstevens@noao.edu>
250 <rstevens@noao.edu>... Recipient ok

>>> DATA
354 Enter mail, end with "." on a line by itself

>>> .
250 Mail accepted

>>> QUIT
221 noao.edu delivering mail

rstevens@noao.edu... Sent
sent.                                        this is output by user agent
```

Only five SMTP commands are used to send the mail: HELO, MAIL, RCPT, DATA, and QUIT.

We type `mail` to invoke our user agent. We're then prompted for a subject, and after typing that, we type the body of the message. Typing a period on a line by itself completes the message and the user agent passes the mail to the MTA for delivery.

The client does the active open to TCP port 25. When this returns, the client waits for a greeting message (reply code 220) from the server. This server's response must start with the fully qualified domain name of the server's host: `noao.edu` in this example. (Normally the text that follows the numeric reply code is optional. Here the domain name is required. The text beginning with `Sendmail` is optional.)

Next the client identifies itself with the HELO command. The argument must be the fully qualified domain name of the client host: `sun.tuc.noao.edu`.

The MAIL command identifies the originator of the message. The next command, RCPT, identifies the recipient. More than one RCPT command can be issued if there are multiple recipients.

The contents of the mail message are sent by the client using the DATA command. The end of the message is specified by the client sending a line containing just a period. The final command, QUIT, terminates the mail exchange.

Figure 28.2 is a time line of the SMTP connection between the sender SMTP (the client) and the receiver SMTP (the server). We have removed the connection establishment and termination, and the window size advertisements.

The amount of data we typed to our user agent was a one-line message ("1, 2, 3."), yet 393 bytes of data are sent in segment 12. The following 12 lines comprise the 393 bytes that are sent by the client:

```
Received: by sun.tuc.noao.edu. (4.1/SMI-4.1)
        id AA00502; Mon, 19 Jul 93 12:47:32 MST
Message-Id: <9307191947.AA00502@sun.tuc.noao.edu.>
From: rstevens@sun.tuc.noao.edu (Richard Stevens)
Date: Mon, 19 Jul 1993 12:47:31 -0700
Reply-To: rstevens@noao.edu
X-Phone: +1 602 676 1676
X-Mailer: Mail User's Shell (7.2.5 10/14/92)
To: rstevens@noao.edu
Subject: testing

1, 2, 3.
```

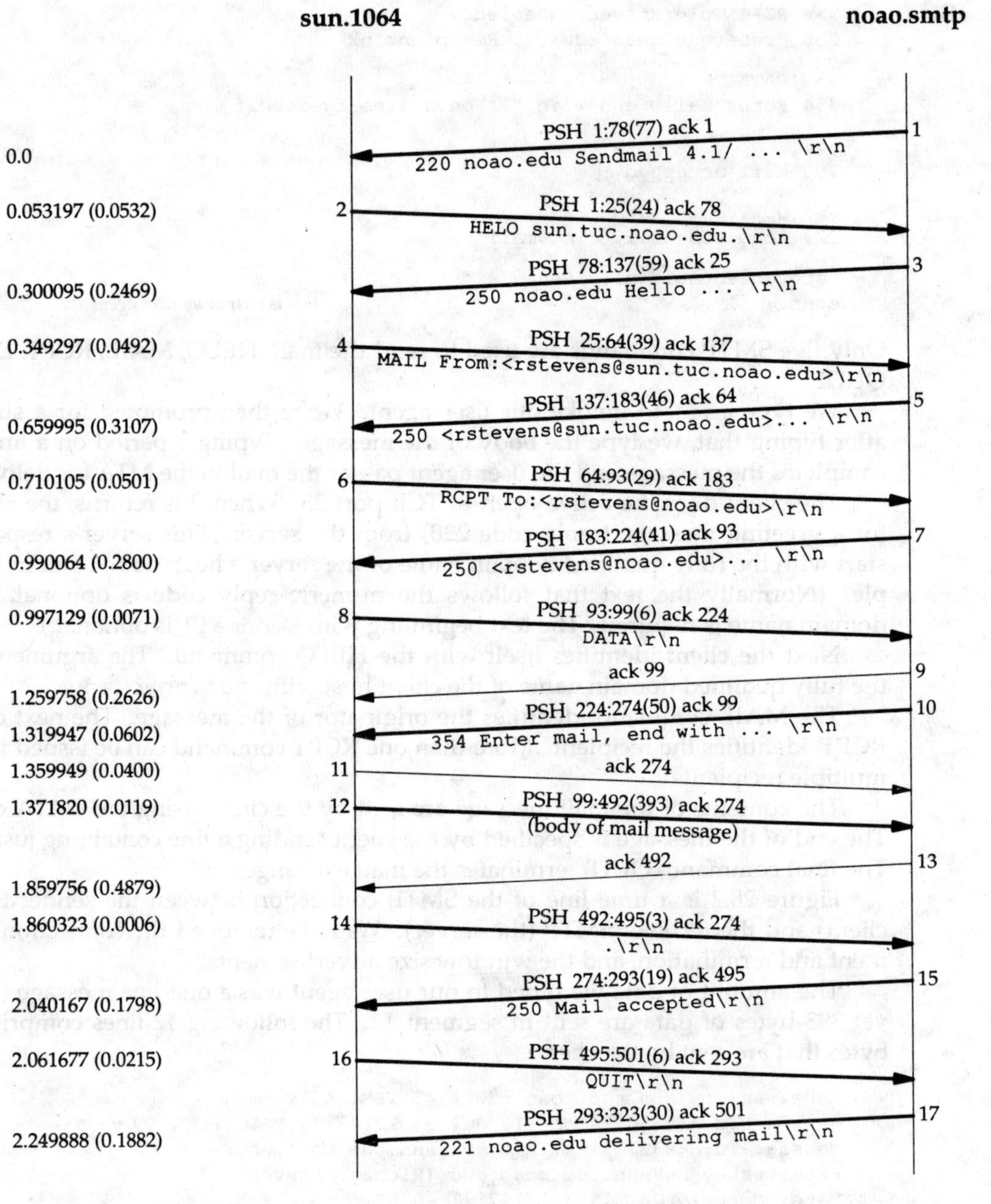

Figure 28.2 Basic SMTP mail delivery.

The first three lines, `Received:` and `Message-Id:`, are added by the MTA, and the next nine are generated by the user agent.

SMTP Commands

The minimal SMTP implementation supports eight commands. We saw five of them in the previous example: HELO, MAIL, RCPT, DATA, and QUIT.

The RSET command aborts the current mail transaction and causes both ends to reset. Any stored information about sender, recipients, or mail data is discarded.

The VRFY command lets the client ask the sender to verify a recipient address, without sending mail to the recipient. It's often used by a system administrator, by hand, for debugging mail delivery problems. We'll show an example of this in the next section.

The NOOP command does nothing besides force the server to respond with an OK reply code (200).

There are additional, optional commands. EXPN expands a mailing list, and is often used by the system administrator, similar to VRFY. Indeed, most versions of Sendmail handle the two identically.

> Version 8 of Sendmail in 4.4BSD no longer handles the two identically. VRFY does not expand aliases and doesn't follow `.forward` files.

The TURN command lets the client and server switch roles, to send mail in the reverse direction, without having to take down the TCP connection and create a new one. (Sendmail does not support this command.) There are three other commands (SEND, SOML, and SAML), which are rarely implemented, that replace the MAIL command. These three allow combinations of the mail being delivered directly to the user's terminal (if logged in), or sent to the recipient's mailbox.

Envelopes, Headers, and Body

Electronic mail is composed of three pieces.

1. The *envelope* is used by the MTAs for delivery. In our example the envelope was specified by the two SMTP commands:

   ```
   MAIL From:<rstevens@sun.tuc.noao.edu>
   RCPT To:<rstevens@noao.edu>
   ```

   RFC 821 specifies the contents and interpretation of the envelope, and the protocol used to exchange mail across a TCP connection.

2. *Headers* are used by the user agents. We saw nine header fields in our example: `Received`, `Message-Id`, `From`, `Date`, `Reply-To`, `X-Phone`, `X-Mailer`, `To`, and `Subject`. Each header field contains a name, followed by a colon, followed by the field value. RFC 822 specifies the format and interpretation of the header fields. (Headers beginning with an `X-` are user-defined fields. The others are defined by RFC 822.) Long header fields, such as `Received` in the example, are folded onto multiple lines, with the additional lines starting with white space.

3. The *body* is the content of the message from the sending user to the receiving user. RFC 822 specifies the body as lines of NVT ASCII text. When transferred

using the DATA command, the headers are sent first, followed by a blank line, followed by the body. Each line transferred using the DATA command must be less than 1000 bytes.

The user agent takes what we specify as the body, adds some headers, and passes the result to the MTA. The MTA adds a few headers, adds the envelope, and sends the result to another MTA.

The term *content* is often used to describe the combination of headers and the body. The content is sent by the client with the DATA command.

Relay Agents

The first line of informational output by our local MTA in our example is "Connecting to mailhost via ether." This is because the author's system has been configured to send all nonlocal outgoing mail to a relay machine for delivery.

This is done for two reasons. First, it simplifies the configuration of all MTAs other than the relay system's MTA. (Configuring an MTA is not simple, as anyone who has ever worked with Sendmail can attest to.) Second, it allows one system at an organization to act as the mail hub, possibly hiding all the individual systems.

In this example the relay system has a hostname of `mailhost` in the local domain (`.tuc.noao.edu`) and all the individual systems are configured to send their mail to this host. We can execute the `host` command to see how this name is defined to the DNS:

```
sun % host mailhost
mailhost.tuc.noao.edu    CNAME    noao.edu          canonical name
noao.edu                 A        140.252.1.54      its real IP address
```

If the host used as the relay changes in the future, only its DNS name need change—the mail configuration of all the individual systems does not change.

Most organizations are using relay systems today. Figure 28.3 is a revised picture of Internet mail (Figure 28.1), taking into account that both the sending host and the final receiving host probably use a relay host.

In this scenario there are four MTAs between the sender and receiver. The local MTA on the sender's host just delivers the mail to its relay MTA. (This relay MTA could have a hostname of `mailhost` in the organization's domain.) This communication uses SMTP across the organization's local internet. The relay MTA in the sender's organization then sends the mail to the receiving organization's relay MTA across the Internet. This other relay MTA then delivers the mail to the receiver's host, by communication with the local MTA on the receiver's host. All the MTAs in this example use SMTP, although the possibility exists for other protocols to be used.

NVT ASCII

One feature of SMTP is that it uses NVT ASCII for everything: the envelope, the headers, and the body. As we said in Section 26.4, this is a 7-bit character code, transmitted as 8-bit bytes, with the high-order bit set to 0.

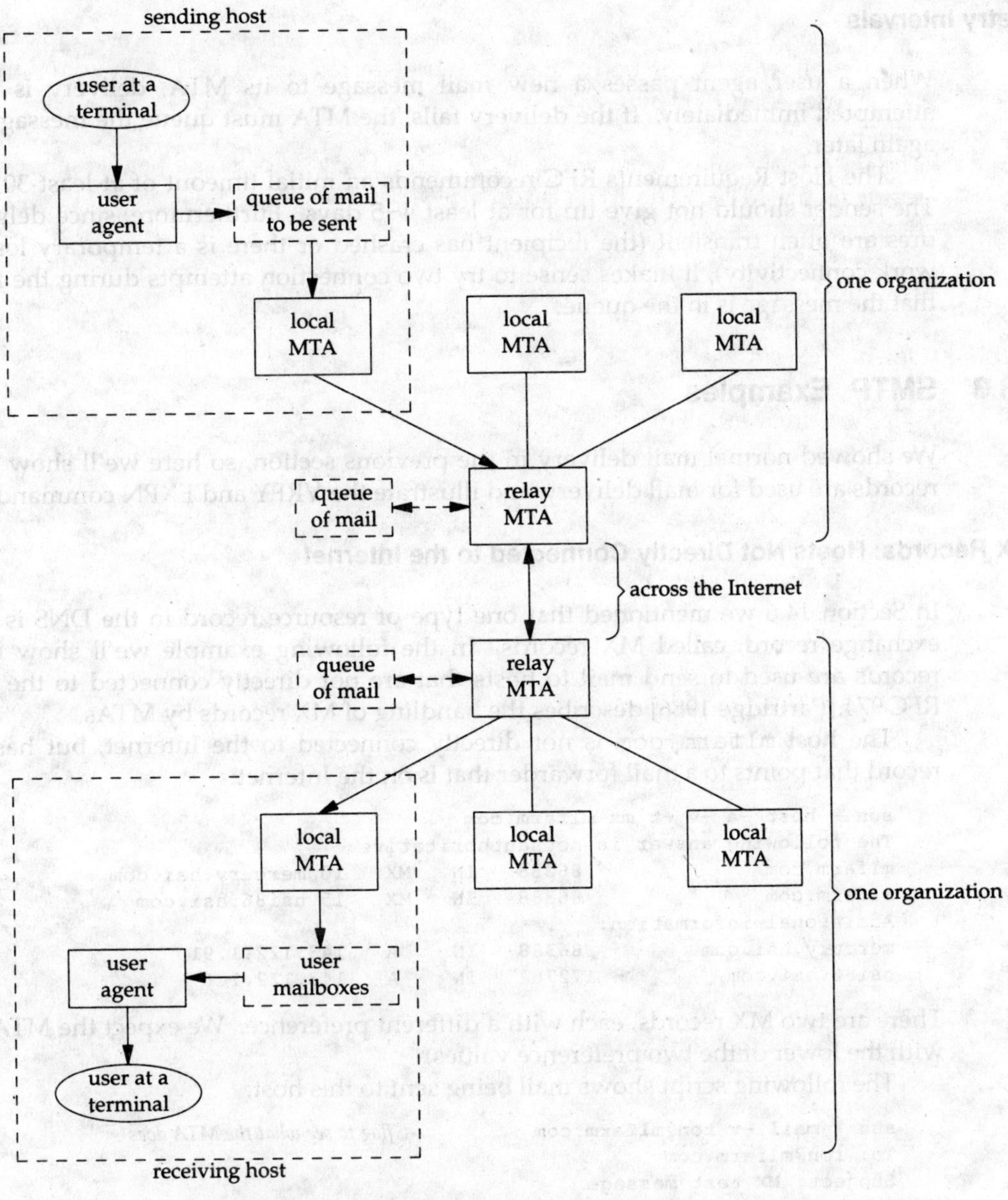

Figure 28.3 Internet electronic mail, with a relay system at both ends.

In Section 28.4 we discuss some newer features of Internet mail, extended SMTP and multimedia mail (MIME), that allow the sending and receiving of data such as audio and video. We'll see that MIME works with NVT ASCII for the envelope, headers, and body, with changes required only in the user agents.

Retry Intervals

When a user agent passes a new mail message to its MTA, delivery is normally attempted immediately. If the delivery fails, the MTA must queue the message and try again later.

The Host Requirements RFC recommends an initial timeout of at least 30 minutes. The sender should not give up for at least 4–5 days. Furthermore, since delivery failures are often transient (the recipient has crashed or there is a temporary loss of network connectivity), it makes sense to try two connection attempts during the first hour that the message is in the queue.

28.3 SMTP Examples

We showed normal mail delivery in the previous section, so here we'll show how MX records are used for mail delivery, and illustrate the VRFY and EXPN commands.

MX Records: Hosts Not Directly Connected to the Internet

In Section 14.6 we mentioned that one type of resource record in the DNS is the mail exchange record, called MX records. In the following example we'll show how MX records are used to send mail to hosts that are not directly connected to the Internet. RFC 974 [Partridge 1986] describes the handling of MX records by MTAs.

The host `mlfarm.com` is not directly connected to the Internet, but has an MX record that points to a mail forwarder that is on the Internet:

```
sun % host -a -v -t mx mlfarm.com
The following answer is not authoritative:
mlfarm.com                86388    IN    MX    10 mercury.hsi.com
mlfarm.com                86388    IN    MX    15 hsi86.hsi.com
Additional information:
mercury.hsi.com           86388    IN     A    143.122.1.91
hsi86.hsi.com            172762    IN     A    143.122.1.6
```

There are two MX records, each with a different preference. We expect the MTA to start with the lower of the two preference values.

The following script shows mail being sent to this host:

```
sun % mail -v ron@mlfarm.com                  -v flag to see what the MTA does
To: ron@mlfarm.com
Subject: MX test message
                                              the body of the message is typed here (not shown)
                                              period on a line by itself to terminate message
Sending letter ... ron@mlfarm.com...
Connecting to mlfarm.com via tcp...
mail exchanger is mercury.hsi.com             the MX records are found
Trying 143.122.1.91... connected.             first tries the one with lower preference
220 mercury.hsi.com ...
                                              remainder is normal SMTP mail transfer
```

We can see in this output that the MTA discovered that the destination host had an MX record and used the MX record with the lowest preference value.

Before running this example from the host sun, it was configured not to use its normal relay host, so we could see the mail exchange with the destination host. It was also configured to use the name server on the host `noao.edu` (which is across its dialup SLIP link), so we could capture both the mail transfer and the DNS traffic using `tcpdump` on the SLIP link. Figure 28.4 shows the starting portion of the `tcpdump` output.

```
1  0.0                   sun.1624 > noao.edu.53: 2+ MX? mlfarm.com. (28)
2  0.445572 (0.4456)     noao.edu.53 > sun.1624: 2* 2/0/2 MX
                                    mercury.hsi.com. 10 (113)
3  0.505739 (0.0602)     sun.1143 > mercury.hsi.com.25: S 1617536000:1617536000(0)
                                                        win 4096
4  0.985428 (0.4797)     mercury.hsi.com.25 > sun.1143: S 1832064000:1832064000(0)
                                                        ack 1617536001 win 16384
5  0.986003 (0.0006)     sun.1143 > mercury.hsi.com.25: . ack 1 win 4096
6  1.735360 (0.7494)     mercury.hsi.com.25 > sun.1143: P 1:90(89) ack 1 win 16384
```

Figure 28.4 Sending mail to a host that uses MX records.

In line 1 the MTA queries its name server for an MX record for `mlfarm.com`. The plus sign following the 2 means the recursion-desired flag is set. The response in line 2 has the authoritative bit set (the asterisk following the 2) and contains 2 answer RRs (the two MX host names), 0 authority RRs, and 2 additional RRs (the IP addresses of the two hosts).

In lines 3–5 a TCP connection is established with the SMTP server on the host `mercury.hsi.com`. The server's initial 220 response is shown in line 6.

Somehow the host `mercury.hsi.com` must deliver this mail message to the destination, `mlfarm.com`. The UUCP protocols are a popular way for a system not connected to the Internet to exchange mail with its MX site.

In this example the MTA asks for an MX record, gets a positive result, and sends the mail. Unfortunately the interaction between an MTA and the DNS can differ between implementations. RFC 974 specifies that an MTA should ask for MX records first, and if none are found, attempt delivery to the destination host (i.e., ask the DNS for an A record for the host, for its IP address). MTAs must also deal with CNAME records in the DNS (canonical names).

As an example, if we send mail to `rstevens@mailhost.tuc.noao.edu` from a BSD/386 host, the following steps are executed by the MTA (Sendmail).

1. Sendmail asks the DNS for CNAME records for `mailhost.tuc.noao.edu`. We see that a CNAME record exists:

   ```
   sun % host -t cname mailhost.tuc.noao.edu
   mailhost.tuc.noao.edu    CNAME    noao.edu
   ```

2. A DNS query is issued for CNAME records for `noao.edu` and the response says none exist.

3. Sendmail then asks the DNS for MX records for `noao.edu` and gets one MX record:

```
sun % host -t mx noao.edu
noao.edu                MX        noao.edu
```

4. Sendmail queries the DNS for an A record (IP address) for `noao.edu` and gets back the value 140.252.1.54. (This A record was probably returned by the name server for `noao.edu` as an additional RR with the MX reply in step 3.)
5. An SMTP connection is initiated to 140.252.1.54 and the mail is sent.

A CNAME query is not tried for the data returned in the MX record (`noao.edu`). The data in the MX record cannot be an alias—it must be the name of a host that has an A record.

The version of Sendmail distributed with SunOS 4.1.3 that uses the DNS only queries for MX records, and gives up if an MX record isn't found.

MX Records: Hosts That Are Down

Another use of MX records is to provide an alternative mail receiver when the destination host is down. If we look at the DNS entry for our host sun we see that it has two MX records:

```
sun % host -a -v -t mx sun.tuc.noao.edu
sun.tuc.noao.edu        86400     IN     MX      0 sun.tuc.noao.edu
sun.tuc.noao.edu        86400     IN     MX      10 noao.edu
Additional information:
sun.tuc.noao.edu        86400     IN     A       140.252.1.29
sun.tuc.noao.edu        86400     IN     A       140.252.13.33
noao.edu                86400     IN     A       140.252.1.54
```

The MX record with the lowest preference indicates that direct delivery to the host itself should be tried first, and the next preference is to deliver the mail to the host `noao.edu`.

In the following script we send mail to ourself at the host `sun.tuc.noao.edu`, from the host `vangogh.cs.berkeley.edu`, after turning off the destination's SMTP server. When a connection request arrives for port 25, TCP should respond with an RST, since no process has a passive open pending for that port.

```
vangogh % mail -v rstevens@sun.tuc.noao.edu
A test to a host that's down.
.
EOT
rstevens@sun.tuc.noao.edu... Connecting to sun.tuc.noao.edu. (smtp)...
rstevens@sun.tuc.noao.edu... Connecting to noao.edu. (smtp)...
220 noao.edu ...
                                remainder is normal SMTP mail transfer
```

We see that the MTA tries to contact `sun.tuc.noao.edu` and then gives up and contacts `noao.edu` instead.

Figure 28.5 is the `tcpdump` output that shows that TCP responds to the incoming SYNs with an RST.

```
1 0.0                   vangogh.3873 > 140.252.1.29.25: S 2358303745:2358303745(0) ...
2 0.000621 (0.0006) 140.252.1.29.25 > vangogh.3873: R 0:0(0) ack 2358303746 win 0

3 0.300203 (0.2996) vangogh.3874 > 140.252.13.33.25: S 2358367745:2358367745(0) ...
4 0.300620 (0.0004) 140.252.13.33.25 > vangogh.3874: R 0:0(0) ack 2358367746 win 0
```

Figure 28.5 Attempt to connect to an SMTP server that is not running.

In line 1 `vangogh` sends a SYN to port 25 at the primary IP address for `sun`: 140.252.1.29. This is rejected in line 2. The SMTP client on `vangogh` then tries the next IP address for `sun`: 140.252.13.33 (line 3), and it also causes an RST to be returned (line 4).

The SMTP client doesn't try to differentiate between the different error returns from its active open on line 1, which is why it tries the other IP address on line 3. If the error had been something like "host unreachable" for the first attempt, it's possible that the second attempt could work.

If the reason the SMTP client's active open fails is because the server host is down, we would see the client retransmit the SYN to IP address 140.252.1.29 for a total of 75 seconds (similar to Figure 18.6), followed by the client sending another three SYNs to IP address 140.252.13.33 for another 75 seconds. After 150 seconds the client would move on to the MX record with the next higher preference.

VRFY and EXPN Commands

The VRFY command verifies that a recipient address is OK, without actually sending mail. EXPN is intended to expand a mailing list, without sending mail to the list. Many SMTP implementations (such as Sendmail) consider the two the same, but we mentioned that newer versions of Sendmail do differentiate between the two.

As a simple test we can connect to a newer version of Sendmail and see the difference. (We have removed the extraneous Telnet client output.)

```
sun % telnet vangogh.cs.berkeley.edu 25
220-vangogh.CS.Berkeley.EDU Sendmail 8.1C/6.32 ready at Tue, 3 Aug 1993 14:
59:12 -0700
220 ESMTP spoken here
helo bsdi.tuc.noao.edu
250 vangogh.CS.Berkeley.EDU Hello sun.tuc.noao.edu [140.252.1.29], pleased
to meet you
vrfy nosuchname
550 nosuchname... User unknown
vrfy rstevens
250 Richard Stevens <rstevens@vangogh.CS.Berkeley.EDU>
expn rstevens
250 Richard Stevens <rstevens@noao.edu>
```

First notice that we purposely typed the wrong hostname on the HELO command: `bsdi` instead of `sun`. Most SMTP servers take the IP address of the client and perform a DNS pointer query (Section 14.5) and compare the hostnames. This allows the server to log the client connection based on the IP address, not the name that a user might have mistyped. Some servers respond with humorous messages, such as "You are a charlatan," or "why do you call yourself ...". We see in this example that this server just prints our real domain name from the pointer query along with our IP address.

We then type a VRFY command for an invalid name, and the server responds with a 550 error. Next we type a valid name, and the server responds with the username on the local host. Next we try the EXPN command and get a different response. The EXPN command determines that the mail for this user is being forwarded, and prints the forwarding address.

Many sites disable the VRFY and EXPN commands, sometimes for privacy, and sometimes in the belief that it's a security hole. For example, we can try these commands with the SMTP server at the White House:

```
sun % telnet whitehouse.gov 25
220 whitehouse.gov SMTP/smap Ready.
helo sun.tuc.noao.edu
250 (sun.tuc.noao.edu) pleased to meet you.
vrfy clinton
500 Command unrecognized
expn clinton
500 Command unrecognized
```

28.4 SMTP Futures

Changes are taking place with Internet mail. Recall the three pieces that comprise Internet mail: the envelope, headers, and body. New SMTP commands are being added that affect the envelope, non-ASCII characters can be used in the headers, and structure is being added to the body (MIME). In this section we consider the extensions to each of these three pieces in order.

Envelope Changes: Extended SMTP

RFC 1425 [Klensin et al. 1993a] defines the framework for adding extensions to SMTP. The result is called *extended SMTP* (ESMTP). As with other new features that we've described in the text, these changes are being added in a backward compatible manner, so that existing implementations aren't affected.

A client that wishes to use the new features initiates the session with the server by issuing an EHLO command, instead of HELO. A compatible server responds with a 250 reply code. This reply is normally multiline, with each line containing a keyword and an optional argument. These keywords specify the SMTP extensions supported by the server. New extensions will be described in an RFC and will be registered with the IANA. (In a multiline reply all lines except the last have a hyphen after the numeric reply code. The last line has a space after the numeric reply code.)

We'll show the initial connection to four SMTP servers, three of which support extended SMTP. We connect to them using Telnet, but have removed the extraneous Telnet client output.

```
sun % telnet vangogh.cs.berkeley.edu 25
220-vangogh.CS.Berkeley.EDU Sendmail 8.1C/6.32 ready at Mon, 2 Aug 1993 15:
47:48 -0700
220 ESMTP spoken here

ehlo sun.tuc.noao.edu
250-vangogh.CS.Berkeley.EDU Hello sun.tuc.noao.edu [140.252.1.29], pleased
to meet you
250-EXPN
250-SIZE
250 HELP
```

This server gives a multiline 220 reply for its greeting message. The extended commands listed in the 250 reply to the EHLO command are EXPN, SIZE, and HELP. The first and last are from the original RFC 821 specification, but they are optional commands. ESMTP servers state which of the optional RFC 821 commands they support, in addition to newer commands.

The SIZE keyword that this server supports is defined in RFC 1427 [Klensin, Freed, and Moore 1993]. It lets the client specify the size of the message in bytes on the MAIL FROM command line. This lets the server verify that it will accept a message of that size, before the client starts to send it. This command was added since the size of Internet mail messages is growing, with the support for message content other than ASCII lines (i.e., images, audio, etc.).

The next host also supports ESMTP. Notice that the 250 reply specifying that the SIZE keyword is supported contains an optional argument. This indicates that this server will accept a message size up to 461 Mbytes.

```
sun % telnet ymir.claremont.edu 25
220 ymir.claremont.edu -- Server SMTP (PMDF V4.2-13 #4220)

ehlo sun.tuc.noao.edu
250-ymir.claremont.edu
250-8BITMIME
250-EXPN
250-HELP
250-XADR
250 SIZE 461544960
```

The keyword 8BITMIME is from RFC 1426 [Klensin et al. 1993b]. This allows the client to add the keyword BODY to the MAIL FROM command, specifying whether the body contains NVT ASCII characters (the default) or 8-bit data. Unless the client receives the 8BITMIME keyword from the server in response to an EHLO command, the client is forbidden from sending any characters other than NVT ASCII. (When we talk about MIME in this section, we'll see that an 8-bit SMTP transport is *not* required by MIME.)

This server also advertises the XADR keyword. Any keyword that begins with an X refers to a local SMTP extension.

The next server also supports ESMTP, advertising the HELP and SIZE keywords that we've already seen. It also supports three local extensions that begin with an X.

```
sun % telnet dbc.mtview.ca.us 25
220 dbc.mtview.ca.us Sendmail 5.65/3.1.090690, it's Mon, 2 Aug 93 15:48:50
-0700
ehlo sun.tuc.noao.edu
250-Hello sun.tuc.noao.edu, pleased to meet you
250-HELP
250-SIZE
250-XONE
250-XVRB
250 XQUE
```

Finally we see what happens when the client tries to use ESMTP by issuing the EHLO command to a server that doesn't support it.

```
sun % telnet relay1.uu.net 25
220 relay1.UU.NET Sendmail 5.61/UUNET-internet-primary ready at Mon, 2 Aug
93 18:50:27 -0400
ehlo sun.tuc.noao.edu
500 Command unrecognized
rset
250 Reset state
```

Instead of receiving a 250 reply to the EHLO command, the client receives a 500 reply. The client should then issue the RSET command, followed by a HELO command.

Header Changes: Non-ASCII Characters

RFC 1522 [Moore 1993] specifies a way to send non-ASCII characters in RFC 822 message headers. The main use of this is to allow additional characters in the sender and receiver names, and in the subject.

The header fields can contain encoded words. They have the following format:

=? *charset* ? *encoding* ? *encoded-text* ?=

charset is the character set specification. Valid values are the two strings `us-ascii` and `iso-8859-X`, where `X` is a single digit, as in `iso-8859-1`.

encoding is a single character to specify the encoding method. Two values are supported.

1. `Q` encoding means *quoted-printable*, and is intended for Latin character sets. Most characters are sent as NVT ASCII (with the high-order bit set to 0, of course). Any character to be sent whose eighth bit is set is sent instead as three characters: first the character =, followed by two hexadecimal digits. For example, the character é (whose binary 8-bit value is `0xe9`) is sent as the three characters `=E9`. Spaces are always sent as either an underscore or the three characters `=20`. This encoding is intended for text that is mostly ASCII, with a few special characters.

2. B means base-64 encoding. Three consecutive bytes of text (24 bits) are encoded as four 6-bit values. The 64 NVT ASCII characters used to represent each of the possible 6-bit values are shown in Figure 28.6.

6-bit value	ASCII char	6-bit value	ASCII char	6-bit value	ASCII char	6-bit value	ASCII char
0	A	10	Q	20	g	30	w
1	B	11	R	21	h	31	x
2	C	12	S	22	i	32	y
3	D	13	T	23	j	33	z
4	E	14	U	24	k	34	0
5	F	15	V	25	l	35	1
6	G	16	W	26	m	36	2
7	H	17	X	27	n	37	3
8	I	18	Y	28	o	38	4
9	J	19	Z	29	p	39	5
a	K	1a	a	2a	q	3a	6
b	L	1b	b	2b	r	3b	7
c	M	1c	c	2c	s	3c	8
d	N	1d	d	2d	t	3d	9
e	O	1e	e	2e	u	3e	+
f	P	1f	f	2f	v	3f	/

Figure 28.6 Encoding of 6-bit values (base-64 encoding).

When the number of characters to encode is not a multiple of three, equal signs are used as the pad characters.

The following example of these two encodings is from RFC 1522:

```
From: =?US-ASCII?Q?Keith_Moore?= <moore@cs.utk.edu>
To: =?ISO-8859-1?Q?Keld_J=F8rn_Simonsen?= <keld@dkuug.dk>
CC: =?ISO-8859-1?Q?Andr=E9_?= Pirard <PIRARD@vm1.ulg.ac.be>
Subject: =?ISO-8859-1?B?SWYgeW91IGNhbiByZWFkIHRoaXMgeW8=?=
 =?ISO-8859-2?B?dSB1bmRlcnN0YW5kIHRoZSBleGFtcGxlLg==?=
```

A user agent capable of handling these headers would output:

```
From: Keith Moore <moore@cs.utk.edu>
To: Keld Jørn Simonsen <keld@dkuug.dk>
CC: Andre  Pirard <PIRARD@vm1.ulg.ac.be>
Subject: If you can read this you understand the example.
```

To see how base-64 encoding works, look at the first four encoded characters in the subject line: `SWYg`. Write out the 6-bit values for these four characters from Figure 28.6 (`S=0x12`, `W=0x16`, `Y=0x18`, and `g=0x20`) in binary:

```
010010 010110 011000 100000
```

Then regroup these 24 bits into three 8-bit bytes:

```
01001001 01100110 00100000
 =0x49     =0x66    =0x20
```

which are the ASCII representations for `I`, `f`, and a space.

Body Changes: Multipurpose Internet Mail Extensions (MIME)

We've said that RFC 822 specifies the body as lines of NVT ASCII text, with no structure. RFC 1521 [Borenstein and Freed 1993] defines extensions that allow structure in the body. This is called MIME, for *Multipurpose Internet Mail Extensions*.

MIME does *not* require any of the extensions that we've described previously in this section (extended SMTP or non-ASCII headers). MIME just adds some new headers (in accordance with RFC 822) that tell the recipient the structure of the body. The body can still be transmitted using NVT ASCII, regardless of the mail contents. While some of the extensions we've just described might be nice to have along with MIME—the extended SMTP SIZE command, since MIME messages can become large, and non-ASCII headers—these extensions are not required by MIME. All that's required to exchange MIME messages with another party is for both ends to have a user agent that understands MIME. No changes are required in any of the MTAs.

MIME defines the five new header fields:

```
Mime-Version:
Content-Type:
Content-Transfer-Encoding:
Content-ID:
Content-Description:
```

As an example, the following two header lines can appear in an Internet mail message:

```
Mime-Version: 1.0
Content-Type: TEXT/PLAIN; charset=US-ASCII
```

The current MIME version is 1.0 and the content type is plain ASCII text, the default for Internet mail. The word `PLAIN` is considered a subtype of the content type (`TEXT`), and the string `charset=US-ASCII` is a parameter.

`Text` is just one of MIME's seven defined content types. Figure 28.7 summarizes the 16 different content types and subtypes defined in RFC 1521. Numerous parameters can be specified for certain content types and subtypes.

The content type and the transfer encoding used for the body are independent. The former is specified by the `Content-Type` header field, and the latter by the `Content-Transfer-Encoding` header field. There are five different encoding formats defined in RFC 1521.

1. `7bit`, which is NVT ASCII, the default.
2. `quoted-printable`, which we saw an example of earlier with non-ASCII headers. It is useful when only a small fraction of the characters have their eighth bit set.
3. `base64`, which we showed in Figure 28.6.
4. `8bit` containing lines of characters, some of which are non-ASCII and have their eighth bit set.
5. `binary` encoding, which is 8-bit data that need not contain lines.

Content-Type	Subtype	Description
text	plain	Unformatted text.
	richtext	Text with simple formatting, such as bold, italic, underline, and so on.
	enriched	A clarification, simplification, and refinement of `richtext`.
multipart	mixed	Multiple body parts to be processed sequentially.
	parallel	Multiple body parts that can be processed in parallel.
	digest	An electronic mail digest.
	alternative	Multiple body parts are present, all with identical semantic content.
message	rfc822	Content is another RFC 822 mail message.
	partial	Content is a fragment of a mail message.
	external-body	Content is a pointer to the actual message.
application	octet-stream	Arbitrary binary data.
	postscript	A PostScript program.
image	jpeg	ISO 10918 format.
	gif	CompuServe's Graphic Interchange Format.
audio	basic	Encoded using 8-bit ISDN μ-law format.
video	mpeg	ISO 11172 format.

Figure 28.7 MIME content types and subtypes.

Only the first three of these are valid for an RFC 821 MTA, since these three generate a body containing only NVT ASCII characters. Using extended SMTP with 8BITMIME support allows `8bit` encoding to be used.

Although the content type and encoding are independent, RFC 1521 recommends `quoted-printable` for `text` with non-ASCII data, and `base64` for `image`, `audio`, `video`, and `octet-stream application` data. This allows maximum interoperability with RFC 821 conformant MTAs. Also, the `multipart` and `message` content types must be encoded as `7bit`.

As an example of a `multipart` content type, Figure 28.8 shows a mail message from the RFC distribution list. The subtype is `mixed`, meaning each of the parts should be processed sequentially, and the boundary between the parts is the string `NextPart`, preceded by two hyphens at the start of a line.

Each boundary can be followed with a line specifying the header fields for the next part. Everything in the message before the first boundary is ignored, as is everything following the final boundary.

Since a blank line follows the first boundary, and not header fields, the content type of the data between the first and second boundaries is assumed to be `text/plain` with a character set of `us-ascii`. This is a textual description of the new RFC.

The second boundary, however, is followed by header fields. It specifies another `multipart` message, with a boundary of `OtherAccess`. The subtype is `alternative`, and two different alternatives are present. The first `OtherAccess` alternative is to fetch the RFC using electronic mail, and the second is to fetch it using anonymous FTP. A MIME user agent would list the two alternatives, allow us to choose one, and then automatically fetch a copy of the RFC using either mail or anonymous FTP.

```
To: rfc-dist@nic.ddn.mil
Subject: RFC1479 on IDPR Protocol
Mime-Version: 1.0
Content-Type: Multipart/Mixed; Boundary="NextPart"
Date: Fri, 23 Jul 93 12:17:43 PDT
From: "Joyce K. Reynolds" <jkrey@isi.edu>

--NextPart                                  the first boundary

A new Request for Comments is now available in online RFC libraries.

. . .                                       (details here on the new RFC)

Below is the data which will enable a MIME compliant Mail Reader
implementation to automatically retrieve the ASCII version
of the RFCs.

--NextPart                                  the second boundary
Content-Type: Multipart/Alternative; Boundary="OtherAccess"
                                  a nested multipart message with a new boundary

--OtherAccess
Content-Type:  Message/External-body;
        access-type="mail-server";
        server="mail-server@nisc.sri.com"

Content-Type: text/plain

SEND rfc1479.txt

--OtherAccess
Content-Type:   Message/External-body;
        name="rfc1479.txt";
        site="ds.internic.net";
        access-type="anon-ftp";
        directory="rfc"

Content-Type: text/plain

--OtherAccess--
--NextPart--                                the final boundary
```

Figure 28.8 Example of a MIME multipart message.

This section has been a brief overview of MIME. For additional details and examples of MIME, see RFC 1521 and [Rose 1993].

28.5 Summary

Electronic mail involves a user agent at both ends (the sender and receiver) and two or more message transfer agents. We can divide a mail message into three parts: the envelope, the headers, and the body. We've seen how all three parts are exchanged using SMTP, the Internet standard. All three are exchanged as NVT ASCII characters.

We've also looked at newer extensions for all three parts: extended SMTP for the envelope, non-ASCII headers, and the addition of structure to the body using MIME. The structure and encoding used by MIME allow arbitrary binary data to be exchanged, using existing 7-bit SMTP MTAs.

Exercises

28.1 Read RFC 822 to find out what a *domain literal* is. Try sending mail to yourself using one.

28.2 Excluding the connection establishment and termination, what is the minimum number of network round trips to send a small mail message?

28.3 TCP is a full-duplex protocol, yet SMTP uses TCP in a half-duplex fashion. The client sends a command then stops and waits for the reply. Why doesn't the client send multiple commands at once, for example, a single write that contains the HELO, MAIL, RCPT, DATA, and QUIT commands (assuming the body isn't too large)?

28.4 How can this half-duplex operation of SMTP fool the slow start mechanism when the network is running near capacity?

28.5 When multiple MX records exist with the same preference value, should they always be returned by a name server in the same order?

29

NFS: Network File System

29.1 Introduction

In this chapter we describe NFS, the Network File System, another popular application that provides transparent file access for client applications. The building block of NFS is Sun RPC: Remote Procedure Call, which we must describe first.

Nothing special need be done by the client program to use NFS. The kernel detects that the file being accessed is on an NFS server and automatically generates the RPC calls to access the file.

Our interest in NFS is not in all the details on file access, but in its use of the Internet protocols, especially UDP.

29.2 Sun Remote Procedure Call

Most network programming is done by writing application programs that call system-provided functions to perform specific network operations. For example, one function performs a TCP active open, another performs a TCP passive open, another sends data across a TCP connection, another sets specific protocol options (enable TCP's keepalive timer), and so on. In Section 1.15 we mentioned that two popular sets of functions for network programming (called APIs) are sockets and TLI. The API used by the client and the API used by the server can be different, as can the operating systems running on the client and server. It is the communication protocol and application protocol that determine if a given client and server can communicate with each other. A Unix client written in C using sockets and TCP can communicate with a mainframe server written in COBOL using some other API and TCP, if both hosts are connected across a network and both have a TCP/IP implementation.

Typically the client sends commands to the server, and the server sends replies back to the client. All the applications we've looked at so far—Ping, Traceroute, routing daemons, and the clients and servers for the DNS, TFTP, BOOTP, SNMP, Telnet, FTP, and SMTP—are built this way.

RPC, *Remote Procedure Call*, is a different way of doing network programming. A client program is written that just calls functions in the server program. This is how it appears to the programmer, but the following steps actually take place.

1. When the client calls the remote procedure, it's really calling a function on the local host that's generated by the RPC package. This function is called the *client stub*. The client stub packages the procedure arguments into a network message, and sends this message to the server.
2. A *server stub* on the server host receives the network message. It takes the arguments from the network message, and calls the server procedure that the application programmer wrote.
3. When the server function returns, it returns to the server stub, which takes the return values, packages them into a network message, and sends the message back to the client stub.
4. The client stub takes the return values from the network message and returns to the client application.

The network programming done by the stubs and the RPC library routines uses an API such as sockets or TLI, but the user application—the client program, and the server procedures called by the client—never deal with this API. The client application just calls the server procedures and all the network programming details are hidden by the RPC package, the client stub, and the server stub.

An RPC package provides numerous benefits.

1. The programming is easier since there is little or no network programming involved. The application programmer just writes a client program and the server procedures that the client calls.
2. If an unreliable protocol such as UDP is used, details like timeout and retransmission are handled by the RPC package. This simplifies the user application.
3. The RPC library handles any required data translation for the arguments and return values. For example, if the arguments consist of integers and floating point numbers, the RPC package handles any differences in the way integers and floating point numbers are stored on the client and server. This simplifies coding clients and servers that can operate in heterogeneous environments.

Details of RPC programming are provided in Chapter 18 of [Stevens 1990]. Two popular RPC packages are Sun RPC and the RPC package in the Open Software Foundation's (OSF) Distributed Computing Environment (DCE). Our interest in RPC is to see what the procedure call and procedure return messages look like for the Sun RPC package, since it's used by the Network File System, which we describe in this chapter. Version 2 of Sun RPC is defined in RFC 1057 [Sun Microsystems 1988a].

Sun RPC

Sun RPC comes in two flavors. One version is built using the sockets API and works with TCP and UDP. Another, called TI-RPC (for "transport independent"), is built using the TLI API and works with any transport layer provided by the kernel. From our perspective the two are the same, although we talk only about TCP and UDP in this chapter.

Figure 29.1 shows the format of an RPC procedure call message, when UDP is used.

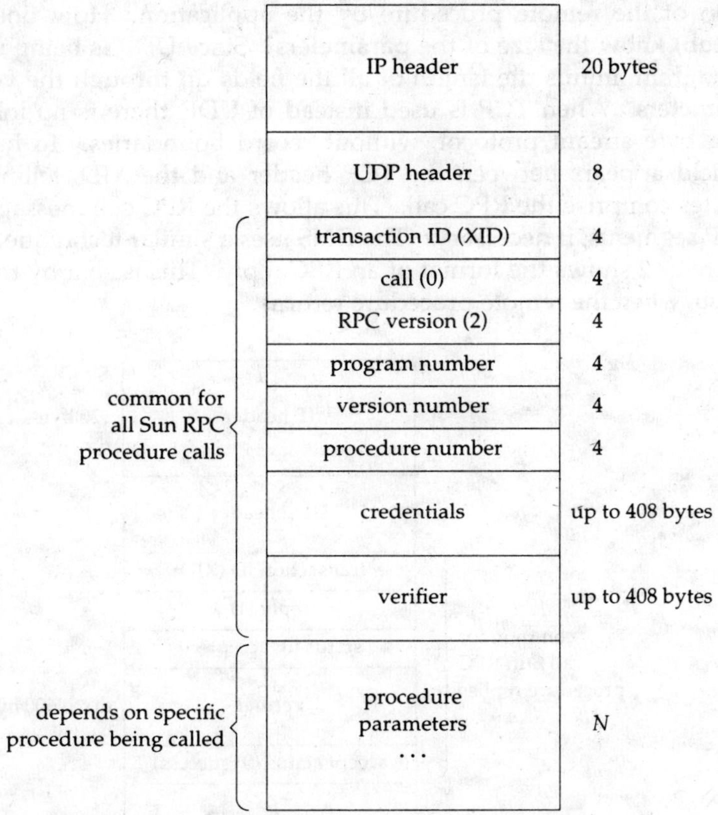

Figure 29.1 Format of RPC procedure call message as a UDP datagram.

The IP and UDP headers are the standard ones we showed earlier (Figures 3.1 and 11.2). What follows after the UDP header is defined by the RPC package.

The *transaction ID* (XID) is set by the client and returned by the server. When the client receives a reply it compares the XID returned by the server with the XID of the request it sent. If they don't match, the client discards the message and waits for the next one from the server. Each time the client issues a new RPC, it changes the XID. But if the client retransmits a previously sent RPC (because it hasn't received a reply), the XID does not change.

The *call* variable is 0 for a call, and 1 for a reply. The current *RPC version* is 2. The next three variables, *program number*, *version number*, and *procedure number*, identify the specific procedure on the server to be called.

The *credentials* identify the client. In some instances nothing is sent here, and in other instances the numeric user ID and group IDs of the client are sent. The server can look at the credentials and determine if it will perform the request or not. The *verifier* is used with Secure RPC, which uses DES encryption. Although the credentials and verifier are variable-length fields, their length is encoded as part of the field.

Following this are the procedure parameters. The format of these depends on the definition of the remote procedure by the application. How does the receiver (the server stub) know the size of the parameters? Since UDP is being used, the size of the UDP datagram, minus the length of all the fields up through the verifier, is the size of the parameters. When TCP is used instead of UDP, there is no inherent length, since TCP is a byte stream protocol, without record boundaries. To handle this, a 4-byte length field appears between the TCP header and the XID, telling the receiver how many bytes comprise the RPC call. This allows the RPC call message to be sent in multiple TCP segments, if necessary. (The DNS uses a similar technique; see Exercise 14.4.)

Figure 29.2 shows the format of an RPC reply. This is sent by the server stub to the client stub, when the remote procedure returns.

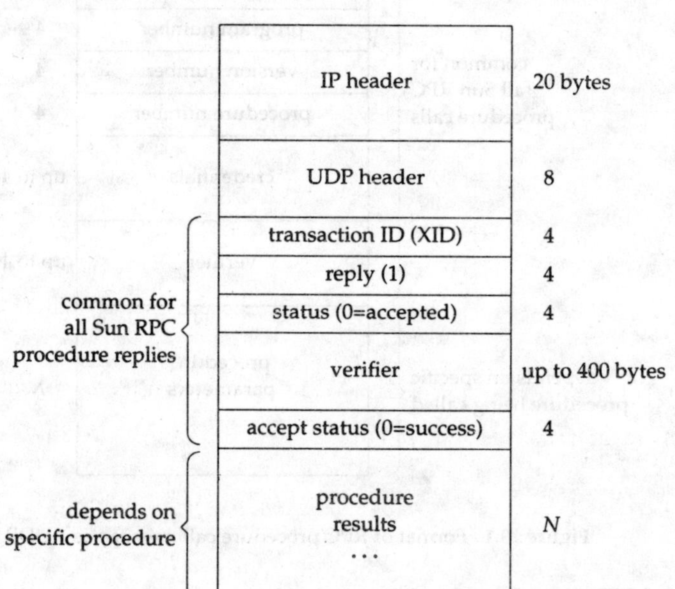

Figure 29.2 Format of RPC procedure reply message as a UDP datagram.

The XID in the reply is just copied from the XID in the call. The *reply* is 1, which we said differentiates this message from a call. The *status* is 0 if the call message was accepted. (The message can be rejected if the RPC version number isn't 2, or if the server cannot authenticate the client.) The *verifier* is used with secure RPC to identify the server.

The *accept status* is 0 on success. A nonzero value can indicate an invalid version number or an invalid procedure number, for example. As with the RPC call message, if TCP is used instead of UDP, a 4-byte length field is sent between the TCP header and the XID.

29.3 XDR: External Data Representation

XDR, *External Data Representation*, is the standard used to encode the values in the RPC call and reply messages—the RPC header fields (XID, program number, accept status, etc.), the procedure parameters, and the procedure results. Having a standard way of encoding all these values is what lets a client on one system call a procedure on a system with a different architecture. XDR is defined in RFC 1014 [Sun Microsystems 1987].

XDR defines numerous data types and exactly how they are transmitted in an RPC message (bit order, byte order, etc.). The sender must build an RPC message in XDR format, then the receiver converts the XDR format into its native representation. We see, for example, in Figures 29.1 and 29.2, that all the integer values we show (XID, call, program number, etc.) are 4-byte integers. Indeed, all integers occupy 4 bytes in XDR. Other data types supported by XDR include unsigned integers, booleans, floating point numbers, fixed-length arrays, variable-length arrays, and structures.

29.4 Port Mapper

The RPC server programs containing the remote procedures use ephemeral ports, not well-known ports. This requires a "registrar" of some form that keeps track of which RPC programs are using which ephemeral ports. In Sun RPC this registrar is called the *port mapper*.

> The term "port" in this name originates from the TCP and UDP port numbers, features of the Internet protocol suite. Since TI-RPC works over any transport layer, and not just TCP and UDP, the name of the port mapper in systems using TI-RPC (SVR4 and Solaris 2.2, for example) has become `rpcbind`. We'll continue to use the more familiar name of port mapper.

Naturally, the port mapper itself must have a well-known port: UDP port 111 and TCP port 111. The port mapper is also just an RPC server program. It has a program number (100000), a version number (2), a TCP port of 111, and a UDP port of 111. Servers register themselves with the port mapper using RPC calls, and clients query the port mapper using RPC calls. The port mapper provides four server procedures:

1. PMAPPROC_SET. Called by an RPC server on startup to register a program number, version number, and protocol with a port number.
2. PMAPPROC_UNSET. Called by server to remove a previously registered mapping.
3. PMAPPROC_GETPORT. Called by an RPC client on startup to obtain the port number for a given program number, version number, and protocol.

4. PMAPPROC_DUMP. Returns all entries (program number, version number, protocol, and port number) in the port mapper database.

When an RPC server program starts, and is later called by an RPC client program, the following steps take place.

1. The port mapper must be started first, normally when the system is bootstrapped. It creates a TCP end point and does a passive open on TCP port 111. It also creates a UDP end point and waits for a UDP datagram to arrive for UDP port 111.
2. When the RPC server program starts, it creates a TCP end point and a UDP end point for each version of the program that it supports. (A given RPC program can support multiple versions. The client specifies which version it wants when it calls a server procedure.) An ephemeral port number is bound to both end points. (It doesn't matter whether the TCP port number is the same or different from the UDP port number.) The server registers each program, version, protocol, and port number by making a remote procedure call to the port mapper's PMAPPROC_SET procedure.
3. When the RPC client program starts, it calls the port mapper's PMAPPROC_GETPORT procedure to obtain the ephemeral port number for a given program, version, and protocol.
4. The client sends an RPC call message to the port number returned in step 3. If UDP is being used, the client just sends a UDP datagram containing an RPC call message (Figure 29.1) to the server's UDP port number. The server responds by sending a UDP datagram containing an RPC reply message (Figure 29.2) back to the client.

   If TCP is being used, the client does an active open to the server's TCP port number, and then sends an RPC call message across the connection. The server responds with an RPC reply message across the connection.

The program `rpcinfo(8)` prints out the port mapper's current mappings. (It calls the port mapper's PMAPPROC_DUMP procedure.) Here is some typical output:

```
sun % /usr/etc/rpcinfo -p
program vers proto   port
 100005    1   tcp    702  mountd      mount daemon for NFS
 100005    1   udp    699  mountd
 100005    2   tcp    702  mountd
 100005    2   udp    699  mountd
 100003    2   udp   2049  nfs         NFS itself
 100021    1   tcp    709  nlockmgr    NFS lock manager
 100021    1   udp   1036  nlockmgr
 100021    2   tcp    721  nlockmgr
 100021    2   udp   1039  nlockmgr
 100021    3   tcp    713  nlockmgr
 100021    3   udp   1037  nlockmgr
```

We see that some programs do support multiple versions, and each combination of a program number, version number, and protocol has its own port number mapping maintained by the port mapper.

Both versions of the mount daemon are accessed through the same TCP port number (702) and the same UDP port number (699), but each version of the lock manager has its own port number.

29.5 NFS Protocol

NFS provides transparent *file access* for clients to files and filesystems on a server. This differs from FTP (Chapter 27), which provides *file transfer*. With FTP a complete copy of the file is made. NFS accesses only the portions of a file that a process references, and a goal of NFS is to make this access *transparent*. This means that any client application that works with a local file should work with an NFS file, without any program changes whatsoever.

NFS is a client–server application built using Sun RPC. NFS clients access files on an NFS server by sending RPC requests to the server. While this could be done using normal user processes—that is, the NFS client could be a user process that makes explicit RPC calls to the server, and the server could also be a user process—NFS is normally not implemented this way for two reasons. First, accessing an NFS file must be transparent to the client. Therefore the NFS client calls are performed by the client operating system, on behalf of client user processes. Second, NFS servers are implemented within the operating system on the server for efficiency. If the NFS server were a user process, every client request and server reply (including the data being read or written) would have to cross the boundary between the kernel and the user process, which is expensive.

In this section we look at version 2 of NFS, as documented in RFC 1094 [Sun Microsystems 1988b]. A better description of Sun RPC, XDR, and NFS is given in [X/Open 1991]. Details on using and administering NFS are in [Stern 1991]. The specifications for version 3 of the NFS protocol were released in 1993, which we cover in Section 29.7.

Figure 29.3 shows the typical arrangement of an NFS client and an NFS server. There are many subtle points in this figure.

1. It is transparent to the client whether it's accessing a local file or an NFS file. The kernel determines this when the file is opened. After the file is opened, the kernel passes all references to local files to the box labeled "local file access," and all references to an NFS file are passed to the "NFS client" box.
2. The NFS client sends RPC requests to the NFS server through its TCP/IP module. NFS is used predominantly with UDP, but newer implementations can also use TCP.
3. The NFS server receives client requests as UDP datagrams on port 2049. Although the NFS server could use an ephemeral port that it then registers with the port mapper, UDP port 2049 is hardcoded into most implementations.

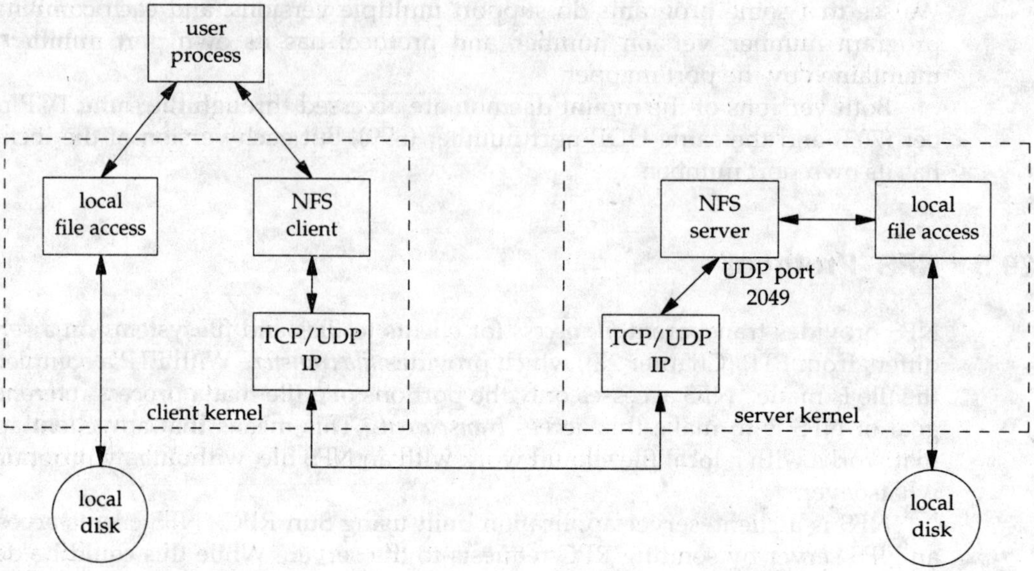

Figure 29.3 Typical arrangement of NFS client and NFS server.

4. When the NFS server receives a client request, the requests are passed to its local file access routines, which access a local disk on the server.
5. It can take the NFS server a while to handle a client's request. The local filesystem is normally accessed, which can take some time. During this time, the server does not want to block other client requests from being serviced. To handle this, most NFS servers are multithreaded—that is, there are really multiple NFS servers running inside the server kernel. How this is handled depends on the operating system. Since most Unix kernels are not multithreaded, a common technique is to start multiple instances of a user process (often called `nfsd`) that performs a single system call and remains inside the kernel as a kernel process.
6. Similarly, it can take the NFS client a while to handle a request from a user process on the client host. An RPC is issued to the server host, and the reply is waited for. To provide more concurrency to the user processes on the client host that are using NFS, there are normally multiple NFS clients running inside the client kernel. Again, the implementation depends on the operating system. Unix systems often use a technique similar to the NFS server technique: a user process named `biod` that performs a single system call and remains inside the kernel as a kernel process.

Most Unix hosts can operate as either an NFS client, an NFS server, or both. Most PC implementations (MS-DOS) only provide NFS client implementations. Most IBM mainframe implementations only provide NFS server functions.

NFS really consists of more than just the NFS protocol. Figure 29.4 shows the various RPC programs normally used with NFS.

Application	Program number	Version numbers	Number of procedures
port mapper	100000	2	4
NFS	100003	2	15
mount	100005	1	5
lock manager	100021	1, 2, 3	19
status monitor	100024	1	6

Figure 29.4 Various RPC programs used with NFS.

The versions we show in this figure are the ones found on systems such as SunOS 4.1.3. Newer implementations are providing newer versions of some of the programs. Solaris 2.2, for example, also supports versions 3 and 4 of the port mapper, and version 2 of the mount daemon. SVR4 also supports version 3 of the port mapper.

The mount daemon is called by the NFS client host before the client can access a filesystem on the server. We discuss this below.

The lock manager and status monitor allow clients to lock portions of files that reside on an NFS server. These two programs are independent of the NFS protocol because locking requires state on both the client and server, and NFS itself is stateless on the server. (We say more about NFS's statelessness later.) Chapters 9, 10, and 11 of [X/Open 1991] document the procedures used by the lock manager and status monitor for file locking with NFS.

File Handles

A fundamental concept in NFS is the *file handle.* It is an *opaque* object used to reference a file or directory on the server. The term opaque denotes that the server creates the file handle, passes it back to the client, and then the client uses the file handle when accessing the file. The client never looks at the contents of the file handle—its contents only make sense to the server.

Each time a client process opens a file that is really a file on an NFS server, the NFS client obtains a file handle for that file from the NFS server. Each time the NFS client reads or writes that file for the user process, the file handle is sent back to the server to identify the file being accessed.

Normal user processes never deal with file handles—it is the NFS client code and the NFS server code that pass them back and forth. In version 2 of NFS a file handle occupies 32 bytes, although with version 3 this changes from a fixed-length field to a variable-length field of up to 68 bytes.

Unix servers normally store the following information in the file handle: the filesystem identifier (the major and minor device numbers of the filesystem), the i-node number (a unique number within a filesystem), and an i-node generation number (a number that changes each time an i-node is reused for a different file).

Mount Protocol

The client must use the NFS mount protocol to mount a server's filesystem, before the client can access files on that filesystem. This is normally done when the client is bootstrapped. The end result is for the client to obtain a file handle for the server's filesystem.

Figure 29.5 shows the sequence of steps that takes place when a Unix client issues the `mount(8)` command, specifying an NFS mount.

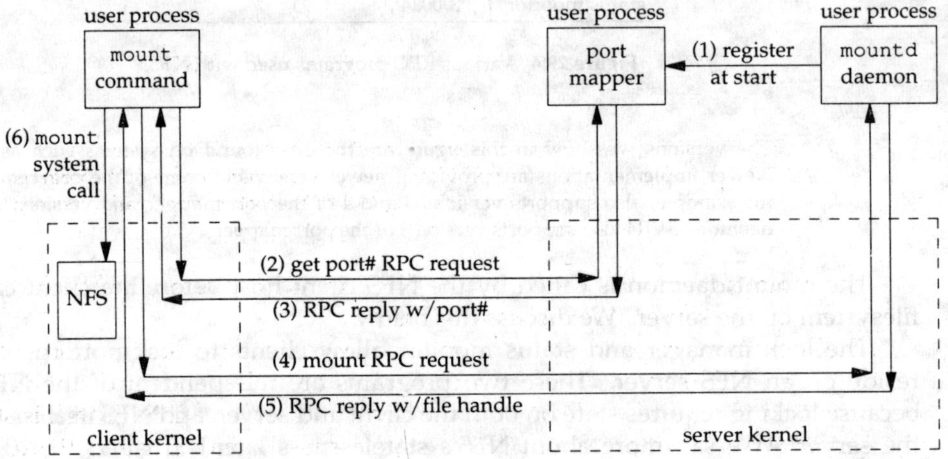

Figure 29.5 Mount protocol used by Unix `mount` command.

The following steps take place.

0. The port mapper is started on the server, normally when the server bootstraps.
1. The mount daemon (`mountd`) is started on the server, after the port mapper. It creates a TCP end point and a UDP end point, and assigns ephemeral port number to each. It then registers these port numbers with the port mapper.
2. The `mount` command is executed on the client and it issues an RPC call to the port mapper on the server to obtain the port number of the server's mount daemon. Either TCP or UDP can be used for this client exchange with the port mapper, but UDP is normally used.
3. The port mapper replies with the port number.
4. The `mount` command issues an RPC call to the mount daemon to mount a filesystem on the server. Again, either TCP or UDP can be used, but UDP is typical. The server can now validate the client, using the client's IP address and port number, to see if the server lets this client mount the specified filesystem.
5. The mount daemon replies with the file handle for the given filesystem.
6. The `mount` command issues the `mount` system call on the client to associate the file handle returned in step 5 with a local mount point on the client. This file

handle is stored in the NFS client code, and from this point on any references by user processes to files on that server's filesystem will use that file handle as the starting point.

This implementation technique puts all the mount processing, other than the mount system call on the client, in user processes, instead of the kernel. The three programs we show—the mount command, the port mapper, and the mount daemon—are all user processes.

As an example, on our host sun (the NFS client) we execute

```
sun # mount -t nfs bsdi:/usr /nfs/bsdi/usr
```

This mounts the directory /usr on the host bsdi (the NFS server) as the local filesystem /nfs/bsdi/usr. Figure 29.6 shows the result.

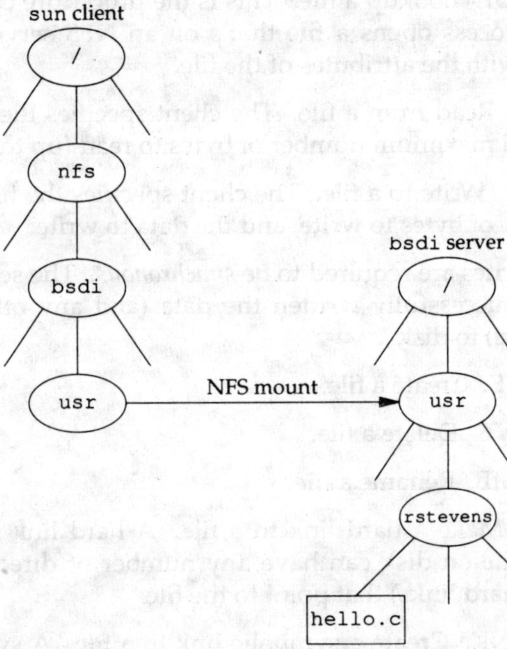

Figure 29.6 Mounting the bsdi:/usr directory as /nfs/bsdi/usr on the host sun.

When we reference the file /nfs/bsdi/usr/rstevens/hello.c on the client sun we are really referencing the file /usr/rstevens/hello.c on the server bsdi.

NFS Procedures

The NFS server provides 15 procedures, which we now describe. (The numbers we use are not the same as the NFS procedure numbers, since we have grouped them according to functionality.) Although NFS was designed to work between different operating systems, and not just Unix systems, some of the procedures provide Unix functionality that might not be supported by other operating systems (e.g., hard links, symbolic links, group owner, execute permission, etc.). Chapter 4 of [Stevens 1992] contains additional information on the properties of Unix filesystems, some of which are assumed by NFS.

1. GETATTR. Return the attributes of a file: type of file (regular file, directory, etc.), permissions, size of file, owner of file, last-access time, and so on.
2. SETATTR. Set the attributes of a file. Only a subset of the attributes can be set: permissions, owner, group owner, size, last-access time, and last-modification time.
3. STATFS. Return the status of a filesystem: amount of available space, optimal size for transfer, and so on. Used by the Unix `df` command, for example.
4. LOOKUP. Lookup a file. This is the procedure called by the client each time a user process opens a file that's on an NFS server. A file handle is returned, along with the attributes of the file.
5. READ. Read from a file. The client specifies the file handle, starting byte offset, and maximum number of bytes to read (up to 8192).
6. WRITE. Write to a file. The client specifies the file handle, starting byte offset, number of bytes to write, and the data to write.

   NFS writes are required to be *synchronous*. The server cannot respond OK until it has successfully written the data (and any other file information that gets updated) to disk.
7. CREATE. Create a file.
8. REMOVE. Delete a file.
9. RENAME. Rename a file.
10. LINK. Make a hard link to a file. A hard link is a Unix concept whereby a given file on disk can have any number of directory entries (i.e., names, also called hard links) that point to the file.
11. SYMLINK. Create a symbolic link to a file. A symbolic link is a file that contains the name of another file. Most operations that reference the symbolic link (e.g., open) really reference the file pointed to by the symbolic link.
12. READLINK. Read a symbolic link, that is, return the name of the file to which the symbolic link points.
13. MKDIR. Create a directory.
14. RMDIR. Delete a directory.
15. READDIR. Read a directory. Used by the Unix `ls` command, for example.

These procedure names actually begin with the prefix NFSPROC_, which we've dropped.

UDP or TCP?

NFS was originally written to use UDP, and that's what all vendors provide. Newer implementations, however, also support TCP. TCP support is provided for use on wide area networks, which are getting faster over time. NFS is no longer restricted to local area use.

The network dynamics can change drastically when going from a LAN to a WAN. The round-trip times can vary widely and congestion is more frequent. These characteristics of WANs led to the algorithms we examined with TCP—slow start and congestion avoidance. Since UDP does not provide anything like these algorithms, either the same algorithms must be put into the NFS client and server or TCP should be used.

NFS Over TCP

The Berkeley Net/2 implementation of NFS supports either UDP or TCP. [Macklem 1991] describes this implementation. Let's look at the differences when TCP is used.

1. When the server bootstraps, it starts an NFS server that does a passive open on TCP port 2049, waiting for client connection requests. This is usually in addition to the normal NFS UDP server that waits for incoming datagrams to UDP port 2049.
2. When the client mounts the server's filesystem using TCP, it does an active open to TCP port 2049 on the server. This results in a TCP connection between the client and server for this filesystem. If the same client mounts another filesystem on the same server, another TCP connection is created.
3. Both the client and server set TCP's keepalive option on their ends of the connection (Chapter 23). This lets either end detect if the other end crashes, or crashes and reboots.
4. All applications on the client that use this server's filesystem share the single TCP connection for this filesystem. For example, in Figure 29.6 if there were another directory named `smith` beneath `/usr` on `bsdi`, references to files in `/nfs/bsdi/usr/rstevens` and `/nfs/bsdi/usr/smith` would share the same TCP connection.
5. If the client detects that the server has crashed, or crashed and rebooted (by receiving a TCP error of either "connection timed out" or "connection reset by peer"), it tries to reconnect to the server. The client does another active open to reestablish the TCP connection with the server for this filesystem. Any client requests that timed out on the previous connection are reissued on the new connection.
6. If the client crashes, so do the applications that are running when it crashes. When the client reboots, it will probably remount the server's filesystem using TCP, resulting in another TCP connection to the server. The previous connection

between this client and server for this filesystem is half-open (the server thinks it's still open), but since the server set the keepalive option, this half-open connection will be terminated when the next keepalive probe is sent by the server's TCP.

Over time, additional vendors plan to support NFS over TCP.

29.6 NFS Examples

Let's use `tcpdump` to see which NFS procedures are invoked by the client for typical file operations. When `tcpdump` detects a UDP datagram containing an RPC call (*call* equals 0 in Figure 29.1) with a destination port of 2049, it decodes the datagram as an NFS request. Similarly if the UDP datagram is an RPC reply (*reply* equals 1 in Figure 29.2) with a source port of 2049, it decodes the datagram as an NFS reply.

Simple Example: Reading a File

Our first example just copies a file to the terminal using the `cat(1)` command, but the file is on an NFS server:

```
sun % cat /nfs/bsdi/usr/rstevens/hello.c        copy file to terminal
main()
{
        printf("hello, world\n");
}
```

On the host `sun` (the NFS client) the filesystem `/nfs/bsdi/usr` is really the `/usr` filesystem on the host `bsdi` (the NFS server), as shown in Figure 29.6. The kernel on `sun` detects this when `cat` opens the file, and uses NFS to access the file. Figure 29.7 shows the `tcpdump` output.

```
 1  0.0                  sun.7aa6 > bsdi.nfs: 104 getattr
 2  0.003587 (0.0036)    bsdi.nfs > sun.7aa6: reply ok 96

 3  0.005390 (0.0018)    sun.7aa7 > bsdi.nfs: 116 lookup "rstevens"
 4  0.009570 (0.0042)    bsdi.nfs > sun.7aa7: reply ok 128

 5  0.011413 (0.0018)    sun.7aa8 > bsdi.nfs: 116 lookup "hello.c"
 6  0.015512 (0.0041)    bsdi.nfs > sun.7aa8: reply ok 128

 7  0.018843 (0.0033)    sun.7aa9 > bsdi.nfs: 104 getattr
 8  0.022377 (0.0035)    bsdi.nfs > sun.7aa9: reply ok 96

 9  0.027621 (0.0052)    sun.7aaa > bsdi.nfs: 116 read 1024 bytes @ 0
10  0.032170 (0.0045)    bsdi.nfs > sun.7aaa: reply ok 140
```

Figure 29.7 NFS operations to read a file.

When `tcpdump` decodes an NFS request or reply, it prints the XID field for the client, instead of the port number. The XID field in lines 1 and 2 is `0x7aa6`.

The filename /nfs/bsdi/usr/rstevens/hello.c is processed by the open function in the client kernel one element at a time. When it reaches /nfs/bsdi/usr it detects that this is a mount point to an NFS mounted filesystem.

In line 1 the client calls the GETATTR procedure to fetch the attributes of the server's directory that the client has mounted (/usr). This RPC request contains 104 bytes of data, exclusive of the IP and UDP headers. The reply in line 2 has a return value of OK and contains 96 bytes of data, exclusive of the IP and UDP headers. We see in this figure that the minimum NFS message contains around 100 bytes of data.

In line 3 the client calls the LOOKUP procedure for the file rstevens and receives an OK reply in line 4. The LOOKUP specifies the filename rstevens and the file handle that was saved by the kernel when the remote filesystem was mounted. The reply contains a new file handle that is used in the next step.

In line 5 the client does a LOOKUP of hello.c using the file handle from line 4. It receives another file handle in line 6. This new file handle is what the client uses in lines 7 and 9 to reference the file /nfs/bsdi/usr/rstevens/hello.c. We see that the client does a LOOKUP for each component of the pathname that is being opened.

In line 7 the client does another GETATTR, followed by a READ in line 9. The client asks for 1024 bytes, starting at offset 0, but receives less. (After subtracting the sizes of the RPC fields, and the other values returned by the READ procedure, 38 bytes of data are returned in line 10. This is indeed the size of the file hello.c.)

In this example the user process knows nothing about these NFS requests and replies that are being done by the kernel. The application just calls the kernel's open function, which causes 3 requests and 3 replies to be exchanged (lines 1–6), and then calls the kernel's read function, which causes 2 requests and 2 replies (lines 7–10). It is transparent to the client application that the file is on an NFS server.

Simple Example: Creating a Directory

As another simple example we'll change our working directory to a directory that's on an NFS server, and then create a new directory:

```
sun % cd /nfs/bsdi/usr/rstevens        change working directory
sun % mkdir Mail                       and create a directory
```

Figure 29.8 shows the tcpdump output.

```
 1  0.0                      sun.7ad2 > bsdi.nfs: 104 getattr
 2  0.004912 ( 0.0049)       bsdi.nfs > sun.7ad2: reply ok 96

 3  0.007266 ( 0.0024)       sun.7ad3 > bsdi.nfs: 104 getattr
 4  0.010846 ( 0.0036)       bsdi.nfs > sun.7ad3: reply ok 96

 5  35.769875 (35.7590)      sun.7ad4 > bsdi.nfs: 104 getattr
 6  35.773432 ( 0.0036)      bsdi.nfs > sun.7ad4: reply ok 96

 7  35.775236 ( 0.0018)      sun.7ad5 > bsdi.nfs: 112 lookup "Mail"
 8  35.780914 ( 0.0057)      bsdi.nfs > sun.7ad5: reply ok 28

 9  35.782339 ( 0.0014)      sun.7ad6 > bsdi.nfs: 144 mkdir "Mail"
10  35.992354 ( 0.2100)      bsdi.nfs > sun.7ad6: reply ok 128
```

Figure 29.8 NFS operations for cd to NFS directory, then mkdir.

Changing our directory causes the client to call the GETATTR procedure twice (lines 1–4). When we create the new directory, the client calls the GETATTR procedure (lines 5 and 6), followed by a LOOKUP (lines 7 and 8, to verify that the directory doesn't already exist), followed by a MKDIR to create the directory (lines 9 and 10). The reply of OK in line 8 doesn't mean that the directory exists. It just means the procedure returned. `tcpdump` doesn't interpret the return values from the NFS procedures. It normally prints OK and the number of bytes of data in the reply.

Statelessness

One of the features of NFS (critics of NFS would call this a wart, not a feature) is that the NFS server is stateless. The server does not keep track of which clients are accessing which files. Notice in the list of NFS procedures shown earlier that there is not an open procedure or a close procedure. The LOOKUP procedure is similar to an open, but the server never knows if the client is really going to reference the file after the client does a LOOKUP.

The reason for a stateless design is to simplify the crash recovery of the server after it crashes and reboots.

Example: Server Crash

In the following example we are reading a file from an NFS server when the server crashes and reboots. This shows how the stateless server approach lets the client "not know" that the server crashes. Other than a time pause while the server crashes and reboots, the client is unaware of the problem, and the client application is not affected.

On the client `sun` we start a `cat` of a long file (`/usr/share/lib/termcap` on the NFS server `svr4`), disconnect the Ethernet cable during the transfer, shut down and reboot the server, then reconnect the cable. The client was configured to read 1024 bytes per NFS read. Figure 29.9 shows the `tcpdump` output.

Lines 1–10 correspond to the client opening the file. The operations are similar to those shown in Figure 29.7. In line 11 we see the first READ of the file, with 1024 bytes of data returned in line 12. This continues (a READ of 1024 followed by a reply of OK) through line 129.

In lines 130 and 131 we see two requests that time out and are retransmitted in lines 132 and 133. The first question is why are there two read requests, one starting at offset 65536 and the other starting at 73728? The client kernel has detected that the client application is performing sequential reads, and is trying to prefetch data blocks. (Most Unix kernels do this *read-ahead*.) The client kernel is also running multiple NFS block I/O daemons (`biod` processes) that try to generate multiple RPC requests on behalf of clients. One daemon is reading 8192 bytes starting at 65536 (in 1024-byte chunks) and the other is performing the read-ahead of 8192 bytes starting at 73728.

Client retransmissions occur in lines 130–168. In line 169 we see the server has rebooted, and it sends an ARP request before it can reply to the client's NFS request in line 168. The response to line 168 is sent in line 171. The client READ requests continue.

```
  1   0.0                  sun.7ade > svr4.nfs: 104 getattr
  2   0.007653 ( 0.0077)   svr4.nfs > sun.7ade: reply ok 96

  3   0.009041 ( 0.0014)   sun.7adf > svr4.nfs: 116 lookup "share"
  4   0.017237 ( 0.0082)   svr4.nfs > sun.7adf: reply ok 128

  5   0.018518 ( 0.0013)   sun.7ae0 > svr4.nfs: 112 lookup "lib"
  6   0.026802 ( 0.0083)   svr4.nfs > sun.7ae0: reply ok 128

  7   0.028096 ( 0.0013)   sun.7ae1 > svr4.nfs: 116 lookup "termcap"
  8   0.036434 ( 0.0083)   svr4.nfs > sun.7ae1: reply ok 128

  9   0.038060 ( 0.0016)   sun.7ae2 > svr4.nfs: 104 getattr
 10   0.045821 ( 0.0078)   svr4.nfs > sun.7ae2: reply ok 96

 11   0.050984 ( 0.0052)   sun.7ae3 > svr4.nfs: 116 read 1024 bytes @ 0
 12   0.084995 ( 0.0340)   svr4.nfs > sun.7ae3: reply ok 1124
                           reading continues
128   3.430313 ( 0.0013)   sun.7b22 > svr4.nfs: 116 read 1024 bytes @ 64512
129   3.441828 ( 0.0115)   svr4.nfs > sun.7b22: reply ok 1124

130   4.125031 ( 0.6832)   sun.7b23 > svr4.nfs: 116 read 1024 bytes @ 65536
131   4.868593 ( 0.7436)   sun.7b24 > svr4.nfs: 116 read 1024 bytes @ 73728

132   4.993021 ( 0.1244)   sun.7b23 > svr4.nfs: 116 read 1024 bytes @ 65536
133   5.732217 ( 0.7392)   sun.7b24 > svr4.nfs: 116 read 1024 bytes @ 73728

134   6.732084 ( 0.9999)   sun.7b23 > svr4.nfs: 116 read 1024 bytes @ 65536
135   7.472098 ( 0.7400)   sun.7b24 > svr4.nfs: 116 read 1024 bytes @ 73728
136  10.211964 ( 2.7399)   sun.7b23 > svr4.nfs: 116 read 1024 bytes @ 65536
137  10.951960 ( 0.7400)   sun.7b24 > svr4.nfs: 116 read 1024 bytes @ 73728
138  17.171767 ( 6.2198)   sun.7b23 > svr4.nfs: 116 read 1024 bytes @ 65536
139  17.911762 ( 0.7400)   sun.7b24 > svr4.nfs: 116 read 1024 bytes @ 73728
140  31.092136 (13.1804)   sun.7b23 > svr4.nfs: 116 read 1024 bytes @ 65536
141  31.831432 ( 0.7393)   sun.7b24 > svr4.nfs: 116 read 1024 bytes @ 73728
142  51.090854 (19.2594)   sun.7b23 > svr4.nfs: 116 read 1024 bytes @ 65536
143  51.830939 ( 0.7401)   sun.7b24 > svr4.nfs: 116 read 1024 bytes @ 73728
144  71.090305 (19.2594)   sun.7b23 > svr4.nfs: 116 read 1024 bytes @ 65536
145  71.830155 ( 0.7398)   sun.7b24 > svr4.nfs: 116 read 1024 bytes @ 73728
                           retransmissions continue
167 291.824285 ( 0.7400)   sun.7b24 > svr4.nfs: 116 read 1024 bytes @ 73728
168 311.083676 (19.2594)   sun.7b23 > svr4.nfs: 116 read 1024 bytes @ 65536
                           server reboots
169 311.149476 ( 0.0658)   arp who-has sun tell svr4
170 311.150004 ( 0.0005)   arp reply sun is-at 8:0:20:3:f6:42

171 311.154852 ( 0.0048)   svr4.nfs > sun.7b23: reply ok 1124

172 311.156671 ( 0.0018)   sun.7b25 > svr4.nfs: 116 read 1024 bytes @ 66560
173 311.168926 ( 0.0123)   svr4.nfs > sun.7b25: reply ok 1124
                           reading continues
```

Figure 29.9 Client reading a file when an NFS server crashes and reboots.

The client application never knows that the server crashes and reboots, and except for the 5-minute pause between lines 129 and 171, this server crash is transparent to the client.

To examine the timeout and retransmission interval in this example, realize that there are two client daemons with their own timeouts. The intervals for the first daemon (reading at offset 65536), rounded to two decimal points, are: 0.68, 0.87, 1.74, 3.48, 6.96, 13.92, 20.0, 20.0, 20.0, and so on. The intervals for the second daemon (reading at offset 73728) are the same (to two decimal points). It appears that these NFS clients are using a timeout that is a multiple of 0.875 seconds with an upper bound of 20 seconds. After each timeout the retransmission interval is doubled: 0.875, 1.75, 3.5, 7.0, and 14.0.

How long does the client retransmit? The client has two options that affect this. First, if the server filesystem is mounted *hard*, the client retransmits forever, but if the server filesystem is mounted *soft*, the client gives up after a fixed number of retransmissions. Also, with a hard mount the client has an option of whether to let the user interrupt the infinite retransmissions or not. If the client host specifies interruptibility when it mounts the server's filesystem, if we don't want to wait 5 minutes for the server to reboot after it crashes, we can type our interrupt key to abort the client application.

Idempotent Procedures

An RPC procedure is called *idempotent* if it can be executed more than once by the server and still return the same result. For example, the NFS read procedure is idempotent. As we saw in Figure 29.9, the client just reissues a given READ call until it gets a response. In our example the reason for the retransmission was that the server had crashed. If the server hasn't crashed, and the RPC reply message is lost (since UDP is unreliable), the client just retransmits and the server performs the same READ again. The same portion of the same file is read again and sent back to the client.

This works because each READ request specifies the starting offset of the read. If there were an NFS procedure asking the server to read the *next* N bytes of a file, this wouldn't work. Unless the server is made stateful (as opposed to stateless), if a reply is lost and the client reissues the READ for the next N bytes, the result is different. This is why the NFS READ and WRITE procedures have the client specify the starting offset. The client maintains the state (the current offset of each file), not the server.

Unfortunately, not all filesystem operations are idempotent. For example, consider the following steps: the client NFS issues the REMOVE request to delete a file; the server NFS deletes the file and responds OK; the server's response is lost; the client NFS times out and retransmits the request; the server NFS can't find the file and responds with an error; the client application receives an error saying the file doesn't exist. This error return to the client application is wrong—the file did exist and was deleted.

The NFS operations that are idempotent are: GETATTR, STATFS, LOOKUP, READ, WRITE, READLINK, and READDIR. The procedures that are not idempotent are: CREATE, REMOVE, RENAME, LINK, SYMLINK, MKDIR, and RMDIR. SETATTR is normally idempotent, unless it's being used to truncate a file.

Since lost responses can always happen with UDP, NFS servers need a way to handle the nonidempotent operations. Most servers implement a recent-reply cache in which they store recent replies for the nonidempotent operations. Each time the server receives a request, it first checks this cache, and if a match is found, returns the previous reply instead of calling the NFS procedure again. [Juszczak 1989] provides details on this type of cache.

This concept of idempotent server procedures applies to any UDP-based application, not just NFS. The DNS, for example, provides an idempotent service. A DNS server can execute a resolver's request any number of times with no ill effects (other than wasted network resources).

29.7 NFS Version 3

During 1993 the specifications for version 3 of the NFS protocol were released [Sun Microsystems 1994]. Implementations are expected to become available during 1994.

Here we summarize the major differences between versions 2 and 3. We'll refer to the two as V2 and V3.

1. The file handle in V2 is a fixed-size array of 32 bytes. With V3 it becomes a variable-length array up to 64 bytes. A variable-length array in XDR is encoded with a 4-byte count, followed by the actual bytes. This reduces the size of the file handle on implementations such as Unix that only need about 12 bytes, but allows non-Unix implementations to maintain additional information.
2. V2 limits the number of bytes per READ or WRITE RPC to 8192 bytes. This limit is removed in V3, meaning an implementation over UDP is limited only by the IP datagram size (65535 bytes). This allows larger read and write packets on faster networks.
3. File sizes and the starting byte offsets for the READ and WRITE procedures are extended from 32 to 64 bits, allowing larger file sizes.
4. A file's attributes are returned on every call that affects the attributes. This reduces the number of GETATTR calls required by the client.
5. WRITEs can be asynchronous, instead of the synchronous WRITEs required by V2. This can improve WRITE performance.
6. One procedure was deleted (STATFS) and seven were added: ACCESS (check file access permissions), MKNOD (create a Unix special file), READDIRPLUS (returns names of files in a directory along with their attributes), FSINFO (returns the static information about a filesystem), FSSTAT (returns the dynamic information about a filesystem), PATHCONF (returns the POSIX.1 information about a file), and COMMIT (commit previous asynchronous writes to stable storage).

29.8 Summary

RPC is a way to build a client–server application so that it appears that the client just calls server procedures. All the networking details are hidden in the client and server stubs, which are generated for an application by the RPC package, and in the RPC library routines. We showed the format of the RPC call and reply messages, and mentioned that XDR is used to encode the values, allowing RPC clients and servers to run on machines with different architectures.

One of the most widely used RPC applications is Sun's NFS, a heterogeneous file access protocol that is widely implemented on hosts of all sizes. We looked at NFS and the way that it uses UDP and TCP. Fifteen procedures define the NFS Version 2 protocol.

A client's access to an NFS server starts with the mount protocol, returning a file handle to the client. The client can then access files on the server's filesystem using that file handle. Filenames are looked up on the server one element at a time, returning a new file handle for each element. The end result is a file handle for the file being referenced, which is used in subsequent reads and writes.

NFS tries to make all its procedures idempotent, so that the client can just reissue a request if the response gets lost. We saw an example of this with a client reading a file while the server crashed and rebooted.

Exercises

29.1 In Figure 29.7 we saw that `tcpdump` interpreted the packets as NFS requests and replies, printing the XID. Can `tcpdump` do this for any RPC request or reply?

29.2 On a Unix system, why do you think RPC server programs use ephemeral ports and not well-known ports?

29.3 An RPC client calls two server procedures. The first server procedure takes 5 seconds to execute, and the second procedure takes 1 second to execute. The client has a timeout of 4 seconds. Draw a time line of what's exchanged between the client and server. (Assume it takes no time for messages from the client to the server, and vice versa.)

29.4 What would happen in the example shown in Figure 29.9 if, while the NFS server were down, its Ethernet card were replaced?

29.5 When the server reboots in Figure 29.9, it handles the request starting at byte offset 65536 (lines 168 and 171), and then handles the next request starting at offset 66560 (lines 172 and 173). What happened to the request starting at offset 73728 (line 167)?

29.6 When we described idempotent NFS procedures we gave an example of a REMOVE reply being lost in the network. What happens in this case if TCP is used, instead of UDP?

29.7 If the NFS server used an ephemeral port instead of 2049, what would happen to an NFS client when the server crashes and reboots?

29.8 Reserved port numbers (Section 1.9) are scarce, since there are a maximum of 1023 per host. If an NFS server requires its clients to have reserved ports (which is common) and an NFS client using TCP mounts N filesystems on N different servers, does the client need a different reserved port number for each connection?

30

Other TCP/IP Applications

30.1 Introduction

In this chapter we describe additional TCP/IP applications that many implementations support. Some are simple and easy to cover completely (Finger and Whois), while another is complex (the X Window System). We provide only a brief overview of this complex application, focusing on its use of the TCP/IP protocols.

Additionally we provide an overview of some Internet resource discovery tools. These are tools to help us navigate our way around the Internet, searching for items whose location and exact name we don't know.

30.2 Finger Protocol

The Finger protocol returns information on one or more users on a specified host. It's commonly used to see if someone is currently logged on, or to figure out someone's login name, to send them mail. RFC 1288 [Zimmerman 1991] specifies the protocol.

Many sites do not run a Finger server for two reasons. First, a programming error in an earlier version of the server was one of the entry points used by the infamous Internet worm of 1988. (RFC 1135 [Reynolds 1989] and [Curry 1992] describe the worm in more detail.) Second, the Finger protocol can reveal detailed information on users (login names, phone numbers, when they last logged in, etc.) that many administrators consider private. Section 3 of RFC 1288 details the security aspects of this service.

From a protocol perspective, the Finger server has a well-known port of 79. The client does an active open to this port and sends a one-line query. The server processes the query, sends back the output, and closes the connection. The query and response are NVT ASCII, similar to what we saw with FTP and SMTP.

While most Unix users access the Finger server using the `finger(1)` client, we'll start by using the Telnet client to connect directly to the server and see the one-line commands issued by the client. If the client query is an empty line (which in NVT ASCII is transmitted as a CR followed by an LF), it is a request for information on all online users.

```
sun % telnet slip finger
Trying 140.252.13.65 ...                      first three lines are output by Telnet client
Connected to slip.
Escape character is '^]'.
                                              here we type RETURN as the Finger client command
Login    Name              Tty  Idle  Login Time    Office   Office Phone
rstevens Richard Stevens   *co   45   Jul 31 09:13
rstevens Richard Stevens   *c2   45   Aug  5 09:41
Connection closed by foreign host.            output by Telnet client
```

The blank output fields for the office and office phone are taken from optional fields in the user's password file entry (which aren't present in this example).

The server must be the end that does the active close, since a variable amount of information is returned by the server, and the reception of the end-of-file by the client is how the client knows when the output is complete.

When the client request consists of a username, the server responds with information only about that user. Here's another example, with the Telnet client output removed:

```
sun % telnet vangogh.cs.berkeley.edu finger
rstevens                                      this is the client request we type
Login: rstevens                               Name: Richard Stevens
Directory: /a/guest/rstevens                  Shell: /bin/csh
Last login Thu Aug  5 09:55 (PDT) on ttyq2 from sun.tuc.noao.edu
Mail forwarded to: rstevens@noao.edu
No Plan.
```

When a system has the Finger service completely disabled, the client's active open will receive an RST from the server, since no process has a passive open on port 79:

```
sun % finger @svr4
[svr4.tuc.noao.edu] connect: Connection refused
```

Some sites provide a server on port 79, but it just outputs information to the client, and doesn't honor any client requests:

```
sun % finger @att.com
[att.com]                      this line output by Finger client; remainder from server
--------------------------------------------------------------
There are no user accounts on the AT&T Internet gateway.
To send email to an AT&T employee, send email to their name
separated by periods at att.com. If the employee has an email
address registered in the employee database, they will receive
email - otherwise, you'll receive a non-delivery notice.
For example: John.Q.Public@att.com
```

```
sun % finger clinton@whitehouse.gov
[whitehouse.gov]

          Finger service for arbitrary addresses on whitehouse.gov is not
supported. If you wish to send electronic mail, valid addresses are
"PRESIDENT@WHITEHOUSE.GOV", and "VICE-PRESIDENT@WHITEHOUSE.GOV"
```

Another possibility is for an organization to implement a *firewall gateway*: a router between the organization and the Internet that filters out (i.e., discards) certain IP datagrams. ([Cheswick and Bellovin 1994] discuss firewall gateways in detail.) The firewall gateway can be configured to discard incoming datagrams that are TCP segments for port 79. In this case the Finger client times out after about 75 seconds.

There are additional options for the Finger server, and for the Unix `finger` client. Refer to RFC 1288 and the `finger(1)` manual page for the details.

RFC 1288 states that vending machines with TCP/IP connections that provide a Finger server should reply to a client request consisting of a blank line with a list of all items currently available. They should reply to a client request consisting of a name with a count or list of available items for that product.

30.3 Whois Protocol

The Whois protocol is another information service. Although any site can provide a Whois server, the one at the InterNIC, `rs.internic.net`, is most commonly used. This server maintains information about all registered DNS domains and many system administrators responsible for systems connected to the Internet. (Another server is provided at `nic.ddn.mil`, but contains information only about the MILNET.) Unfortunately the information can be out of date or incomplete. RFC 954 [Harrenstien, Stahl, and Feinler 1985] documents the Whois service.

From a protocol perspective, the Whois server has a well-known TCP port of 43. It accepts connection requests from clients, and the client sends a one-line query to the server. The server responds with whatever information is available and then closes the connection. The requests and replies are transmitted using NVT ASCII. This is almost identical to the Finger server, although the requests and replies contain different information.

The common Unix client is the `whois(1)` program, although we can use Telnet and type in the commands ourself. The starting place is to send a request consisting of just a question mark, which returns more detailed information on the supported client requests.

When the NIC moved to the InterNIC in 1993, the site for the Whois server moved from `nic.ddn.mil` to `rs.internic.net`. Many vendors still ship versions of the `whois` client with the name `nic.ddn.mil` built in. You may need to specify the command-line argument `-h rs.internic.net` to contact the correct server.

Alternately, we can Telnet to `rs.internic.net` and login as `whois`.

We'll use the Whois server to track down the author. (We've removed the extraneous Telnet client output.) Our first request is for all names that match "stevens."

```
sun % telnet rs.internic.net whois
stevens                               this is the client command we type
                                      information on 25 other "stevens" that we omit
Stevens, W. Richard (WRS28)    stevens@kohala.com    +1 602 297 9416

The InterNIC Registration Services Host ONLY contains Internet
Information (Networks, ASN's, Domains, and POC's).
Please use the whois server at nic.ddn.mil for MILNET Information.
```

The three uppercase letters followed by a number in parentheses after the name, (WRS28), are the person's NIC handle. The next query contains an exclamation point and a NIC handle, to fetch more information about this person.

```
sun % telnet rs.internic.net whois
!wrs28                                client request that we type
Stevens, W. Richard (WRS28)              stevens@kohala.com
   Kohala Software
   1202 E. Paseo del Zorro
   Tucson, AZ 85718
   +1 602 297 9416

   Record last updated on 11-Jan-91.
```

Lots of additional information about Internet variables can also be queried. For example, the request net 140.252 returns information about the class B address 140.252.

White Pages

Using the VRFY command of SMTP, along with the Finger protocol and the Whois protocol to locate users on the Internet is similar to using the white pages of a telephone book to find someone's phone number. At the present time ad hoc tools such as these are all that's widely available, but research is under way to improve this type of service.

[Schwartz and Tsirigotis 1991] contains additional information on various white pages services being tried on the Internet. The particular tool, called Netfind, can be accessed by using Telnet to either bruno.cs.colorado.edu or ds.internic.net and logging in as netfind.

RFC 1309 [Weider, Reynolds, and Heker 1992] provides an overview of the OSI directory service, called X.500, and compares and contrasts it with current Internet techniques (Finger and Whois).

30.4 Archie, WAIS, Gopher, Veronica, and WWW

The tools that we described in the previous two sections—Finger, Whois, and a white pages service—are for locating information on people. Other tools exist to locate files and documents, and this section gives an overview of these tools. We only provide an overview, because examining the details of each tool is beyond the scope of this book. Methods are given for accessing these tools across the Internet, and you are encouraged to do so, to find which tool can help you. Additional tools are continually being developed. [Obraczka, Danzig, and Li 1993] provide an overview of resource discovery services on the Internet.

Archie

Many of the resources used in this text were obtained using anonymous FTP. The problem is finding which FTP site has the program we want. Sometimes we don't even know the exact filename, but we know some keywords that probably appear in the filename.

Archie provides a directory of thousands of FTP servers across the Internet. We can access this directory by logging into an Archie server and searching for files whose name contains a specified regular expression. The output is a list of servers with matching filenames. We then use anonymous FTP to that site to fetch the file.

There are many Archie servers across the world. One starting point is to use Telnet to `ds.internic.net`, login as `archie`, and execute the command `servers`. This provides a list of all the Archie servers, and their location.

WAIS: Wide Area Information Servers

Archie helps us locate filenames that contain keywords, but sometimes we're looking for a file or database that contains a keyword. That is, we want to search for a file that contains a keyword, not a filename containing a keyword.

WAIS knows about hundreds of databases that contain information on both computer-related topics and other general topics. To use WAIS we select the databases to search and specify the keywords. To try WAIS Telnet to `quake.think.com` and login as `wais`.

Gopher

Gopher is a menu-driven front end to other Internet resource services, such as Archie, WAIS, and anonymous FTP. Gopher is one of the easiest to use, since its user interface is the same, regardless of which resource service it's using.

To use Gopher, Telnet into `is.internic.net` and login as `gopher`.

Veronica: Very Easy Rodent-Oriented Netwide Index to Computerized Archives

Just as Archie is an index of anonymous FTP servers, Veronica is an index of titles of Gopher items. A Veronica search typically searches hundreds of Gopher servers.

To access Veronica we must go through a Gopher client. Select the Gopher menu item "Beyond InterNIC: Virtual Treasures of the Internet" and then select Veronica from the next menu.

WWW: World Wide Web

World Wide Web lets us browse a large, worldwide set of services and documents using a tool called *hypertext*. As information is displayed, certain keywords are highlighted, and we can select more information on those keywords.

To access WWW, Telnet to `info.cern.ch`.

30.5 X Window System

The X *Window System*, or just X, is a client–server application that lets multiple clients (applications) use the bit-mapped display managed by a server. The server is the software that manages a display, keyboard, and mouse. The client is an application program that runs on either the same host as the server or on a different host. In the latter case the common form of communication between the client and server is TCP, although other protocols such as DECNET can be used. In some instances the server is a dedicated piece of hardware (an X terminal) that communicates with clients on other hosts. In another instance, a stand-alone workstation, the client and server are on the same host and communicate using interprocess communication on that host, without any network involvement at all. Between these two extremes is a workstation that supports clients on the same host and clients on other hosts.

X requires a reliable, bidirectional stream protocol, such as TCP. (X was not designed for an unreliable protocol such as UDP.) The communication between the client and server consists of 8-bit bytes exchanged across this connection. [Nye 1992] gives the format of the more than 150 messages exchanged between the client and server across their TCP connection.

On a Unix system, when the X client and X server are on the same host, the Unix domain protocols are normally used instead of TCP, because there is less protocol processing than if TCP were used. The Unix domain protocols are a form of interprocess communication that can be used between clients and servers on the same host. Recall in Figure 2.4 (p. 28) that when TCP is used for communication between two processes on the same host, the loopback of this data takes place below the IP layer, implying that all the TCP and IP processing takes place.

Figure 30.1 shows one possible scenario with three clients using one display. One client is on the same host as the server, using the Unix domain protocols. The other two clients are on different hosts, using TCP. One client is normally a *window manager* that has authority for the layout of windows on the display. The window manager allows us to move windows around the screen, or change their size, for example.

On first glance the terms *client* and *server* appear backward. With applications such as Telnet and FTP we think of the client as the interactive user at the keyboard and display. But with X, the keyboard and display belong to the server. Think of the server as the end providing the service. The service provided by X is access to a window, keyboard, and mouse. With Telnet the service is logging in to the remote host. With FTP the service is the filesystem on the server.

The X server is normally started when the X terminal or workstation is bootstrapped. The server creates a TCP end point and does a passive open on port $6000 + n$,

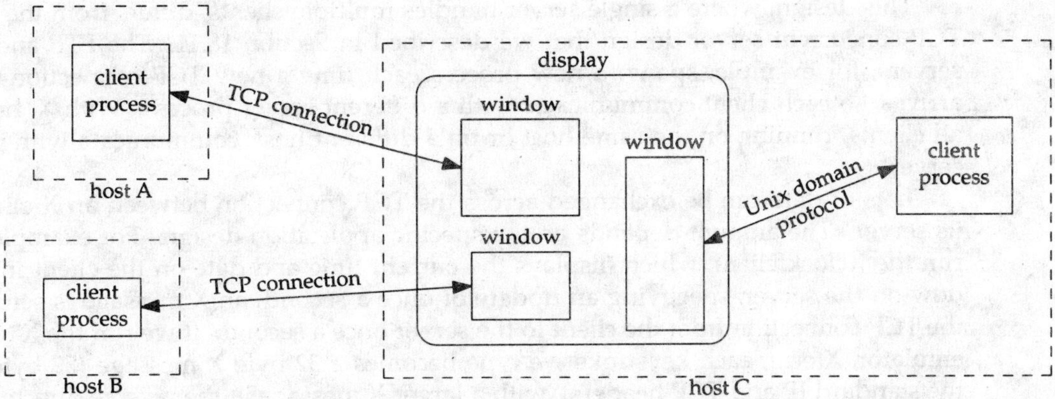

Figure 30.1 Three X clients using one display.

where *n* is the display number (normally 0). Most Unix servers also create a Unix domain socket with the name `/tmp/.X11-unix/Xn`, where *n* is again the display number.

When a client is started on another host, it creates a TCP end point and performs an active open to port 6000 + *n* on the server. Each client gets its own TCP connection to the server. It is the server's responsibility to multiplex all the clients. From this point on the client sends requests to the server across the TCP connection (e.g., create a window), the server sends back replies, and the server also sends events to the client (mouse button pushed, keyboard key pressed, window exposed, window resized, etc.).

Figure 30.2 is a redo of Figure 30.1, emphasizing that the clients communicate with the X server process, which in turn manages the windows on the display. Not shown here is that the X server also manages the keyboard and mouse.

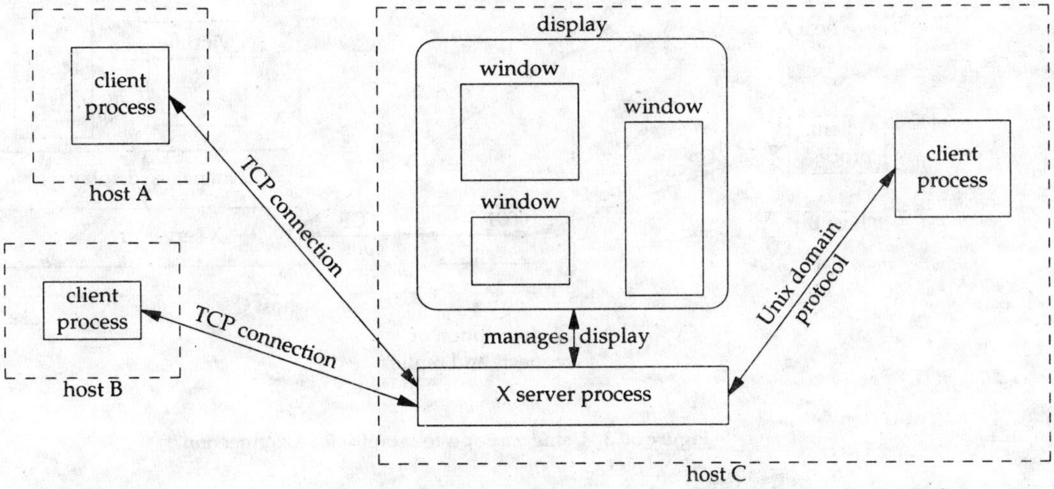

Figure 30.2 Three clients using one display.

This design, where a single server handles multiple clients, differs from the normal TCP concurrent server design that we described in Section 18.11. The FTP and Telnet servers, for example, spawn a new process each time a new TCP connection request arrives, so each client communicates with a different server process. With X, however, all clients, running on the same host or on a different host, communicate with a single server.

Lots of data can be exchanged across the TCP connection between an X client and its server. The amount depends on the specific application design. For example, if we run the Xclock client, which displays the current time and date on the client in a window on the server, specifying an update of once a second, an X message is sent across the TCP connection from the client to the server once a second. If we run the X terminal emulator, Xterm, each keystroke we type becomes a 32-byte X message (72 bytes with the standard IP and TCP headers), with a larger X message in the reverse direction with the character echo. [Droms and Dyksen 1990] measure the TCP traffic between various X clients and one particular server.

Xscope Program

A handy program for examining what's exchanged between an X client and its server is Xscope. It's provided with most X window implementations. It sits between a client and server, passing everything in both directions, and also deciphering all the client requests and server replies. Figure 30.3 shows the setup.

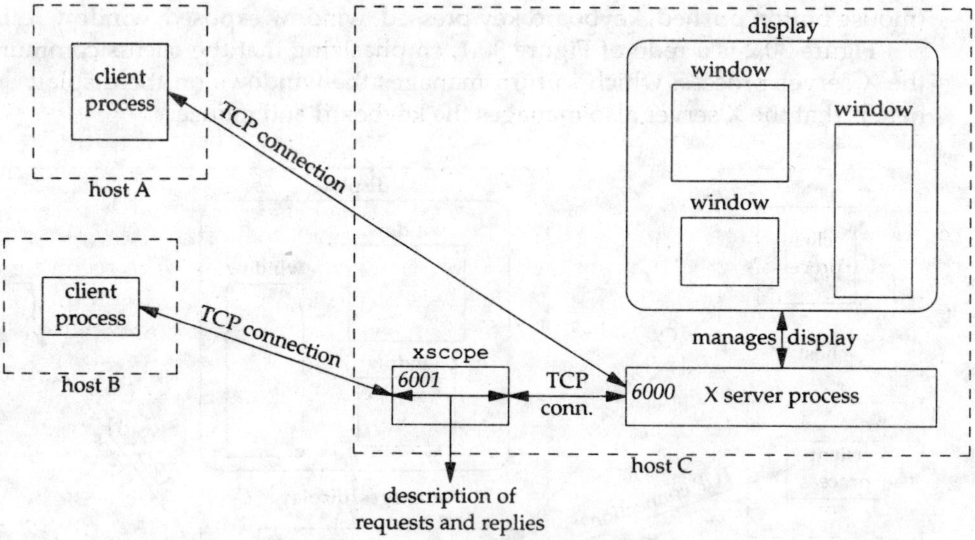

Figure 30.3 Using `xscope` to monitor an X connection.

We first start the `xscope` process on the same host as the server, but `xscope` listens for TCP connection requests on port 6001, not 6000. We then start a client on another host and specify display number 1, not 0, so the client connects to xscope, not directly to the server. When the connection request from the client arrives, xscope creates a TCP connection to the real server at port 6000, and copies everything between the client and server, and produces a readable description of the requests and replies.

We'll start xscope on our host sun and then run the xclock client on the host svr4.

```
svr4 % DISPLAY=sun:1 xclock -digital -update 5
```

This displays the time and date in the digital format

```
Thu Sep  9 10:32:55 1993
```

in a window on the host sun. We specify an update time of once every 5 seconds.

We specify the -q option for xscope to produce minimal output. Various levels of verbosity are available, to see all the fields in each message. The following output shows the first three requests and replies.

```
sun % xscope -q
0.00: Client --> 12 bytes
0.02:                                 152 bytes <-- X11 Server
0.03: Client --> 48 bytes
          ............REQUEST: CreateGC
          ............REQUEST: GetProperty
0.20:                                 396 bytes <-- X11 Server
                                  ..............REPLY: GetProperty
0.30: Client -->  8 bytes
0.38: Client --> 20 bytes
          ............REQUEST: InternAtom
0.43:                                  32 bytes <-- X11 Server
                                  ..............REPLY: InternAtom
```

The first client message at time 0.00 and the server's response at time 0.02 are the standard connection setup between the client and server. The client identifies its byte ordering and the version of the server that it expects. The server responds with various information about itself.

The next message at time 0.03 contains two client requests. The first request creates a graphics context in the server in which the client will draw. The second gets a property from the server (the RESOURCE_MANAGER property). Properties provide for communication between clients, often between an application and the window manager. The server's 396-byte reply at time 0.20 contains this property.

The next two messages from the client at times 0.30 and 0.38 form a single request to return an atom. (Each property has a unique integer ID called an atom.) The server replies at time 0.43 with the atom.

It is impossible to delve farther into this example without providing lots of details about the X window system, which isn't the purpose of this section. In this example a total of 12 segments comprising 1668 bytes is sent by the client and a total of 10 segments comprising 1120 bytes is sent by the server, before the window is displayed. The elapsed time was 3.17 seconds. From this point the client sent a small request every 5 seconds, averaging 44 bytes, with an update to the window. This continued until the client was terminated.

LBX: Low Bandwidth X

The encoding used by the X protocol is optimized for LANs, where the time spent encoding and decoding the data is more important than minimizing the amount of data transmitted. While this is OK for an Ethernet, it becomes a problem for slow serial lines, such as SLIP and PPP links (Sections 2.4 and 2.6).

Work is progressing to define a standard called *Low Bandwidth X* (LBX) that uses the following techniques to reduce the amount of network traffic: caching, sending differences from previous packets, and compression. Specifications should appear early in 1994 with a sample implementation in the X window system Release 6.

30.6 Summary

The first two applications that we covered, Finger and Whois, are for obtaining information on users. Finger clients query a server, often to find someone's login name (for sending them mail) or to see if someone is currently logged in. The Whois client normally contacts the server run by the InterNIC, looking for information on a person, institution, domain, or network number.

The other Internet resource discovery services that we briefly described, Archie, WAIS, Gopher, Veronica, and WWW, help us locate files and documents across the Internet. Other resource discovery tools are currently being developed.

This chapter finished with a brief look at the X Window System, another heavy user of TCP/IP. We saw that the X server manages multiple windows on a display, and handles the communication between a client and its window. Each client has its own TCP connection to the server and a single server manages all the clients for a given display. With the Xscope program we saw how it's possible to place another program between a client and server to output information about the messages exchanged between the two.

Exercises

30.1 Use Whois to find the owner of the class A network ID 88.

30.2 Use Whois to find the DNS servers for the `whitehouse.gov` domain. Does the reply match the answer given by the DNS?

30.3 In Figure 30.3, do you think the `xscope` process must be run on the same host as the X server?

Appendix A

The tcpdump Program

The tcpdump program was written by Van Jacobson, Craig Leres, and Steven McCanne, all of Lawrence Berkeley Laboratory, University of California, Berkeley. Version 2.2.1 (June 1992) is used in this text.

tcpdump operates by putting the network interface card into *promiscuous mode* so that every packet going across the wire is captured. Normally interface cards for media such as Ethernet only capture link level frames addressed to the particular interface or to the broadcast address (Section 2.2).

The underlying operating system must allow an interface to be put into promiscuous mode and let a user process capture the frames. tcpdump support is provided or can be added to the following Unix systems: 4.4BSD, BSD/386, SunOS, Ultrix, and HP-UX. Consult the README file that accompanies the tcpdump distribution for the details on what operating system and which versions are supported.

There are alternatives to tcpdump. In Figure 10.8 (p. 135) we use the Solaris 2.2 program snoop to look at some packets. AIX 3.2.2 provides the program iptrace, which provides similar features.

A.1 BSD Packet Filter

Current BSD-derived kernels provide the *BSD Packet Filter* (BPF), which is one method used by tcpdump to capture and filter packets from a network interface that has been placed into promiscuous mode. BPF also works with point-to-point links, such as SLIP (Section 2.4), which require nothing special to capture all packets going through the interface, and with the loopback interface (Section 2.7).

BPF has a long history. The Enet packet filter was created in 1980 by Mike Accetta and Rick Rashid at Carnegie Mellon University. Jeffrey Mogul at Stanford ported the code to BSD and continued its development from 1983 on. Since then, it has evolved into the Ultrix Packet Filter at DEC, a STREAMS NIT module under SunOS 4.1, and BPF. Steven McCanne, of Lawrence Berkeley Laboratory, implemented BPF in Summer 1990. Much of the design is from Van Jacobson. Details of the latest version, and a comparison with Sun's NIT, are given in [McCanne and Jacobson 1993].

Figure A.1 shows the features of BPF when used with an Ethernet.

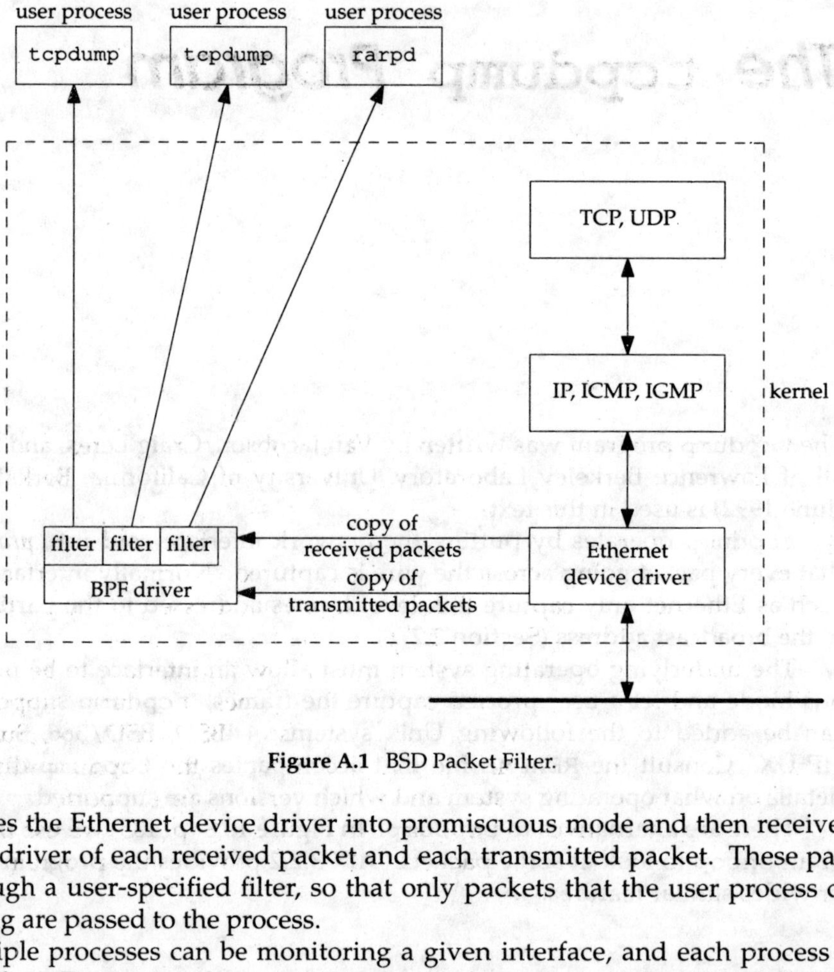

Figure A.1 BSD Packet Filter.

BPF places the Ethernet device driver into promiscuous mode and then receives a copy from the driver of each received packet and each transmitted packet. These packets are run through a user-specified filter, so that only packets that the user process considers interesting are passed to the process.

Multiple processes can be monitoring a given interface, and each process specifies its own filter. Figure A.1 shows two instances of tcpdump and an RARP daemon (Section 5.4) both monitoring the same Ethernet. Each instance of tcpdump specifies its own filter. The filter for tcpdump can be specified by the user on the command line, while rarpd always uses the same filter to capture only RARP requests.

In addition to specifying a filter, each user of BPF also specifies a timeout value. Since the data rate of the network can easily outrun the processing power of the CPU, and since it's costly for a user process to issue small reads from the kernel, BPF tries to pack multiple frames into a single read buffer and return only when the buffer is full, or the user-specified timeout has expired. `tcpdump` sets the timeout to 1 second since it normally receives lots of data from BPF, while the RARP daemon receives few frames, so `rarpd` sets the timeout to 0 (which returns when a frame is received).

The user-specified filter to tell BPF what frames the process considers interesting is a list of instructions for a hypothetical machine. These instructions are interpreted by the BPF filter in the kernel. Filtering in the kernel, and not in the user process, reduces the amount of data that must pass from the kernel to the user process. The RARP daemon always uses the same filter program, which is built into the program. `tcpdump`, on the other hand, lets the user specify a filter expression on the command line each time it's run. `tcpdump` converts the user-specified expression into the corresponding sequence of instructions for BPF. Examples of the `tcpdump` expressions are:

```
% tcpdump tcp port 25
% tcpdump 'icmp[0] != 8 and icmp[0] != 0'
```

The first prints only TCP segments with a source or destination port of 25. The second prints only ICMP messages that are not echo requests or echo replies (i.e., not ping packets). This expression specifies that the first byte of the ICMP message, the *type* field from Figure 6.2, not equal 8 or 0, an echo request or echo reply from Figure 6.3. As you can see, fancy filtering requires knowledge of the underlying packet structure. The expression in the second example has been placed in single quotes to prevent the Unix shell from interpreting the special characters.

Refer to the `tcpdump`(1) manual page for complete details of the expression that the user can specify. The `bpf`(4) manual page details the hypothetical machine instructions used by BPF. [McCanne and Jacobson 1993] compare the design and performance of this machine against other approaches.

A.2 SunOS Network Interface Tap

SunOS 4.1.x provides a STREAMS pseudo-device driver called the *Network Interface Tap* or NIT. ([Rago 1993] contains additional details on streams device drivers. We'll call the feature "streams.") NIT is similar to the BSD Packet Filter, but not as powerful or as efficient. Figure A.2 shows the streams modules involved in using NIT. One difference between this figure and Figure A.1 is that BPF can capture packets received from and transmitted through the network interface, while NIT only captures packets received from the interface. Using `tcpdump` with NIT means we only see packets sent by other hosts on the network—we never see packets transmitted by our own host. (Although BPF works with SunOS 4.1.x, it requires source code changes to the Ethernet device driver, which are impossible for most users who don't have access to the source code.)

When the device `/dev/nit` is opened, the streams driver `nit_if` is opened. Since NIT is built using streams, processing modules can be pushed on top of the `nit_if` driver. `tcpdump` pushes the module `nit_buf` onto the STREAM. This module aggregates multiple network frames into a single read buffer, with the user process specifying a timeout value. This is similar to what we described with BPF. The RARP daemon doesn't push this module onto its stream, since it deals with a low volume of packets.

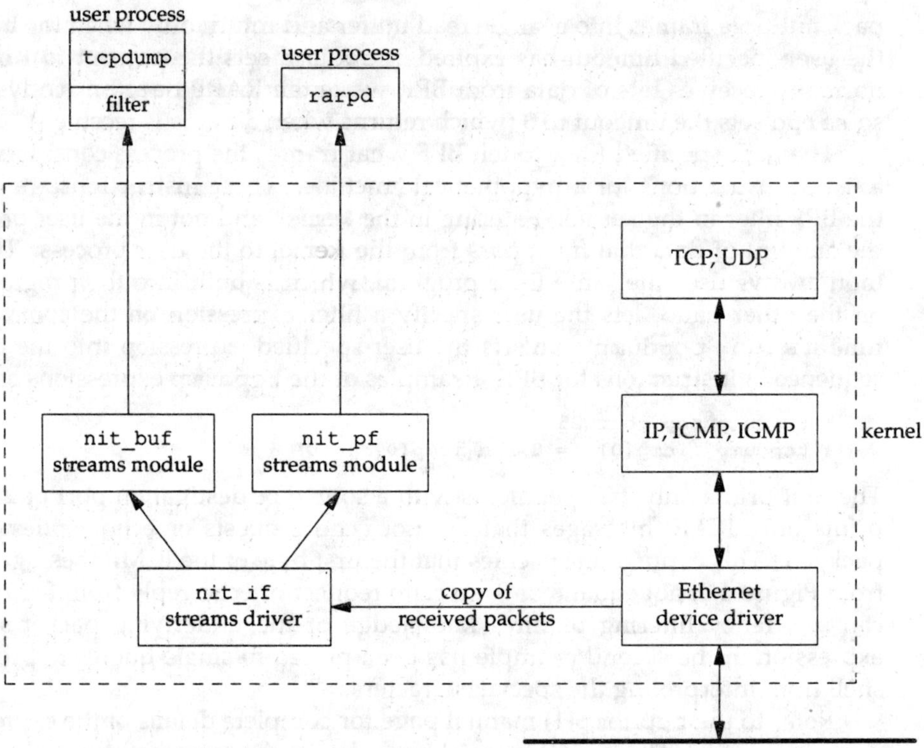

Figure A.2 SunOS Network Interface Tap.

The user-specified filtering is done by the streams module `nit_pf`. Notice in Figure A.2 that this module is used by the RARP daemon, but not by `tcpdump`. Instead, under SunOS `tcpdump` performs its own filtering in the user process. The reason is that the hypothetical machine instructions used by `nit_pf` are different (and not as powerful) as those supported by BPF. This means that when the user specifies a filter expression to `tcpdump` more data crosses the kernel-to-user boundary with NIT than with BPF.

A.3 SVR4 Data Link Provider Interface

SVR4 supports the *Data Link Provider Interface* (DLPI) which is a streams implementation of the OSI Data Link Service Definition. Most versions of SVR4 still support version 1 of the DLPI, SVR4.2 supports both versions 1 and 2, and Sun's Solaris 2.x supports version 2, with additional enhancements.

Network monitoring programs such as `tcpdump` must use the DLPI for raw access to the data-link device drivers. In Solaris 2.x the packet filter streams module has been renamed `pfmod` and the buffer module has been renamed `bufmod`.

Although Solaris 2.x is still new, an implementation of `tcpdump` should appear someday. Sun also supplies a program named `snoop` that performs functions similar to `tcpdump`. (`snoop` replaces the SunOS 4.x program named `etherfind`.) The author is not aware of any port of `tcpdump` to vanilla SVR4.

A.4 tcpdump Output

The output produced by `tcpdump` is "raw." We'll modify it for inclusion in the text to make it easier to read.

First, it always outputs the name of the network interface on which it is listening. We'll delete this line.

Next, the timestamp output by `tcpdump` is of the form `09:11:22.642008` on a system with microsecond resolution, or `09:11:22.64` on a system with only 10-ms clock resolution. (In Appendix B we talk more about computer clock resolution.) In either case the HH:MM:SS format is not what we want. Instead we are interested in both the relative time of each packet from the start of the dump, and the time difference between successive packets. We'll modify the output to show these two differences. The first difference we print with six digits to the right of the decimal point when microsecond resolution is available (two digits when only 10-ms resolution is provided), and the second difference we print with either four digits or two digits to the right of the decimal point (depending on the clock resolution).

> In this text most `tcpdump` output was collected on the host `sun`, which provides microsecond resolution. Some output was collected on the host `bsdi` running BSD/386 Version 0.9.4, which only provided 10-ms resolution (e.g., Figure 5.1). Some output was also collected on `bsdi` when it was running BSD/386 Version 1.0, which provides microsecond resolution.

`tcpdump` always prints the name of the sending host, then a greater than sign, then the name of the destination host. This makes it hard to follow the flow of packets between two hosts. Although our `tcpdump` output will still show the direction of data flow like this, we'll often take this output and produce a time line instead. (The first of these in the text is Figure 6.11, p. 80.) In our time lines one host will be on the left, and the other on the right. This makes it easier to see which side sends and which side receives each packet.

We add line numbers to the `tcpdump` output, allowing us to reference specific lines in the text. We also add additional space between certain lines, to separate some packet exchanges.

Finally, `tcpdump` output can exceed the width of the page. We wrap long lines around at convenient points in the line.

As an example, the output produced by `tcpdump` corresponding to Figure 4.4 (p. 58) is shown in Figure A.3, assuming an 80-column terminal window.

We won't show our typing the interrupt key (which terminates `tcpdump`) and we won't show the number of packets received and dropped. (Dropped packets are those that arrived faster than `tcpdump` could keep up with. Since the examples in the text were often run on an otherwise idle network, this is always 0.)

```
sun % tcpdump -e
tcpdump: listening on le0
09:11:22.642008 0:0:c0:6f:2d:40 ff:ff:f f:ff:ff:ff arp 60: arp who-has svr4 tell
bsdi
09:11:22 .644182 0:0:c0:c2:9b:26 0:0:c0:6f:2d:40 arp 60: arp reply svr4 is-at 0:0
:c0:c2:9b:26
09:11:22.644839 0:0:c0:6f:2d:40 0:0:c0:c2:9b:26  ip 60: bsdi.1030 > svr4.discard:
 S 596459521:596459521(0) win 4096 <mss 1024> [tos 0x10]
09:11:22. 649842 0:0:c0:c2:9b:26 0:0:c0:6f:2d:40 ip 60: svr4.discard > bsdi.1030:
 S 3562228225:3562228225(0) ack 596459522 win 4096 <mss 1024>
09:1 1:22.651623 0:0:c0:6f:2d:40 0:0:c0:c2:9b:26 ip 60: bsdi.1030 > svr4.discard:
 . ack 1 win 4096 [tos 0x10]
                                        4 other packets that we don't show
^?                                      type our interrupt key to terminate
9 packets received by filter
0 packets dropped by kernel
```

Figure A.3 tcpdump output for Figure 4.4 (p. 58).

A.5 Security Considerations

It should be obvious that tapping into a network's traffic lets you see many things you shouldn't see. For example, the passwords typed by users of applications such as Telnet and FTP are transmitted across the network exactly as the user enters them. (This is called the *cleartext* representation of the password, in comparison to the *encrypted* representation. It is the encrypted representation that is stored in the Unix password file, normally /etc/passwd or /etc/shadow.) Nevertheless, there are many times when a network administrator needs to use a tool such as tcpdump to diagnose network problems.

Our use of tcpdump is as a learning tool, to see what really gets transmitted across the network. Access to tcpdump, and similar vendor-supplied utilities, depends on the system. Under SunOS, for example, access to the NIT device is restricted to the superuser. The BSD Packet Filter uses a different technique: access is controlled by the permissions on the devices /dev/bpf*XX*. Normally these devices are readable and writable only by the owner (which should be the superuser) and readable by the group (often the system administration group). This means normal users can't run programs such as tcpdump, unless the system administrator makes the program set-user-ID.

A.6 Socket Debug Option

Another way to see what's going on with a TCP conne ction is to enable socket debugging, on systems that support this feature. This feature works only with TCP (not with other protocols) and requires application support (to enable a socket option when it's started).

Most Berkeley-derived implementations support thi s, including SunOS, 4.4BSD, and SVR4.

The program enables a socket option, and the kernel then keeps a trace record of what happens on that connection. At some later time all this information can be output by running the program trpt(8). It doesn't require special permission to enable the socket debug option, but it requires special privileges to run trpt, since it accesses the kernel's memory.

Our sock program (Appendix C) supports this feature with its -D option, but the information output is harder to decipher and understand than the corresponding tcpdump output. We do, however, use it in Section 21.4 to look at kernel variables in the TCP connection block that tcpdump cannot access.

Appendix B

Computer Clocks

Since most of the examples in this text measure a time interval, we need to describe in more detail the type of timekeeping used by current Unix systems. The following description applies to the systems being used for the examples in this book, and for most Unix systems. Additional details are given in Sections 3.4 and 3.5 of [Leffler et al. 1989].

The hardware generates a clock interrupt at some frequency. For Sun SPARCs and Intel 80386s the interrupts occur every 10 ms.

It should be noted that most computers use an uncompensated crystal oscillator to generate these interrupts. As noted in Table 7 of RFC 1305 [Mills 1992], you don't want to ask what the drift per day of such an oscillator is. This means few computers keep accurate time (i.e., the interrupts don't occur exactly every 10 ms). A 0.01% tolerance gives an error of 8.64 seconds per day. To keep better time requires (1) a better oscillator, (2) an external time source with greater precision (e.g., the time source supplied by the Global Positioning Satellites), or (3) access across the Internet to systems with more precise clocks. The latter is provided by the Network Time Protocol, as described in detail in RFC 1305, which is beyond the scope of this book.

Another common source of time errors in Unix systems is that the 10-ms clock interrupts only cause the kernel to increment a variable that keeps track of the time. If the kernel loses an interrupt (i.e., it's too busy for the 10 ms between two consecutive interrupts), the clock will lose 10 ms. Lost interrupts of this type often cause Unix systems to lose time.

Even though the clock interrupts arrive approximately every 10 ms, newer systems such as SPARCs provide a higher resolution timer to measure time differences. `tcpdump`, through the NIT driver (described in Appendix A) has access to this higher resolution timer. On SPARCs this timer provides microsecond resolution. Access to this higher resolution timer is also provided for user processes through the `gettimeofday`(2) function.

The author ran the following experiment. A program was run that called the `gettimeofday` function 10,000 times in a loop, saving each return value in an array. At the end of the loop the 9,999 differences were printed out. For a SPARC ELC the distribution of the differences are shown in Figure B.1.

Microseconds	Count
36	4,914
37	4,831
38	167
39	8
other	79

Figure B.1 Distribution of time required to call `gettimeofday` 10,000 times on SPARC ELC.

The total clock time required to run the program was 0.38 seconds, on an otherwise idle system. From this we can say that the time for the process to call `gettimeofday` is about 37 microseconds. Since the ELC is rated around 21 MIPS (million instructions per second), 37 microseconds corresponds to about 800 instructions. This seems reasonable for the kernel to handle a system call from a user process, execute the system call, copy back 8 bytes of results, and return to the user process. (MIPS ratings are questionable, and it's hard to try to measure instruction times on current systems. All we're trying to do is get a rough idea and see if the values make sense.)

From this simple experiment we can say that the values returned by `gettimeofday` do contain microsecond resolution.

If we run similar tests under SVR4/386, however, the results are different. This is because many 386 Unix systems, such as SVR4, only count the 10-ms clock interrupts, and don't try to provide any higher resolution. Figure B.2 is the distribution of the 9,999 differences under SVR4 on an 25 Mhz 80386.

Microseconds	Count
0	9,871
10,000	128

Figure B.2 Distribution of time required to call `gettimeofday` 10,000 times under SVR4/386.

These values are worthless, since the differences are normally less than 10 ms, which is treated as 0. About all we can do on these systems is measure the clock time on an idle system, and divide by the number of loops. This provides an upper bound, since it includes the time required to call `printf` 9,999 times, writing the results to a file. (In the SPARC case, Figure B.1, the differences did not include the `printf` times since all 10,000 values were first obtained, and then the results were printed.) Under SVR4 the clock time was 3.15 seconds, yielding 315 microseconds per system call. This system call time, about 8.5 times slower than the SPARC, seems about right.

BSD/386 Version 1.0 provides microsecond resolution similar to the SPARC. It reads the 8253 clock register and calculates the number of microseconds since the last clock tick. This is made available to processes that call `gettimeofday` and to kernel modules such as the BSD Packet Filter.

In relation to tcpdump these numbers mean that we can believe the millisecond and submillisecond values that are printed on the SPARC and BSD/386 systems, but the values printed by tcpdump under SVR4/386 will always be a multiple of 10 ms. For other programs that print round-trip times, such as ping (Chapter 7) and traceroute (Chapter 8), on the SPARC and BSD/386 systems we can believe the millisecond values that are output, but the values printed under SVR4/386 will always be multiples of 10. To measure anything like the ping time on a LAN, which we show in Chapter 7 to be around 3 ms, requires running ping on the SPARC or BSD/386.

Some of the examples in this text were run under BSD/386 Version 0.9.4, which was similar to SVR4 in that it provided only 10-ms clock resolution. When we show tcpdump output from this system, we show only two numbers to the right of the decimal point, since that's the resolution provided.

Appendix C

The sock Program

A simple test program named sock is used throughout the book to generate TCP and UDP data. It is used as both a client and server process. Having a test program like this, which is executable from a shell prompt, prevents us from having to write new client and server C programs for each specific feature that we want to examine. Since the purpose of this book is to understand the networking protocols, and not network programming, in this Appendix we only describe the program and its various options.

There are numerous other programs with functionality similar to sock. Juergen Nickelsen wrote a program named socket and Dave Yost wrote a program named sockio. Both contain many similar features. Pieces of the sock program have also been inspired by the public domain ttcp program, written by Mike Muuss and Terry Slattery.

The sock program operates in one of four modes:

1. Interactive client: the default. The program connects to a server and then copies standard input to the server and copies everything received from the server to standard output. This is shown in Figure C.1.

Figure C.1 Default operation of sock as interactive client.

We must specify the name of the server host and the name of the service to connect to. The host can also be specified as a dotted-decimal number, and the service can be specified as an integer port number. Connecting to the standard echo server (Section 1.12), from sun to bsdi echoes everything we type:

```
sun % sock bsdi echo
a test line                 we type this line
a test line                 and the echo server returns a copy
^D                          type our end-of-file character to terminate
```

2. Interactive server: the `-s` option is specified. The service name (or port number) is required:

   ```
   sun % sock -s 5555          act as server listening on port 5555
   ```

   The program waits for a connection from a client and then copies standard input to the client and copies everything received from the client to standard output. An Internet address can precede the port number on the command line, to specify on which local interface connections are accepted:

   ```
   sun % sock -s 140.252.13.33 5555     accept connections only on Ethernet
   ```

   The default mode is to accept a connection request on any local interface.

3. Source client: the `-i` option is specified. By default a 1024-byte buffer is written to the network 1024 times. The `-n` and `-w` options can change these defaults. For example,

   ```
   sun % sock -i -n12 -w4096 bsdi discard
   ```

   writes 12 buffers, each containing 4096 bytes of data, to the discard server on host `bsdi`.

4. Sink server: the `-i` and `-s` options are specified. Data is read from the network and discarded.

Although these examples used TCP (the default), the `-u` option specifies UDP.

There are a multitude of options that provide finer control over exactly how the program operates. These options are needed to generate all the test conditions used throughout the text.

`-b` *n* Bind *n* as the client's local port number. (By default an ephemeral port number assigned by the system is used by the client.)

`-c` Convert newline characters that are read on standard input into a carriage return and a linefeed. Similarly, when reading from the network, convert the sequence <carriage return, linefeed> into a single newline character. Many Internet applications expect NVT ASCII (Section 26.4), which uses the carriage return and linefeed to terminate each line.

`-f` *a.b.c.d.p*
Specify the foreign IP address (*a.b.c.d*) and the foreign port number (*p*) for a UDP end point (Section 11.12).

`-h` Implement TCP's half-close facility (Section 18.5). That is, do not terminate when an end-of-file is encountered on standard input. Instead, issue a half-close on the TCP connection but continue reading from the network until the peer closes the connection.

`-i` Source client or sink server. Either write data to the network (default) or if used in conjunction with the `-s` option, read data from the network. The `-n` option can specify the number of buffers to write (or read), the `-w` option can specify the size of each write, and the `-r` option can specify the size of each read.

`-n` *n* When used with the `-i` option, *n* specifies the number of buffers to read or write. The default value of *n* is 1024.

`-p` *n* Specify the number of seconds to pause between each read or write. This can be used with the source client (`-i`) or sink server (`-is`) to delay between each read or write of network. Also see the `-P` option to pause before the first read or write.

`-q` *n* Specify the size of the pending connection queue for the TCP server: the number of accepted connections that TCP will queue for the application (Figure 18.23). The default is 5.

`-r` *n* When used with the `-is` options, *n* specifies the size of each read from the network. The default is 1024 bytes per read.

`-s` Operate as a server instead of as a client.

`-u` Use UDP instead of TCP.

`-v` Verbose. Print additional details (such as the client and server ephemeral port numbers) onto standard error.

`-w` *n* When used with the `-i` option, specifies the size of each write to the network. The default is 1024 bytes per write.

`-A` Enable the `SO_REUSEADDR` socket option. With TCP this allows the process to assign itself a port number that is part of a connection that is in the 2MSL wait. With UDP on a system that supports multicasting, it allows multiple processes to use the same local port to receive broadcast or multicast datagrams.

`-B` Enable the `SO_BROADCAST` socket option to allow UDP datagrams to be sent to a broadcast IP address.

`-D` Enable the `SO_DEBUG` socket option. This causes additional debugging information to be maintained by the kernel for this TCP connection (Section A.6). This information can be output later by running the `trpt`(8) program.

`-E` Enable the `IP_RECVDSTADDR` socket option, if supported by the implementation (Section 11.12). This is intended for UDP servers, to print the destination IP address of the received UDP datagram.

`-F` Specifies a concurrent TCP server. That is, the server creates a new process using the `fork` function for each client connection.

`-K` Enable TCP's `SO_KEEPALIVE` socket option (Chapter 23).

`-L` *n* Set the linger time (`SO_LINGER` socket option) for a TCP end point to *n*. A linger time of 0 means when the network connection is closed, any data still queued for sending is discarded and a reset is sent to the peer (Section 18.7).

A positive linger time is the time (in 100ths of a second) that a close on the network connection should wait for all outstanding data to be sent and acknowledged. If, after closing the network connection, all the pending data has not been sent and acknowledged when this timer expires, the close will return an error.

`-N` Set the `TCP_NODELAY` socket option to disable the Nagle algorithm (Section 19.4).

`-O` *n* Specify the number of seconds for a TCP server to pause before accepting the first client connection.

`-P` *n* Specify the number of seconds to pause before the first read or write of the network. This can be used with the sink server (`-is`) to delay after accepting the connection request from the client but before performing the first read from the network. When used with the source client (`-i`) it delays after the connection has been established, but before the first write to the network. Also see the `-p` option to pause between each successive read or write.

`-Q` *n* Specify the number of seconds for a TCP client or server to pause after receiving an end-of-file from the other end, but before closing its end of the connection.

`-R` *n* Set the socket's receive buffer (`SO_RCVBUF` socket option) to *n*. This can directly affect the size of the receive window advertised by TCP. With UDP this specifies the largest UDP datagram that can be received.

`-S` *n* Set the socket's send buffer (`SO_SNDBUF` socket option) to *n*. With UDP this specifies the largest UDP datagram that can be sent.

`-U` *n* Enter TCP's urgent mode after write number *n* to the network. One byte of data is written to initiate urgent mode (Section 20.8).

Appendix D

Solutions to Selected Exercises

Chapter 1

1.1 The value is $2^7 - 2$ (126) plus $2^{14} - 2$ (16,382) plus $2^{21} - 2$ (2,097,150) for a total of 2,113,658. We subtract 2 in each calculation since a network ID of all zero bits or all one bits is invalid.

1.2 Figure D.1 shows a plot of the values through August 1993.

Figure D.1 Number of networks announced to NSFNET.

The dashed line estimates that the maximum number of networks will be reached in the year 2000, if the exponential growth continues.

1.3 "Be liberal in what you accept, and conservative in what you send."

Chapter 3

3.1 No, any class A address with a network ID of 127 is OK, although most systems use 127.0.0.1.

3.2 `kpno` has five interfaces: three point-to-point links and two Ethernets. R10 has four Ethernet interfaces. `gateway` has three interfaces: two point-to-point links and one Ethernet. Finally, `netb` has one Ethernet interface and two point-to-point links.

3.3 There's no difference: both have a subnet mask of 255.255.255.0, as does a class C address that is not subnetted.

3.5 It's valid and it's called a *noncontiguous subnet mask* since the 16 bits for the subnet mask are not contiguous. The RFCs, however, recommend against using noncontiguous subnet masks.

3.6 It's a historical artifact. The value is $1024+512$ but the MTU values printed include any required headers. Solaris 2.2 sets the MTU of the loopback interface to 8232 $(8192+40)$, which allows room for 8192 bytes of user data along with the normal 20-byte IP header and 20-byte TCP header.

3.7 First, datagrams eliminate the need for connection state in the routers. Second, datagrams provide the basic building block on which unreliable (UDP) and reliable (TCP) transport layers can be built. Third, datagrams represent the minimal network layer assumption, allowing a wide range of data-link layers to be used.

Chapter 4

4.1 Issuing an `rsh` command establishes a TCP connection with the other host. Doing that causes IP datagrams to be exchanged between the two hosts. This requires the ARP cache on the other host to have an entry for our host. Therefore, even if the ARP cache was empty before we executed the `rsh` command, it's guaranteed to have an entry for our host when the `rsh` server executes the `arp` command.

4.2 Make sure that your host does not have an entry in its ARP cache for some other host on its Ethernet, say `foo`. Make sure `foo` sends a gratuitous ARP request when it bootstraps, perhaps running `tcpdump` on another host when `foo` bootstraps. Then shut down the host `foo` and enter an incorrect entry into the ARP cache on your system for `foo`, using the `arp` command and being sure to specify the `temp` option. Bootstrap `foo` and when it's up, look at your host's ARP cache entry for it to see whether the incorrect entry has been corrected.

4.3 Read Section 2.3.2.2 of the Host Requirements RFC and Section 11.9 of this text.

4.4 Assuming that a completed ARP entry existed for the server on the client when the server was taken down, if we continually try to contact the (down) server, the

ARP timeout gets extended for another 20 minutes. When the server finally reboots with a new hardware address, if it doesn't issue a gratuitous ARP, the old, invalid ARP entry will still exist on the client. We won't be able to contact the server at its new hardware address until we either manually delete the ARP cache entry or stop trying to contact it for 20 minutes.

Chapter 5

5.1 A separate frame type is not an absolute requirement, since the *op* field in Figure 4.3 has a different value for all four operations (ARP request, ARP reply, RARP request, and RARP reply). But the implementation of an RARP server, separate from the kernel's ARP server, is made easier with the different frame type field.

5.2 Each RARP server can delay for a small random time before sending a response.

As a refinement, one RARP server can be designated the primary and the others as secondaries. The primary server can respond without a delay, and the secondaries with random delays.

As yet another refinement, with a primary and secondaries, the secondaries can be programmed to respond only to a duplicate request received in a short time frame. This assumes that the reason for the duplicate request is that the primary is down.

Chapter 6

6.1 If there were one hundred hosts on the local cable, each could try to send an ICMP port unreachable at about the same time. Many of these transmissions could lead to collisions (if an Ethernet is being used), which can render the network useless for a second or two.

6.2 It is a "should."

6.3 An ICMP error is always sent with a TOS of 0, as we indicated in Figure 3.2. An ICMP query request can be sent with any TOS, and the corresponding reply should be sent with the same TOS.

6.4 `netstat -s` is the common way to see the per-protocol statistics. On a SunOS 4.1.1 host (`gemini`) that has received 48 million IP datagrams, the ICMP statistics are:

```
Output histogram:
        echo reply: 1757
        destination unreachable: 700
        time stamp reply: 1
Input histogram:
        echo reply: 211
        destination unreachable: 3071
        source quench: 249
```

```
routing redirect: 2789
echo: 1757
#10: 21
time exceeded: 56
time stamp: 1
```

The 21 input messages of type 10 are router solicitations that SunOS 4.1.1 doesn't support.

SNMP can also be used (Figure 25.26) and some systems, such as Solaris 2.2, generate `netstat -s` output that uses SNMP variable names.

Chapter 7

7.2 86 bytes divided by 960 bytes/sec, times 2 gives 179.2 ms. When `ping` is run at this speed, the printed values are 180 ms.

7.3 (86 + 48) bytes divided by 960 bytes/sec, times 2 gives 279.2 ms. The additional 48 bytes are because the final 48 bytes of the 56 bytes in the data portion must be escaped: `0xc0` is the SLIP END character.

7.4 CSLIP only compresses the TCP and IP headers for TCP segments. It has no effect on the ICMP messages used by `ping`.

7.5 On a SPARCstation ELC a ping of the loopback address yields an RTT of 1.310 ms, while a ping of the host's Ethernet address yields an RTT of 1.460 ms. This difference is the additional processing done by the Ethernet driver, to determine that the datagram is really destined for the local host. You need a version of `ping` that outputs microsecond resolution to measure this.

Chapter 8

8.1 If an incoming datagram has a TTL of 0, doing the decrement and then test would set the TTL to 255 and let the datagram continue. Although a router should never receive a datagram with a TTL of 0, it has occurred.

8.2 We noted that `traceroute` stores 12 bytes of data in the data portion of the UDP datagram, part of which is the time the datagram was sent. From Figure 6.9, however, we see that ICMP only returns the first 8 bytes of the IP datagram that was in error, and we noted there that this is the 8-byte UDP header. Therefore the time value stored by `traceroute` is not returned in the ICMP error message. `traceroute` saves the time when it sends a packet, and when an ICMP reply is received, fetches the current time and subtracts the two value to get the RTT.

Recall from Chapter 7 that `ping` stored the time in the outgoing ICMP echo request and this data was echoed by the server. This allowed `ping` to print the correct RTT, even if the packets were returned out of order.

8.3 The first line of output is correct and identifies R1. The next probe starts with a TTL of 2, and this is decremented by R1. When R2 receives this it decrements the

TTL from 1 to 0 but incorrectly forwards it to R3. R3 sees that the incoming TTL is 0 and sends back the time exceeded. This means the second line of output (for the TTL of 2) identifies R3, not R2. The third line of output correctly identifies R3. The clue that this bug is present is two consecutive lines of output that identify the same router.

8.4 In this case the TTL of 1 identifies R1, the TTL of 2 identifies R2, and the TTL of 3 identifies R3; but when the TTL is 4 the UDP datagram gets to the destination with an incoming TTL of 1. The ICMP port unreachable is generated, but its TTL is 1 (incorrectly copied from the incoming TTL). This ICMP message goes to R3 where the TTL is decremented and the message discarded. An ICMP time exceeded is *not* generated, since the datagram that was discarded was an ICMP error message (port unreachable). A similar scenario occurs for the probe with a TTL of 5, but this time the outgoing port unreachable starts with a TTL of 2 (the incoming TTL) and makes it back to R2, where it's discarded. The port unreachable corresponding to the probe with a TTL of 6 makes it back to R1, where it's discarded. Finally the port unreachable for the probe with a TTL of 7 makes it all the way back, where it arrives with an incoming TTL of 1. (`traceroute` considers an arriving ICMP message with a TTL of 0 or 1 to be suspicious, so it prints an exclamation point after the RTT.) In summary, the lines for a TTL of 1, 2, and 3 correctly identify R1, R2, and R3, followed by three lines each containing three timeouts, followed by the line for a TTL of 7 that identifies the destination.

8.5 It appears that all these routers initialize the outgoing TTL of an ICMP message to 255. This is common. The incoming value of 255 from `netb` is what we expect, but the value of 253 from `butch` means there is probably a missing router between it and `netb`. Otherwise we would expect an incoming TTL of 254 at this point. Similarly, from `enss142.UT.westnet.net` we expect a value of 252, not 249. It appears these missing routers are not handling the outbound UDP datagram correctly, but they are decrementing the TTL on the returned ICMP message correctly.

We must be careful when looking at the incoming TTL, since sometimes a value other than what we expect can be caused by the return ICMP message taking a different path from the outbound UDP datagram. In this example, however, it confirms what we suspect—there are missing routers that `traceroute` is not finding when the loose source routing option is used.

8.7 The `ping` client sets the identifier field in the ICMP echo request message (Figure 7.1, p. 86) to its process ID. The ICMP echo reply contains this identifier field. Each client looks at this returned identifier field and handles only those that it sent.

The `traceroute` client sets its UDP source port number to the logical-OR of its process ID and 32768. Since the returned ICMP message always contains the first 8 bytes of the IP datagram that generated the error (Figure 6.9, p. 78), which includes the entire UDP header, this source port number is returned in the ICMP error.

8.8 The `ping` client sets the optional data portion of the ICMP echo request message to the time at which the packet is sent. This optional data must be returned in the ICMP echo reply. This allows `ping` to calculate the accurate round-trip time, even if packets are returned out of order.

The `traceroute` client can't operate this way because all that's returned in the ICMP error is the UDP header (Figure 6.9, p. 78), none of the UDP data. Therefore `traceroute` must remember when it sends a request, wait for the reply, and calculate the time difference.

This illustrates another difference between Ping and Traceroute: Ping sends one packet a second, regardless of whether it receives any replies, while Traceroute sends a request and then waits for either a reply or a timeout before sending the next request.

8.9 Since Solaris 2.2 starts ephemeral UDP port numbers at 32768 by default, there is a much greater chance that the destination port is in use on the destination host.

Chapter 9

9.1 When the ICMP standard was first specified, RFC 792 [Postel 1981b], subnetting was not in use. Also, using a single network redirect instead of *N* host redirects (for all *N* hosts on the destination network) saves some space in the routing table.

9.2 The entry is not required, but if it is removed, all IP datagrams to `slip` are sent to the default router (`sun`), which then forwards them to the router `bsdi`. Since `sun` is forwarding a datagram out the same interface on which it was received, it sends an ICMP redirect to `svr4`. This creates the same routing table entry on `svr4` that we removed, although this time it is created by a redirect instead of being added at bootstrap time.

9.3 When the 4.2BSD host receives the datagram destined for 140.1.255.255 it finds that it has a route to the network (140.1) so it tries to forward the datagram. To do this it sends an ARP broadcast looking for 140.1.255.255. No reply is received for this ARP request, so the datagram is eventually discarded. If there are many of these 4.2BSD hosts on the cable, every one sends out this ARP broadcast at about the same time, swamping the network temporarily.

9.4 This time a reply is received for each ARP request, telling each 4.2BSD host to send the datagram to the specified hardware address (the Ethernet broadcast). If there are *k* of these 4.2BSD hosts on the cable, all receive their own ARP reply, causing each one to generate another broadcast. Each host receives each broadcast IP datagram destined to 140.1.255.255, and since every host now has an ARP cache entry, the datagram is forwarded again to the broadcast address. This continues and generates an *Ethernet meltdown*. [Manber 1990] describes other forms of chain reactions in networks.

Chapter 10

10.1 Thirteen of the routes came from `kpno`: all except 140.252.101.0 and 140.252.104.0, the other networks to which `gateway` is directly connected.

10.2 Sixty seconds will pass before the 25 routes advertised in the lost datagram are updated. This isn't a problem because RIP normally requires 3 minutes without an update before it declares a route dead.

10.3 RIP runs on top of UDP, and UDP provides an optional checksum for the data portion of the UDP datagram (Section 11.3). OSPF, however, runs on top of IP. The IP checksum covers only the IP header, so OSPF must add its own checksum field.

10.4 Load balancing increases the chances of packets being delivered out of order, and possibly distorts the round-trip times calculated by the transport layer.

10.5 This is called simple split horizon.

10.6 In Figure 12.1 we show that each of the 100 hosts processes the broadcast UDP datagram through the device driver, IP layer, and UDP layer, where it'll finally be discarded when it's discovered that UDP port 520 is not in use.

Chapter 11

11.1 Since there are 8 additional bytes of header when IEEE 802 encapsulation is used, 1465 bytes of user data is the smallest size that causes fragmentation.

11.3 There are 8200 bytes of data for IP to send, the 8192 bytes of user data and the 8-byte UDP header. Using the `tcpdump` notation, the first fragment is 1480@0+ (1480 bytes of data, offset of 0, with the "more fragments" bit set). The second is 1480@1480+, the third is 1480@2960+, the fourth is 1480@4440+, the fifth is 1480@5920+, and the sixth is 800@7400. $1480 \times 5 + 800 = 8200$, which is the number of bytes to send.

11.4 Each 1480-byte fragment is divided into three pieces: two 528-byte fragments and one 424-byte fragment. The largest multiple of 8 less than 532 (552 – 20) is 528. The 800-byte fragment is divided into two pieces: a 528-byte fragment and a 272-byte fragment. Thus, the original 8192-byte datagram becomes 17 frames across the SLIP link.

11.5 No. The problem is that when the application times out and retransmits, the IP datagram generated by the retransmission has a new identification field. Reassembly is done only for fragments with the same identification field.

11.6 The identification field in the IP header (47942) is the same.

11.7 First, from Figure 11.4 we see that `gemini` does not have outgoing UDP checksums enabled. It's highly probable that the operating system on this host (SunOS 4.1.1) is one that never verifies an incoming UDP checksum unless outgoing UDP checksums are enabled. Second, it could be that most of the UDP traffic is local traffic, instead of WAN traffic, and therefore not subject to all the vagaries of WANs.

11.8 The loose and strict source routing options are copied into each fragment. The timestamp option and the record route option are not copied into each fragment—they appear only in the first fragment.

11.9 No. We saw in Section 11.12 that many implementations can filter incoming datagrams destined for a given UDP port number based on the destination IP address, source IP address, and source port number.

Chapter 12

12.1 Broadcasting by itself does not add to network traffic, but it adds extra host processing. Broadcasting can lead to additional network traffic if the receiving hosts incorrectly respond with errors such as ICMP port unreachables. Also, routers normally don't forward broadcast packets, whereas bridges normally do, so broadcasts on a bridged network can travel much farther than they would on a routed network.

12.2 Every host receives a copy of every broadcast. The interface layer receives the frame, and passes it to the device driver. If the type field is for some other protocol, it is the device driver that discards the frame.

12.3 First execute `netstat -r` to see the routing table. This shows the names of all the interfaces. Then execute `ifconfig` (Section 3.8) for each interface: the flags tell if the interface supports broadcasting, and if so the broadcast address is also output.

12.4 Berkeley-derived implementations do not allow a broadcast datagram to be fragmented. When we specified the length of 1472 bytes, the resulting IP datagram was exactly 1500 bytes, the Ethernet MTU. Refusing to allow a broadcast datagram to be fragmented is a policy decision—there is no technical reason (other than a desire to reduce the number of broadcast packets).

12.5 Depending on the multicasting support in the various Ethernet interface cards in the 100 hosts, the multicast datagram can be ignored by the interface card, or discarded by the device driver.

Chapter 13

13.1 Use some host-unique value when generating the random value. The IP address and link-layer address are two values that should differ on every host. The time-of-day is a bad choice, especially if all the hosts run a protocol such as NTP to synchronize their clocks.

13.2 They added an application protocol header that included a sequence number and a timestamp.

Chapter 14

14.1 A resolver is always a client, but a name server is both a client and server.

14.2 The question is returned, which accounts for the first 44 bytes. The single answer occupies the remaining 31 bytes: a 2-byte pointer for the domain name (i.e., a pointer to the domain name in the question), 10 bytes for the fixed-size fields (type, class, TTL, and resource length), and 19 bytes for the resource data (a domain name). Notice that the domain name in the resource data (`svr4.tuc.noao.edu.`) doesn't share a suffix with the domain name in the question (`34.13.252.140.in-addr.arpa.`) so a pointer can't be used.

14.3 Reversing the order means using the DNS first, and if that fails, trying to convert the argument as a dotted-decimal number. This means every time a dotted-decimal number is specified, the DNS is used, involving a name server. This is a waste of resources.

14.4 Section 4.2.2 of RFC 1035 specifies that a 2-byte length precedes the actual DNS message.

14.5 When a name server starts it normally reads the (possibly out of date) list of root servers from a disk file. It then tries to contact one of these root servers, requesting the name server records (a query type of NS) for the root domain. This returns the current up-to-date list of root servers. Minimally this requires one of the root server entries in the start-up disk file to be current.

14.6 The registration services of the InterNIC updates the root servers three times a week.

14.7 Since the resolver comes and goes, as applications come and go, if the system is configured to use multiple name servers and the resolver maintains no state, the resolver cannot keep track of the round-trip times to its various name servers. This can lead to timeouts for resolver queries that are too short, causing unnecessary retransmissions.

14.8 Sorting the A records should be done by the resolver, not the name server, since the resolver normally knows more than the server about the network topology of the client. (Newer releases of BIND provide for resolver sorting of A records.)

Chapter 15

15.1 TFTP requests sent to the broadcast address should be ignored. As stated in the Host Requirements RFC, responding to a broadcast request can create a significant security hole. A problem, however, is that not all implementations and APIs provide the destination address of a UDP datagram to the process that receives the datagram (Section 11.12). For this reason many TFTP servers don't enforce this restriction.

15.2 Unfortunately, the RFC says nothing about this block number wrap. Implementations should be able to transfer files up through 33,553,920 bytes (65535 × 512).

Many implementations fail when the size of the file exceeds 16,776,704 (32767×512) since they incorrectly maintain the block number as a signed 16-bit integer instead of an unsigned integer.

15.3 This simplifies coding a TFTP client to fit in read-only memory, because the server is the sender of the bootstrap files, so the server must implement the timeout and retransmission.

15.4 With its stop-and-wait protocol, TFTP can transfer a maximum of 512 bytes per client–server round trip. The maximum throughput of TFTP is then 512 bytes divided by the round-trip time between the client and server. On an Ethernet, assuming a round-trip time of 3 ms, the maximum throughput is around 170,000 bytes/sec.

Chapter 16

16.1 A router could forward an RARP request to some other host on one of the router's other attached networks, but sending a reply then becomes a problem. The router would also have to forward RARP replies.

BOOTP doesn't have this reply problem since the address to reply to is a normal IP address that the routers know how to forward anyway. The problem is that RARP uses only link-layer addresses, and routers don't normally know these values for hosts on other, nonattached, networks.

16.2 It could use its own hardware address, which should be unique, and which is set in the request and returned in the reply.

Chapter 17

17.1 All are mandatory except the UDP checksum. The IP checksum covers only the IP header, while the others start immediately after the IP header.

17.2 The source IP address, source port number, or protocol field might have been corrupted.

17.3 Many Internet applications use a carriage return and linefeed to mark the end of each application record. This is NVT ASCII coding (Section 26.4). An alternative technique is to prefix each record with a byte count, which is used by the DNS (Exercise 14.4) and Sun RPC (Section 29.2).

17.4 As we saw in Section 6.5, an ICMP error must return at least the first 8 bytes beyond the IP header of the IP datagram that caused the error. When TCP receives an ICMP error it needs to examine the two port numbers to determine which connection the error corresponds to, so the port numbers must be in the first 8 bytes of the TCP header.

17.5 There are options at the end of the TCP header, but there are no options in the UDP header.

Chapter 18

18.1 The ISN is a 32-bit counter that wraps around from 4,294,912,000 to 8,704 approximately 9.5 hours after the system was bootstrapped. After approximately another 9.5 hours it will wrap around to 17,408, then 26,112 after another 9.5 hours, and so on. Since the ISN starts at 1 when the system is bootstrapped, and since the lowest order digit cycles through 4, 8, 2, 6, and 0, the ISN should always be an odd number.

18.2 In the first case we used our `sock` program, and by default it transmits the Unix newline character as itself—the single ASCII character 012 (octal). In the second case we used the Telnet client and it converts the Unix newline into two ASCII characters—a carriage return (octal 015) followed by a linefeed (octal 012).

18.3 On a half-closed connection one end has sent a FIN and is waiting for either data or a FIN from the other end. A half-open connection is when one end crashes, unbeknown to the other end.

18.4 The 2MSL wait state is only entered for a connection that has gone through the ESTABLISHED state.

18.5 First, the daytime server does the active close of the TCP connection after writing the time and date to the client. This is indicated by the message printed by our `sock` program: "connection closed by peer." The client's end of the connection goes through the passive close states. This puts the socket pair in the TIME_WAIT state on the server, not the client.

Next, as shown in Section 18.6, most Berkeley-derived implementations allow a new connection request to arrive for a socket pair currently in the TIME_WAIT state, which is exactly what's happening here.

18.6 A reset is sent in response to the FIN, because the FIN arrived for a connection that was CLOSED.

18.7 The party that dials the number does the active open. The party whose telephone rings does the passive open. Simultaneous opens are not permitted, but a simultaneous close is OK.

18.8 We would only see ARP requests, not TCP SYN segments, but the ARP requests would have the same timing as in the figure.

18.9 The client is on the host `solaris` and the server is on the host `bsdi`. The client's ACK of the server's SYN is combined with the first data segment from the client (line 3). This is perfectly legal under the rules of TCP, although most implementations don't do this. Next, the client sends its FIN (line 4) before waiting for the ACK of its data. This allows the server to acknowledge both the data and the FIN in line 5.

This exchange (sending one segment of data from the client to the server) requires seven segments. The normal connection establishment and termination (Figure 18.13), along with a single data segment and its acknowledgment, requires nine segments.

18.10 First, the server's ACK of the client's FIN is normally not delayed (we discuss delayed ACKs in Section 19.3) but sent as soon as the FIN arrives. It takes the application a while to receive the EOF and tell its TCP to close its end of the connection. Second, the server that receives the FIN does not have to close its end of the connection on receiving the FIN from the client. As we saw in Section 18.5, data can still be sent.

18.11 If an arriving segment that generates an RST has an ACK field, the sequence number of the RST is the arriving ACK field. The ACK value of 1 in line 6 is relative to the ISN of 26368001 in line 2.

18.12 See [Crowcroft et al. 1992] for comments on layering.

18.13 Five queries are issued. Assume there are three packets to establish the connection, one for the query, one to ACK the query, one for the response, one to ACK the response, and four to terminate the connection. This means 11 packets per query, for a total of 55 packets. Using UDP reduces this to 10 packets.

This can be reduced to 10 packets per query if the ACK of the query is combined with the response (Section 19.3).

18.14 The limit is about 268 connections per second: the maximum number of TCP port numbers (65536 – 1024 = 64512, ignoring the well-known ports) divided by the TIME_WAIT state of 2MSL.

18.15 The duplicate FIN is acknowledged and the 2MSL timer is restarted.

18.16 The receipt of an RST while in the TIME_WAIT state causes the state to be prematurely terminated. This is called *TIME_WAIT assassination.* RFC 1337 [Braden 1992a] discusses this in detail and shows the potential problems. The simple fix proposed by this RFC is to ignore RST segments while in the TIME_WAIT state.

18.17 It's when the implementation does not support a half-close. Once the application causes a FIN to be sent, the application can no longer read from the connection.

18.18 No. Incoming data segments are demultiplexed using the source IP address, source port number, destination IP address, and destination port number. For incoming connection requests we saw in Section 18.11 that a TCP server can normally prevent connections from being accepted based on the destination IP address.

Chapter 19

19.1 Two application writes, followed by a read, cause a delay because the Nagle algorithm will probably be invoked. The first segment (with 8 bytes of data) is sent and its ACK is waited for before sending the 12 bytes of data. If the server implements delayed ACKs, there can be a delay of up to 200 ms (plus the RTT) before this ACK is received.

19.2 Assuming 5-byte CSLIP headers (IP and TCP) and 2 bytes of data, the RTT across the SLIP link for these segments is about 14.5 ms. We have to add to this the RTT across the Ethernet (normally 5–10 ms), plus the routing time on `sun` and `bsdi`. So yes, the observed times do appear correct.

19.3 In Figure 19.6 the time difference between segments 6 and 9 is 533 ms. In Figure 19.8 the time difference between segments 8 and 12 is 272 ms. (We measured the time for the F2 key, not the F1 key, since the first echo of the F1 key was lost in the second figure.)

Chapter 20

20.1 Byte number 0 is the SYN and byte number 8193 is the FIN. The SYN and FIN each occupy 1 byte in the sequence number space.

20.2 The first application write causes the first segment to be sent with the PUSH flag. Since BSD/386 always uses slow start, it waits for the first ACK before sending any more data. During this time the next three application writes occur, and the sending TCP buffers the data to send. The next three segments do not contain the PUSH flag since there is more data in the buffer to send. Eventually slow start catches up with the application writes and every application write causes a segment to be sent, and since that segment is the last one in the buffer, the PUSH flag is set.

20.3 Solving the bandwidth-delay equation for the capacity, it is 1,920 bytes for the first case, and 2,062 for the satellite case. It appears that the receiving TCP is only advertising a window of 2,048 bytes.

A window greater than 16,000 bytes should be able to saturate the satellite link.

20.4 No, because TCP can repacketize data after a timeout, as we'll see in Section 21.11.

20.5 Segment 15 is a window update sent automatically by the TCP module as a result of the application reading data, which causes the window to open. This is similar to segment 9 in that figure. Segment 16, however, is a result of the application closing its end of the connection.

20.6 This can cause the sender to inject packets into the network at a rate faster than the network can really handle. This is called *ACK compression* or *ACK smashing* [Mogul 1993, Sec. 15.8.13]. This reference indicates that ACK compression occurs on the Internet, although it rarely leads to congestion.

Chapter 21

21.1 The next timeout is for 48 seconds: $0 + 4 \times 12$. The factor of 4 is the next multiplier in the exponential backoff.

21.2 It appears SVR4 still uses the factor $2D$ instead of $4D$ in the calculation of *RTO*.

21.3 The stop-and-wait protocol used by TFTP is limited to 512 bytes of data per round trip. $32768/512 \times 1.5$ is 96 seconds.

21.4 Show four segments, numbered 1, 2, 3, and 4. Assume the order of receipt is 1, 3, 2, and 4. The ACKs generated by the receiver will be ACK 1 (a normal ACK), ACK 1 (a duplicate ACK when segment 3 is received out of order), ACK 3 when segment 2 is received (acknowledging both segments 2 and 3), and then ACK 4. Here one duplicate ACK is generated. If the order of receipt were 1, 3, 4, 2, two duplicate ACKs would be generated.

21.5 No, because the slope is still up and to the right, not downward.

21.6 See Figure E.1, p. 526.

21.7 In Figure 21.2 the segments contain 256 bytes of data, which takes approximately 250 ms to transfer across the 9600 bits/sec CSLIP link between `slip` and `bsdi`. Assuming the data segments are not queued somewhere between `bsdi` and `vangogh`, they arrive at `vangogh` about 250 ms apart. Since this exceeds the 200-ms delayed ACK timer, each segment is acknowledged when the next delayed ACK timer expires.

Chapter 22

22.1 The ACKs are probably all delayed on the host `bsdi`, because there is no reason to send them immediately. That's why the relative times have 0.170 and 0.370 as the fractional part. It also appears that the 200-ms timer on `bsdi` is running about 18 ms behind the same timer on `sun`.

22.2 The FIN flag, just like the SYN flag, occupies 1 byte in the sequence number space. The advertised window appears to be 1 byte smaller because TCP allows room for the 1 byte of sequence number space occupied by the FIN flag.

Chapter 23

23.1 It is usually simpler to invoke the keepalive option than explicitly coding application probes; the keepalive probes take less network bandwidth than application probes (since keepalive probes and answers contain no data); no probes are sent unless the connection is idle.

23.2 The keepalive option can cause a perfectly good connection to be dropped because of a temporary network outage; the probe interval (2 hours) is normally not configurable on an application basis;

Chapter 24

24.1 It means the sending TCP supports the window scale option, but doesn't need to scale its window for this connection. The other end (that receives this SYN) can then specify a window scale factor (that can be 0 or nonzero).

24.2 64000: the receive buffer size (128000) right shifted 1 bit. 55000: the receive buffer size (220000) right shifted 2 bits.

24.3 No. The problem is that acknowledgments are not reliably delivered (unless they're piggybacked with data) so a scale change appearing on an ACK could get lost.

24.4 $2^{32} \times 8$ / 120 equals 286 Mbits/sec, 2.86 times the FDDI data rate.

24.5 Each TCP would have to remember the last timestamp received on any connection from each host. Read Appendix B.2 of RFC 1323 for additional details.

24.6 The application must set the size of the receive buffer *before* establishing the connection with the other end, since the window scale option is sent in the initial SYN segment.

24.7 If the receiver ACKs every second data segment, the *throughput* is 1,118,881 bytes/sec. Using a window of 62 segments, with an ACK for every 31 segments, the value is 1,158,675.

24.8 With this option the timestamp echoed in the ACK is always from the segment that caused the ACK. There is no ambiguity about which retransmitted segment the ACK is for, but the other part of Karn's algorithm, dealing with the exponential backoff on retransmission, is still required.

24.9 The receiving TCP queues the data, but it cannot be passed to the application until the three-way handshake is complete: when the receiving TCP moves into the ESTABLISHED state.

24.10 Five segments are exchanged:

1. Client to server: SYN, data (request), and FIN. The server must queue the data as described in the previous exercise.
2. Server to client: SYN and ACK of client's SYN.
3. Client to server: ACK of server's SYN and client FIN (again). This causes the server to move to the ESTABLISHED state, and the queued data from segment 1 is passed to the server application.
4. Server to client: ACK of client FIN (which also acknowledges client data), data (server's reply), and server's FIN. This assumes that the SPT is short enough to allow this delayed ACK. When the client TCP receives this segment, the reply is passed to the client application, but the total time has been twice the RTT plus the SPT.
5. Client to server: ACK of server's FIN.

24.11 16,128 transactions per second (64,512 divided by 4).

24.12 The transaction time using T/TCP cannot be faster than the time required to exchange a UDP datagram between the two hosts. T/TCP should always take longer, since it still involves state processing that UDP doesn't do.

Chapter 25

25.1 If a system is running both a manager and agent, they are probably different processes. The manager listens on UDP port 162 for traps, and the agent listens on UDP port 161 for requests. If the same port were used for both traps and requests, separating the manager from the agent would be hard.

25.2 Refer to the section "Table Access" in Section 25.7.

Chapter 26

26.1 We expect segments 2, 4, and 9 from the server to be delayed. The time difference between segments 2 and 4 is 190.7 ms and the time difference between segments 2 and 9 is 400.7 ms.

All the ACKs from the client to the server appear to be delayed: segments 6, 11, 13, 15, 17, and 19. The time differences of the last five from segment 6 are 400.0, 600.0, 800.0, 1000.0, and 2.600 ms.

26.2 If one end of a connection is in TCP's urgent mode, then every time a segment is received, one is sent. This segment does not tell the receiver anything new (it is not acknowledging new data, for example), and it contains no data, it just reiterates that urgent mode has been entered.

26.3 There are only 512 of these reserved ports (512–1023), limiting a host to 512 Rlogin clients. The limit is normally less than 512 in real life, since some of the port numbers in this range are used as well-known ports by various servers, such as the Rlogin server.

TCP's limitation is that the socket pair defining a connection (the 4-tuple) must be unique. Since the Rlogin server always uses the same well-known port (513) multiple Rlogin clients on a given host can use the same reserved port only if they're connected to different server hosts. Rlogin clients, however, don't use this technique of trying to reuse reserved ports. If this technique were used, the theoretical limit is a maximum of 512 Rlogin clients at any one time that are all connected to the same server host.

Chapter 27

27.1 Theoretically the connection cannot be established while the socket pair is in the 2MSL wait on either end. Realistically, however, we saw in Section 18.6 that most Berkeley-derived implementations do accept a new SYN for a connection in the TIME_WAIT state.

27.2 These lines are not part of a server reply that begins with a 3-digit reply code, so they cannot be from the server.

Chapter 28

28.1 A *domain literal* is a dotted-decimal IP address within square brackets. For example: `mail rstevens@[140.252.1.54]`.

28.2 Six round trips: the HELO command, MAIL, RCPT, DATA, body of the message, and QUIT.

28.3 This is legal and is called *pipelining* [Rose 1993, Sec. 4.4.4]. Unfortunately there exist brain-damaged SMTP receiver implementations that clear their input buffer after each command is processed, causing this technique to fail. If this technique is used, naturally the client cannot discard the message until all the replies have been checked to verify that the message was accepted by the server.

28.4 Consider the first five network round trips from Exercise 28.2. Each is a small command (probably a single segment) that places little load on the network. If all five make it through to the server without retransmission, the congestion window could be six segments when the body is sent. If the body is large, the client could send the first six segments at once, which the network might not be able to handle.

28.5 Newer releases of BIND shuffle the MX records with the same value, as a form of load balancing.

Chapter 29

29.1 No, because `tcpdump` cannot distinguish an RPC request or reply from any other UDP datagram. The only time it interprets the contents of UDP datagrams as NFS packets is when the source or destination port number is 2049. Random RPC requests and replies can use an ephemeral port number on each end.

29.2 From Section 1.9 recall that a process must have superuser privileges to assign itself a port number less than 1024 (a well-known port). While this is OK for system-provided servers, such as the Telnet server, the FTP server, and the Port Mapper, we wouldn't want this restriction for all RPC servers.

29.3 Two concepts in this example are that the client ignores any server reply that doesn't have the XID that the client is waiting for, and UDP queues received datagrams (up to some limit) until the application reads the datagram. Also, the XID does not change on a timeout and retransmission, it changes only when another server procedure is called.

The events performed by the client stub are as follows: time 0: send request 1; time 4: time out and retransmit request 1; time 5: receive server's reply 1, return reply to application; time 5: send request 2; time 9: time out and retransmit request 2; time 10: receive server's reply 1, but ignore it since we're waiting for reply 2; time 11: receive server's reply 2, return reply to application.

The events at the server are as follows: time 0: receive request 1, start operation; time 5: send reply 1; time 5: receive request 1 (from client's retransmission at time 4), start operation; time 10: send reply 1; time 10: receive request 2 (from client's transmission at time 5), start operation; time 11: send reply 2; time 11: receive request 2 (from client's retransmission at time 9), start operation; time 12: send reply 2. This final server reply is just queued by the client's UDP for the next receive done by the client. When the client reads it, the XID will be wrong, and the client will ignore it.

29.4 Changing the server's Ethernet card changes its physical address. Even though we noted in Section 4.7 that SVR4 does not send a gratuitous ARP on bootstrap, it still must send an ARP request for the physical address of `sun` before it can reply to its NFS requests. Since `sun` already has an ARP entry for `svr4`, it updates this entry with the sender's (new) hardware address from the ARP request.

29.5 The second of the client's block I/O daemons (reading at offset 73728) is out of sync with the first by about 0.74 seconds. That is, this second daemon times out 0.74 seconds after the first in lines 131–145. It appears the server never saw the request in line 167, but did see the request in line 168. The second block I/O daemon won't retransmit until 0.74 seconds after line 168, and in the mean time the first block I/O daemon continues issuing requests.

29.6 If TCP is used, and the TCP segment containing the server's reply is lost in the network, the server's TCP will time out and retransmit the reply when it doesn't receive an ACK from the client's TCP. Eventually the segment will arrive at the client's TCP. The difference here is that the two TCP modules do the timeout and retransmission, not the NFS client and server. (When UDP is used, the NFS client code performs the timeout and retransmission.) Therefore the NFS client never knows that the reply was lost and had to be retransmitted.

29.7 It is possible for the NFS server to obtain a different port number after the reboot. This would complicate the client, because it would have to know that the server crashed and contact the server's port mapper after the reboot to find the NFS server's new port number.

This scenario, where the server crashes and reboots and a server RPC application obtains a new ephemeral port, can happen to any RPC application that doesn't use a well-known port.

29.8 No. The NFS client can reuse the same local, reserved port number for different servers. TCP requires the 4-tuple of local IP address, local port, foreign IP address, and foreign port to be unique, and the foreign IP address is different for each server host.

Chapter 30

30.1 Type `whois "net 88"`. Class A network IDs 64 through 95 are reserved.

30.2 Type `whois whitehouse-dom`. Either the `host` command or `nslookup` can query the DNS.

30.3 No, `xscope` can run on a different host from the server. If the hosts are different, then `xscope` can also use TCP port 6000 for its incoming connection.

Appendix E

Configurable Options

We've seen many features of TCP/IP that we've had to describe with the qualifier "it depends on the configuration." Typical examples are whether or not UDP checksums are enabled (Section 11.3), whether destination IP addresses with the same network ID but a different subnet ID are local or nonlocal (Section 18.4), and whether directed broadcasts are forwarded or not (Section 12.3). Indeed, many operating characteristics of a given TCP/IP implementation can be modified by the system administrator.

This appendix lists some of the configurable options for the various TCP/IP implementations that have been used throughout the text. As you might expect, every vendor does things differently from all others. Nevertheless, this appendix gives an idea of the types of parameters different implementations allow one to modify. A few options that are highly implementation specific, such as the low-water mark for the memory buffer pool, are not described.

These variables are described for informational purposes only. Their names, default values, or interpretation can change from one release to the next. Always check your vendor's documentation (or bug them for adequate documentation) for the final word on these variables.

This appendix does not cover the initialization that takes place every time the system is bootstrapped: the initialization of each network interface using `ifconfig` (setting the IP address, the subnet mask, etc.), entering static routes into the routing table, and the like. Instead, this appendix focuses on the configuration options that affect how TCP/IP operates.

E.1 BSD/386 Version 1.0

This system is an example of the "classical" BSD configuration that has been used since 4.2BSD. Since the source code is distributed with the system, configuration options are specified by the administrator, and the kernel is recompiled. There are two types of options: constants that are defined in the kernel configuration file (see the `config`(8) manual page), and variable initializations in various C source files. Brave and knowledgeable administrators can also change the values of these C variables in either the running kernel or the kernel's disk image, using a debugger, to avoid rebuilding the kernel.

Here are the constants that can be changed in the kernel's configuration file.

`IPFORWARDING`
: The value of this constant initializes the kernel variable `ipforwarding`. If 0 (default), IP datagrams are not forwarded. If 1, forwarding is always enabled.

`GATEWAY`
: If defined, causes `IPFORWARDING` to be set to 1. Additionally, defining this constant causes certain system tables (the ARP cache and the routing table) to be larger.

`SUBNETSARELOCAL`
: The value of this constant initializes the kernel variable `subnetsarelocal`. If 1 (default), a destination IP address with the same network ID as the sending host but a different subnet ID is considered local. If 0, only destination IP addresses on an attached subnet are considered local. This is summarized in Figure E.1.

Network IDs	Subnet IDs	`subnetsarelocal` 1	`subnetsarelocal` 0	Comment
same	same	local	local	always local
same	different	local	nonlocal	depends on configuration
different		nonlocal	nonlocal	always nonlocal

Figure E.1 Interpretation of `subnetsarelocal` kernel variable.

This affects the MSS selected by TCP. When sending to local destinations, TCP chooses the MSS based on the MTU of the outgoing interface. When sending to nonlocal destinations, TCP uses the variable `tcp_mssdflt` as the MSS.

`IPSENDREDIRECTS`
: The value of this constant initializes the kernel variable `ipsendredirects`. If 1 (default), the host will send ICMP redirects when forwarding IP datagrams. If 0, ICMP redirects are not sent.

`DIRECTED_BROADCAST`
: If 1 (default), received datagrams whose destination address is the directed broadcast address of an attached interface are forwarded as a link-layer broadcast. If 0, these datagrams are silently discarded.

The following variables can also be modified. These variables are spread throughout different files in the /usr/src/sys/netinet directory.

tcprexmtthresh	The number of consecutive ACKs that triggers the fast retransmit and fast recovery algorithm. The default value is 3.
tcp_ttl	The default value for the TTL field for TCP segments. Default value is 60.
tcp_mssdflt	The default TCP MSS for nonlocal destinations. Default value is 512.
tcp_keepidle	Number of 500-ms clock ticks before sending a keepalive probe. Default value is 14400 (2 hours).
tcp_keepintvl	Number of 500-ms clock ticks between successive keepalive probes, when no response is received. Default value is 150 (75 seconds).
tcp_sendspace	The default size of the TCP send buffer. Default value is 4096.
tcp_recvspace	The default size of the TCP receive buffer. This affects the window size that is offered. Default value is 4096.
udpcksum	If nonzero, UDP checksums are calculated for outgoing UDP datagrams, and incoming UDP datagrams containing nonzero checksums have their checksum verified. If 0, outgoing UDP datagrams do not contain a checksum, and no checksum verification is performed on incoming UDP datagrams, even if the sender calculated a checksum. Default is 1.
udp_ttl	The default value for the TTL field in UDP datagrams. Default value is 30.
udp_sendspace	The default size of the UDP send buffer. Defines the maximum UDP datagram that can be sent. Default is 9216.
udp_recvspace	The default size of the UDP receive buffer. The default is 41600, allowing for 40 1024-byte datagrams.

E.2 SunOS 4.1.3

The method used with SunOS 4.1.3 is similar to what we saw with BSD/386. Since most of the kernel sources are not distributed, all the C variable initializations are contained in a single C source file that is provided.

The administrator's kernel configuration file (see the config(8) manual page) can define the following variables. After modifying your configuration file, a new kernel must be made and rebooted.

`IPFORWARDING`
The value of this constant initializes the kernel variable `ip_forwarding`. If –1, IP datagrams are never forwarded. Furthermore, the variable is never changed. If 0 (default), IP datagrams are not forwarded, but the variable's value is changed to 1 if multiple interfaces are up. If 1, forwarding is always enabled.

`SUBNETSARELOCAL`
The value of the kernel variable `ip_subnetsarelocal` is initialized from this constant. If 1 (default), a destination IP address with the same network ID as the sending host but a different subnet ID is considered local. If 0, only destination IP addresses on an attached subnet are considered local. This is summarized in Figure E.1. When sending to local destinations, TCP chooses the MSS based on the MTU of the outgoing interface. When sending to nonlocal destinations, TCP uses the variable `tcp_default_mss`.

`IPSENDREDIRECTS`
The value of this constant initializes the kernel variable `ip_sendredirects`. If 1 (default), the host will send ICMP redirects when forwarding IP datagrams. If 0, ICMP redirects are not sent.

`DIRECTED_BROADCAST`
The value of this constant initializes the kernel variable `ip_dirbroadcast`. If 1 (default), received datagrams whose destination address is the directed broadcast address of an attached interface are forwarded as a link-layer broadcast. If 0, these datagrams are silently discarded.

The file `/usr/kvm/sys/netinet/in_proto.c` defines the following variables that can be changed. Once these variables are changed, a new kernel must be made and rebooted.

`tcp_default_mss`	The default TCP MSS for nonlocal destinations. Default value is 512.
`tcp_sendspace`	The default size of the TCP send buffer. Default value is 4096.
`tcp_recvspace`	The default size of the TCP receive buffer. This affects the window size that is offered. Default value is 4096.
`tcp_keeplen`	A keepalive probe to a 4.2BSD host must contain a single byte of data to get a response. Set the variable to 1 for compatibility with these older implementations. Default value is 1.
`tcp_ttl`	The default value for the TTL field for TCP segments. Default value is 60.
`tcp_nodelack`	If nonzero, ACKs are not delayed. Default value is 0.
`tcp_keepidle`	Number of 500-ms clock ticks before sending a keepalive probe. Default value is 14400 (2 hours).

`tcp_keepintvl` Number of 500-ms clock ticks between successive keepalive probes, when no response is received. Default value is 150 (75 seconds).

`udp_cksum` If nonzero, UDP checksums are calculated for outgoing UDP datagrams, and incoming UDP datagrams containing nonzero checksums have their checksum verified. If 0, outgoing UDP datagrams do not contain a checksum, and no checksum verification is performed on incoming UDP datagrams, even if the sender calculated a checksum. Default is 0.

`udp_ttl` The default value for the TTL field in UDP datagrams. Default value is 60.

`udp_sendspace` The default size of the UDP send buffer. Defines the maximum UDP datagram that can be sent. Default is 9000.

`udp_recvspace` The default size of the UDP receive buffer. The default is 18000, allowing for two 9000-byte datagrams.

E.3 System V Release 4

The TCP/IP configuration of SVR4 is similar to the previous two systems, but fewer options are available. In the file `/etc/conf/pack.d/ip/space.c` two constants can be defined, and the kernel must then be rebuilt and rebooted.

`IPFORWARDING`
The value of this constant initializes the kernel variable `ipforwarding`. If 0 (default), IP datagrams are not forwarded. If 1, forwarding is always enabled.

`IPSENDREDIRECTS`
The value of this constant initializes the kernel variable `ipsendredirects`. If 1 (default), the host will send ICMP redirects when forwarding IP datagrams. If 0, ICMP redirects are not sent.

Many of the variables that we've described in the previous two sections are defined in the kernel, but one must patch the kernel to modify them. For example, there is a variable named `tcp_keepidle` with a value of 14400.

E.4 Solaris 2.2

Solaris 2.2 is typical of the newer Unix systems that provide a program for the administrator to run to change the configuration options of the TCP/IP system. This allows reconfiguration without having to modify source files and rebuild a kernel.

The configuration program is ndd(1). We can run the program to see what parameters we can examine or modify in the UDP module:

```
solaris % ndd /dev/udp \?
udp_wroff_extra                    (read and write)
udp_def_ttl                        (read and write)
udp_first_anon_port                (read and write)
udp_trust_optlen                   (read and write)
udp_do_checksum                    (read and write)
udp_status                         (read only)
```

There are five modules we can specify: /dev/ip, /dev/icmp, /dev/arp, /dev/udp, and /dev/tcp. The question mark argument (which we have to prevent the shell from interpreting by preceding it with a backslash) tells the program to list all the parameters for that module. An example that queries the value of a variable is:

```
solaris % ndd /dev/tcp tcp_mss_def
536
```

To change the value of a variable we need superuser privilege and type:

```
solaris # ndd -set /dev/ip ip_forwarding 0
```

These variables can be divided into three categories:

1. Configuration variables that a system administrator can change (e.g., ip_forwarding).
2. Status variables that can only be displayed (e.g., the ARP cache). Normally this information is provided in an easier to understand format by the commands ifconfig, netstat, and arp.
3. Debugging variables intended for those with kernel source code. Enabling some of these generates kernel debug output at runtime, which can degrade performance.

We now describe the parameters in each module. All parameters are read–write, unless marked "(Read only)." The read-only parameters are the status variables from case 2 above. We also mark the "(Debug)" variables from case 3. Unless otherwise noted, all the timing variables are specified in milliseconds, which differs from the other systems that normally specify times as some number of 500-ms clock ticks.

/dev/ip

`ip_cksum_choice`
(Debug) Selects between two independent implementations of the IP checksum algorithm.

`ip_debug`
(Debug) Enables printing of debug output by the kernel, if greater than 0. Larger values generate more output. Default is 0.

`ip_def_ttl`
Default TTL for outgoing IP datagrams, if not specified by transport layer. Default is 255.

`ip_forward_directed_broadcasts`
If 1 (default), received datagrams whose destination address is the directed broadcast address of an attached interface are forwarded as a link-layer broadcast. If 0, these datagrams are silently discarded.

`ip_forward_src_routed`
If 1 (default), received datagrams containing a source route option are forwarded. If 0, these datagrams are discarded.

`ip_forwarding`
Specifies whether the system forwards incoming IP datagrams: 0 means never forward, 1 means always forward, and 2 (default) means only forward when two or more interfaces are up.

`ip_icmp_return_data_bytes`
The number of bytes of data beyond the IP header that are returned in an ICMP error. Default is 64.

`ip_ignore_delete_time`
(Debug) Minimum lifetime of an IP routing table entry (IRE). Default is 30 seconds. (This parameter is in seconds, not milliseconds.)

`ip_ill_status`
(Read only) Displays the status of each IP lower layer data structure. There is one lower layer structure for each interface.

`ip_ipif_status`
(Read only) Displays the status of each IP interface data structure (IP address, subnet mask, etc.). There is one of these structures for each interface.

`ip_ire_cleanup_interval`
(Debug) The interval at which the IP routing table entries are scanned for possible deletions. Default is 30000 ms (30 seconds).

`ip_ire_flush_interval`
The interval at which ARP information in unconditionally flushed from the IP routing table. Default is 1200000 ms (20 minutes).

`ip_ire_pathmtu_interval`
The interval at which the path MTU discovery algorithm tries to increase the MTU. Default is 30000 ms (30 seconds).

`ip_ire_redirect_interval`
The interval at which IP routing table entries that are from ICMP redirects are deleted. Default is 60000 ms (60 seconds).

`ip_ire_status`
(Read only) Displays all the IP routing table entries.

`ip_local_cksum`
If 0 (default), IP does not calculate the IP checksum or the higher layer protocol checksum (i.e., TCP, UDP, ICMP, or IGMP) for datagrams sent or received through the loopback interface. If 1, these checksums are calculated.

`ip_mrtdebug`
(Debug) Enables printing of debug output concerning multicast routing by the kernel, if 1. Default is 0.

`ip_path_mtu_discovery`
If 1 (default), path MTU discovery is performed by IP. If 0, IP never sets the "don't fragment" bit in outgoing datagrams.

`ip_respond_to_address_mask`
If 0 (default), the host does not respond to ICMP address mask requests. If 1, it does respond.

`ip_respond_to_echo_broadcast`
If 1 (default), the host responds to ICMP echo requests that are sent to a broadcast address. If 0, it does not respond.

`ip_respond_to_timestamp`
If 0 (default), the host does not respond to ICMP timestamp requests. If 1, the host responds.

`ip_respond_to_timestamp_broadcast`
If 0 (default), the host does not respond to ICMP timestamp requests that are sent to a broadcast address. If 1, it responds if `ip_respond_to_timestamp` is also set.

`ip_rput_pullups`
(Debug) Count of number of buffers from the network interface driver that needed to be pulled up to access the full IP header. Initialized to 0 at bootstrap time, and can be reset to 0.

`ip_send_redirects`
If 1 (default), the host sends ICMP redirects when acting as a router. If 0, these are not sent.

`ip_send_source_quench`
If 1 (default), the host generates ICMP source quench errors when incoming datagrams are discarded. If 0, these are not generated.

`ip_wroff_extra`
(Debug) Number of bytes of extra space to allocate in buffers for IP headers. Default is 32.

/dev/icmp

`icmp_bsd_compat`
(Debug) If 1 (default), the length field in the IP header of received datagrams is adjusted to exclude the length of the IP header. This is compatible with Berkeley-derived implementations and is for applications reading raw IP or raw ICMP packets. If 0, the length field is not changed.

`icmp_def_ttl`
The default TTL for outgoing ICMP messages. Default is 255.

`icmp_wroff_extra`
(Debug) Number of bytes of extra space to allocate in buffers for IP options and data-link headers. Default is 32.

/dev/arp

`arp_cache_report`
(Read only) The ARP cache.

`arp_cleanup_interval`
The interval after which ARP entries are discarded from ARP's cache. Default is 300000 ms (5 minutes). (IP maintains its own cache of completed ARP translations; see `ip_ire_flush_interval`.)

`arp_debug`
(Debug) If 1, enables printing of debug output by the ARP driver. Default is 0.

/dev/udp

`udp_def_ttl`
The default TTL for outgoing UDP datagrams. Default value is 255.

`udp_do_checksum`
If 1 (default), UDP checksums are calculated for outgoing UDP datagrams. If 0, outgoing UDP datagrams do not contain a checksum. (Unlike most other implementations, this UDP checksum flag does not affect incoming datagrams. If a received datagram has a nonzero checksum, it is always verified.)

`udp_largest_anon_port`
Largest port number to allocate for UDP ephemeral ports. Default is 65535.

`udp_smallest_anon_port`
Starting port number to allocate for UDP ephemeral ports. Default is 32768.

`udp_smallest_nonpriv_port`
A process requires superuser privilege to assign itself a port number less than this. Default is 1024.

`udp_status`
(Read only) The status of all local UDP end points: local IP address and port, foreign IP address and port.

`udp_trust_optlen`
(Debug) No longer used.

`udp_wroff_extra`
(Debug) Number of bytes of extra space to allocate in buffers for IP options and data-link headers. Default is 32.

/dev/tcp

`tcp_close_wait_interval`
The 2MSL value: the time spent in the TIME_WAIT state. Default is 240000 ms (4 minutes).

`tcp_conn_grace_period`
(Debug) Additional time added to the timer interval when sending a SYN. Default is 500 ms.

`tcp_conn_req_max`
The maximum number of pending connection requests queued for any listening end point. Default is 5.

`tcp_cwnd_max`
The maximum value of the congestion window. Default is 32768.

`tcp_debug`
(Debug) If 1, enables printing of debug output by TCP. Default is 0.

`tcp_deferred_ack_interval`
The time to wait before sending a delayed ACK. Default is 50 ms.

`tcp_dupack_fast_retransmit`
The number of consecutive duplicate ACKs that triggers the fast retransmit, fast recovery algorithm. Default is 3.

`tcp_eager_listeners`
(Debug) If 1 (default), TCP completes the three-way handshake before returning a new connection to an application with a pending passive open. This is the way most TCP implementations operate. If 0, TCP passes an incoming connection request (received SYN) to the application, and does not complete the three-way handshake until the application accepts the connection. (Setting this to 0 might break many existing applications.)

`tcp_ignore_path_mtu`
(Debug) If 1, path MTU discovery ignores received ICMP fragmentation needed messages. If 0 (default), path MTU discovery is enabled for TCP.

`tcp_ip_abort_cinterval`
The total retransmit timeout value when TCP is performing an active open. Default is 240000 ms (4 minutes).

`tcp_ip_abort_interval`
The total retransmit timeout value for a TCP connection after it is established. Default is 120000 ms (2 minutes).

`tcp_ip_notify_cinterval`
The timeout value when TCP is performing an active open after which TCP notifies IP to find a new route. Default is 10000 ms (10 seconds).

`tcp_ip_notify_interval`
The timeout value for an established connection after which TCP notifies IP to find a new route. Default is 10000 ms (10 seconds).

`tcp_ip_ttl`
The TTL to use for outgoing TCP segments. Default is 255.

`tcp_keepalive_interval`
The time that a connection must be idle before a keepalive probe is sent. Default is 7200000 ms (2 hours).

`tcp_largest_anon_port`
Largest port number to allocate for TCP ephemeral ports. Default is 65535.

`tcp_maxpsz_multiplier`
(Debug) Specifies the multiple of the MSS into which the stream head packetizes the application's write data. Default is 1.

`tcp_mss_def`
Default MSS for nonlocal destinations. Default is 536.

`tcp_mss_max`
The maximum MSS. Default is 65495.

`tcp_mss_min`
The minimum MSS. Default is 1.

`tcp_naglim_def`
(Debug) Maximum value of the per-connection Nagle algorithm threshold. Default is 65535. The per-connection value starts out as the minimum of the MSS or this value. The per-connection value is set to 1 by the `TCP_NODELAY` socket option, which disables the Nagle algorithm.

`tcp_old_urp_interpretation`
(Debug) If 1 (default), the older (but more common) BSD interpretation of the urgent pointer is used: it points 1 byte beyond the last byte of urgent data. If 0, the Host Requirements RFC interpretation is used: it points to the last byte of urgent data.

`tcp_rcv_push_wait`
(Debug) Maximum number of bytes received without the PUSH flag set before the data is passed to the application. Default is 16384.

`tcp_rexmit_interval_initial`
(Debug) Initial retransmit timeout interval. Default is 500 ms.

`tcp_rexmit_interval_max`
(Debug) Maximum retransmit timeout interval. Default is 60000 ms (60 seconds).

`tcp_rexmit_interval_min`
(Debug) Minimum retransmit timeout interval. Default is 200 ms.

`tcp_rwin_credit_pct`
(Debug) Percentage of receive window that must be buffered before flow control is checked on every received segment. Default is 50%.

`tcp_smallest_anon_port`
Starting port number to allocate for TCP ephemeral ports. Default is 32768.

`tcp_smallest_nonpriv_port`
A process requires superuser privilege to assign itself a port number less than this. Default is 1024.

`tcp_snd_lowat_fraction`
(Debug) If nonzero, the send buffer low-water mark is the send buffer size divided by this value. Default is 0 (disabled).

`tcp_status`
(Read only) Information on all TCP endpoints.

`tcp_sth_rcv_hiwat`
(Debug) If nonzero, the value to set the stream head high-water mark to. Default is 0.

`tcp_sth_rcv_lowat`
(Debug) If nonzero, the value to set the stream head low-water mark to. Default is 0.

`tcp_wroff_xtra`
(Debug) Number of bytes of extra space to allocate in buffers for IP options and data-link headers. Default is 32.

E.5 AIX 3.2.2

AIX 3.2.2 allows network options to be set at runtime using the `no` command. It can display the value of an option, set the value of an option, or set an option value back to its default. For example, to display an option we type:

```
aix % no -o udp_ttl
udp_ttl = 30
```

The following options can be modified.

`arpt_killc`
The time (in minutes) before an inactive completed ARP entry is removed. Default is 20.

`ipforwarding`
If 1 (default), IP datagrams are always forwarded. If 0, forwarding is disabled.

`ipfragttl`
The time to live (in seconds) for IP fragments awaiting reassembly. Default is 60.

`ipsendredirects`
If 1 (default), the host will send ICMP redirects when forwarding IP datagrams. If 0, ICMP redirects are not sent.

`loop_check_sum`
If 1 (default), the IP checksum is calculated for datagrams sent through the loopback interface. If 0, this checksum is not calculated.

`nonlocsrcroute`
If 1 (default), received datagrams containing a source route option are forwarded. If 0, these datagrams are discarded.

`subnetsarelocal`
If 1 (default), a destination IP address with the same network ID as the sending host but a different subnet ID is considered local. If 0, only destination IP addresses on an attached subnet are considered local. This is summarized in Figure E.1. When sending to local destinations, TCP chooses the MSS based on the MTU of the outgoing interface. When sending to nonlocal destinations, TCP uses the default (536) as the MSS.

`tcp_keepidle`
Number of 500-ms clock ticks before sending a keepalive probe. Default value is 14400 (2 hours).

`tcp_keepintvl`
Number of 500-ms clock ticks between successive keepalive probes, when no response is received. Default value is 150 (75 seconds).

`tcp_recvspace`
The default size of the TCP receive buffer. This affects the window size that is offered. Default value is 16384.

`tcp_sendspace`
The default size of the TCP send buffer. Default value is 16384.

`tcp_ttl`
The default value for the TTL field for TCP segments. Default value is 60.

`udp_recvspace`
The default size of the UDP receive buffer. The default is 41600, allowing for 40 1024-byte datagrams.

`udp_sendspace`
The default size of the UDP send buffer. Defines the maximum UDP datagram that can be sent. Default is 9216.

`udp_ttl`
The default value for the TTL field in UDP datagrams. Default value is 30.

E.6 4.4BSD

4.4BSD is the first of the Berkeley releases to provide dynamic configuration for numerous kernel parameters. The `sysctl(8)` command is used. The names for the parameters were chosen to look like MIB names from SNMP. To examine a parameter we type:

```
vangogh % sysctl net.inet.ip.forwarding
net.inet.ip.forwarding = 1
```

To change a parameter we need superuser privilege and then type:

```
vangogh # sysctl -w net.inet.ip.ttl=128
```

The following parameters can be changed.

`net.inet.ip.forwarding`
: If 0 (default), IP datagrams are not forwarded. If 1, forwarding is enabled.

`net.inet.ip.redirect`
: If 1 (default), the host will send ICMP redirects when forwarding IP datagrams. If 0, ICMP redirects are not sent.

`net.inet.ip.ttl`
: The default TTL for both TCP and UDP. The default is 64.

`net.inet.icmp.maskrepl`
: If 0 (default), the host does not respond to ICMP address mask requests. If 1, it does respond.

`net.inet.udp.checksum`
: If 1 (default), UDP checksums are calculated for outgoing UDP datagrams, and incoming UDP datagrams containing nonzero checksums have their checksum verified. If 0, outgoing UDP datagrams do not contain a checksum, and no checksum verification is performed on incoming UDP datagrams, even if the sender calculated a checksum.

Additionally, numerous variables that we've described earlier in this appendix are scattered among various source files (`tcp_keepidle`, `subnetsarelocal`, etc.) and can be modified.

Appendix F

Source Code Availability

This book uses many publicly available software packages. This appendix provides additional details on how to obtain this software.

The technique used to obtain this software is called *anonymous FTP*, where FTP is the standard Internet File Transfer Protocol (Chapter 27). Section 27.3 shows an example of anonymous FTP. For a background on Internet resources in general, and specifically anonymous FTP, refer to any of the recently available books on the Internet, such as [LaQuey 1993] or [Krol 1992].

The hosts listed here are believed to be the primary site where the package is available. There may be many other sites where the software is also available. The Internet Archie service can locate additional versions. Also, the versions listed below are the ones used for the examples in the text.

Newer versions may have been released by the time you read this.

You should use the FTP `dir` command to see if newer versions exist on that specified host.

This appendix is ordered by the chapter or section number where the resource was used in this text.

RFCs (Section 1.11)

Section 1.11 provides the electronic mail address to send a request to. The reply details numerous sites from which the RFCs can be obtained using either e-mail or anonymous FTP.

Remember that the starting place is to obtain the current index and look up the RFC that you want in the index. This entry tells you if that RFC has been obsoleted or updated by a newer RFC.

BSD Net/2 Source Code (Section 1.14)

The BSD Net/2 source code, which includes the kernel implementation of the TCP/IP protocols, along with the standard utilities (Telnet client and server, FTP client and server, etc.), is available from `ftp.uu.net` in the directory tree starting at `systems/unix/bsd-sources`.

SLIP (Section 2.4)

The version of SLIP used in this text is available from `ftp.ee.lbl.gov`. The filename begins with `cslip`, since it supports compressed SLIP (Section 2.5).

`icmpaddrmask` Program (Section 6.3)

Refer to the final entry of this section.

`icmptime` Program (Section 6.4)

Refer to the final entry of this section.

`ping` Program (Chapter 7)

The BSD version of `ping` normally has more options and features than the version supplied by many vendors. The host `ftp.uu.net` contains the latest BSD version in the file `systems/unix/bsd-sources/sbin/ping`.

`traceroute` Program (Chapter 8)

The `traceroute` program is available from `ftp.ee.lbl.gov`. Refer to the final entry of this section for the version used in Section 8.5 that allows loose and strict source routing.

Router Discovery Daemon (Section 9.6)

A program is available that provides host support and router support for the router discovery messages. The host is `gregorio.stanford.edu` and the file is `gw-discovery/nordmark-rdisc.tar`. The program was written by Sun Microsystems and made publicly available.

`gated` Daemon (Section 10.3)

The `gated` routing daemon, mentioned in Section 10.3, is available from the host `gated.cornell.edu`.

`traceroute.pmtu` Program (Section 11.7)

Refer to the final entry of this section.

IP Multicasting Software (Chapter 13)

The modifications required to support IP multicasting for SunOS 4.x and Ultrix are available from `gregorio.stanford.edu` in the directory `vmtp-ip`. This directory also contains the source code modifications required to implement IP multicasting in a Berkeley Unix system.

BIND Name Server (Chapter 14)

The BIND name server, the `named` daemon, is available from the host `ftp.uu.net` in the file `networking/ip/dns/bind/bind.4.8.3.tar.Z`.

A newer version, 4.9, is available from `gatekeeper.dec.com` in the directory `pub/BSD/bind/4.9`.

`host` Program (Chapter 14)

The `host` program is available from the host `nikhefh.nikhef.nl` in the file `host.tar.Z`.

`dig` and `doc` Programs (Chapter 14)

The `dig` and `doc` programs mentioned in Chapter 14 are available from the host `isi.edu` in the files `dig.2.0.tar.Z` and `doc.2.0.tar.Z`.

BOOTP Server (Chapter 16)

Various versions of the commonly used Unix BOOTP server are available from the host `lancaster.andrew.cmu.edu`, in the `pub` directory.

TCP High-Speed Extensions (Chapter 24)

A publicly available source code implementation of the TCP window scale option, timestamp option, and PAWS algorithm is available as a set of patches to the BSD Net/2 release from the host `uxc.cso.uiuc.edu` in the file `pub/tcplw.shar.Z`.

ISODE SNMP Manager and Agent (Chapter 25)

The SNMP manager and agent described in Section 25.7 are part of the ISODE 8.0 distribution. This is available from many FTP archive sites, such as `ftp.uu.net` in the `networking/osi/isode` directory.

MIME Software and Examples (Section 28.4)

A program named MetaMail that provides MIME capabilities for many different user agents is available on the host `thumper.bellcore.com` in the `pub/nsb` directory. Also in this directory is additional information on MIME.

Sun RPC (Section 29.2)

A version of the RPC 4.0 sources (which use the sockets API) is available from the host `ftp.uu.net` in the `systems/sun/sextape/rpc4.0` directory. A version of the TI-RPC sources (which use the TLI API) is available from the host `ftp.uu.net` in the `networking/rpc` directory.

Sun NFS (Chapter 29)

A publicly available implementation of an NFS client and server is provided as part of the BSD Net/2 Source Code described earlier in this appendix.

`tcpdump` Program (Appendix A)

The version of `tcpdump` used in this text is from the host `ftp.ee.lbl.gov` in the file `tcpdump-2.2.1.tar.Z`.

BSD Packet Filter (Section A.1)

The BSD packet filter is part of the `tcpdump` distribution.

`sock` Program (Appendix C)

Refer to the final entry of this section.

`ttcp` Program

(This program was not used in the text, but is a useful tool of which readers should be aware.) `ttcp` is a benchmarking tool for measuring TCP and UDP performance between two systems. It was created at the U.S. Army Ballistics Research Lab (BRL) and is in the public domain. Copies are available from many anonymous FTP sites but an enhanced version is available from `ftp.sgi.com` in the directory `sgi/src/ttcp`.

Author-Written Software

The author-written software used in the book is available from the host `ftp.uu.net` in the file `published/books/stevens.tcpipiv1.tar.Z`.

Bibliography

All the RFCs are available at no charge through electronic mail or using anonymous FTP across the Internet as described in Section 1.11.

Albitz, P., and Liu, C. 1992. *DNS and BIND*. O'Reilly & Associates, Sebastopol, Calif.

Lots of details on the administrative tasks required to configure and run a name server.

Alexander, S., and Droms, R. 1993. "DHCP Options and BOOTP Vendor Extensions," RFC 1533, 30 pages (Oct.).

Almquist, P. 1992. "Type of Service in the Internet Protocol Suite," RFC 1349, 28 pages (July).

How to use the type-of-service field in the IP header.

Almquist, P., ed. 1993. "Requirements for IP Routers," Internet Draft (Mar.).

This is the draft of an RFC to replace RFC 1009 [Braden and Postel 1987]. The new RFC will probably appear in four volumes. Volume 1: Internet architecture, terminology, and general considerations. Volume 2: link layer, internet layer, transport layer, and application layer. Volume 3: forwarding and routing protocols. Volume 4: operations and maintenance, and network management.

This draft is available via anonymous FTP from the host `jessica.stanford.edu` in the directory `rreq`. Ignore this draft once the final RFC is published.

Bellovin, S. M. 1993. Private Communication.

Bhide, A., Elnozahy, E. N., and Morgan, S. P. 1991. "A Highly Available Network File Server," *Proceedings of the 1991 Winter USENIX Conference*, pp. 199–205, Dallas, Tex.

Describes a use of gratuitous ARP (Section 4.7).

Borenstein, N., and Freed, N. 1993. "MIME (Multipurpose Internet Mail Extensions) Part One: Mechanisms for Specifying and Describing the Format of Internet Message Bodies," RFC 1521, 81 pages (Sept.).

This RFC obsoletes the earlier RFC 1341. Appendix H of this RFC lists the differences from RFC 1341.

Borman, D. A., ed. 1990. "Telnet Linemode Option," RFC 1184, 23 pages (Oct.).

Borman, D. A. 1991. "IP Bandwidth Limits," Message-ID <91011437.AA17276@berserkly.cray.com>, Usenet, comp.protocols.tcp-ip Newsgroup (Jan.).

States the three practical limits on TCP performance that we listed at the end of Section 24.8.

Borman, D. A. 1992. "TCP/IP Performance at Cray Research," *Proceedings of the Twenty-third Internet Engineering Task Force*, pp. 492–493 (Mar.), San Diego Supercomputer Center, San Diego, Calif.

Borman, D. A., ed. 1993a. "Telnet Environment Option," RFC 1408, 7 pages (Jan.).

The Telnet option for passing environment variables from the client to the server.

Borman, D. A. 1993b. "A Practical Perspective on Host Networking," in *Internet System Handbook*, eds. D. C. Lynch and M. T. Rose, pp. 309–367. Addison-Wesley, Reading, Mass.

A practical look at the Host Requirements RFCs (1122 and 1123).

Braden, R. T., ed. 1989a. "Requirements for Internet Hosts—Communication Layers," RFC 1122, 116 pages (Oct.).

The first half of the Host Requirements RFC. This half covers the link layer, IP, TCP, and UDP.

Braden, R. T., ed. 1989b. "Requirements for Internet Hosts—Application and Support," RFC 1123, 98 pages (Oct.).

The second half of the Host Requirements RFC. This half covers Telnet, FTP, TFTP, SMTP, and the DNS.

Braden, R. T. 1989c. "Perspective on the Host Requirements RFCs," RFC 1127, 20 pages (Oct.).

An informal summary of the discussions and conclusions of the IETF working group that developed the Host Requirements RFC.

Braden, R. T. 1992a. "TIME-WAIT Assassination Hazards in TCP," RFC 1337, 11 pages (May).

Shows how the receipt of an RST while in the TIME_WAIT state can lead to problems.

Braden, R. T. 1992b. "Extending TCP for Transactions—Concepts," RFC 1379, 38 pages (Nov.).

The concepts and history behind the development of T/TCP.

Braden, R. T. 1992c. "Extending TCP for Transactions—Functional Specification," Internet Draft, 32 pages (Dec.).

The functional specification and a discussion of the implementation issues in T/ TCP.

Braden, R. T., Borman, D. A., and Partridge, C. 1988. "Computing the Internet Checksum," RFC 1071, 24 pages (Sept.).

Provides techniques and algorithms for calculating the checksum used by IP, ICMP, IGMP, UDP, and TCP.

Braden, R. T., and Postel, J. B. 1987. "Requirements for Internet Gateways," RFC 1009, 55 pages (June).

The equivalent of the Host Requirements RFC for routers. This RFC is being replaced; see [Almquist 1993].

Caceres, R., Danzig, P. B., Jamin, S., and Mitzel, D. J. 1991. "Characteristics of Wide-Area TCP/IP Conversations," *Computer Communication Review*, vol. 21, no. 4, pp. 101–112 (Sept.).

Callon, R. 1992. "TCP and UDP with Bigger Addresses (TUBA), A Simple Proposal for Internet Addressing and Routing," RFC 1347, 9 pages (June).

Case, J. D., Fedor, M. S., Schoffstall, M. L., and Davin, C. 1990. "Simple Network Management (SNMP)," RFC 1157, 36 pages (May).

The protocol specification for SNMP.

Case, J. D., McCloghrie, K., Rose, M. T., and Waldbusser, S. 1993. "An Introduction to Version 2 of the Internet-Standard Network Management Framework," RFC 1441, 13 pages (Apr.).

An introduction to SNMPv2 along with references to the other 11 RFCs defining SNMPv2.

Case, J. D., and Partridge, C. 1989. "Case Diagrams: A First Step to Diagrammed Management Information Bases," *Computer Communication Review*, vol. 19, no. 1, pp. 13–16 (Jan.).

Defines diagrams that are useful for visualizing the relationship between SNMP variables in a given module.

Casner, S., and Deering, S. E. 1992. "First IETF Internet Audiocast," *Computer Communication Review*, vol. 22, no. 3, pp. 92–97 (July).

Describes how live audio for an IETF meeting was audiocast using multicasting over the Internet. A PostScript copy of this paper is available via anonymous FTP from the host `venera.isi.edu` in the file `pub/ietf-audiocast-article.ps`. Also, the file `mbone/faq.txt` on that host contains the frequently asked questions regarding the Internet multicast backbone (MBONE).

Cheriton, D. P. 1988. "VMTP: Versatile Message Transaction Protocol," RFC 1045, 123 pages (Feb.).

Cheswick, W. R., and Bellovin, S. M. 1994. *Firewalls and Internet Security: Repelling the Wily Hacker*. Addison-Wesley, Reading, Mass.

Describes how to set up and administer a firewall gateway and the security issues involved.

Clark, D. D. 1982. "Window and Acknowledgment Strategy in TCP," RFC 813, 22 pages (July).

The original RFC that identified the silly window syndrome and how to avoid it.

Clark, D. D. 1988. "The Design Philosophy of the DARPA Internet Protocols," *Computer Communication Review*, vol. 18, no. 4, pp. 106–114 (Aug.).

Describes the early reasoning that shaped the Internet protocols.

Comer, D. E., and Stevens, D. L. 1993. *Internetworking with TCP/IP: Vol. III: Client–Server Programming and Applications, BSD Socket Version*. Prentice-Hall, Englewood Cliffs, N.J.

Cooper, A. W., and Postel, J. B. 1993. "The US Domain," RFC 1480, 47 pages (June).

Describes the `.us` domain in the DNS.

Crocker, D. H. 1982. "Standard for the Format of ARPA Internet Text Messages," RFC 822, 47 pages (Aug.).

Defines the format of electronic mail messages transmitted using SMTP.

Crocker, D.H. 1993. "Evolving the System," in *Internet System Handbook*, eds. D. C. Lynch and M. T. Rose, pp. 41–76. Addison-Wesley, Reading, Mass.

Some history on the development of standards in the ARPANET, along with details on the current structure of the Internet technical community. Also defines the current Internet standards process.

Croft, W., and Gilmore, J. 1985. "Bootstrap Protocol (BOOTP)," RFC 951, 12 pages (Sept.).

Crowcroft, J., Wakeman, I., Wang, Z., and Sirovica, D. 1992. "Is Layering Harmful?," *IEEE Network*, vol. 6, no. 1, pp. 20–24 (Jan.).

The seven missing figures from this paper appear in the next issue, vol, 6, no. 2 (March).

Curry, D. A. 1992. *UNIX System Security: A Guide for Users and System Administrators*. Addison-Wesley, Reading, Mass.

A book on Unix security. Chapters 4 and 5 deal with network security.

Dalton, C., Watson, G., Banks, D., Calamvokis, C., Edwards, A., and Lumley, J. 1993. "Afterburner," *IEEE Network*, vol. 7, no. 4, pp. 36–43 (July).

Describes how to speed up TCP by reducing the number of data copies performed, and a special purpose interface card that supports this design.

Danzig, P. B., Obraczka, K., and Kumar, A. 1992. "An Analysis of Wide-Area Name Server Traffic," *Computer Communication Review*, vol. 22, no. 4, pp. 281–292 (Oct.).

An analysis of the traffic to one of the root name servers over two 24-hour periods. Shows how DNS traffic from faulty implementations can consume 20 times more WAN bandwidth than necessary. A PostScript copy of this paper is available via anonymous FTP from the host `caldera.usc.edu` in the file `pub/danzig/dns.ps.Z`.

Deering, S. E. 1989. "Host Extensions for IP Multicasting," RFC 1112, 17 pages (Aug.).

The specification of IP multicasting and IGMP.

Deering, S. E., ed. 1991. "ICMP Router Discovery Messages," RFC 1256, 19 pages (Sept.).

Deering, S. E., and Cheriton, D. P. 1990. "Multicast Routing in Datagram Internetworks and Extended LANs," *ACM Transactions on Computer Systems*, vol. 8, no. 2, pp. 85–110 (May).

Proposes extensions to common routing techniques to support multicasting.

Dixon, T. 1993. "Comparison of Proposals for Next Version of IP," RFC 1454, 15 pages (May).

A comparison and summary of SIP, PIP, and TUBA.

Droms, R. 1993. "Dynamic Host Configuration Protocol," RFC 1541, 39 pages (Oct.).

Droms, R., and Dyksen, W. R. 1990. "Performance Measurements of the X Window System Communication Protocol," *Software Practice & Experience*, vol. 20, pp. 119–136 (Oct.).

Measurements of the TCP communication involved when using various X clients.

Fedor, M. S. 1988. "GATED: A Multi-routing Protocol Daemon for UNIX," *Proceedings of the 1988 Summer USENIX Conference*, pp. 365–376, San Francisco, Calif.

Finlayson, R. 1984. "Bootstrap Loading using TFTP," RFC 906, 4 pages (June).

Finlayson, R., Mann, T., Mogul, J. C., and Theimer, M. 1984. "A Reverse Address Resolution Protocol," RFC 903, 4 pages (June).

Floyd, S. 1994. Private Communication.

Ford, P. S., Rekhter, Y., and Braun, H-W. 1993. "Improving the Routing and Addressing of IP," *IEEE Network*, vol. 7, no. 3, pp. 10–15 (May).

A description of CIDR (classless interdomain routing).

Fuller, V., Li, T., Yu, J. Y., and Varadhan, K. 1993. "Classless Inter-Domain Routing (CIDR): An Address Assignment and Aggregation Strategy," RFC 1519, 24 pages (Sept.).

The specification of CIDR (classless interdomain routing).

Gerich, E. 1993. "Guidelines for Management of IP Address Space," RFC 1466, 10 pages (May).

The specification of how IP addresses will be allocated in the future (i.e., class B addresses will be hard to obtain and normally a block of class C addresses will be allocated instead).

Gurwitz, R., and Hinden, R. 1982. "IP—Local Area Network Addressing Issues," IEN 212, 11 pages (Sept.).

One of the earliest references to IP broadcast addresses.

Harrenstien, K., Stahl, M. K., and Feinler, E. J. 1985. "NICNAME/WHOIS," RFC 954, 4 pages (Oct.).

Hedrick, C. L. 1988a. "Routing Information Protocol," RFC 1058, 33 pages (June).

Hedrick, C. L. 1988b. "Telnet Terminal Speed Option," RFC 1079, 3 pages (Dec.).

Hedrick, C. L., and Borman, D. A. 1992. "Telnet Remote Flow Control Option," RFC 1372, 6 pages (Oct.).

Hornig, C. 1984. "Standard for the Transmission of IP Datagrams over Ethernet Networks," RFC 894, 3 pages (Apr.).

Huitema, C. 1993. "IAB Recommendation for an Intermediate Strategy to Address the Issue of Scaling," RFC 1481, 2 pages (July).

The IAB recommendation for the implementation of CIDR.

Jacobson, V. 1988. "Congestion Avoidance and Control," *Computer Communication Review*, vol. 18, no. 4, pp. 314–329 (Aug.).

A classic paper describing the slow start and congestion avoidance algorithms for TCP. A PostScript copy of this paper is available via anonymous FTP from the host `ftp.ee.lbl.gov` in the file `congavoid.ps.Z`.

Jacobson, V. 1990a. "Compressing TCP/IP Headers for Low-Speed Serial Links," RFC 1144, 43 pages (Feb.).

Describes CSLIP, a version of SLIP with the TCP and IP headers compressed.

Jacobson, V. 1990b. "Modified TCP Congestion Avoidance Algorithm," April 30, 1990, end2end-interest mailing list (Apr.).

Describes the fast retransmit and fast recovery algorithms.

Jacobson, V. 1990c. "Berkeley TCP Evolution from 4.3-Tahoe to 4.3-Reno," *Proceedings of the Eighteenth Internet Engineering Task Force*, p. 365 (Sept.), University of British Columbia, Vancouver, B.C.

Jacobson, V., and Braden, R. T. 1988. "TCP Extensions for Long-Delay Paths," RFC 1072, 16 pages (Oct.).

Describes the selective acknowledgment option for TCP, which was removed from the later RFC 1323.

Jacobson, V., Braden, R. T., and Borman, D. A. 1992. "TCP Extensions for High Performance," RFC 1323, 37 pages (May).

Describes the window scale option, the timestamp option, and the PAWS algorithm, along with the reasons these modifications are needed.

Jacobson, V., Braden, R. T., and Zhang, L. 1990. "TCP Extensions for High-Speed Paths," RFC 1185, 21 pages (Oct.).

Despite this RFC being obsoleted by RFC 1323, the appendix on protection against old duplicate segments in TCP is worth reading.

Juszczak, C. 1989. "Improving the Performance and Correctness of an NFS Server," *Proceedings of the 1989 Winter USENIX Conference*, pp. 53–63, San Diego, Calif.

Provides implementation details on an NFS server cache.

Kantor, B. 1991. "BSD Rlogin," RFC 1282, 5 pages (Dec.).

The specification of the Rlogin protocol.

Karn, P., and Partridge, C. 1987. "Improving Round-Trip Time Estimates in Reliable Transport Protocols," *Computer Communication Review*, vol. 17, no. 5, pp. 2–7 (Aug.).

Details of Karn's algorithm to handle the retransmission timeout for segments that have been retransmitted. A PostScript copy of this paper is available via anonymous FTP from the host `sics.se` in the file `pub/craig/karn-partridge.ps`.

Katz, D. 1990. "Proposed Standard for the Transmission of IP Datagrams Over FDDI Networks," RFC 1188, 11 pages (Oct.).

Specifies the encapsulation of IP datagrams and ARP requests and replies on FDDI networks, including multicasting.

Kent, C. A., and Mogul, J. C. 1987. "Fragmentation Considered Harmful," *Computer Communication Review*, vol. 17, no. 5, pp. 390–401 (Aug.).

Kent, S. T. 1991. "U.S. Department of Defense Security Options for the Internet Protocol," RFC 1108, 17 pages (Nov.).

Kleinrock, L. 1992. "The Latency/Bandwidth Tradeoff in Gigabit Networks," *IEEE Communications Magazine*, vol. 30, no. 4, pp. 36–40 (Apr.).

Klensin, J., Freed, N., and Moore, K. 1993. "SMTP Service Extension for Message Size Declaration," RFC 1427, 8 pages (Feb.).

Klensin, J., Freed, N., Rose, M. T., Stefferud, E. A., and Crocker, D. 1993a. "SMTP Service Extensions," RFC 1425, 10 pages (Feb.).

Klensin, J., Freed, N., Rose, M. T., Stefferud, E. A., and Crocker, D. 1993b. "SMTP Service Extension for 8bit-MIME Transport," RFC 1426, 6 pages (Feb.).

Krol, E. 1992. *The Whole Internet*. O'Reilly & Associates, Sebastopol, Calif.

A beginner's introduction to the Internet.

LaQuey, T. 1993. *The Internet Companion: A Beginner's Guide to Global Networking*. Addison-Wesley, Reading, Mass.

A beginner's introduction to the Internet.

Leffler, S. J., and Karels, M. J. 1984. "Trailer Encapsulations," RFC 893, 3 pages (Apr.).

Leffler, S. J., McKusick, M. K., Karels, M. J., and Quarterman, J. S. 1989. *The Design and Implementation of the 4.3BSD UNIX Operating System*. Addison-Wesley, Reading, Mass.

An entire book on the 4.3BSD Unix system. This book describes the Tahoe release of 4.3BSD.

Lougheed, K., and Rekhter, Y. 1991. "A Border Gateway Protocol 3 (BGP-3)," RFC 1267, 35 pages (Oct.).

Lynch, D. C. 1993. "Historical Perspective," in *Internet System Handbook*, eds. D. C. Lynch and M. T. Rose, pp. 3–14. Addison-Wesley, Reading, Mass.

A description of the early days of the Internet: the ARPANET.

Macklem, R. 1991. "Lessons Learned Tuning the 4.3BSD Reno Implementation of the NFS Protocol," *Proceedings of the 1991 Winter USENIX Conference*, pp. 53–64, Dallas, Tex.

Describes an implementation of NFS that uses both UDP and TCP.

Malkin, G. S. 1993a. "RIP Version 2: Carrying Additional Information," RFC 1388, 7 pages (Jan.).

Malkin, G. S. 1993b. "Traceroute Using an IP Option," RFC 1393, 7 pages (Jan.).

Proposed modifications to ICMP for a new version of traceroute.

Mallory, T., and Kullberg, A. 1990. "Incremental Updating of the Internet Checksum," RFC 1141, 2 pages (Jan.).

Describes an implementation technique for incrementally updating the internet checksum.

Manber, U. 1990. "Chain Reactions in Networks," *IEEE Computer*, vol. 23, no. 10, pp. 57–63 (Oct.).

Describes types of broadcast storms and network meltdowns, similar to those demonstrated in Exercises 9.3 and 9.4.

McCanne, S., and Jacobson, V. 1993. "The BSD Packet Filter: A New Architecture for User-Level Packet Capture," *Proceedings of the 1993 Winter USENIX Conference*, pp. 259–269, San Diego, Calif.

A detailed description of the BSD Packet Filter (BPF) and comparisons with Sun's Network Interface Tap (NIT). A PostScript copy of this paper is available via anonymous FTP from the host `ftp.ee.lbl.gov` in the file `papers/bpf-usenix93.ps.Z`.

McCloghrie, K., and Rose, M. T. 1991. "Management Information Base for Network Management of TCP/IP-based Internets: MIB-II," RFC 1213 (Mar.).

McGregor, G. 1992. "PPP Internet Protocol Control Protocol (IPCP)," RFC 1332, 12 pages (May).

A description of the NCP for PPP that is specific to TCP/IP.

Mills, D. L. 1992. "Network Time Protocol (Version 3): Specification, Implementation, and Analysis," RFC 1305, 113 pages (Mar.).

Mockapetris, P. V. 1987a. "Domain Names: Concepts and Facilities," RFC 1034, 55 pages (Nov.).

An introduction to the DNS.

Mockapetris, P. V. 1987b. "Domain Names: Implementation and Specification," RFC 1035, 55 pages (Nov.).

The specification of the DNS.

Mogul, J. C. 1990. "Efficient Use of Workstations for Passive Monitoring of Local Area Networks," *Computer Communication Review*, vol. 20, no. 4, pp. 253–263 (Sept.).

Describes the use of workstations to monitor local area networks, instead of purchasing dedicated network analyzer hardware.

Mogul, J. C. 1992. "Holy Turbocharger Batman, (evil cheating), NFS async writes," Message-ID <1992Mar2.191711.9935@PA.dec.com>, Usenet, comp.protocols.nfs Newsgroup (Mar.).

Some interesting statistics on internet checksum errors collected on a busy NFS server over 40 days.

Mogul, J. C. 1993. "IP Network Performance," in *Internet System Handbook*, eds. D. C. Lynch and M. T. Rose, pp. 575–675. Addison-Wesley, Reading, Mass.

Covers numerous topics in the TCP/IP protocols that are candidates for tuning to obtain optimal performance.

Mogul, J. C., and Deering, S. E. 1990. "Path MTU Discovery," RFC 1191, 19 pages (Apr.).

Mogul, J. C., and Postel, J. B. 1985. "Internet Standard Subnetting Procedure," RFC 950, 18 pages (Aug.).

Moore, K. 1993. "MIME (Multipurpose Internet Mail Extensions) Part Two: Message Header Extensions for Non-ASCII Text," RFC 1522, 10 pages (Sept.).

Describes a way to send non-ASCII characters in RFC 822 mail headers, using 7-bit ASCII.

Moy, J. 1991. "OSPF Version 2," RFC 1247, 189 pages (July).

Nagle, J. 1984. "Congestion Control in IP/TCP Internetworks," RFC 896, 9 pages (Jan.).

Description of the Nagle algorithm.

Nye, A., ed. 1992. *The X Window System, Volume 0: X Protocol Reference Manual, Third Edition.* O'Reilly & Associates, Sebastopol, Calif.

Obraczka, K., Danzig, P. B., and Li, S. 1993. "Internet Resource Discovery Services," *IEEE Computer*, vol. 26, no. 9, pp. 8–22 (Sept.).

Presents an overview of current Internet resource discovery tools: Alex, Archie, Gopher, Indie, Knowbot Information Service, Netfind, Prospero, WAIS, WWW, and X.500. A PostScript copy of this paper is available via anonymous FTP from the host `caldera.usc.edu` in the file `/pub/kobraczk/ieeecomputer.ps.Z`.

Papadopoulos, C., and Parulkar, G. M. 1993. "Experimental Evaluation of SunOS IPC and TCP/IP Protocol Implementation," *IEEE/ACM Transactions on Networking*, vol. 1, no. 2, pp. 199–216 (Apr.).

Measures the overhead involved at different layers of the protocol suite as data is sent and received.

Partridge, C. 1986. "Mail Routing and the Domain System," RFC 974, 7 pages (Jan.).

How to use DNS MX records for mail routing.

Partridge, C. 1994. *Gigabit Networking*. Addison-Wesley, Reading, Mass.

Describes the issues involved when network speeds exceed one gigabit per second.

Partridge, C., and Pink, S. 1993. "A Faster UDP," *IEEE/ACM Transactions on Networking*, vol. 1, no. 4, pp. 429–440 (Aug.).

Describes implementation improvements to the Berkeley sources to speed up UDP performance about 30%.

Paxson, V. 1993. "Empirically-Derived Analytic Models of Wide-Area TCP Connections: Extended Report," LBL-34086, Lawrence Berkeley Laboratory and EECS Division, University of California, Berkeley (June).

Contains an analysis of 2.5 million TCP connections that occurred during 14 wide-area traffic traces. A PostScript copy of this report is available via anonymous FTP from the host `ftp.ee.lbl.gov` in the files `WAN-TCP-models.1.ps.Z` and `WAN-TCP-models.2.ps.Z`.

Perlman, R. 1992. *Interconnections: Bridges and Routers*. Addison-Wesley, Reading, Mass.

A book with lots of details on ways to interconnect networks (bridges and routers) along with various routing algorithms.

Plummer, D. C. 1982. "An Ethernet Address Resolution Protocol," RFC 826, 10 pages (Nov.).

Postel, J. B. 1980. "User Datagram Protocol," RFC 768, 3 pages (Aug.).

Postel, J. B., ed. 1981a. "Internet Protocol," RFC 791, 45 pages (Sept.).

Postel, J. B. 1981b. "Internet Control Message Protocol," RFC 792, 21 pages (Sept.).

Postel, J. B., ed. 1981c. "Transmission Control Protocol," RFC 793, 85 pages (Sept.).

Postel, J. B. 1982. "Simple Mail Transfer Protocol," RFC 821, 68 pages (Aug.).

Postel, J. B. 1987. "TCP and IP Bake Off," RFC 1025, 6 pages (Sept.).

Describes some of the procedures and scoring performed between different implementations of TCP/IP during its early development phases to test for interoperability.

Postel, J. B., ed. 1994. "Internet Official Protocol Standards," RFC 1600, 36 pages (Mar.).

The status of all Internet protocols. This RFC is updated regularly—check the latest RFC index for the current version.

Postel, J. B., and Reynolds, J. K. 1983a. "Telnet Protocol Specification," RFC 854, 15 pages (May).

The basic Telnet protocol specification. Many later RFCs describe specific Telnet options.

Postel, J. B., and Reynolds, J. K. 1983b. "Telnet Binary Transmission," RFC 856, 4 pages (May).

Postel, J. B., and Reynolds, J. K. 1983c. "Telnet Echo Option," RFC 857, 5 pages (May).

Postel, J. B., and Reynolds, J. K. 1983d. "Telnet Suppress Go Ahead Option," RFC 858, 3 pages (May).

Postel, J. B., and Reynolds, J. K. 1983e. "Telnet Status Option," RFC 859, 3 pages (May).

Postel, J. B., and Reynolds, J. K. 1983f. "Telnet Timing Mark Option," RFC 860, 4 pages (May).

Postel, J. B., and Reynolds, J. K. 1985. "File Transfer Protocol (FTP)," RFC 959, 69 pages (Oct.).

Postel, J. B., and Reynolds, J. K. 1988. "Standard for the Transmission of IP Datagrams over IEEE 802 Networks," RFC 1042, 15 pages (Apr.).

The specification for the encapsulation of IP datagrams and ARP requests and replies on IEEE 802 networks.

Pusateri, T. 1993. "IP Multicast Over Token-Ring Local Area Networks," RFC 1469, 4 pages (June).

Rago, S. A. 1993. *UNIX System V Network Programming*. Addison-Wesley, Reading, Mass.

A book on TLI and the streams subsystem.

Rekhter, Y., and Gross, P. 1991. "Application of the Border Gateway Protocol in the Internet," RFC 1268, 13 pages (Oct.).

Rekhter, Y., and Li, T. 1993. "An Architecture for IP Address Allocation with CIDR," RFC 1518, 27 pages (Sept.).

Reynolds, J. K. 1989. "The Helminthiasis of the Internet," RFC 1135, 33 pages (Dec.).

Contains a detailed discussion of the Internet worm of 1988.

Reynolds, J. K., and Postel, J. B. 1992. "Assigned Numbers," RFC 1340, 138 pages (July).

All the magic numbers in the Internet protocol suite. This RFC is updated regularly—check the latest RFC index for the current version.

Romkey, J. L. 1988. "A Nonstandard for Transmission of IP Datagrams Over Serial Lines: SLIP," RFC 1055, 6 pages (June).

Rose, M. T. 1990. *The Open Book: A Practical Perspective on OSI*. Prentice-Hall, Englewood Cliffs, N.J.

A book on the OSI protocols. Chapter 8 provides additional details on ASN.1 and BER.

Rose, M. T. 1993. *The Internet Message: Closing the Book with Electronic Mail.* Prentice-Hall, Englewood Cliffs, N.J.

A book on Internet mail, with details on MIME

Rose, M. T. 1994. *The Simple Book: An Introduction to Internet Management, Second Edition.* Prentice-Hall, Englewood Cliffs, N.J.

A book on SNMPv2. The first edition of this book covered SNMPv1.

Rose, M. T., and McCloghrie, K. 1990. "Structure and Identification of Management Information for TCP/IP-based Internets," RFC 1155, 22 pages (May).

Defines the SMI for SNMPv1.

Rosenberg, W., Kenney, D., and Fisher, G. 1992. *Understanding DCE.* O'Reilly & Associates, Sebastopol, Calif.

Provides an overview of OSF's Distributed Computing Environment.

Routhier, S. A. 1993. "Implementation Experience for SNMPv2," *The Simple Times*, vol. 2, no. 4, pp. 1–4 (July-Aug.).

Describes modifying an SNMPv1 implementation to support SNMPv2.

This journal is distributed electronically at no charge. Send e-mail with a subject of `help` to `st-subscriptions@simple-times.org` to receive subscription information.

Schryver, V. J. 1993. "Info on High Speed Transport Protocols Requested," Message-ID <i0imr8g@rhyolite.wpd.sgi.com>, Usenet, comp.protocols.tcp-ip Newsgroup (May).

Provides TCP performance numbers for some FDDI implementations.

Schwartz, M. F., and Tsirigotis, P. G. 1991. "Experience with a Semantically Cognizant Internet White Pages Directory Tool," *Journal of Internetworking Research and Experience*, vol. 2, no. 1, pp. 23–50 (Mar.).

Also available by anonymous FTP from the host `ftp.cs.colorado.edu` in the file `pub/cs/techreports/schwartz/PostScript/White.Pages.ps.Z`.

Simpson, W. A. 1993. "The Point-to-Point Protocol (PPP)," RFC 1548, 53 pages (Dec.).

Defines PPP and its link control protocol.

Sollins, K. R. 1992. "The TFTP Protocol (Revision 2)," RFC 1350, 11 pages (July).

Stallings, W. 1987. *Handbook of Computer-Communications Standards, Volume 2: Local Network Standards.* Macmillan, New York.

Contains details on the IEEE 802 local area network standards.

Stallings, W. 1993. *SNMP, SNMPv2, and CMIP: The Practical Guide to Network-Management Standards.* Addison-Wesley, Reading, Mass.

Describes the differences between SNMPv1 and SNMPv2.

Stern, H. 1991. *Managing NFS and NIS.* O'Reilly & Associates, Sebastopol, Calif.

Contains lots of details on installing, using, and administering NFS.

Stevens, W. R. 1990. *UNIX Network Programming.* Prentice-Hall, Englewood Cliffs, N.J.

A detailed book on network programming under Unix, using sockets and TLI.

Stevens, W. R. 1992. *Advanced Programming in the UNIX Environment.* Addison-Wesley, Reading, Mass.

A detailed book on Unix programming.

Sun Microsystems. 1987. "XDR: External Data Representation Standard," RFC 1014, 20 pages (June).

Sun Microsystems. 1988a. "RPC: Remote Procedure Call, Protocol Specification, Version 2," RFC 1057, 25 pages (June).

Sun Microsystems. 1988b. "NFS: Network File System Protocol Specification," RFC 1094, 27 pages (Mar.).

The specification of version 2 of Sun NFS.

Sun Microsystems. 1994. *NFS: Network File System Version 3 Protocol Specification*. Sun Microsystems, Mountain View, Calif.

A PostScript copy of this document is available by anonymous FTP from the host `ftp.uu.net` in the file `networking/ip/nfs/NFS3.spec.ps.Z`.

Tanenbaum, A. S. 1989. *Computer Networks, Second Edition*. Prentice-Hall, Englewood Cliffs, N.J.

A general text on computer networks.

Topolcic, C. 1993. "Status of CIDR Deployment in the Internet," RFC 1467, 9 pages (Aug.).

Tsuchiya, P. F. 1991. "On the Assignment of Subnet Numbers," RFC 1219, 13 pages (Apr.).

Recommends assigning subnet IDs from the highest order bit down, and host IDs from the lowest order bit up. This makes it easier to change the subnet mask at some point in the future without having to renumber all the systems.

Ullmann, R. 1993. "TP/IX: The Next Internet," RFC 1475, 35 pages (June).

Another proposal for the next generation of Internet protocols.

VanBokkelen, J. 1989. "Telnet Terminal-Type Option," RFC 1091, 7 pages (Feb.).

Waitzman, D. 1988. "Telnet Window Size Option," RFC 1073, 4 pages (Oct.).

Waitzman, D., Partridge, C., and Deering, S. E. 1988. "Distance Vector Multicast Routing Protocol," RFC 1075, 24 pages (Nov.).

Warnock, R. P. 1991. "Need Help Selecting Ethernet Cards for Very High Performance Throughput Rates," Message-ID <lbhal10@sgi.sgi.com>, Usenet, comp.protocols.tcp-ip Newsgroup (Sept.).

Provides the TCP performance numbers we calculated from Figure 24.9.

Weider, C., Reynolds, J. K., and Heker, S. 1992. "Technical Overview of Directory Services Using the X.500 Protocol," RFC 1309, 16 pages (Mar.).

Wimer, W. 1993. "Clarifications and Extensions for the Bootstrap Protocol," RFC 1542, 23 pages (Oct.).

X/Open. 1991. *Protocols for X/Open Internetworking: XNFS*. X/Open, Reading, Berkshire, U.K.

A better description of Sun RPC, XDR, and NFS. Also contains a description of the NFS lock manager and status monitor protocols, along with appendices detailing the semantic differences that can be encountered using NFS, versus local file access. X/Open document number XO/CAE/91/030.

Zimmerman, D. P. 1991. "Finger User Information Protocol," RFC 1288, 12 pages (Dec.).

Sun Microsystems. 1987. "XDR: External Data Representation Standard," RFC 1014, 20 pages (June).

Sun Microsystems. 1988a. "RPC: Remote Procedure Call Protocol Specification, Version 2," RFC 1057, 25 pages (June).

Sun Microsystems. 1988b. "NFS: Network File System Protocol Specification," RFC 1094, 27 pages (Mar.).

The specification of version 2 of NFS.

Sun Microsystems. 1990. *Network Programming*, Part Number 800-3850-10, Sun Microsystems, Inc., Mountain View, Calif.

A hardcopy of the documentation [illegible]

Tanenbaum, A. S. 1989. *Computer Networks*, Second Edition. Prentice-Hall, Englewood Cliffs, N.J.

A general text on computer networks.

Topolcic, C. 1993. "Status of CIDR Deployment in the Internet," RFC 1467, 9 pages (Aug.).

Tsuchiya, P. F. 1991. "On the Assignment of Subnet Numbers," RFC 1219, 13 pages (Apr.).

Recommends assigning subnet IDs from the most significant bit and host IDs from the least significant bit. [illegible] without having to renumber all the systems.

Ullmann, R. 1993. "TP/IX: The Next Internet," RFC 1475, 35 pages (June).

A proposal for the next generation internet protocol.

VanBokkelen, J. 1989. "Telnet Terminal-Type Option," RFC 1091, 7 pages (Feb.).

Waitzman, D. 1988. "Telnet Window Size Option," RFC 1073, 4 pages (Oct.).

Waitzman, D., Partridge, C., and Deering, S. E. 1988. "Distance Vector Multicast Routing Protocol," RFC 1075, 24 pages (Nov.).

Warnock, R. P. 1991. "Re: Help selecting Internet Card, looking High-Performance [illegible] Rates," Message-ID [illegible], Usenet, comp.protocols.tcp-ip Newsgroup (Sept.).

[illegible] the TCP performance numbers [illegible]

Weider, C., Reynolds, J. K., and Heker, S. 1992. "Technical Overview of Directory Services Using the X.500 Protocol," RFC 1309, 16 pages (Mar.).

Wimer, W. 1993. "Clarifications and Extensions for the Bootstrap Protocol," RFC 1542, 23 pages (Oct.).

X/Open. 1991. *Protocols for X/Open Internetworking: XNFS*. X/Open [illegible] Reading, Berkshire, U.K.

A detailed description of Sun RPC, XDR, and NFS [illegible]

Zimmerman, D. P. 1991. "The Finger User Information Protocol," RFC 1288, 12 pages (Dec.).

Index

Rather than provide a separate glossary (with most of the entries being acronyms), this index also serves as a glossary for all the acronyms used in the book. The primary entry for the acronym appears under the acronym name. For example, all references to the Network Time Protocol appear under NTP. The entry under the compound term "Network Time Protocol" refers the reader back to the main entry under NTP. This is because you are more likely to look up the acronym than the compound term. Additionally, a list of all these acronyms with their compound terms is found in the inside back cover.

ACRONYMS

ACK	acknowledgment flag, TCP header, p. 227
API	application program interface, p. 17
ARP	Address Resolution Protocol, p. 53
ARPANET	Advanced Research Projects Agency network, p. 548
AS	autonomous system, p. 128
ASCII	American Standard Code for Information Interchange, p. 401
ASN.1	Abstract Syntax Notation One, p. 386
BER	Basic Encoding Rules, p. 386
BGP	Border Gateway Protocol, p. 138
BIND	Berkeley Internet Name Domain, p. 188
BOOTP	Bootstrap Protocol, p. 215
BPF	BSD Packet Filter, p. 491
BSD	Berkeley Software Distribution, p. 16
CIDR	classless interdomain routing, p. 140
CIX	Commercial Internet Exchange, p. 119
CLNP	Connectionless Network Protocol, p. 50
CRC	cyclic redundancy check, p. 22
CSLIP	compressed SLIP, p. 25
CSMA	carrier sense multiple access, p. 21
DCE	Distributed Computing Environment, p. 462
DDN	Defense Data Network, p. 8
DF	don't fragment flag, IP header, p. 149
DHCP	Dynamic Host Configuration Protocol, p. 222
DLPI	Data Link Provider Interface, p. 494
DNS	Domain Name System, p. 187
DSAP	Destination Service Access Point, p. 22
DTS	Distributed Time Service, p. 77
DVMRP	Distance–Vector Multicast Routing Protocol, p. 185
EBONE	European IP Backbone, p. 119
EGP	Exterior Gateway Protocol, p. 128
EOL	end of option list, p. 93
FCS	frame check sequence, p. 22
FDDI	Fiber Distributed Data Interface, p. 4
FIFO	first in, first out, p. 259
FIN	finish flag, TCP header, p. 227
FQDN	fully qualified domain name, p. 189
FTP	File Transfer Protocol, p. 419
HDLC	high-level data link control, p. 26
HELLO	routing protocol, p. 128
IAB	Internet Architecture Board, p. 14
IANA	Internet Assigned Number Authority, p. 13
ICMP	Internet Control Message Protocol, p. 69
IDRP	Interdomain Routing Protocol, p. 141
IEEE	Institute of Electrical and Electronics Engineers, p. 21
IEN	Internet Experiment Notes, p. 172
IESG	Internet Engineering Steering Group, p. 14
IETF	Internet Engineering Task Force, p. 14
IGMP	Internet Group Management Protocol, p. 179
IGP	interior gateway protocol, p. 128
IP	Internet Protocol, p. 33
IRTF	Internet Research Task Force, p. 14
IS–IS	Intermediate System to Intermediate System Protocol, p. 141
ISN	initial sequence number, p. 226
ISO	International Organization for Standardization, p. 26
ISOC	Internet Society, p. 14
LAN	local area network, p. 3
LBX	low bandwidth X, p. 490
LCP	link control protocol, p. 26
LFN	long fat network, p. 344
LIFO	last in, first out, p. 259
LLC	logical link control, p. 22